Nepal

Pokhara
p206

**The Terai &
Mahabharat Range**
p237

**Kathmandu to
Pokhara**
p196

Kathmandu
p64

**Around the
Kathmandu Valley**
p120

Bradley Mayhew, Lindsay Brown, Paul Stiles

Contents

PLAN YOUR TRIP

EVEREST BASE CAMP TREK
P294

CHITWAN NATIONAL PARK
P243

ON THE ROAD

Contents

Welcome to Nepal

A trekkers' paradise, Nepal combines Himalayan views, golden temples, charming hill villages and jungle wildlife-watching to offer one of the world's great travel destinations.

Mountain Highs

The Nepal Himalaya is the ultimate goal for mountain lovers. Some of the Himalaya's most iconic and accessible hiking is on offer here, with rugged trails to Everest, the Annapurnas and beyond. Nowhere else can you trek for days in incredible mountain scenery, secure in the knowledge that a hot meal, cosy lodge and warm slice of apple pie await you at the end of the day. Then there's the adrenaline kick of rafting a roaring Nepali river or bungee jumping into a yawning Himalayan gorge. Canyoning, climbing, kayaking, paragliding and mountain biking all offer a rush against the backdrop of some of the world's most dramatic landscapes.

Medieval Cities & Sacred Sites

Other travellers prefer to see Nepal at a more refined pace, admiring the peaks over a sunset gin and tonic from a Himalayan viewpoint, strolling through the medieval city squares of Kathmandu, Patan and Bhaktapur, and joining Tibetan Buddhist pilgrims on a spiritual stroll around centuries-old stupas and monasteries. Even after the 2015 earthquake, Nepal remains the cultural powerhouse of the Himalaya; the Kathmandu Valley in particular offers an unrivalled collection of world-class palaces, hidden backstreet shrines and sublime temple art.

Jungle Adventures

South of Nepal's mountains lies something completely different: a chain of wild and woolly national parks, where nature buffs scan the subtropical treetops for exotic bird species and comb the jungles for rhinos, tigers and crocodiles. Choose from a luxury safari lodge in central Chitwan or go exploring on a wilder trip to remote Bardia or Koshi Tappu, stopping en route to visit the birthplace of Buddha on the steamy plains near Lumbini. Whether you cross the country by mountain bike, motorbike, raft or tourist bus, Nepal offers an astonishingly diverse array of attractions and landscapes.

Travel Nirvana

There are few countries in the world that are as well set up for independent travel as Nepal. Wandering the trekking shops, bakeries and pizzerias of Thamel and Pokhara, it's easy to feel that you have somehow landed in a kind of backpacker Disneyland. Out in the countryside lies a quite different Nepal, where traditional mountain life continues at a slower pace, and a million potential adventures glimmer on the mountain horizons. The biggest problem you might face in Nepal is just how to fit everything in, which is one reason why many people return here over and over again.

ALEXANDEER MAZURKEVICH/SHUTTERSTOCK©

Why I Love Nepal

By Bradley Mayhew, Writer

If, like me, you get your highs from pristine mountain views and the sense of perspective that a Himalayan journey offers, then you are going to like Nepal. But if, also like me, you've always secretly wished that your mountain wilderness came with a warm slice of apple pie instead of a soggy tent, then you will simply love this place. My favourite thing about Nepal? There's always another adventure. Done Annapurna? Try the Gokyo Valley. Done Gokyo? Try a 6000m trekking peak. It's adventure heaven, with an espresso on the side.

For more about our writers, see p416

Above: Annapurna Circuit Trek (p301)

Nepal

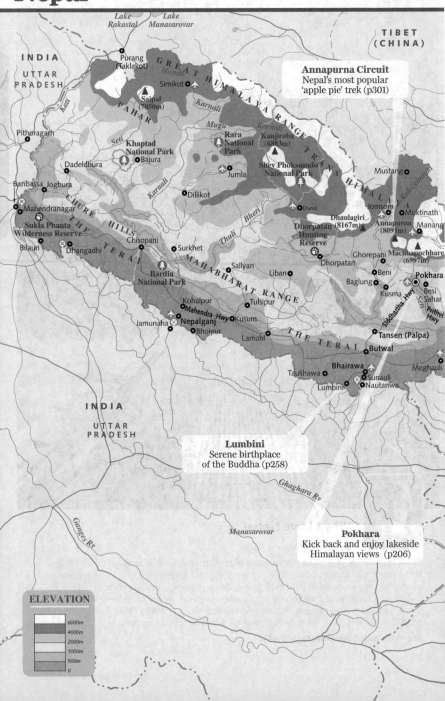

Annapurna Circuit
Nepal's most popular 'apple pie' trek (p301)

Lumbini
Serene birthplace of the Buddha (p258)

Pokhara
Kick back and enjoy lakeside Himalayan views (p206)

ELEVATION

6000m
4000m
2000m
1000m
500m
0

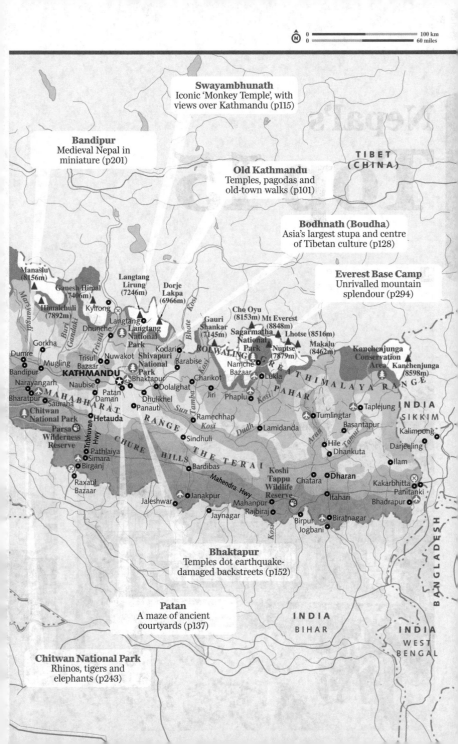

Swayambhunath
Iconic 'Monkey Temple', with
views over Kathmandu (p115)

Bandipur
Medieval Nepal in
miniature (p201)

Old Kathmandu
Temples, pagodas and
old-town walks (p101)

Bodhnath (Boudha)
Asia's largest stupa and centre
of Tibetan culture (p128)

Everest Base Camp
Unrivalled mountain
splendour (p294)

Bhaktapur
Temples dot earthquake-
damaged backstreets (p152)

Patan
A maze of ancient
courtyards (p137)

Chitwan National Park
Rhinos, tigers and
elephants (p243)

Nepal's
Top 15

Old Kathmandu

1 Even after suffering damage in the 2015 earthquake, the historic centre of old Kathmandu (p65) remains an open-air architectural museum of magnificent medieval temples, pagodas, pavilions and shrines. Once occupied by Nepal's cloistered royal family and still home to the Kumari, Kathmandu's very own living goddess, Durbar Sq (pictured below left) is the gateway to a maze of medieval streets that burst even more vividly to life during spectacular festivals. For an introduction to old Kathmandu, follow our walking tours through the hidden backstreet courtyards and temples of the surrounding warren-like old town.

Everest Base Camp Trek

2 Topping many people's travel bucket list is this two-week-long trek (p294) to the base of the world's highest, and most hyped, mountain. Despite only limited views of Mount Everest itself, the surrounding Himalayan peaks are truly awesome, and the half-hour you spend watching the alpenglow ascend beautiful Pumori or Ama Dablam (pictured below right) is worth all the altitude headaches you will likely suffer. The crowds can be thick in October, but the welcome at the Sherpa lodges is as warm as their fresh apple pie.

ANANDART/SHUTTERSTOCK ©

HEATH HOLDEN/GETTY IMAGES ©

LAURA GRIER/GETTY IMAGES ©

JAN COBB PHOTOGRAPHY LTD/GETTY IMAGES ©

Bodhnath Stupa

3 The village of Bodhnath is the centre of Nepal's exiled Tibetan community and home to Asia's largest stupa (p128), a spectacular white dome and spire that draws Buddhist pilgrims from hundreds of kilo-metres away. Equally fascinating are the surrounding streets, bustling with monks with shaved heads and maroon robes, and lined with Tibetan monasteries and shops selling prayer wheels and juniper incense. Come at dusk and join the Tibetan pilgrims as they light butter lamps and walk around the stupa on their daily *kora* (ritual circumambulation).

Bhaktapur

4 Of the three former city-states that jostled for power over the Kathmandu Valley, medieval Bhaktapur (p152) is the most atmospheric. Despite damage in the 2015 quake, its backstreets still burst with temples and pagodas, including the Nyatapola Temple, Nepal's tallest. Winding lanes lined with red-brick buildings lead onto squares used by locals for drying corn and making pottery – this is no museum but a living, breathing town where residents live their lives in public. Stay overnight in a guesthouse or attend one of the city's fantastic festivals. Above: Golden Gate (p156)

Swayambhunath

5 The iconic white-washed stupa of Swayambhunath (p117) is both a Unesco World Heritage Site and one of Nepal's most sacred Buddhist shrines. The great stupa – painted with iconic, all-seeing Buddha eyes – survived the 2015 quake with only minor damage and it remains a focal point for Buddhist devotion. Pilgrims wander the shrines, spinning prayer wheels and murmuring mantras, while nearby astrologers read palms, and shopkeepers sell magic amulets and sacred beads. Come at dusk for spectacular views over the city lights of Kathmandu.

Annapurna Circuit Trek

6 This trek around the 8091m Annapurna massif is Nepal's most popular trek (p301), and it's easy to see why. The lodges are comfortable, there is little earthquake damage, the crossing of the 5416m Thorung La (pictured right) provides a physical challenge and the sense of journey from lowland Nepal to Trans-Himalayan plateau is immensely satisfying. Our best tip is to take your time and explore the spectacular side trips, particularly around Manang. Road construction has eaten away at either end of the trek but alternative footpaths continue to avoid the road.

Chitwan National Park

7 In the 'other Nepal', down in the humid plains, Chitwan (p243) is one of Asia's best wildlife-viewing spots and the place to don your safari togs and head into the dawn mist in search of rhinos and tigers. There's plenty to keep you busy here, from scanning the forest for critters to visiting local Tharu villages, and the brave can even take a guided walk through the jungle, surrounded by the hoots and roars of the forest. If you are lucky, you'll see gharial, spotted deer and wild gaurs, plus plenty of exotic birds. Above: Rhinos in Chitwan National Park

Views from Pokhara

8 Nepal's second-biggest tourist town may lack the historical depth of Kathmandu, but it more than makes up for this with a seductively laid-back vibe and one of the country's most spectacular locations. The dawn views of Machhapuchhare and Annapurna, mirrored in the calm waters of Phewa Tal (pictured above; p208), or seen from the town's hilltop viewpoints, are simply unforgettable. Take them in on a trek, from the saddle of a mountain bike or, best of all, dangling from a paraglider high above the valley floor.

SUBBOTSKY/GETTY IMAGES ©

PETER STUCKINGS/GETTY IMAGES ©

Langtang Valley

9 Nepal's third great teahouse trek is nestled in a lovely Alpine Valley next to the Tibet border. Combing lush bamboo and Himalayan forest with high peaks, pastures and glaciers, Langtang (p310) offers incredible variety, especially if you add on a side trek to the holy Gosainkund lakes, set in a mountain bowl at 4400m. Langtang suffered greatly in the 2015 earthquake but the lodges have been rebuilt, the trails improved and the trek is open for business. The nearby newly opened border with Tibet offers a superb new overland add-on.

Lumbini – Birthplace of the Buddha

10 A pilgrimage to the Maya Devi Temple (pictured; p258), Buddha's birthplace, ranks as one of the subcontinent's great spiritual journeys. You can visit the exact spot where Siddhartha Gautama was born 2500 years ago, rediscovered only a century or so ago, and then tour a multitude of temples. But perhaps the most powerful thing to do is simply find a quiet spot, and a book on Buddhism, and meditate on the nature of existence. Travel experiences don't get much more profound than this.

Momos

11 These little meat- or vegetable-filled dumplings are Nepal's unofficial national dish. Enjoy them in a grandiose Newari restaurant, at a shared table in a backstreet Tibetan kitchen such as Yangling Tibetan Restaurant (p103), or in a trekking lodge overlooking the Annapurnas – they are the quintessential taste of the Himalaya. Join a cooking class to learn how to make these deceptively simple morsels that are savoured from China to Central Asia. Kathmandu's restaurants also fill them with apple and cinnamon, and serve them with ice cream. Yum!

Bandipur

12 Halfway between Kathmandu and Pokhara is this perfectly preserved ridgetop village (p201) of traditional 18th-century Newari houses and temples. Apart from just enjoying the peace and quiet, there are some fine walks to be had in the surrounding hills, while adventurous types can arrange to abseil into the Siddha Gufa cave, paraglide over the village or go canyoning in nearby waterfalls. At the end of the day several well-run guesthouses offer atmospheric accommodation in restored Newari mansions.

Nepal's Fantastic Festivals

13 Nepal has so many spectacular festivals that any visit is almost certain to coincide with at least one. Celebrations range from masked dances designed to exorcise unruly demons to epic bouts of tug-of-war between rival sides of a town. For a full-on medieval experience, time your travel with one of the slightly mad chariot processions, such as the parade of Rato Machhendranath (p145), when hundreds of enthusiastic devotees drag tottering 20m-tall chariots through the crowded city streets of Kathmandu and Patan.
Above: Holi festival (p22)

Patan

14 Kathmandu's sister city (p137) doesn't get the attention it deserves. The city of Newari traders, interconnected Buddhist courtyards and hidden temples has a greater cultural cohesion than any other city in Nepal. Wander the fascinating backstreets, the magnificent Durbar Sq and the Patan Museum, the best museum in the country, plus ancient Ashoka-era stupas and the valley's best collection of international restaurants and it's clear you need a couple of trips to take it all in. Spend the night here and you'll have the backstreets to yourself.

White-Water Rafting

15 Nepal is one of the world's best rafting and kayaking destinations. Fuelled by water rushing down from Himalayan peaks, rivers such as the Trisuli and Bhote Kosi promise thrilling white water for day trippers. Even better are the multiday adventures – liquid journeys that take you down the Karnali, Tamur and Sun Kosi rivers through some of Nepal's remotest corners. Companies such as Ultimate Descents Nepal (p48) offer everything from roller-coaster white water trips to serene floats through jungle wilderness.

ALEKSANDAR TODOROVIC/SHUTTERSTOCK ©

ALEX TREADWAY/GETTY IMAGES ©

Need to Know

For more information, see Survival Guide (p373)

Currency
Nepali rupee (Rs)

Language
Nepali

Visas
Tourist visas (15-, 30- and 90-day) are available on arrival; fill in your details online beforehand or on the spot, and bring cash in US dollars.

Money
It's easy to change cash and access ATMs in Kathmandu, Pokhara and other cities, but almost impossible in rural areas or on treks.

Mobile Phones
Buy SIM cards at Kathmandu airport on arrival or at Nepal Telecom (Namaste) or Ncell outlets across the country.

Time
Nepal Standard Time (GMT/UTC plus 5¾ hours)

When to Go

- Subtropical warm winters, hot wet summers
- Cool winters, warm wet summers
- High altitude freezing winters, cool summers

Jomsom
GO Jun–Nov

Everest Base Camp
GO Mar–May
Oct–Nov

Pokhara
GO Oct–Apr

Chitwan
National Park
GO Oct–Mar

Kathmandu
GO Sep–Apr

High Season
(Oct–Nov)

➡ Clear skies and warm days make autumn the peak season.

➡ Thousands of people hit the trails in the Everest and Annapurna regions.

➡ Accommodation in Kathmandu gets booked up and prices peak.

Shoulder
(Mar–Apr)

➡ The second-best time to visit and trek; spring brings warm weather and spectacular rhododendron blooms.

Low Season
(Jun–Sep)

➡ The monsoon rains (mostly at night) bring landslides, and clouds often obscure mountain views.

➡ Rain, mud and leeches deter most trekkers.

➡ Hefty hotel discounts are common.

Useful Websites

Nepal Tourism Board (www.welcomenepal.com) Government site.

Visit Nepal (www.visitnepal.com) Comprehensive private website with detailed travel tips.

Lonely Planet (www.lonelyplanet.com/nepal) Hotel bookings, traveller forum and more.

Inside Himalayas (www.insidehimalayas.com) Online magazine and blog devoted to travel in Nepal.

kimkim (www.kimkim.com) Booking platform that has lots of good background articles on Nepal.

Important Numbers

Nepal's Country code	☑977
International access code	☑00
Police	☑100
Tourist police	☑01-4247041
Ambulance	☑102

Exchange Rates

Australia	A$1	Rs 83
Canada	C$1	Rs 88
China	Y1	Rs 16
Euro zone	€1	Rs 124
India	₹1	Rs 1.60
Japan	¥100	Rs 80
New Zealand	NZ$1	Rs76
UK	£1	Rs 158
USA	US$1	Rs 102

For current exchange rates see www.xe.com.

Daily Costs

Budget: Less than US$50

➡ Dorm bed in a hostel: US$10

➡ Budget hotel room in Kathmandu: US$15–25

➡ Room, dinner and breakfast in a trekking lodge: US$12–15

➡ Trekking porter/guide: US$17/25 per day

Midrange: US$50–150

➡ Organised camping trek: US$60–80 per person per day

➡ Midrange meal in Kathmandu: US$7–10

➡ Midrange hotel: US$25–80

Top End: More than US$150

➡ Top-end hotel in Kathmandu or lodge in Chitwan: US$150–250

➡ Mountain flight: US$199

➡ Private car hire with driver: US$80 per day

➡ Mustang trekking permit: US$500 for 10 days

Opening Hours

Business hours are year-round for banks and most offices. Many places in the mountains keep slightly longer summer hours and shorter winter hours.

Banks 9am–noon and 2–4pm Sunday to Friday, 10am–noon Saturday

Bars and clubs Usually close by midnight or 1am, even in Kathmandu

Museums generally 10.30am–4.30pm, often closed Tuesday

Restaurants 8am–10pm

Shops 10am–8pm (varies widely, some closed Saturday)

Arriving in Nepal

Tribhuvan International Airport (Kathmandu) Prepaid taxis are available inside the terminal. Many midrange hotels offer free pick-ups from the airport. Long queues at immigration can slow things up if you are getting your visa on arrival.

Sunauli (Indian border) For Kathmandu and Pokhara, take a direct bus from the border. Golden Travels offers the most comfortable service. For other destinations, take a jeep or rickshaw to nearby Bhairawa and change there.

Getting Around

Transport in Nepal is reasonably priced and accessible. Roads are often narrow, overcrowded and poorly maintained and delays should be expected. Sadly, air disasters and bus crashes are not uncommon.

Air Flights to/from major centres are efficient, whereas mountain flights to trailheads are highly weather-dependent and frequently delayed.

Bus Tourist-class buses are comfortable, usually air-conditioned, and relatively safe and reliable. Micro or minibuses are quick but usually overcrowded, and local buses are, without exception, uncomfortable, crowded and slow.

For much more on **getting around**, see p389

What's New

Post-Earthquake Recovery

Nepal is definitely open for business, from trekking trails to architectural sites. You'll still see damage in places like Kathmandu's Durbar Sq, Nuwakot and Bhaktapur, but reconstruction is well under way and the country needs your business like never before.

Langtang Valley

After suffering great damage in the 2015 earthquake, the Langtang trekking route is back. Trekking lodges have been rebuilt, the valley is as gorgeous as ever and the new border with Tibet is open at nearby Rasuwagadhi.

Kathmandu's Durbar Square

The 2015 earthquake toppled several temples in this royal square, but most temples remain standing and reconstruction has started, notably on the towers of Hanuman Dhoka palace.

Annapurna Roads

Four-wheel-drive tracks continue to inch around the Annapurna Circuit, shrinking the famous trekking route. Trekkers now generally start in Chame or Dharapani, and a dirt road now reaches as far as Manang.

Traffic-Free Thamel

A partially pedestrianised Thamel has made walking Kathmandu's main tourist district much more pleasant. We have seen the scheme come and go before, so hopefully it will continue.

Elephant Welfare in Chitwan

In 2017 Tiger Tops announced it was ending its elephant-back safaris in Chitwan due to animal welfare concerns, and many international agents no longer offer elephant safaris. More local companies will likely follow, offering foot safaris instead.

Five-Star Thamel

A rash of new five-star hotels are opening on the edge of Thamel, from the Sheraton Kathmandu and Aloft Kathmandu to the already opened Fairfield Marriott. How far the once-budget-conscious Thamel has come...

International Airports

Airports in Bhairawa (near Lumbini), and eventually Nijgadh in central Nepal and Pokhara, are due to start regional international flights over the next couple of years, opening up some potentially useful air connections with India.

Terrible Roads

The construction of a water pipeline from Melamchi to Kathmandu through the Kathmandu Valley has left roads in both the city and valley in a terrible state. The roads to Bodhnath, Sankhu and Langtang are particularly bad and will remain so for a year or two at least.

Reliable Electricity

Kathmandu's infamous 'load shedding' (power cuts) are finally a thing of the past and electricity supplies are now pretty constant. On the down side, new hydro projects are impacting rafting routes and the environment across the country.

For more recommendations and reviews, see lonelyplanet.com/nepal.

If You Like...

Temples

Nepal's Hindu and Buddhist temples are masterworks in oiled brick, stone and carved wood. Colossal statuary, intricately ornate *toranas* (lintels) and erotic carvings still inspire the desired amount of wonder.

Kathmandu's old town Backstreet temples, local gods and half-hidden stupas make Kathmandu's old town our favourite place for a early-morning walk. (p65)

Bhaktapur Still impressive despite some earthquake damage, this medieval town features the country's tallest temple, a royal palace and even some carved elephant erotica. (p152)

Golden Temple, Patan This 15th-century courtyard is centred on a beautiful Buddha statue and displays fine Tibetan frescoes. (p143)

Changu Narayan Temple Earthquake-damaged but still standing, this World Heritage Site is a treasure house of Himalayan art, including 1500-year-old Licchavi statues and carvings. (p168)

Swayambhunath Monkeys swarm around this glorious gold-topped stupa, which rises like a beacon over Kathmandu (p117)

Trekking

In Nepal you can trek for days through the most incredible mountain scenery, safe in the knowledge that you'll find a hot dinner and a place to stay at the end of each day.

Everest Region Some of the world's most astounding high mountain scenery combined with cosy Sherpa lodges, but try to visit outside of October. (p294)

Annapurna Circuit Nepal's most popular trek offers lots of variety – Tibetan-style villages, Hindu temples, glacier views and a 5500m pass. (p301)

Annapurna Sanctuary A direct trek past Gurung villages and bamboo groves straight into the frozen heart of the Himalaya. (p307)

Langtang Alpine pastures, 7000m peaks, high mountain lakes and epic Himalayan panoramas make this a great option. (p310)

Around Pokhara For treks that take less than a week but still get you into the hills for spectacular mountain views. (p227)

Villages & Day Hikes

Nepal's mountains and valleys are laced with a network of footpaths travelled for centuries by traders and pilgrims. Ready your daypack for a brief encounter of rural Nepali life.

Tansen Follow ancient trade routes, visit a potters' village and explore the eerie ruins of a riverside palace. (p268)

Jomsom Use this hub as a base to visit fabulous nearby Trans-Himalayan villages like Kagbeni and Marpha. (p234)

Bandipur Base yourself in comfortable digs at this charming medieval village and day hike out to temples, viewpoints and caves. (p201)

Pokhara There are loads of options here, including Phewa Tal, Sarangkot and the Peace Pagoda, all offering superb views. (p206)

Chitwan & Bardia National Parks While visiting these parks, explore a Tharu village and experience a stick dance. (p243)

Wildlife Watching

Nepal's subtropical plains host an array of wildlife worthy of *The Jungle Book*. Tiger enthusiasts should visit between March and June and bring their own binoculars.

Chitwan National Park Spot rhinos, gharial (crocodiles) and maybe one of the park's majestic Bengal tigers lurking in the elephant grass. (p243)

Bardia National Park Track wildlife by 4WD, raft or foot, well away from the crowds in Nepal's far west. (p272)

Koshi Tappu Wildlife Reserve A birdwatcher's paradise with 450 species, best spotted from guided canoe trips on the Sapt Kosi. (p283)

Sagarmatha National Park Look for Himalayan tahr (wild mountain goats), yaks and maybe even a yeti in this World Heritage Site in the Everest region. (p294)

Sukla Phanta National Park An uncrowded reserve in Nepal's far west that features birdwatching and more. (p276)

Adrenaline Rushes

Nepal is the ultimate outdoor-sports destination. From climbing and mountaineering to mountain biking and ziplining, Nepal does it all – and at a fraction of the cost of other countries.

Paragliding Ride the thermals over Pokhara, relishing the incredible views of Phewa Tal and the Annapurna mountains. (p213)

Rafting Anything from a whitewater rush on the raging Bhote Kosi to a weeklong expedition on the Sun Kosi. (p326)

Canyoning Abseil down and through a series of rushing waterfalls and pools near the Tibetan border. (p193)

Bungee jumping Follow Asia's highest bungee jump with a giant Tarzan-style swing. (p193)

Climbing a trekking peak Learn the basics of ropework and crampons before summiting a 6000m Himalayan peak. (p300)

Top: Sadhu (wandering Hindu holy man) at Pashupatinath Temple (p124), Kathmandu
Bottom: Valley around Muktinath

Ziplining Brave the world's fastest zipline rushing beneath the Annapurna peaks. (p211)

The Sacred & the Spiritual

The fascinating blend of Indian Hinduism and Tibetan Buddhism is one of Nepal's great draws. From holy lakes to marigold-laden crossroad shrines, the sacred imbues every aspect of Nepali life.

Lumbini Explore Buddhist architecture from across Asia and gaze upon the birthplace of the Buddha. (p258)

Bodhnath Light a butter lamp at the subcontinent's largest stupa, the focal point of Nepal's Tibetan community. (p128)

Kopan Monastery One of the best places in Asia to learn about Tibetan Buddhism and meditation, or to take a short retreat. (p134)

Kathmandu & Pokhara Both good places to practise and learn yoga, with classes lasting from an hour to a week. (p85)

Pashupatinath Nepal's holiest Hindu shrine, beside the cremation ghats of the sacred Bagmati River, draws holy men from across the subcontinent. (p156)

Devghat Join Hindu pilgrims at the auspicious confluence of two mighty rivers. (p242)

Getting Off the Beaten Track

It's not that hard to find a relatively little-visited corner of Nepal. You'll likely have the following towns all to yourself, especially if

you visit outside October/ November.

Budhanilkantha A monumental Vishnu statue reclines on the valley fringe, close to Kathmandu but far from the madding crowds. (p134)

Panauti Overnight at this sacred confluence to visit the many temples and shrines at dawn and dusk. (p188)

Kirtipur Just beyond the Ring Rd, with brick-lined backstreets, good Newari food and a Bhairab temple bristling with swords. (p172)

Pharping A miniature Tibet in the southern valley and a magnet for Tibetan pilgrims; continue to Dakshinkali to see Tantric Hinduism at its most visceral and gory. (p174)

Ilam Darjeeling's quiet younger brother offers strolls through cultivated tea estates and some adventurous DIY trips. (p288)

Himalayan Views

Majestic mountain panoramas are not hard to come by in Nepal. That said, the following stand out for their awe-inspiring views. Come at dawn for a spectacular light show.

Nagarkot The best place close to Kathmandu from which to get Himalayan views from your hotel bed. (p180)

Sarangkot Machhapuchhare, Dhaulagiri and the Annapurnas dominate this viewpoint that's easily accessed from Pokhara. (p227)

Mountain flight Pray for clear weather on this dawn flight along the spine of the Himalaya, or get more personal on an ultralight flight from Pokhara. (p87)

Kala Pattar Breathless views of Everest and the Khumbu Glacier from 5545m on the Everest Base Camp trek. (p298)

Poon Hill Take a short trek from Pokhara right into the lair of the mountain gods for a stunning but popular sunrise. (p309)

Daman Earthquake-shaken but still offering Nepal's widest mountain panorama, revealing a 300km-long chain of peaks from the Annapurnas to Everest. (p269)

A Life of Luxury

There's no need to rough it in Nepal. Top-end accommodation includes luxury jungle lodges, converted traditional mansions and wonderful rural retreats, all offering organic food and spa treatments.

Dwarika's Kathmandu's most romantic hotel is all oiled brick and carved wood, linked by lovely traditional pools. (p99)

Chitwan & Bardia National Parks Both parks have lavish jungle tourism lodges run by Tiger Tops, the pioneers of luxury jungle travel. (p252)

Top-end trekking Prefer your hiking days to end with a cosy lodge and cocktails rather than a campsite latrine? Several companies offer luxury lodges in the Everest and Annapurna regions. (p294)

Tiger Mountain Pokhara Lodge An eco-friendly tourism pioneer with snowy Himalayan peaks reflected in a luxe swimming pool. (p220)

Dwarika's Resort Dhulikhel A Vedic and Buddhist wellbeing spa on the valley fringe with views to die for. (p187)

Month by Month

February

The end of winter is an especially good time for a low-altitude trek or to visit the national parks of the Terai without the crowds. Pokhara is warmer than chilly Kathmandu.

🎊 Losar

Tibetan peoples from Dolpo to the Khumbu celebrate their New Year with parades, pujas (religious offerings or prayers) and prayer flags. Find celebrations in the Kathmandu Valley at Bodhnath, Swayambhunath and Jawalakhel, near Patan.

🎊 Maha Shivaratri

Shiva's birthday heralds festivities at all Shiva temples, but particularly at Pashupatinath, and hundreds of sadhus flock here from all over Nepal and India. The crowds bathing in the Bagmati's holy waters are a colourful sight. (p124)

March

The trekking season kicks in as the days get warmer. The trails are less crowded in spring than in autumn, but cloud is more likely to roll in and obscure the views.

🎊 Holi

Known as the Festival of Colours, when coloured powder and water are riotously dispensed as a reminder of the cooling monsoon days to come. Foreigners get special attention, so keep your camera protected and wear old clothes. Can be in February.

🎊 Seto Machhendranath

Kicking off in the wake of the sacrificial festival of Chaitra Dasain, crowds drag an image of Seto Machhendranath from its temple at Kel Tole in Kathmandu on a towering, tottering *rath* (chariot) through the backstreets of the old town for four days. (p78)

April

It's getting uncomfortably hot in the lowlands and Terai, but the rhododendrons are in full technicolour bloom at higher elevations, making this the third-most-popular month for trekking.

🎊 Bisket Jatra

Nepalis celebrate their New Year as huge crowds drag tottering chariots through the winding backstreets of Bhaktapur, pausing for a quick tug-of-war. (p161)

🎊 Balkumari Jatra

Thimi celebrates New Year by hosting palanquins from 32 nearby villages at the town's Balkumari Temple for three days of festivities. Nearby Bode holds a grisly tongue-piercing ceremony at the same time. (p167)

🎊 Balaju Jatra

Thousands of pilgrims keep an all-night vigil at the Swayambhunath temple during the full moon of Baisakh. The following day they trek to the Baise Dhara (22 waterspouts) at Balaju for a ritual bath. (p117)

May

The dusty run-up to the monsoon pushes the mercury over 30°C (86°F) in the Terai and Kathmandu Valley, and the coming rains hang over the country like a threat. This is the key month for Everest expeditions and a good time to spot tigers.

✸ Rato Machhendranath

Patan's biggest festival involves the spectacular month-long procession of a temple chariot, culminating in the showing of the sacred vest of the god Machhendranath. (p147)

✸ Buddha Jayanti

A full-moon fair at Lumbini marks the Buddha's birth, enlightenment and passing into nirvana, and there are celebrations in Swayambhunath, Bodhnath and Patan. Swayambhunath displays a collection of rare thangkas (Tibetan religious paintings) for one day only. (p258)

August

The monsoon rains lash Nepal from mid-June to September, bringing swollen rivers, muddy trails, landslides and leeches. Tourist levels are at a low, though high Trans-Himalayan valleys such as Mustang and upper Dolpo enjoy perfect weather.

✸ Ghanta Karna

This festival celebrates the destruction of the demon 'bell ears' when a god, disguised as a frog, lured him into a deep well. Ghanta Karna is burnt in effigy on this night throughout Newari villages to cleanse evil from the land.

✸ Naga Panchami

On this day, nagas (serpent deities) are honoured all over the country for their

magical powers over the monsoon rains. Protective pictures of the nagas are hung over doorways of houses, and food is put out for snakes in Bhaktapur. (p164)

✸ Janai Purnima

On the full moon, high-caste men (Chhetri and Brahmin) change the *janai* (sacred thread), which they wear looped over their left shoulder. Janai Purnima also brings Hindu pilgrims to sacred Gosainkund lakes and the Kumbeshwar Temple in Patan. (p317)

✸ Gai Jatra

Newars believe that, after death, cows will guide them to Yama, the god of the underworld, and this 'Cow Festival' is dedicated to those who died during the preceding year. Cows are led through towns and small boys dress up as cows (especially in Bhaktapur).

✸ Krishna Jayanta (Krishna's Birthday)

The birthday (also known as Krishnasthami) of the popular Hindu god Krishna is celebrated with an all-night vigil at the Krishna Mandir in Patan. Oil lamps light the temple and singing continues through the night. (p139)

✸ Teej

The Festival of Women starts with a sumptuous meal and party; at midnight, women commence a 24-hour fast. On the second day women dress in their red wedding saris and head to Shiva temples across the country to pray for a happy marriage.

September

The end of the monsoon brings unpredictable weather but temperatures remain warm, and the land is lush and green. High water levels make for especially exciting rafting.

✸ Indra Jatra

This colourful autumn festival combines homage to Indra with an annual appearance by Kathmandu's Kumari (living goddess), who parades through the streets of the old town in a palanquin. It also marks the end of the monsoon. (p88)

October

Crystal-clear Himalayan views and comfortable temperatures means peak season and competition for airline seats, hotels and trekking lodges, so book ahead. The Dasain festival brings disruptions to some services for a week or more.

✸ Pachali Bhairab Jatra

The fearsome form of Bhairab, Pachali Bhairab, is honoured on the fourth day of the bright fortnight in early October or September. Bhairab's bloodthirsty nature means that there are numerous animal sacrifices.

✸ Dasain

Nepal's biggest festival lasts for 15 days. It celebrates the victory of the goddess Durga over the forces of evil (personified by the buffalo demon

Mahisa-sura). Across the country hundreds of thousands of animals are sacrificed and bamboo swings are erected at the entrances to villages.

🎊 Fulpati (Phulpati)

Fulpati ('Sacred Flowers') is the first really important day of Dasain. A jar of flowers symbolising the goddess Taleju is carried from Gorkha to Kathmandu and presented to the president at the Tundikhel before being transported on a palanquin to Durbar Sq.

🎊 Maha Astami

The 'Great Eighth Day' and Kala Ratri, the 'Black Night', mark the start of the sacrifices to Durga. At midnight, in a temple courtyard near Kathmandu's Durbar Sq, eight buffaloes and 108 goats are beheaded, each with a single stroke of a blade.

🎊 Navami

The sacrifices continue on Kathmandu's Kot Sq the next day; it's a fascinating and gruesome spectacle that certainly won't appeal to all. Blood is sprinkled on the wheels of cars (and Nepal Airlines' aircraft) and goat is on almost everyone's menu.

🎊 Vijaya Dashami

The 10th day of Dasain is a family affair: cards and greetings are exchanged and parents place a *tika* (sandalwood-paste spot) on their children's foreheads, while evening processions and masked dances celebrate the victory of Lord Rama over the demon-king Ravana in the Ramayana.

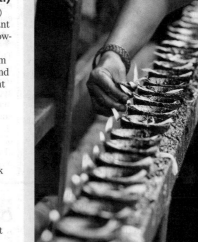

OCEANFISHING/GETTY IMAGES ©

IGNACIO PALACIOS/GETTY IMAGES ©

Top: Butter lamps

Bottom: Masked performers at the Royal Palace (p140), Patan

✨ Kartika Purnima

The full-moon day in September/October marks the end of Dasain. It is celebrated with gambling in many households: you will see even small children avidly putting a few coins down on various local games of chance.

✨ Tihar

Tihar (also called Diwali or Deepawali on the third day of celebrations) is the second-most-important Hindu festival in Nepal. The festival honours certain animals, starting with offerings of rice to the crows ('messengers of death' sent by the god Yama), followed by dogs (who guide departed souls across the river of the dead), cows and bullocks on consecutive days.

✨ Deepawali (Festival of Lights)

The third day of Tihar is when Lakshmi, the goddess of wealth, comes to visit every home that has been suitably lit for her presence. No one likes to turn down a visit from the goddess of wealth and so homes are brightly lit with candles and lamps.

✨ Newari New Year

The fourth day of Tihar is also the start of the New Year for the Newari people of the Kathmandu Valley. The following day marks Bhai Tika, when brothers and sisters meet to offer gifts of sweets and money and place *tikas* on each other's foreheads.

✨ Haribodhini Ekadashi

On the 11th day after the new moon the god Vishnu awakens from his four-month monsoonal slumber. The best place to see the festivities is at the temple of the Sleeping Vishnu in Budhanilkantha. (p134)

November

The continued good weather makes this the second-most-popular month to visit Nepal; conditions are perfect for outdoor activities and trekking, though tourist numbers start to drop off at the end of the month.

☆ Kartik Dances

Patan's Durbar Sq fills with music and dancers for this festival that traces its origins back to human sacrifices during the 17th-century rule of King Siddhinarsingh Malla. Dancers wear masks to represent the god Narsingha and demon Hiranyakashipu. Can fall in late October.

✨ Mani Rimdu

This popular Sherpa festival takes place at Tengboche Monastery in the Solu Khumbu region and features masked dances and dramas. Another Mani Rimdu festival takes place six months later at nearby Thame Gompa.

December

Winter brings chilly nights to Kathmandu, and morning mist sometimes delays flight schedules. Snowfall can close passes on high trekking routes, while visiting Everest Base Camp can be a real feat of endurance.

✨ Bala Chaturdashi

On the new-moon day in late November or early December, pilgrims flock to Pashupatinath, burning oil lamps at night, scattering grain for the dead and bathing in the holy Bagmati River. (p127)

✨ Sita Bibaha Panchami

Tens of thousands of pilgrims from all over the subcontinent flock to Janakpur (the birthplace of Sita) to celebrate the marriage of Sita to Rama. The wedding is re-enacted with a procession carrying Rama's image to Sita's temple by elephant. (p279)

☆ Pokhara Street Festival

Around half a million visitors flock to Pokhara to enjoy street food, parades and cultural performances in the run-up to New Year's Day. Book your accommodation well in advance.

For more information on Nepali holidays and festivals see Nepali Calendars (p381).

Itineraries

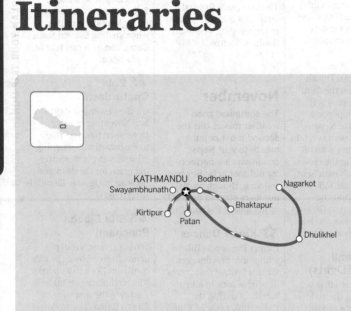

KATHMANDU Bodhnath
Swayambhunath
Kirtipur
Patan
Bhaktapur
Nagarkot
Dhulikhel

1 WEEK The Kathmandu Valley

A week gives you time to see the great cultural highlights of the Kathmandu Valley, including no fewer than six Unesco World Heritage Sites. Start off in **Kathmandu** with our walking tour south from Thamel to the stunning medieval temples and palaces of Durbar Sq. On day two, walk to the towering stupa of **Swayambhunath** and the under-appreciated National Museum. You can fill the afternoon with a walk around the famous stupa at the Tibetan centre of **Bodhnath**.

Make time for a day trip to **Patan** for its spectacular Durbar Sq and Patan Museum, combined with another great backstreet walking tour and dinner at one of the many great restaurants in Jawalakhel. Complete the trilogy of former royal kingdoms with a full-day visit to **Bhaktapur**, ideally with an overnight stay.

Next get your Himalayan kick with dawn mountain views at **Nagarkot** or **Dhulikhel** before returning to Kathmandu on foot or mountain bike via the earthquake-damaged temple at Changu Narayan. Fill another day by visiting **Kirtipur** and neighbouring towns in the southern valley. On your last day, take time for some serious shopping in Kathmandu or the fair-trade shops of Patan.

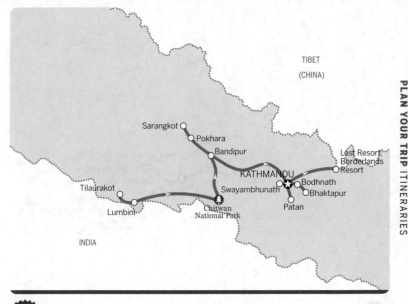

TIBET
(CHINA)

Sarangkot
Pokhara
Bandipur

Last Resort;
Borderlands
Resort

KATHMANDU

Tilaurakot
Swayambhunath
Bodhnath
Bhaktapur

Lumbini
Chitwan
National Park
Patan

INDIA

2 WEEKS — From Buddha to Boudha

Mixing contemplative temple tours with a healthy dose of wilderness and adventure, this 500km route across Nepal is one part meditation mixed with two parts adrenaline.

Kick off at **Lumbini**, the birthplace of the Buddha, 20km from the border crossing with India at Sunauli, or a short flight from Kathmandu. Take your time exploring this world map of Buddhist temples, then spend the next day at the little-visited archaeological site of **Tilaurakot**, where the Buddha once ruled as a pampered prince.

From Lumbini, make a beeline for **Chitwan National Park**, budgeting two or three days to allow dawn and dusk safaris among the tigers and gharial.

From Chitwan take the day-long tourist bus to **Pokhara** for your first proper peek at the mountains. After enjoying the shops and cocktail bars of Lakeside, savour the views of Machhapuchhare from the World Peace Pagoda or lofty **Sarangkot**, or glide past the peaks at eye-level on a tandem paraglide.

Another long bus trip will take you to **Kathmandu**, where you can fill up three or four days with the pick of the Kathmandu Valley itinerary. If you want to break the trip, consider a detour to the charming and historic hill town of **Bandipur**.

Once in the valley, make time to explore the backstreets of **Bhaktapur** on our walking tour, gain a deeper understanding of Buddhist art at **Patan Museum** and enjoy the views over the city at dusk from **Swayambhunath**. To escape Kathmandu's traffic and pollution, consider basing yourself in Bodhnath, Bhaktapur or Patan.

There should just be time for a two-day rafting, canyoning or bungee adrenaline rush near the Tibetan border at the **Last Resort** or **Borderlands Resort**, both a half-day drive from the capital.

On your last day, give thanks for a head-spinning trip at **Bodhnath**, where you can buy a Buddha statue or a bundle of prayer flags to take home.

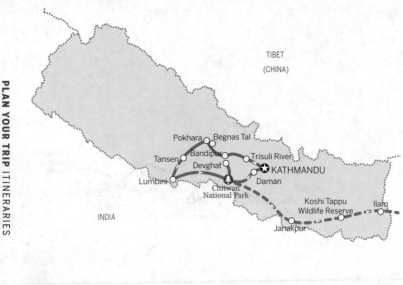

3 WEEKS Once Around the Middle

This off-the-beaten-track, 400km-loop route combines the best of Nepal's seldom-visited Middle Hills and offers lots of opportunities for great day hikes.

Start with a few days visiting the temples and stupas of **Kathmandu**, then book a rafting trip or kayak clinic on the **Trisuli River** en route to Pokhara, staying in one of the riverside adventure camps. Next stop is **Bandipur**, a little-visited gem of a village where you can stroll to eerie caverns and relax among some wonderfully preserved traditional Newari architecture. From here, roll on to **Pokhara** for a row-boat ride around Phew Tal, some good Western food and a quick jaunt across to **Begnas Tal**.

Take the winding Siddhartha Hwy southwest to charming **Tansen**, the base for some great day hikes to nearby temples, villages and viewpoints. Continue south to peaceful **Lumbini**, birthplace of the Buddha, in the sultry Terai plains to rove around the Buddhist monasteries by bicycle.

Having come this far, it would be a shame to miss **Chitwan National Park**. If your budget allows, stay at one of the lodges deep inside the park for the most atmospheric digs. Budget at least one early morning and one late afternoon safari. You might also consider a reflective stroll to the village of **Devghat**, at the sacred confluence of the Trisuli and Kali Gandaki Rivers.

The logical return route to Kathmandu would be to follow the snaking Tribhuvan Hwy north to **Daman**, one of Nepal's most impressive viewpoints, and rise at dawn for a 300km-wide panorama of majestic Himalayan peaks.

Alternatively, if your ultimate destination is India, you could dive off the beaten track, heading east to the temple town of **Janakpur** (aim for the Sita Bibaha Panchami festival in November or December) and then on to **Koshi Tappu Wildlife Reserve** for Nepal's best birdwatching opportunities. Make sure you avoid the monsoon months when much of the area is under floodwater. Continue east to the tranquil tea fields of **Ilam** for some off-map adventure before continuing to the Indian border at Kakarbhitta and the delights of Darjeeling and Sikkim beyond.

4 WEEKS Kathmandu & Everest

With a month to spare, you can explore the Kathmandu Valley and fit in a trek into the mighty Himalaya.

From Kathmandu, fly east to **Lukla** to start the **Everest Base Camp** trek. This is the definitive Himalayan trek, climbing from teahouse to teahouse among neck-craning peaks to the base of the tallest mountain on earth. The trek takes at least two weeks because of the gain in altitude.

With an extra week to play with, consider doing an Everest loop, detouring to the spectacular glaciers and lakes of the **Gokyo Valley** en route to Base Camp for a total trek of 21 days.

Because of the changeable weather in Nepal, it's wise to leave yourself a buffer at the end of the trip in case flights are cancelled. Finish off by exploring the highlights of the Kathmandu Valley itinerary, but do your sightseeing *after* the trek, not before.

After the thrills and chills of the mountains, finish off with a four-day excursion to steamy **Chitwan National Park**, where you can scan the jungle for rhinos and tigers.

3 WEEKS Annapurna Circuit Trek

The most popular alternative to Everest is the Annapurna region. From **Pokhara** (or Kathmandu) take a combination of bus and 4WD to **Dharapani** or Chame to set off on the Annapurna Circuit. The full circuit takes about 17 days, but you can shorten it to 10 days by flying or taking public transport back to Pokhara from Jomsom.

The highlights of the trek are around **Manang**, and it's worth tacking on a few extra days to walk the high route between **Pisang** and the lovely village of **Bragha**. The trek's major physical challenge is crossing the 5416m high pass of **Thorung La**, and it's vital that you acclimatise sufficiently between Manang and the pass.

Muktinath on the other side of the pass is a major Hindu pilgrimage site and there are some fine short walks to the Tibetan-style villages of Jhong and Purang. The medieval village of **Kagbeni** is another highlight, as is the charming village of **Marpha** and nearby Chhairo Gompa.

Back in Pokhara it's worth taking it easy for a couple of days. Get clean clothes, enjoy a hearty yak steak and have a shave and/or head massage at the barber.

Plan Your Trip

Planning Your Trek

Nepal is one of the easiest and most exciting places in the world to trek; nowhere else can you comfortably walk for weeks carrying little more than a day pack. The following classic routes offer a spectacular introduction to trekking in Nepal, but for more routes, see Lonely Planet's Trekking in the Nepal Himalaya.

Best Treks

Most Iconic Trek

Everest Base Camp A minimum two-week trek into the heart of the world's highest mountains, following in the footsteps of mountaineers and Sherpas; 15 days.

Best Mountain Scenery

Everest & Gokyo Lakes Add on a detour to the Gokyo Valley for the most spectacular views in the Everest region; 17 days.

Best Overall Trek

Annapurna Circuit A huge variety of landscapes, charming villages and great lodges make this one of the world's classic walks, despite road construction at either end; from 12 days.

Best Medium Trek

Annapurna Sanctuary A relatively short trek with a powerful punch that leads you into a breathtaking amphitheatre of peaks and glaciers; from 11 days.

Best Trek to Help Earthquake Reconstruction

Langtang Valley A weeklong walk past ever-changing landscapes and newly rebuilt lodges to glorious mountain views, with the option to add on the Gosainkund Lakes; 12 days.

When to Trek

In general the best trekking time is the dry season from October to May; the worst time is the monsoon period from June to September. However, this generalisation doesn't allow for the peculiarities of individual treks.

Several festivals enliven the main trekking trails; in particular, the Mani Rimdu festival in October/November brings particularly colourful masked dances at the Everest region's Tengboche Monastery.

October to November The first two months of the dry season offer the best weather for trekking and the main trails are heaving with trekkers at this time, for good reason. The air is crystal clear, the mountain scenery is superb and the weather is still comfortably warm. Freak winter weather is becoming more frequent in October as global climate patterns change.

December to February Good months for trekking, but the cold can be bitter and dangerous at high altitudes. Getting up to the Everest Base Camp can be a real endurance test, and the Thorung La (Annapurna Circuit) and other high passes are often blocked by snow.

March to April Dry weather and dust means poorer Himalayan views but the compensations are several: fewer crowds, warm weather and spectacular rhododendron blooms. By May it starts to get very hot, dusty and humid at lower altitudes.

June to September Monsoon rains bring landslides, slippery trails and hordes of *jukha* (leeches). Raging rivers often wash away bridges and stretches of trail. Trekking is difficult but still possible and there are hardly any trekkers on the trails. Good for cultural treks and Trans-Himalayan regions like Mustang, Dolpo and around Jomsom.

What Kind of Trek?

There are many different styles of trekking to suit your budget, fitness level and available time. Most independent trekkers plan to sleep and eat in lodges every night and forgo the complications of camping. This is teahouse trekking.

You can carry your own pack and rely on your own navigation skills and research; or you might find it makes sense to hire a local porter to carry your heavy backpack so that you can enjoy walking with only a daypack. A good guide will certainly enhance the trekking experience, though a bad one will just make life more complicated. Most popular trails are not hard to follow in good weather, so you don't strictly need a porter or guide for route-finding alone.

To save time, many people organise a trek through a trekking agency, either in Kathmandu or in their home country. Such organised treks can be simple lodge-to-lodge affairs or extravagant expeditions with the full regalia of porters, guides, portable kitchens, dining tents and even toilet tents.

Trekking is physically demanding. Some preparation is recommended, even for shorter treks. You will need stamina and a certain fitness level to tackle the steep ascents and descents that come with trekking in the world's highest mountain range. It makes sense to start on some kind of fitness program at least a month or two before your trek. That said, Nepal's treks are well within the range of most active people.

On the trail you will begin to realise just how far you are from medical help and the simple comforts that you usually take for granted. For most people isolation is part of the appeal of trekking, but even a twisted ankle or sore knee can become a serious inconvenience if you are several days away from help and your companions need to keep moving.

In October 2014, over 50 trekkers and guides were killed in the Thorung La region after a blizzard descended on the area. In the wake of the tragedy there were calls to make trekking with a guide compulsory, but this is up in the air following the 2015 earthquake. Trekking regulations could change at any time, so check the current situation when planning your trek.

Independent Trekking

Independent trekking does not mean solo trekking; in fact we advise trekkers never to walk alone. It simply means that you are not part of an organised tour. The main trekking trails have accommodation and food along their entire length, often every hour or two, so there's no need to pack a tent, stove or mat.

There are many factors that will influence how much you spend on an independent trek. Accommodation in simple plywood double rooms generally costs between Rs 200 and Rs 500 per room. A simple, filling meal of daal bhaat (rice, lentils and vegetables) costs around Rs 250 at the start of the trek but can rise to Rs 700 just before a high pass. You can double your bill by having a cold beer or slice of apple pie at the end of a long hiking day. A reasonable daily budget in the Annapurna and Everest regions is US$20 per person per day, which should cover the occasional luxury but not a guide or porter. Add on another few dollars for wi-fi access and the occasional hot shower. You can sometimes negotiate a cheaper room if you promise to eat your meals at your lodge.

The bulk of your expenses will be for food. Menu prices are standardised and fixed across most lodges in a particular region and rates are not unreasonable considering the effort it takes to carry the food up there.

Guides & Porters

If you can't (or don't want to) carry a large pack, if you have children or elderly people in your party, or if you plan to walk in regions where you have to carry in food, fuel and tents, you should consider hiring a porter to carry your baggage.

There is a distinct difference between a guide and a porter. A guide should speak English, know the terrain and the trails, and supervise porters, but probably won't carry a load or do menial tasks such as cooking or putting up tents. Porters are generally only hired for load-carrying, although an increasing number speak some English and know the trails well enough to act as porter-guides.

Professional porters employed by camping groups usually carry their loads in a bamboo basket known as a *doko*. Porter-guides used to dealing with independent trekkers normally prefer to carry your backpack on their shoulders. They will likely carry a daypack for their own gear, packed on top of your pack or worn on their front.

If you make arrangements with one of the small trekking agencies in Kathmandu, expect to pay around US$25 per day for a guide and US$17 for a porter. These prices generally include your guide/porter's food and lodging, but not transport to and from the trailhead.

Finding Guides & Porters

To hire a guide, look on bulletin boards, check out forums, such as www.lonely planet.com/thorntree or www.trekinfo.com, hire someone through a trekking agency, or check with the office of Kathmandu Environmental Education Project (KEEP; www.keepnepal.org). It's not difficult to find guides and porters, but it is hard to be certain of their reliability and ability. Don't hire a porter or guide you meet on the street in Kathmandu or Pokhara.

If during a trek you decide you need help, either because of illness, problems with altitude, blisters or weariness, it will generally be possible to find a porter. Most lodges can arrange a porter, particularly in large villages or near an airstrip or road-head, where there are often porters who have just finished working for a trekking party and are looking for another load to carry.

Whether you're making the arrangements yourself or dealing with an agency, make sure you clearly establish your itinerary (write it down and go through it day by day), how long you will take, how much you are going to pay and whether that includes your porter's food and accommodation. It's always easier to agree on a fixed daily inclusive rate for your guide and porter's food and accommodation rather than pay their bills as you go. Note that you will have to pay your porter/guide's transportation to and from the trailhead and will have to pay their daily rate for the time spent travelling.

The 3 Sisters Trekking (p35) company at Lakeside North, Pokhara, organises female porters and guides for female trekkers.

Obligations to Guides & Porters

An important thing to consider when you decide to trek with a guide or porter is that you become an employer. This means that you may have to deal with disagreements over trekking routes and pace, money negotiations and all the other aspects of being a boss. Be as thorough as you can when hiring people and make it clear from the beginning what the requirements and limitations are.

Porters often come from the lowland valleys, are poor and poorly educated, and are sometimes unaware of the potential dangers of the areas they are being employed to work in. Stories abound of porters being left to fend for themselves,

---

THE LOCAL FIREWATER

On trekking routes, look out for the traditional homebrews of the hills. One drink you'll find everywhere is *chang*, a mildly alcoholic Tibetan concoction made from fermented barley or millet and water. It can be drunk hot or cold – local connoisseurs take it hot with a raw egg in it…

In eastern Nepal, look out for *tongba*, a Himalayan brew made by pouring boiling water into a wooden (or metal) pot full of fermented millet. The liquid is slurped through a bamboo straw and more hot water is added periodically to seep extra alcohol from the mash.

Harder spirits include *arak*, fermented from potatoes or grain, and *raksi*, a distilled rice wine that runs the gamut from smooth-sipping schnapps to headache-inducing paint stripper.

Hiking the Himalaya

wearing thin cotton clothes and sandals when traversing high mountain passes in blizzard conditions.

When hiring a porter you are responsible (morally if not legally) for the welfare of those you employ. Many porters die or are injured each year and it's important that you don't contribute to the problem. If you hire a porter or guide through a trekking agency, the agency will naturally pocket a percentage of the fee but it should also provide insurance for the porter (check with the agency).

There are some trekking companies in Nepal, especially at the budget end of the scale, who simply don't look after the porters they hire.

The following are the main points to bear in mind when hiring and trekking with a porter:

➡ Ensure that adequate clothing is provided for any staff you hire. Clothing needs to be suitable for the altitudes you intend to trek to and should protect against bad weather. Equipment should include adequate footwear, headwear, gloves, windproof jacket, trousers and sunglasses.

➡ Ensure that whatever provision you have made for yourself for emergency medical treatment is available to porters working for you.

➡ Ensure that porters who fall ill are not simply paid off and left to fend for themselves (it happens!).

➡ Ensure that porters who fall ill, and are taken down and out in order to access medical treatment, are accompanied by someone who speaks the porter's language and also understands the medical problem.

➡ If you are trekking with an organised group using porters, be sure to ask the company how they ensure the wellbeing of porters hired by them.

In order to prevent the abuse of porters, the International Porter Protection Group (www.ippg.net) was established in 1997 to improve health and safety for porters at work, to reduce the incidence of avoidable illness, injury and death, and to educate trekkers and travel companies about porter welfare.

You can learn a lot about the hardships of life as a porter by watching the excellent BBC documentary *Carrying the Burden*, shown daily at 2pm at KEEP (p36).

EARTHQUAKE-DAMAGED TREKKING ROUTES

The 2015 earthquakes caused massive landslides and avalanches and destroyed whole villages in the Langtang, Helambu, Manaslu and Rolwaling regions, and buildings collapsed across central Nepal, including on the approach to Everest in villages like Thame.

Locals have shown great resilience in rebuilding lodges as quickly as possible, largely without government support. At the time of writing, trekking was possible on all the main teahouse trekking routes in Nepal, including the Everest, Annapurna, Langtang and Manaslu regions, as well as in eastern and western Nepal. Villagers in places such as Langtang have never needed the support of trekkers more.

If you're hiring your own porters, contact the porter clothing bank at KEEP, a scheme that allows you to rent protective gear for your porter. A similar clothing bank operates at Lukla. If you've got gear left over at the end of your Everest trek, consider donating it there (it is well signed and just off the main drag in Lukla).

It's common practice to offer your guide and porter a decent tip at the end of the trek for a job well done. Figure on about one day's wages per week, or about 15% to 20% of the total fee. Always give the tip directly to your porters rather than the guide or trek company.

Organised Trekking

There are hundreds of trekking agencies in Nepal, ranging from big operations connected to international travel companies down to small agencies that specialise in handling independent trekkers. Organised treks can vary greatly in standards and costs, so it's important you understand exactly what you are getting for your money.

Organised treks generally charge solo travellers a supplement if you don't want to share a tent or room.

International Trekking Agencies

At the top of the price range are foreign adventure-travel companies with seductive brochures. The trek cost will probably include accommodation in Kathmandu before and after the trek, tours and other activities, as well as the trek itself. A fully organised trek provides virtually everything: tents, sleeping bags, food and porters, as well as an experienced English-speaking *sirdar* (trail boss), Sherpa guides and sometimes a Western trek leader. You'll trek in real comfort with tables, chairs, dining tents, toilet tents and other luxuries. All you need worry about is a daypack and camera.

Although the trek leaders may be experienced Western walkers from the international company, the on-the-ground organisation in Nepal will be carried out by a reputable local trekking company.

Foreign-run companies that are based in Nepal include the excellent Project Himalaya (www.project-himalaya.com), Kamzang Treks (www.kamzang.com) and Himalayan Trails (www.himalayan-trails.com).

Local Trekking Agencies

It's quite possible (and it can save a lot of money) to arrange a fully organised trip when you get to Nepal. Many trekking companies in Nepal can put together a fully equipped trek if you give them a few days' notice. Organised treks normally cost US$50 to US$100 per person per day for a fully equipped camping trek, or US$40 to US$50 for a teahouse trek, depending on the itinerary, group size and level of service.

Smaller agencies are generally happy to fix you up with individual porters or guides. You can either just pay a daily rate for these and then pay your own food and lodging costs or you can pay a package rate that includes your food, accommodation and transport to and from the trailheads. You gain a measure of protection by booking with an agency that is a member of the Trekking Agencies Association of Nepal (TAAN).

Several agencies run specialist treks: **Nature Treks** (Map p90; ☏01-4381214; www.nature-treks.com; Thamel) focuses on wildlife, birdwatching and community ecolodge treks, while **Purana Yoga & Treks** (Map p210; ☏061-465922; www.nepalyogatrek.com;

Sedi Mathi) is one of several agencies that run yoga treks on all the main trails.

3 Sisters Adventure Trekking (Map p216; ☑061-462066; www.3sistersadventuretrek.com; Lakeside North)

Adventure Pilgrims Trekking (Map p90; ☑01-4424635; www.trekinnepal.com)

Adventure Treks Nepal (Map p90; ☑9851065354; www.adventurenepaltreks.com; Narsingh Gate)

Alpine Adventure Club Treks (Map p70; ☑01-4260765; www.alpineadventureclub.com; Dhobichaur)

Ama Dablam Adventures (Map p70; ☑01-4415372; www.amadablamadventures.com; Kamal Pokhari)

Asian Trekking (Map p90; ☑01-4424249; www.asian-trekking.com; Bhagwan Bahal)

Blue Sheep Journeys (Map p70; ☑01- 4414545; www.bluesheep.com.np; Naxal)

Crystal Mountain Treks (Map p70; ☑01-4416813; www.crystalmountaintreks.com; Kholagal)

Earthbound Expeditions (Map p90; ☑01-4701041; www.enepaltrekking.com; Thamel)

Explore Himalaya (Map p90; ☑01-4418100; www.explorehimalaya.com; Bhagwan Bahal)

Explore Nepal (Map p70; ☑01-4226130; www.xplorenepal.com)

Firante Treks & Expeditions (Map p70; ☑01-4000043; www.firante.com; Lazimpat)

High Spirit Treks (Map p90; ☑01-4701084; www.allnepaltreks.com; Thamel)

Himalaya Journey (Map p90; ☑01-4383184; www.himalayajourneys.com; Paknajol)

Himalayan Glacier (Map p90; ☑01-4411387; www.himalayanglacier.com)

International Trekkers (☑01-4371397; www.everestlodges.com/treks; Dhumbarahi)

Langtang Ri Trekking & Expeditions (Map p90; ☑01-4423360; www.langtang.com; Narsingh Chowk, Thamel)

Makalu Adventure (Map p90; ☑01-4420136; www.makaluadventure.com; Amrit Marg, Thamel)

Miteri Nepal International Trekking (Map p90; ☑01-4437163; www.miterinepaltrekking.com; Bhagwatisthan 29, Thamel)

Nepal Social Treks (Map p90; ☑01-4701070; www.nepalsocialtreks.com; Paknajol)

Peak Promotion (Map p70; ☑01-4263115; www.peakpromotionnepal.com; Jyatha)

Snow Cat Travel/Rural Heritage (Rural Heritage; Map p70; ☑01-44222617; www.snowcattravel.com; Vista Bldg, Nag Pokhari)

Sherpa Society (☑01-4249233, 9851023553; www.sherpasocietytrekking.com)

Sisne Rover Trekking (Map p216; ☑9856020976, 061-461893; www.sisnerover.com; Central Lakeside)

Trek Nepal International (Map p90; ☑01-4700012; www.treknepal.com; Mandala St, Thamel)

Trekking Team Group (Map p90; ☑01-4227506; www.trekkingteamgroup.com; Chaksibari Marg)

What to Pack
Clothing & Footwear

The clothing you require depends on where and when you are trekking. If you're going to Everest Base Camp in the middle of winter you must take down-filled gear, mittens and thermals. If you're doing a short, low-altitude trek early or late in the season the weather is likely to be fine enough for T-shirts during the day and a fleece to pull on in the evenings.

Apart from ensuring you have adequate clothing to keep you warm, it's essential that your feet are comfortable and will stay dry if it rains or snows. Uncomfortable shoes and blistered feet are the worst possible trekking discomforts. Make sure your shoes are broken in, fit well and are comfortable for long periods. Running shoes are adequate for low-altitude (below 3000m), warm-weather treks where you won't encounter snow, otherwise the minimum standard of footwear is lightweight waterproof trekking boots. Don't even think about buying boots in Kathmandu and then heading on a trek.

If you are going on an organised trek, check what equipment is supplied by the company you sign up with.

Buying or Renting in Nepal

It's always best to have your own equipment since you will be familiar with it and know for certain that it works. That said, you can buy almost anything you need these days from Kathmandu's trekking gear stores. Much of what's for sale is fake; the backpacks won't quite fit comfortably, the seams on the Gore-Tex jackets will leak and stitching will start to fray eventually. Even so, most items are reasonably well made and will stand up to the rigours of at least one major trek. The best buys are probably down jackets, fleeces and other jackets. There is also an increasing amount of imported gear, at prices comparable to abroad.

It's possible to rent sleeping bags (four-season) for Rs 120 or a down jacket for Rs 60 in Kathmandu, Pokhara and even Namche Bazaar. Tents are harder to find. Large deposits are often required (never leave your passport). You can purchase sundries, such as sunblock, shampoo and woolly hats, on the main trails in places like Chame and Namche Bazaar.

Butane gas canisters are available in Kathmandu for Rs 650 to Rs 1150, depending on the percentage of propane (propane is better suited to higher altitudes). Prices are double this in Namche Bazaar, but remember that gas cannisters can't be taken on aeroplanes.

Equipment Checklist for Teahouse Trekking

Clothing

➡ spare socks (minimum three pairs)

➡ hiking trousers

➡ quick-drying T-shirts (not cotton)

➡ down vest or jacket

➡ fleece

➡ rain shell or poncho

➡ fleece hat

➡ sun hat

Equipment

➡ sleeping bag (three- or four-season)

➡ daypack

➡ head torch and spare batteries

➡ trekking poles

➡ polarised sunglasses

➡ sunscreen (SPF 30+)

➡ water bottle

➡ water purification items

➡ camera, batteries and memory cards

➡ phone and charger, plus battery pack or solar charger

Miscellaneous

➡ lip balm

➡ toiletries

➡ toilet paper and lighter

➡ camp towel (quick-drying)

➡ laundry soap (biodegradable)

➡ hand sanitiser

➡ medical kit (p394)

➡ blister kit with moleskin, scissors and strong tape

➡ playing cards, book or Kindle

➡ stuff sacks and garbage bags

➡ padlock

➡ emergency whistle

Information

The Himalayan Rescue Association (HRA), Kathmandu Environmental Education Project (KEEP) and Trekking Agencies' Association of Nepal (TAAN) offer free, up-to-date information on trekking conditions, health risks and minimising your environmental impact. They are also excellent places to visit and advertise for trekking companions.

Kathmandu Environmental Education Project
(KEEP; Map p90; ☏01-4267471; www.keepnepal. org; Jyatha, Thamel; ⊙10am-5pm Sun-Fri; ☎) Has a library, some useful trekkers notebooks, a water refill service, an excellent noticeboard and a small cafe. It also sells iodine tablets (Rs 1000), biodegradable soap and other environmentally friendly equipment. It's a good place to find a trek partner, donate clothes to or hire a set of clothes for your porter from the Porter's Clothing Bank (Rs 500, with a Rs 2000 to Rs 5000 deposit). It shifts location frequently, so check before heading out.

Trekking Agencies' Association of Nepal
(TAAN; Map p70; ☏01-4427473; www.taan.org. np; Maligaun Ganeshthan, Kathmandu) Details trekking regulations and can mediate in disputes with trekking agencies.

MOUNTAIN LITERATURE

Trekking offers plenty of time to catch up on your reading. Pack the following titles for those long teahouse evenings:

➡ *Annapurna* by Maurice Herzog, a controversial mountaineering classic from 1950.

➡ *Into Thin Air* by Jon Krakauer, the gripping story of the 1996 Everest disaster.

➡ *The Ascent of Rum Doodle* by WE Bowman, a highly enjoyable spoof of all those serious mountaineering tomes.

➡ *The Snow Leopard* by Peter Matthiessen, a profound metaphysical description of a trek through Dolpo in the company of grumpy naturalist George Schaller.

➡ *Nepal Himalaya* by WH Tilman, British wit from the 1950s trekking pioneer.

➡ *Everest* by Walt Unsworth, the ultimate but hefty Everest reference, if you have a porter to carry it.

➡ *Into the Silence* by Wade Davis, a similarly encyclopedic history of the earliest attempts to scale Everest, mostly from the Tibet side.

➡ *Himalaya* by Michael Palin, tales of travel on Annapurna and Everest by the charming ex-Python.

➡ *Chomolungma Sings the Blues* by Ed Douglas, a thought-provoking 'state-of-the-mountain' address detailing the dirtier side of Everest mountaineering.

Maps

Most trekkers are content to get one of the trekking route maps produced locally by companies like Himalayan Map House (www.himalayan-maphouse.com), Nepa Maps or Shangrila Maps (www.shangrila maps.com). They are relatively inexpensive (Rs 400 to Rs 800) and are adequate for the popular trails, though not for off-route travel. They are found everywhere in map and bookshops in Thamel. Be aware that there is a great deal of repackaging going on; don't buy two maps with different covers and names assuming you are getting significantly different maps.

The best series of maps of Nepal is the 1:50,000 series produced by Erwin Schneider and now published by Nelles Verlag. They cover the Kathmandu Valley and the Everest region from Jiri to the Hongu Valley, as well as the Khumbu region. You may also find older 1:100,000 Schneider maps of Annapurna and other regions. All are somewhat dated in terms of road construction.

National Geographic produces 1:125,000 trekking maps to the Khumbu, Everest Base Camp, Annapurna and Langtang areas, as part of its Trails Illustrated series.

All of these maps are available at bookshops in Kathmandu and at some speciality map shops overseas, including the following:

Melbourne Map Centre (www.melbmap.com.au)

Omni Resources (www.omnimap.com)

Stanfords (www.stanfords.co.uk)

There are several excellent online map resources. Google Earth is an incredible resource for trekkers, and it's also worth rummaging through Digital Himalaya (www.digitalhimalaya.com).

If you are headed on the Annapurna Sanctuary Trek then visit the interactive maps at www.4dgraphics.net/abc.

Useful Websites

Great Himalayan Trail (www.greathimalayatrail. com, www.greathimalayatrails.com) Excellent website detailing different sections of the epic trail, with articles, practical advice and a forum board.

Lonely Planet Thorn Tree (www.lonelyplanet.com/ thorntree) Both the Nepal and Trekking branches of this forum are good places to get the latest trail information and track down trekking partners.

Missing Trekker Nepal (www.missingtrekker. com) Has a list of missing trekkers in Nepal and safety tips on how to not become one yourself.

Nepal Mountaineering Association (www. nepalmountaineering.org) Everything you need to know about climbing and trekking to the top of Nepal's mountains.

Trekinfo.com (www.trekinfo.com) Some of the information is dated but there's a useful forum board.

Trekking Agencies' Association of Nepal (www.taan.org.np) Details current trekking regulations.

Trekking Partners (www.trekkingpartners.com) Great place to meet a trekking partner or read trip reports.

Documents & Fees

TIMS Card

All trekkers are required to register their trek by obtaining a Trekking Information Management System (TIMS; www.timsnepal.com) card. The card costs the equivalent of US$20 for individual trekkers or US$10 if you are part of a group. SAARC trekkers pay US$6 (US$3 for groups). You need to show the TIMS card at the start of the Annapurna and Langtang treks.

At the time of research, the local authorities in the Khumbu had introduced a Rs 2000 'entry fee' to the Everest region, doing away with the need for a TIMS card, but this could change, so check before heading out to Lukla.

The place to get a TIMS card in Kathmandu is from the Tourist Service Centre (p383), mainly because you can also get conservation-area and national park tickets in this building. Bring your passport and two passport photos (though you can get free digital photos here). The card is issued on the spot; green for individuals and blue for group trekkers.

National Park & Conservation Fees

If your trek enters a national park such as Sagarmatha (Everest) or Langtang, you will need to pay a national-park fee. You can pay the fee at the entry to the parks, or in advance from the **national parks office** (Map p70; ☑01-4224406; www.dnpwc.gov.np; ☺9.15am-2pm Sun-Fri), which is located at the Tourist Service Centre, a 20-minute walk from Thamel in Kathmandu. The fee is Rs 3390 for each park. If trekking to Helambu you need to pay a Rs 565 entry to Shivapuri Nagarjun National Park. No photo is required.

If you are trekking in the Annapurna, Manaslu or Gauri Shankar (Rolwaling) regions you must pay a conservation-area fee to the **Annapurna Conservation Area Project** (ACAP; Map p70; ☑01-4222406; www.ntnc.org.np; Bhrikuti Mandap; ☺9am-1pm & 2-3pm), which is also at the Tourist Service Centre. Bring Rs 2000 and two photographs. The permit is issued on the spot.

Conservation fees for the Annapurna area are also payable in Pokhara at ACAP (p225), at Damside inside the Nepal Tourism Board (NTB) office, or in Besi Sahar at the start of the Annapurna Circuit Trek. Note that if you arrive at another ACAP checkpoint without a permit you will be charged double for the permit.

Trekking Permits

Other than the TIMS card, trekking permits are not required for the main treks in the Everest, Annapurna and Langtang regions.

The following treks require trekking permits, which can only be obtained through registered trekking agencies:

AREA	TREKKING FEE
Humla	US$50 for 1st week, then US$7 per day
Kanchenjunga & Lower Dolpo	US$10 per week
Manaslu	US$70 for 1st week, then US$10 per day Sep-Nov, US$50 for 1st week then US$7 per day Dec-Aug
Nar-Phu	US$90 per week Sep-Nov, US$75 per week Dec-Aug
Tsum Valley	US$35 per week Sep-Nov, US$20 Dec-Aug
Upper Mustang & Upper Dolpo	US$500 for 1st 10 days, then US$50 per day

Responsible Trekking

Nepal faces several environmental problems as a result of, or at least compounded by, tourists' actions and expectations. These include the depletion of forests for firewood; the build-up of nonbiodegradable waste, especially plastic bottles; and the pollution of waterways. You can help by choosing an environmentally and socially

PRACTICALITIES

➡ Rechargeable batteries can be charged at many trekking lodges for a fee of around Rs 300 per hour. To charge batteries or an iPod off the beaten track, consider bringing a battery pack or solar charger.

➡ Tip: batteries lose their juice quickly in cold temperatures so keep them in your sleeping bag overnight at higher elevations.

➡ You can change cash in Namche Bazaar, Chame and at some trailheads, and access ATMs in Jomsom and Namche Bazaar, but you should generally bring all the cash rupees you will need with you, plus a stash of US dollars and a credit card in case you need to arrange an emergency flight out.

➡ Bring something for water purification – either chemical tablets, a filter or a UV steriliser like a Steripen.

➡ Wi-fi is available at many lodges on the main teahouse treks, normally for a couple of hundred rupees. Mobile phone connections (including data) are available at lower altitudes.

responsible company and being responsible with garbage, water and firewood.

KEEP is a good resource for tips on responsible trekking.

Firewood & Forest Depletion

➡ Minimise the use of firewood by staying in lodges that use kerosene or fuel-efficient wood stoves and solar-heated hot water. Avoid using large open fires for warmth – wear additional clothing instead.

➡ Consolidate cooking time by ordering the same items at the same time as other trekkers. Daal bhaat (rice and lentils) is usually readily available for large numbers of people, does not require lengthy cooking time, and is nutritious.

➡ Those travelling with organised groups should ensure kerosene is used for cooking, including by porters. In alpine areas ensure that all members are outfitted with enough clothing so that fires are not a necessity for warmth.

Garbage & Waste

➡ Purify your own water instead of buying mineral water in nonbiodegradable plastic bottles.

➡ Bring a couple of spare stuff sacks and use them to compact litter that you find on mountain trails to be disposed of down in Kathmandu.

➡ Independent trekkers should always carry their garbage out or dispose of it properly. You can burn it, but you should remember that the fireplace in a Nepali home is sacred and throwing rubbish into it would be a great insult. Don't bury your rubbish. Try to ensure your guide also follows these guidelines.

➡ Carry out all your batteries, as they will eventually leak toxins.

➡ Toilet paper is a particularly unpleasant sight along trails; if you must use it, carry it in a plastic bag until you can burn it. Those travelling with organised camping groups should ensure that toilet tents are properly organised, that everyone uses them (including porters) and that rubbish is carried out. Check on a company's policies before you sign up and let them know this is a priority for you.

Water

➡ Don't soap up your clothes and wash them in streams. Instead, use a bowl or bucket and discard the dirty water away from watercourses.

➡ On the Annapurna Circuit, the ACAP has introduced the Safe Drinking Water Scheme – a chain of 16 outlets selling purified water to trekkers. Its aim is to minimise the estimated one million plastic bottles brought into the Annapurna Conservation Area each year. A litre of water here costs a fraction of the cost of bottled water.

Health & Safety

For the majority of trekkers health problems are likely to be minor, such as stomach upsets and blisters, and commonsense precautions are all that are required to avoid illness.

Make sure you and your teeth are in good health before departing, as there is very little medical or dental attention along the trails. For more information on health, see p393.

HEALTH ON THE TRAIL

AMS (Altitude Sickness)

Acute Mountain Sickness (AMS), or altitude sickness, is the major concern on all high-altitude treks – be ever-alert to the symptoms (p398).

Diarrhoea

This is a fairly minor problem but it can ruin a trek, so watch what you eat and ensure your medical kit contains antidiarrhoeal medicine such as Lomotil or Imodium (for emergencies only) and a broad-spectrum antibiotic like Azithromycin or Norfloxacin, available without a prescription at pharmacies in Kathmandu and Pokhara. Always treat your water.

Trekker's Knee

Many people suffer from knee and ankle strains, particularly if they're carrying their own pack. Elastic supports or bandages can help, as can anti-inflammatories such as Ibuprofen tablets and analgesic cream, and using collapsible trekking poles.

Blisters

Always carry moleskin, plasters (Band-Aids) and tape in your daypack in case of blisters. Investigate any hot spot as soon as you feel it. Wear clean socks.

Sunburn & Snowblindness

The high-altitude Himalayan sun is incredibly strong. Bring plenty of high-factor suncreen, a brimmed hat and a good pair of sunglasses for pass crossings.

Trekking Safely

Fired up by the gung-ho stories of adventurous travellers, it is also easy to forget that mountainous terrain carries an inherent risk. There are posters plastered around Kathmandu with the faces of missing trekkers.

In rural areas of Nepal rescue services are limited and medical facilities are primitive or nonexistent. Helicopter evacuations are possible, but the costs run into the thousands of US dollars.

Only a tiny minority of trekkers end up in trouble, but accidents can often be avoided or risks minimised if people have a realistic understanding of trekking requirements. Don't take on a Himalayan trek lightly.

Several basic rules should be followed:

➡ Never trek alone.

➡ Always carry an emergency supply of food, water purification tablets/gear, warm clothes, a whistle and map.

➡ Manage altitude sickness risks and don't skip the acclimatisation days.

➡ Register with your embassy before setting off and make sure someone knows your itinerary.

➡ Tell your lodge if attempting a day-trip detour.

➡ Make sure you have comprehensive health and evacuation insurance.

Embassy Registration

Officials of all embassies in Nepal stress the benefits of registering with them, telling them where you are trekking, and reporting in again when you return. You can register online with embassies of the following countries:

Australia (www.smartraveller.gov.au)

Canada (www.voyage.gc.ca/register)

New Zealand (https://register.safetravel.govt.nz)

USA (https://step.state.gov/step/)

Choosing Companions

➡ Never trek alone. You'll appreciate having someone around when you're lost, sick or suffering from altitude sickness. It's also useful to have someone to occasionally watch your pack or valuables when you visit the bathroom or take a shower.

➡ Solo women travellers should choose companions and guides carefully, as there have been repeated reports of harassment and isolated instances of assault – ask fellow travellers for recommendations.

➡ To find a fellow trekking companion, check the bulletin board at KEEP or post a message on www.trekinfo.com, www.trekkingpartners.com or www.lonelyplanet.com/thorntree.

➡ Unless you are an experienced trekker or have a friend to trek with, you should at least take a porter or guide.

Trail Conditions

➡ Walking at high altitudes on rough trails can be dangerous. Watch your footing on narrow, slippery trails and keep your eyes on the trail not the mountains. Never underestimate the changeability of the weather at high altitude – at any time of the year.

➡ If you are crossing high passes where snow is a possibility, never walk with fewer than three people.

➡ Carry a supply of emergency rations, have a map and compass (and know how to use them), and have sufficient clothing and equipment to deal with cold, wet, blizzard conditions.

➡ You will be sharing the trail with porters, mules and yaks, all usually carrying heavy loads, so give them the right of way. If a mule or yak train approaches, always move to the high side of the trail to avoid being knocked over the edge.

Rescue Insurance

➡ Check that your travel insurance policy does not exclude mountaineering or 'alpinism' or what it's definitions for these are, especially if you are tackling a trekking peak. Check what insurance is available through your foreign trekking company, if using one.

➡ Rescue insurance will need to cover an emergency helicopter evacuation or a charter flight from a remote airstrip, as well as international medical evacuation. A helicopter evacuation from 4000m near Mt Everest will cost you up to US$10,000 and payment must be cleared in advance. Your embassy can help with this if you have registered with it. Bring a credit card as you will likely have to prepay the helicopter company.

➡ Disreputable companies sometimes push fast-paced budget treks that don't allow for adequate acclimatisation in order to earn generous commission from helicopter evacuations. Make sure your itinerary includes acclimatisation days and don't be persuaded to trek higher if you are feeling unwell.

Altitude

Walking the trails of Nepal often entails a great deal of altitude gain and loss; even the base camps of Nepal's great peaks can be very high. Most treks that go through populated areas stick to between 1000m and 3000m, although the Everest Base Camp Trek and the Annapurna Circuit Trek both reach over 5000m. On high treks like these, ensure adequate acclimatisation by limiting altitude gain above 3000m to 500m per day. The maxim of 'walking high, sleeping low' is good advice; your night halt should be at a lower level than the highest point reached in the day.

Make a point of catching the free altitude lectures given by the Himalayan Rescue Association health posts at Manang, Pheriche and Everest Base Camp on the Annapurna and Everest treks.

Plan Your Trip

Outdoor Activities

Nepal is a playground for lovers of adventure sports and high-adrenaline activities. The country offers some of the best mountain biking and rafting trips in the world, as well as canyoning, bungee jumping, zip wires and rock climbing. The options are almost limitless.

Best Outdoor Activities

Best Wilderness Rafting Trip

Sun Kosi or Tamur Exciting expedition-style trips that last for a week and traverse a huge range of remote terrain.

Best Place for a Kayak Clinic

Sun Kosi or Seti River Base yourself at a comfortable riverside camp or float down the Seti River, while learning about Eskimo rolls and eddies.

Best Place to Scare Yourself

Bhote Kosi Plunge 160m towards earth on a bungee jump at Last Resort.

Best Mountain-Biking Trip

Jomsom to Pokhara Downhill trail that follows 4WD tracks down the western half of the spectacular Annapurna Circuit.

Best Place to Learn to Climb

Astrek Climbing Wall Offers rock-climbing courses at its wall in Kathmandu and on rock at nearby Nagarjun. Organises trekking peak climbs from a base in Lobuche.

Mountain Biking

Fat tyres, a soft padded seat and 17 more gears than the average Nepali bike – the mountain bike is an ideal, go-anywhere, versatile machine for exploring Nepal. These attributes make it possible to escape sealed roads, and to ride tracks and ancient walking trails to remote, rarely visited areas of the country. Importantly, they allow a liberating freedom of travel – you can stop whenever you like – and they free you from crowded buses and claustrophobic taxis.

While the heart of the Kathmandu Valley is too hectic and traffic-congested nowadays to truly offer a fun biking experience, the fringes of the valley are another story and they quite possibly offer some of the best and most consistent biking in Nepal, with a dense network of tracks, trails and back roads. A mountain bike really allows you to get off the beaten track and discover idyllic Newari villages that have preserved their traditional lifestyle.

Many trails are narrow, century-old walkways that are not shown on maps, so you need a good sense of direction when venturing out without a guide. To go unguided entails some risks, and you should learn a few important words of Nepali to assist in seeking directions. Bring a map and compass or at least a GPS-enabled smartphone with a map app.

Nepa Maps and Himalayan Maphouse produce the useful maps *Mountain Biking the Kathmandu Valley* and *Biking around Annapurna,* though they aren't to be relied on completely.

Guided Tours

A booming number of Nepali companies offer guided mountain-bike trips. They provide high-quality bicycles, local and Western guides, helmets and all the necessary equipment. There is usually a minimum of four cyclists required per trip, although for shorter tours two is often sufficient. For the shorter tours (two to three days) vehicle support is not required, while for longer tours vehicles are provided at an extra cost.

Local group tours range from US$55 to US$65 for a simple day trip with bike rental, such as the loop routes north from Kathmandu to Tinpiple, Tokha and Budhanilkantha, or south to the traditional village of Bungamati. Expect to pay around US$25 a day if you just want a mountain-bike guide.

A faster-paced downhill day trip with vehicle support costs around US$100 per person. Options include driving to Nagarkot and riding down to Sankhu and Bodhnath or Bhaktapur, or driving to Kakani and taking the Scar Rd down through Shivapuri National Park. Dawn Till Dusk (p86) and Chhango (p86) offer exhilarating downhill runs from the top of Phulchowki and Nagarjun peaks.

Multiday trips around the Kathmandu Valley cost around US$55 per day without vehicle backup (US$75 with vehicle support) and range from two to 10 days. Prices include bike hire, a guide, hotel accommodation and meals.

Longer guided trips include the back road route from Kathmandu to Pokhara and a four-day ride from Jomsom to Beni.

Tour Companies

A number of companies have good-quality imported mountain bikes that can also be hired independently of a tour.

Alternative Nepal (p86) Mountain-bike hire and guided trips.

Annapurna Mountain Bikes (Map p90; ☑9841436811, 01-6912195; www.annapurna biking.com; Chaksibari Marg) The young team

members behind this Thamel venture offer trips around the Kathmandu Valley, Annapurna area and Upper Mustang. Charges are around US$75 to US$85 per day for overnight trips. Bike hire and repairs available.

Chain 'n' Gear Mountain Bikes (p212) In Pokhara.

Dawn Till Dusk (p86) Local mountain bike and country-wide tours, with a desk at the Kathmandu Guest House office.

Himalayan Single Track (Map p90; ☑01-4700619; www.himalayansingletrack.com; Annapurna Market, Saatgumthi) Offers an exciting and comprehensive array of bike tours taking in all the favourites, plus Upper Mustang, Manaslu, the Jomsom–Muktinath Trail and even overland cycling trips to Tibet and helibiking. Giant bike rental, sales and full servicing is available. It also runs weekly social rides and women's rides from Kathmandu. Contact Santosh Rai. Located in Thamel.

Nepal Mountain Bike Tours (p86) Kathmandu Valley trips and more.

Transporting Your Own Bicycle

If you plan to do a mountain-biking trip of more than a day or two, it may be a good idea to bring your own bicycle from home. Your bicycle can be carried as part of your baggage allowance on international flights. You are required to deflate the tyres, turn the handlebars parallel with the frame and remove the pedals. Passage through Nepali customs is quite simple once you reassure airport officers that it is 'your' bicycle and it will also be returning with you, though this requirement is never enforced.

On most domestic flights, if you pack your bicycle correctly, removing wheels and pedals, it is possible to load it in the cargo hold. Check with the airline first.

Local buses are useful if you wish to avoid some of the routes that carry heavy traffic. You can place your bicycle on the roof for an additional charge (Rs 50 to Rs 100 depending on the length of the journey and the bus company). Keep in mind that more baggage is likely to be loaded on top once you're inside. A lock and chain is a wise investment.

Equipment

Most of the bicycles for rent in Nepal are low-quality, Indian and Chinese mountain bikes, not suitable for the rigours of trail

SARO17/GETTY IMAGES ©

EYAL COHEN/500PX ©

Top: Mountainbiker on the Annapurna Circuit Trek (p301)

Bottom: Indian rhino, Bardia National Park (p272)

riding. The better operators rent high-quality front-shock, 18-gear mountain bikes made by Giant or Trek for around US$12 to US$15 per day, with discounts for a week's hire. Any decent rental shop will supply a helmet, lock and basic repair kit.

If you bring your own bicycle, it is essential to bring tools and spare parts, as these are largely unavailable outside of Kathmandu. Established mountain-bike tour operators have mechanics, workshops and a full range of bicycle tools at their offices in Kathmandu.

Road Conditions

Nepali roads carry a vast array of vehicles: buses, motorcycles, cars, trucks, tractors, holy cows, wheelbarrows, dogs, wandering children and chickens, all moving at different speeds and in different directions. Traffic generally travels on the left-hand side, though it's not uncommon to find a vehicle approaching you head-on. In practice, smaller vehicles give way to larger ones, and bicycles are definitely at the bottom of the heap.

A few intrepid mountain bikers have taken bicycles into trekking areas such as the Annapurna Circuit and, more recently, the Mansalu Circuit, hoping to find great riding, but you have to be prepared to carry your bicycle for at least 30% of the time. In addition, there are always trekkers, porters and local people clogging up the trails. Sagarmatha National Park doesn't allow mountain bikes. Courtesy and care on the trails should be a high priority when cycling.

Trail Etiquette

Clothing

Tight-fitting lycra bicycle clothing might be functional, but it's a shock to locals, who maintain a very modest approach to dressing. Such clothing is embarrassing and also offensive to Nepalis.

A simple way to overcome this is by wearing a pair of comfortable shorts and a T-shirt over your bicycle gear. This is especially applicable to female cyclists, as women in Nepal generally dress conservatively.

Safety

Trails are often filled with locals going about their daily work. A small bell attached to your handlebars and used as a warning of your approach, reducing your speed, and a friendly call or two of '*cycle ioh!*' (cycle coming!) go a long way in keeping everyone on the trails happy and safe. Children love the novelty of the bicycles, the fancy helmets, the colours and the strange clothing, and will come running from all directions to greet you. They also love to grab hold of the back of your bicycle and run with you. You need to maintain a watchful eye so no one gets hurt.

Rafting

When to Go

In general the best times for rafting and kayaking are September to early December, and March to early June.

March to May The summer season has long, hot days and lower water flows, which generally means the rapids are a grade lower than they are from September to November. The rivers rise again in May with the pre-monsoon storms and some snowmelt.

June to August Monsoon rains mean the rivers carry 10 times their low-water flows, and can flood with 60 to 80 times the low-water levels, making most rivers insanely difficult. Only parts of the Seti, Upper Sun Kosi and Trisuli are commercially run during the monsoon.

September to early October and May to June Rivers can be extremely high with monsoon run-off. Any expeditions attempted at this time require a very experienced rafting company with an intimate knowledge of the river and strong teams, as times of high flows are potentially the most dangerous times to be on a river.

Mid-October to November One of the most popular times to raft or kayak, with warm, settled weather and exciting runs.

December Many of the rivers become too cold to enjoy unless you have a wetsuit, and the days are short with the start of winter – the time to consider shorter trips.

What to Bring

If you go on an organised rafting or kayaking trip, all specialised equipment is supplied, as well as tents. Roll-top dry bags keep your gear dry even if the vessel flips.

Usually you will only need light clothing, with a warmer change for cool nights. A swimsuit, a towel, a sunhat, insect repellent, sunscreen and light tennis shoes or sandals (that will stay on your feet) are all necessary. In winter you will need thermal clothing, especially on rivers like the Bhote Kosi. Check if companies provide paddle jackets and wetsuits.

Waterproof camera containers are useful to take photos along the river – ask your company if they have any for hire or, better, bring your own.

Information

Anyone who is seriously interested in rafting and kayaking should get *White Water Nepal* by Peter Knowles. It has very detailed information on river trips, with 60 maps, river profiles and hydrographs, plus advice on equipment and health. Check out www.riverspublishing.co.uk or get a copy of the book in Kathmandu.

Himalayan Maphouse and Peter Knowles have produced three river maps for kayakers and rafters: *Whitewater Rafting and Kayaking for Western Nepal, Central Nepal* and *Eastern Nepal*.

The website of the Nepal Association of Rafting Agencies (www.raftingassociation. org.np) has listings of rafting companies, overviews of river routes and information on the annual Himalayan Whitewater Challenge.

The Nepal River Conservation Trust (www.nrct.org.np) is a worthy organisation that lobbies to protect Nepal's rivers. Its campaigns include protection of the

RIVER TRIPS IN NEPAL

Note that in the 'Season/Grade' column, the number in brackets refers to the grade when the high river flows, which is normally at the beginning and end of the season.

RIVER	DURATION (DAYS)	APPROXIMATE COST (US$)	TRANSPORT	SEASON/ GRADE	ADD-ONS
Bhote Kosi	1	60	3hr from Kathmandu	late Oct-May/ 4 (5-)	bungee jumping, canyoning, kayak clinics, day trips possible
Upper Sun Kosi	2	140	2hr from Kathmandu	Oct-May/ 3 (4), Jun-Sep/4 (4+)	
Trisuli	2	110	2hr from Kathmandu	Oct-May/3 (4), Jun-Sep/ 4 (4+)	excursions to Bandipur or Pokhara, day trips possible
Seti	2-3	110-130	1½hr from Pokhara	Sep-May/ 2 (3+)	kayak clinics are popular here
Kali Gandaki	3	180	2hr from Pokhara	late Sep-May/ 3 (4)	Chitwan National Park
Marsyangdi	4	280	5hr from Kathmandu	late Oct-Apr/ 4 (5-)	Annapurna Circuit Trek
Sun Kosi	8-9	630	3hr from Kathmandu, then 16hr bus back to Kathmandu, or fly from Biratnagar	Sep-Nov/3+ (4+), Dec-Apr/ 3 (4)	Koshi Tappu Wildlife Reserve or continue on to Darjeeling in India
Karnali	10	800-950	16hr bus ride from Kathmandu, or flight and 4hr bus ride	late Sep-May/ 3 (4+)	Bardia National Park
Tamur	12	920-1300	18hr bus ride from Kathmandu, or flight then three-day trek; flight or 16hr bus back (six days of rafting in total)	Oct-Dec/ 4 (5-)	trek to Kanchenjunga

Karnali, Nepal's last free-flowing river, and clean-up campaigns of Kathmandu's Bagmati River.

Choosing a River

Before you decide on a river (p325), you need to decide what it is that you want out of your trip. There are trips available from two to 12 days on different rivers, all offering dramatically different experiences.

First, don't believe that just because it's a river it's going to be wet 'n' wild. Some rivers, such as the Sun Kosi, which is a full-on white-water trip in September and October, are basically flat in the low water of early spring. On the flip side, early spring can be a superb time to raft rivers such as the Marsyangdi, which would be suicidal during high flows. The Karnali is probably the only river that offers continually challenging white water at all flows, though during the high-water months of September and May it's significantly more challenging than in the low-water months.

Longer trips such as the Sun Kosi (in the autumn), the Karnali and the Tamur offer some real heart-thumping white water with the sense of journey inherent in a long river trip. With more time on the river, things are more relaxed, relationships progress at a more natural pace, and memories become entrenched for a lifetime. River trips are much more than gravity-powered roller-coaster rides; they're liquid journeys traversed on very special highways.

For a shorter float combined with some premier wildlife-watching, consider also the two- to three-day raft from Mugling to Chitwan National Park and a day raft on the Geruwa River near Bardia National Park.

Dam construction is having a big impact on the quality of rafting on many rivers in Nepal. Check locally to see how this has affected runs before booking a trip.

Safety

Safety is the most important part of any river trip. Unfortunately, there are no minimum safety conditions enforced by any official body in Nepal. This makes it very important to choose a professional rafting and kayaking company. Your guide should give you a comprehensive safety talk and paddle training before you launch off downstream. If you don't get this, it is probably cause for concern.

➡ Modern self-bailing rafts, good life jackets and helmets are essential.

➡ There should be a minimum of two rafts per trip. In higher water, three rafts are safer than two.

➡ Good safety kayakers are invaluable on steeper rivers where they can often get to swimmers in places no other craft could manage.

➡ If possible, speak with the guide who will lead the trip to get an impression of the people you will be spending time with and the type of trip they run.

➡ All guides should have a current first-aid certificate and be trained in cardiopulmonary resuscitation. International accreditation such as the Swiftwater Rescue Technician (SRT) qualification is a bonus.

➡ Always wear your life jacket in rapids. Wear your helmet whenever your guide tells you, and make sure that both the helmet and jacket are properly adjusted and fitted.

➡ Keep your feet and arms inside the raft. If the raft hits a rock or wall and you are in the way, the best you'll escape with is a laceration.

➡ If you do swim in a rapid, get into the 'white-water swimming position'. You should be on your back, with your feet downstream and up where you can see them. Hold on to your paddle as this will make you more visible. Relax and breathe when you aren't going through waves. Then turn over and swim at the end of the rapid when the water becomes calmer. Self-rescue is the best rescue.

Organised Trips

There are dozens of companies in Kathmandu claiming to be rafting and kayaking operators. A few are well-established companies with good reputations, and the rest are newer companies, often formed by guides breaking away and starting their own operations. Although these new companies can be enthusiastic and good, they can also be shoestring operations that may not have adequate equipment and staff. Most of the small travel agencies simply sell trips on commission; often they have no real idea about the details of what they are selling and are only interested in getting bums on seats.

If a group has recently returned from a trip, speak to its members. This will give you reliable information about the quality of equipment, the guides, the food and the transportation. Question the company about things such as how groups get to and from the river, the number of hours spent paddling or rowing, where the camps are set up, what food is provided (rafting promotes a very healthy appetite), who does the cooking and work around the camp, the cooking fuel used (wood isn't convenient or responsible), what happens to rubbish, hygiene precautions and night-time activities. Check how many people have booked and paid for a trip, as well as the maximum number that will be taken.

Shorter trips depart every few days, but the longer rafting trips only depart every week or so, so it's worth contacting a company in advance to see when they are planning a trip. The best companies will refer you to a friendly competitor if they don't have any suitable dates.

Generally you'll be rafting or kayaking for around five to six hours a day, and you can expect to be running rapids about 30% of the time depending on the river. The first and last days will most likely be half days. Longer trips of a week or more will probably have one rest day when you can relax or explore the surroundings.

Trips booked in Nepal range in price from US$60 to US$120 a day, depending on the standard of service, number of people on the trip, and the river. Generally you get what you pay for. It is better to pay a bit more and have a good, safe trip than to save US$100 and have a lousy, dangerous trip.

With the constant change in rafting and kayaking companies it's difficult to make individual recommendations; the fact that a company is not recommended here does not necessarily mean it will not deliver an excellent trip. Nonetheless, a number of companies have been recommended for their professionalism.

Adrenaline Rush (Map p90; ☎01-4701056; www. adrenalinenepal.com; Thamel) Trisuli rafting and kayaking trips, including tubing and 'ducky' (inflatable kayak) trips, from a simple camp at Kuringhat on the Trisuli. Shares an office with Chhango.

Adventure Aves (Map p90; ☎01-4700230; www. adventureaves.com; Saatghumti) Thamel-based Nepali-British operation focused on rafting and kayaking, with a camp on the Trisuli River. Contact Dil Bahadur Gurung.

Drift Nepal (Map p90; ☎01-4700797; www. driftnepalexpedition.com) All the major rivers are represented, as well as kayak clinics and treks. Based in Thamel. Contact Sanjay Gurung.

Equator Expeditions (Map p90; ☎01-4700854; www.equatorexpeditionsnepal.com; Thamel) This company specialises in long participatory rafting/ kayaking trips and kayak instruction at the Sukute Beach Resort on the Bhote Khosi.

GRG Adventure Kayaking (Map p90; ☎01-4700928, 01-4266277; www.grgadventurekayaking.com) Run by Nepal's best kayaker. Operates rafting and kayaking trips and a four-day kayak clinic at a tented camp close to Fishling, near Kuringhat. Also rents kayaks.

Paddle Nepal (p213) As well as several white-water rafting options, there are beginner kayak clinics and combined canyoning/rafting expeditions at this Pokhara-based operation.

Rapidrunner Expeditions (p213) Offers kayak clinics and 'ducky trips', in addition to serious white-water rafting trips. Pokhara based.

Ultimate Descents Nepal (Map p90; ☎01-4381214; www.udnepal.com) Near Northfield Cafe in Thamel and part of the Borderlands group; it also has an office in Pokhara. Specialises in long participatory rafting trips as well as kayak instruction and clinics on the Seti River or at its Sun Koshi Beach Camp.

Ultimate Rivers (Map p90; www.ultimaterivers. com.np; Mandala St, Thamel) Associated with the New Zealand company Ultimate Descents International. The Kathmandu office is shared with Last Resort.

Kayaking

There has been a continuous increase in the number of kayakers coming to Nepal over the last few years, and it is justifiably recognised as a mecca for paddlers. Several companies offer trips that cater specifically to kayakers, where you get to explore the river with rafts carrying all your gear and food, and often camp near choice play spots.

The opportunities for kayak expeditions are exceptional. Of note, at the right flows, are the Mardi Khola, Tamba Kosi, Karnali headwaters, Thuli Bheri, Balephi Khola and tributaries of the Tamur.

WHIT RICHARDSON/GETTY IMAGES ©

Rafting on the Tamur river (p328)

The upper Modi Khola is also good for experienced kayakers. The side creek of the Bhurungdi Khola, by Birethani village, hides several waterfalls that are runnable by experienced kayakers.

Kayak Clinics

Nepal is an ideal place to learn to kayak and several companies offer learner kayak clinics. Due to the high levels of communication required to teach, the best instruction clinics tend to be staffed by both Western and Nepali instructors. Kayak clinics normally take about four days, which gives you time to get a good grounding in the basics of kayaking, safety and river dynamics.

The clinics are a pretty laid-back introduction to kayaking, with around four to six hours of paddling a day. On day one you'll learn self-rescue, T-rescue and the Eskimo roll, which will help you to right yourself when you capsize. Day two sees you on the river, learning to ferry glide (cross the river), eddy in and eddy out (entering and leaving currents) and perfecting your paddling strokes. Day three is when you start really having fun on the river,

running small (class 2) rapids and journeying down the river, learning how to read the rapids. Expect one instructor for every three people.

Equator Expeditions and Ultimate Rivers operate clinics on the upper Sun Kosi. Equator runs the Sukute Beach Resort, just north of Sukute village between kilometre markers 69 and 70. It's fairly comfortable, but has squat toilets and cold showers, and it has a great spot on the river, with a private beach, a bar area with pool tables and a lovely stretch of river nearby. It also has a pool, which is a real bonus when learning Eskimo rolls.

Ultimate Rivers uses the Ultimate Rivers Bhote Koshi Resort, between kilometre markers 83 and 84, which is a similarly basic camp. Equator charges US$200 for a four-day clinic if you don't mind taking the bus to get there. For both trips check what kind of transportation is included. You may find yourself flagging down local buses and putting your kayak on the roof for short rides after a trip down the river.

The Royal Beach Camp (p198) offers two- to seven-day kayak clinics from its

WARREN/500PX ©

Paragliding above Sarangkot (p213)

fixed camp and swimming pool at Kataudi on the Trisuli River, 85km from Kathmandu. Packages include two- to seven-day kayak clinics, combination kayaking, rafting and canyoning trips, and family-friendly expeditions.

Ultimate Descents Nepal (p48) operates its four-day clinics on the gentle Seti River, for around US$260, from Pokhara to Pokhara. The first day's training takes place on Phewa Tal and the remaining three days are on the Seti, with two nights' riverside camping. The advantage to learning on the Seti is that you get to journey down a wilderness river. Upper Sun Kosi kayak clinics can also be structured for instruction from one to four days from its base at the Sun Koshi Beach Camp.

Kayaking specialists like GRG Adventure Kayaking (p48) can often arrange kayaking tuition during the quieter sections of a Sun Kosi rafting run.

Drift Nepal (p48) also offers a four-day kayak clinic where you get your tuition while paddling down the lower Seti and staying in temporary beach camps; figure on US$280 per person.

Pokhara-based operations including Paddle Nepal (p213) and Rapidrunner Expeditions (p213) also offer kayaking courses.

Nose plugs are useful for those practise Eskimo rolls and you should bring a warm change of clothes as you are going to get wet. The bulk of kayak clinics operate in late October, November, March and April. December to February clinics are still possible, but with shorter days, and there's a lot less sunlight to warm you up at the beginning and end of the day.

Rock Climbing

Perhaps surprisingly, rock climbing is still in its infancy in Nepal and caving is even less developed. Most of the climbing is around the Kathmandu Valley. Hardcore Nepal (p203) offers a four-day climbing course for US$420, and Kathmandu's Astrek Climbing Wall (p86) offers guided weekly climbs for all levels at nearby Nagarjun.

Climbing Nepal's trekking peaks (p300) as part of a multiday training course is a popular activity.

If you prefer to get under rocks, then Hardcore offers combined climbing, abseiling and caving trips to the Siddha Gufa, a huge cave near Bandipur, as well as three-day multi-activity trips (US$250) that combine caving and canyoning.

Bungee Jumping

For those who want to up the adrenaline ante there are two established bungee jumps in Nepal. Last Resort (p192), on the road between Kathmandu and Tibet, offers a 160m plunge (one of the 10 highest bungee jumps in the world) off a bridge spanning a gorge through which the Bhote Kosi rages. It charges US$99 for a bungee day package that includes lunch and transportation.

Further west more elastic-band 'fun' can be had just outside Pokhara, where Zip-Flyer Nepal (p211) offers a 70m-high tower bungee jump (US$68). The same fiendish minds also offer an 1800m-long zipline ride (US$68) where speeds of 120km/h can be reached.

Canyoning

This wet-and-wild sport is a combination of abseiling, climbing, swimming and jumping into rivers. The best known canyoning area is on the turbulent Bhote Kosi north of Kathmandu on the road to Tibet, but there are more canyons in Sundarijal in the Kathmandu Valley and at Jalbiri en route to Chitwan. September, October, April and May offer the best conditions.

Canyoning trips are organised by Borderlands Resort (p192), Last Resort (p192) and Chhango (p86); expect to pay around US$100/150 for a one-/two-day trip, which can be combined with other activities.

Paragliding & Ultralights

Paragliding, where you strap yourself to a tandem parachute and silently sail on the thermals with incredible views of Annapurna and Macchapuchhare, is available just outside Pokhara and in Bandipur.

One of the longest-established paragliding companies, Sunrise Paragliding (p213) offers flights and courses from its Pokhara base.

Frontiers Paragliding (p213) is also based in Pokhara; if you enjoy its tandem flights you can sign up for a multiday package or take a pilot's course.

There's little regulation in the paragliding industry and injuries such as broken ankles or worse are not unheard of. Ask to see your pilot's licence before committing; a pilot with a minimum of three years' experience is what you are looking for.

An ultralight, which is like a paraglider with a lawnmower strapped to it, is a fabulous way to view the mountain peaks. Flights are available through Avia Club Nepal (p214) and Pokhara Ultralight (p214), both based in Pokhara. The 60-minute option gets you thrillingly close to the peaks; less than this and you'll just be flying around Phewa Tal. Open cockpits are more exciting but colder; a fixed-wing option gets you higher quicker.

Other Activities

Not all activities in Nepal involve a head for heights, a love of speed or a desire to get soaked in freezing river rapids. The three big national parks of the Terai – Chitwan, Bardia and Koshi Tappu – all offer safaris, forest walks and boat/canoe rides, all of which are delightfully relaxing and calm.

Plan Your Trip

Volunteering & Responsible Travel

Tourism certainly brings revenue and other benefits to the people of Nepal, and can play an important part in post-earthquake reconstruction. Sadly, negative impacts also follow in tourism's wake, from begging in city streets to deforestation along trekking trails. Read on to see how you can maximise your contribution while minimising your footprint.

Volunteering Tips

Choosing Where to Volunteer
Consider honestly how your skill set may best benefit an organisation and community, and then do some research to ensure your potential organisation is reputable and transparent.

Time is Valuable
Think realistically about how much time you can devote to a project. You are unlikely to be of lasting help if you stay for less than a couple of months.

Paying to Volunteer
It may surprise you to have to pay to volunteer, but many companies charge substantial placement fees and ask you to cover your own costs, including accommodation, food and transport.

Resources
Ethical Volunteering (www.ethicalvolunteering.org) has useful tips on selecting an ethical volunteer agency. *Volunteer: A Traveller's Guide to Making a Difference Around the World* offers invaluable one-stop information and directory; a Lonely Planet publication.

Volunteering

Hundreds of travellers volunteer in Nepal every year, working on an incredible range of development and conservation projects, covering everything from volunteering with street children in Kathmandu to counting the tracks of endangered animals in the high Himalaya. The potential for personal growth and the opportunity to forge a connection with a local community can give a profoundly deeper significance to the notion of travel. In the wake of Nepal's 2015 earthquake, volunteers have never been in greater need.

However, it is important to remember the principles of ethical volunteering – good volunteer agencies match a volunteer's skill sets to suitable projects that result in real and lasting benefit to local communities, rather than simply offering travellers the chance to feel better about themselves during a fleeting two-week placement.

As so-called 'voluntourism' has grown in popularity, dozens of organisations have sprung up to take advantage of a new source of revenue, muddying an already murky issue. You'll need to do serious research to ensure that your time and money are genuinely going to help the cause you are trying to advance. Do it right though, and an extended time spent volunteering will bring you much closer to the country. Dare we say it, it may even change your life.

Voluntrekking

A number of trekking and tour agencies use the proceeds from their trips to support charitable projects around Nepal, and many travellers also undertake sponsored treks and climbing expeditions in Nepal to raise money for specific charities and projects.

There are a number of organisations that set up expeditions of this kind, including the following:

Australian Himalayan Foundation (www. australianhimalayanfoundation.org.au) Offers fundraising treks to its aid projects.

Community Action Treks (www.catreks.com) Offers various treks that contribute to the work of Community Action Nepal.

Crooked Trails (www.crookedtrails.com) Runs fundraising treks and volunteer programs.

Himalayan Healthcare (www.himalayan-health care.org) Arranges medical and dental treks around Nepal.

Nepal Trust (www.nepaltrust.org) British agency that runs treks in Humla to support its development work.

Red Panda Network (www.redpandanetwork.org) Runs an annual nine-day trip to eastern Nepal to photograph red pandas, with proceeds going to panda conservation.

Summit Climb (www.summitclimb.com) Runs an annual service trek providing health care in remote parts of Solu Khumbu.

Volunteer Work

Voluntourism has become a booming business in Nepal, with travel companies co-opting the idea as a branch of their for-profit enterprises. To avoid the bulk of your placement fees going into the pockets of third-party agencies, it's important to do your research on the hundreds of organisations that now offer volunteer work and find a suitable one that supports your skills.

Although you give your time for free, you will be expected to pay for food and lodging, and you may also be asked to pay a placement fee. Volunteers should try to find out exactly how much of their placement fees is going into Nepal, and how much is going towards company profit and administrative costs. Fees paid to local agencies tend to be much lower than those charged by international volunteer agencies.

Nepal's orphanages in particular have come under a critical spotlight in recent years, with several operations linked to child trafficking and adoption scandals. Conor Grennan's book *Little Princes* is an inspiring account of time volunteering in a Nepali orphanage that touches on the corruption and murky moral dilemmas inherent in trying to do the right thing in Nepal. Following a damning UNICEF report in 2014, many foreign governments now advise their citizens against volunteering at orphanages unless they have been verified as legitimate by the Nepali Central Child Welfare Board (CCWB; www.ccwb.gov.np).

When looking for a volunteer placement, it is essential to investigate what your chosen organisation does and, more importantly, how it goes about it. If the focus is not primarily on your skills, and how these can be applied to help local people, then this should ring alarm bells. Any organisation that promises to let you do any kind of work, wherever you like, for as long as you like, is unlikely to be putting the needs of local people first.

For any organisation working with children, child protection is a serious concern; places that do not conduct background checks on volunteers should be regarded with extreme caution. For some sobering perspectives on the volunteering industry, see www.nextgenerationnepal.org/ethical-volunteering and www.just-one.org/your-chance/volunteering.

Following is a list of organisations offering volunteering opportunities in Nepal, but Lonely Planet does not endorse any organisations that we do not work with directly, so it is essential that you do your own thorough research before agreeing to volunteer with anyone.

Butterfly Foundation (www.butterflyfoundation. org) Accepts volunteers to help with administration and child care in Pokhara; linked to Butterfly Lodge (p215).

Nepali children play with foreign volunteers at a Kathmandu earthquake relief camp

Child Environment Nepal (www.cennepal.org.np) Accepts child-care volunteers at its premises at Naya Bazaar in Kathmandu.

Child Rescue Nepal (www.childrescuenepal.org) Can arrange placements working to improve the lives of trafficked and abandoned children.

Ford Foundation (www.fordnepal.org) Arranges volunteer work focusing on teaching and child care.

Global Vision International (www.gvi.co.uk) Offers both short- and long-term internships and volunteer placements, some combined with trekking.

Helping Hands (www.helpinghandsusa.org) Places medical volunteers at clinics around Nepal.

Himalayan Children Care Home (www.hchmustang.org) Accepts volunteers to help with the care and education of kids from remote Mustang who are attending schools in Pokhara.

Insight Nepal (www.insightnepal.org) Combines a cultural and education program near Pokhara with a volunteer placement and a trek in the Annapurna region; lasts seven weeks or three months.

Kathmandu Environmental Education Project (KEEP; www.keepnepal.org) Placements in education and training in and around Kathmandu; minimum two-month placements preferred and a US$50 administration fee.

Mountain Fund (www.mountainvolunteer.org) Education, media, agriculture and health-care opportunities at Her Farm.

Mountain Trust Nepal (www.mountain-trust. org) British NGO that can arrange volunteer placements in social projects around Pokhara.

Nepal Trust (www.nepaltrust.org) Has a focus on Humla in western Nepal.

Nepali Children's Trust (www.nepalichildrenstrust.com) Works with disabled Nepali children.

People & Places (www.travel-peopleandplaces. co.uk) Placements for responsible and ethical volunteering.

Prisoners Assistance Nepal (www.panepal. org) Kathmandu-based organisation that needs volunteers to help with social justice and look after children whose parents are in prison.

Rokpa (www.rokpa.org) Swiss-Tibetan organisation that needs volunteers for its medical tent at Bodhnath for six or more weeks (December to March).

Rural Assistance Nepal (www.rannepal.org) UK-based charity that places volunteers in education and health care.

Sustainable Agriculture Development Program (www.sadpnepal.org) Arranges placements in sustainable agriculture and social programs near Pokhara.

Volunteers Initiative Nepal (www.volunteering nepal.org) Wide range of opportunities; see also www.friendsofvin.nl.

Responsible Travel

In the 65 years since Nepal opened its borders to outsiders, tourism has brought many benefits, in terms of wealth generation, employment opportunities, infrastructure, health care, education and transport, creating a level of social mobility that would have been unthinkable in the past. Many of the Nepalis who own trekking companies today worked as porters themselves 20 or 30 years ago.

Sadly, the negative effects of tourism are also clear to see. Begging is widespread, litter chokes mountain trails, and forests are diminished as lodge owners collect ever more firewood to keep trekkers supplied with warm showers and hot meals.

There is endless discussion about the most environmentally and culturally sensitive way to travel. What is certain is that making a positive contribution is as much about the way you behave as the money you spend. Independent travellers may spend less money, but they have a much greater impact on poverty alleviation by contributing directly to the local economy.

Drop into the Kathmandu office of the Kathmandu Environmental Education Project (KEEP; www.keepnepal.org) for more advice. And if you have any clothes, equipment or medications left at the end of your trip, consider donating them to the porter's clothing bank at KEEP.

Economic Choices

Don't underestimate your power as an informed consumer. By choosing local trekking agencies, tour companies and lodges that have a policy of reducing their environmental and cultural impact, you are providing an example to other travellers and an incentive for other companies to adopt the same practices. Hiring guides on treks also helps; as well as improving your cultural understanding, it provides employment, infusing money into the hill economy.

For more on the general issues of responsible travel check out Tourism

---

DONATING IN NEPAL

While travelling in Nepal, many people are struck by the challenges faced by ordinary people. As one of the poorest nations on earth, Nepal has few public services provided by government, and access to even basic essentials such as health care, sanitation and education is limited, particularly in rural areas, leaving many local people in a desperate position. The 2015 earthquake has only worsened the plight of Nepal's poor, with many families still living in temporary accommodation over two years after the earthquake.

Just by visiting Nepal and spending money in businesses owned by local people, you are making a contribution to their future, but should you wish to make a more lasting contribution, consider making a donation to a non-government organisation that is working long-term to improve the lives of people in Nepal. Dozens of Nepali and international organisations are working in areas as diverse as installing water pumps and reuniting trafficked children with their families, and almost all rely on support from donations as well as funding from international governments.

As in any sphere, some organisations are more effective than others, so it is important to investigate the options carefully before you contribute. Seek out organisations that spend the bulk of donations on local projects, rather than on administration costs and salaries for their staff. The website www.ethicalconsumer. org has some useful information on ethical giving – search the site for 'comparing charities'. For listings of charities working in Nepal, visit www.charity-charities.org/Nepal-charities/Nepal.html.

RESPONSIBLE TRAVELLER'S ETIQUETTE

➡ When visiting monasteries or temples, avoid smoking and remove your shoes and hat before you enter. Don't sit with the soles of your feet pointing towards a person or a Buddha image.

➡ Some Hindu temples are closed to non-Hindus (this is normally indicated by a sign) and others will not allow you to enter with any leather items (mainly shoes and belts).

➡ Locals always leave a donation in a gompa or temple and you should follow their example.

➡ If you are introduced to a Buddhist lama it is customary to give them a *kata* (white scarf). Place it in the lama's hands, not around their neck.

➡ Avoid touching children on the head, particularly young monks.

➡ Short shorts, sleeveless tops and other revealing items of clothing are unsuitable for women or men; nudity is unacceptable anywhere. Women should carry a sarong with them if they will be bathing at local water taps.

➡ Public displays of affection between men and women are frowned upon.

➡ Never point at someone, or beckon them with a single finger. If you do need to beckon someone over to you, use your whole hand instead of one finger, and be careful to keep your palm facing downwards.

➡ Never step over someone's legs – politely ask them to move their legs so you can get past.

➡ Food becomes ritually *jhuto* (polluted) if touched by someone else's hand, plate or utensils, so only eat off your own plate and never use your own fork or spoon to serve food off a communal plate.

➡ When using water from a communal jug or cup, pour it straight into your mouth without touching the sides (and without pouring it all over your shirt!).

➡ When hiring porters and guides for treks, ensure they are properly equipped and have insurance; as their employer, you are responsible for their wellbeing.

Concern (www.tourismconcern.org.uk) and World Expedition's *Responsible Travel* guidebook, available at www.world expeditions.com.

To get a different perspective on Nepal, Hidden Journeys (www.hiddenjourneys nepal.com) specialises in connecting visitors with Nepal's new generation of social entrepreneurs, artists and activists aiming to bring change to their country. To book a tour contact the company well in advance.

Ethical Shopping

Many species in Nepal are being driven towards extinction by the trade in animal parts. Although most products made from endangered species are sent to China or Tibet for use in traditional medicine, travellers also contribute to the problem by buying souvenirs made from wild animals.

In particular, avoid anything made from fur, and the metal-inlaid animal skulls and tortoise shells. Another item to avoid is the *shahtoosh* shawl, a form of pashmina that comes from (and results in the death of) the endangered *chiru* (Tibetan antelope). *Shahtoosh* is illegal in Nepal.

Fair Trade

Fair-trade principles can make a genuine difference in Nepal, a nation where 83% of the population live in underdeveloped rural areas. A number of nonprofit organisations support local cooperatives that pay artisans a fair wage to produce traditional crafts in safe working conditions, using sustainable materials, without child labour. Many of these organisations provide work, training and education for workers from neglected economic groups, including women, the disabled and members of the 'untouchable' castes.

Established by the Nepali philanthropist Tulsi Mehar, Mahaguthi (p108) provides employment and rehabilitation for destitute women, funded through the sale of quality handicrafts at its shops in Patan and Lazimpat (in Kathmandu). In Pokhara, the Women's Skills Development Organisation (p224) has two outlets in Lakeside selling woven and stitched bags and toys.

The workshops run by Tibetan refugees at Jawalakhel in Patan also contribute directly to the welfare of disadvantaged people.

More information on fair trade can be found at www.fairtradegroupnepal.org.

Begging

Hinduism and Buddhism have a long tradition of giving alms to the needy. However, begging in Nepal today is also fuelled by the perception that foreigners will hand out money on demand. In areas frequented by tourists, some groups of beggars work specific street corners using tried-and-tested scams to separate tourists from their money. Among all this, there are also many people who are genuinely in need and there are likely to be many more people who fit this description following the 2015 earthquake.

At many religious sites you will see long lines of beggars, and pilgrims customarily give a coin to everyone in the line (there are moneychangers nearby who will change notes for loose change). Sadhus (holy men) are also dependent on alms, though there are plenty of con artists among their ranks.

In tourist areas, you can expect to be hit with requests for 'one pen, one chocolate, one rupee' by children and even sometimes by adults. Don't encourage this behaviour. Most Nepalis find it offensive and demeaning (as do most visitors), and it encourages a whole range of unhealthy attitudes.

Ways to Help

You only need to look at the standards of dentistry in Nepal to realise that handing out sweets to children is neither appropriate nor responsible. If you want to give something to local people, make the donation to an adult, preferably someone in authority, such as a teacher or a lama at a local monastery. Appropriate gifts include toothbrushes and toothpaste, pens and paper, biodegradable soap, and school books, preferably with lessons in Nepali.

Many international NGOs working in Nepal rely on support from international donors. The late Sir Edmund Hillary's Himalayan Trust (www.hillaryhimalayantrust.org) supports health care, cultural projects and afforestation in Nepal and has rebuilt hundreds of school destroyed by the earthquake. Similar work is carried out by the Sir Edmund Hillary Foundation (www.thesiredmundhillaryfoundation.ca) in Canada, the Australian Himalayan Foundation (www.australianhimalayanfoundation.org.au) and the American Himalayan Foundation (www.himalayan-foundation.org).

Cultural Considerations

Travellers may find the traditional lifestyle of people in Nepal to be picturesque, but in many places it is a meagre, subsistence-level existence that could be improved in numerous ways. The challenge faced by many charitable organisations working in Nepal is how to bring a modern standard of living without destroying the traditional culture.

You can do your bit by showing respect for local traditions – this will also demonstrate to local people that the relationship between locals and foreigners is one of equals. Many of the problems experienced by travellers in Nepal have been caused by past travellers who have treated locals as second-class citizens.

The behaviour of some photographers at places such as Pashupatinath (the most holy cremation site in Nepal) is shameful – imagine the outrage if a busload of scantily clad, camera-toting tourists invaded a family funeral in the West. Do not intrude with a camera, unless it is clearly OK with the people you are photographing. Ask first, and respect the wishes of local people. Photography is prohibited at many temples and monasteries, and it is plainly inappropriate at cremations or where people are washing in public at riverbanks or cisterns.

Plan Your Trip

Eat & Drink Like a Local

Nepali food blends Indian and Newari influences with Tibetan and foreign imports. In Kathmandu and Pokhara you can eat an unparalleled range of dishes from around the globe, but the choice becomes much more limited once you head into the countryside or along trekking trails.

Where to Eat

Tourist Restaurants Kathmandu and Pokhara boast an astounding range of global cuisines, from Mexican to Thai, plus great bakeries and cafes.

Newari Restaurants Several Kathmandu restaurants serve traditional Newari food in grand restored surroundings, accompanied by traditional dance and music.

Bhojanalaya Local restaurants serve up daal bhaat and snacks such as chow mein, but often no English menus.

Misthan Bhandar These Indian-style sweet shops serve tea, sweets and vegetarian snacks like *dosa* (South-Indian style fried lentil-flour pancakes) and samosas.

Trekking Teahouses These offer a carb-heavy selection of daal bhaat tarkari, fried potatoes, pasta, soup and even a 'Snickers roll' (deep-fried Snickers in batter!).

Nepali Food

The staple meal of Nepal is *daal bhaat tarkari* – literally lentil soup, rice and curried vegetables. If you are lucky it will be spiced up with *achar* (pickles) and maybe some *dahi* (curd or yoghurt) or *papad* (pappadam – a crispy fried lentil-flour pancake). To eat daal bhaat the local way, pour the soupy daal onto the rice, mix it into balls with your fingers, add a pinch of pickle and vegetables and shovel it into your mouth with your right hand. If you order daal bhaat, someone will come around offering free extra helpings of rice, daal and *tarkari*. Only very occasionally does it come with *masu* (meat).

Most Hindu Nepalis are vegetarians, some out of choice and some out of necessity. However, the Newars of the Kathmandu Valley are great meat eaters – *buff* (water buffalo) is the meat of choice, but goat is also common. Cows are sacred to Hindus and are never eaten. Some Kathmandu restaurants import real beef from India and you can also get yak steaks at some trekking lodges.

Spices feature heavily in Newari food, especially chilli, and Newari dishes are usually served with *chiura* (dry, beaten rice), which looks, and frankly tastes, like dry oatmeal porridge.

Top: Traditional Nepali *thali* (set meal), including lentil soup and rice

Bottom: Spices and teas for sale in Asan Tole (p78), Kathmandu

Many Newari dishes are only eaten at celebrations or family events, but several upmarket restaurants in Kathmandu now offer good Newari cuisine.

Nepal is also one of the best places to try Tibetan cuisine, though most dishes are simple variations on momos (dumplings) or *thuk* noodle stews (*thukpa* are long noodles, whereas *thenthuk* is more like torn pasta).

Nepali has some decent street food. A couple of samsa (samosas – potato curry, fried in a lentil-dough parcel) or papad make a great light meal. Newari beer snacks are legendary – try a plate of seku-wa (spiced, barbecued meat) or 'masala peanuts' (with chilli and spices) when you have a beer.

Many Nepalis round off a meal with a digestif of *pan* (betel nut and leaf mixture). Those little spots of red on the pavement that look like little pools of blood are (generally!) *pan*.

Recipes

Food Nepal (www.food-nepal.com) offers an excellent introduction to Nepali food and ingredients, with recipes from mango lassi to chicken chilli.

The Nepal Cookbook, by the Association of Nepalis in the Americas, is a good collection of home recipes, or take a look at *Taste of Nepal,* by Jyoti Pathak.

Desserts

Like their Indian neighbours, Nepalis enjoy a huge range of sticky sweets, mostly based on milk curd, *jaggery* (palm sugar) and nuts. Top treats include *barfi* (milk fudge), *rasbari* (milk balls), *lal mohan* (deep-fried milky dough balls), *kheer* (rice pudding) and *julebi* (orange-coloured, syrupy, fried dough swirls).

Anyone who visits Bhaktapur should try the *juju dhau* (king of curds), which is wonderfully creamy thick yoghurt. *Sikarni* is a popular traditional dessert of whipped yoghurt with cinnamon, nuts and dried fruit.

Drinks
Alcoholic

Nepali beer is pretty good, especially after a hard day's trek. Tuborg (Danish), Carlsberg (Danish) and San Miguel (Spanish) are brewed under licence in Nepal; local brands include the excellent Sherpa, as well as Gorkha, Everest and Kathmandu Beer. The local Khukri Rum goes down well with mixers. Also available is Abominable Snowman gin, a British-Nepal collaboration.

Officially, alcohol is not sold by retailers on the first two days (full-moon days) and the last two Saturdays of the Nepali month, but this rarely affects tourist restaurants.

Nonalcoholic

The golden rule in Nepal is *don't drink the water*. Cheap bottled water is available everywhere, but every bottle contributes to Nepal's mountain of waste plastic. See p396 for more about water purification.

Tea is almost always safe. For proper Nepali *chiya* (sometimes called masala tea), the leaves are boiled with milk, sugar and spices. If you want Western-style tea, ask for 'milk separate'. Kathmandu and Pokhara now have dozens of places to get proper espresso coffee.

In Tibetan-influenced areas the drink of choice is black tea churned with salt and butter – providing useful metabolites for dealing with high altitude and cold weather. It's an acquired taste – locals often pour it over their *tsampa* (roasted barley flour).

In Indian-influenced areas, look out for *lassi* – a refreshing drink of curd (yoghurt) mixed with sugar and what may be untreated water (proceed with caution).

Regions at a Glance

Kathmandu

Architecture
Food
Shopping

Malla Masterpieces

Kathmandu's medieval old town is stuffed with ancient stupas, hidden courtyards and millennium-year-old sculptures at every crossroad; each turn reveals a new masterpiece of medieval Malla architecture.

Global Tastes

The Thamel district is a global mash-up of Tibetan, Japanese, Thai and Italian restaurants, separated only by bakeries offering espresso and lemon cheesecake. For something special, the city's Newari restaurants offer the more refined tastes of the Rana court.

Shopper's Nirvana

Where to start? World-class outdoor gear, Asia's best bookshops, bargain-priced pashminas, Tibetan thang-kas (religious paintings) and prayer flags...the list is endless. Bring a spare bag – you'll need it.

p64

Around the Kathmandu Valley

Temples
Outdoor Activities
Traditional Architecture

Temple Art

The valley boasts the world's densest collection of World Heritage Sites, with almost every town here blessed with stunning temples and exquisite statuary, even after the 2015 earthquake.

Hiking & Biking

The valley's web of fine hiking and mountain-biking trails offer the best way to explore this area. To up the ante, head for the Tibetan border for some wild rafting and canyoning.

Newari Architecture

Bhaktapur and Patan top the list, but there are dozens of other charming villages to explore, from Kirtipur in the south to sleepy Budhanilkantha in the north. All offer fine traditional architecture and village squares that seem lifted from the 15th century.

p120

Kathmandu to Pokhara

History
Extreme Sports
Traditional Towns

Forts & Sacrifices

Despite earthquake damage, Nepal's first capital at Gorkha boasts a historically important and impressive royal fort palace, with historic temples littering the backstreets. Gruesome sacrifices to honour the goddess Durga take place here and at the nearby hilltop temple at Manakamana.

River Fun

Rafting runs and kayaking clinics on the warm waters of the Trisuli River are the most popular excursions, and there are some exciting canyoning, caving and ziplining add-ons.

Restored Bandipur

Bandipur's Newari-style old town is one of the most atmospheric in Nepal's Middle Hills, with outdoor teahouses, good accommodation options and excellent day hikes.

p196

Pokhara

Relaxation
Vistas
Trekking

The Easy Life

With a warm climate, little pollution, and backpacker comforts, Pokhara is the perfect place to take a break, preferably over a leisurely lakeshore breakfast or an ambitious round of yoga and massage.

Mountain Panoramas

It's all about Machhapuchhare and the Annapurnas, with spectacular dawn views from atop Sarangkot ridge, the World Peace Pagoda or while paddling a *dhunga* rowboat around serene Phewa Tal.

Annapurna Trails

A superb range of treks kick off from Pokhara, from short teahouse hikes into the foothills around Ghorepani and Ghandruk to the alpine splendour of the Annapurna Sanctuary, Tibet-style Trans-Himalayan deserts around Jomsom or the full monty: the Annapurna Circuit.

p206

The Terai & Mahabharat Range

Temples
Wildlife
Outdoor Activities

Buddha's Birthplace

There are two major religious sites in the Terai. Buddhists celebrate the birthplace of the Buddha at Lumbini, while Hindus flock to the colourful temple complex at Janakpur to commemorate the marriage of Rama to Sita.

Tigers, Rhinos & Elephants

Fabulous Chitwan and remote Bardia National Parks both offer big-game wildlife watching in sultry river deltas and grasslands, while Koshi Tappu Wildlife Reserve is ground zero for birdwatchers.

Safaris & Hiking

Scanning the jungle for wildlife is the major activity in the Terai, though there's also some good off-the-beaten-track walking around Ilam and non-touristy Tansen.

p237

On the Road

Pokhara
p206

**The Terai &
Mahabharat Range**
p237

**Kathmandu to
Pokhara**
p196

Kathmandu
p64

**Around the
Kathmandu Valley**
p120

Kathmandu

01 / POP 1.3 MILLION / ELEV 1337M

Best Places to Eat

➡ Gaia Restaurant (p103)

➡ Third Eye (p103)

➡ Kaiser Cafe (p104)

➡ Fire & Ice Pizzeria (p104)

➡ Roadhouse Cafe (p100)

Best Places to Stay

➡ Hotel Ganesh Himal (p96)

➡ Dwarika's (p99)

➡ Kantipur Temple House (p95)

➡ Kathmandu Guest House (p89)

Why Go?

For many, stepping off a plane into Kathmandu is a pupil-dilating experience, a riot of sights, sounds and smells that can quickly lead to sensory overload. Whether you're barrelling through the traffic-jammed alleyways of the old town in a rickshaw, marvelling at the medieval temples or dodging trekking touts in the backpacker district of Thamel, Kathmandu can be an intoxicating, amazing and exhausting place.

The 2015 earthquake destroyed several temples in Kathmandu's Unesco-listed Durbar Sq, but most areas emerged unscathed. Stroll through the backstreets and Kathmandu's timeless cultural and artistic heritage still reveals itself in hidden temples overflowing with marigolds, courtyards full of drying chillies and rice, and tiny hobbit-sized workshops.

This endlessly fascinating, sometimes infuriating city has enough sights to keep you busy for a week, but be sure to leave its backpacker comforts and explore the 'real Nepal' before your time runs out.

When to Go
Kathmandu

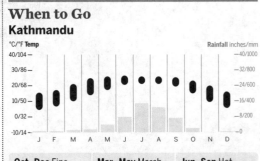

Oct–Dec Fine mountain views and warm days until December, with high-season crowds.

Mar–May March brings the Seto Machhendranath festival. Days can be hot in May.

Jun–Sep Hot days and frequent monsoon showers, but also the spectacular Indra Jatra festival.

History

The history of Kathmandu is really a history of the Newars, the main inhabitants of the Kathmandu Valley. While the documented history of the valley goes back to the Kiratis, around the 7th century BC, the foundation of Kathmandu itself dates from the 12th century AD, during the time of the Malla dynasty.

The original settlements of Yambu and Yangala, at the confluence of the Bagmati and Vishnumati Rivers in what is now the southern half of the old town, grew up around the trade route to Tibet. Traders and pilgrims stayed at rest houses such as the now destroyed Kasthamandap, which lent its name to the city.

Originally known as Kantipur, the city flourished during the Malla era, and the bulk of its superb temples, buildings and other monuments date from this time. Initially, Kathmandu was an independent city within the valley, but in the 14th century the valley was united under the rule of the Malla king of Bhaktapur. The 15th century saw division once more, this time into three independent kingdoms: Kathmandu, Patan and Bhaktapur. Rivalry between the three city-states led to a series of wars that left each state weakened and vulnerable to the 1768 invasion of the valley by Prithvi Narayan Shah.

The ensuing Shah dynasty unified Nepal and made the expanded city of Kathmandu its new capital – a position the city has held ever since. In 1934 a massive earthquake reshaped parts of Kathmandu, and the reconstruction created a network of modern boulevards such as New Rd.

Kathmandu escaped the worst of the Maoist uprising in the 1990s, though the city was frequently crippled by demonstrations and strikes. Tens of thousands of Nepalis flooded into the rapidly expanding city to escape the political violence, and the city infrastructure is still struggling to cope even a decade after the end of the conflict.

On 25 April 2015, history repeated itself as another massive earthquake shook the Kathmandu Valley. Several of Kathmandu's most famous monuments were reduced to rubble and the city swelled with rural refugees whose homes had been destroyed. While life is slowly returning to normal in the Nepali capital after the disaster, the repercussions of the earthquake are likely to be felt for generations.

KATHMANDU

⊙ Sights

Most of the interesting things to see in Kathmandu are clustered in the old part of town, focused on the majestic Durbar Sq and its surrounding backstreets.

In terms of tourism, the effect of the 2015 earthquake in Kathmandu was largely limited to the Dharahara Tower and the city's famous Durbar Sq, where several major temples at the south end were toppled. Most other sights were relatively untouched and have since been restored.

◉ Durbar Square

Kathmandu's **Durbar Square** (Map p74; foreigner/SAARC Rs 1000/150, no student tickets) was where the city's kings were once crowned and legitimised, and from where they ruled ('durbar' means palace). Tragically, parts of the square were seriously damaged during the 2015 earthquake. As the first tremor hit, palaces crumbled and temples tumbled from their plinths, reducing several temples in this Unesco World Heritage–listed site to a mound of splintered timber and brick dust. Despite this, much still endures amid the destruction and rebuilding has already started. Many key monuments such as the palace of the Kumari – Nepal's living goddess – stand in defiance of the disaster.

> ### ⓘ DURBAR SQUARE TICKETS
>
> The admission ticket to Durbar Sq gives access to all the temples in the square, as well as Hanuman Dhoka and technically the museums inside it (though the museums are currently closed for renovation). The ticket is only valid for the date stamped. If you want a longer duration you need to go to the **site office** (Map p74; ☏ 01-4268969; www.kathmandu.gov.np; Basantapur Sq; ◷ 6am-7pm), on the south side of Basantapur Sq, to get a free visitor pass, which allows you access for as long as your visa is valid (if you extend your visa you can extend your visitor pass). You will need your passport and one photo and the process takes about two minutes. You generally need to show your ticket even if you are just transiting the square to New Rd or Freak St. There is a toilet near the site office.

Kathmandu Highlights

1 Kathmandu's Old Town (p77) Wandering labyrinthine backstreets, little-known temples and hidden courtyards such as the Kathesimbhu Stupa.

2 Kumari Bahal (p69) Marvelling at the ornate courtyard and at how much survived the 2015 earthquake in Kathmandu's regal Durbar Sq.

3 Newari restaurants (p102) Dining on momos (dumplings) and wild boar to the beat of *madal* (drums) and *bansari* (flutes) at a traditional restaurant.

4 Thamel (p109) Shopping for pashminas, thangkas and trekking gear for family and friends.

5 Swayambhunath Stupa (p117) Dodging the monkeys at the sacred stupa of this Unesco World Heritage Site.

6 Garden of Dreams (p82) Escaping the traffic in this peaceful and beautifully restored Rana-era garden.

7 Asan Tole (p78) Feeling the energy of Kathmandu's busiest market junction.

8 Seto Machhendranath Temple (p78) Watching the interplay between Buddhism and Hinduism against a backdrop of chiming bells.

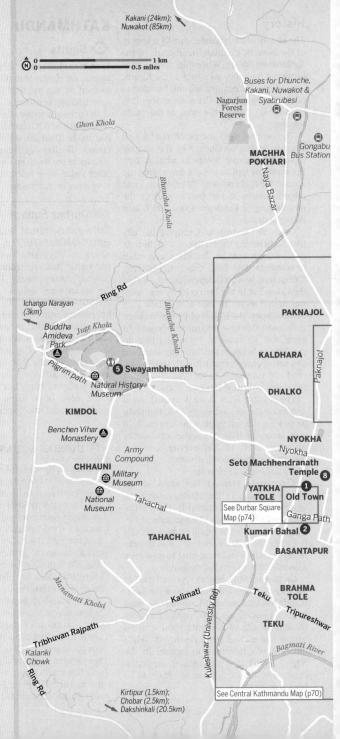

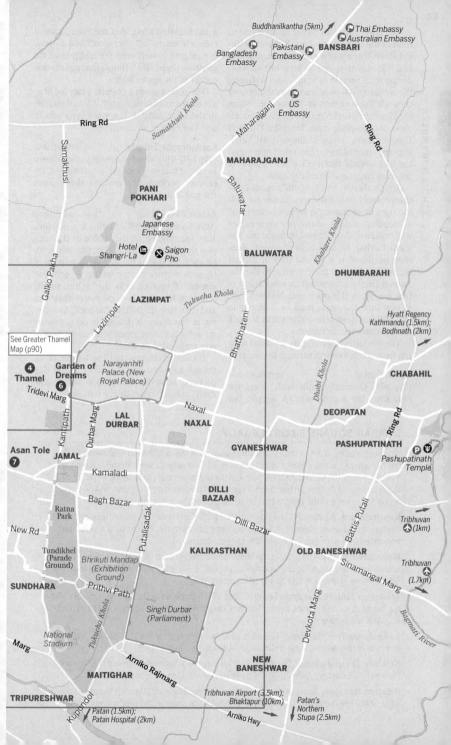

The government of Nepal has pledged to rebuild the lost monuments, but even without these, there is still a huge amount to see, and it is easy to spend an hour or two wandering from temple to temple and watching the continuous flow of humanity that moves through these streets as it has done since the time of Prithvi Narayan Shah. Although most of the square dates from the 17th and 18th centuries (many of the original buildings are much older), a great deal of rebuilding had already taken place here following the even larger earthquake of 1934.

The Durbar Sq area is actually made up of three loosely linked squares. To the south is the open Basantapur Sq area, a former royal elephant stables whose northern palace wall remains unstable and is closed off. The main Durbar Sq area is to the west. Running northeast is a second part of Durbar Sq, which contains the entrance to the Hanuman Dhoka palace and an assortment of temples. From this open area Makhan Tole, at one time the main road in Kathmandu and still the most interesting street to walk down, continues northeast.

The Durbar Sq monuments are listed moving from south to north through the square.

Singh Sattal   HISTORIC BUILDING

(Map p74) Originally built with wood left over from the Kasthamandap Temple, this squat building was called the Silengu Sattal (*silengu* means 'left over wood' and a *sattal* is a pilgrim hostel) until the addition of the golden-winged *singh* (lions) that guard each corner of the upper floor.

The building was a popular place for *bhajan* (devotional music) until it was damaged in the earthquake. It has since been rebuilt and looks oddly unweathered.

Kabindrapur Temple   HINDU TEMPLE

(Map p74) This wooden temple, also known as the Dhansa Dega, is an ornate 17th-century performance pavilion that houses the god of music.

Ashok Binayak   HINDU SHRINE

(Maru Ganesh; Map p74) At the top of Maru Tole, surrounded by the rubble of the temples that used to surround it, this tiny golden shrine is one of the four most important Ganesh shrines in the valley. A constant stream of visitors help themselves to the self-serve *tika* (sandalwood paste) dispenser and then ring the bells at the back. An offering at this shrine is thought to ensure safety on a forthcoming journey, so come here if you are headed on a trek.

It's uncertain how old the temple is, although its gilded roof was added in the 19th century. Look for the golden shrew (Ganesh's vehicle) opposite the temple.

DURBAR SQUARE'S LOST LEGACY

Nowhere are the scars of the 2015 earthquake more obvious than in Kathmandu's Durbar Sq, where a succession of landmark temples and palaces were literally shaken apart by the force of the tremor. In time, some of these monuments may be reconstructed, but the grandeur of Durbar Sq has been somewhat diminished by their loss. As you wander around, you will see the plinths that once supported the following temples.

Kasthamandap (Map p74) The building that gave Kathmandu its name, built in the 12th century as a pilgrim shelter but with roots dating back to the 7th century. It was later converted into a temple to Goraknath. Largely destroyed.

Maju Deval (Map p74) A handsome, three-tiered step-roofed temple that was formerly one of Kathmandu's principal landmarks, built in 1690 by the mother of Bhaktapur's king Bhupatindra Malla. Only the 10-tiered base remains.

Trailokya Mohan Narayan Temple (Map p74) A three-tiered temple to Narayan/Vishnu, formerly famous for its carved timbers; only the fine carved Garuda statue in front survived the quake.

Kakeshwar Temple (Map p74) Built in 1681, but damaged in the 1934 quake and rebuilt in a hybrid Newari and India shikhara style. Under reconstruction.

Krishna Temple (Chyasin Dega; Map p74) An elegant octagonal temple in the Newari tiered style, constructed in 1648–49 by Pratap Malla. Under reconstruction.

Krishna Narayan Temple (Map p74) A three-tiered Narayan (Vishnu) temple to the west of the Shiva-Parvati Temple. A pile of bricks sits unattended on the empty plinth.

ⓘ ORIENTATION & ADDRESSES IN KATHMANDU

The most interesting part of Kathmandu is the crowded backstreets of the rectangular-shaped old town. This is bordered to the east by the sprawling modern new town and to the north by the main tourist and backpacker district of Thamel (pronounced tha-*mel*). With over 2500 tourist-related companies jammed into half a dozen narrow streets, Thamel boasts a collection of hotels, restaurants, trekking agencies, bakeries and shops that is rivalled only by Bangkok's Khao San Rd. Thamel is 15 to 20 minutes' walk north from Durbar Sq.

East of Thamel is Durbar Marg, a wide street flanked by airline offices, restaurants and expensive hotels. Further north are the embassy and NGO districts of Lazimpat and Maharajganj. To the south of town is Patan, a historically distinct city, which has now partially merged with Kathmandu's southern sprawl. Both Kathmandu and Patan are encircled by the Ring Rd.

In old Kathmandu, streets are only named after their district, or *tole*. The names of these districts, squares and other landmarks (perhaps a monastery or temple) form the closest thing to an address. For example, the address for everyone living within a 100m radius of Thahiti Tole is Thahiti Tole. 'Thamel' is now used to describe a sprawling area with at least a dozen roads and several hundred hotels and restaurants.

Given this anarchic approach it is amazing that any mail gets delivered – it does, but slowly. If you're trying to find a particular house, shop or business, make sure you get detailed directions.

Maru Tole
STREET

This *tole* (street) leads you away from Durbar Sq down to the Vishnumati River, where a footbridge continues the pathway to Swayambhunath. This was a busy street in the hippie era, but the famous pastry shops that gave it the nickname 'Pie Alley' have long gone. It's worth strolling down to see **Maru Hiti**, one of the city's many sunken water conduits.

Shiva-Parvati Temple
HINDU TEMPLE

(Nawa Jogini Temple; Map p74) Looking north from the plinth of the wrecked Maju Deval, a pair of much-photographed white images of Shiva and his consort look out from the upstairs window. The temple was built in the late 1700s by Bahadur Shah, the son of Prithvi Narayan Shah. It stands on a two-stage platform that may have been an open dancing stage hundreds of years earlier. There are some worrying cracks in the brick walls, which are supported by braces.

Kumari Bahal
COURTYARD

(Map p74) At the junction of Durbar and Basantapur squares, this red-brick, three-storey building is home to the Kumari, the girl who is selected to be the town's living goddess and a symbol of *devi* – the Hindu concept of female spiritual energy. Inside the building is **Kumari Chowk**, a three-storey courtyard. It is enclosed by magnificently carved wooden balconies and windows, making it quite possibly the most beautiful courtyard in Nepal.

The Kumari (p79) generally shows her face between 9am and 11am. Photographing the goddess is forbidden, but you are quite free to photograph the courtyard when she is not present. In 2005 the Kumari went on strike, refusing to appear at her window for tourists, after authorities denied her guardians' request for a 10% cut of Durbar Sq's admission fees!

The building, in the style of the Buddhist *vihara* (monastic abodes) of the valley, was built in 1757 by Jaya Prakash Malla. The courtyard contains a miniature stupa carrying the symbols of Saraswati, the goddess of learning. Amazingly, the *bahal* escaped with only minor damage during the 2015 earthquake despite the destruction all around – a sign some Nepalis see as the Kumari's benign influence.

The large yellow gate to the right of the Kumari Bahal conceals the huge chariot that transports the Kumari around the city during the annual Indra Jatra festival. Look for the huge wooden runners with their sacred painted tips in front of the Kumari Bahal that are used to transport the chariot.

Gaddhi Baithak
PALACE

(Map p74) Dominating the eastern side of Durbar Sq, this white neoclassical building lost large chunks of its once elegant facade during the earthquake and is scheduled for renovation. It stands as a memorial to the imported European style that became fashionable in Nepal during the Rana period.

Central Kathmandu

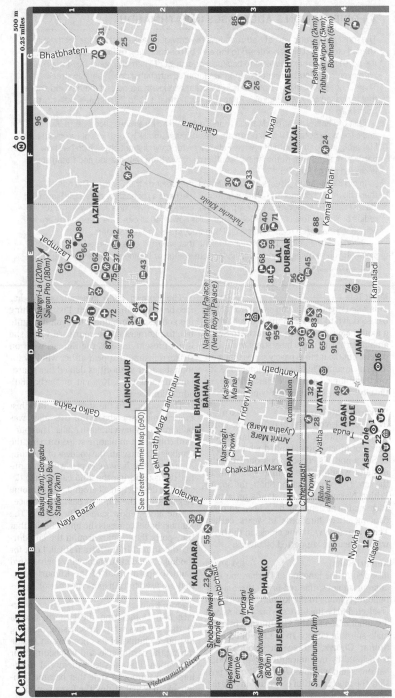

N
0   500 m
0   0.25 miles

Bhatbhateni

LAZIMPAT

Hotel Shangri-La (120m);
Saigon Pho (180m)

Lazimpat

Balaju (3km); Gongabu
(Kathmandu) Bus
Station (2km)

Naya Bazar

Galko Pakha

LAINCHAUR

Lekhnath Marg Lainchaur

THAMEL

PAKNAJOL

Paknajol

See Greater Thamel Map (p90)

BHAGWAN
BAHAL

Narsingh
Chowk

Chaksibari Marg

KALDHARA

Dhobichaur

Indrani
Temple

DHALKO

Shobabaghwati
Temple

BIJESHWARI

Bijeshwari
Temple

Swayambhunath (800m)

Swayambhunath (1km)

Vishnumati River

Narayanhiti Palace
(New Royal Palace)

Tukucha Khola

Gairidhara

Naxal

NAXAL

GYANESHWAR

Pashupatinath (2km);
Tribhuvan Airport (5km);
Bodhnath (6km)

Kamal Pokhari

Kamaladi

LAL
DURBAR

Kaiser
Mahal

Tridevi Marg

Amrit Marg
(Jyatha Marg)

Commission

Jyatha

Teuda

CHHETRAPATI

Chhetrapati
Chowk

Ikha
Pokhari

ASAN
TOLE

Asan Tole

JAMAL

JYATHA

Kantipath

Nyokha

Kilagal

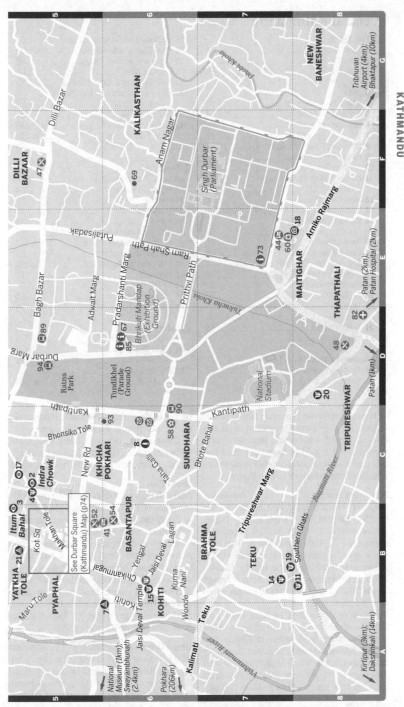

Central Kathmandu

Built as part of the Hanuman Dhoka palace in 1908, it makes a strange contrast to the traditional Nepali architecture that dominates the square. It is said to have been modelled on London's National Gallery following Prime Minister Jung Bahadur's visit to Europe.

Bhagwati Temple   HINDU TEMPLE
(Map p74) On the northwest corner of the Gaddhi Baithak, this triple-storey, triple-roofed temple is easily missed because it surmounts the building below it. The temple is actually part of the Hanuman Dhoka palace courtyard. Like the nearby Gaddhi Baithak, the temple sustained some damage in the 2015 earthquake, but the main structure is intact.

The temple was built by King Jagat Jaya Malla and originally had an image of Naryan. The image was stolen in 1766; when Prithvi Narayan Shah conquered the valley two years later, he simply substituted it with an image of the goddess Bhagwati. In April each year the image of the goddess is transported to the valley of Nuwakot, 65km to the north, then returned a few days later.

The building below is lined with shops selling thangkas (Tibetan religious paintings) and their Newari equivalents, called *paubha*.

Great Bell   MONUMENT
(Map p74) On your left as you leave the southern part of Durbar Sq along Makhan Tole is the Great Bell. The bell's ring drives off evil spirits, but it is only rung during puja (worship) at the nearby Degutaleju Temple. Across from the Great Bell is a very ornate corner balcony, decorated in gorgeous copper and ivory, from where members of the royal court could view the festival action taking place in Durbar Sq. The bell is elevated atop a white building erected by Rana Bahadur Shah (son of Prithvi Narayan Shah) in 1797.

Great Drums & Kot Square   MONUMENT
(Map p74) Once used to warn the city of impending danger, the Great Drums still stand in a restored pavilion to the north of Hanuman Dhoka. Traditionally, a goat and a buffalo

must be sacrificed to the drums twice a year. Just behind is the closed-off Kot Sq, where Jung Bahadur Rana perpetrated the famous 1846 massacre that led to a hundred years of Rana rule. Kot means 'armoury' or 'fort'.

During the Dasain festival each year, blood again flows in Kot Sq as hundreds of buffaloes and goats are sacrificed. Young soldiers are supposed to lop off each head with a single blow.

King Pratap Malla's Column MONUMENT
(Map p74) The square stone pillar, known as the Pratap Dhvaja, was previously topped by a famous statue of King Pratap Malla (r 1641–74), looking towards his private prayer room on the 3rd floor of the Degutaleju Temple, but though the column remains, the statue was topped and crushed in the earthquake. Similar pillars were erected in the Malla era in Patan and Bhaktapur.

This area and its monuments are usually covered in hundreds if not thousands of pigeons; you can buy grain to feed them.

Seto (White) Bhairab STATUE
(Map p74) Seto (White) Bhairab's horrible face is hidden away behind a grille in an earthquake-damaged pavilion opposite King Pratap Malla's Column. The huge mask dates from 1794, during the reign of Rana Bahadur Shah, the third Shah-dynasty king. Each September during the Indra Jatra festival the gates are opened to reveal the mask for a few days. At other times of the year you can peek through the lattice to see the mask, which is used as the symbol of Nepal Airlines.

During Indra Jatra, Bhairab's face is covered in flowers and rice; at the start of the festivities beer is poured through the horrific mouth as crowds of men fight to get a drink of the blessed brew.

Jagannath Temple HINDU TEMPLE
(Map p74) This temple, noted for the erotic carvings on its roof struts, is the oldest structure in this part of Durbar Sq. Pratap Malla claimed to have constructed the temple during his reign, but it may actually date

Durbar Square (Kathmandu)

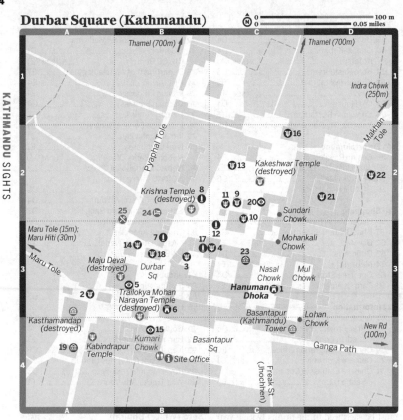

Durbar Square (Kathmandu)

⊙ Top Sights
1 Hanuman Dhoka C3

⊙ Sights
2 Ashok Binayak..A3
3 Bhagwati Temple....................................B3
4 Degutaleju Temple.................................C3
5 Durbar Square..B3
6 Gaddhi Baithak.......................................B3
7 Great Bell...B3
8 Great Drums & Kot Square..................B2
9 Indrapur Temple.....................................C2
10 Jagannath Temple..................................C2
11 Kala (Black) Bhairab.............................C2
12 King Pratap Malla's Column................C3
13 Kotilingeshwar Mahadev Temple C2

14 Krishna Narayan Temple.......................B3
15 Kumari Bahal...B4
16 Mahendreshwar Temple.......................C2
17 Seto (White) Bhairab.............................B3
18 Shiva-Parvati Temple............................B3
19 Singh Sattal...A4
20 Stone Inscription....................................C2
21 Taleju Temple..D2
22 Tana Deval Temple.................................D2
23 Tribhuvan Museum.................................C3

⊜ Sleeping
24 World Heritage Hotel.............................B2

⊗ Eating
25 Cosmo de Café Restaurant.................B2

back to 1563, during the rule of Mahendra Malla. The temple has a three-tiered platform and two storeys. There are three doors on each side of the temple, but only the centre door opens. There are worrying cracks in the upper-storey brickwork.

Degutaleju Temple HINDU TEMPLE

(Map p74) This triple-roofed temple is actually part of the darker, red-brick Hanuman Dhoka, surmounting the buildings below it, but it is most easily seen from outside the palace walls. Despite some earthquake damage, the painted roof struts are particularly fine. Degutaleju is another manifestation of the Malla's personal goddess Taleju.

Kala (Black) Bhairab HINDU MONUMENT

(Map p74) North of the Jagannath Temple is the figure of Kala (Black) Bhairab. Bhairab is Shiva in his most fearsome aspect, and this huge stone image of the terrifying Kala Bhairab has six arms, wears a garland of skulls and tramples a corpse, which is symbolic of human ignorance. It is said that telling a lie while standing before Kala Bhairab will bring instant death and it was once used as a form of trial by ordeal.

The figure is said to have been brought here by Pratap Malla, having been found in a field to the north of the city. The image was originally cut from a single stone but the upper left-hand corner has since been repaired.

Indrapur Temple HINDU TEMPLE

(Map p74) Little is known about this mysterious temple. Even the god to which it is dedicated is controversial – the lingam inside indicates that it is a Shiva temple, but the Garuda image half-buried on the southern side connects it to Vishnu. To compound the puzzle, the temple's name clearly indicates it is dedicated to Indra! The temple's unadorned design and plain roof struts, together with the lack of an identifying *torana* (pediment above the temple doors), offer no further clues.

Stone Inscription HISTORIC SITE

(Map p74) On the outside of the white palace wall, opposite the Vishnu Temple, is a long, low stone inscription to the goddess Kalika written in 15 languages, including one word of French. King Pratap Malla, renowned for his linguistic abilities, set up this inscription in 1664 and a Nepali legend tells that milk will flow from the spout in the middle if somebody is able to decipher all 15 languages!

Kotilingeshwar Mahadev Temple HINDU TEMPLE

(Map p74) This distinctive early stone Malla temple dates from the reign of Mahendra Malla in the 16th century. The three-stage plinth is topped by a temple in the *gumbhaj* style, which basically means a square structure topped by a bell-shaped dome. The bull facing the temple on the west side indicates that it is dedicated to Shiva.

Mahendreshwar Temple HINDU TEMPLE

(Map p74) At the extreme northern end of Durbar Sq, this popular temple dates from 1561, during the reign of Mahendra Malla, and is always bustling with pilgrims. The temple was clumsily restored with marble in 1963 and is dedicated to Shiva. At the northeastern corner there is an image of Kama Deva. The temple has a wide, two-level plinth and a spire topped by a golden umbrella.

Taleju Temple HINDU TEMPLE

(Map p74) Durbar Sq's most magnificent temple stands at its northeastern extremity but is not open to the public. Even for Hindus, admission is restricted; they can only visit it briefly during the annual Dasain festival. The 35m-high temple was built in 1564 by Mahendra Malla. Taleju Bhawani was originally a goddess from the south of India, but she became the titular deity, or royal goddess, of the Malla kings in the 14th century.

Perhaps because of the influence of the royal goddess, the temple escaped with only minor damage in the 2015 earthquake. The temple stands on a 12-stage plinth, dominating the Durbar Sq area. The eighth stage of the plinth forms a wall around the temple, in front of which are 12 miniature temples. Four more miniature temples stand inside the wall, which has four beautifully carved wide gates.

Tana Deval Temple HINDU TEMPLE

(Map p74) Directly north of the Taleju Temple is a 10th-century kneeling **Garuda statue** facing a small Vishnu temple. To the east, in a walled courtyard just past the long row of stalls, is the neglected Tana Deval Temple, with three carved doorways and multiple garishly painted struts that depict the multi-armed Ashta Matrikas (Mother Goddesses). It's possible to enter the temple.

Crowded and fascinating **Makhan Tole** (*makhan* is the Nepali word for butter; *tole* means street) runs from here towards the busy marketplace of Indra Chowk; it was at one time the main street in Kathmandu and the start of the main caravan route to Tibet.

★Hanuman Dhoka PALACE

(Map p74; admission free with Durbar Sq ticket; ⊙10.30am-4pm Tue-Sat Feb-Oct, to 3pm Tue-Sat Nov-Jan, to 2pm Sun) Kathmandu's royal palace, known as the Hanuman Dhoka, was originally founded during the Licchavi period (4th to 8th centuries AD), but the compound was expanded considerably by King Pratap Malla in the 17th century. Sadly, the sprawling palace was hit hard by the 2015 earthquake and damage was extensive. At the time of research, the main Nasal Chowk courtyard was open but the palace buildings remain closed for reconstruction.

Even from the outside, the palace is impressive. Hanuman's assistance to the noble Rama during the exciting events of the Ramayana has led to the monkey god's appearance guarding many important entrances. Here, cloaked in red and sheltered by an umbrella, a **Hanuman statue** marks the *dhoka* (entrance) to the Hanuman Dhoka and has even given the palace its name. The statue dates from 1672; the god's face has long disappeared under a coating of orange vermillion paste applied by generations of devotees.

Standards bearing the double-triangle flag of Nepal flank the statue, while on each side of the palace gate are gaudy stone lions, one ridden by Shiva, the other by his wife Parvati. Above the gate a brightly painted niche is illustrated with a central figure of a ferocious Tantric version of Krishna. On the left side is the gentler Hindu Krishna in his traditional blue colour accompanied by two of his comely *gopi* (milkmaids). On the other side are King Pratap Malla and his queen.

The Hanuman Dhoka originally housed 35 courtyards (chowks), but the 1934 earthquake reduced the palace to today's 10 chowks.

➡ *Nasal Chowk*

Your main taste of the royal palace will be this handsome courtyard inside the main entrance. Nasal Chowk was constructed in the Malla period, but many of the buildings around the square are later Rana constructions. During the Rana period, Nasal Chowk was used for coronations, a practice that continued until as recently as 2001 with the crowning of King Gyanendra here. The former **coronation platform** stands in the centre of the courtyard, while the damaged Basantapur (Kathmandu) Tower looms over the southern end of the courtyard.

Beyond the door is the large **Narsingha Statue**, Vishnu in his man-lion incarnation, in the act of disembowelling a demon. The stone image was erected by Pratap Malla in 1673 and the inscription on the pedestal explains that he placed it here for fear that he had offended Vishnu by dancing in a Narsingha costume. The Kabindrapur Temple in Durbar Sq was built for the same reason.

Next is the Sisha Baithak, or **Audience Chamber**, of the Malla kings. The open verandah houses the Malla throne and contains portraits of the Shah kings.

At the northeastern corner of Nasal Chowk stands the damaged **Panch Mukhi Hanuman Temple**, with its five circular roofs. Each of the valley towns has a five-storey temple, although it is the great Nyatapola Temple of Bhaktapur that is by far the best known. Hanuman is worshipped in the temple in Kathmandu, but only the priests may enter.

In Nepali *nasal* means 'dancing one', and Nasal Chowk takes its name from the **Dancing Shiva statue** hidden in the whitewashed chamber on the northeastern side of the square.

On display along the east side of the courtyard are the palanquins used to carry Queen Aishwarya during her wedding to Birendra in 1970 and later to transport her body to her cremation in 2001. Also displayed here is the royal throne.

➡ *Tribhuvan Museum*

The palace wing to the west of Nasal Chowk, overlooking the main Durbar Sq area, was constructed by the Ranas in the middle to late part of the 19th century after they wrested power from the royal Shah dynasty. Ironically, it later became a museum celebrating King Tribhuvan (r 1911–55) and his successful revolt against their regime, along with memorials to Kings Mahendra (r 1955–72) and Birendra (r 1972–2001). Sadly, this wing of the palace bore the brunt of the damage in the 2015 earthquake. Many exhibits were destroyed and the Department of Archaeology has estimated that reconstruction will take years. It is unclear at this stage whether such unusual treasures as the king's favourite stuffed bird and his Land Rover, with the scars of an attempted assassination, survived the disaster.

Rising above the museum is the nine-storey **Basantapur (Kathmandu) Tower** (Map p74) (1770), which once stood like a beacon at the end of Freak St. Unfortunately, the upper tiers collapsed during the earthquake and the tower is closed to visitors while it is repaired with Chinese assistance.

➡ *Lohan Chowk & Mul Chowk*

These two courtyards are currently under renovation but should eventually reopen. The first square you reach after the Tribhuvan Museum is Lohan Chowk. This courtyard was formerly ringed by four

KATHMANDU IN...

Two Days

Start off the day with a walking tour (p80) south from Thamel to Durbar Sq. Grab lunch overlooking Basantapur Sq or in nearby Freak St and then spend the afternoon soaking up the architectural grandeur of Durbar Square (p65). Finish the day with a cold beer and dinner in the Thamel area.

Next day head out to Swayambhunath Stupa (p117) in the morning and spend the afternoon shopping in Thamel (p109). For your final meal, splurge at one of the blowout Newari restaurants such as Bhojan Griha (p102) or Thamel House (p102).

Four Days

If you have an extra couple of days, take a short taxi ride out to Patan (p137) for a full day exploring its Durbar Sq and Patan Museum (the best in the country); take a fascinating backstreet walking tour. For dinner, dine in one of Jhamsikhel's excellent restaurants.

On day four take a taxi to Pashupatinath Temple (p124) and then take the short walk out to Bodhnath Stupa (p128) to soak up some Tibetan culture as the pilgrims gather at dusk.

One Week

With a week up your sleeve, you can spend a day (and preferably a night) at Bhaktapur. If stress levels build, fit in some quiet time at the delightful Garden of Dreams (p82).

Seven days gives you the chance to gorge on Thai (Yin Yang; p103), Indian (Third Eye; p103), Korean (Hankook Sarang; p101), steak (K-Too; p103), felafel (Or2k; p100) and maybe even some Nepali food! Don't get us started on lunch...

---

red-coloured towers constructed by King Prithvi Narayan Shah, representing the four ancient cities of the valley. The upper parts of the Basantapur (Kathmandu) Tower and Bhaktapur Tower (Lakshmi Bilas) collapsed in 2015, but the Kirtipur Tower and Patan (Lalitpur) Tower (known more evocatively as the Bilas Mandir, or House of Pleasure) are still standing.

North of Lohan Chowk, Mul Chowk was completely dedicated to religious functions within the palace and is configured like a *vihara,* with a two-storey building surrounding the courtyard. Mul Chowk is dedicated to Taleju Bhawani, the royal goddess of the Mallas, and sacrifices are made to her in the centre of the courtyard during the Dasain festival. Non-Hindus are not allowed in the square, but you can get views from the doorway in the northeastern corner of Nasal Chowk.

→ *Mohankali Chowk & Sundari Chowk*

On the northern side of Nasal Chowk, a beautifully carved doorway leads to the Malla kings' private quarters, which rank as the oldest parts of Hanuman Dhoka. This area was also damaged and reconstruction may take some years. Until then, both courtyards remain closed.

The first courtyard is Mohankali (Mohan) Chowk, which dates from 1649. At one time,

a Malla king had to be born here to be eligible to wear the crown. (The last Malla king, Jaya Prakash Malla, had great difficulties during his reign, even though he was the legitimate heir, because he was born elsewhere.) Impressive wood carvings line the wall alcoves, many of them depicting the exploits of young Krishna, and the central hiti (water reservoir) is the palace's finest.

Pride of place in the intimate black-and-white Sundari Chowk behind is the ritual bathing pool with its Lichhavi-era carving of Krishna subduing the coils of the Kaliya serpent, hewn from a single block of stone in the 6th century. The Malla kings would ritually bathe each morning at the golden waterspout, whose waters allegedly flow from Budhanilkantha in the north of the valley.

◉ North of Durbar Square

Hidden in the fascinating backstreets north of Durbar Sq is a dense sprinkling of colourful temples, courtyards and shrines. The best way to get a feel for this area is on our walking tour (p80).

Kathesimbhu Stupa   BUDDHIST STUPA

(Map p70; Naghal Tole) The most popular Tibetan pilgrimage site in the old town is this lovely stupa, a small copy dating from around

1650 of the great Swayambhunath complex. The stupa is set in a hidden courtyard. Just as at Swayambhunath, there is a two-storey pagoda to Hariti, the goddess of smallpox, in the northwestern corner of the square. In the northeast corner is the Tibetan-style **Drubgon Jangchup Choeling Monastery**. It's just a couple of minutes' walk south of Thamel.

Bangemudha
SHRINE

(Map p70) At the southern end of the Sikha Narayan Temple square, just across the crossroads on the corner, you will see a lump of wood into which thousands of coins have been nailed. The coins are offerings to the toothache god, which is represented by a tiny image in the grotesque lump of wood. The square at the junction is known as Bangemudha, which means 'Twisted Wood'.

Also in Bangemudha Sq is the small, double-roofed **Sikha Narayan Temple**, easily identified by the kneeling Garuda figure and the modern clock on the wall. The temple houses a beautiful 10th- or 11th-century four-armed Vishnu figure.

On the north side of the square, in the middle of the northern frontage, directly beneath the 'Raj Dental Clinic' sign, is a standing **Buddha statue** framed by modern blue and white tilework. The image is only about 60cm high but dates from the 5th or 6th century. It's a reminder of how casually artistic treasures lie strewn around Kathmandu.

SETO MACHHENDRANATH FESTIVAL

Kathmandu's Seto (White) Machhendranath festival kicks off a month prior to the larger Rato (Red) Machhendranath festival in Patan. The festival starts with removing the white-faced image of Seto Machhendranath from the temple (p78) at Kel Tole and placing it on a towering and creaky wooden temple chariot known as a *rath*. For the next four evenings, the chariot totters slowly from one historic location to another, eventually arriving at Lagan in the south of Kathmandu's old town, where the chariot is hauled three times around the square. The image is taken down from the chariot and carried back to its starting point in a palanquin while the chariot is disassembled and put away until next year.

★ Asan Tole
SQUARE

(Map p70) From dawn until dusk the six-spoked junction of Asan Tole is jammed with vegetable and spice vendors selling everything from yak tails to dried fish. It's the busiest square in the city and a fascinating place to linger, if you can stand the crowds. Cat Stevens allegedly wrote his hippie-era song 'Kathmandu' in a smoky teahouse in Asan Tole.

Every day, produce is carried to this popular marketplace from all over the valley, so it is fitting that the three-storey **Annapurna Temple** (Map p70) in the southeast corner is dedicated to the goddess of abundance; Annapurna is represented by a silver *purana,* a bowl full of grain. At most times, but especially on Sundays, you'll see locals walk around the shrine, touch a coin to their heads, throw it into the temple and ring the bell above them.

Nearby the red-faced **Ganesh shrine** is coated in bathroom tiles. The historic **Yita Chapal (Southern Pavilion)** (Map p70), which was once used for festival dances, was damaged in the 2015 earthquake but still stands, supported by buttresses.

On the western side of the square are spice shops. In the centre of the square, between two potted trees, is a small **Narayan shrine** (Narayan is a form of Vishnu).

Krishna Temple
HINDU TEMPLE

(Map p70) This old building, jammed between gleaming brass shops just southwest of Asan Tole, looks decrepit at first glance. Look closer and you'll notice some fabulously elaborate woodcarvings, depicting beaked monsters and a tiny Tibetan protector, holding a tiger on a chain like he's taking the dog for a walk. Look also for the turn-of-the-century plaques depicting marching troops on the building to the left and the ornately carved entryway just below it.

Seto Machhendranath Temple (Jan Bahal)
TEMPLE

(Map p70) Southwest of Asan Tole at the junction known as Kel Tole, this temple attracts both Buddhists and Hindus – Buddhists consider Seto (White) Machhendranath to be a form of Avalokiteshvara, while to Hindus he is a rain-bringing incarnation of Shiva. The arched entrance to the temple was destroyed in the 2015 earthquake and the temple is currently closed for repairs.

In the courtyard there are lots of small shrines, chaitya (small stupas) and statues,

KUMARI DEVI

Not only does Nepal have hundreds of gods, goddesses, deities, bodhisattvas, Buddhas, avatars (incarnations of deities) and manifestations – which are worshipped and revered as statues, images, paintings and symbols – but it also has a real, living goddess. The Kumari Devi is a young girl who lives in the building known as the Kumari Bahal (p69), right beside Kathmandu's Durbar Sq.

The practice of having a living goddess probably came about during the reign of the last of the Malla kings of Kathmandu, and although there are actually a number of living goddesses around the Kathmandu Valley, the Kumari Devi of Kathmandu is the most important. The Kumari is selected from a particular caste of Newari gold- and silversmiths. Customarily, she is somewhere between four years old and puberty, and must meet 32 strict physical requirements ranging from the colour of her eyes and shape of her teeth to the sound of her voice. Her horoscope must also be appropriate, of course. The most recent Kumari, three-year-old Trishna Shakya, took on her role in September 2017.

Once suitable candidates have been found they are gathered together in a darkened room where terrifying noises are made, while men dance by in horrific masks and 108 gruesome buffalo heads are on display. These goings-on are thought unlikely to frighten an incarnation of Durga, so the young girl who remains calm and collected throughout this ordeal is deemed the new Kumari. In a process similar to the selection of the Dalai Lama, as a final test the Kumari then chooses items of clothing and decoration worn by her predecessor.

Once chosen as the Kumari Devi, the young girl moves into the Kumari Bahal with her family and makes only a half-dozen ceremonial forays into the outside world each year, mainly during the September Indra Jatra festival, when she travels through the city on a huge temple chariot.

The Kumari's reign ends with her first period, or any serious accidental loss of blood. Once this first sign of puberty is reached she reverts to the status of a normal mortal, and the search must start for a new Kumari. On retirement the old Kumari is paid a handsome dowry but readjusting to normal life can be hard. It is said that marrying an ex-Kumari is unlucky, perhaps because taking on a spoilt ex-goddess is likely to be too much hard work!

including a mysteriously European-looking female figure surrounded by candles who faces the temple. It may well have been an import from Europe that has simply been accepted into the pantheon of gods. Facing the other way, just in front of the temple, are two graceful bronze figures of the Taras seated atop pillars. Buy some grain to feed the pigeons and boost your karma.

Inside the temple you can see the white-faced image of the god covered in flowers. The image is taken out during the Seto Machhendranath festival in March/April each year and paraded around the city in a chariot. You can follow the interior path that circles the central building. The temple's age is not known, but it was restored during the 17th century.

In the courtyard you may see men standing around holding what looks like a bizarre stringed instrument. This tool is used to separate and fluff up the downlike cotton padding that is sold in bulk nearby. The string is plucked with a twang by a wooden double-headed implement that looks like a cross between a dumb-bell and a rolling pin.

As you leave the temple, to the left (north) you'll see the small, triple-roofed **Lunchun Lunbun Ajima**, a Tantric temple that's red-tiled around the lower level and has some erotic carvings at the base of the struts at the back.

Just to the north of the temple on the side street known as Bhedasingh is a collection of shops selling *topi* (cloth hats) and the Nepali traditional dress known as a *daura suruwal* (a long shirt over tapered drainpipe trousers), including adorable miniature versions for children.

★ **Indra Chowk**   SQUARE
(Map p70) The busy street of Makhan Tole spills into Indra Chowk, the courtyard named after the ancient Vedic deity, Indra. Locals crowd around the square's newspaper sellers, scanning the day's news. Indra Chowk is traditionally a centre for the sale of blankets and cloth, and merchants cover

the platforms of the **Mahadev Temple** to the north. The next-door black stone **Shiva Temple** to the northeast is a smaller and simplified version of Patan's Krishna Temple.

On the west side of the square is the facade of the **Akash Bhairab Temple** (Map p70), or Bhairab of the Sky Temple. From the balcony four metal lions rear out over the street. The temple's entrance is on the right-hand side of the building, guarded by two more brass lions, but non-Hindus cannot enter. The silver image inside is visible through the open windows from out in the street, and during important festivals the image is displayed in the square. In a small niche just to the left of the Akash Bhairab Temple is a very small but much-visited brass Ganesh shrine.

Before you leave the chowk, look for the market hidden in the alleyways to the east, crowded with stalls selling the lurid beads and bangles that are so popular with married Nepali women.

★**Itum Bahal**   COURTYARD

(Map p70; www.itumbaha.org) The long, rectangular courtyard of the Itum Bahal is the largest bahal (Buddhist monastery courtyard) in the old town and remains a haven of tranquillity in the chaotic surroundings. On the western side of the courtyard is the **Kichandra Bahal**, one of the oldest bahals in the city, dating from 1381. A chaitya in front of the entrance has been completely shattered by a Bodhi tree, which has grown right up through its centre.

Inside the Kichandra Bahal (or Keshchandra Paravarta Mahar Bihar) is a central pagoda-like sanctuary, and to the south is a small chaitya decorated with graceful standing bodhisattvas.

On the northern side of the courtyard are four brass plaques mounted on the upper-storey wall. The one on the extreme left shows a demon known as Guru Mapa taking a misbehaving child from a woman and stuffing it greedily into his mouth. Eventually the demon was bought off with the promise of an annual feast of buffalo meat, and the plaque to the right shows him sitting down and dipping into a pot of food. With such a clear message on juvenile misbehaviour it is fitting that the courtyard for many years housed a primary school – right under the Guru Mapa plaques!

To this day, every year during the festival of Holi the inhabitants of Itum Bahal sacrifice a buffalo to Guru Mapa on the banks of the Vishnumati River, cook it in the afternoon in the courtyard and in the middle of

🚶 Walking Tour
South from Thamel to Durbar Square

START THAHITI TOLE
END DURBAR SQ
LENGTH 2KM; TWO HOURS

This walk fits perfectly before or after a trip to Durbar Sq. To get to Thahiti Tole, walk south from Thamel on the road from the main Thamel Chowk; the first square you come to is Thahiti.

Thahiti Tole wraps around a 15th-century ❶ **stupa** encircled by prayer wheels. The ❷ **Nateshwar Temple**, on the northern side of the square, is dedicated to a form of Shiva that doubles as the local Newari god of music; the brass doorway depicts animal-headed creatures busily playing a variety of musical instruments.

Take the road heading south past shops selling prayer flags, Tibetan-style khata (ritual scarves) and Buddhist brocade, then bear west to the impressive ❸ **Kathesimbhu Stupa** (p77), radiating colourful prayer flags.

About 30m down on the left, past a Ganesh statue, is a small recessed area and a dark grilled doorway marking a small but intricate central ❹ **stone relief** dating from the 9th century. It shows Shiva sitting with Parvati on Mt Kailash, her hand resting proprietarily on his knee in the pose known as Uma Maheshwar. To the right of the door is an almost unrecognisable orange-coloured Ganesh head. Incidentally, the impressive wooden balcony across the road is said to have had the first glass windows in Kathmandu (it looks like it's the same glass!).

Continue south past a string of dentists' shops (the reason will soon become clear), until you get to ❺ **Bangemudha Square**. Don't miss the wooden shrine to the ❻ **toothache god** on the main crossroads, that gives the square its name.

Head 50m east to the triple-roofed ❼ **Ugratara Temple** by a small square known as Nhhakantalla; a prayer at the half-sunken shrine is said to work wonders for the eyes. Just further on your right you will pass the Krishna Music Emporium (maker and repairer of harmoniums), before spotting a gated entrance on the right that leads into ❽ **Haku Bahal**. Look for

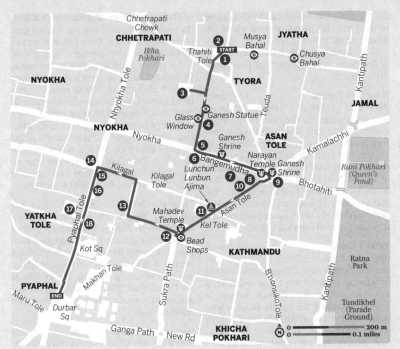

the next-door glasses shop. This tiny bahal has some fine carvings, including an ornate wooden window overlooking the courtyard, which doubles as motorbike parking.

You'll soon come to the bustling chowk of **9 Asan Tole** (p78), old Kathmandu's busiest junction and an utterly fascinating place to linger. The diagonal southwest-to-northeast main road was for centuries the start of the caravan route to Tibet.

The street continues southwest past brassware shops and the ornate and octagonal **10 Krishna Temple** (p78) into Kel Tole, where you'll find one of the most important and ornate temples in Kathmandu, the **11 Seto Machhendranath Temple** (p78), currently closed for post-earthquake renovations.

After 50m the busy shopping street spills into **12 Indra Chowk** (p79), marked by the stepped Mahadev Temple and Akash Bhairab Temple.

Take the quiet alleyway west from Indra Chowk, past *bindi* (forehead decoration) shops and bangle stalls, and after 200m or so, by a small square, look for a tiny entryway to the right, by a triple shrine and under the sign for 'Jenisha Beauty Parlour'. The entryway leads into the long, rectangular

courtyard of **13 Itum Bahal** (p80), one of the oldest and largest bahals in the city, with some lovely architecture and stupas.

Exit the courtyard at the north end and turn left (west). On your right at the next junction is the **14 Nara Devi Temple** (p82). On the south side of the **15 dance platform** is a small shop occupied by one of Kathmandu's many marching bands, mainly used for weddings – look for gleaming tubas, red uniforms and tuneless trumpeting.

At the Nara Devi corner, turn left (south); after 30m or so you come to a corner photocopy/magazine shop on your left with a magnificent **16 wooden window** above it. It has been called *deshay madu* in Nepali, which means 'there is not another one like it'.

Further south, on the right is the entrance to the **17 Yatkha Bahal** (p82), one of the old town's many Buddhist squares, with its eye-catching white central stupa.

Back on the road you'll see the deep redbrick **18 temple** to Chaumanda, a Newari mother goddess, which features a six-pointed star in the upper window frame. Head south again, past the drum and marching-band shops on the right, to Durbar Sq, your final destination for this walk.

the night carry it in huge cauldrons to a tree in the Tundikhel parade ground where the demon is said to live.

In autumn and winter the main square is decorated in ornate swirling patterns of drying grain.

Nara Devi Temple HINDU TEMPLE

(Map p70) Halfway between Chhetrapati and Durbar Sq, the Nara Devi Temple is dedicated to Kali, Shiva's destructive consort. It's also known as the Seto (White) Kali Temple. It is said that Kali's powers protected the temple from the 1934 and 2015 earthquakes. A Malla king once stipulated that a dancing ceremony should be held for the goddess every 12 years, and dances are still performed on the small dance platform that is across the road from the temple.

Yatkha Bahal BUDDHIST TEMPLE

(Map p70) Hidden off the main road just north of Durbar Sq is a large open courtyard set around a central stupa that resembles a mini-Swayambhunath. Directly behind it is an old building, the Yatkha Bahal, whose upper storey is supported by four superb carved-wood struts. Dating from the 12th to 13th century, they are carved in the form of *yaksha* (attendant deities or nymphs), one of them gracefully balancing a baby on her hip.

◉ East of Thamel

There are a couple of interesting sites in the modern new town bordering Thamel district.

★ Garden of Dreams GARDENS

(Swapna Bagaicha; Map p90; ☑ 01-4425340; www.gardenofdreams.org.np; adult/child Rs 200/100; ⊙ 9am-10pm, last entry 9pm) The beautifully restored Swapna Bagaicha, or Garden of Dreams, remains one of the most serene and beautiful enclaves in Kathmandu. It's two minutes' walk and a million miles from central Thamel.

Field marshal Kaiser Shamser (1892–1964), whose palace the gardens complement, built the Garden of Dreams in the 1920s after a visit to several Edwardian estates in England, using funds won from his father (the prime minister) in an epic Rs 100,000 game of cowrie shells. The gardens and its pavilions suffered neglect to the point of collapse before they were lovingly brought back to life over a six-year period (finishing in 2007) by the same Austrian-financed team that created the Patan Museum.

There are dozens of gorgeous details in the small garden, including the original gate, a marble inscription from Omar Khayam's *Rubaiyat*, the new fountains and ponds, and a quirky 'hidden garden' to the south. Of the original 1.6 hectares and six pavilions (named after the six Nepali seasons), only half a hectare and three pavilions remain. To truly savour the serenity, come armed with a book or picnic to distract you from the amorous Nepali couples and relax on one of the supplied lawn mats. Wi-fi is available (Rs 50 per hour). Dwarika's hotel operates the serene Kaiser Cafe (p104) here and there are occasional cultural events and exhibitions.

Three Goddesses Temples TEMPLE

(Map p90) Next to the modern Sanchaya Kosh Bhawan Shopping Centre in Thamel are the often ignored Three Goddesses Temples. The street on which the temples are located is Tridevi Marg – *tri* means 'three' and *devi* means 'goddesses'. The goddesses are Dakshinkali, Manakamana and Jawalamai, and the roof struts have some creative erotic carvings.

Narayanhiti Palace Museum MUSEUM

(Map p70; ☑ 01-4227844; Durbar Marg; foreigner/SAARC & Chinese Rs 500/250; ⊙ 11am-4pm Thu-Mon, to 3pm Nov-Jan) Few things speak clearer to the political changes that have transformed Nepal over the last 15 years than this walled palace at the northern end of Durbar Marg. King Gyanendra was given 15 days to vacate the property in 2008 and within two years the building was reopened as a people's museum by then prime minister Prachandra, the very Maoist guerrilla leader who had been largely responsible for the king's spectacular fall from grace. The palace walls and gates were damaged in the 2015 earthquake, but the palace itself dates from the 1960s and was largely unaffected.

Full of chintzy meeting rooms and faded 1970s glamour, the palace interior is more outdated than opulent; it feels a bit like the lair of a B-grade *Thunderball*-era James Bond villain. The highlights are the impressive throne and banquet halls and the surprisingly modest royal bedrooms. Stuffed gharial, tigers and rhino heads line the halls next to towering portraits of earlier Shahs and photos of the royal family taken with other doomed leaders – Yugoslavia's Tito, Romania's Ceaușescu and Pakistan's Zia ul-Haq.

The locations where Prince Dipendra massacred his family in 2001 are rather morbidly

EROTIC ART (OR HOW THEY DID IT IN ANCIENT TIMES)

The most eye-catching decorations on Nepali temples are the erotic scenes, often quite explicit, that decorate the *tunala* (roof struts). These scenes are rarely the central carving on the strut; they're usually the smaller carving at the bottom of the strut, like a footnote to the larger image, and in a crude, even cartoonlike style.

The purpose of the images is unclear. Are they simply a celebration of an important part of the life cycle? Are they a more explicit reference to Shiva's and Parvati's creative roles than the enigmatic lingams (phallic symbols) and yonis (female sexual symbols) scattered around so many temples? Or are they supposed to play some sort of protective role for the temple? It's popularly rumoured that the goddess of lightning is a shy virgin who wouldn't dream of striking a temple with such goings-on, although that's probably more a tour-guide tale than anything else.

Whatever the reason for their existence, these Tantric elements can be found on temples throughout the valley. Some temples reveal just the odd sly image, while others are plastered with the 16th-century equivalent of hard-core pornography, ranging from impressively athletic acts of intercourse to medieval *ménages à trois*, scenes of oral or anal intercourse or couplings with demons or animals.

The temples you may want to avoid showing your kids include Kathmandu's Jagannath Temple, the damaged Basantapur (Kathmandu) Tower and Ram Chandra Temple; Patan's Jagannarayan Temple; and Bhaktapur's Erotic Elephants and Pashupatinath Temples.

marked, though the actual building was rather suspiciously levelled after the crime. Bullet holes are still visible on some of the walls. Just as interesting as the building are the locals' reactions to it, as they peek behind the wizard's curtain at a regal lifestyle that for centuries they could only have dreamed about. Cameras and bags are not allowed inside the complex but lockers are available.

Rani Pokhari   POND
(Map p70) This large fenced tank just off Kantipath is said to have been built by King Pratap Malla in 1667 to console his queen over the death of their son (who was trampled by an elephant). The pool (*pokhari* means pool or small lake) was apparently used during the Malla era for trials by ordeal and later became a favourite suicide spot.

Siddhartha Art Gallery   GALLERY
(Map p70; ☑01-4218048; www.siddharthaart gallery.com; Baber Mahal Revisited; ⊙11am-5pm Sun-Fri, noon-5pm Sat) FREE This is the city's best gallery for contemporary Nepali art, with a wide range of top-notch exhibitions. It is worth a visit if you're shopping at Baber Mahal Revisited (p108).

◉ South of Durbar Square

The southern part of Kathmandu's old city was the heart of the ancient city in the Licchavi period (4th to 8th centuries AD). Unfortunately, several monuments were lost here in the 2015

earthquake, including the historic Jaisi Deval Temple, a triple-tiered Shiva temple that played an important part in the city's ceremonial life. Further south, the **Bhimsen Tower (Dharahara)** (Map p70; Sundhara) became the unfortunate symbol of the earthquake in the international media when it collapsed to its foundations, showering rubble onto crowded shopping streets and killing 180 people, many of whom were sightseers who had climbed the tower to admire the views. Today just the base remains as a shrouded unofficial memorial to the disaster.

Bhimsen Temple   BUDDHIST TEMPLE
(Map p70) The Newari deity Bhimsen is said to watch over traders and artisans, so it's quite appropriate that the ground floor of this well-kept temple is devoted to shop stalls. An image of Bhimsen used to be carried to Lhasa in Tibet every 12 years to protect those vital trade routes, until the route was closed by the flight of the Dalai Lama in 1959.

Tourists are not allowed inside the temple, which is fronted by a brass lion on a pedestal holding a spotlight on the building.

Ram Chandra Temple   HINDU TEMPLE
(Map p70) Reached through an innocuous entryway to the southwest of the ruined Jaisi Deval platform, this courtyard is named after Ram, an incarnation of Vishnu and the hero of the Hindu epic, the *Ramayana*. This small temple is notable for the tiny erotic scenes on its roof struts; it looks as if the

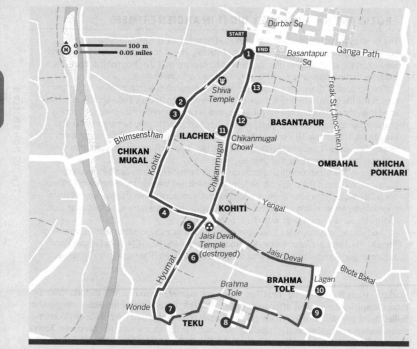

Walking Tour
South from Durbar Square

START DURBAR SQ
END DURBAR SQ
LENGTH 2KM; ONE HOUR

Starting from the damaged southwestern corner of Durbar Sq, fork right at the rebuilt ❶ **Singh Sattal**, and follow the road for 50m past a stone Shiva temple with a finely carved pilgrim shelter. Soon you come to a large sunken ❷ **hiti**, or water tank, beside the highly decorated ❸ **Bhimsen Temple** (p83).

Continue south beyond the Bhimsen Temple, then continue straight (ie left) at the junction, instantly losing most of the traffic. Swing left and pass the deep and ornate ❹ **Kohiti water tank**. At the top of the hill you'll come out by the ruined seven-tiered base of the 17th-century Jaisi Deval Temple, destroyed in the 2015 earthquake; just southwest is the damaged ❺ **Ram Chandra Temple** (p83).

Heading southwest you pass through the small and lived-in courtyard of ❻ **Tukan Bahal**, with its Swayambhunath-style 14th-century stupa in the centre.

The road continues with a few bends, then turns sharply left (east) at Wonde junction, which is marked by temples, including a tall, white ❼ **shikhara temple**.

Our walk continues past Brahma Tole to the ❽ **Musum Bahal**, with its phallic-shaped Licchavi-style chaityas, an enclosed well and three parallel courtyards. Take a right back at the main road and then a sharp left (north) at the next main junction. After 25m look out for the ❾ **Ta Bahal**, with its lovely stone chaityas, hidden down an alley on the right.

The road turns into an open square, known as Lagan, featuring the 5m-high ❿ **Machhendranath Temple** and its white-faced deity.

Continue straight out of Lagan, swinging left back to the ruins of Jaisi Deval Temple, then turn right (northeast) back towards Durbar Sq. Pass the red-brick ⓫ **Hari Shankar Temple** (1637) and continue north past a ⓬ **Vishnu (Narayan) Temple** to the ⓭ **Adko Narayan Temple**, one of the four most important Vishnu temples in Kathmandu. There's a particularly ornate *path* (pilgrim's shelter) on the street corner. Just 50m further lies Durbar Sq.

carver set out to illustrate 16 different positions, starting with the missionary position, and just about made it before running out of ideas (there's one particularly ambitious, back-bending position).

The temple suffered cracks, bows and a serious lean during the 2015 earthquake, but is still open.

Pachali Bhairab & the Southern Ghats HINDU TEMPLE
(Map p70) The northern banks of the Bagmati River south of the old town are home to several little-visited temples and shrines, as well as the worst urban poverty in Kathmandu; rarely do such splendour and squalor sit so close. The banks are worth a stroll, especially as an extension of a walking tour (p84). There are plans to redevelop the ghats with new pedestrian walkways.

Between Tripureshwar Marg and the Bagmati River at Pachali Bhairab a huge, ancient pipal tree forms a natural sanctuary for an image of Bhairab Pachali, surrounded by tridents (Pachali is a form of Shiva). To the side lies the brass body of Baital, one of Shiva's manifestations. Worshippers gather here on Tuesday and Saturday. It is particularly busy here during the festival of Pachali Bhairab Jatra, held during the time of Dasain.

From the temple, head south towards the ghats (riverside steps) on the holy riverbank. To the right is the Newari-style pagoda of the **Lakshmi Mishwar Mahadev Temple** (Map p70); to the left (southeast) is the damaged but striking **Tin Deval Temple** (Map p70), easily recognised by its three shikhara-style spires.

From here you can continue west along footpaths to cremation ghats and a temple at the holy junction of the Bagmati and Vishnumati Rivers; or east past some of Kathmandu's poorest and lowest-caste communities to the triple-roofed **Tripureshwar Mahadev Temple** (Map p70), currently a museum of Nepali folk musical instruments. The nearby Mughal-style **Kalmochan Temple**, built in 1873, was destroyed in the 2015 earthquake.

🏃 Activities

The swimming pools at the Annapurna, Shanker and Radisson hotels are open to non-guests for around Rs 1000. The Hyatt charges Rs 1250 for its pool, or Rs 1700 for its pool, gym, tennis court and sauna. Add tax to all these.

For golf near the capital, head to Gokarna Forest Resort Golf Course (p171).

Pranamaya Yoga YOGA
(Map p90; ✆9802045484; www.pranamaya-yoga.com; Tridevi Marg; classes Rs 700; ⊘8am-8pm) Faced with one too many hairy male yoga teachers displaying contortive poses in their underpants, the owners of this centre decided to set up a modern, comfortable environment for drop-in practitioners. Classes take place in the studio on Tridevi Marg above Himalayan Java, as well as in Patan and Bodhnath. See the website for a schedule. It also runs three-day retreats at Pharping in the southern Kathmandu Valley, yoga treks and a free 30-minute guided meditation on Mondays at 7.30am.

Charak Yoga YOGA
(Map p90; ✆9818148030; www.charakyoga.com; Chaksibari Marg; classes Rs 700) This bright, clean space above Jatra in central Thamel runs three classes daily (Friday mornings are good for beginners), and offers a week-long beginner's course for US$200.

Himalayan Buddhist Meditation Centre MEDITATION
(HBMC; Map p70; ✆9808296590; www.fpmt-hbmc.org; Naryan Chaur, Naxal) This Buddhist organisation offers hour-long introductory meditation classes once or twice a week (donation requested), as well as a program of talks and multiday Buddhist and reiki courses; check the website for the program. It's above the 1905 Suites restaurant out in Naxal, but shifts location frequently.

Seeing Hands MASSAGE
(Map p90; ✆01-4253513; www.seeinghandsnepal.org; Jyatha; massage 60/90min Rs 1800/2600; ⊘10am-6pm) A branch of the Pokhara-based organisation that offers massage from blind masseurs, providing employment to some of Nepal's 600,000 blind people. Choose between a relaxing post-trek Swedish massage or remedial sports therapy for specific issues. The environment is functional rather than luxuriant.

Himalayan Healers MASSAGE
(Map p90; ✆01-4437183; saira.tphi@gmail.com; Tilicho Bldg, Tridevi Marg; ⊘10am-8pm) This impressive operation trains 'untouchables', war widows and victims of human trafficking or domestic violence in 500 hours of massage therapy and then organises a placement. It's a relaxing place that has a spa feel.

Treatments are a flat rate of Rs 2400/3000 for 60/90 minutes of massage (Swedish or Nepali), reflexology, body wraps or scrubs.

Hot stone treatments and *shirodhara* (a treatment involving a stream of warm oil on your forehead) are a bit pricier. You can get a discount of up to 30% for morning treatments. There's a also a steam room and sauna (Rs 700).

Adventure Sports

Borderlands ADVENTURE SPORTS
(Map p90; ☑01-4701295; www.borderland resorts.com; by Northfield Cafe, Thamel) Rafting, canyoning and trekking based at the resort (p192) near the Tibetan border, together with Ultimate Descents Nepal. Also has mountain bike trips across the country.

Last Resort ADVENTURE SPORTS
(Map p90; ☑01-4700525; www.thelastresort.com. np; Mandala St, Thamel) Rafting, canyoning, bungee jumping and accommodation near Borderlands on the road to Tibet, together with Ultimate Rivers.

Astrek Climbing Wall CLIMBING
(Map p90; ☑01-4419265; www.facebook.com/ Astrek.Climbing; 8am-4pm Sun-Fri Rs 350, 4-8pm Sun-Fri & all day Sat Rs 450) If you need to polish your climbing skills before heading to the big peaks, or if you just want to learn some free-climbing techniques, you can do so here at Nepal's tallest artificial climbing wall. It also runs guided climbs in nearby Nagarjun (Rs 5500) every Saturday, suitable for all levels. A six-day training course on the wall costs around Rs 15,000. Add Rs 250 for shoes (limited sizes) and a harness. There's a pleasant cafe here. Contact Niraj.

Chhango CANYONING
(Map p90; ☑01-4701251; www.canyoninginnepal. com; Thamel) Offers canyoning day trips to Sundarijal (US$110) and rock climbing day trips in Nagarjun (US$99), including transportation and equipment. It also offers mountain bike trips and a five-day Kathmandu Valley 'ultimate adventure' package of climbing, hiking, biking and canyoning. Contact Kishor Shahi.

Nepal Mountain Bike Tours CYCLING
(Map p90; ☑01-4701701; www.nepalmountain biketours.com; 321 Chaksibari Marg) Mountain bike hire from Rs 800 to Rs 1500 per day, including helmet, lock and repair kits. Also runs day trips (US$65 per person) and multiday bike tours around the valley. It's in the same compound as Equator Expeditions. Contact Ranjan Rajbhandari.

Dawn Till Dusk CYCLING
(Map p90; ☑01-4700286; www.nepalbiking.com; Kathmandu Guest House, Thamel) Local mountain bike and country-wide tours, with a desk at the Kathmandu Guest House office. For bike rentals (Rs 1000 to Rs 3000 per day), spare parts and servicing, visit the **workshop** (Map p90; www.nepalbiking.com; Tridevi Marg) a five-minute walk east, just off Tridevi Marg, below Himalayan Healers.

Alternative Nepal CYCLING, KAYAKING
(Map p90; ☑01-4700170; www.alternativenepal. com; Mandala St) Mountain-bike hire in Thamel with guided day/overnight trips throughout the country, plus climbing, kayak clinics and rafting on the Trisuli River.

Courses

Nepal is a particularly popular place for people to take up spiritual pursuits. Check the noticeboards in Thamel for up-to-date information about yoga and Buddhism courses and shop around before you commit yourself.

Nepal Cooking School COOKING
(Map p90; ☑9860941107; www.nepalcooking school.com; Saatghumti; course Rs 3500) From shopping for fresh produce and spices to learning to make Nepali tea and then five Nepali dishes, this half-day course is a fun and sociable way to learn some cooking skills. Come hungry as you get to eat the fruit (or rather chicken momos) of your labours. Classes start at 9.30am and 1.30pm. Book in advance by phone or online. Classes aren't cheap but profits go to funding the school rebuilding and student sponsorship work of Journey Nepal (www.journey-nepal.org).

Nepal Vipassana Centre HEALTH & WELLBEING
(Map p70; ☑01-4250581; www.dhamma.org.np; Jyoti Bhawan Bldg, Kantipath; ⊙10am-5.30pm Sun-Fri) This office is the place to sign up for the 10-day retreats held twice a month (starting on the 1st and 14th of the month) at the Dharmashringa centre just north of Budhanilkantha outside Kathmandu. There are also occasional shorter courses for intermediate students.

These are serious meditation courses that involve rising at 4am every morning, not talking or making eye contact with anyone over 10 days, and not eating after midday. The fee is donation only.

Himalayan Yoga Resort HEALTH & WELLBEING
(☑01-2021259; www.yogainnepal.com; Gairigaon; s/d tent US$50/90, bungalow US$65/110, house

US$85/150) In a peaceful location between Swayambhunath and Nagarjun hill, this small but comfortable centre offers residential yoga and guided meditation to help you decompress. Overnight rates include accommodation, vegetarian meals, a morning yoga and evening guided meditation lesson and one massage. Day rates without accommodation cost US$44 per person. It also runs Hatha and Vinaysa yoga teacher training.

Gandharba Culture & Art Organisation
MUSIC

(Map p90; ☑01-4700292; Thamel) This organisation represents the city's musician caste and members offer lessons in the *sarangi* (four-stringed instrument played with a bow), *madal* (drum) and *bansari* (flute). Expect to pay around Rs 500 per hour. The office is located in central Thamel (on the 3rd floor).

Social Tours
COOKING

(Map p90; ☑01-4412508, 9801123401; www.socialtours.com) This innovative and responsible company runs a half-day 'Cook Like a Local' Nepali cookery course that involves a trip to a local market to get ingredients for momos, spinach curry, *alu gobi* (potato and cauliflower), tomato pickle and *alu paratha* (fried chapatti with potato). Pay what you think the experience is worth and then eat your homework.

The company also runs great day tours, including a Newari culture and snack tour in Kirtipur, a weave your own souvenir trip in Bungamati, a local market walk to Asan Tole, and a 'lunch with nuns' hike to Nagi Gompa in Shivapuri Nagarjun National Park.

Backstreet Academy
COURSE

(Map p70; ☑9818421646; www.backstreet academy.com; Laxmi Bank Building, Thirbam Sadak, Bhatbhateni; tours from Rs 1300) This organisation uses English-speaking facilitators to link travellers with local craftspeople, many of whom are from disadvantaged backgrounds. Crash courses including mask carving, pottery making, stone carving, silk weaving, sari wearing and momo making are available, or just tour Swayambhunath with a local monk. Facilitators meet you at your hotel.

🌟 Festivals & Events

Kathmandu has an endless supply of religious festivals, of which the most outrageous is probably Indra Jatra (p"Kathmandu's Indra Jatra Festival" on page 88) in Septem-

MOUNTAIN FLIGHTS

A popular activity from Kathmandu is to take an early-morning scenic mountain flight (US$199) along the spine of the Himalaya for close-up views of Mt Everest and other peaks from a distance of just 9.3km. Major airlines like Buddha Air and Yeti Airlines offer the hour-long flights and each passenger on the six- to 30-seat turbo props is guaranteed a window seat.

The quality of the views depends on weather conditions. If the flight is cancelled due to bad weather, airlines offer a full refund or a seat on a later flight. In 2011 a Buddha Air mountain flight crashed outside Kathmandu, killing 19.

ber, closely followed by the Seto Machhendranath (p78) chariot festival in March/April, Dasain (p23) in October, and the Pachali Bhairab Jatra (p23), also in October.

Kathmandu International Marathon
SPORTS

(www.prosports.com.np; ⊙Sep) This annual road race attracts over 6000 runners in September, with courses ranging from 5km to 42km. Registration costs US$40 for foreigners. Amazingly, the police hold back Kathmandu's revving traffic for a full five hours to let the race take place.

Jazzmandu Festival
MUSIC

(www.jazzmandu.org; tickets around Rs 900; ⊙Oct) This annual music event is a week-long program of local and international jazz, fusion and world music acts that is staged in venues across town in mid-October (sometimes early November). See the website for details.

Kathmandu International Film Festival
FILM

(www.kimff.org; ⊙Dec) An interesting week-long festival of international and Nepali documentary and short films, held in December.

Kathmandu Triennale
ART

(www.kt.artmandu.org; ⊙Mar) Every three years (most recently in 2017) artists from three dozen countries exhibit works at venues across the city. It's normally held at the end of March.

🛌 Sleeping

Kathmandu has a huge range of places to stay, from luxurious international-style hotels to cheap and cheerful lodges. Most budget and some midrange places are found in the bustling Thamel district. Midrange and top-end places are widely scattered around Kathmandu, some quite a way from the centre.

It's difficult to recommend hotels in the budget and midrange brackets, as rooms in each hotel can vary widely. Many of these hotels have multiple wings and, while some rooms may be very gloomy and run-down, others (generally the upper floors) might be bright and pleasant. In general, roadside rooms are brighter but noisier than interior rooms, and top-floor rooms are the best as you stand a chance of getting a view and have easy access to the roof garden.

Budget places generally don't have heating so in winter, you'll want the warmer south-facing rooms and garden access, as it's always pleasant to sit outside during the cool, but sunny, autumn and winter days.

Quite a few hotels bridge the budget and midrange categories by having a range of room standards – these places have been grouped according to their lowest price.

It's always worth asking for a discount, particularly during low season when most places offer discounts of between 20% and 40%. Midrange and top-end places add on an extra 23% tax, but most budget places offer inclusive rates. If you email a reservation in advance many places offer a free airport pick-up.

Some travellers base themselves further afield, outside Kathmandu in Patan or Bodhnath, to escape the increasingly unpleasant traffic, pollution and commercialism of Thamel, and this isn't a bad idea. For something quieter still, an increasing number of midrange and top-end resorts around the Kathmandu Valley offer a peaceful rural atmosphere less than an hour from the centre of Kathmandu.

Thamel

For budget and midrange places, the tourist ghetto of Thamel is the main locale. It's a convenient area to stay for a short time, especially to meet fellow travellers or indulge in some last-minute shopping, but you are likely to tire of the noise and congestion in a couple of days.

In an attempt to establish some order in this sprawling chaos, we have somewhat arbitrarily divided the Greater Thamel area as follows: central Thamel, around the two central intersections; Paknajol, to the north; Bhag-

---

KATHMANDU'S INDRA JATRA FESTIVAL

Indra, the ancient Aryan god of rain, was once captured in the Kathmandu Valley while stealing a flower for his mother, Dagini. He was imprisoned until Dagini revealed his identity and his captors swiftly released him. The festival in September celebrates this remarkable achievement (villagers don't capture a real god every day of the week). In return for his release Dagini promised to spread dew over the crops for the coming months and to take back with her to heaven all those who had died in the past year.

The Indra Jatra festival thus honours the recently deceased and pays homage to Indra and Dagini for the coming harvests. It begins when a huge wooden pole, carried via the Tundikhel, is erected outside the Hanuman Dhoka. At the same time images and representations of Indra, usually as a captive, are displayed and sacrifices of goats and roosters are made; the screened doors obscuring the horrific face of Seto (White) Bhairab are also opened and for the next three days his gruesome visage will stare out at the proceedings.

The day before all this activity, three golden temple chariots are assembled in Basantapur Sq, outside the home of the Kumari living goddess. In the afternoon the Kumari (p79) appears to a packed crowd, either walking on a rolled-out carpet or carried by attendants so that her feet do not touch the ground. The Kumari mounts the central chariot, flanked by two boys also in chariots, playing the roles of Ganesh and Bhairab.

The chariots move off and the Kumari is greeted from the balcony of the old palace by the president, before continuing to the huge Seto (White) Bhairab mask. The Kumari greets the image of Bhairab and then, with loud musical accompaniment, beer starts to pour from Bhairab's mouth! Getting a sip of this beer is guaranteed to bring good fortune, but one lucky individual will also get the small fish that has been put to swim in the beer – this brings especially good luck (though probably not for the fish).

Numerous other processions also take place around the town until the final day, when the great pole is lowered and carried down to the river. A similar pole is erected in Bhaktapur as part of the Bisket Jatra festival, celebrating the Nepali New Year.

wan Bahal, to the northeast; Jyatha, to the southeast; and Chhetrapati, to the southwest.

Several top-end international chains are building properties on the edge of Thamel, including Aloft Kathmandu (2018) in the new 15-storey Chhaya Center building (www.chhayacenter.com) and a nearby Sheraton (in 2019).

Central Thamel

Karma Travellers Home
GUESTHOUSE $
(Map p90; ☑ 01-4417897; www.karmatravellershome.com; Bhagawati Marg; s/d US$12/16, deluxe US$20/25; ❄ 🛜) This popular central place has decent rooms, several nice terrace sitting areas and helpful owners. The air-conditioned deluxe rooms are more spacious and some rooms come with a balcony. You can get a 20% discount online and a free airport pick-up. Rates include tax.

Hotel Potala
GUESTHOUSE $
(Map p90; ☑ 01-4700159; www.potalahotelnepal.com; s/d incl breakfast US$12/18, deluxe US$15/20, without bathroom US$8/13; @ 🛜) Bang in the beating heart of Thamel, this small backpacker place has a nice rooftop area and a convenient vegetable momo restaurant overlooking Thamel's main drag. Rooms are certainly simple but clean and decent, with sunny corner deluxe rooms. It's down an alleyway near the Maya Cocktail Bar and suffers from weekend music noise. Don't confuse it with Potala Guest House. Rates include tax.

Hotel Silver Home
GUESTHOUSE $
(Map p90; ☑ 01-4262986; www.hotelsilverhome.com; dm US$6, s/d US$10/14, deluxe US$15/18; @ 🛜) The positives here include a quiet but central backstreet location, friendly helpful management and a free airport pick-up if you book three or more nights. The rooms are simple but come with proper mattresses and hot water in the bathroom. Sunny south-facing rooms are best.

Hotel Florid
GUESTHOUSE $
(Map p90; ☑ 01-4701055; www.hotelflorid.com.np; Z St; r without air-con US$17, r with air-con US$20-25; ❄ 🛜) There's a pleasant garden restaurant at the rear of this guesthouse, giving a feeling of space that is often lacking in Thamel. The suite-like deluxe rooms overlooking the garden are sunny and spacious. Doubles overlooking the road are noisier but come with a shared balcony. You'll need to negotiate a discount to get good value here. Rates include breakfast and tax.

★ Kathmandu Guest House
HOTEL $$
(Map p90; ☑ 01-4700800; www.ktmgh.com; s/d standard US$44/55, garden-facing US$66/77, deluxe US$90/100; ❄ @ 🛜) The KGH is an institution. A former Rana palace, it was the first hotel to open in Thamel in the late 1960s and still serves as the central landmark. Everyone from Jeremy Irons to Ricky Martin has stayed here. Despite losing a couple of buildings in the earthquake, the relaxing garden is still Kathmandu's social hub, so book rooms well in advance. Rates include tax and breakfast.

Ambassador Garden Home
BOUTIQUE HOTEL $$
(Map p90; ☑ 01-4700724; www.aghhotel.com; s/d US$51/63, deluxe US$63/72, super deluxe US$87/105; ❄ @ 🛜) Right in the eye of the Thamel storm but surprisingly peaceful, this place has splashes of style and a nice garden and lobby reading area. Standard rooms are a bit small; deluxe rooms come with air-con and minibar and are more spacious. What you are paying for is the location. The hotel is named after the owner's great grandfather, once the Nepali ambassador to China.

Thamel Eco Resort
HOTEL $$
(Map p90; ☑ 01-4263810; www.thamelecoresort.com; Chibahal; s/d US$40/45, deluxe US$50/55; ❄ 🛜) A complex set back from the road, it has fresh modern rooms of varying size placed around a pleasant central stupa courtyard decorated with carved wood and Newari brick. A good breakfast buffet and central location are a bonus and the hotel is building Nepal's first craft beer bar, with ales imported from Colorado. Rates include breakfast and tax. This place is popular with trekking groups and so can feel crowded when it's full. Reception can put you in touch with a yoga teacher for a private class at the hotel.

Hotel Horizon
HOTEL $$
(Map p90; ☑ 01-4220904; www.hotelhorizon.com; Chaksibari Marg; s/d US$20/25, deluxe US$25/30; ❄ @ 🛜) The Horizon is a good upper budget choice down an alley off the main street in southern Thamel, making it a quiet and central option. Most rooms are bright and spacious, although the bathrooms are slightly dingy, and there are some nice terrace seating areas, including around the newly designed courtyard.

Thorong Peak Guest House
GUESTHOUSE $$
(Map p90; ☑ 01-4253458; www.thorongpeak.com; s/d US$20/28, superior US$28/36, ste US$50;

Greater Thamel

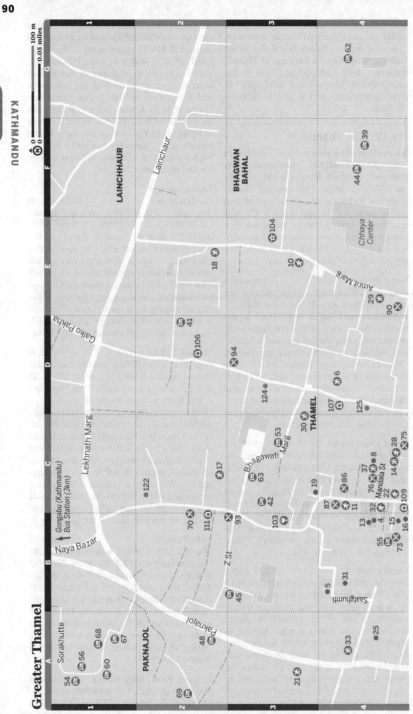

Greater Thamel

❀@⊛) A clean and well-tended place, off the main street in a small cul-de-sac. Deluxe rooms are comfortable enough (superior rooms are the same rooms but with air-con), if a little bland, and have super-clean bathrooms. Bonuses include nice communal balconies and a decent courtyard restaurant, though without a discount it's a bit overpriced.

Dalai-la Boutique Hotel BOUTIQUE HOTEL **$$$**
(Map p90; ☎01-4701436; www.dalailaboutique hotel.com; Chaksibari Marg; deluxe s/d US$80/90, super deluxe US$120/130; ❀⊛) An impressive Tibetan-run place set around a charming prayer-flag-strewn courtyard that offers romantic al fresco dining. Rooms in the new

wing are best, and come with a small balcony, though none are very spacious. There are some stylish Tibetan touches with crafts collected from across the valley, and environmental efforts such as plastic-free shampoo containers are commendable.

🛏 Paknajol (Northern Thamel)

This area lies to the northwest of central Thamel and can be reached by continuing north from the Kathmandu Guest House, or by approaching from Lekhnath Marg to the north.

Not far from the steep Paknajol intersection with Lekhnath Marg (northwest of Thamel) are half a dozen pleasant guesthouses grouped together in a district known as Sorakhutte. They're away from traffic, a short walk from Thamel (but it could be a million miles), and they have fine views across the valley towards Balaju and Swayambhunath.

Kathmandu Garden House　GUESTHOUSE $
(Map p90; ☏01-4381239; www.hotel-in-nepal.com; Sorakhutte; s/d Rs 1200/1500; 🛜) This small and intimate guesthouse is cosy and deservedly popular. The views from the roof are excellent, the place is impeccably clean, mattresses are comfortable and there is a pleasant garden where you can sit back and marvel at the staff cutting the grass by hand (literally!).

Zostel　HOSTEL $
(Map p90; ☏01-4383579; www.zostel.com; Pipalbot Marg, Kaldhara; dm Rs 650-850, r Rs 2500-3000; 🛜) Part of an Indian chain of hostels, Zostel is a clean, comfortable and well-run place a stone's throw from Thamel. The thick comfortable mattresses, well thought-out design (individual bed lights and electricity outlets) and services like bag storage and bus ticketing have made it the most popular hostel in the city.

Dorms have four to eight beds, with one female-only dorm; some dorms have en suite bathroms, while others share a clean, spacious bathroom down the hall. Check out the amazing rooftop cube-shaped hammock, from where you can take in the mountain views in clear weather, hidden down an alley off Paknajol Marg – look for the building-sized mural of the Kumari. Rates include tax.

Yellow House GUESTHOUSE **$**
(Map p90; ☎01-4381186; theyellowhouse2007@gmail.com; Sorakhutte; r Rs 600-1500; 📶) This friendly Swiss-Nepali place is a good addition to the expanding budget Paknajol scene. There's a big range of bright rooms, a concrete terrace and the house restaurant dishes up decent Thai food, Swiss rösti and wine by the glass. One downer: the mattresses are thin and hard.

Kathmandu Peace Guest House GUESTHOUSE **$**
(Map p90; ☎01-4380369; www.ktmpeaceguesthouse.com; Sorakhutte; s Rs 1000-1500, d Rs 1200-2200, s/d without bathroom Rs 500/800; ❄@📶) Rooms at this slightly old-fashioned but friendly place come with satellite TV in either the slightly ramshackle old wing or the fresher new block. The pricier rooms come with air-con and the ground floor and rooftop garden are pleasant. Rates include taxes.

Tibet Peace Guest House GUESTHOUSE **$**
(Map p90; ☎01-4381026; www.tibetpeace.com; Sorakhutte; s Rs 700-1400, d Rs 900-1600; 📶) This is a quiet and mellow hang-out with a small garden and restaurant. There's a wide range of rooms – some ramshackle with the tiniest bathrooms in Kathmandu and others with private balconies – so have a dig around before committing. If you get a dud room there are plenty of other budget options within 100m.

Nirvana Peace Home GUESTHOUSE **$**
(Map p90; ☎01-4383053; www.nirvanapeacehome.net; Sorakhutte; r Rs 1200-1500, without bathroom Rs 1000; 📶) One of half a dozen good places in budget-friendly Paknajol, the rooms are simple but clean with thick mattresses and an upstairs lounge hang-out that makes it a decent choice in this area.

Shree Tibet Family Guest House GUESTHOUSE **$**
(Map p90; ☎01-4700902; www.hotelshreetibet.com; Bhagawati Marg; r Rs 1000-1500; @📶) It's easy to miss this budget place and most people do (it's often deserted). It's clean, quiet and friendly, with simple but cosy rooms, although most are dark and smallish due to the buildings being very close together. As always, the back rooms on the higher floors are best. Prayer wheels mark the entrance.

Hotel Moonlight HOTEL **$$**
(Map p90; ☎01-4380452; www.hotelmoonlight.com; Paknajol; s/d incl breakfast from US$60/70; ❄📶) The modern Moonlight is a good mid-range choice, with a calming interior garden courtyard, lobby cafe and spa, all punctuated with some nice design touches. Single-bed rooms are easily the biggest; others can be a bit pokey. The 67 rooms are spread over two buildings and construction work continues apace.

International Guest House HOTEL **$$**
(Map p70; ☎01-4252299; www.ighouse.com; Kaldhara; s/d US$28/32, deluxe US$38/42, superior deluxe US$50/54; 📶) This is a solid and quietly stylish place that boasts century-old carved woodwork, terraced sitting areas and a lovely, spacious garden complete with sun loungers that makes up for somewhat plain rooms.

Though none of the rooms are exactly luxurious, the superior rooms in the renovated wing are generally bright, spacious and well decorated, while the best deluxe rooms in the old building come with a garden view. The smaller and plainer standard rooms vary.

The hotel is west from the Saatghumti (Seven Bends St) in an area known as Kaldhara. This area is quieter and much less of a scene than Thamel, but still close to plenty of restaurants. Rates include tax, breakfast, wi-fi and airport pick-up.

Bhagwan Bahal (Northeastern Thamel)

This area is quieter than central Thamel, offers more space and is closer to transport options and access to the rest of the city. There are several huge new five-star developments under construction here.

Alobar 1000 HOSTEL **$**
(Map p90; ☎01-4410114; www.alobar1000; 214 Keshar Mahal Marg; dm Rs 350-550, r Rs 1400-2700) If you are looking to hook up with other young backpackers, this well-run and oddly named place (taken from a Tom Robbins novel) is one the most popular hostels in the city. The travel desk offers treks, free weekly language classes and city walks, and there's fair-priced laundry and airport transfers. The sociable rooftop restaurant is the place to meet a trekking buddy.

Dorm rooms have between four and 12 beds, all of which come with a locker, and there are two women-only dorms. For a private room you can get better value elsewhere.

Annapurna Guest House
GUESTHOUSE $

(Map p90; ☑ 01-4420510; www.annapurnaguest house.com; Gahiti Marg; s/d/tr US$15/20/25, deluxe US$20/25/30; 🛜) The rooms at this recently relocated family guesthouse are split between large three-bed rooms and smaller doubles, with deluxe air-conditioned rooms. The side street in the north of Thamel is quieter than the centre and there's a small rooftop sitting areas. Rates include tax.

Hotel Blue Horizon
HOTEL $$

(Map p90; ☑ 01-4421971; www.hotelbluehorizon. com; Keshar Mahal Marg; s/d budget US$15/20, standard US$20/25, deluxe US$30/35; ✳ @ 🛜) Renovations have revitalised this old favourite, adding a spacious garden and a new block of midrange rooms. There's a wide range of options spread over multiple floors and terraces; the deluxe rooms offer the best value. Best of all is the secluded location down an alleyway off Tridevi Marg, which makes it super easy for transport around the city.

Mi Casa
BOUTIQUE HOTEL $$

(Map p90; ☑ 01-4415149; www.micasanepal.com; Keshar Mahal Marg; r US$50-70; ✳ 🛜) For a stylish, cosy option with good personal service this place has just nine rooms with splashes of colour from Nepali fabrics and potted plants. The pricier rooms come with kitchenette and terrace; others are smallish but there's a courtyard cafe that serves breakfast. The location is useful for both Thamel and the new town. Prices include tax.

Sheraton
LUXURY HOTEL $$$

(Map p90; www.starwoodhotels.com; Kantipath) One of several big hotels currently under construction on the fringes of Thamel, this will be the closest luxury hotel to central Kathmandu when it opens in 2019.

🛏 Jyatha (Southeastern Thamel)

The neighbourhood southeast of Thamel is traditionally known as Jyatha. The southern section has evolved into a popular area with Chinese tourists. Turn east a short way down Jyatha Rd, and a couple of twists and turns will bring you to a neat little cluster of modern guesthouses, whose central but quiet location feels a million miles from the Thamel hustle.

Imperial Guest House
GUESTHOUSE $

(Map p90; ☑ 01-4249339; http://imperial.idia.ru; s/d US$12/15; 🛜) At the end of a quiet cul-de-

sac, this simple but friendly guesthouse has a boarding-school feel, with threadbare but functional and clean rooms and narrow beds with elephant-grey blankets. The pleasant garden rooftop overlooks a small leafy shrine.

Fuji Hotel
HOTEL $$

(Map p90; ☑ 01-4250435; www.fujihotel.com.np; Jyatha; s/d from US$30/40, deluxe US$40/50, super deluxe US$50/60; ✳ @ 🛜) The well-run Fuji is popular with budget groups and rooms are neat, quiet and spotlessly clean. Some rooms have a small balcony and the sunny rooms on the rooftop are particularly spacious (there's a lift). Rates are somewhat overpriced without the frequent 25% discount.

Hotel Holy Himalaya
HOTEL $$

(Map p90; ☑ 01-4258648; www.holyhimalaya. com; 117 Brahmakumari Marg; s/d US$35/40, deluxe US$45/55, ste US$75/85; ✳ @ 🛜) This is a good midrange find frequented by small in-the-know tour groups. The rooms are simple but reassuring and some come with a balcony. Perks include organic coffee, a nice rooftop garden and free guided meditation in the mornings. The spacious deluxe rooms in the new building across the road offer the best value. Rates include tax and breakfast.

Sacred Valley Home
HOTEL $$

(Map p90; ☑ 01-4251063; www.hotelthesacred valleyhome.com; r US$30, deluxe US$40; 🛜) This is a good upper-budget choice. The carpeted rooms are clean, modern and fresh and some have sunny balconies, though there are no single rates for solo travellers. The excellent rooftop garden and the ground-floor lounge and library are a bonus, as is the quiet but central location, tucked away in a lane behind Hotel Utse. Rates include tax.

★ Kantipur Temple House
BOUTIQUE HOTEL $$$

(Map p70; ☑ 01-4250131; www.kantipurtemple house.com; s/d US$95/120, deluxe US$130/155) 🌱 Hidden down an alley on the southern edge of Thamel, this Newari temple–style hotel has been built with meticulous attention to detail. The spacious rooms are tastefully decorated, with traditional carved wood, terracotta floor tiles, window seats and fair-trade *dhaka* (hand-woven) cloth bedspreads. Due to the traditional nature of the building, rooms tend to be a little dark.

This place is also doing its best to be eco-friendly – guests are given cloth bags to use when shopping and bulk mineral water is available free of charge in traditional bronze pitchers (in fact, there's no plastic anywhere in the hotel). The rooms encircle a traditional brick courtyard and there's free yoga in the garden at 8am. Don't expect TVs, air-con or heating. The old-town location is close to almost anywhere in town, but taxi drivers might have a hard time finding it. There are 50% discounts from December to February and May to September.

Hotel Mulberry HOTEL $$$
(Map p90; ☑ 01-4218899; www.mulberyynepal. com; Jyatha; s/d deluxe US$90/110, executive US$130/150; ✳ 🛜 ⛱) One of new breed of sleek, modern and somewhat impersonal top-end hotels on the edge of Thamel. The 67 rooms are spacious, modern and fresh and include a good buffet breakfast, but the highlight is the small but breathtaking rooftop infinity pool, gym and lounge bar, which is a memorable place for a drink.

🛏 Chhetrapati (Southwest Thamel)

This area is named after the important five-way intersection (notable by its distinctive bandstand) to the southwest of Thamel. The further you get from Thamel, the more traditional the surroundings become.

Khangsar Guest House HOTEL $
(Map p90; ☑ 01-4260788; www.khangsarguest house.com; s/d US$14/18; 🛜) This friendly and central backpacker option was undergoing major renovation in 2018, so expect rates to rise. Rooms come with a narrow but clean bathroom and there's a pleasant garden rooftop bar for cold beers under the stars. The upper-floor rooms are best, especially the sunny corner ones away from the road.

★ Hotel Ganesh Himal HOTEL $$
(Map p70; ☑ 01-4263598; www.hotelganesh himal.com; old building US$20-35, deluxe r US$30-60; ✳ 🛜) Our pick for midrange comfort on a budget is this well-run and super-friendly place. The rooms are among the best value in Kathmandu, with endless hot water and lots of balcony and relaxing garden seating. Throw in free airport pick-up and this place is hard to beat. The best standard rooms are in the side building (and are the sunniest in winter). The deluxe rooms are more spacious, while a little quieter and the spacious new Nepali-style super-deluxe rooms have brick floors and traditional decor. It's a 10-minute walk southwest of Thamel – far enough to be out of range of the tiger-balm

salesmen but close enough to restaurants for dinner. Bring earplugs, as this residential neighbourhood can be noisy.

Tibet Guest House HOTEL $$
(Map p90; ☑ 01-4251763; www.tibetguesthouse. com; s/d US$16/20, standard US$40/45, deluxe US$50/60, superior US$70/80, ste US$90/100; ✳ @ 🛜) This busy, efficient and popular hotel has functional rooms that are looking a bit worn in places, but it's a solid choice so book in advance. There's a lovely breakfast patio, a lobby espresso bar and the superb views of Swayambhunath from the rooftop cry out to be appreciated at sunset with a cold beer.

All but the cheapest rooms here are comfortable, though lower floors can be dark; the superior rooms have a lot more space. Some of the simple standard rooms are in a separate block across the street and come with a balcony. Discounts of 20% are standard.

Nirvana Garden Hotel HOTEL $$
(Map p90; ☑ 01-4256200; www.nirvanagarden. com; s/d US$40/50, deluxe US$50/60; @ 🛜) The relaxing garden here is a real oasis, making this hotel a decent choice close to the centre. The deluxe rooms with sunny balcony and garden view are the ones to opt for, though these don't have air-con and all rooms are getting a bit tired and overpriced these days. Aim for a 20% discount.

🛏 Freak Street (Jhochhen) & Durbar Square

Although Freak St's glory days have passed, a few determined budget restaurants and lodges have clung on. Staying here offers three pluses – you won't find rooms much cheaper, there are fewer crowds and you're right in the heart of the fascinating old city. On the downside, the pickings are slimmer and the lodges are generally grungier than in Thamel.

Monumental Paradise HOTEL $
(Map p70; ☑ 01-4240876; mparadise52@hotmail. com; Jhochhen; s/d from Rs 600/1200, ste Rs 2000; 🛜) Most places in Freak St are old and grungy, but this newish place has clean rooms with a tiled bathroom, and there's a pleasant rooftop bar-restaurant hangout. The single suite in the crow's nest has its own private balcony with views towards Durbar Sq. It's good value for solo travellers.

World Heritage Hotel BOUTIQUE HOTEL $$
(Map p74; ☑ 01-4261862; www.dwarikaschhen. com; Hanuman Dhoka; r without bathroom US$20, r

FREAK STREET – THE END OF THE ROAD

Running south from Basantapur Sq, Freak St dates from the overland days of the late 1960s and early 1970s, when it was one of the great gathering places on 'the road east'. In its hippie prime, this was the place for cheap hotels (Rs 3 a room!), colourful restaurants, hash and 'pie' (pastry) shops, the sounds of Jimi and Janis blasting from eight-track players and, of course, the weird and wonderful foreign 'freaks' who gave the street its name. Along with Bodhnath and Swayambhunath, Freak St was a magnet for those in search of spiritual enlightenment, cheap dope and a place where the normal boundaries no longer applied.

Times change and Freak St (better known these days by its real name, Jhochhen) is today only a pale shadow of its former funky self. While there are still cheap hotels and restaurants, it's the Thamel area in the north of the city that is the main gathering place for a new generation of travellers. However, for those people who find Thamel too slick and commercialised, Freak St retains a faint echo of those mellower days.

standard/deluxe US$55/75) Well away from the Thamel bustle, this traditional-style hotel is right next to the splendours of Durbar Sq and some rooms even offer views over the temple rooftops. The 12 rooms are decked out in stone and carved wood and come with ikat bedspreads and window seats.

The deluxe rooms are much larger than the pokey attic standard rooms but all suffer from a lack of natural light. The three plywood-walled budget rooms in the back courtyard share a single bathroom. A good range of Newari snacks and set meals is available from the pleasant courtyard restaurant. Note that this hotel is sometimes called Dwarika's Chhen. Rates include tax and breakfast.

Central Kathmandu

These hotels are within walking distance of Durbar Marg and the Thamel area, and fall into the top-end price range.

Three Rooms   BOUTIQUE HOTEL $$$

(Map p70; ☑9860378515; www.thepaulines. com/3rooms; Baber Mahal Revisited; r US$89-94, ste US$109; ☜) There are actually four rooms at this intimate French-run secret in the stylish Baber Mahal complex. Another surprise is just how spacious and charming the rooms are, with traditional dark slate and brass sinks given a cool modern twist by some well-chosen black-and-white photographs. One room even has its own fabulous private terrace. Rates include breakfast and tax.

Yak & Yeti Hotel   HOTEL $$$

(Map p70; ☑01-4248999; www.yakandyeti. com; Lal Durbar Marg; d US$240-280; ☒☜☳) This hotel is probably the best known in Nepal, due to its connections with the near-legendary Boris Lissanevitch (p98), who

ran the original restaurant. The recently renovated Newari wing incorporates wood-carvings, oil brick walls and local textiles, while the deluxe rooms in the Durbar wing are fresh, modern and stylish.

The oldest section of the hotel is part of the Lal Durbar, a former Rana palace that is worth a look for traces of an overblown but spectacular baroque decor and some excellent old black-and-white photos of Rana royalty. The borscht at the famous Chimney Restaurant here retains a tenuous link with its Russian past. The back garden (ask for a garden-facing room), two pools and tennis courts provide a rare sense of space. Online discounts of 30% are standard.

Maya Manor Hotel   HOTEL $$$

(Map p70; ☑01-4428028; www.mayamanor hotel.com; Hattisar Sadak; s/d US$90/100, ste US$120/150; ☒☜) This colonial-style villa in buttercup yellow was once the family home of the owners of Kathmandu Guest House, who manage the place. Rooms are modern and fresh and the spacious Rana-era suites are named after such illustrious house guests as George Schaller and Jane Goodall. There's a small but pleasant garden and a hidden upper terrace; the service is excellent. The only downside is the location, which lacks the central convenience of the Kathmandu Guest House. A side building houses the room where Jimmy Carter had his office when observing recent elections. Rates include breakfast and tax.

Lazimpat

North of central Kathmandu is the Lazimpat embassy area, popular with NGO staff, repeat visitors and business people.

BORIS LISSANEVITCH

Boris Lissanevitch is known as the godfather of tourism in Nepal. He was a fascinating figure, a white Russian émigré who fled the Bolshevik Revolution and worked at various times as a ballet dancer, chef, tiger hunter, fighter pilot, Shanghai club owner and trapeze artist. A friend of Ingrid Bergman, he acted in a film with Jean-Paul Belmondo.

Boris was running the Club 300 in Calcutta when he first met King Tribhuvan in 1944 (some even whisper that Boris helped pass secret messages between the king and Nehru, helping overthrow the Rana regime). Tribhuvan later invited him to Nepal to open Nepal's first hotel, the Royal, in a former royal palace (now the Electoral Commission Building). He brought the first tour group to the kingdom and hosted early mountaineering groups who would camp on the front lawn. The hotel and its famous Chimney Restaurant closed in the 1970s but would later morph into the Yak & Yeti Hotel (p97), where to this day you can sip on Russian borscht at the Chimney Restaurant.

Hotel Manaslu   HOTEL $$
(Map p70; ☑01-4410071; www.hotelmanaslu.com; Lazimpat; s/d incl breakfast US$70/80; ❄🖗🌊) The big draw at this comfortable, modern hotel is the lovely terrace garden and its pool fed by Newari-style fountains. The glorious carved windows in the restaurant were brought in from Bhaktapur. Rooms have been freshened up in recent years, making this a good choice, especially if you get a room in the back block overlooking the garden.

Hotel Ambassador   BUSINESS HOTEL $$
(Map p70; ☑01-4410432; www.ambassadornepal.com; Lazimpat; s/d from US$80/90; ❄🖗) This fresh, modern and comfortable hotel has a useful location between Thamel and Lazimpat that makes it good for both tourists and business travellers, with good double glazing to block out the busy junction noise. Head to the 9th-floor rooftop bar and sun deck for great 360-degree views. Good restaurants include Kotetsu (p105) and the lobby Flat Iron Grill for American-style sandwiches and salads. Unusually for Kathmandu, there are two wheelchair-accessible rooms.

★ Hotel Tibet   HOTEL $$$
(Map p70; ☑01-4429085; www.hotel-tibet.com.np; Lazimpat; s/d US$85/95, ste US$115/125; ❄🖗) Tibetophiles and tour groups heading to or from Tibet like the Tibetan vibe of this recommended place. The 54 quiet and comfortable rooms are plain compared to the opulent Tibetan-style lobby, but several of the larger front-facing rooms have a balcony. There's also a great rooftop terrace bar-restaurant and a side garden cafe.

The hotel is building the huge 17-storey top-end Lhasa International Hotel next door so you can expect front-facing rooms to suffer from construction noise until 2020. Hikers with sore legs can try the 90-minute 'trekkers' recovery massage' (Rs 3850) at the attached Shambhala Spa.

Shanker Hotel   HISTORIC HOTEL $$$
(Map p70; ☑01-4410151; www.shankerhotel.com.np; Lazimpat; s/d incl breakfast US$75/80; ❄🖗🌊) There's nowhere in town quite like this creaky 19th-century former Rana residence – the kind of place where you expect to bump into some whiskered old Rana prince shuffling around one of the wooden corridors. The entry columns of neoclassical whipped cream overlook a palatial manicured garden and one of the city's nicest swimming pools.

The palace conversion means that rooms are idiosyncratic, with some rooms featuring hobbit-sized half-windows, and others comfortably modern and spacious. The '400' number rooms offer the most historical touches. For real grandeur you'll have to track down the dining halls and Durbar Hall conference space. There was minor damage during the earthquake, but renovations are almost finished.

Radisson   HOTEL $$$
(Map p70; ☑01-4423888; www.radisson.com/kathmandune; Lazimpat; r US$195-260; ❄@🖗🌊) A favourite of embassy staff and business travellers, the Radisson is a modern if somewhat soulless five-star choice, with a 5th-floor pool, spa and a good gym. The premium rooms in the new building are the freshest option. Several good cafes and bars loiter outside the main gates. Online discounts of at least 30% are standard.

Hotel Shangri-La
HOTEL $$$

(☑ 01-4412999; www.hotelshangrila.com; Lazimpat; s/d incl breakfast US$100/110; ✳@🛜🏊) The real draw at this five-star place is the large relaxing garden, with its terrace restaurant and small but nice pool. Come for the Friday barbecue or Saturday champagne brunch, or try a *Lost Horizon*–themed cocktail during happy hour (4pm to 6pm) at the cosy James Hilton Bar. Request a garden-view room. It's not connected to the Shangri-La chain.

🛏 Elsewhere

The edges of the city offer a quietish escape if you don't mind a drive into the city each day. The eastern Swayambhunath region offers a distinctly Tibetan flavour.

Hotel Vajra
BOUTIQUE HOTEL $$

(Map p70; ☑ 01-4271545; www.hotelvajra.com; Bijeshwari; s/d from US$33/38, without bathroom US$16/18, ste US$90/100) Across the Vishnumati River on the way to Swayambhunath, this is one of Kathmandu's most interesting hotels in any price category. The brick complex feels more like an artists' retreat than a hotel, with lush gardens, a library, a rooftop bar and an ayurvedic massage room. The only catch is the location, which, though peaceful, makes it tricky for getting a taxi.

All the rooms in the old wing are different (the cheapest share bathrooms), so take a look at more than one. If you are in the new wing (single/double US$65/70), try to score a balcony. Some rooms are looking a bit tired and the service is somewhat begrudging, but it's still a good option.

★ Dwarika's
BOUTIQUE HOTEL $$$

(☑ 01-4479488; www.dwarikas.com; Battis Putali; s/d US$275/295, ste from US$400; 🛜🏊) For stylish design and sheer romance, this outstanding hotel is unbeatable; if you're on your honeymoon, look no further. Over 40 years the owners have rescued thousands of woodcarvings from around the valley and incorporated them into the hotel design. The end result is a beautiful hybrid – a cross between a museum and a boutique hotel, with a lush, pampering ambience.

The hotel consists of clusters of traditional Newari buildings separated by brick-paved courtyards. All rooms are unique and some have sensuous open-plan black-slate bathrooms. Highlights include a lovely library lounge, back pool, a spa where they make their own inhouse soaps, a good Japanese restaurant and a bar in the hotel's original building. The location on a busy street east of town, a short walk southwest of Pashupatinath, is a horror, but finding a taxi is never a problem. Book well in advance.

★ Hyatt Regency Kathmandu
LUXURY HOTEL $$$

(☑ 01-4491234; www.kathmandu.regency.hyatt. com; Taragaon; d from US$165; 🛜🏊) No expense has been spared on this superb palace-style building, from the dramatic entrance of Newari water pools to the modern Malla-style architecture. It's worth popping in just to admire the gorgeous Patan-style chaitya in the foyer. As you'd expect, the spacious rooms are furnished tastefully, with huge bathrooms, and you can pay an extra US$20 for views over nearby Bodhnath stupa.

The large swimming pool, good restaurants and Sunday brunch make this the perfect spot for a splurge: after a tough day's sightseeing unwind with a *shirodhara* ayurvedic treatment at the spa. Extra touches like a 24-hour gym and good room security make this the best hotel in Kathmandu. The Hyatt is a couple of kilometres outside Kathmandu, on the road to Bodhnath. The club rooms can be great value for couples; for US$55 extra you can often get breakfast for two, airport transfers, cocktails and wi-fi.

Soaltee Crowne Plaza
LUXURY HOTEL $$$

(☑ 01-4273999; www.crowneplaza.com/Kath mandu; Tahachal; r from US$180; 🏊) Space and tranquillity are precious commodities in Kathmandu, but the Soaltee has acres of both; 4.5 hectares, to be precise. Spread around the palatial grounds are excellent restaurants, a lovely poolside area and even a bowling alley. The price you pay is a crummy location on the western edge of town, a 15-minute taxi ride from the centre.

🍴 Eating

Kathmandu has an astounding array of restaurants. Indeed, with the possible exception of the canteen at the UN building, there are many places where you can have the choice of Indian, Chinese, Japanese, Mexican, Korean, Middle Eastern, Italian or Irish cuisines, all within a five-minute walk. After weeks trekking in the mountains, Kathmandu feels like a culinary paradise.

Thamel's restaurant scene has been sliding upmarket for a few years now, with most places now charging US$5 to US$7 per main course, plus 24% tax. A bottle of beer will double your bill in most places. Finding a budget meal is still possible but it involves some hunting.

Many restaurants in Kathmandu try to serve something from everywhere – pizzas, momos, Indian curries, a bit of Thai here, some Mexican there. Predictably, the ones that specialise generally serve the finest food.

If you can't face battling Kathmandu's traffic, Foodmandu (www.foodmandu.com) is an online service and app that will bring you food from 170 restaurants in Kathmandu. Delivery cost depends on the distance, but is generally less than Rs 100; orders are taken until 8.30pm.

Central Thamel

The junction outside the Kathmandu Guest House is the epicentre of Thamel dining and you'll find dozens of excellent restaurants within a minute's walk in either direction. You should make dinner reservations at most of these places in October's high season.

Pumpernickel Bakery   BAKERY **$**
(Map p90; pastries/sandwiches Rs 100/350; ⊙7am-7pm) Bleary-eyed tourists crowd in here every morning for fresh croissants, quality breads and reviving espresso in the pleasant garden area at the back. Lunchtime brings good sandwiches.

Momo Hut   TIBETAN **$**
(Map p90; Narsingh Chowk; momos Rs 200-250; ⊙10am-10pm) Buff (water buffalo) momos, mushroom momos, cheese and spinach momos, ostrich momos, chocolate momos – sweet or savoury, steamed or fried... Honestly, you'd be silly not to order the momos. We recommend paying an extra Rs 50 to get them in a delicious sesame peanut sauce (*jhol momo*). You can even sign up for the 8am momo-making class (Rs 1500). Momos.

Mustang Thakali Chulo   NEPALI **$**
(Map p90; ☑01-4248083; daal bhaat from Rs 245; ⊙10am-3.30pm & 5.30-9.30pm) Located on the 2nd floor, this is a good option for local Thakali daal bhaat (rice, curry and lentil soup) or a curry with rice, and is popular with local Manangis. It's quiet, intimate (with booth seating) and, best of all, authentic. The exotic special thali comes with pumpkin curry and *gidiful* (goat's brains).

Thakali Bhanchha   NEPALI **$**
(Map p90; ☑01-4701910; Chaksibari Marg; daal bhaat from Rs 300; ⊙10am-11pm) If, after having travelled all the way to Nepal, you actually fancy some Nepali food(!), this upstairs restaurant is a good bet and popular with local Thamel workers on their lunch break. Most opt for the favourful and bottomless daal bhaat, but there's also a range of Thakali beer snacks such as fried *bandel* (boar) and roasted *bhatmas* (soybeans).

For the full-on local experience, swap the rice for *dhido,* the doughy buckwheat paste eaten daily by millions of Nepalis.

Dream Garden Restaurant   INTERNATIONAL **$$**
(Map p90; mains Rs 500-600) The outdoor garden restaurant at the Kathmandu Guest House has easily the classiest ambience in town, with prices on par with Thamel's other restaurants. The menu ranges from Indian dishes such as fish tikka to sandwiches, steaks and sizzlers and it's a peaceful place for a pre-dinner drink.

Roadhouse Cafe   PIZZA **$$**
(Map p90; ☑01-4262768; www.roadhouse.com.np; Arcadia Building, Chaksibari Marg; pizzas Rs 600-650; ⊙11am-10pm; ☎) The big attractions at this well-run place are the pizzas from the wood-fired oven and the warm and intimate decor, with an open-air courtyard located out the back. The salads, sandwiches, desserts (sizzling brownie with ice cream) and espresso coffees are all top-notch.

Or2k   MIDDLE EASTERN **$$**
(Map p90; ☑01-4422097; www.or2k.net; Mandala St; mains Rs 300-500; ⊙9am-11pm; ☎🍴) This bright, buzzy and ever-popular Israeli vegetarian restaurant is a favourite for fresh and light Middle Eastern dishes, with plenty of vegan and gluten-free dishes. The menu spreads to fatoush salad, zucchini and mushroom pie and *ziva* (pastry fingers filled with cheese), as well as a great meze sampler of hummus, felafel and *labane* (sour cream cheese).

Seating is on cushions on the floor and you have to take your shoes off, so make sure you're wearing clean socks. A popular stand at street level serves takeaway felafel wraps.

New Orleans Cafe   INTERNATIONAL **$$**
(Map p90; ☑01-4700736; www.neworleanscafe ktm.com; mains Rs 370-500; ⊙8am-10.30pm; ☎🍴) Hidden down an alley near the Kathmandu Guest House, New Orleans boasts an intimate candlelit vibe, a classy blues and

---

DON'T MISS

WALKING KATHMANDU'S OLD TOWN

Kathmandu's backstreets are dense with beautiful temples, shrines and sculptures, especially in the crowded maze of streets and courtyards in the area north of Durbar Sq, and exploring these half-hidden sights is a real highlight.

The old town is bursting with traditional markets, temples, *tole* (streets), *bahal* (Buddhist monastery courtyards), *bahil* (residential courtyards) and chowk (intersections), which remain the focus of traditional Nepali life. You only really appreciate Kathmandu's museum-like quality when you come across a 1000-year-old statue – something that would be a prized possession in many Western museums – being used as a plaything or a washing line in some communal courtyard.

For the best markets and most important temples explore with our backstreets walking tour (p80) between Thamel and Durbar Sq. For fewer spectacular sights but where the everyday life of city dwellers goes on and tourists are few and far between, follow our walking tour (p84) south of Durbar Sq.

If walking tours leave you wanting more, pick up Annick Holle's book *Kathmandu the Hidden City* or John Child's *Streets of Silver, Streets of Gold*, both of which detail dozens of backstreet courtyards across town.

---

jazz soundtrack and live music on Wednesdays and Saturdays. It's a popular spot for a drink, but the menu also ranges far and wide, from Thai curries to Creole jambalaya and oven-roasted veggies. You need to book a table in the high season.

Forest & Plate   HEALTH FOOD $$
(Map p90; ☏01-4701161; Sagarmatha Bazaar, Mandala St; salads Rs 490-590; ⊙11am-9.30pm; ☏⁄) Healthy foodies pining for their kale and quinoa will breathe a sigh of relief at this well-run place specialising in organic salads. The inventive combinations burst with fresh flavours and quality ingredients, while some steak and chicken dishes are thrown in for the carnivores. The pleasant rooftop location above Himalayan Java and the full bar makes it a good place for a cocktail.

Friends Restaurant   INTERNATIONAL $$
(Map p90; ☏01-4700063; Mandala St; mains Rs 300-600; ⊙9am-10pm; ☏) Run by the same people as Or2k, but a less grungy, more grown-up option, Friends shows its Israeli roots through its hummus, *shawarma* and *borek* (filo pastry pies), but the menu also stretches to breakfasts, burgers, pizza and a particularly fine Thai beef salad. The decor is warm and relaxed, with exposed brick and farmhouse tables, and the service is normally good. Rates include tax but not service.

Black Olives   INTERNATIONAL $$
(Map p90; ☏01-4700956; www.blackolives cafethamel.com; Chaksibari Marg; mains Rs 500-600; ⊙7am-10.30pm; ☏) Maybe it's because of

happy hour's free *papad* (pappadam) with salsa or perhaps it's the super-friendly staff – either way, we like this reliable courtyard restaurant. The menu offers something for everyone, with good burgers and salads, and there are seasonal dishes, wines by the glass and live music on Saturdays.

Hankook Sarang   KOREAN $$
(Map p90; ☏01-4256615; mains Rs 350-750; ⊙10am-10pm) The Hankook is that rare combination of authentic taste and good value. The spicy Korean main dishes come with crunchy kimchi, salad, soup, dried fish, sweet beans and green tea. Alternatively, fire up the barbecue for some *bulgogi* (barbecued beef), cooked at your table and eaten with lettuce, or try the good-value *kimbap* (vegetarian rice rolls). Government tax included.

If you are new to Korean food try the *bibimbap* – rice and vegetables in a stone pot, to which you add egg and sweet chilli sauce and mix it all together. The service is friendly and there's a choice of floor seating or pleasant al fresco garden dining. It's down an alley near Tamas Spa Lounge.

Furusato   JAPANESE $$
(Map p90; ☏01-4265647; set meals Rs 380-520; ⊙10am-9pm) Bright and calming, Furusato is perfect for a light dinner. Dishes include udon or cold soba noodles, *donburi* (rice bowls), bento boxes and *gyoza* dumplings (the Japanese version of a momo), but most people opt for one of the set meals, which come with sesame-flavoured salad, miso

soup and pickles. It's hidden down an alley opposite Weizen Bakery.

Northfield Cafe
INTERNATIONAL $$

(Map p90; ☎ 01-4700884; www.northfieldcafe.net; Chaksibari Marg; breakfast Rs 200-315, mains Rs 415-650; ☺ 7am-10.30pm; 🛜 💧) This pleasant, spacious spot is the place for serious breakfast devotees (think waffles and *huevos rancheros*), with the useful option of half or full portions. The Mexican and Indian tandoori dishes (dinner only) are also excellent (you'll have to ask if you want them spicy) and the American comfort food spreads to burgers, nachos and even chilli cheese fries.

There's a sense of space here missing in many of Thamel's other restaurants. The outdoor firepit is a real plus in winter and there's traditional Nepali music in the evenings. It's also one of the few places to offer kids' meals.

Revolution Cafe
INTERNATIONAL $$

(Map p90; www.revocafenp.com; mains Rs 450-600; ☺ 7am-10pm; 🛜) Revolution is a decent option if you need a break in northern Thamel. It's a pretty cool place, with courtyard, indoor or traditional seating, all grooving to a solid blues soundtrack. The coffee and fruit juices are good and the menu offers a taste of everything, from an organic goat's cheese salad to chicken tikka masala. Prices include tax and service.

★ Third Eye
INDIAN $$$

(Map p90; ☎ 01-4260160; www.thirdeye.com.np; Chaksibari Marg; mains Rs 475-650; ☺ 11am-10pm) This long-running favourite is popular with well-heeled tourists. Indian food is the speciality and the tandoori dishes are especially good, even if the portions are a bit small. Spice levels are set at 'tourist' so let the efficient (if not friendly) suited waiters know if you'd like extra heat.

NEPALI & NEWARI RESTAURANTS

A growing number of restaurants around town specialise in Nepali (mostly Newari) food. Several are in converted Rana-era palaces that offer a set meal, either veg or nonveg, and you dine on cushions at low tables. All offer a cultural show that consists of musicians and dancers performing 'traditional' song and dance routines. The whole thing is a bit touristy, but it's a classy night out nonetheless. At most places it's a good idea to make a reservation during the high season.

The food stretches to half a dozen courses that generally include a starter of momos and such main dishes as *alu tareko* (fried potato with cumin and tumeric), *bandhel* (boar), *kukhura ko ledo* (chicken in gravy), *chicken sekuwa* (barbecued or smoked meat), *alu tama kho jhol* (bamboo shoot stew) and *gundruk* (sour soup with dried greens), finished off with *shikarni* (sweet yoghurt with dried fruit and cinnamon) and masala tea. Look out also for *kwati*, a soup consisting of a dozen types of sprouted beans that is prepared during Newari festivals.

Bhojan Griha (Map p70; ☎ 01-4416423; www.bhojangriha.com; Dilli Bazaar; set menus Rs 2000; ☺ 11am-2pm & 5-10pm) The most ambitious of the city's traditional Newari restaurants, Bhojan Griha is located in a restored 150-year-old mansion in Dilli Bazaar, just east of the city centre. It's worth eating here just to see the imaginative renovation of this beautiful old building, once the residence of the caste of royal priests. There's a cultural show at 7pm.

Most of the seating is traditional (ie on cushions on the floor), although these are actually legless chairs, which saves your back and knees. In an effort to reduce waste, plastic is not used in the restaurant and mineral water is bought in bulk and sold by the glass.

Thamel House (Map p90; ☎ 01-4410388; Paknajol; mains Rs 300-700, set meals veg/nonveg Rs 1050/1150; ☺ 10am-4pm & 6-10pm) This place is set in a traditional old Newari building and has bags of atmosphere, as well as a dance show at 7pm. Choose between the downstairs courtyard or upper-floor balcony seating. The food is traditional Nepali and Newari, and there are à la carte options. It's particularly convenient for Thamel.

Krishnarpan Restaurant (☎ 01-4470770; www.dwarikas.com; set meals US$40-65; ☺ 6-9.30pm) One of the best places for traditional Nepali food is this impressive place at Dwarika's hotel. The atmosphere is superb and the organic food gets consistent praise from diners. Set meals range from six courses to the blowout 22-course option (US$65). Reservations required. The hotel's Friday barbecue buffet (US$30) is also popular.

Reserve a window seat at the sit-down section at the front or try the more informal section with low tables and cushions at the back; both are candlelit to create an intimate vibe.

La Dolce Vita   ITALIAN $$$

(Map p90; ☑ 01-4700612; Chaksibari Marg; pastas Rs 485-560, mains Rs 750-850, house wine per glass Rs 410; ◔ 11am-10pm) Life is indeed sweet at Thamel's best Italian bistro, offering up such delights as parmesan gnocchi; goat's cheese and spinach ravioli; and sinfully rich chocolate torta. Choose between the rustic red-and-white tablecloths and terracotta tiles of the main restaurant, the breezy rooftop terrace or the lounge space with its two tables overlooking Thamel Chowk; either way the atmosphere and food are excellent.

Yin Yang Restaurant   THAI $$$

(Map p90; ☑ 01-4425510; www.yinyang.com.np; curries Rs 600, rice Rs 125; ◔ 10am-10pm) Yin Yang is one of Thamel's most highly regarded restaurants, serving authentic Thai food that is a definite cut above the imitation Thai food found elsewhere. The green curry is authentically spicy; for something sweeter try the massaman curry (with onion, peanut and potato). There's a good range of vegetable choices, as well as Continental alternatives.

K-Too Steakhouse   STEAK $$$

(Map p90; ☑ 01-4700043; www.kilroygroup.com; mains Rs 460-760; ◔ 10am-10pm; ☏) The food and warm and buzzy atmosphere here are excellent. Dishes range from chilli lemongrass chicken to healthy salads, but it's really all about the steaks. The pepper steak sizzler (Rs 760) followed by fried apple momos and an Everest Beer is a post-trekking classic. For a quieter vibe, head for the garden.

✖ Elsewhere in Thamel

Yangling Tibetan Restaurant   TIBETAN $

(Map p70; Kaldhara; momos Rs 150-250; ◔ noon-9pm Sun-Fri) Both locals and tourists flock to this unpretentious family-run place for possibly the best momos in town (try the chicken ones). The ground-floor kitchen here is a nonstop momo production line. You can also get soupy Tibetan butter tea and tasty *then-thuk* (noodle soup). It recently relocated to a less central location west of Thamel.

Yak Restaurant   TIBETAN $

(Map p90; mains Rs 170-350; ◔ 7am-9.30pm; ☏) We always find ourselves returning to this unpretentious and reliable local place at the southern end of Thamel. The booths give it a 'Tibetan diner' vibe and the clientele is a mix of trekkers, Sherpa guides and local Tibetans who come to shoot the breeze over a tube of *tongba* (hot millet beer) and a plate of *kothey* (fried momos). Government tax included.

★ Gaia Restaurant   INTERNATIONAL $$

(Map p90; Jyatha; mains Rs 400-550; ◔ 7am-9pm; ☏) This popular and dependable place combines good breakfasts, salads, sandwiches and organic coffee in a pleasant garden courtyard with global music, reasonable prices (tax included) and good service. The Thai red curry is surprisingly good and the chicken *choiyla* (spicy barbecued meat) packs a punch; you're bound to find something good in a menu that ranges from daal bhaat to carrot cake.

Utse Restaurant   TIBETAN $$

(Map p90; ☑ 01-4257614; Amrit Marg; mains Rs 200-485; ◔ 6am-9pm; ☏) In the hotel of the same name, this is one of the longest-running restaurants in Thamel (since 1971!) and still turns out excellent Tibetan dishes, including authentic butter tea and hard-to-find Tibetan desserts such as *dhay-shi* (sweet rice, curd and raisins). The mellow, old-school decor feels lifted straight from an old Lhasa backstreet.

For a group blowout, *gacok* (also spelt *gyakok*) is a form of hotpot named after the brass tureen that is heated at the table (Rs 1250 for two). The set meals are also a worthy extravagance. If you like the food you can buy its Tibetan cookbook.

Mitho Restaurant   INTERNATIONAL $$

(Map p90; www.facebook.com/mithorestaurant; JP Marg; mains Rs 400-500; ◔ 7am-10pm; ☑) A friendly and cool place on the edge of Thamel that is trying to offer something more than the bog-standard tourist restaurant options. There are lots of fresh choices like aubergine tagine, chicken tikka wraps and a watermelon and feta salad, alongside a good range of Indian dishes.

The decor is modern with brushed concrete and blonde wood and there's a pleasant upstairs balcony. Prices include all taxes.

Rosemary Kitchen   INTERNATIONAL $$

(Map p90; ☑ 01-4267554; www.rosemary-kitchen. net; mains Rs 400-700; ◔ 7am-10pm; ☏) There's a little bit of everything here, from Nepali choela chicken and tasty Thai curries to fresh salads, homemade bread and wine by the glass. Choose from the classy interior or little garden; either way book in high season. Prices include government tax, with an Everest Beer going for just Rs 299 during happy hour (4pm to 7pm).

Dechenling   TIBETAN, BHUTANESE $$
(Map p90; ✆01-4412158; mains Rs 350-600, set meals Rs 800; ☺8am-9.30pm; ☎) Quality Himalayan food and one of Kathmandu's most relaxing courtyards are the draws of this charming garden restaurant-bar. It's also one of the few places in town to offer interesting Bhutanese dishes such as *kewa dhatsi* (potato and cheese curry). If you can't decide, opt for one of the grand Tibetan or Bhutanese set meals.

★ Fire & Ice Pizzeria   PIZZA $$$
(Map p90; ✆01-4250210; www.fireandicepizzeria.com; 219 Sanchaya Kosh Bhawan, Tridevi Marg; pizzas Rs 580-750; ☺8am-11pm) This excellent and informal Italian place serves the best pizzas in Kathmandu (wholewheat crusts available, as well as combo pizzas), alongside breakfasts, smoothies, crêpes and good espresso, all to a cool soundtrack of Cuban son or Italian opera. The ingredients are top-notch, from the imported anchovies to the house-made tomato sauce. It's very popular so make a reservation and expect to share one of the tavern-style wooden tables.

✕ Freak Street (Jhochhen) & Durbar Square

Freak St has a small number of budget restaurants where you can find simple food at lower prices than Thamel. Even if you're staying in other areas of the city, you might need a place for lunch if you're sightseeing around Durbar Sq.

Kumari Restaurant   INTERNATIONAL $
(Map p70; Freak St; mains Rs 150-300; ☺9am-9pm; ☎) Next to the Century Lodge, this basic but friendly hang-out is one of few places that seems to have hung onto some of the mellowness of times past. Grab a seat outside if the interior is too glum. All the travellers' favourites are here at Kathmandu's cheapest prices.

Snowman Restaurant   BAKERY $
(Map p70; Freak St; cakes Rs 80-100) A long-running and relaxed place, perhaps too dingy for some, this is one of those rare Kathmandu hang-outs that attracts both locals and nostalgic former hippies. The chocolate cake has been drawing overland travellers for close to 40 years now. When Lennon starts singing 'I am the Walrus' on the eight-track, it feels like 1967 all over again...

Cosmo de Café Restaurant   INTERNATIONAL $$
(Map p74; Durbar Sq; mains Rs 350-500; ☺10am-8pm) This is perhaps the best value of the several rooftop tourist restaurants that overlook Durbar Sq. The views over the destroyed Maju Deval temple are not what they once were, but the range of food is good and prices are reasonable.

✕ Central Kathmandu

The restaurants in the Kantipath and Durbar Marg areas are generally more expensive than around Thamel, but the quality is higher and there are are several worthwhile splurges.

Dudh Sagar   INDIAN $
(Map p70; ✆01-4232263; Kantipath; dosas Rs 100-200; ☺8am-8pm) This bustling local sweets house is the place to reacquaint yourself with South Indian vegetarian snacks such as dosas, *idly* (pounded rice cakes) and *uthapam* (pizza-like rice-and-daal pancake), topped off by a vast range of milk-based Indian sweets. A masala dosa followed by *dudh malai* (cream-cheese balls in chilled pistachio milk) makes a great meal for Rs 215.

Baan Thai   THAI $$
(Map p70; ✆01-4231931; Durbar Marg; curries Rs 375-420; ☺11am-10pm) This unpretentious place overlooking Durbar Marg is a good choice for authentic Thai food. Starters include squid salad and *som tam thai* (young papaya and dried shrimp salad), the curries are creamy and the *tom kha ghai* (chicken coconut milk soup) comes served in a hotpot big enough for two.

★ Kaiser Cafe   INTERNATIONAL, AUSTRIAN $$$
(Map p90; ✆01-4425341; Garden of Dreams, Tridevi Marg; mains Rs 600-1650; ☺9am-10pm) This cafe-restaurant in the Garden of Dreams is run by Dwarika's so quality is high. It's a fine place for a light meal (such as savoury crêpes or build-your-own sandwiches), a quiet breakfast or to linger over a pot of tea or something stiffer. More than anything else, it's one of the city's most romantic locations, especially at dusk.

Austrian-inspired dishes such as Wiener schnitzel and Sachertorte are a nod to the country that financed and oversaw the

OFF THE BEATEN TRACK

QUIRKY KATHMANDU

Kathmandu has more than its fair share of quirk and, as with most places in the subcontinent, a 10-minute walk in any direction will throw up numerous curiosities.

The corridors of the Natural History Museum (p119) are full of bizarre moth-eaten animals and jars that lie somewhere between a school science experiment and *The Texas Chainsaw Massacre*. The 20ft python skin and nine-month-old baby rhino in a jar are guaranteed to give you nightmares. The other exhibits are a bit slapdash, including the line of stuffed birds nailed carelessly to a bit of wood to indicate their distribution, or the big pile of elephant dung deposited randomly in the front corner.

The nearby National Museum (p119) also houses more than its fair share of weirdness, including the skin of a two-headed calf, a creepy doll collection and a portrait of King Prithvi Narayan Shah giving everyone the finger (apparently symbolising the unity of the nation...).

Once it reopens following earthquake repairs, the **Tribhuvan Museum** (Map p74) in Hanuman Dhoka should still be the place to see such quirky gems of royal paraphernalia as the king's personal parachuting uniform, his film projector and his walking stick with a spring-loaded sword inside – very '007'.

Kathmandu's **Kaiser Library** (Map p90; ☑ 01-4411318; Ministry of Education & Sports compound, cnr Kantipath & Tridevi Marg; ⊙ 10.30am-4.30pm Sun-Thu, to 2.30pm Fri) is definitely worth a visit, partly for its remarkable collection of antique travel books but also for the main reading room, which has antique globes, a stuffed tiger and suits of armour that you expect to spring to life at any moment.

Compared to all this funkiness, Kathmandu's old town is pretty docile. Look for the antique **fire engines** hidden behind a grille just west of the junction of New Rd and Sukra Path. If you get a toothache during your trip, be sure to visit the old town's toothache god (p80) across from Sikha Narayan Temple – the god is represented by a tiny image in a raggedy old stump of wood covered with hundreds of nails and coins.

garden's restoration. The house meatballs are described modestly (by themselves) as 'one of the greatest bar snacks in the world'. You'll have to pay the garden's admission fee to eat here.

Mezze   MEDITERRANEAN $$$
(Map p70; ☑ 01-4223087; Mercantile Plaza, Durbar Marg; mains Rs 350-700; ⊙ 10am-11pm) This hip rooftop bar-restaurant on Durbar Marg has an urban warehouse vibe, with an open kitchen and a striking rooftop location providing a splash of glamour. There are good salads, mezze platters, paninis and pizza, but it's also a great place for a summer sangria or a cocktail under the stars.

Old House   FRENCH $$$
(Map p70; ☑ 01-4250931; www.theoldhouse.
com.np; Lal Durbar Marg; mains Rs 800-1250; ⊙ 9am-11pm) This easily missed but charming 200-year-old Rana residence features French-Nepali food. Dishes range from light lunch sandwiches (Rs 400 to Rs 500) and salads to set five-course tasting menus (Rs 2900), with standout dishes including the lime trout, Mediterranean-style chicken leg with olives, bacon and wine sauce, and fine desserts such as lime curd on almond cream.

It's also a stylish place for a coffee in the peaceful garden or something stiffer in the patio bar area.

Koto Restaurant   JAPANESE $$$
(Map p70; ☑ 01-4226025; Durbar Marg; sushi Rs 370-690, set menus Rs 980; ⊙ 11.30am-3pm & 6-9.30pm) There are now two branches of long-running Koto next to each other on Durbar Marg; the southern one has the larger selection of sushi and nigiri rolls, and the northern has more sukiyaki and fresh mackerel. Both branches have a wide range of other Japanese dishes, plus several set menus and bento boxes.

Kotetsu   JAPANESE $$$
(Map p70; ☑ 01-6218513; Lainchaur; sushi Rs 800-900, set meal Rs 1600; ⊙ noon-2pm & 5.30-9.30pm Mon-Fri, 5.30-9.30pm Sun) It takes a brave person to order sushi in the Himalaya, but raw-fish experts (afishionados?) generally rate Koketsu as the best Japanese place in town. The seafood is flown in fresh from Thailand. The focal point of the restaurant is the counter seating at the teppanyaki grill. It's inside the Ambassador Hotel at the southern end of Lazimpat.

Ghar-e-Kebab INDIAN $$$

(Map p70; Durbar Marg; mains Rs 550-850, rice Rs 300; ☺noon-10pm) Located inside the Hotel de l'Annapurna on Durbar Marg, this has some of the best north Indian and tandoori food in the city. Indian miniatures hang on the walls underneath an ornate carved-wood ceiling and in the evenings classical Indian music is played and traditional Urdu *ghazals* (love songs) are sung. Try the pistachio sherbet for dessert.

✗ Elsewhere

Saigon Pho VIETNAMESE $$

(☑01-4443330; Lazimpat; mains Rs 350-550; ☺10am-10pm; ☎) This authentic Vietnamese-run place in Lazimpat is bursting with the flavours of coriander, lemongrass and fish sauce. The light and tasty dishes include shrimp rice wraps, spring rolls, green papaya salad, lots of *pho* noodles and a tasty *ca kho gung* (fish stew with ginger and onion). Grab a seat in the house's upper balcony. Branches are opening all over town, including in the south end of Thamel in 2018.

Chez Caroline FRENCH $$$

(Map p70; ☑01-4263070; www.chezcarolinenepal. com; mains Rs 600-1600; ☺9.30am-10pm) In the Baber Mahal Revisited complex, Caroline's is a sophisticated outdoor bistro popular with expat foodies. It offers French-influenced main courses such as wild-mushroom tart with walnut sauce, Roquefort salad, and crêpes Suzette with passionfruit sorbet, plus fine quiches and pastries, daily specials and a lazy weekend brunch (Rs 1250), all with a wide range of desserts, teas and wines. Try a swift glass of pastis (liquorice-flavoured liqueur) with mint syrup: it's the perfect aperitif to an afternoon's shopping.

1905 Suites INTERNATIONAL $$$

(Map p70; ☑01-4411348; www.1905suites.com; Naryanchaur; lunch mains Rs 600, dinner Rs 1000-1500; ☺8am-10pm) This classy restaurant is set in a charming former residence of a Rana court musician, with a lovely garden set off by a modern glass pavilion. Food ranges from tapas snacks and an all-day breakfast menu to lunch wraps and salads and heavier dinner mains. It's a wonderfully romantic place for drinks (30% discount 5pm to 7pm).

Self-Catering

For trekking food such as noodles, nuts, dried fruit and cheese, there are several well-stocked supermarkets grouped around central Thamel Chowk. For cheaper supermarkets try the various branches of **Bluebird Mart** (Map p70; www.bluebirdmart.com.np; ☺9am-9pm), one of which is just east of Durbar Sq; **Big Mart** (Map p70; Lazimpat; ☺7am-9pm) in Lazimpat, near the Radisson Hotel; and **Bhat Bhateni Supermarket** (Map p70; www.bbsm. com.np; Bhatbhateni; ☺7.30am-8.30pm), south of the Chinese embassy.

Garet Express SANDWICHES $

(Map p90; baguettes from Rs 250; ☺9am-11pm) There are several sandwich shops in Thamel, but this French-style épicerie is a definite grade above them all. Choose from nak cheese from Jiri, French chorizo or bacon fillers. Alternatively, raid the deli section for a top-shelf DIY picnic of French Camembert, pâté, organic jams and baguettes.

Weizen Bakery BAKERY $

(Map p90; Chaksibari Marg; pastries Rs 70-120, mains Rs 400-500) This bakery-restaurant has decent cakes, breads and pastries, with bakery goods (but not cakes) discounted by 50% after 8pm. The pleasant, attached garden-style **Rickshaw Cafe** is a quiet place for breakfast and offers interesting dishes such as beetroot, feta and walnut salad and a feta and bacon burger.

Curry Kitchen/Hot Bread BAKERY $

(Map p90; pastries Rs 70-120; ☺6am-10pm) This bakery on the main Thamel junction does a roaring trade in sandwiches, bread rolls, pizza slices and pastries. Add an espresso and head upstairs to the sunny terrace for a leisurely breakfast or pack a ham-and-veg roll for lunch on the run. Bakery items are discounted by 50% after 9.30pm.

Organic Farmers Market MARKET $$

(www.lesherpa.com.np; Restaurant Le Sherpa, Maharajganj; ☺9am-noon Sat) This weekly organic food market in the Le Sherpa Restaurant is popular with foreign residents who come here for the French cheese, jams, breads and organic vegetables. The location is a bit inconvenient for most Thamel-based visitors.

♟ Drinking & Nightlife

There are bars scattered around Thamel, all within a short walk of each other. Just poke your nose in to see which has the crowd and style that appeals. Many have live bands, though the playlists can get monotonously familiar. Most bars in Thamel close by 11pm, or midnight on Fridays and Saturdays.

A beer costs between Rs 450 and Rs 550, plus 23% tax. Most places have a happy hour between 5pm and 8pm, with two-for-one cocktails, and a modest beer discount.

Be wary of Thamel's sleazy 'dance bars' or 'shower dance' bars. At first glance many seem quite tame, but many are fronts for the prostitution of trafficked women.

Himalayan Java   CAFE

(Map p90; ☏ 01-4422519; www.himalayanjava. com; Tridevi Marg; coffee/snacks Rs 130/400; ⊘7am-9pm; ☏) The various branches of this modern and buzzing coffeehouse are the place to lose yourself in a sofa, a laptop and a pulse-reviving Caffè Americano. There are also breakfasts, paninis, salads and cakes. The main Tridevi Marg branch has a balcony, lots of sofas and a big-screen TV for the football, but feels a bit like a hotel foyer; the smaller Mandala St **branch** (Map p90; Mandala St; ⊘7am-9pm) in Thamel is quieter.

Jatra   LOUNGE

(Map p90; ☏ 01-4211010; Chaksibari Marg; cocktails Rs 400; ⊘10am-11pm; ☏) A quiet, intimate and pretty cool venue for a beer accompanied by Newari snacks or a full dinner (mains Rs 450 to Rs 600), with spacious indoor and terrace seating, a global soundtrack and live music on Fridays. Happy hour brings two-for-one cocktails from 5-7pm.

Sam's Bar   BAR

(Map p90; ⊘4pm-1am) A long-time favourite with trek leaders, mountain guides and other Kathmandu regulars. There's reggae every Saturday. It's hidden upstairs just north of the Saatghumti junction.

Maya Cocktail Bar   COCKTAIL BAR

(Map p90; cocktails Rs 600, mains Rs 570-715; ⊘11am-midnight) A long-running favourite; the two-for-one cocktails between 4pm and 10pm (some only until 7pm) and salsa music on the stereo are a guaranteed jump-start to a good evening, plus there are decent Mexican enchiladas and chimichangas if you get peckish (a main course gets you another free cocktail). Weekend happy hours bring free snacks.

Tom & Jerry Pub   BAR

(Map p90; ☏ 9851072794; www.tomnjerryktm. com; Chaksibari Marg; beer from Rs 450; ⊘3pm-1am Sun-Thu, to 2am Fri & Sat) This is a long-running, rowdy upstairs place that has pool tables and a dance floor. There's live music most weekends, frequent parties and Thursday is ladies' night.

★ Entertainment

Nepal is an early-to-bed country and even in Kathmandu you'll find few people on the streets after 10pm, especially when the capital's political situation is tense.

Major sporting events such as English Premier League football and the Formula 1 grand prix are televised in all the major bars.

Casinos

Kathmandu's casinos are attached to most of the five-star hotels and are open 24 hours, though they are sometimes closed by the government due to disputes over unpaid taxes. You can play in either Indian rupees or US dollars, and winnings (in the same currency) can be taken out of the country when you leave. The main games offered are roulette and blackjack. Most clients are Indian; Nepalis are officially forbidden from entering.

Casino Royale   CASINO

(Map p70; ☏ 01-4271244; ⊘24hr) Pull your tuxedo out of your backpack, polish up your best Sean Connery impersonation ('Aaah, Mish Moneypenny...') and make a beeline for this former Rana palace at the Yak & Yeti Hotel. Hang around the tables (not the slots) long enough and staff may ply you with a dinner buffet, though sadly the Russian dancing girls have gone back to Moscow.

Music

Duelling cover bands compete for aural supremacy at various Thamel restaurants on Friday and Saturday nights in the high season – just follow the sounds of Bryan Adams and Coldplay covers.

There are a few cultural performances in the restaurants of the top-end hotels, which generally involve local youths wearing a variety of dress over their jeans and performing traditional dances from Nepal's various ethnic groups, accompanied by a live band that includes a tabla, harmonium and singer.

House of Music   LIVE MUSIC

(Map p90; ☏ 9851075172; www.houseofmusic nepal.com; Amrit Marg; cover Rs 300-500; ⊘11am-11pm Tue-Sun) This beery bar is the best place in Kathmandu to listen to original Nepali rock, reggae and R'n'B music, mostly on Friday and Saturday. It's in northern Thamel but miles away from the cover bands of the centre. Upcoming concerts are posted on the venue's Facebook page (www.facebook.com/houseof

musicnepal). It's part-owned by the drummer of 1974AD, one of Nepal's biggest bands.

Jazz Upstairs
LIVE MUSIC

(Map p70; ☏ 01-4416983; www.jazzupstairs.com; Lazimpat; concerts Rs 600; ⊙ noon-midnight) It's worth schlepping out to Lazimpat on a Wednesday and Saturday night (from 8pm) to catch the live jazz in this tiny upstairs bar, recently relocated to new top-floor digs. The stage is intimate, the vibe is friendly and the clientele is an interesting mix of locals and expats. Monday brings live blues.

Cinemas

Sadly, the video cafes made famous by the title of Pico Iyer's book *Video Night in Kathmandu* have disappeared, replaced by fake DVD stores.

QFX Jai Nepal Cinema
CINEMA

(Map p70; ☏ 01-4442220; www.qfxcinemas.com; 315 Narayanhiti Marg; tickets Rs 230-340) This is the most convenient place to catch the latest Bollywood-style Hindi or Nepali hit. Not understanding the dialogue is really only a minor hindrance to enjoying these comedy-musical 'masala movies'.

QFX Civil Mall
CINEMA

(Map p70; ☏ 01-4442220; www.qfxcinemas.com; 7th fl, Civil Mall, Sundhara; tickets Rs 310-560) The main cinema for English-language Hollywood blockbusters, with 50% weekday morning discounts.

🔒 Shopping

Kathmandu offers the best shopping in the country. Everything that is turned out in the various centres around the valley can be found here. The recent pedestrianisation of parts of Thamel has made it a much more pleasant place to shop; hopefully the traffic-free status will be maintained. Other streets still suffer from chaotic traffic; dive into a side street or garden haven when stress levels start to rise.

Thamel has some excellent trekking gear for sale, but don't think that you are necessarily getting the genuine article. Most of the 'Columbia' fleeces and 'North Face' jackets are Chinese knock-offs or made locally but with imported fleece and Gore-Tex.

Kathmandu has dozens of excellent bookshops with a great selection of Himalaya titles, including books that are not usually available outside the country. Many dealers will buy back books for 50% of what you paid.

An endless supply of curios, art pieces and plain old junk is churned out for the tourist trade. Most does not come from Tibet but from the local Tamang community. Prayer flags and prayer wheels are a popular buy in Durbar Sq, Bodhnath and Swayambhunath, but be prepared to bargain.

In general you'll often find a better choice of crafts, or more unusual items, in the centres that produce the items – Jawalakhel (southern Patan) for Tibetan carpets, Patan for cast-metal statues, Bhaktapur for woodcarvings, and Thimi for masks. Head over to Patan to find well-stocked fair-trade shops.

Remember that antiques (over 100 years old) cannot be taken out of the country. Get a receipt and a description of any major purchase from the shop where you bought it. If in doubt get your item verified at the **Department of Archaeology** (Map p70; ☏ 01-4250683; www.doa.gov.np; Ramshah Path, Kathmandu; ⊙ 10am-2pm Sat, to 3pm Sun-Thu).

Mahaguthi
HOMEWARES

(Map p70; ☏ 01-4438760; www.mahaguthi.org; Lazimpat; ⊙ 10am-6.30pm Sun-Fri, to 5pm Sat) Good range of crafts and home furnishings, much of it made by disadvantaged or minority groups, with transparent pricing on pashminas (Rs 2325 for a pashmina-silk blend). Credit cards accepted. There's a larger outlet (p151) and collection of other fair-trade stores in Kopundol in Patan.

One Tree Stop
DESIGN

(Map p70; www.facebook.com/onetreestop; Durbar Marg; ⊙ 11am-7pm) 🖋 It's worth popping in to peruse this small but interesting collection of quality and unique gifts produced by a hand-picked roster of women's groups, NGOs and local design studios. After a browse, head upstairs for a coffee and break at the charming **One Tree Café**, set around an old banyan tree and employing mostly hearing-impaired waiters.

Baber Mahal Revisited
ARTS & CRAFTS

(Map p70; www.babermahal-revisited.com) Originally built in 1919 by the then prime minister for his son, this unique complex of neoclassical Rana palace outbuildings has been redeveloped to house a warren of chic clothes shops, designer galleries and handicraft shops, as well as a couple of top-end restaurants and stylish bars. The classiest shopping experience in the city, prices are as high as the quality.

Paper Park PAPER PRODUCTS
(Map p90; ☑01-4700475; www.handmadepaper
park.com; Chaksibari Marg; ☺10am-9pm) One
of the best of several shops in Thamel that
sell handmade paper products, from photo
albums to paper lamps. The paper comes
from the *lokta* (daphne) plant, whose bark
is boiled and beaten with wooden mallets
before the pulp is spread over a frame to dry.
The finished product folds without creasing
and is used for all official Nepali documents.

Shona's Alpine Rental SPORTS & OUTDOORS
(Map p90; ☑01-4265120; Amrit Marg; ☺10am-
9pm) Reliable rentals and gear shop that
makes its own sleeping bags and offers advice on the best trekking gear for your trip.
Get a season warmer than they recommend.
Sleeping bags (Rs 70 to Rs 120 per day) and
down jackets (Rs 50 to Rs 60) are available
for rent, with a deposit of around Rs 8000.

Tibet Book Store BOOKS
(Map p90; ☑01-4415788; Tridevi Marg;
☺10am-7pm) The best collection of Tibet-
related titles, once owned by the Tibetan
government-in-exile.

Tara Oriental CLOTHING
(Map p70; ☑01-4436315; www.taraoriental.com;
Lazimpat; ☺10am-6pm) This designer's stu-
dio is the best place for top-end designer

THE ESSENTIAL THAMEL SHOPPING GUIDE

From Kashmiri carpets to trekking poles and yak-milk soap, Thamel offers the best collection of shops in the country. Bring an extra bag (or buy one here!) and stock up early
on Christmas presents.

Spices Plenty of shops and supermarkets in Thamel sell small packets of spices, from
momo mixes to chai spices, or head to Asan Tole, where the locals buy their freshly
ground masalas.

Embroidery Sewing machines around Thamel whirr away late into the night adding logos and Tibetan symbols to jackets, hats and T-shirts. Trekkers can commission badges
and T-shirts commemorating their successful trek or even get a business logo made.

Jewellery Kathmandu is a great place for jewellery, particularly silver. Buy it ready-made,
ask the jeweller to create a design for you or bring in something you would like copied.
The price of silver is quoted per *tola* (11.7g) in the daily newspaper.

Puppets Puppets make good gifts for children and are made in Bhaktapur as well as other
centres. They're often of multi-armed deities clutching little wooden weapons in each
hand. The puppet heads may be made of easily broken clay or more durable papier mâché.

Pashminas A shawl or scarf made from fine pashmina (the underhair of a mountain
goat) is a popular buy. The cost of a shawl depends on the percentage of pashmina in the
mix and from which part of the goat's body the hair originated, starting from the cheapest back wool and rising through the belly and chest to neck hair, which is about five
times more expensive than back hair. The cheapest shawls are a 70/30% cotton/pash-
mina blend, silk-pashmina blends cost around 30% more and pure pashmina shawls
range from around US$50 to US$275 for a top-end ring shawl (named because they are
fine enough to be pulled through a finger ring; also known as a water shawl).

Tea Ilam, Ontu, Kanyan and Mai Valley teas are the best Nepali teas, from the east of
the country near Darjeeling. Expect to pay anything from Rs 600 (in Ilam) to Rs 3000
(in Thamel) per kilogram for good Ilam tea. The excellently named 'super fine tipi gold-
en flower orange pekoe' tea is about as good as it gets. Connoisseurs choose the first
(March) or second (May) flush, rather than the substandard monsoon flush. Lemon tea
flavoured with lemongrass is another favourite, as is pre-spiced masala tea.

Clothes There are lots of funky wool hats, felt bags, embroidered T-shirts (our favourite
has 'Same Same...' on the front and '...But Different' on the back!), jumpers etc, particularly
on the twisting road known as Saatghumti. Always try clothes on before handing over the
cash. Impossibly cute baby-sized North Face fleeces and down jackets are hard to pass by.

Prayer flags The best place to buy is the street in front of the Kathesimbhu Stupa south
of Thamel. Choose between cheaper polyester and better-quality cotton flags and remember, this is your karma that we are talking about.

pashmina throws, scarves and sweaters, retailing at around US$160. Yes, it's expensive but it's top-end stuff. Show your LP guide for a 20% discount.

North Face
SPORTS & OUTDOORS
(Map p90; Tridevi Marg) One of several *pukka* (not fake) gear shops on Tridevi Marg, offering imported gear at foreign prices. These shops sell everything from Black Diamond climbing gear to US Thermarests. Other brands such as Mountain Hard Wear, Marmot and the Kathmandu-based Sherpa brand are nearby.

Sonam Gear
SPORTS & OUTDOORS
(Map p90; ☑ 01-4259191; Jyatha; ☺ 10am-9pm) Sonam makes its own brand of quality trekking gear, with this the larger of its two shops in Thamel.

Holyland Hiking Shop
SPORTS & OUTDOORS
(Map p90; ☑ 01-4248104; ☺ 10am-9pm) The better trekking gear shops are at the southern end of Thamel, and Holyland is one of the better choices.

Hi-Himal Sports Wear International
SPORTS & OUTDOORS
(Map p90; ☑ 01-4444085; www.hi-himal.com) This friendly gear shop makes its own down products and offers equipment rental, including down jackets (Rs 60 to Rs 100 per day), sleeping bags (Rs 150 to Rs 200) and Chinese-made tents (Rs 150).

Amrita Craft Collection
ARTS & CRAFTS
(Map p90; ☑ 01-4240757; www.amritacraft.com; Chaksibari Marg) This broad collection of mass-produced crafts and clothing is a good place to start your souvenir shopping. Quality isn't top-notch, but subtract 20% from its fixed prices and you get a good benchmark for what you should aim to pay on the street if you don't mind haggling.

Aroma Garden
INCENSE
(Map p90; ☑ 01-4420724; www.aromagarden.biz; ☺ 10am-8.30pm) As the name suggests, this is Thamel's sweetest-smelling shop. It's a good one-stop shop for *dhoop* (incense), essential oils, Himalayan soaps and almost anything else that smells heavenly.

Pilgrims Book House
BOOKS
(Map p90; ☑ 01-4221546; www.pilgrimsonline shop.com; ☺ 10am-9pm) Kathmandu's best bookstore tragically burned down in 2013. Its reincarnation has risen from the ashes and still has a good selection of titles.

Vajra Books
BOOKS
(Map p90; ☑ 01-4220562; www.vajrabooks.com. np; Amrit Marg) This knowledgeable local publisher offers an excellent selection of academic books and is a magnet for local writers and researchers. Ask to see the expanded section upstairs.

Nepal Book Depot
BOOKS
(Map p90; ☑ 01-4700975; Chaksibari Marg; ☺ 9am-9pm) Good prices, a central location and a huge selection of new and secondhand titles.

Curio Arts
ARTS & CRAFTS
(Map p70; ☑ 01-4224871; www.devasarts.com; Durbar Marg) Durbar Marg has several top-end showrooms concentrating on statues, Tibetan furniture and other crafts. Curio Arts is a good place to start.

ℹ Information

EMERGENCY & IMPORTANT NUMBERS

Police	☑ 100
Tourist Police	☑ 01-4247041
Ambulance	☑ 102

INTERNET ACCESS
There are a few cybercafes in Thamel, though almost all cafes, restaurants and hotels offer free wi-fi.

LAUNDRY
Several laundries across Thamel will machine-wash laundry for Rs 80 to Rs 100 per kilo. Get it back the next day or pay double for a three-hour service. Amazingly, it all comes back relatively clean, even after a three-week trek.

MEDICAL SERVICES
Dozens of pharmacies on the fringes of Thamel offer all the cheap antibiotics you can pronounce.

CIWEC Clinic Travel Medicine Center (Map p70; ☑ 01-4435232, 01-4424111; www.ciwec-clinic.com; Kapurdhara Marg, Lazimpat; ☺ emergency 24hr, clinic 9am-noon & 1-4pm Mon-Fri) In operation since 1982 and has an international reputation for research into travellers' medical problems. Staff are mostly foreigners and a doctor is on call round the clock. Credit cards are accepted and the centre is used to dealing with insurance claims.

CIWEC Dental Clinic (Map p70; ☑ 01-4440100, emergency 01-4424111; www.ciwec-clinic.com; Kapurdhara Marg, Lazimpat) US dentist on the top floor of the CIWEC Clinic.

Healthy Smiles (Map p70; ☑ 01-4420800; www.healthysmiles.com.np; Lazimpat; ☺ 10am-

5pm Sun-Fri) UK-trained dentist, opposite the Hotel Ambassador, with a branch in Patan.

Nepal International Clinic (Map p70; ☑ 01-4435357, 01-4434642; www.nepalinternational clinic.com; Lal Durbar; ⏱ 9am-1pm & 2-5pm) Just south of the New Royal Palace, east of Thamel. It has an excellent reputation and is slightly cheaper than the CIWEC Clinic. Credit cards accepted.

NORVIC International Hospital (Map p70; ☑ 01-4258554; www.norvichospital.com; Thapathali) Private Nepali hospital with a good reputation for cardiology.

Patan Hospital (p152) Perhaps the best hospital in the Kathmandu Valley.

MONEY

There are dozens of licensed moneychangers in Thamel. Their hours are longer than those of the banks (generally until 8pm or so) and rates are similar, perhaps even slightly higher if you don't need a receipt.

There are ATMs everywhere in Thamel. Useful locations include beside Yin Yang (p103) Restaurant, Ganesh Man Singh Building and Roadhouse Cafe (p100).

Himalayan Bank (Map p90; ☑ 01-4250208; www.himalayanbank.com; Tridevi Marg; ⏱ 10am-7pm Sun-Fri, 9am-noon Sat) The most convenient bank for travellers in Thamel, this kiosk on Tridevi Marg changes cash until 2.30pm (1.30pm on Friday) without commission; after this time head to the main branch in the basement of the nearby Sanchaya Kosh Bhawan shopping centre. There's a useful ATM next to the kiosk. It's in front of the Three Goddesses Temples.

Standard Chartered Bank (Map p70; ☑ 01-4418456; Lazimpat; ⏱ 9.45am-7pm Sun-Thu, 9.45am-4.30pm Fri, 9.30am-12.30pm Sat & holidays) has well-located ATMs opposite the Third Eye restaurant and in the compound of the Kathmandu Guest House. They dispense up to Rs 35,000 per transaction but charge a Rs 500 commission. The main branch in Lazimpat charges Rs 200 per transaction for cash.

POST

Most bookshops in Thamel sell stamps and deliver postcards to the post office, which is much easier than making a special trip to the post office yourself.

Main Post Office (Map p70; Sundhara; ⏱ 10am-5pm Sun-Thu, to 3pm Fri) Facing the Tundikhel near the ruins of the Bhimsen Tower (Dharadhara). Stalls in the courtyard sell airmail and padded envelopes. You can post packages up to 2kg at counter 16; beyond

---

ⓘ DANGERS & ANNOYANCES

Kathmandu is a fairly safe city, but what it lacks in dangers it more than makes up for in annoyances:

➡ The combination of ancient vehicles, low-quality fuel and lack of emission controls makes the streets of Kathmandu particularly dirty, noisy and unpleasant.

➡ Avoid the city's seedy dance bars and street corner hashish sellers.

Pedestrians account for over 40% of all traffic fatalities in Nepal. Bear in mind the following:

➡ Traffic rules exist, but are rarely followed or enforced; be especially careful when crossing streets or riding a bicycle.

➡ Traffic is supposed to travel on the left side of the road, but many drivers simply choose the most convenient side, which can make walking in Kathmandu a deeply stressful experience.

➡ Consider buying a face mask to filter out dust and emission particles, especially if you plan to ride a bicycle or motorcycle in Kathmandu. After a few days in the city you will likely feel the onset of a throat infection.

➡ Post-earthquake repairs are ongoing and there is lots of rubble piled up in the streets, creating additional hazards for pedestrians.

Other annoyances in Thamel are the crazy motorcyclists, and the barrage of irritating flute sellers, tiger-balm hawkers, chess-set sellers, musical-instrument vendors, travel-agency touts, hashish suppliers, freelance trekking guides and rickshaw drivers.

Note that the colourful sadhus (itinerant holy men) who frequent Durbar Sq and Pashupatinath will expect baksheesh (a tip) if you take a photo, as will the Thamel 'holy men' who anoint you with a *tika* on your forehead.

Kathmandu has in the past been the focus of political demonstrations and *bandhs* (strikes), which close shops and shut down transport.

that you need to go to the next-door building. Parcels have to be examined and sealed by a customs officer. Start the process before 2pm.

Express Mail Service (EMS; Map p70; Sundhara; ⊙10am-2.30pm Sun-Thu, 10am-1.30pm Fri) Express documents can be sent from the separate building just north of the main post office (but in the same compound). A 500g package to the USA or UK costs Rs 1800.

DHL (Map p70; ☑01-2298124; www.dhl.com. np; Kamaladi; ⊙9.30am-6pm Sun-Fri) The closest service centre to Thamel is in Kamaladi, a 15-minute walk away.

Fedex (Map p70; ☑01-4269248; www.fedex. com/np; Kantipath; ⊙9am-7pm Sun-Fri, to 1pm Sat) As a guide, 1kg of documents costs around Rs 3350 to the USA and takes three days.

TELEPHONE

If for some reason you don't have a mobile phone or access to Skype or Viber, you can make international telephone calls from internet cafes for around Rs 20 per minute.

There are dozens of Ncell offices around town where you can buy or top up a SIM card.

TOURIST INFORMATION

Tourist Service Centre (Map p70; ☑01-4256909 ext 223; www.welcomenepal.com; Bhrikuti Mandap; ⊙10am-1pm & 2-5pm Sun-Fri, TIMS card 10am-5.30pm, national parks tickets 9am-2pm Sun-Fri) On the eastern side of the Tundikhel parade ground; has an inconvenient location but is the place for trekkers to get a TIMS card (p38), and pay national park and conservation area fees (p38).

There are a number of good noticeboards in Thamel that are worth checking for information on apartments, travel and trekking partners, courses and cultural events. The Kathmandu Guest House (p89) has a good noticeboard, as do the Pumpernickel Bakery (p100) and Fire & Ice Pizzeria (p104).

TRAVEL AGENCIES

Flight Connection International (Map p90; ☑domestic flights 01-4258282, international flights 01-4233111; www.flightconnectionintl. com; Jyatha, Thamel) Good for air tickets; in the courtyard of the Gaia Restaurant.

President Travel & Tours (Map p70; ☑01-4220245; www.pttnepal.com; Durbar Marg) Professional agency favoured by expats and wealthy Nepalis; particularly good at getting seats on heavily booked flights.

Wayfarers (Map p90; ☑01-4266010; www.wayfarers.com.np; Chaksibari Marg, Thamel; ⊙9am-6pm Mon-Fri, to 5pm Sat & Sun) For straight-talking ticketing, bespoke Nepal tours and Kathmandu Valley walking trips.

VISA EXTENSIONS

Visa extensions of 30 to 60 days are fairly painless at the **Central Immigration Office** (Map p70; ☑01-4429659; www.nepalimmigration. gov.np; Kalikasthan, Dilli Bazaar; ⊙10am-4pm Sun-Thu, 10am-3pm Fri, 11am-1pm Sat). You need to make your application online and upload a photo up to 15 days before arriving at the office, though there is currently a computer in the hall in case you forget. The process generally takes less than one hour. Extensions cost US$30 for a minimum 15 days, plus US$2 per additional day.

❶ Getting There & Away

AIR

It's a good idea to double-check the departure time of your return flight before flying, especially for unreliable Nepal Airlines, with whom you should reconfirm at least once.

The ageing **Tribhuvan International Airport** (☑01-4472256; www.tiairport.com.np), about 6km east of the centre, is the main international hub in Nepal. The airport's former name of Gaucher (literally 'cow pasture') speaks volumes about Kathmandu's rapid urban expansion – early flights did indeed land on the grass amid the cattle.

Domestic Airlines

Kathmandu is the main hub for domestic flights, including to Pokhara (US$121), Lukla (US$177), Bharatpur (US$109; for Chitwan) and Bhairawa (US$111; for Lumbini). The most reliable airlines are **Buddha Air** (Map p70; ☑01-5542494; www. buddhaair.com; Hattisar), **Yeti** (Map p90; ☑01-4213012; www.yetiairlines.com; Thamel Chowk) and Tara Air (www.taraair.com); others seem to change with the weather. It's far less hassle to buy tickets through a travel agency, and you'll probably get a better deal this way. You can generally change the date of the ticket up to two days before departure without charge.

Nepal Airlines domestic office (Map p70; ☑01-4227133; www.nepalairlines.com.np; Kantipath; ⊙10am-5pm) has flights to remoter airstrips, but only has computerised booking on some of its flights. The other domestic carriers are much more reliable if you have a choice. Again, book at a travel agent. If for some reason you need to come to the office it is down an alley to the side of the main international **Nepal Airlines international booking centre** (☑01 4248614; www.nepalairlines.com.np; New Rd; ⊙10am-1pm & 2-5pm).

Be aware that Nepali airlines don't have the best safety record (p390). You may want to do some online research into the record of specific airlines before committing to a flight.

BUS
Long-Distance Buses

The **Gongabu bus station** (Ring Rd, Balaju) is north of the city centre, on the Ring Rd. It is also called the Kathmandu Bus Terminal, or simply 'new bus park'. This bus station is basically for all long-distance buses, including to destinations in the Terai. It's a huge and confusing place and there are very few signs in English, but most of the ticket sellers are helpful. There's often more than one reservation counter for each destination.

Bookings for long trips should be made a day in advance – Thamel travel agents will do this for a fee and this will save you both time and the taxi fare. Bus 23 (Rs 20) runs to Gongabu bus station from Lekhnath Marg on the northern edge of Thamel, but it takes an age. Be careful travelling in the other direction as only some of the buses route via Thamel. A taxi from Thamel costs around Rs 250.

Buses serving the Langtang region leave from the **Pasang Lhamo Transport** (☎01-4356342) stand at Machha Pokhari (Fish Pond), diagonally across the Ring Rd from Gongabu bus station. There are daily tourist buses (Rs 600, 6.30am and 8am) and local services (Rs 450, 6.20am and 7am) to Syabrubesi via Dhunche. The 6.30am and 7am buses continue to Rasuwagadhi on the China–Tibet border (Rs 550 to Rs 700).

Minibuses and buses also run frequently from near Machha Pokhari to Kakani (Rs 50 to Rs 100, every 30 minutes) and at 7am, 9am and 1pm to Nuwakot (Rs 250).

Popular tourist buses to Pokhara (Rs 600 to Rs 750, seven hours) and Sauraha for Chitwan National Park (Rs 600, six hours) depart daily at 7am from a far more conveniently located **tourist bus stand** (Map p90; Kantipath) at the Thamel end of Kantipath. Buses are comfortable and you get a fixed seat number with your ticket (buy these a day or two in advance).

Greenline (Map p90; ☎01-4417199; www.greenline.com.np; Tridevi Marg; ☉6am-6pm) offers air-con deluxe services that are considerably more expensive than the tourist buses (but include lunch). There are daily morning buses at 7.30am to Pokhara (US$23, six hours). A daily service to Chitwan (US$20, six hours) should resume in 2018, with a lunch break and bus change in Kurintar. Book a day or two in advance.

Golden Travels (Map p70; ☎01-4220036; Woodlands Complex, Durbar Marg) runs a similar service, departing at 7am from Kantipath to Pokhara (Rs 950). On the return you will likely be dropped at Sundhara on the eastern edge of Kathmandu's old town. Buy tickets at any travel agency.

BUSES FROM GONGABU BUS STATION

DESTINATION	DISTANCE (KM)	DEPARTURES	DURATION (HR)	COST (RS)	TICKET WINDOW
Besi Sahar	150	7am (tourist bus), 8am, 8.40am (AC) & 9am	6	360-430 (AC 500)	26, 27, 30, 32
Beni	290	7am (tourist bus)	10	850 (AC)	40
Bhairawa/ Sunauli	282	every 30min 5am-2pm & 4-8.30pm (ordinary bus); 6am, 7am & 8am (tourist bus)	8	510 (tourist bus 675)	28, 29, 30
Bharatpur	150	7am, noon	5	350	17, 16, 37
Bhulbhule		6.45am, 8.30am	7	450	26, 27, 30
Birganj	300	7pm	8	550	15, 37
Gorkha	140	6am-1pm	5	300	38, 39
Hile (via Dharan)	635	2pm	17	1150-1300	13, 39
Kakarbhitta	610	5am, hourly 1-5pm	14	1065-1280 (AC 1550)	13, 26, 39
Lumbini	260	6.30am (AC), 7.15am, 7.30pm	9-10	550 (AC 790)	28, 29, 30
Nepalganj	530	6am & 6pm (deluxe); 4pm, 5pm & 7pm (ordinary)	12	900-1140 (AC 1350)	11, 24, 25, 20, 36, 39
Pokhara	200	9am, 10am & 11am (tourist bus); others every 15min to 3pm	6-8	390 (tourist bus 550-600)	26, 27, 28
Tansen (Palpa)	300	6.40am, 5.30pm	10	560 (AC 770)	29, 30

To/From Kathmandu Valley

Buses for most destinations within the Kathmandu Valley, and for those on or accessed from the Arniko Hwy (for Jiri and Barabise near the Tibetan border), operate from the **Ratna Park bus station** (Map p70; Durbar Marg), also known as the old or city bus stand, in the centre of the city on the eastern edge of Tundikhel parade ground.

The station is currently being rebuilt as part of a multistorey complex, so for the time being buses leave from a temporary lot just to the northwest. The lot is a bit of a horror, drenched in diesel fumes, with no English signs and not much English spoken. Keep shouting out your destination and someone will eventually direct you to the right bus.

Frequent departures include Banepa (Rs 45, two hours), Dhulikhel (Rs 55, two hours), Panauti (Rs 60, two hours) and Barabise (Rs 200, four hours). Buses run frequently to Patan, though most people just take a taxi. There are also early-morning departures at 6am and 8am for Jiri (Rs 580) and Shivalaya (Rs 690), if you are trekking to Lukla.

Some services leave from other stops around Kathmandu. Buses to Bhaktapur (Rs 25, one hour) run from a **stand** (Map p70) on Bagh Bazar. Drivers sometimes try to charge foreigners double on this route.

Buses to Pharping and Dakshinkali leave from a **stand** (Map p70) at Shahid Gate (Martyrs' Memorial) at the southern end of the Tundikhel parade ground, as well as the Ratna Park station.

Buses heading to Bungamati, Godavari and Chapagaon in the southern valley leave from Patan's Lagankhel bus station.

CAR

Although you cannot hire cars on a drive-yourself basis, they can be readily hired with a driver from a number of travel agencies. The rental cost is relatively high, both in terms of the initial hiring charge and fuel. Charges can be up to US$50 per day, although they can be lower, especially if you are not covering a huge distance.

TAXI

A better option to renting a car is to hire a taxi for the day. Between several people, longer taxi trips around the valley, or even outside it, are affordable. A half-/full-day sightseeing trip within the valley starts at around Rs 1000/1800.

For longer journeys outside the valley, count on about Rs 3000 per day plus fuel, which is generally cheaper than hiring a car through a travel agency.

ℹ Getting Around

Most of the sights in Kathmandu itself can easily be covered on foot, and this is by far the best way to appreciate the city, even with the atrocious traffic. When you run out of steam, there are plenty of reasonably priced taxis, but agree a price before you get in.

TO/FROM THE AIRPORT

Getting into town from Tribhuvan International Airport is quite straightforward. Both the international and domestic terminals offer a fixed-price prepaid taxi service, currently Rs 750 to Thamel.

Once outside the international terminal you will be confronted by hotel touts, who are often taxi drivers making commission on taking you to a particular hotel. Many hold up a signboard of the particular hotel they are connected with and, if the one you want is there, you can get a free lift. The drawback with the taxis is that the hotel is then much less likely to offer you a discount, as it will be paying a hefty commission to the taxi driver.

If you book a room in advance for more than one night, many hotels will pick you up for free.

Public buses leave from the main road – about 300m from the terminal – but they're only really practical if you have very little luggage and know exactly how to get to where you want to go.

From Kathmandu to the airport you should be able to get a taxi for Rs 500, or a bit more for a late or early flight.

BICYCLE

Cycling is a good way to explore parts of the Kathmandu Valley and many companies offer bike rentals and tours. You need to be selective about your routes to avoid heavy traffic.

Mountain bikes cost from around Rs 800 per day for simple models. For longer trips around the valley, the major mountain-bike companies such as Dawn Till Dusk (p86) and Nepal Mountain Bike Tours (p86) hire out high-quality bikes with front suspension and disc brakes for around US$10 to US$15 per day.

If you want to make an early start, most places are happy to give you the bike the evening before. For all bikes, negotiate discounts for rentals of more than a day. You should get a helmet, lock and repair kit. Check the brakes before committing and be certain to lock the bike whenever you leave it.

CYCLE-RICKSHAW

Cycle-rickshaws cost around Rs 80 for short rides around Thamel or the old town, but you can expect to haggle hard. It's essential to agree on a price before you start.

MOTORCYCLE

There are a number of motorcycle rental operators in Thamel. You will have to leave your passport as deposit. For Rs 800 per day you'll get a 150cc Indian-made Hero Honda or Pulsar road bike, which is generally fine for road trips in the Kathmandu Valley.

Reputable rental companies will require you to have an international driving licence to ride a motorbike in Nepal. On the road, this regulation hasn't been enforced for years, but recent reports suggest traffic police are targeting foreigners on this and other hitherto disregarded traffic violations in an attempt to raise funds. A traffic fine will set you back around Rs 1000.

Motorcycles can be great fun outside town, once you master the traffic. The main problem is getting out of Kathmandu, which can be a stressful, choking and dangerous experience. You will need a pair of goggles and some kind of face mask (available in most pharmacies).

Fuel currently costs Rs 100 per litre; you'll only need a couple of litres for a day trip. Beyond the ring road petrol stations are few and far between.

Singh Motorbike Centre (Map p90; ☑ 01-4418594; singh.motorbike@gmail.com; Bhagawatisthan, Thamel; ⊙ 8am-7pm) A reliable place for bike hire. New Indian-made Pulsar 200cc motorbikes (Rs 1500) are most commonly available, though you might find a cheaper Hero Honda (Rs 700) or an Enfield Bullet (Rs 3000).

Pheasant Transportation Service (Map p90; ☑ 01-4701090; www.biketournepal.com; Thamel Chowk) Down a side street off the central Thamel junction, this tiny office has somewhat elastic prices, with a Honda 150cc starting at Rs 800, a Pulsar 220cc around Rs 1200 and an Enfield Bullet 350cc costing Rs 2000.

TAXI

Taxis are quite reasonably priced, though few taxi drivers use the meters in these days of rising fuel prices. Shorter rides around town (including to the bus station) cost around Rs 200. Night-time rates (between 10pm and 6am) cost 50% more.

Most taxis are tiny Suzuki Marutis, which can just about fit two backpackers and their luggage.

The closest **taxi stand** (Map p90; Tridevi Marg) to Thamel is on Tridevi Marg, close to the junction with Jyatha Rd. Taxis can be booked in advance on 01-4420987; at night call 01-4224374.

Approximate taxi fares from Thamel include the following:

➡ Bhaktapur Rs 700
➡ Bodhnath Rs 600
➡ Budhanilkantha Rs 700
➡ Changu Narayan Rs 1600
➡ Nagarkot Rs 3000
➡ Pashupatinath Rs 500
➡ Patan Rs 500
➡ Swayambhunath Rs 300

AROUND KATHMANDU

There are several outlying attractions inside the ring road that surrounds Kathmandu. All can be reached by taxi, rented bicycle or motorcycle, or on foot.

Swayambhunath

A journey up to the Buddhist temple and Unesco World Heritage Site of Swayambhunath is one of the definitive experiences of Kathmandu. Mobbed by monkeys and soaring above the city on a lofty hilltop, the 'Monkey Temple' is a fascinating jumble of Buddhist and Hindu iconography. Even the 2015 earthquake failed to topple Kathmandu's best loved temple, though a couple of outlying buildings crumbled in the tremor.

The compound is centred on the gleaming white stupa, topped by a gilded spire painted with the eyes of the Buddha. Depictions of these eyes appear all over the Kathmandu Valley. The atmosphere is heightened in the morning and evening by local devotees who make a ritual circumnavigation of the stupa, spinning the prayer wheels set into its base. It is also a great place to watch the sun set over Kathmandu.

According to legend, the Kathmandu Valley was once a lake – geological evidence supports this – and the hill now topped by Swayambhunath rose spontaneously from the waters, hence the name *swayambhu*, meaning 'self-arisen'.

The emperor Ashoka allegedly visited 2000 years ago, but the earliest confirmed activity here was in AD 460. During the 14th century, Mughal invaders from Bengal broke open the stupa in the search for gold, but the stupa was restored and expanded over the following centuries.

◉ Sights

Eastern Stairway   BUDDHIST MONUMENT
There are two ways to approach Swayambhunath Temple, but by far the most atmospheric is the stone pilgrim stairway that climbs the eastern end of the hill. Constructed by King Pratap Malla in the 17th century, this steep stone staircase is mobbed by troops of rhesus macaques, who have made an artform of sliding down the steep handrails. A word of advice: keep foodstuffs out of sight of these simian hoodlums!

From a collection of brightly painted Buddha statues at the bottom of the hill, the steps climb past a series of chaitya and bas-reliefs, including a stone near the entrance showing the birth of the Buddha, with his mother Maya Devi grasping a tree branch. You can often see Tibetan astrologers reading fortunes here. At the top, the steps are lined with pairs of Garudas, lions, elephants, horses and peacocks: the 'vehicles' of the Dhyani Buddhas. Near the end of the climb is the ticket office (there's another one at the western entrance, near the tourist bus park). When you reach the top, remember to walk around the stupa in a clockwise direction.

Great Thunderbolt   BUDDHIST MONUMENT

At the top of the eastern stairway is an enormous, brass-plated *dorje* (thunderbolt), one of the core symbols of Tibetan Buddhism. Known as a *vajra* in Sanskrit, the thunderbolt is a Tantric symbol of the power of enlightenment, which destroys ignorance but is itself indestructible. In rituals the *dorje* is used to indicate male power, while female power is represented by a ceremonial bell.

Around the pedestal supporting the symbol are the animals of the Tibetan calendar. The plinth was formerly flanked by the **Anantapura** and **Pratapura** temples, two slender, Indian-style shikhara towers built

Swayambhunath

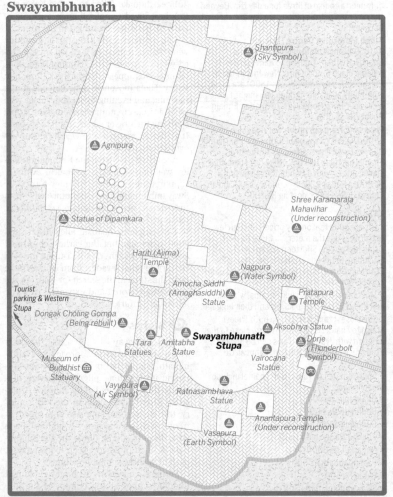

WALKING OR CYCLING TO SWAYAMBHUNATH

There are two possible walking or bicycle routes to Swayambhunath – using both offers a useful circuit, either in the direction described or in reverse, though traffic can make walking hard work.

Starting at the Chhetrapati Tole junction near Thamel, the road runs west to the Vishnumati River (with Swayambhunath clearly visible in the distance), passing the earthquake-damaged **Indrani Temple**, which is surrounded by ghats used for cremations.

Cross the river and detour right to the **Shobabaghwati Temple**, with its gaudy painted statues of Shiva and other Hindu deities. Return to the bridge and follow the steps uphill past the courtyard-style **Bijeshwari Temple**, following an arcade of shops selling *malas* (prayer beads) and fabulous *gau* (Tibetan-style amulets) that lead to the statue-lined stairway at the east end of Swayambhunath hill.

You can return to the centre of old Kathmandu via the National Museum. From the bottom of the eastern stairway, go west around the base of the hill and turn left at the first major junction, past the Benchen Vihar monastery and cafe, then left again at the large T-junction to reach the museum. Continue southeast along this road to reach Tank-eshwor, then turn left again and cross the Vishnumati River. On the other side, it's a short walk north to the bottom of Durbar Sq.

by King Pratap Malla in the 17th century, but sadly the Anantapura temple collapsed in the 2015 earthquake (it's currently being rebuilt). Nearby is a viewpoint and a raised area with telescopes for hire.

⭐**Swayambhunath Stupa**   BUDDHIST STUPA (foreigner/SAARC Rs 200/50; ⊘ dawn-dusk) The Swayambhunath Stupa is one of the crowning glories of Kathmandu Valley architecture. This perfectly proportioned monument rises through a whitewashed dome to a gilded spire, from where four iconic faces of the Buddha stare out across the valley in the cardinal directions. The site was shaken severely by the 2015 earthquake, but the main stupa sustained only superficial damage.

The entire structure of the stupa is deeply symbolic: the white dome represents the earth, while the 13-tiered, tower-like structure at the top symbolises the 13 stages to nirvana. The nose-like squiggle below the piercing eyes is actually the Nepali number *ek* (one), signifying unity, and above is a third eye signifying the all-seeing insight of the Buddha.

The base of the central stupa is ringed by prayer wheels embossed with the sacred mantra *om mani padme hum* ('hail to the jewel in the lotus'). Pilgrims circuiting the stupa spin each one as they pass by. Fluttering above the stupa are thousands of prayer flags, with similar mantras, which are said to be carried to heaven by the Wind Horse. Set in ornate plinths around the base of the stupa are statues representing the five Dhyani

Buddhas – Vairocana, Ratnasambhava, Amitabha, Amoghasiddhi and Aksobhya – and their consorts. These deities represent the five qualities of Buddhist wisdom.

Stupa Platform   BUDDHIST MONUMENT The great stupa is surrounded on all sides by a veritable sculpture garden of religious monuments. Several buildings were destroyed by the earthquake and rebuilding will continue for some years, but it's still a charming place to explore.

At the rear of the stupa is a small, poorly lit **museum** of Buddhist statuary. The adjacent Kagyud-school **Dongak Chöling gompa** was badly damaged by the earthquake and is currently being rebuilt.

North of the pilgrim shelter is the golden pagoda-style **Hariti (Ajima) Temple**, with a beautiful image of Hariti, the goddess of smallpox. This Hindu goddess, who is also responsible for fertility, illustrates the seamless interweaving of Hindu and Buddhist beliefs in Nepal.

On the west side of the stupa are two figures of the goddess Tara, attached to stone columns. The **White and Green Tara** are said to symbolise the Chinese and Nepali wives of King Songtsen Gampo, the first royal patron of Buddhism in Tibet, and are also female consorts to two of the Dhyani Buddhas.

Northwest of these statues is a garden of ancient chaityas, and at the back of this group is a slick **black statue of Dipankara**, carved in the 7th century. Also known as the

DAY TRIPS FROM KATHMANDU

The great thing about Kathmandu is that there are so many fantastic sights just a couple of kilometres outside the city centre. You can check out any of the following sites by bus, motorbike or taxi and still be back in Thamel for the start of happy hour:

➡ Bhaktapur (p152)

➡ Patan (p137)

➡ Bodhnath (p128)

➡ Budhanilkantha (p134)

'Buddha of Light', Dipankara is one of the 'past Buddhas' who achieved enlightenment before the time of Siddhartha Gautama, the historical Buddha. Also note the black chaityas set atop a yoni – a clear demonstration of the mingling of Hindu and Buddhist symbology.

Back at the northeast corner of the complex, the Buddhist temple known as **Shree Karmaraja Mahavihar** became structurally unsound after the earthquake and was carefully taken down following a ritual prayer ceremony, but devotees hope to eventually raise a new temple on the site.

Symbols of the five elements – earth, air, water, fire and ether – can be found around the hilltop, though several were damaged by the earthquake. Behind the newly rebuilt **Anantapura** temple are shrines dedicated to **Vasupura**, the earth symbol, and **Vayupura**, the air symbol. The **Nagpura**, the symbol for water, is a stone set in a muddy pool just north of the stupa, while **Agnipura**, the symbol for fire, is the red-faced god on a polished boulder on the northwestern side of the platform. **Shantipura**, the symbol for the sky, is north of the platform, part of the damaged Shantipura building.

Buddha Amideva Park   BUDDHIST STATUE

This compound frequented by Tibetan pilgrims contains three enormous shining golden statues of Sakyamuni Buddha, a four-armed Chenresig and Guru Rinpoche, constructed in 2003.

Western Stupa   BUDDHIST STUPA

If you follow either path leading west from the main stupa, you will reach a smaller stupa near the tourist parking. Just behind is a **gompa** surrounded by rest houses for

pilgrims and an important **shrine** to Saraswati, the goddess of learning. At exam time, many scholars come here to improve their chances, and school children fill the place during Basanta Panchami, the Festival of Knowledge.

🛏 Sleeping

Benchen Vihar Guest House   GUESTHOUSE $

(☏01-4284204; www.benchen.org; Chhauni, Swayambhunath; r Rs 600-800; @🛜) If you've ever fancied staying in a Tibetan monastery, try this guesthouse attached to the Benchen Phuntsok Dargyeling Monastery, 10 minutes' walk from Swayambhunath. It's surprisingly comfortable, with en suite bathrooms, a garden cafe and fine city views from the upper floors. There are opportunities to join the monks for prayers at 6am and 4pm. Profits go to the monastery.

ℹ Getting There & Away

You can approach Swayambhunath by taxi (Rs 250 to Rs 300 from Thamel), by bicycle or as part of a 45-minute stroll from Kathmandu. Taxis generally drop you at the steep pilgrim stairway at the eastern end of the hill, though groups sometimes start at the tourist parking at the upper western end of the hill.

Cramped minivans and less frequent *safa* (electric) tempo No 20 shuttle between Swayambhunath's eastern stairway and Kathmandu's Sundhara district (near the main post office), via the National Museum.

Around Swayambhunath

There are several other sights scattered around Swayambhunath. Before moving on, get a taste of Tibet by joining the old pilgrims on a clockwise kora (pilgrim circuit) around the base of the hill, spinning the line of prayer wheels past a series of gigantic chörtens (reliquary stupas), *mani dungkhor* (room-sized prayer wheels) and Buddhist chapels.

Starting from the eastern gateway to Swayambhunath, follow the prayer wheels (not the road) around the southwest side of the hill, passing the road turn-off to the tourist parking and the Natural History Museum. The path meets the Ring Rd at Buddha Amideva Park, a compound containing three enormous shining golden statues of Sakyamuni Buddha, four-armed Chenresig and Guru Rinpoche, constructed in 2003. Chenresig is the Tibetan bodhisattva of compassion, of whom the Dalai Lama is considered an emanation. Guru Rinpoche was a wonder-working saint who helped bring Buddhism to Tibet. Return past the string of chörtens and chapels along the north side of the hill.

◉ Sights

National Museum MUSEUM
(☎01-4271504; www.nationalmuseum.gov.np; Chhauni; foreigner/SAARC Rs 150/50, camera/video Rs 100/200; ◷10.30am-4.30pm Wed-Sun, to 2.30pm Mon) Around 800m south of Swayambhunath at Chhauni, this sprawling museum set in a walled compound looks a little moth-eaten and overgrown, but there are some fabulous treasures on dusty display and it never gets crowded. It's well worth a visit.

As you enter the compound, turn left to reach the **Judda Art Gallery**, which contains some exquisite stone, metal and terracotta statues of Nepali deities and fabulous *paubha* cloth paintings. Look out for the 1800-year-old life-sized statue of standing Jayavarma, discovered while digging house foundations in 1992, as well as the bronze statue of buffalo-headed Sukhavara Samvara with 34 arms, 16 feet and nine faces.

At the back of the compound is the temple-style **Buddhist Art Gallery**. As well as some archaeological displays from Buddha's birthplace at Lumbini, some fine Buddhist statues, votive objects, thangkas (religious paintings) and manuscripts, there are some informative upstairs displays on mandalas (geometric Buddhist diagrams). A highlight here is the 8th-century stone depiction of the birth of Buddha, showing Queen Maya holding onto the branch of a tree.

Don't miss the antique **Hudson Phantom** just around the corner, made in Detroit and believed to be the first car to arrive in Nepal, carried across the Himalaya by a team of porters in the early 1900s.

To the north of the main compound, the handsome Rana-era palace building was damaged in the 2015 earthquake. The ground floor **Natural History Gallery** is still open, with its arthritic-looking stuffed animals and old whale bones, but the upper storey collection of weapons, coins and stamps remains off limits.

Ticket sales stop an hour before closing time; bags must be left in the free lockers at the gate. The museum closes an hour earlier in winter (November to January).

Military Museum MUSEUM
(☎01-4271504; Tahachal; foreigner/SAARC Rs 100/40, camera/video Rs 50/200; ◷10am-4pm Wed-Sun, to 2pm Mon) Opposite the National Museum in an army compound, this will likely appeal only to fans of military history. Lined up on parade outside the museum are a two-person tank, Nepal's first ever Rolls-Royce, gifted by Queen Elizabeth II in 1961, and a Skyvan transport plane.

The interior displays lead past endless paintings of death and mayhem depicting Nepali battles over the centuries, including several against British and Tibetans, as well as an armoury, including a fine bazooka and circular weapon rack. Look for the portrait of the intriguing 18th-century queen Rajendra Laxmi Devi Shah, who trained as a soldier and led her army on three campaigns.

The museum closes an hour earlier between November and March.

Natural History Museum MUSEUM
(foreigner/SAARC Rs 50/20, camera Rs 50; ◷10am-5pm Sun-Fri) Below Swayambhunath, on the road to the tourist parking, this neglected museum offers a faded but quirky collection of exhibits, including varnished crocodiles, model dinosaurs and mounted animal heads that look suspiciously like hunting trophies.

Around the Kathmandu Valley

Best Places to Eat

→ Mayur Restaurant (p165)

→ Peaceful Restaurant
(p165)

→ Newa Lahani Restaurant
(p174)

Best Places to Stay

→ Shivapuri Heights Cottage
(p135)

→ Famous Farm (p195)

→ Neydo Tashi Choeling
Monastery Guest House
(p176)

→ Milla Guest House (p162)

Why Go?

In many ways the Kathmandu Valley *is* Nepal. Created from the bed of a sacred lake by the deity Manjushri, according to Buddhist legend, the basin is a patchwork of terraced fields and sacred temple towns that showcase the glory of the architects and artisans of Nepal. Sadly, the area also bore the brunt of the 2015 earthquake. This has taken its toll on the valley's medieval villages, but there is still much to see, from centuries-old temples to Himalayan viewpoints and an adventurous road to Tibet.

Aside from the exceptional Unesco World Heritage Sites of Patan and Bhaktapur, there are numerous Newari villages that are off the tourist circuit. Many attractions can be explored by minibus, taxi, mountain bike, motorcycle and even on foot, following a web of ancient trails. You'll likely see fewer tourists just 10km outside Kathmandu than you will if you trek for days through the Himalaya.

When to Go
Nagarkot

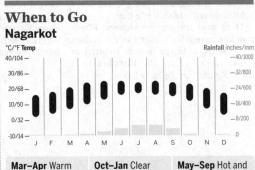

Mar–Apr Warm weather, green farmland and spectacular chariot festivals.

Oct–Jan Clear views and sunny days, but chilly nights at Nagarkot and Dhulikhel.

May–Sep Hot and humid, regular rainfall and temperatures peaking over 30°C (86°F).

Around the Kathmandu Valley Highlights

1 Patan (p137) Wandering Patan's courtyards on a walking tour, soaking in the glorious Newari architecture of Durbar Sq and visiting Patan Museum, the best in the country.

2 Bhaktapur (p152) Exploring the fascinating backstreets of Bhaktapur, Nepal's best preserved medieval city.

3 Panauti (p188) Having a medieval mini-adventure in this historic city, which escaped the earthquake's destruction.

4 Last Resort (p192) Getting your pulse racing on a bungee, canyoning or rafting trip at this adventure resort, just a stone's throw from the Tibet border.

5 Dakshinkali (p175) Finding Nepal's spiritual side on the monastery-strewn road to Dakshinkali, where Tibetan Buddhism merges with Tantric Hinduism.

6 Nuwakot (p194) Escaping the crowds and relaxing at this little-visited, historically significant village with fine architecture.

History

The legend that the Kathmandu Valley was formed when the Buddhist deity Manjushri drained a sacred lake with his flaming sword has its roots in reality. The uprising of the Himalaya trapped rivers draining south from Tibet, creating a vast lake that eventually burst its banks and drained away around 10,000 years ago.

As people settled from the north and south, the valley became the biggest clearinghouse on the trade route from India to Tibet. Himalayan missionaries and saints transferred Buddhism across the Himalaya into Tibet, and centuries later migrating Tibeto-Burman tribes carried Buddhism back into Nepal, fusing Tantric Indian beliefs with the ancient Bön religion of Tibet. This

THE 2015 EARTHQUAKE

At 11.56am on 25 April 2015, Nepal was hit by a massive earthquake measuring 7.8 on the Richter scale, causing devastation to the central parts of the country. Three years later tourism has bounced back, but many Nepalis will be living with the repercussions of that day for years.

Thousands of buildings collapsed in the initial tremor and in subsequent aftershocks, killing more than 8500 people, and destroying 600,000 homes. Landslides destroyed entire villages, notably at Langtang where almost 200 villagers and 41 foreign trekkers were killed, while an avalanche at Everest Base Camp killed 18 climbers in Nepal's worst mountaineering disaster. Aftershocks followed for weeks, including a major tremor on 12 May that killed hundreds more. The earthquake has been described as the worst disaster to hit Nepal since the deadly Bihar-Nepal earthquake of 1934.

The focus has shifted from immediate emergency relief to the reconstruction of lost homes, schools, monuments and livelihoods, but this is likely to be a slow and drawn-out process, especially given the notorious bureaucracy and lassitude of Nepal's government.

Counting the Cost of the Disaster

While the earthquake was one of the worst disasters to have hit the Himalayan region, it is important to note that damage was localised.

In Gorkha, Dhading, Sindapulchowk, Rasuwa and Dolakha districts, damage was severe; many communities were devastated and centuries-old monuments were reduced to rubble. Kathmandu and other towns in the Kathmandu Valley were also seriously affected, but little damage was recorded in Pokhara and the Annapurna region, and only mild shocks were felt in the Terai and in eastern and western Nepal.

Whole villages were destroyed by landslides and avalanches in Langtang, Helambu, Manaslu, Rolwaling and parts of the Everest region, but other trekking areas were mostly untouched by the disaster. Most trekking lodge owners have been quick to rebuild their lodges (largely without government funds) and the major trekking routes in Langtang, Helambu and Manaslu are now all back up and running, and as beautiful as they ever were.

The cultural damage was also patchy. Some historic temples, palaces and monuments in Kathmandu's Durbar Sq and Bhaktapur were reduced to piles of bricks and broken timbers, but the majority escaped with minor damage. It will take several years to reconstruct or stabilise all the monuments in Kathmandu and beyond.

Where Now for Nepal?

Three years after the earthquake many thousands of rural Nepalis are still living in temporary accommodation. Most homeowners have the received at least the first of three government payments to help rebuild their houses, after having their building plans authorised by government officials. However, even the total payment of US$3000 will only cover a fraction of the cost of rebuilding. Trekking lodges and hotels do not qualify for government payments, nor do many houses in national parks like Langtang. The face of traditional villages across Nepal is changing as villagers rebuild in sturdy concrete rather than traditional brick.

Tourism has largely rebounded after the earthquake and is more economically important than ever. If you visit today, and spend your money in rural communities with local businesses, you will be contributing directly to the reconstruction effort, providing valuable revenue that has the real potential to change lives.

has resulted in a fascinating hybrid culture, where Hindu and Buddhist beliefs jointly infuse Nepali life.

Historically, the Kathmandu Valley has been the homeland of the Newars, great traders and craftspeople of mixed Indian and Tibeto-Burman origin. Much of the iconography, architecture and culture associated with Nepal today is actually based on Newari culture.

The first formal records of Newari history come from the Licchavi era (AD 400 to 750), but the golden age of the Newars came in the 17th century when the valley was dominated by three city-states – Kantipur (Kathmandu), Lalitpur (Patan) and Bhadgaon (Bhaktapur) – all of which competed to outshine each other with architectural brilliance. The reign of the Malla kings saw the construction of many of Nepal's most iconic palaces, temples and monuments.

The unification of Nepal in 1768–69 by Prithvi Narayan Shah signalled the end of this three-way scramble for supremacy. Nepali, an Indo-European language spoken by the Khas of western Nepal, replaced Newari as the country's language of administration and Kathmandu became the undisputed capital of the nation.

Tragically, many of the historic towns in the Kathmandu Valley were devastated by the 2015 earthquake, with huge loss of life. Reconstruction is under way and local people are rebuilding their lives and livelihoods, but the scars of the earthquake will be visible on the landscape for many years to come.

🛈 Dangers & Annoyances

Women in particular should avoid hiking alone in remote corners of the valley. Nagarjun Hill (p136) near Kathmandu and Pulchowki Mountain south of Godavari have historically seen robberies and worse.

If you plan to explore the Kathmandu Valley on a rented motorcycle, be wary of the traffic police, particularly after dark. Locals are routinely stung with fines for trumped-up traffic offences and foreigners are increasingly being targeted.

Be aware of the risk of landslides on the roads to Langtang and Kodari.

🛈 Getting Around

If you intend to do any biking, hiking or motorcycling, it's worth investing in Nepa Maps' useful 1:50,000 *Around the Kathmandu Valley* or 1:60,000 *Biking Around Kathmandu Valley*. Both are available from bookshops in Kathmandu.

LORD OF THE ANIMALS

Elsewhere in Nepal, Shiva is worshipped in his wrathful form as the destructive Bhairab, but at Pashupatinath he is celebrated as Pashupati, Lord of the Animals. Shiva is said to have wandered the banks of the Bagmati River here in the form of a deer and one legend claims the main temple's lingam originates from the divine deer's broken horn.

Sadhus and devotees of Shiva flock to Pashupatinath from across the subcontinent and many Nepalis choose to be cremated on the banks of the holy river. Even the kings of Nepal used to come here to ask for a blessing from Pashupati before commencing any important journey. Nepal's Dalit ('untouchable') community was only allowed access to the shrine in 2001.

BICYCLE & MOTORBIKE

By far the most efficient and economical way of getting around the valley is by rented bicycle or motorbike. Once you get beyond the Kathmandu Ring Rd, there is less traffic and the valley offers some charming riding country, as long as you choose your routes wisely.

It's not all plain sailing though. Traffic and road conditions can be terrible, especially on the main roads, so it's worth getting advice on the best routes from Kathmandu's many bike rental and tour companies. Take corners slowly as buses and trucks will not give way. Be sure to securely lock your bike or motorcycle when you stop, and carry plenty of petrol from Kathmandu as rural petrol stations regularly run dry. On day trips, give yourself time to get back to Kathmandu by nightfall – you really don't want to ride these roads after dark.

BUS & TAXI

From Kathmandu's Ratna Park bus station, inexpensive public buses run to every town in the valley, though you may need to change in Patan or Bhaktapur. However, the buses can be incredibly crowded, and they are glacially slow.

As a more comfortable alternative to travelling by bus, consider hiring a car or taxi from Kathmandu – as a guide, a day hire to Changu Narayan and Bhaktapur or to Dakshinkali, Chobar and Kirtipur costs around Rs 3500.

HIKING

A web of footpaths around the valley links its villages and towns and there are many interesting day hikes and overnight treks, allowing you to take shortcuts that are not accessible by bicycle or motorcycle. You can easily link several towns on foot and could even put together a five- or six-day hike linking Kakani to Budhanil-kantha, Chisopani, Nagarkot, Dhulikhel, Balthali, Namobuddha and Panauti.

See the Nepal Environment and Tourism Initiative Foundation website (www.netifnepal.org) for details of multiday hikes around the valley.

ORGANISED TOURS

Many of the travel agents in Thamel, in Kathmandu, can arrange day trips around the valley, but standards vary. If you prefer a guided walk, Wayfarers (p112) offers guided day hikes through Kirtipur, Khokana and Bungamati (US$35 per person), which include lunch and local transport. Three-day mini-treks to Panauti, Namobuddha, Dhulikhel (overnight), Nagarkot (overnight), Changu Narayan and Sankhu operate with a minimum of two people (US$175 per person with guide, meals and accommodation).

AROUND THE RING ROAD

There are several interesting sights just outside the Kathmandu Ring Rd, all accessible by public transport or by rented bike or motorcycle, and all easy day trips from the capital. Pashupatinath and Bodhnath rank among Nepal's most famous and emotionally compelling religious sites.

Pashupatinath

Nepal's most important Hindu temple stands on the banks of the holy Bagmati River, surrounded by a bustling market of religious stalls selling marigolds, *prasad* (offerings), incense, rudraksha beads, conch shells, pictures of Hindu deities and temples, *tika* powder in rainbow colours, glass lingams, models of Mt Meru and other essential pilgrim paraphernalia.

At first glance, Pashupatinath might not look that sacred – the temple is just a few hundred metres from the end of the runway at Tribhuvan Airport, overlooking a particularly polluted stretch of the Bagmati. However, in religious terms this is a powerhouse of Hindu spiritual energy, and is closely connected to Shiva in the form of Pashupati, the Lord of Animals.

Some surrounding minor shrines were damaged in the 2015 earthquake, but the main *mandir* (temple) was unscathed.

Non-Hindus cannot enter the main temple, but the surrounding complex of Shaivite shrines, lingams and riverside ghats (stone steps) is fascinating and highly photogenic. Groups of photogenic sadhus loiter around in outlandish paraphernalia hoping to make a little money posing for tourist photos (Rs 50 to Rs 100 per photo). Be respectful with your camera at the funeral ghats – you wouldn't take snaps of bereaved relatives at a funeral back home, so don't do it here. Keep a respectful distance.

The entry fee for foreigners is surprisingly high, considering non-Hindus are not allowed into the two main temples; some travellers consider it overpriced. All the sights are covered by a single Pashupatinath entry ticket. Guides can be hired from the ticket office on a rota basis. Figure on Rs 500 for an hour-long tour, though guides will ask for Rs 1000.

The best times to visit are early in the morning or around 6pm during evening prayers.

◉ Sights

Pashupatinath Temple   HINDU TEMPLE
(Map p125; foreigner/SAARC Rs 1000/free, child under 10yr free; ◷ 24hr) Undiminished by the earthquake, the pagoda-style Pashupatinath Temple was constructed in 1696, but has been a site of Hindu and Buddhist worship for far longer. Only Hindus are allowed to enter the compound of the famous main temple, but you can catch tantalising glimpses of what is going on inside from several points around the perimeter wall.

From the main gate on the west side of the compound, you can view the mighty golden behind of an enormous brass **statue of Nandi** (Map p125), Shiva's bull. Inside the shrine, hidden from view, is a black, four-headed image of Pashupati. There are good views of the gilded rooftop from the top of the terraces on the east side of the Bagmati.

If you follow the road running south from the side entrance to the temple, you will pass the **Panch Deval** (Map p125), a former temple complex that survived the quake and acts as a social welfare centre for destitute elderly Nepalis.

Western Cremation Ghats   HINDU SITE
(Map p125) Despite being clogged with garbage and black with pollution, the fetid Bagmati River is actually an extremely sacred river; Pashupatinath is the Nepali equivalent of Varanasi on the sacred River Ganges. The cremation ghats along the Bagmati are the city's

Pashupatinath

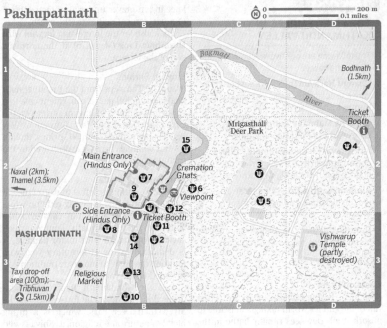

N 0 / 0 ——— 200 m / 0.1 miles

Pashupatinath

◉ Sights

1	Bachhareshwari Temple	B2
2	Eastern Ghats	B3
3	Gorakhnath Temple	C2
4	Guhyeshwari Temple	D2
5	Lingam Shrines	C2
6	Lingam with Shiva Face	C2
7	Nandi Statue	B2
8	Panch Deval	B3
9	Pashupatinath Temple	B2
10	Raj Rajeshwari Temple	B3
11	Ram Temple	B3
12	Shiva Shrines	B2
13	Standing Buddha Image	B3
14	Western Cremation Ghats	B3
15	Yogi Caves	B2

most important location for open-air cremations. Fires burned here day and night after
the 2015 earthquake as hundreds of families
dealt with the human cost of the disaster.

Only members of the royal family can be
cremated immediately in front of Pashupatinath Temple; the funerals of 10 members of
the Nepali royal family took place here after
the massacre in 2001. Funerals of ordinary
Nepalis take place daily on the ghats to the
south of the temple. Bodies are wrapped in
shrouds and laid out along the riverbank,
then cremated on a wooden pyre in a surprisingly businesslike way. This is the most
interesting aspect to Pashupatinath and it's
a powerful place to contemplate notions of
death and mortality. Needless to say, this is a
private time for relatives to grieve and tourists
intruding with cameras is not appropriate.

At the north end of the ghats, visible from
across the river, are a series of **yogis' caves**
(Map p125), used as shelters since medieval
times and still occupied by meditators today.

If you walk south along the west bank,
you will see a 7th-century **standing Buddha image** (Map p125), next to the damaged
Raj Rajeshwari Temple (Map p125), with its
unusual curved stucco outbuildings.

Bachhareshwari Temple   HINDU TEMPLE
(Map p125) Between the two groups of ghats
on the west bank of the Bagmati is this
small, 6th-century temple, decorated with
Tantric figures, skeletons and erotic scenes.
It is said that human sacrifices were once
made at this temple as part of the Maha
Shivaratri Festival (p127).

TOP FIVE TEMPLES IN THE KATHMANDU VALLEY

The following are our five favourite temples in the valley:

Changu Narayan (p168) A treasure house of sculpture at this Unesco World Heritage Site.

Gokarna Mahadev Temple (p170) A visual A to Z of Hindu iconography.

Indreshwar Mahadev Temple (p189) A perfect temple by a mystical river confluence south of the highway to Tibet.

Budhanilkantha (p134) Impressive monolithic stone carving of a sleeping Vishnu.

Dakshinkali (p175) Spooky defile where blood sacrifices to a wrathful goddess take place.

Eastern Ghats   HINDU SITE

(Map p125) Pashupatinath's ghats are often full of life and it's worth taking some time to absorb it all. Devotees ritually bathe in the dubious-looking waters of the Bagmati, holy men perform rituals on the stone steps and children fish for coins from the murky river using a magnet on the end of a string. You may also see families preparing the funeral pyres across the river.

Two footbridges cross the Bagmati in front of the Pashupatinath Temple, entering a garden of stone terraces covered in dozens of small **Shiva shrines** (Map p125). These one-room temples are often used as lodgings by wandering sadhus and each contains a central Shiva lingam. Although the shrines are built in many styles, all share certain design features – note the mask of Bhairab, Shiva's fearsome incarnation, on the south wall, the Nandi statue on the west and the bull-head water spout to the north.

Two flights of steps lead up the hillside between the shrines, passing the damaged but still elaborately frescoed wooden **Ram Temple** (Map p125), which is often thronged by visiting sadhus, especially during the Maha Shivaratri Festival. At the top, where the path enters the forest, a side track leads north along the top of the terraces to an excellent **viewpoint** (Map p125) over the Pashupatinath Temple. Look for the enormous golden trident on the northern side of the temple and the golden figure of the king

kneeling in prayer under a protective hood of *naga* (serpent deities) to the south.

Look also for the interesting **lingam with the Shiva face** (Map p125) at the northern end of the terrace.

Lingam Shrines   HINDU SITE

(Map p125) The steps from the Pashupatinath ghats lead uphill past a convenient cafe to a sprawling complex of lingam shrines on the edge of the forest that is well worth exploring. There are more than 50 shrines, though several buildings here were destroyed by the earthquake.

Gorakhnath Temple   HINDU TEMPLE

(Map p125) Continuing left at the top of the hill will take you to the towering red-and-white shikhara (temple with tall corn cob–like spire) of the Gorakhnath Temple, which survived the quake with minor damage. It is dedicated to the 11th-century yogi who founded the Shaivite monastic tradition and invented Hatha yoga.

Past the Gorakhnath Temple, the path drops down through the forest, passing the Mrigasthali Deer Park, which is a fitting blend of nature and religion, as Shiva is said to have frolicked here once in the shape of a golden deer.

Guhyeshwari Temple   HINDU TEMPLE

(Map p125) The path drops out of the forest to the large, courtyard-style Guhyeshwari Temple, built by King Pratap Malla in 1653 and dedicated to Parvati (the wife of Shiva) in her terrible manifestation as Kali. Entry is banned to non-Hindus, but from the path you can see the four huge gilded snakes that support the central finial, as well as the Bodhnath Stupa in the distance.

The temple's curious name comes from the Nepali words *guhya* (vagina) and *ishwari* (goddess) – literally, it's the temple of the goddess' vagina. According to legend, the father of Parvati insulted Shiva and the goddess became so incensed that she burst into flames, providing the inspiration for the practice of *sati*, where widows were burned alive on the funeral pyres of their husbands. The grieving Shiva wandered the earth with the disintegrating corpse of Parvati and her genitals fell at Guhyeshwari. Indian Hindus make the same claim for the Kamakhya Temple at Guwahati in Assam.

The riverbank in front of the temple is lined with Shiva shrines and bell-roofed octagonal pavilions for ritual bathing.

✨ Festivals & Events

Pashupatinath is generally busiest with genuine pilgrims on *ekadashi* days, which fall 11 days after the full and new moon each month. As night falls, pilgrims release butter lamps on boats made of leaves onto the Bagmati as part of the *arati* (light) ceremony.

Sadhus congregate on Pashupatinath year-round to meditate in the vicinity of the sacred shrine, but the number of holy men goes into overdrive during Maha Shivaratri in February or March, the most important Shiva festival in the Hindu calendar.

Maha Shivaratri Festival   RELIGIOUS

(☉Feb/Mar) In the Nepali month of Falgun (Feb or March), tens of thousands of pilgrims throng to Pashupatinath from all over Nepal and India to celebrate Shiva's birthday. It's an incredible spectacle, and a chance to see members of some of the more austere Shaivite sects performing rituals through the night.

Bala Chaturdashi   RELIGIOUS

(☉Nov/Dec) During the new moon of November/December, pilgrims hold a lamp-lit vigil and bathe in the holy Bagmati the following morning. Pilgrims then scatter sweets and seeds around the compound for their deceased relatives to enjoy in the afterlife.

ℹ Information

Entry tickets for Pashupatinath are sold at the tourist booths at the **main entrance** (Map p125) and by the **northern gate** (Map p125).

ℹ Getting There & Away

You can visit Pashupatinath as a half-day trip from central Kathmandu, or combine a visit with nearby Bodhnath.

From Kathmandu, the most convenient way to Pashupatinath is by taxi (Rs 500 from Thamel) – taxis often drop you just south of the temple complex, near the Ring Rd at Gaushala, but you can also approach from the west or north. Heading away from Pashupatinath, there's a taxi stand a short walk south of the temple complex.

If you are walking or cycling, head east from the Narayanhiti Palace through Naxal, meeting the Ring Rd near the Jayabageshwari Temple, with its fine painting of Bhairab. To reach Pashupatinath Temple, cross the Ring Rd and follow the winding lanes lined with religious stalls towards the Bagmati.

If you want to walk on from Pashupatinath to Bodhnath, it's a pleasant 20-minute stroll through villages and farmland, offering a window onto ordinary life in the Kathmandu suburbs. Take the footbridge across the river in front of the Guhyeshwari Temple and head north for five minutes, then turn right by a temple surrounding a large pipal tree. At the next junction follow the Buddha's example and take the middle (straight) path, which eventually emerges on the main Bodhnath road, right across from the stupa.

Chabahil

East of the centre of Kathmandu, on the way to Bodhnath, the suburb of Chabahil has a number of historic temples and shrines that warrant a brief stop.

STUPAS

The Kathmandu Valley is dotted with impressive stupas (*chörten* in Tibetan). The most impressive are at Bodhnath (p128) and Swayambhunath (p117), but there are also substantial examples at little-visited Chabahil (p128) and Kathesimbhu (p77) in Kathmandu. The oldest stupas are the four in Patan that were allegedly built by emperor Ashoka. You'll pass smaller chörtens and chorten-shaped *kani* (arch-like gateways) on almost every trek in Nepal.

The very first stupas were built to house the ashes and relics of Siddhartha Gautama (the Historical Buddha) and became a powerful early symbol of the new faith at a time when images of the Buddha had not yet become popular. Many Tibetan-style chörtens still house religious relics or the ashes of lamas. The range of styles is immense, from the huge platforms of Bodhnath to the fragile stone chörtens atop a mountain pass.

Each of the elements of a stupa has a symbolic meaning, from the square base (earth) and the hemispherical dome (water) to the tapering spire (fire), whose 13 step-like segments can symbolise the steps leading to Buddhahood. On top of the 13 steps is an ornament shaped like a crescent moon (air), and a vertical spike, which represent ether or the sacred light of Buddha.

In Nepal, the central rectangular tower is painted with the all-seeing eyes of Buddha. What appears to be a nose is actually the Sanskrit character for the number one, symbolising the absoluteness of Buddha.

◉ Sights

Chabahil Stupa
BUDDHIST STUPA

(Ring Rd) **FREE** Right on the Ring Rd is this imposing stupa, the fourth largest in the Kathmandu area after Bodhnath, Swayambhunath and the Kathesimbhu Stupa near Thahiti Chowk. According to legend, the stupa was constructed by Charumati, the daughter of Ashoka, but it has been rebuilt numerous times, most recently in 2015, after damage from the Gorkha earthquake.

The spire is covered by brass plates and the surrounding courtyard has some graceful chaitya from the Licchavi period.

Chandra Binayak
Ganesh Temple
HINDU TEMPLE

This revered temple enshrines a tiny silver image of Ganesh and is currently being rebuilt after sustaining damage during the 2015 earthquake. The courtyard is full of tika-powder-covered statues – note the Budhanilkantha-style statue of Narayan reclining on his serpent bed, next to a human figure made of beaten brass panels. It's a two-minute walk from Chabahil Stupa; take the lane to the north past a small white stupa then go through the white arch.

Charumati Vihar
BUDDHIST TEMPLE

The Charumati Vihar is a medieval Buddhist monastery that used to house the monks who tended the Chabahil Stupa. To get here from the Chabahil Stupa, take the lane just to the north and turn left at a smaller white stupa.

ⓘ Getting There & Away

Chabahil is an easy stop on either public transport or a hired taxi en route between Kathmandu and either Bodhnath or Pashupatinath.

Bodhnath (Boudha)
📷 01

There is nowhere quite like Bodhnath. Asia's largest stupa pulses with life as thousands of pilgrims gather daily to make a *kora* (ritual circumnavigation) of the dome, beneath the watchful eyes of the Buddha, which gaze out from the gilded central tower. Tibetan monks in maroon robes wander the prayer flag–decked streets while pilgrims spin prayer wheels and stock up on yak butter and *tsampa* (roasted barley flour).

This is one of the few places in the world where Tibetan Buddhist culture is accessible and unfettered, and the lanes around the stupa are crammed with monasteries and workshops producing butter lamps, ceremonial horns, Tibetan drums, monks' headgear and the other accessories essential for Tibetan Buddhist life.

Many of the monasteries around the stupa have opened their doors to foreign students, so you'll see plenty of Western dharma students in maroon robes as you stroll around the backstreets.

Historically, the stupa was an important staging post on the trade route between Lhasa and Kathmandu, and Tibetan traders would pray here for a safe journey before driving their yaks on to the high passes of the Himalaya. Originally a Tamang settlement, today most of the people living in the village of Boudha (pronounced boe-da) are Tibetan refugees who fled China after 1959. The stupa also attracts many Sherpas, descendants of eastern Tibetans who migrated to the Everest region of Nepal in the 16th century.

The best time to visit Bodhnath is late afternoon, when the tour groups head home and elderly exiles stroll down to the stupa to light butter lamps, spin prayer wheels, chant mantras, socialise and stroll clockwise around the monument as part of their daily spiritual workout. Try to visit on the evening of the full moon, when the plaza surrounding the stupa is lit up by thousands of butter lamps.

◉ Sights

★ Bodhnath Stupa
BUDDHIST STUPA

(Map p129; foreigner/SAARC Rs 400/100) The first stupa at Bodhnath was built sometime after AD 600, when the Tibetan king, Songtsen Gampo, converted to Buddhism. In terms of grace and purity of line, no other stupa in Nepal comes close to Bodhnath. From its whitewashed dome to its gilded tower painted with the all-seeing eyes of the Buddha, the monument is perfectly proportioned.

Jamchen Lhakhang
BUDDHIST MONASTERY

(Map p129) This Sakya-school monastery on the west side of the stupa circuit houses a huge three-storey statue of Jampa (Maitreya), the Future Buddha. Look for the unusual murals depicting former King Tribhuvan and his wife.

Guru Lhakhang
BUDDHIST MONASTERY

(Map p129) This prominent *lhakhang* (chapel) houses an impressive three-storey statue of Guru Rinpoche (Padmasambhava), the 7th-century magician and holy man who helped establish Buddhism in Tibet.

Bodhnath (Boudha)

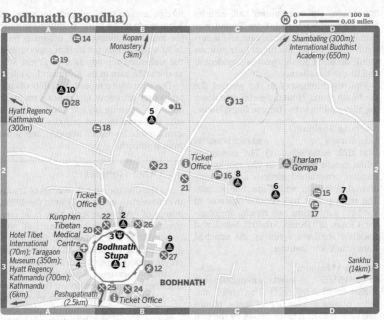

Bodhnath (Boudha)

◎ Top Sights
1 Bodhnath Stupa B3

◎ Sights
2 Guru Lhakhang B3
3 Harati (Ajima) Shrine...........................B3
4 Jamchen Lhakhang...............................A3
5 Ka-Nying Sheldrup Ling Gompa B1
6 Pal Dilyak Gompa..................................C2
7 Pal Nye Gompa.....................................D2
8 Sakya Tharig Gompa.............................C2
9 Samtenling Gompa................................B3
10 Shechen Gompa....................................A1

◎ Activities, Courses & Tours
11 Rangjung Yeshe Institute.....................B1
12 Responsible Treks.................................B3
13 Seeing Hands...C1

◎ Sleeping
14 Dragon Guest House A1
15 Lotus Guest House D2

16 Pal Rabten Khansar Guest House C2
17 Pema Guest House................................D2
18 Rokpa Guest House...............................B2
19 Shechen Guest House A1

◎ Eating
20 Café du Temple B3
21 Double Dorjee Restaurant....................B2
22 Flavors Café..B3
23 Garden Kitchen.....................................B2
24 La Casita de Boudhanath B3
25 Pho 99 ....B3
   Rabsel Garden Cafe......................(see 19)
26 Stupa View Restaurant.........................B3
27 White Dzambala Tibetan
   Restaurant...B3

◎ Shopping
28 Tsering Art School Shop........................A1

Look also for the **plaque** to the right of the *lhakhang* that commemorates Ekai Kawaguchi, the Japanese monk and traveller who stayed here in 1899 before heading off on a remarkable journey to Mustang and Tibet.

Shechen Gompa BUDDHIST MONASTERY
(Shechen Tengyi Dargyeling Gompa; Map p129; www. shechen.org) This huge complex was established by the famous Nyingmapa lama Dilgo Khyentse Rinpoche to replace the destroyed Shechen Gompa in eastern Tibet. Today the monastery has a thriving community of over

300 monks. The main prayer hall, with its fabulous murals by artists from Bhutan, was damaged by the 2015 earthquake and is currently under repair. You might hear raucous monk debating in the western residential building in the afternoons.

Find the monastery to the west of the Bodhnath Stupa, behind a metal gate down the alley leading to the Dragon Guest House.

Ka-Nying Sheldrup Ling Gompa
BUDDHIST MONASTERY

(Map p129; www.shedrub.org) The handsome 'white gompa' is home to 225 monks and features ornamental gardens and a richly decorated interior with some fine murals. The main prayer hall became unstable in the 2015 earthquake and repairs are ongoing. Classes in Tibetan, Sanskrit, Nepali and Buddhist studies are run by the attached Rangjung Yeshe Institute.

Taragaon Museum
MUSEUM

(☏01-4497505; www.taragaonmuseum.com; ☉10am-5pm Sun-Fri) FREE This small museum houses a collection of maps, photos and archaeological plans drawn by the first foreign architectural advisers to arrive in Kathmandu in the 1970s. Highlights include the museum building itself, originally built in 1974 as a hostel for foreign experts, and the wall-sized reproduction of Erwin Schneider's first map of the Kathmandu Valley.

There are also temporary exhibits of contemporary art, occasional cultural events, a Saturday morning organic food market, a cafe and some top-end galleries. It's in the grounds of the Hyatt Regency, accessible from Bodhnath.

◉ Other Gompas

Since the Chinese sent thousands of troops to enforce their claim on Tibet in the 1950s, dozens of new monasteries have been constructed at Bodhnath by refugees. All welcome visitors but many close their doors in the middle of the day. Most places have prayer sessions around 5am and 3pm.

Minor backstreet monasteries worth tracking down are **Samtenling Gompa** (Map p129), which is damaged but under restoration, **Sakya Tharig Gompa** (Map p129; www.sakyatharig.org.np), **Pal Dilyak Gompa** (Map

---

VISITING TIBETAN MONASTERIES

Most Tibetan Buddhist monasteries welcome visitors and entering these atmospheric buildings can be a powerful and evocative experience. During the morning and evening prayers, the lamas (high-ranking Tibetan Buddhist monks) and novices gather to chant Buddhist texts, normally accompanied by a cacophony of crashing cymbals, thumping drums and booming Tibetan horns.

From Ladakh to Lhasa, Tibetan gompas (monasteries) follow a remarkably consistent layout. The main prayer hall is invariably decorated with intricate murals depicting the life of Buddha, alongside various bodhisattvas and protectors, who also appear on dangling thangkas (Tibetan religious paintings) edged with brocade and in statue form behind the main altar.

Many gompas also have a library of cloth-wrapped, loose-leafed Buddhist manuscripts, known as the Kangyur and Tengyur, set into alcoves around the altar. The altar itself is covered in offerings, including butter lamps and seven bowls of water. The throne of the abbot is often surrounded by pictures of past abbots and the Dalai Lama, the spiritual leader of Tibetan Buddhism and the representation on earth of Chenresig (Avalokiteshvara), the deity of compassion.

As you enter a monastery you will see murals of the four guardian protectors – fearsome-looking deities who scare away ignorance – and the Wheel of Life, a highly complex diagram representing the Buddha's insights into the way humans are chained by desire to the endless cycle of life, death and rebirth.

The front of a monastery may also feature enormous *mani dungkhor* – giant prayer wheels stuffed with thousands of copies of the Buddhist mantra *om mani padme hum* ('hail to the jewel in the lotus').

This mantra also appears on the smaller prayer wheels around the outer wall and on the fluttering prayer flags outside. On the monastery roof you may see a statue of two deer on either side of the Wheel of Law, symbolising the Buddha's first sermon at the deer park of Sarnath.

p129) and **Pal Nye Gompa** (Map p129). There's little to choose between them, so follow the sounds of booming trumpets and crashing cymbals to see which are open.

🏃 Activities

International Buddhist Academy
HEALTH & FITNESS

(☑ 01-4915218, 9803372212; www.internation albuddhistacademy.org; Tinchuli) Alongside more heavyweight courses, free 90-minute dharma talks on aspects of Buddhism are held here most Saturdays at 9.30am, aimed squarely at foreign tourists and residents. Look for a schedule on flyers plastered around Bodhnath. The centre is a 20-minute walk northeast of the Bodhnath Stupa.

Responsible Treks
TREKKING

(Map p129; ☑ 01-4916101; www.responsibletreks. com; Bodhnath) This agency offers a full range of treks, as well as tours and day hikes in the Bodhnath area. Enquire about the free Thursday walk to Kopan and Pullahari monasteries.

Seeing Hands
MASSAGE

(Map p129; ☑ 01-4910780; www.seeinghands nepal.org; massage per hr Rs 1500) A branch of the Kathmandu blind centre, offering Swedish-style massage from blind masseurs.

🐘 Courses

Rangjung Yeshe Institute
LANGUAGE

(Map p129; ☑ 01-4483575; www.ryi.org) Located at Ka-Nying Sheldrup Ling Gompa, this Buddhist institute offers a seven-day seminar on Tibetan Buddhist teachings, practice and meditation, led by the monastery's abbot Chokyi Nyima Rinpoche. The popular course is held in mid-November and fees are by donation. A follow-up three-day retreat is held at Nagi Gompa (US$85).

The institute also offers a university-accredited summer course in Buddhist theory and meditation in June/July, as well as eight-week summer Tibetan and Nepali language courses, staying with local families.

🎆 Festivals & Events

Buddha Jayanti (Saga Dawa)
RELIGIOUS

(☉ Apr/May) During the full moon of April/ May Buddhists everywhere commemorate the birth, enlightenment and death of the Buddha. Thousands of butter lamps are lit by devotees and an image of the Buddha is paraded around the Bodhnath Stupa. Tibetans know the festival as Saga Dawa.

Losar
RELIGIOUS

(☉ Feb/Mar) Bodhnath goes into spiritual overdrive every year in February or March for the Tibetan New Year. Long copper horns are blown, a portrait of the Dalai Lama is paraded around, thousands of pilgrims throng the stupa, and monks from the surrounding monasteries perform masked *chaam* (religious dances).

🛏 Sleeping

The guesthouses in the tangle of lanes north and east of the stupa offer an interesting and much more peaceful alternative to basing yourself in Kathmandu. It's a good idea to book ahead in October.

Flyers and online forums often advertise homestays and long-term apartments aimed at dharma students. Airbnb also offers furnished apartments in Bodhnath.

Lotus Guest House
GUESTHOUSE $

(Map p129; ☑ 01-4915320; lotusguesthouse boudha@gmail.com; s/d/tr Rs 700/1000/1500, s/d without bathroom Rs 600/1000; ☎) This calm, contemplative budget guesthouse is located close to Pal Dilyak Gompa. Rooms are spread over two floors around a marigold-fringed garden lawn and the shared bathrooms are clean.

Shechen Guest House
GUESTHOUSE $

(Map p129; ☑ 01-5178209; www.shechenguest house.com.np; s/d/tr Rs 1200/1650/2200; ☎) Located in the back of the Shechen Gompa compound, this agreeable guesthouse caters to a mix of long-term dharma students, Buddhist groups and ordinary travellers. Nepali bedspreads add a dash of colour to the otherwise plain rooms and the attached Rabsel Garden Cafe (p133) cooks up excellent vegetarian food in a peaceful garden.

To get here, enter the Shechen Monastery compound and turn left, then right beside a line of giant white chörten (Tibetan-style stupas). Profits go to the monastery.

Dragon Guest House
GUESTHOUSE $

(Map p129; ☑ 01-5178162; dragon@ntc.net.np; Mahankal; s/d without bathroom Rs 800/1000; ☎) This friendly, family-run place is set in a peaceful location north of Shechen Gompa. Staff keep the rooms spick and span and there's a vegetarian restaurant in the pleasant garden. Avoid the hot upper rooms in summer, especially as wi-fi is limited to the lower floors. To get here, walk north through the gate beside the Shechen Guest House.

AROUND THE KATHMANDU VALLEY BODHNATH (BOUDHA)

Pal Rabten Khansar Guest House
GUESTHOUSE $

(Map p129; ☎01-4915955; www.sakyatharig.org.np; s/d Rs 1250/1500, deluxe r Rs 2000; @ 🛜) This simple guesthouse is run by the next-door Sakya Tharig Gompa. The spacious carpeted deluxe rooms are comfortable and offer the best value; other rooms are smaller but still comfortable. Out the back is a small ornamental garden with a large stupa, plus there's a library and a nice rooftop with a kitchen for guests.

Pema Guest House
GUESTHOUSE $

(Map p129; ☎01-4915862; pemagurung@gmail.com; r from Rs 1800, without bathroom from Rs 1200, deluxe Rs 2500; 🛜) This tidy house is set in a neat courtyard garden. The spacious rooms on the upper levels get lots of natural light and there are terraces on each level where you can sit and enjoy some sun or a coffee from the attached cafe. Ground-floor rooms are darker. Not the best value in town.

★ Rokpa Guest House
HOTEL $$

(Map p129; ☎01-4479705; www.rokpaguesthouse.org; s/d US$30/40, deluxe US$40/50, ste US$50/60; 🛜) 🍃 Even if guests here didn't get a warm glow from knowing that their money was funding a nearby children's home (see www.rokpa.org), it would still be a great place to stay. The rooms are modern and spacious, staff are helpful and there's a relaxing garden restaurant that boasts its own bakery. Prices include breakfast and government tax.

Seven new-block rooms should be available from 2018. There are good monthly rates for long-term visitors.

Shambaling
BOUTIQUE HOTEL $$$

(☎01-4916868; www.shambaling.com; r standard/deluxe from US$70/110, ste from US$170; @ 🛜) This former pilgrim rest house has been reincarnated by its Tibetan owners into Bodhnath's most stylish boutique option. Each floor is designed in a different colour scheme to reflect the colours of Tibetan prayer flags. The more spacious deluxe rooms are easily the best bet, especially those that overlook the quiet and spacious garden centred around a bodhi tree.

Rates include breakfast in the excellent garden restaurant, where you can relax with an espresso or a shot of house-made spiced rum infused with cardamom and ginger. The

property is hard to find the first time; taxis approach from the Mahankal road to the north.

Hotel Tibet International
LUXURY HOTEL $$$

(☎01-4488188; www.hoteltibetintl.com.np; Main Rd; r from US$200; ✳ @ 🛜) A lot of thought has gone into this top-of-the-line Tibetan hotel, from the stylish Tibetan decor, including hand-knotted carpets from its own factory (check out the on-site showroom) to the choice of room pillows and the meditation room. The views of the Bodhnath Stupa from the 6th-floor breakfast buffet are fabulous. Request a room away from the busy main road. Online discounted rates normally hover around US$135 for a standard room.

🍴 Eating

Buddhist Bodhnath is nirvana for vegetarians. Traveller-oriented rooftop restaurants ring the stupa and offer superlative views, or for cheaper eats head to the back lanes radiating out from the stupa, where any building with a curtain across an open door is a local cafe serving Tibetan momos (dumplings) and *thukpa* (noodle soup). Most restaurants open from 8am to 9pm.

Garden Kitchen
INTERNATIONAL $

(Map p129; ☎01-4470760; mains Rs 250-400; ⊗8am-9pm) A partly open-air place serving the usual globe-trotting menu in a quiet and pleasant garden. Reasonable prices attract many long-term dharma students.

Double Dorjee Restaurant
TIBETAN $

(Map p129; ☎01-4488947; mains Rs 200-300) On the lane north of the stupa, this border-line dingy Tibetan-run old-timer caters to backpackers and the dharma crowd with rock-bottom prices, tasty Tibetan and Western food, and soft sofas that you'll have to prise yourself out of. Go local with bowl of *tsampa* (roasted barley flour) and milk for breakfast.

White Dzambala Tibetan Restaurant
CHINESE $

(Map p129; ☎9861988888; mains Rs 250-400; ⊗8am-8.30pm) It's hard not to feel a twinge of guilt eating Chinese food in Tibetan Bodhnath, but this doesn't seem to deter the local Tibetan businessmen and monks who come here to tuck into authentic Sichuanese *gongbao jiding* (spicy chicken with peanuts) or to nurse a *wanzi* fruit tea in the garden pavilions. It's just 40m from the stupa and sees almost no tourists.

Pho 99   VIETNAMESE **$$**
(Map p129; ☏01-2239773; mains Rs 350-550; ⊙11am-9pm; ☏) This new place is a stylish take on light and fresh Vietnamese dishes such as summer spring rolls, a spicy green papaya salad and plenty of pho noodles. There are also good cakes, coffee and, unexpectedly, French cheese.

Flavors Café   INTERNATIONAL **$$**
(Map p129; ☏01-4495484; mains Rs 400-540; ⊙7.30am-9pm; ☏☏) There's something for everyone here, from baked mushroom and spinach to Thai curries, pizzas and steak. There are no views from the pleasant interior courtyard just off the stupa, but it's a quiet, secluded place and the service is good.

Rabsel Garden Cafe   INTERNATIONAL **$$**
(Map p129; mains Rs 360-500; ⊙7am-9pm; ☏) This restaurant in the Shechen Guest House (p131) offers espresso coffee and cooks up excellent vegetarian food in a peaceful garden.

Café du Temple   INTERNATIONAL **$$**
(Map p129; ☏01-4489002; mains Rs 375-500, set meals Rs 675-775; ⊙9am-8.30pm) Run by the same people as the Café du Temple in Patan, this smart and efficient place targets tour groups with a variety of Indian, Chinese and Tibetan dishes, plus unbeatable rooftop views that shine in the afternoon light.

La Casita de Boudhanath   SPANISH **$$$**
(Map p129; ☏9813614384; mains Rs 700-1000; ⊙noon-9pm Sun-Fri) For something a bit different, climb the narrow stairs at this tiny place and grab a romantic perch for wine and tapas overlooking the stupa. The authentic gazpacho, paella (for two) and toast with imported chorizo are best washed down with a glass of Rioja wine or hot chocolate with churros. Tax is included.

Stupa View Restaurant   INTERNATIONAL **$$$**
(Map p129; ☏01-4914962; mains Rs 500-600, meze platters Rs 915; ⊙8am-8.30pm; ☏) The stupa views are as good as they claim at this superior traveller-oriented vegetarian place, so come early to nab one of the coveted top-floor seats. The meze and sampler platters are excellent, with fresh and tasty dishes such as chickpea balls in peanut sauce.

🛍 Shopping

The stupa is ringed by shops selling Tibetan crafts, thangkas, Buddhist statues, jewellery and souvenirs, but you'll get better prices by exploring the winding side streets. For monk's clothing, butter lamps, prayer flags and juniper incense, try the shops on the alleyway leading north from the stupa. Listen out for the tap-tap of metal-workers creating intricate *repoussé* designs using hammers and punches, a technique used for centuries to create panels for Nepal's temples and monasteries.

Tsering Art School Shop   ARTS & CRAFTS
(Map p129; Shechen Gompa; ⊙8-11.15am & 1-5pm Mon-Sat) The shop at Shechen Gompa has an on-site workshop that produces painted and embroidered thangkas and incense. The shop also sells Buddhist reference books.

CHINA'S LONG REACH

China's influence is on the rise globally, and Nepal is no exception. China has become an increasingly vital investor and aid donor in the country, funding everything from roads to hydroelectric plants. In the last decade China has built five new roads from Tibet into Nepal and there are even plans to connect the Tibet train line to the Nepal border.

One group eyeing this growing economic and political clout with apprehension is Nepal's 20,000-strong community of Tibetan refugees. Organisations such as Human Rights Watch claim that China's growing influence has led to increased pressure on Tibetans in Nepal amid increasingly violent crackdowns on pro-Tibetan demonstrations. Between 2008 and 2013 over 100 Tibetans set themselves on fire in Tibet protesting China's policies there. In 2013 two Tibetan protestors set themselves alight in front of the Bodhnath stupa, causing alarm that protests would spread abroad.

Chinese advisors have allegedly played a role in suppressing anti-Chinese demonstrations in Bodhnath and training Nepali border guards to catch and send back Tibetan refugees crossing the border into Nepal. The success of Communist parties in Nepal's 2017 elections is likely to strengthen ties between Nepal and China, with implications for Nepal's Tibetan community.

❶ Information

There are ticket offices at the **southern** (Map p129), **northern** (Map p129) and **north-eastern** (Map p129) approaches to the stupa plaza.

If you fancy trying out Tibetan traditional medicine, pay a visit to the **Kunphen Tibetan Medical Centre** (Map p129; ☑ 01-4251920; consultation Rs 300; ☺ 2-5pm Sun-Fri) on the west side of the stupa square, near Tsamchen Gompa. Diagnosis is based on the speed and regularity of the pulse and the condition of the tongue, and illnesses are treated with pills of Himalayan herbs available for purchase at the attached pharmacy.

❶ Getting There & Away

From Kathmandu, the easiest way to reach Bodhnath is by taxi (Rs 500 one way), but you can also come by bus from Ratna Park bus station (Rs 15, 30 minutes) or by tempo from Kantipath (Rs 15, routes 2 and 28).

There's also a pleasant short walk (p127) between Bodhnath and Pashupatinath, or you could combine Bodhnath with a visit to Kopan Monastery and Gokarna Mahadev Temple (p171).

Kopan

On a hilltop north of Bodhnath, **Kopan Monastery** (☑ 01-4821268; www.kopan-monastery.com) was founded by Lama Thubten Yeshe, who died in 1984, leading to a worldwide search for his reincarnation. A young Spanish boy, Osel Torres, was declared to be the reincarnated lama, providing the inspiration for Bernardo Bertolucci's film *Little Buddha*. Lama Tenzin Osel Rinpoche no longer resides at Kopan (he recently renounced his vows to become a cinematographer in Ibiza!), but visitors are welcome to explore the monastery. Accommodation is available and many people come here to study Buddhist psychology and philosophy.

You can visit Kopan on the pleasant walk between Bodhnath and the Gokarna Mahadev Temple (p171) or even from Nagi Gompa in Shivapuri Nagarjun National Park. A taxi here from Kathmandu costs around Rs 600, or Rs 300 from Bodhnath.

❖ Courses

Kopan Monastery   HEALTH & WELLBEING
(☑ 01-4821268; www.kopan-monastery.com) Kopan is probably the best place in the Himalaya to learn the basics of meditation and Tibetan Buddhism. The reasonably priced and popular 10-day courses (US$140), with a two-day silent retreat, are generally presented six or seven times a year by foreign teachers. There's also a very popular annual one-month course (US$510, booking essential) held in November, followed by an optional seven-day retreat. Visitors can also attend the daily dharma talks at 10am

The monastery is closed to visitors between 11 November and 20 December.

THE NORTHERN & WESTERN VALLEY

There are several interesting detours to the north and northwest of the capital, which can easily be visited by bus, tempo, taxi, rented bicycle or motorcycle, or even on foot. These include the temples of Budhanilkantha and Ichangu Narayan, plus the wilds of Shivapuri Nagarjun National Park.

Budhanilkantha

The Kathmandu Valley is awash with ancient temples and sacred sites, but Budhanilkantha is a little bit special. For one thing, it lies off the main traveller circuit, so most visitors are local devotees. This gives Budhanilkantha a uniquely mystical air – come on a busier day and you'll discover butter lamps flickering in the breeze, incense curling through the air, and devotees tossing *tika* powder around like confetti. For both devotees and sightseers, the focus is the impressive 5m-long reclining statue of Vishnu that floats in a sacred tank in the middle of the village.

❖ Sights

Reclining Statue of Vishnu   STATUE
(☺ dawn-dusk) **FREE** Budhanilkantha's focal point for devotions is a large reclining statue of Vishnu as Narayan, the creator of all life. From his navel grew a lotus and from the lotus came Brahma, who in turn created the world. The 5m-long Licchavi-style image was created in the 7th or 8th century from one piece of black stone and hauled here from outside the valley by devotees. It's one of the most impressive pieces of sculpture in Nepal, and that's saying something!

Only Hindus can approach the statue to leave offerings of fruit and flower garlands, but visitors can view the statue through the fence that surrounds the sacred tank. Narayan slumbers peacefully on the knotted coils of Ananta (or Shesha), the 11-headed snake god who symbolises eternity. In each hand, Narayan holds one of the four symbols of Vishnu: a chakra disc (representing the mind), a conch shell (the four elements), a mace (primeval knowledge) and a lotus seed (the moving universe).

Vaishnavism (the worship of Vishnu) was the main sect of Hinduism in Nepal until the early Malla period, when Shiva became the most popular deity. The Malla king Jayasthithi is credited with reviving the Vishnu cult by claiming to be the latest incarnation of this oft-incarnated god. Every subsequent king of Nepal has made the same claim, and because of this they are forbidden, on pain of death, from seeing the image at Budhanilkantha.

Vishnu is supposed to sleep through the four monsoon months and a great festival takes place at Budhanilkantha for Haribodhini Ekadashi – the 11th day of the Hindu month of Kartik (October/November) – when Vishnu is said to awaken from his annual slumber.

Sleeping & Eating

The road to the sacred pavilion is lined with bhojanalayas serving *sel roti* (rice-flour doughnuts), *channa puri* (fried bread with chickpeas), pakora (battered vegetables) and outsized pappadams.

★ **Shivapuri Heights Cottage**   GUESTHOUSE $$$
(☑ 9802012245, 9841371927; www.shivapuricottage.com; half-board tents US$45, r per person US$65-85; ☎) Perched on the hillside above Budhanilkantha, Shivapuri Heights offers a peaceful, private bolthole far away from the chaos of Kathmandu. Rooms are divided into three cottages, all decked out with charming living rooms and flower-fringed terraces that offer excellent views over the Kathmandu Valley. There are also safari-style tents for a more rustic stay.

You can rent a whole cottage (each housing four to six guests, so great for families) or just a room if you don't mind sharing the living room. The Jasmine House cottage offers the most luxury. The location makes it a great base for guided forest hikes to Namkha Dzong Monastery or Nagi Gompa, or just relax with sunrise yoga, a gentle massage or a cooling dip in the plunge pool. It's worth staying for two or three nights.

The compound is a 15-minute uphill walk from Budhanilkantha; staff can arrange

OFF THE BEATEN TRACK

ICHANGU NARYAN

About 3km northwest of Swayambhunath, **Ichangu Narayan Temple** (☉ dawn-dusk) is one of several important temples dedicated to Vishnu in his incarnation as Narayan, the 'eternal man'. Built in the two-tiered pagoda style, the temple was founded in around AD 1200 and its courtyard is dotted with ancient Garuda statues and other Vaishnavite symbols. The complex was shaken by the 2015 earthquake, but most structures have been stabilised and repaired.

Microvans (route 23) go to Ichangu Narayan (Rs 25) about every half hour from Kathmandu's Ratna Park or New Road Gate (near the Nepal Airlines office). They stop at the Aadeswor Temple, from where you have to walk about 2km to the temple. A taxi from Thamel to Ichangu Narayan costs Rs 500.

transport from Budhanilkantha, Kathmandu or the airport on request.

Park Village Resort   RESORT $$$
(☑ 01-4375280; www.ktmgh.com; s/d incl breakfast from US$80/90, ste US$175; ✳☎⬤) This delightful hotel feels like a country retreat, despite being smack in the middle of Budhanilkantha. The tidy but cosy standard rooms and the much smarter super-deluxe rooms are surrounded by gardens and there's a lovely pool (possibly the best in Kathmandu Valley). The hotel also offers spa treatments and activities, including bird-spotting tours to Shivapuri Nagarjun National Park.

❶ Getting There & Away

From Kathmandu, No 5 minibuses run from the northern end of Kantipath to the main junction in Budhanilkantha (Rs 20, 35 minutes). There are also tempos (from Sundhara) and buses (from both Gongabu and Ratna Park bus stations). The shrine is about 100m uphill from the junction. From Thamel, a taxi costs around Rs 700 one way or Rs 1000 return.

Shivapuri Nagarjun National Park

The northern part of the Kathmandu Valley rises to the sprawling forests of **Shivapuri Nagarjun National Park** (☑ 01-4370355; foreigner/SAARC/Nepalese Rs 565/339/56, mountain

OFF THE BEATEN TRACK

ASHOKA STUPAS

Legend has it that the four ancient stupas marking the boundaries of Patan were built when the great Buddhist emperor Ashoka visited the valley 2500 years ago. All are worth a quick visit, especially during the auspicious full moon of August when Buddhist and Tibetan pilgrims walk around all four stupas in a single day.

Northern Stupa (Map p138) Just beyond the Kumbeshwar Temple, on the way to the Sankhamul ghats.

Lagan (Southern) Stupa Just south of the Lagankhel bus station, crowning a hilltop and offering good views over southern Patan.

Western Stupa (Map p138; Pulchowk) Covered in grass beside the main road at Pulchowk. A set of steps leads uphill to the Aksheshwar Mahavihar, a courtyard-style Buddhist monastery on the hilltop.

Eastern Stupa Well to the east of the centre, across Kathmandu's Ring Rd.

bike foreigner/Nepalese Rs 1000/100, compulsory guide half/full day Rs 800/1500; ⊘ entry 7am-2pm, latest exit 5pm), upgraded to national park status in 2002 to protect the valley's main water source, as well as 177 species of birds and numerous rare orchids. This is one of the last areas of primary woodland left in the valley, and the forest is alive with monkeys, and maybe even leopards and bears.

The park is split into two distinct zones by the roads running north from Kathmandu. The bulk of the park lies immediately north of Buddhanilkantha, on the trekking route to Helambu, but there's a second forested zone, the erstwhile Rani Ban, uphill from Balaju on the road towards Trisuli Bazaar, encircling 2095m Nagarjun Hill.

◎ Sights

Nagarjun Hill   NATIONAL PARK
(Rani Ban; foreigner/SAARC/Nepalese Rs 565/339/56, mountain bike foreigner/Nepalese Rs 1000/100, compulsory guide half/full day Rs 800/1500; ⊘ entry 7am-2pm, latest exit 5pm) Now formally part of Shivapuri Nagarjun National Park, Nagarjun Hill, also known as the Rani Ban (Queen's Forest), is west of the main park, beside the road to Trisuli

Bazaar. This protected woodland provides a home for pheasants, deer and monkeys. It's a peaceful spot, but safety is a consideration. Visitors are discouraged from walking here alone after two foreign tourists were murdered in the reserve in 2005. In 2016 guides were made compulsory.

The 2095m summit of the hill – accessible by the winding unpaved road or a two-hour hike on the footpath leading directly up the hill – is a popular Buddhist pilgrimage site and there's a small shrine to Padmasambhava. The viewing tower offers one of the Kathmandu Valley's widest mountain panoramas, stretching all the way from the Annapurnas to Langtang Lirung (a plaque identifies the peaks).

Several Kathmandu-based adventure companies run introductory rock-climbing courses here. Astrek Climbing Wall (p86) runs guided climbing (Rs 5500) every Saturday, suitable for all levels.

🏃 Activities

In the past the Shivapuri Peak section of the park was mainly visited by trekkers en route to Helambu, but today the reserve is a popular destination for birdwatching tours from Kathmandu. Several trekking and mountain-bike routes criss-cross the park, including the challenging Scar Rd cycle path (p31).

You can combine a nature-spotting tour with a trip to the Tibetan nunnery of **Nagi Gompa**, about 3km uphill from the main gate above Budhanilkantha. Around 100 nuns are resident and there are soaring valley views – you can walk here from Budhanilkantha in 1½ hours or drive in 20 minutes by motorcycle or hired 4WD.

From the gompa it's possible to climb steeply for about three hours to reach **Shivapuri Peak** (2725m), via Baghdwar (where the source of the holy Bagmati River pours out of two stone tiger mouths), returning to the park entrance via the Pani Muhan water tank, for a very long day of around seven hours. This is a serious hike that you shouldn't attempt alone (in any case, guides are now compulsory). Take a map, food and plenty of water.

There are several easier walks from Nagi Gompa. Consider the relaxing downhill stroll to Budhanilkantha, or continue south along the ridgeline for three hours to reach Kopan Monastery and Bodhnath. Another good option on foot or by mountain bike is to follow the dirt track east to Mulkarkha and then descend to Sundarijal – a mostly level 11km trip.

A regulation introduced in 2016 requires visitors to both sections of the park to hire a guide (foreigner Rs 800/1500 per half/full day). A half day is a maximum of three hours; a full day is any period more than three hours.

ⓘ Getting There & Away

The main gate to the Shivapuri Peak section, Pani Mohan Gate, is about 3km north of the Budhanilkantha temple, an easy 45-minute walk uphill. Trails lead from the gate to Shivapuri Peak and Nagi Gompa. A taxi from Thamel to the gate will cost Rs 700.

The main entrance to the Nagarjun Hill section is at Phulbari, about 2km north of Balaju. A ride up to the summit makes for a fine motorbike excursion. A taxi from Thamel will cost Rs 2500 including some waiting time.

PATAN

📄 01 / POP 227,000

Once a fiercely independent city-state, Patan (*pah*-tan) is now almost a suburb of Kathmandu, separated only by the murky Bagmati River. Many locals still call the city by its original Sanskrit name of Lalitpur (City of Beauty) or by its Newari name, Yala. Almost everyone who comes to Kathmandu also visits Patan's spectacular Durbar Sq – even after the 2015 earthquake, this remains the finest collection of temples and palaces in the whole of Nepal.

Another good reason to come here is to take advantage of the shops and restaurants set up to cater to the NGO workers and diplomats who live in the surrounding suburbs. Then there are Patan's fair-trade shops, selling superior handicrafts at fair prices and channelling tourist dollars to some of the most needy people in Nepal.

History

Patan has a long Buddhist history, which has even influenced the town's Hindu temples. The four corners of the city are marked by stupas said to have been erected by the great Buddhist emperor Ashoka in around 250 BC. Today there are still around 1200 Buddhist monuments scattered around the city.

The town was ruled by local noblemen until King Shiva Malla of Kathmandu conquered the city in 1597, temporarily unifying the valley. Patan's major building boom took place under the Mallas in the 16th, 17th and 18th centuries.

The 2015 earthquake did not spare Patan. Many temples were damaged and several collapsed in Durbar Sq, but as in previous quakes, the city fared better than Kathmandu and Bhaktapur.

◉ Sights

Most of the famous sights are centred on Durbar Sq. Ticket offices at either end of the square charge a combined Durbar Sq and Patan Museum (p141) entry fee. For repeat visits ensure that your visa validity date is written on the back of your ticket.

◉ Durbar Square

As in Kathmandu, the ancient Royal Palace of Patan faces on to a magnificent **Durbar Square** (Royal Square; Map p142; foreigner/SAARC Rs 1000/250; ⊙ticket office 7am-6pm). Temple construction in the square went into overdrive during the Malla period (14th to 18th centuries), particularly during the reign of King Siddhinarsingh Malla (1619–60). Despite the 2015 earthquake, this concentrated mass of temples is perhaps the most visually stunning display of Newari architecture to be seen in Nepal.

Bhimsen Temple   HINDU TEMPLE
(Map p142) At the northern end of Durbar Sq (p137) the Bhimsen Temple is dedicated to the god of trade and business, which may explain its prosperous appearance. One of the five Pandavas from the Mahabharata, Bhimsen is credited with superhuman strength – he is often depicted as a red muscleman, lifting a horse or crushing an elephant under his knee.

The three-storey pagoda has an unusual rectangular plan that sets it apart from other temples in Patan. The current temple was completely rebuilt in 1682 after a fire and was later restored after the 1934 earthquake, and again in 1967. Once repairs following the 2015 quake are complete, non-Hindus may once again be able to climb to the upper level (the inner sanctum is usually upstairs in Bhimsen temples) to view the wild-eyed statue of Bhimsen.

Manga Hiti   RELIGIOUS SITE
(Map p142) Immediately across from Bhimsen Temple is the sunken Manga Hiti, one of the water conduits with which Patan is liberally endowed. The tank contains a cruciform-shaped pool and three wonderfully carved *dhara* (water spouts) in the shape

Patan

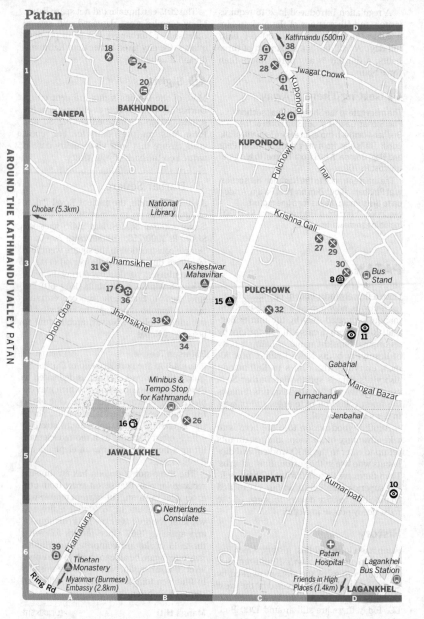

of makara (mythical crocodile-like beasts). The two wooden ceremonial pavilions that overlook the tank – known as the **Mani Mandap** (Map p142) – collapsed in the 2015 earthquake and are under repair.

Vishwanath Temple   HINDU TEMPLE
(Map p142) South of the Bhimsen Temple (p137) stands the Vishwanath Temple, dedicated to Shiva. This elaborately decorated two-tiered pagoda was built in 1627 and it features some particularly ornate woodcarv-

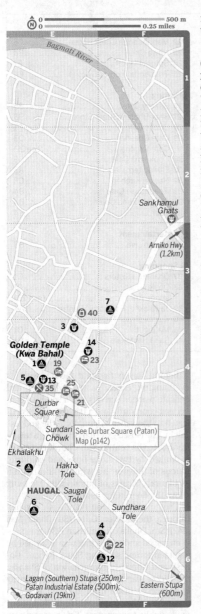

foot. When the doors are open, you can view the enormous lingam inside.

★ Krishna Mandir HINDU TEMPLE

(Map p142) Heading into Durbar Sq (p137), you can't miss the splendid Krishna Mandir built by King Siddhinarsingh Malla in 1637. Constructed from carved stone – in place of the usual brick and timber – this fabulous architectural confection shows the clear influence of Indian temple design and is the earliest stone temple of its type in Nepal. The temple stayed intact through the 2015 earthquake.

The temple consists of three tiers, fronted by columns and supporting a northern Indian-style shikhara spire. The distinctive temple is often depicted on the ornate brass butter lamps hung in Nepali homes. Non-Hindus cannot enter to view the statue of Krishna, the goatherd, but you'll often hear temple musicians playing upstairs. Vishnu's mount, the man-bird Garuda, kneels with folded arms on top of a column facing the temple. The delicate stone carvings along the beam on the 1st floor recount events from the Mahabharata, while the hard-to-see beam on the 2nd floor features scenes from the Ramayana.

A major festival, Krishna Jayanta, also known as Krishnasthami, is held here in the Nepali month of Bhadra (August to September) for Krishna's birthday.

King Yoganarendra Malla's Statue MONUMENT

(Map p142) South of the Jagannarayan Temple (Char Narayan Temple; Map p142) is a tall column topped by a striking brass statue of King Yoganarendra Malla (r 1684–1705) and his queens. Installed in 1700, the column toppled in the 2015 earthquake but was one of the first items to be restored. Looming over the king's head is a cobra, and alighted on the head of the cobra is a small brass bird.

Legend has it that as long as the bird remains, the king may still return to his palace. Accordingly a door and window of the palace are always kept open and a hookah pipe is kept ready. A rider to the legend adds that when the bird flies off, the elephants in front of the Vishwanath Temple will stroll over the Manga Hiti (p137) for a drink.

Behind the statue of the king are three smaller Vishnu temples (Map p142; Durbar Sq), including a brick-and-plaster shikhara temple, built in 1590 to enshrine an image of Narsingha, Vishnu's man-lion incarnation.

ing, especially on the torana (lintel) above the colonnade.

On the west side is a statue of Shiva's loyal mount, Nandi the bull, while the east side features two stone elephants with mahouts, one elephant crushing a man beneath its

Patan

⊙ Top Sights

1	Golden Temple (Kwa Bahal)	E4

⊙ Sights

	Gauri Shankar Temple	(see 13)
2	I Baha Bahi	E5
3	Kumbeshwar Temple	E4
4	Mahabouddha Temple	F6
5	Maru Mandapa Mahavihar	E4
6	Minnath Temple	E5
7	Northern Stupa	F3
8	Peace Gallery	D3
9	Pim Bahal Pokhari	D4
10	Rato Machhendranath Temple	D5
11	Sulima Square	D4
12	Uku Bahal	F6
13	Uma Maheshwar Temple	E4
14	Uma Maheshwar Temple	E4
15	Western Stupa	C3
16	Zoo	B5

☺ Activities, Courses & Tours

17	Pranamaya Yoga	B3
18	Summit Nepal Trekking	A1

⌂ Sleeping

19	Cosy Nepal	E4
20	Hotel Greenwich Village	B1
21	Inn Patan	E4
22	Mahabuddha Guest House	F6
23	Newa Chén	E4
24	Summit Hotel	B1
25	Traditional Homes Swotha	E4

⊗ Eating

26	Bakery Café	B5
27	Bhat Bheteni Super Store	D3
28	Bricks Cafe	C1
29	Café Cheeno	D3
	Cafe Swotha	(see 21)
30	Dhokaima Café	D3
31	El Mediterraneo	A3
32	Newari Kitchen	C3
33	Roadhouse Cafe	B4
34	Sing Ma Food Court	B4
35	Yala	E4

⊙ Entertainment

36	Moksh Live	B3

⌂ Shopping

37	Dhankuta Sisters	C1
38	Dhukuti	C1
	Image Ark	(see 23)
39	Jawalakhel Handicraft Centre	A6
40	Kumbeshwar Technical School	E3
41	Mahaguthi	C1
42	Sana Hastakala	C1

Taleju Bell　　　　　MONUMENT
(Map p142) Facing the Royal Palace is a huge, ancient bell, hanging between two stout pillars, erected by King Vishnu Malla in 1736. Petitioners could ring the bell to alert the king to their grievances. It's said the bell tolled ominously during the 2015 earthquake. Behind the bell pavilion is a small ornamental water feature.

Krishna Temple　　　　HINDU TEMPLE
(Chyasim Deval; Map p142) This attractive, octagonal stone temple completes the 'front line' of temples in Durbar Sq (p137). It has strong architectural similarities to the Krishna temple at the north end of the square. The tiered structure was built in 1723 in a style clearly influenced by the stone temples of northern India.

Royal Palace　　　　PALACE
(Map p142) Forming the entire eastern side of Durbar Sq (p137), the Royal Palace of Patan was originally built in the 14th century, and expanded during the 17th and 18th centuries by Siddhinarsingh Malla, Srinivasa Malla and Vishnu Malla. The Patan palace predates the palaces in Kathmandu and Bhaktapur and is one of the architectural highlights of Nepal.

Behind the extravagant facade, with its overhanging eaves, carved windows and delicate wooden screens, are a series of connecting courtyards and a trip of temples dedicated to the valley's main deity, the goddess Taleju. The closed external **Bhairab gateway** leading to the central Mul Chowk courtyard is flanked by two stone lions and colourful murals of Shiva in his wrathful incarnation as Bhairab. Strings of buffalo guts are hung above the door in his honour.

The northern courtyard is reached through the **Golden Gate** (Sun Dhoka; Map p142) (Sun Dhoka). Installed in 1734, this finely engraved and gilded gateway is topped by a golden torana showing Shiva, Parvati, Ganesh and Kumar (an incarnation of Skanda, the god of war). Directly above the gateway is a window made from gold foil wrapped around a timber frame, where the king once made public appearances. This gateway now forms the entrance to the Patan Museum and northern ticket office.

Restoration works following the 2015 earthquake are not the first to take place at the palace. Reconstruction followed the conquest of the valley by Prithvi Narayan Shah in 1768, and again after the earthquake of 1934.

★**Patan Museum**   MUSEUM
(Map p142; ☎ 01-5521492; www.patanmuseum.gov.
np; admission with Durbar Sq foreigner/SAARC Rs
1000/250; ☺8am-6pm) Formerly the residence
of the Malla kings, the section of the Royal
Palace surrounding Keshav Narayan Chowk
now houses one of the finest collections of
religious art in Asia. The museum is a national
treasure and an invaluable introduction to
the art, symbolism and architecture of the
valley. You need at least an hour, and preferably
two, to do this place justice, and it's worth
taking a break at the Museum Café (p149)
before diving in for another round.

The collection is displayed in a series of
brick and timber rooms, linked by steep and
narrow stairways. There are informative
labels on each of the hundreds of statues,
carvings and votive objects, allowing you to
put a name to many of the deities depicted
at temples around the valley.

There are also some interesting displays
on the techniques used to create these wonderful
objects, including the art of repoussé
and the 'lost-wax' method of casting. The
top floor houses some fascinating photos of
Patan at the end of the 19th century.

The museum has a shop selling reproductions
of some of the works displayed inside.
For a sneak preview of the museum's
highlights and the story of its renovation, go
to www.asianart.com/patan-museum. Photography
is allowed.

★**Mul Chowk**   COURTYARD
(Map p142; Durbar Sq; admission with Durbar
Sq/Patan Museum ticket foreigner/SAARC Rs
1000/250) South of the Patan Museum, a
gateway opens onto the stately Mul Chowk,
the largest and oldest of the Royal Palace's
three main chowk (squares). The original
buildings were destroyed by fire in 1662 but
rebuilt just three years later by Srinivasa
Malla. The temples in the courtyard were
restored in 2014 and the surrounding walls
and buildings were quickly restored after
the 2015 earthquake.

In the centre of the square is the small,
gilded, central **Bidyapith Temple** (Map
p142), beside a wooden post used to secure
animals for sacrifices. The central deity is
Yantaju, a form of Durga, and a personal deity
to the Malla kings.

On the south side of the square is the
Taleju Bhawani Temple (Map p142; Durbar
Sq), flanked by statues of the river goddesses
Ganga, on a tortoise, and Jamuna, on a
makara. The upper galleries now form part

of the museum's architectural displays, with
fine examples of carved wooden struts.

At the northeastern corner of the square is
the **Degutalle Temple**, topped by an octagonal
triple-roofed tower. The larger, triple-roofed
Taleju Temple is directly north,
looking over Durbar Sq, and dedicated to
Taleju, another protective deity of the Malla
kings.

★**Sundari Chowk**   COURTYARD
(Map p142) South of Mul Chowk (p141) is the
smaller Sundari Chowk, arranged around a
superbly carved sunken water tank known
as the **Tusha Hiti** (Map p142; Durbar Sq). The
chowk was restored in 2014, and again after
the 2015 earthquake. Built in 1647, the
renovated water tank has 72 carved stone
plaques depicting Tantric deities and was
used by the king for ritual ablutions. The
spout is new; the original was stolen in 2010
(and recovered). Ancient carved wooden
struts lie scattered in the corners.

On the way out look at the restored
Bhandarkhal water tank (Map p142), once
the main water supply for the palace, featuring
a charming meditation pavilion.

Back in Durbar Sq (p137), the traditional
gateway to Sundari Chowk features three
magnificent statues of **Hanuman** (barely
recognisable beneath layers of orange
paint), **Ganesh** and Vishnu as **Narsingha**,
the man-lion, tearing out the entrails of a
demon.

EARTHQUAKE DAMAGE IN PATAN

Although Patan weathered the 2015
earthquake better than Kathmandu
and Bhaktapur – as was the case in the
1934 quake – several iconic temples
completely collapsed. The government,
with the help of foreign governments and
local organisations, has begun to restore
the damaged monuments, including
the Jagannarayan Temple (p139), **Hari
Shankar Temple** (Map p142), Mani
Mandap (p138) pavilions and statue of
King Yoganarendra Malla (p139). The
latter was one of the first completed, and
rebuilding of the others was ongoing in
2017. Nevertheless, enough buildings remain
to ensure that Patan's Durbar Sq is
still spectacular, and a world-class repository
of medieval art and architecture.

Durbar Square (Patan)

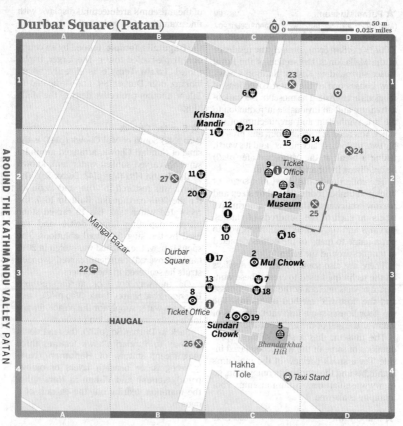

Durbar Square (Patan)

◎ **Top Sights**

◎ North of Durbar Square

★ Golden Temple

(Kwa Bahal) BUDDHIST TEMPLE
(Hiranya Varna Mahavihara; Map p138; foreigner/SAARC Rs 50/20; ☺5am-6pm) This unique Buddhist monastery is just north of Durbar Sq (p137). It was allegedly founded in the 12th century, and it has existed in its current form since 1409. The temple gets its name from the gilded metal plates that cover most of its frontage and it is one of the most beautiful in Patan.

Entry is via an ornate narrow stone doorway to the east, or a wooden doorway to the west from one of the interlinked courtyards on the north side of Nakabhil.

Entering from the east, note the gaudy lions and the 1886 signature of Krishnabir, the master stonemason who sculpted the fine doorway with its frieze of Buddhist deities. This second doorway leads to the main courtyard of the Golden Temple; shoes and leather articles must be removed to enter the lower courtyard. The main priest of the temple is a young boy under the age of 12, who serves for 30 days before handing the job over to another young boy.

The temple itself is a magnificent example of courtyard temple architecture. Two elephant statues guard the doorway and the facade is covered by a host of gleaming Buddhist figures. Inside the main shrine is a beautiful statue of Sakyamuni (no photos allowed). To the left of the courtyard is a statue of Green Tara and in the right corner is a statue of the Bodhisattva Vajrasattva wearing an impressive silver-and-gold cape. Both are inside inner shrines.

Facing the main temple is a smaller shrine containing a 'self-arisen' *(swayambhu)* chaitya. The four corners of the courtyard have statues of four Lokeshvaras (incarnations of Avalokiteshvara) and four monkeys, which hold out jackfruits as an offering. A stairway leads to an upper-floor chapel dedicated to a white eight-armed Avalokiteshvara, lined with Tibetan-style frescoes including a wheel of life. Finally, as you leave the temple at the eastern exit, look up to see an embossed mandala mounted on the ceiling. Outside of winter, look for the tortoises pottering around the compound – these are the temple guardians.

It's worth ducking south towards Durbar Sq to see the small, two-tiered **Uma Maheshwar Temple** (Map p138) and the handsome stone **Gauri Shankar Temple** (Map p138), in the Indian shikhara style. Across the road, the Buddhist **Maru Mandapa Mahavihar** (Map p138) is set in a small courtyard.

Kumbeshwar Temple HINDU TEMPLE
(Map p138) Due north of Durbar Sq (p137) is the eye-catching Kumbeshwar Temple, one of the valley's three five-storey temples. This tall, thin mandir (temple) features some particularly artistic woodcarving, and it seems to defy gravity as it towers above the surrounding houses. Amazingly, this precarious structure survived the earthquake, though the top tier toppled in May 2015 and the tower is now leaning slightly. A large Nandi statue and central lingam indicate that the shrine is sacred to Shiva.

The temple platform has two ponds whose water is said to come straight from the holy lake at Gosainkund, a weeklong trek north of the valley. Bathing in the tank at Kumbeshwar Temple is said to be as meritorious as making the arduous walk to Gosainkund.

The surrounding square is dotted with temples sacred to Bhairab and Baglamukhi (Parvati). Local women gather at the tank known as **Konti Hiti** to socialise, wash clothes and fill up their water jugs. Down an alley to the north of the temple is the Kumbeshwar Technical School (p151).

From here you can detour north to see the Northern Stupa (p136), one of four marker shrines showing the old city limits of Patan.

Uma Maheshwar Temple HINDU TEMPLE
(Map p138) Peer inside this temple to see a very beautiful black-stone relief of Shiva and Parvati in the pose known as Uma Maheshwar – the god sitting cross-legged with his consort leaning against him rather seductively.

Pim Bahal Pokhari POND
(Map p138) This large pond is a hidden gem centred around a charming lakeshore pavilion. On the north side is three-tiered **Chandeswari Temple** built in 1663. Walk around the pond clockwise and you'll pass a 600-year-old whitewashed stupa that was damaged by Muslim invaders in 1357.

Sulima Square COURTYARD
(Map p138) Northeast of the Pim Bahal Pokhari is Sulima Sq, a crumbling brick-lined space with a 17th-century Mahadev (Shiva) shrine. On the east side of the square is the derelict house of a famous 16th-century Tantric master.

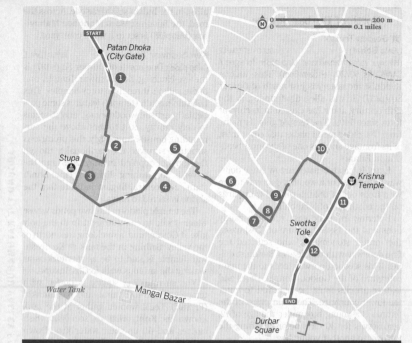

Town Walk
Patan: North of Durbar Square

START PATAN DHOKA
END DURBAR SQ
LENGTH 1.5KM; TWO HOURS

From Patan Dhoka, stroll southeast to a handsome two-storey **1 Ganesh shrine**, then swing right past **2 Sulima Square** to the **3 Pim Bahal Pokhari** (p143) pond, which is flanked by a large stupa. A sign on the stupa's southern side describes its history.

At the road junction on the southeast corner of the pond, walk northeast past fine wooden windows to a large square at Nakabhil. On the south side is the courtyard-style **4 Lokakirti Mahavihar**, a former Buddhist monastery. An old retired runner for the chariot used during the Rato Machhendranath Festival sits by the front door. Masked dances are performed on the *dabali* (platform) in front of the monastery during festival time. An alley ('Bhaskar Varna Mahavihar') leads north off the square to the courtyard of **5 Nyakhuchowk Bahal**.

Head past a row of stupas to the eastern wall and go through the covered entrance

(signed 'please mind your head'), straight across an alley, into another chaitya-filled courtyard, the **6 Naga Bahal**. Head left then right to walk past the Hindu statue of a bull to a caged-off painting of a naga on a wall.

Go through the eastern passageway to the Ilanani Courtyard with the red-walled Harayana Library in the southwestern corner. Follow a diagonal path to the southeastern corner and walk beneath a wooden torana to enter the **7 Golden Temple** (p143).

Exit east onto a street, then turn left. A few doors down you'll see a small blue sign for the courtyard-style **8 Manjushri Temple** on your left. From here, continue north past a group of ancient **9 megaliths**, possibly the oldest objects of worship in the Kathmandu Valley, and continue to the impressive **10 Kumbeshwar Temple** (p143).

Head east and take a right (south) to Durbar Sq. This road is lined with shrines to Vishnu, including the two-tiered **11 Uma Maheshwar Temple** (p143). Further south, at Swotha Tole is the Garuda-fronted **12 Narayan Temple**. It's a few more steps to Durbar Sq.

◉ South of Durbar Square

Most sights south of Durbar Sq (p137) are in the backstreets south of Mangal Bazar, the main local shopping street. If you continue south, you will reach the busy marketplace surrounding the Lagankhel bus stand.

I Baha Bahi   BUDDHIST MONASTERY

(Map p138) Just a one-minute walk south of Durbar Sq (p137), a large doorway flanked by black lions with Cheshire-cat grins leads to a quiet bahal containing the I Baha Bahi. This handsome Buddhist monastery was founded in 1427 and the structure was restored in the 1990s by a team of architects from Japan.

Minnath Temple   BUDDHIST TEMPLE

(Map p138) Just 200m south of I Baha Bahi, a large water tank marks the entrance to a courtyard strewn with wooden beams. In the centre is the brightly painted, two-tiered Minnath Temple, dedicated to the Bodhisattva Jatadhari Lokesvara, who is considered to be the little brother of Rato Machhendranath. The temple was founded in the Licchavi period (3rd to 9th centuries), but the multi-armed goddesses on the roof struts were added much later.

Note the metal pots and pans nailed to the temple rafters by devotees. The timbers surrounding the temple are assembled into a chariot every year to haul the statue of Minnath around town as part of the Rato Machhendranath Festival (p147).

Rato Machhendranath Temple   TEMPLE

(Map p138) Almost directly across the road from the Minnath Temple, down an alley, a white-columned gateway leads to the wide, open square containing the revered Rato Machhendranath Temple. Dedicated to the god of rain and plenty, the temple, like so many in Nepal, blurs the line between Buddhism and Hinduism. Buddhists regard Rato (Red) Machhendranath as an incarnation of Avalokiteshvara, while Hindus see him as an incarnation of Shiva.

Set inside a protective metal fence, the towering three-storey temple dates from 1673, but there has been some kind of temple on this site since at least 1408. The temple's four ornate doorways are guarded by stone snow lions, and at ground level on the four corners of the temple plinth are yeti-like demons known as *kyah*.

Mounted on freestanding pillars at the front of the temple is a curious collection of metal animals in protective cages, including a peacock, Garuda, horse, buffalo, lion, elephant, fish and snake. Look up to see the richly painted roof struts of the temple, which show Avalokiteshvara standing above figures being tortured in hell.

The main image of Machhendranath resides here for six months a year, before moving to Bungamati during the spectacular Rato Machhendranath Festival (p147) in April/May.

Mahabouddha Temple   BUDDHIST TEMPLE

(Map p138; Rs 50; ◷9am-5.30pm) As you step through the entryway of this hard-to-find courtyard in the southeast of Patan, the temple suddenly looms above you, crammed in like a plant straining to get some sunlight. Built in the Indian shikhara style, the shrine takes its name from the hundreds of terracotta tiles that cover it, each bearing an image of the Buddha. The shikhara is upright, although it was cloaked in heavy-duty scaffolding when we last visited.

The temple dates from 1585, but was totally rebuilt after the 1934 earthquake. Unfortunately, without plans to work from, the builders ended up with a different-looking temple, and had enough bricks and tiles left over to construct a smaller shrine to Maya Devi, the Buddha's mother, in the courtyard.

NARSINGHA

The image of Vishnu in his man-lion incarnation as Narsingha (or Narsimha) can be seen all over the Kathmandu Valley. The deity is normally depicted gleefully disembowelling the demon Hiranyakashipu with his bare hands, recalling a famous legend from the Bhagavata Purana. Because of a deal made with Brahma, the demon was granted special powers – he could not be killed by man or beast, either inside or outside, on the ground or in the air, by day or by night, nor by any weapon. Vishnu neatly got around these protections by adopting the form of a man-lion and killing the demon with his fingernails, at dusk, on his lap, on the threshold of the house. You can see statues of Narsingha at his grisly work at the Gokarna Mahadev Temple, in front of the palace in Patan and just inside the Hanuman Dhoka entrance in Kathmandu.

DON'T MISS

IMAGES OF WAR

Nepal's decade-long civil war has been marked by a photo exhibition that brings the conflict poignantly to life. Based on the book *A People War* by *Nepali Times* editor Kunda Dixit, the exhibition is on display at the **Peace Gallery** (Map p138; ☑ school office 01-5522614; ⊙ 10am-4pm) inside the Rato Bangla School. It's possible the exhibition will find a new home, in which case contact the **Bhaktapur Tourism Development Committee** (Map p158; www.btdc.org.np; Taumadhi Tole) for updates.

Images include portraits of schoolchildren giving the Maoist red salute, of siblings who faced each other on either side of the front line and a teacher who continued to teach despite having his hands cut off by Maoists. It's everything photojournalism should be – nuanced, moving, surprising and never simplistic.

Enter the school, just behind Dhokaima Café (p150), and ask for directions. The gallery is on the 4th floor of an administration building.

The temple is loosely modelled on the Mahabouddha Temple at Bodhgaya in India, where the Buddha gained enlightenment.

The surrounding lanes are full of shops selling high-quality Patan-style metal statues. The roof terrace of the shop at the back of the courtyard has a good view of the temple.

To reach the Mahabouddha Temple, you must walk southeast from Durbar Sq along Hakha Tole, passing a series of small Vaishnavite and Shaivite temples. When you reach Sundhara Tole, with its temple and sunken hiti (water tank) with three brass water spouts, turn right and look for the tiny doorway leading to the temple.

Uku Bahal   BUDDHIST MONASTERY
(Rudra Varna Mahavihar; Map p138; Rs 50; ⊙ 9am-5.30pm) South of the Mahabouddha Temple (p145), this ancient Buddhist monastery is one of the best known in Patan. The main courtyard is jam-packed with statuary and metalwork – dorje (thunderbolt symbols), bells, peacocks, elephants, Garudas, rampant goats, kneeling devotees, a regal-looking statue of a Rana general and, rather incongruously, a pair of Victorian-style British lions that look like they could have been lifted straight from London's Trafalgar Sq.

The monastery has been used for centuries, and the wooden roof struts are some of the oldest in the valley, but much of what you can see today dates back to the 19th century. Behind the monastery is a Swayambhunath-style stupa accessed by a side door.

◎ West of Durbar Square

Zoo   ZOO
(Map p138; ☑ 01-5528323; adult/child foreigner Rs 750/375, SAARC Rs 250/125, Nepali Rs 150/90; ⊙ 10am-5pm, to 4pm Dec-Mar) Nepal's only zoo is in southwestern Patan by the Jawalakhel roundabout. The animals live in better conditions than you might expect and there are always crowds of local kids being wowed by such exotic creatures as elephants, tigers, leopards, hyenas, gaur, blue bulls, gharial, langur monkeys and some very noisy hippos.

🏃 Activities

Pranamaya Yoga   YOGA
(Map p138; ☑ 9851002920; www.pranamaya-yoga.com; ground fl, Moksh Complex, Gyanmandala, Jhamsikhel; classes from Rs 700; ⊙ 8am-8pm) Branch of the well-run chain of yoga centres, inside a courtyard. See the website for a schedule.

🎊 Festivals & Events

Rato Machhendranath Festival   RELIGIOUS
See boxed text opposite.

Janai Purnima Festival   RELIGIOUS
(⊙ Jul/Aug) Thousands of pilgrims visit the Kumbeshwar Temple (p143) in July/August, as members of the Brahmin and Chhetri castes replace the sacred thread they wear looped over their left shoulder. A silver-and-gold lingam is set up in the tank and devotees take a ritual bath while jhankri (faith healers) in colourful headdresses dance around the temple beating drums.

🛏 Sleeping

Most people visit Patan on a day trip from Kathmandu, which is a shame because there's a small but stylish spread of accommodation, including some charming traditional options, especially in the upper midrange category. The city becomes a different place once the crowds of day-trippers retreat across the Bagmati. Stay overnight and you'll be able to explore the myriad *tole* (squares) and bahal (courtyards) at your leisure.

Café de Patan HOTEL $
(Map p142; ☏ 01-5537599; www.cafedepatan.com; s/d Rs 1490/1865, without bathroom Rs 870/1120) This courtyard hotel is almost on Durbar Sq (p137) and there's a rooftop garden and a pleasant downstairs cafe. The rooms are simple, with thin mattresses, but there's plenty of common seating. Six rooms have attached bathrooms.

Mahabuddha Guest House GUESTHOUSE $
(Map p138; ☏ 01-5540575; mhg@mos.com.np; s/d Rs 600/800, ste Rs 1200; ☎) Southeast of Durbar Sq (p137), across the road from the Mahabouddha Temple (p145), this is a simple, somewhat grim budget choice. The location is a bit inconvenient and there are no common sitting areas, but the tidy rooms are acceptable and there's wi-fi. Rooms are named after Nepal's highest peaks, with the better ones higher up. Rates include tax.

Cosy Nepal ACCOMMODATION SERVICES $$
(Map p138; ☏ 9860111757; www.cosynepal.com; Swotha Sq 18; s US$35, d US$45-70; ☎) This French-Nepali agency manages several traditional houses in the old town, all renovated with modern touches. The website details the different options, from simple single crash pads to family suites with kitchenettes. All strike a great balance between traditional architecture and modern style. Discounts are available for long-term stays. The office is in a hidden courtyard next to the main Yala Chhen address at Swotha Sq, behind Cafe Swotha (p149). Book in advance.

Newa Chén BOUTIQUE HOTEL $$
(Map p138; ☏ 01-5533532; www.newachen.com; s/d US$35/50, without bathroom US$25/40, deluxe US$45/60; @☎) Housed inside the Unesco-restored Shestha House mansion, this place is more traditional than most and offers a window onto what it must have been like to be a well-to-do resident of Patan in centuries past. Rooms are all different but are decked out in traditional style, with divan seating areas and coir matting, and there's a nice communal living room.

On a practical level the roadside rooms are noisy during the day, while anyone over 5ft 6in tall will feel a bit cramped. Rates include breakfast.

Inn Patan BOUTIQUE HOTEL $$$
(Map p138; ☏ 01-5547834; www.theinnpatan.com; s/d US$80/90, ste s/dUS$90/100; ☎) This century-old residence has been converted into a stylish and well-run boutique hotel, albeit with original low doorways and ceilings. The harmonious use of cream tones and natural fibres gives a sense of calm, while designer touches like niche lighting and walk-in showers bring hints of luxury. The suite room is worth it for the extra space and private balcony.

RATO MACHHENDRANATH FESTIVAL

The image in the Rato Machhendranath Temple (p145) may look like a crudely carved piece of painted wood, but each year it forms the centrepiece for the Rato Machhendranath Festival in the Nepali month of Baisakh (April/May). Machhendranath is considered to have powers over rain and, since the monsoon is approaching at this time, this festival is essentially a plea for generous rains. Buddhists regard Rato (Red) Machhendranath as an incarnation of Avalokiteshvara, while Hindus see him as an incarnation of Shiva.

Immediately prior to the festival, the scattered timbers of Rato Machhendranath's chariot are gathered and assembled and the statue is installed on his awesome coach. It takes a full month to move the chariot across Patan to Jawalakhel, where the chariot is finally dismantled. The main chariot is so large and the route is so long that the Nepali army is often called in to help transport it.

The towering main chariot is accompanied for much of its journey by a smaller chariot, which contains the image of Rato Machhendranath's companion, Jatadhari Lokesvara, which normally resides in the Minnath Temple (p145). The highlight of the festival is the **Bhoto Jatra**, or showing of the sacred vest. According to the legend, the jewelled vest was given to the god for safe keeping after a dispute between two potential owners. Every year, the vest is displayed three times in order to give the owner the chance to claim it.

From Jawalakhel, Rato Machhendranath is conveyed on a khat (palanquin) to his second home in the village of Bungamati, 6km to the south, where he spends the next six months of the year, before returning to Patan.

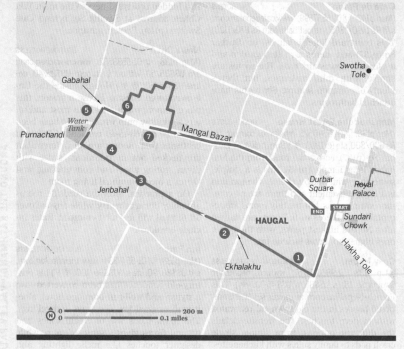

🚶 Town Walk
Patan: South of Durbar Square

START DURBAR SQ
END DURBAR SQ
LENGTH 1.25KM; ONE HOUR

Start this walk by heading south from Durbar Sq (p137), then take the lane leading west to the **1 Bishwakarma (Bishokarma) Temple**, whose facade is covered with embossed copper. The temple is dedicated to the patron deity of carpenters and craftspeople, many of whom you'll hear banging away in the surrounding workshops.

Continuing northwest past the **2 Vishnu shrines** of Ekhalakhu junction, you next pass a Ganesh shrine, a Shiva shrine, another three-tiered **3 Ganesh Temple** at Jenbahal junction and then a shikhara-style **4 Narayan Temple**.

At Purnachandi junction, turn right past a collapsed **5 Vaishnavite Temple** to the junction at Gabahal. Turn right and look for a small gateway on the left, guarded by a pair of snow lions, leading to **6 Bubahal**, a courtyard full of Buddhist statues and chaityas in front of the ornate Yasodhar Mahabihar Temple.

Here's where things get fun! It's possible to continue east along the main road to reach the Haka Bahal but it's much better to detour through the maze of interconnecting courtyards. Follow our instructions, leave a popcorn trail and if in doubt turn right.

From the Bubahal courtyard take the far right (northeastern) entryway through a courtyard into a second hidden courtyard with ornate wooden windows. Continue through the far (northeastern) corner into a third courtyard with a black chaitya. Exit through a door in the eastern side, through a dark alleyway to another courtyard. Take the southeastern exit and swing right into another courtyard that has a well and a small printing press. Continue south through a small courtyard to a larger courtyard with a Vishnu Temple. From here you can rejoin the main road to the south and take a right to see the Haka Bahal.

Assuming you aren't hopelessly lost (well done!), pop into **7 Haka Bahal**, the restored courtyard of the Ratnakar Mahavihar. Continue east through Mangal Bazar to finish at the south end of Durbar Sq.

Traditional Homes Swotha BOUTIQUE HOTEL **$$$**
(Map p138; ☑01-5551184; www.traditionalhomes.
com.np; s/d US$80/90, ste US$120-160; ☎) Just
50m from Durbar Sq (p137), this 70-year-old
house has been revamped into stylish accom-
modation. Unlike most traditional homes,
the nine rooms here are bright and spacious,
with pressed-concrete floors, reclaimed wood
and gas heaters. Bathrooms are small due to
the nature of the house, but eight rooms en-
joy a private balcony. The attached Cafe Swo-
tha is also recommended.

Summit Hotel RESORT **$$$**
(Map p138; ☑01-5522843; www.summit-nepal.
com; r from US$110; ❋@☎☳) Expats and
NGOs like to keep the Summit secret so that
there is room when relatives and friends
come to visit. The Dutch-founded resort-
style hotel is built in mock-Newari style,
with lots of red brick and carved timber, and
the atmosphere is superbly romantic and relaxed. The Garden Wing and larger and pricier Himalayan View rooms are delightful.

The swimming pool comes into its own in
summer, while multiple fireplaces keep things
snug in winter, especially in the cosy bar. The
hotel is tucked away in the quiet lanes west of
Kupondol, offering fine views over Kathmandu. Weekend barbecues are a highlight.

Hotel Greenwich Village HOTEL **$$$**
(Map p138; ☑01-5521780; www.greenwichnepal.
com; s/d from US$85/95, deluxe r US$110; ❋☎☳)
The oddly named Greenwich Village is
peaceful and secluded, though less luxurious
than the rates might suggest. The modern
rooms are smart and comfortable, but you'll
probably spend most of your time at the love-
ly poolside patio and cafe. Foreign exchange
and airport pick-up are available on request.

✖ Eating

Several restaurants overlook Durbar Sq, of-
fering bland food but magical views, and are
aimed squarely at day-tripping tour groups.
In general, the further you get from Durbar
Sq the better the food becomes. Most places
open from 8am to 8pm.

For a classy dinner for two while in Patan,
consider the expat-oriented restaurants
around Pulchowk.

✖ Durbar Square

Third World Restaurant INTERNATIONAL **$**
(Map p142; ☑01-5543206; Durbar Sq; mains Rs
180-350; ◷9am-8pm) Located on the qui-

et western side of Durbar Sq (p137), with
budget prices, Newari set meals and good
rooftop views of the Krishna Mandir (p139).

Patan Museum Café INTERNATIONAL **$$**
(Map p142; ☑01-5526271; snacks Rs 200-400,
mains Rs 400-650, coffee Rs 175-225; ◷10am-
5pm) In the rear courtyard of the Patan Museum (p141), this pleasant open-air place is
a good spot to take a break from museum
and temple-gazing. The garden setting feels
elegant and refined, though the service can
suffer during the lunchtime group rush. You
don't need to buy a museum ticket to eat at
the cafe. Tables can be reserved.

Si Taleju Restaurant & Bar INTERNATIONAL **$$**
(Map p142; ☑01-5538358; Durbar Sq; mains Rs
300-500; ◷10am-9pm) A narrow, towering
place with four floors, each with a different
feel. Best is the top-floor dining room with
magical views north across Durbar Sq (p137)
to the mountains beyond. You'll find all your
favourites (momos, burgers, noodles, pasta,
curries) on the menu.

Café de Patan INTERNATIONAL **$$**
(Map p142; ☑01-5537599; www.cafedepatan.com;
dishes Rs 250-500; ◷8am-10pm) Southwest of
Durbar Sq behind a small Uma Maheshwar Temple, this quiet place is a long-running travellers' favourite, with an open-air
courtyard and a rooftop garden (though no
views). The menu runs to momos, Chinese
and Italian, plus numerous Newari dishes
including set meals.

Café du Temple INTERNATIONAL **$$**
(Map p142; ☑01-5527127; www.cafedutemple.
com.np; mains Rs 325-420, set meals Rs 675-775;
◷9am-9pm) A tour-group favourite at the
north end of Durbar Sq (p137). The airy roof-
top tables are covered by red-and-white sun
umbrellas and the menu runs from Chinese
fried rice to daal bhaat (traditional Nepali
dish of rice and vegetables), via chicken stro-
ganoff. The nearby sister restaurant **Casa
Pagoda** (Map p142; ☑01-5538980; mains Rs
295-595, set meals Rs 695; ◷8am-9pm) runs a
similar menu.

Cafe Swotha INTERNATIONAL **$$$**
(Map p138; mains Rs 520-1100; ◷9am-10pm)
Fresh and modern with lots of glass and
a tiny garden, Swotha serves light salads,
quiches and sandwiches made with seasonal
ingredients, plus daily specials. It's attached
to Traditional Homes Swotha.

Yala

INTERNATIONAL $$$

(Map p138; ☑ 01-5522395; www.yalamandala.com; mains Rs 550-1400; ⊙ 10am-9.30pm; ☎) An island of calm in the courtyard of the Unesco-restored Rajbhandari House, this stylish cafe and art gallery has a peaceful back terrace and a fine menu of Nepali, Newari and continental food.

✖ Elsewhere

Bakery Café

CAFE $

(Map p138; ☑ 01-5522949; www.nanglo.com.np; mains Rs 150-400; ⊙ 10.30am-9.30pm; ☎) All the branches of this excellent chain provide work for deaf Nepalis. This one by the main roundabout at Jawalakhel offers good-value coffee, momos, *dosas*, sizzlers and sandwiches.

Bhat Bhateni Super Store

SUPERMARKET $

(Map p138; www.bhatbhatenionline.com; Krishna Gali; ⊙ 7.30am-8.30pm) The largest and best-stocked supermarket in town.

★ Newari Kitchen

NEPALI $$

(Map p138; ☑ 01-5530570; www.newarikitchen. com.np; Gabahal Rd, Pulchowk; set meals Rs 170-520; ⊙ noon-10pm; ☎) This excellent-value restaurant is a great place to start exploring Newari food. The set meals are a good choice, or combine a *wo* (lentil) or *chatamari* (rice) savoury pancake with the excellent *pancha kwa* (stew with bamboo shoots, potato and dried mushrooms) for a light lunch. The patrons are mostly local Newaris, so you know the food is good.

If you really want to dive in face-first, try the *shapo mhicha* (bone marrow wrapped in tripe and deep fried). It's next to Labin Mall, just off the Pulchowk junction, a short walk from Durbar Sq.

Dhokaima Café

INTERNATIONAL $$

(Map p138; ☑ 01-5522113; mains Rs 320-600; ⊙ 7am-10pm; ☎) A sophisticated cafe set inside a Rana-era storehouse by the Patan Dhoka gateway. Shaded by a sprawling walnut tree, the courtyard garden is a peaceful place to enjoy a good range of light and healthy dishes, such as organic salads, momos or a sandwich and soup combo, plus good coffee and cakes.

Café Cheeno

INTERNATIONAL $$

(Map p138; Krishna Gali; mains Rs 350-700; ⊙ 7.30am-8pm) A great place just outside Patan Dhoka with a charming garden (sadly next door to the noisy bus stand), good salads and soups, tasty breakfast crêpes and an upper floor 'Wellness Sanctuary' for beauty treatments and massage.

Bricks Cafe

INTERNATIONAL $$

(Map p138; ☑ 01-5521756; www.brickscafe.com.np; mains Rs 250-650; ⊙ noon-10pm) This convert-

---

EXPAT EATS

The area around Kupondol, Pulchowk and Jhamsikhel is a favourite hang-out of diplomats, NGO staff and other expats, and it feels a long way from the tourist crowds of Thamel or Patan's Durbar Sq. There are now so many restaurants here that locals have dubbed the area 'Jhamel'. And when you can't face battling the traffic, there's **Foodmandu** (☑ 01-4444177; www.foodmandu.com; ⊙ 11am-8.30pm) which offers delivery to Patan or Kathmandu from over 170 local restaurants.

Sing Ma Food Court (Map p138; ☑ 01-5509092; Jhamsikhel; mains Rs 320-495; ⊙ 8.30am-9pm Sun-Fri) For the authentic tastes of Malaysia, head to this busy food court south of Pulchowk. The noodle soups, *nasi lemak* (coconut rice with anchovies) and beef rendang (dry coconut curry with lime leaves) are the real *mamak* (Malay Tamil) deal. It also does a surprisingly good cheesecake.

El Mediterraneo (Map p138; ☑ 01-5527059; Jhamsikhel; mains Rs 400-700; ⊙ 12.30-9pm) This local tapas bar feels surprisingly authentic thanks to the attentive owner, a Spanish-speaking Nepali who lived in Spain for several years. Dishes range from paella and risotto to chicken with *pisto* (tomato, peppers, onion and garlic sauce) and a particularly delicious gazpacho (available until the end of October).

Perhaps the best bet is to order a sangria and linger over the 13-course tapas menu (Rs 1080), featuring imported *jamón* and chorizo.

Roadhouse Cafe (Map p138; ☑ 01-5521755; Jhamsikhel; pizza Rs 525-675; ⊙ 11am-10pm) A stylish branch of the ever-popular Thamel pizza parlour, with a relaxed, family vibe. Pasta and other dishes are also available.

ed century-old traditional house is a great place to take a break from shopping at the nearby interior design shops of Kupondol. You can relax in the peaceful courtyard, and the food, from wood-fired pizzas and *seku-wa* (barbecued meat) to salads and burgers, is excellent. Good coffee too.

☆ Entertainment

Moksh Live LIVE MUSIC
(Map p138; ☑ 01-5528362; Gyanmandala, Jhamsik-hel; ⊙ 11am-11pm Tue-Sun) Moksh has some of the best live rock, funk and folk music in town (not just the standard cover bands), most frequently on Friday from 7.30pm but also some acoustic bands on Tuesday. Other nights there are pizzas from the outdoor oven.

🔒 Shopping

Patan is a famous centre for bronze casting, repoussé work and other metal arts. Most of the statues that you see on sale in Kathmandu are actually made in Patan, and you can save money by buying them at their source.

There are dozens of metalwork shops north and west of Durbar Sq (p137), and more around the Mahabouddha Temple (p145). The price of a bronze statue of a Buddhist or Hindu deity can range from Rs 3000 to more than Rs 100,000, depending on the size, the complexity of the casting, the level of detail and the amount of gilding and enamelling on the finished statue.

Patan is the best place in the valley for interior design and fair-trade products, specifically along Kupondol Rd, which is lined with shops that support the work of Nepali craft cooperatives, channelling money directly from travellers to disadvantaged and neglected communities.

The Jawalakhel area around the zoo has the best selection of carpet shops.

Jawalakhel Handicraft Centre CARPETS
(Map p138; ☑ 01-5521305; ⊙ 9am-noon & 1-5pm Sun-Fri) Anyone who appreciates carpets should visit this Tibetan refugee cooperative, where Nepal's enormous carpet industry was essentially born in 1960. You can watch the carpet-makers at work (the centre employs 1000 refugees) before shopping upstairs for the finished article. The quality is high, there is a good selection, the prices are transparent and staff can arrange shipping.

Carpet quality depends on knots per inch and the price is worked out per square metre. The size of a traditional Tibetan carpet

is 1.8m by 90cm (around US$500). They also sell fixed-price cashmere and yak-hair shawls. Credit cards are accepted for a 4% fee.

Image Ark ART
(Map p138; ☑ 01-5006665; www.image-ark.com; Kulimha Tole; ⊙ 10am-5pm Sun-Fri, 11am-4pm Sat) This bright and colourful modern gallery in Patan's old town casts a light on Nepali multimedia and pop art, selling both limited-edition prints and cheaper cards. It's next to the Uma Maheshwar Temple (p143) and makes for a nice break from temple gazing.

Mahaguthi FAIR TRADE
(Map p138; ☑ 01-5521607; www.mahaguthi.org; Kupondol; ⊙ 10am-6pm) Mahaguthi was founded by a Nepali disciple of Mahatma Gandhi and its Kupondol showroom is a treasure house of dhaka weavings, handmade paper, ceramics, block prints, pashminas, woodcrafts, jewellery, knitwear, statues, leather bags, embroidery and Mithila paintings. There's a smaller branch in Kathmandu's Lazimpat district. Credit cards are accepted.

Dhukuti FAIR TRADE
(Map p138; ☑ 01-5535107; Kupondol; ⊙ 9am-7pm) Dhukuti packs in three floors of home furnishings, textiles, shawls, scarves, bags and rugs from the Nupri region of Manaslu, and even has Christmas decorations, created by over 1200 low-income producers. It's probably the single best shop on Kupondol. Credit cards are accepted.

Sana Hastakala FAIR TRADE
(Map p138; ☑ 01-5522628; www.sanahastakala.com; ⊙ 9.30am-6pm Sun-Fri, 10am-5pm Sat) A recommended place for paper, batiks, Mithila crafts, felt products and clothing woven from natural fibres. Credit cards accepted.

Dhankuta Sisters FAIR TRADE
(Map p138; ☑ 9841555990; Kupondol; ⊙ 11am-6.30pm Sun-Fri) Come here for tablecloths, cushion covers and clothing made from dhaka-style cloth from eastern Nepal. Most items are cotton, but silk, banana and nettle fibres are also used.

Kumbeshwar Technical School FAIR TRADE
(Map p138; ☑ 01-5537484; www.kumbeshwar.com; Kumbeshwar 22, Lalitpur; ⊙ 9am-1pm & 2-5pm Sun-Thu, 9am-1pm Fri) Near the Kumbeshwar Temple (p143) in the backstreets of Patan, this small workshop provides disadvantaged low-caste families (primarily the *pode* or streetsweepers' caste) with training, education and a livelihood,

producing carpets, knitwear and furniture. Sales from the showroom help fund the attached primary school.

Patan Industrial Estate   ARTS & CRAFTS
(☑01-5521367; www.patan.com.np; ⊘10am-5pm Sun-Fri) Despite the unpromising name, this tourist-oriented crafts complex boasts a number of workshop showrooms selling high-quality carpets, woodcarvings and metalwork, if you have a special interest. It's around 500m southeast of Lagankhel bus stand.

❶ Information

There are banks with ATMs at Mangal Bazar, at the south end of Durbar Sq, and at Pulchowk and the restaurant street of Jawalakhel.

Probably the best hospital in the Kathmandu Valley is **Patan Hospital** (Map p138; ☑01-5522278), in the Lagankhel district of Patan. Partly staffed by Western missionaries.

❶ Getting There & Away

You can get to Patan from Kathmandu by bicycle, taxi, bus or tempo. The trip costs around Rs 400 by taxi. There's a **taxi stand** (Map p142) near Hakha Tole. **Minibuses and tempos** (Map p138) for Kathmandu congregate at Jawalakhel near the zoo.

Local buses and minibuses run frequently between Kathmandu's Ratna Park bus station and the Patan Dhoka **bus stand** (Map p138) or the chaotic **Lagankhel Bus Station** (Map p138) (Rs 15 to Rs 20, 30 minutes).

Buses and faster minibuses to the southern valley towns leave when full from Lagankhel Bus Station. There are regular services to Godavari (Rs 25, 45 minutes), Bungamati (Rs 20, 40 minutes) and Chapagaon (Rs 25, 45 minutes). Buses run until around 6.30pm. There are also frequent buses to Bhaktapur (Rs 25, 30 minutes).

An interesting route back to Kathmandu on foot or bike is to continue northeast from the Northern Stupa (p136) down to the riverside ghats at Sankhamul, across the footbridge over the Bagmati River and then up to the Arniko Hwy near the big convention centre, from where you can take a taxi or minibus back to Thamel.

BHAKTAPUR

☑01 / POP 81,728
The third of the medieval city-states in the Kathmandu Valley, Bhaktapur was always described as the best preserved. Tragically, however, the 2015 earthquake caused terrible devastation and loss of life. Nevertheless, only a few temples were destroyed, there is still much to see here and tourism is vital to the community.

Many Nepalis use the old name of Bhadgaon (pronounced bud-gown) or the Newari name Khwopa, which means City of Devotees. The name fits – Bhaktapur has three major squares full of towering temples that comprise some of the finest religious architecture in the country.

Cultural life is also proudly on display. Along narrow alleys, artisans weave cloth and chisel timber, squares are filled with drying pots, and locals gather in courtyards to bathe, collect water, play cards and socialise. To view this tapestry of Nepali life, visitors must pay a town entry fee, which helps fund temple repair and maintenance.

When it comes to sightseeing post-earthquake, the attractions remain the same as they ever were: temple-studded medieval squares, narrow cobblestone streets winding between red-brick houses, and hidden courtyards peppered with temples, statues, cisterns and wells. And Bhaktapur remains refreshingly devoid of the traffic and pollution of Kathmandu and Patan, though more and more motorbikes and cars are beginning to threaten its pedestrian charms.

However, many traditional buildings that survived the earthquake have since been declared uninhabitable and are slowly being torn down. The scars of the disaster are still clearly visible and it will take years for the city to fully recover. As you wander the streets – the best way to experience Bhaktapur – you may have to pick your way through damaged streets and rubble, and duck under temporary props securing precariously leaning walls.

History

As with many other towns in the valley, Bhaktapur grew up to service the old trade route from India to Tibet, but the city became a formal entity under King Ananda Malla in the 12th century. The oldest part of town, around Tachupal Tole, was laid out at this time.

From the 14th to the 16th century, Bhaktapur became the most powerful of the valley's three Malla kingdoms, and a new civic square was constructed at Durbar Sq in the west of the city.

Many of the city's most iconic buildings date from the rule of King Yaksha Malla (1428–82), but there was another explosion of temple-building during the reign of King Bhupatindra Malla in the 18th century. At its

ℹ ENTRY TICKETS

To enter Bhaktapur you must pay a hefty fee of US$15 (or Rs 1500). SAARC nationalities and Chinese pay Rs 500 and children under 10 are free. This fee is collected at **ticket offices** (Map p154; Palpasa Marg; ⊘ 6am-7.30pm) at over a dozen entrances to the city and your ticket will be checked whenever you pass one of the checkpoints. If you are staying here for up to a week, you need only pay the entrance fee once, but you must ask the ticket desk to write your passport number on the back of the ticket.

For longer stays (up to one year or the duration of your visa), a Bhaktapur Visitor Pass is available within a week of purchasing your entry ticket. You need to bring two passport photos and a photocopy of your visa and passport details to the **tourist information centre** (Map p158; Durbar Sq; ⊘ 6am-7.30pm) next to the **Central Ticket Booth** (Map p158; Durbar Sq; ⊘ 6am-7.30pm), which also offers maps and free internet for 30 minutes. Look out for the booklet *Bhaktapur: A Guide Book*, published by the Bhaktapur Tourism Development Committee (p146) and sold in local shops.

peak the city boasted 172 temples and monasteries, 77 water tanks, 172 pilgrim shelters and 152 wells.

The 15th-century Royal Palace in Durbar Sq was the principal seat of power in the valley until the city was conquered by Prithvi Narayan Shah in 1768 and relegated to the status of a secondary market town. An earthquake that hit in 1934 caused major damage to the city but locals were able to restore most of the buildings, though you can still see the occasional unoccupied temple plinth.

Bhaktapur's streets were paved and extensively restored in the 1970s by the German-funded Bhaktapur Development Project, which also established proper sewerage and waste-water management facilities. Reconstruction after the 2015 earthquake is altering the appearance of Bhaktapur significantly as families tear down damaged houses and rebuild ever higher with 'earthquake proof' reinforced concrete.

◉ Sights

◉ Durbar Square

Bhaktapur's Durbar Sq was once much more crowded than it is today. Victorian-era illustrations show the square packed with temples and buildings, but the disastrous earthquake of 1934 reduced many of the temples to empty brick plinths, with lion-guarded stairways leading to nowhere. More structures were destroyed in the deadly earthquake of 2015, including the iconic Vatsala Durga Temple (p156) and the **Fasidega Temple** (Map p158), and many village houses collapsed at the entrance to the square. However, there is still plenty of stunning medieval architecture on display.

Expect to be approached by a string of freelance guides as you walk around; they charge Rs 300 per hour.

Erotic Elephants Temple   HINDU TEMPLE
(Map p158) Outside the main Durbar Sq entrance gate is this little piece of architectural whimsy on the roof of the small Shiva Parvati Temple. Giving graphic representation to the lyrics 'birds do it, bees do it...', the temple roof struts feature camels, cows, armadillos and even elephants engaged in the act of making sweet love. Missionary style!

Shiva Parvati Temple   HINDU TEMPLE
(Map p158) With a plinth similar to Nyatapola Temple (p157), this much smaller version also features pairs of statues of elephants, lions, bulls and the wrestlers Jayamel and Phattu leading up the stairs. On top, a simple statue of Shiva and Parvati awaits reconstruction of the temple roof and walls.

Indrayani Temple   HINDU TEMPLE
(Map p154) Just outside Durbar Sq, head down the path near the hiti that leads down the stairs to this atmospheric Kali temple that was built around a gnarled pipal tree. Blood flows on Saturdays with animal sacrifices.

Ugrachandi & Bhairab Statues   MONUMENT
(Map p158) As you enter Durbar Sq through the western gate, look left to a gateway flanked by two stocky stone lions, erected by King Bhupatindra Malla in 1701. On either side are statues of the terrible Bhairab (right), the rending, sundering incarnation of Shiva, and his consort on the left side, the equally terrible Ugrachandi (Durga). It is said that the unfortunate sculptor had his hands cut off afterwards, to prevent him from duplicating his masterpieces.

Bhaktapur

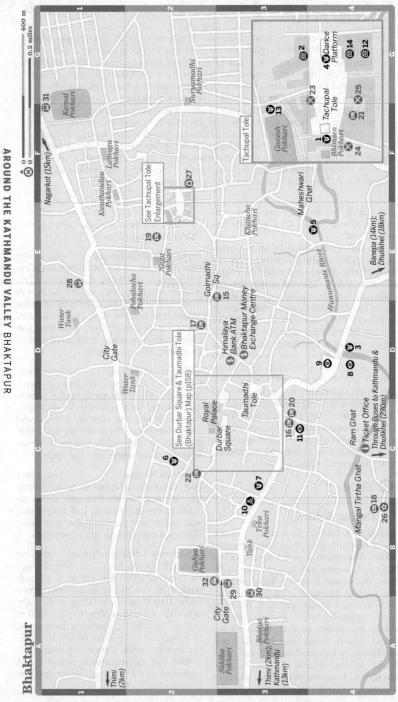

Bhaktapur

⊙ Sights
1	Bhimsen Temple	F4
2	Brass & Bronze Museum	G3
3	Cremation Plinths	D4
4	Dattatreya Temple	G4
5	Hanuman Ghat	E4
6	Indrayani Temple	C2
7	Jaya Varahi Temple	C3
8	Kathmandu University Department of Music	D4
9	Khalna Tole	D4
10	Ni Bahal	B3
	Peacock Window	(see 12)
11	Potters' Square	C3
12	Pujari Math	G4
13	Salan Ganesh Temple	F3
14	Woodcarving Museum	G4

⊜ Sleeping
15	City Guest House	E3
16	Cosy Hotel	C3
17	Ganesh Guest House	D2
18	Hotel Heritage	B4
19	Milla Guest House	E2
20	Nyatapola Guest House	C3
21	Peacock Guesthouse	F4
22	Thagu Chhen	C2

⊗ Eating
	Mayur Restaurant	(see 21)
23	New Café dé Peacock	G4
24	Newa Chhen Restaurant	F4
25	Peaceful Restaurant	G4

⊛ Entertainment
26	Downtown Pub & Grill	B4

⊜ Shopping
27	Peacock Shop	F2

⊙ Transport
28	Buses to Changu Narayan	E1
29	Buses to Kathmandu & Patan	B3
30	Buses to Kathmandu & Thimi	B3
31	Buses to Nagarkot	F1
32	Taxis	B2

Ugrachandi has 18 arms holding various Tantric weapons symbolising the multiple aspects of her character. She is depicted casually killing a demon with a trident to symbolise the victory of wisdom over ignorance. Bhairab gets by with just 12 arms, one holding two heads impaled on a trident and another holding a cup made from a human skull. The statues originally guarded a courtyard that was destroyed in the 1934 quake.

Char Dham Temples   HINDU TEMPLE
(Map p158) Standing at the western end of Durbar Sq, the four Char Dham temples were constructed to provide spiritual merit for pilgrims who were unable to make the journey to the Indian state of Uttaranchal to visit its famed Char Dham temples. After the 2015 earthquake, only three remained. The shikhara-style **Kedarnath Temple**, dedicated to Shiva, was shaken apart by the tremor, but was under reconstruction when we visited.

Although damaged, the three remaining temples are still worth visiting. The two-roofed **Gopi Nath Temple** (Jagarnath Temple; Map p158; Durbar Sq), also called Jagarnath, features different incarnations of Vishnu on the ceiling struts and a statue of Garuda on the pillar at the entrance.

The small **Rameshwar Temple** (Map p158; Durbar Sq), topped by an ornate dome, is still standing on its four repaired but cracked pillars. The **Badrinath Temple** (Map p158; Durbar Sq) is sacred to Vishnu in his incarnation as Narayan.

National Art Gallery   GALLERY
(Map p158; Durbar Sq; foreigner/SAARC Rs 150/50, camera/video Rs 100/200; ⊙10am-5pm Wed-Sun, to 3pm Mon, to 4pm Wed-Sun mid-Oct–mid-Jan) The western end of Bhaktapur's Royal Palace contains the best of the three museums in Bhaktapur. You can view an extensive collection of Tantric cloth paintings – the Hindu version of Buddhist thangkas – as well as palm-leaf manuscripts, and metal, stone and wooden votive objects, some of which date from the 12th century. Keep your ticket as this also covers the Woodcarving Museum (p159) and Brass & Bronze Museum (p160) in Tachupal Tole.

The entrance to the gallery is flanked by two huge guardian lions, one male and one female. Beside the lions are some imposing 17th-century statues of Hanuman the monkey god, in his four-armed Tantric form, and Vishnu, as the gut-ripping Narsingha.

Inside the gallery are portraits of all the Shah kings, including a surly Gyanendra (the last of the Nepali kings) following the abolition of the monarchy in 2008. In the first gallery look out for depictions of the nightmarish Maha Sambhara, with 21 faces and an unbelievable number of arms, and then turn around on the spot for scenes from the Kama Sutra.

★ **Golden Gate** HISTORIC BUILDING

(Sun Dhoka; Map p158; Durbar Sq) The magnificent Golden Gate is a visual highlight of Durbar Sq. Set into a bright red gatehouse surrounded by white palace walls, the fabulous golden portal boasts some of Nepal's finest repoussé metalwork. The gilded torana features a fabulous Garuda wrestling with a number of supernatural serpents, while below is a four-headed and 10-armed figure of the goddess Taleju Bhawani, the family deity of the Malla kings.

Construction of the gate began during the reign of King Bhupatindra Malla (r 1696–1722), and the project was completed by his successor, Jaya Ranjit Malla, in 1754. The death of Jaya Ranjit Malla marked the end of the Malla dynasty and the end of the golden age of Newari architecture in Nepal.

The gate opens to the inner courtyards of the **Royal Palace**, a once vast compound until the 1934 earthquake levelled all but a handful of its 99 courtyards. More walls toppled during the 2015 earthquake. To the right of the Golden Gate is the **55 Window Palace** (Map p158; Durbar Sq), which, you guessed it, has 55 intricate wooden windows stretching along its upper level.

As you enter the palace complex, hidden behind grills in the darkness on either side of the inner gate is a pair of enormous **war drums** (Map p158; Durbar Sq), which were used to rouse the city in the event of attack. From here you'll pass the two statues of traditionally dressed guards standing either side of an ornate door, brought here from Rajasthan.

Continuing on you'll reach the main entrance to Mul Chowk, the oldest part of the palace and the site of **Taleju Temple** (Map p158; Durbar Sq), built in 1553. Damaged in the quake but not destroyed, it is one of the most sacred temples in Bhaktapur. Only Hindus can enter, but you can peer in and admire its entrance, which is fronted by magnificent woodcarvings. Photography is prohibited.

Continuing on around the corner from Mul Chowk is the **Naga Pokhari** (Map p158), a 17th-century water tank used for the ritual immersion of the idol of Taleju. The pool is encircled by a writhing stone cobra and other serpents rise up in the middle and at the end of the tank, where water pours from a magnificent *dhara* (spout) in the form of a goat being eaten by a makara.

King Bhupatindra Malla's Column MONUMENT

(Map p158) With hands folded in a prayer position, the bronze statue of King Bhupatindra Malla sits atop a column in front of the **Vatsala Durga Temple** (Map p158; Durbar Sq). The statue was created in 1699 and similar statues were erected in the Durbar Sqs of Kathmandu and Patan. Both of the latter collapsed in 2015; Patan's was restored, but Kathmandu's was awaiting restoration at the time of research. Bhupatindra was the best known of the Malla kings of Bhaktapur, and contributed to much of the architecture in town.

Taleju Bell MONUMENT

(Map p158) In front of what once was the Vatsala Durga Temple is a large bell, which was erected by King Jaya Ranjit Malla in 1737 to mark morning and evening prayers at the Taleju Temple. A smaller bell on the plinth of the Vatsala Durga Temple was known as the 'barking bell'. According to legend, it was erected by King Bhupatindra Malla in 1721 to counteract a vision he had in a dream, and dogs were said to bark and whine when the bell was rung. Unfortunately it was damaged when the temple collapsed in 2015 and it now sits forlornly in a corner of the entrance to Mul Chowk. Behind the bell pavilion is an ornate sunken hiti containing a fine stone *dhara* in the form of a makara, topped by a crocodile and a frog – the only part of the famous Vatsala Durga Temple to survive the 2015 earthquake.

Chyasilin Mandap MONUMENT

(Map p158) 'Chyasilin' refers to the eight-cornered roof of this pavilion. It was rebuilt in 1990 using old photos and paintings and components from the original building, which was destroyed in the 1934 earthquake. With modern steel-frame technology underpinning it, it survived the 2015 earthquake. The original was used to receive royal guests, the upper floor used as a viewing platform during festivals, and at least once it was the venue of a poetry competition.

Pashupatinath Temple HINDU TEMPLE

(Map p158) Behind the Vatsala Durga Temple, the Pashupatinath Temple is dedicated to Shiva as Pashupati and is a replica of the main shrine at Pashupatinath. Originally built by King Yaksha Malla in 1475 (or 1482), it is the oldest temple in Durbar Sq. Like many temples, the roof struts feature erotic images, but what exactly the dwarf is doing with that bowl takes things to a new level.

Siddhi Lakshmi Temple HINDU TEMPLE

(Map p158) The attractive 17th-century stone Siddhi Lakshmi Temple stood by the southeastern corner of Bhaktapur palace until it collapsed in the 2015 earthquake. The steps up to where the temple once stood remain and are flanked by male and female attendants, each leading a child and a rather eager-looking dog. On successive levels the stairs are flanked by horses, garlanded rhinos, human-faced lions and camels. The temple itself was built in the classic shikhara style, commonly seen in northern India.

Behind the temple is a neglected corner of Durbar Sq that contains a pair of massive, lost-looking curly haired **stone lions** (Map p158; Durbar Sq). The small red-brick Vatsala Temple was destroyed in the 2015 earthquake.

Tadhunchen Bahal BUDDHIST TEMPLE

(Chatur Varna Mahavihara; Map p158) Walking east from Durbar Sq, you'll pass the gateway to the restored Tadhunchen Bahal monastery, tucked between souvenir shops. This Buddhist temple is linked to the cult of the Kumari, Bhaktapur's living goddess. Bhaktapur actually has three Kumaris, but they lack the political importance of Kathmandu's.

⊙ Taumadhi Tole

★ Nyatapola Temple HINDU TEMPLE

(Map p158; Taumadhi Tole) You should be able to see the sky-high rooftop of the Nyatapola Temple long before you reach Taumadhi Tole. With five storeys towering 30m above the square, this is the tallest temple in all of Nepal and one of the tallest buildings in the Kathmandu Valley. This perfectly proportioned temple was built in 1702 during the reign of King Bhupatindra Malla, and the construction was so sturdy that the 1934 and 2015 earthquakes caused only minor damage.

The temple is reached by a stairway flanked by stone figures of the temple guardians. At the bottom are the legendary Rajput wrestlers Jayamel and Phattu, depicted kneeling with hefty maces. Subsequent levels are guarded by elephants with floral saddles, lions adorned with bells, beaked griffons with rams' horns and finally two goddesses – Baghini and Singhini. Each figure is said to be 10 times as strong as the figure on the level below.

The temple is dedicated to Siddhi Lakshmi, a bloodthirsty incarnation of the goddess Durga (Parvati). The idol of the goddess is so fearsome that only the temple's priests are allowed to enter the inner sanctum, but less brutal incarnations of the goddess appear on the torana above the door, beneath a canopy of braided snakes, and also on the temple's 180 carved roof struts. In a classic piece of religious crossover, the Buddhist eight lucky signs are carved beside the temple doorways.

Look for the chariot runners piled up on the north side of the temple.

Bhairabnath Temple HINDU TEMPLE

(Kasi Vishwanath, Akash Bhairab; Map p158; Taumadhi Tole) The broad-fronted, triple-roofed Bhairabnath Temple is dedicated to Bhairab, the fearsome incarnation of Shiva, whose consort occupies the Nyatapola Temple across the square. Despite Bhairab's fearsome powers and his massive temple, the deity is depicted here as a disembodied head just 15cm high! Casually stacked against the north wall of the temple are the enormous wheels and runners from the chariot used to haul the image of Bhairab around town during the Bisket Jatra (p161) festival in mid-April.

The first temple on this site was a modest structure built in the early 17th century, but King Bhupatindra Malla added an extra storey in 1717 and a third level was added when the temple was rebuilt after the 1934 earthquake. The final version of the temple has a similar rectangular plan to the Bhimsen Temple (p137) in Patan's Durbar Sq.

A small hole in the temple's central door (below a row of carved boar snouts) is used to push offerings into the temple's interior; prior to the 2015 earthquake, priests accessed the interior through the small **Betal Temple**, on the south side of the main pagoda, but this collapsed entirely, and restoration work is under way.

The temple's facade is guarded by two brass lions holding the Nepali flag, the only national flag that is not rectangular or square. To the right of the door is an image of Bhairab painted on rattan, decorated with a gruesome garland of buffalo guts. Head here at dusk to hear traditional devotional music.

Next to the temple is a sunken **hiti** with a particularly fine spout in the form of a makara (mythical crocodile-like beast).

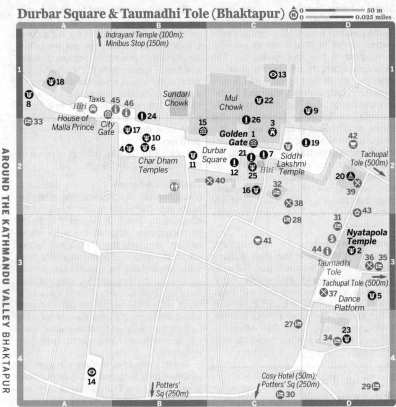

AROUND THE KATHMANDU VALLEY BHAKTAPUR

Til Mahadev Narayan Temple   HINDU TEMPLE

(Map p158; Taumadhi Tole) This interesting temple at Taumadhi Tole is hidden away behind the buildings at the south end of the square. The Til Mahadev Narayan Temple is set in an untidy courtyard, but this is actually an important place of pilgrimage and one of the oldest temples in the city. An inscription states that the site has been in use since 1080 and that the image of Til Mahadev was installed here in 1170.

The double-tiered temple is fronted by an elegant kneeling Garuda statue on a pillar and two columns bearing the sacred sankha and chakra symbols of Vishnu. In case Shiva was feeling left out, a lingam symbol on a yoni base (the Shaivite symbol for the male and female genitals) stands behind a wooden grill in front and to one side of the temple. A plaque to the right of the door depicts the Buddhist deity Vajrayogini in a characteristic pose with her left leg high in the air.

Tachupal Tole

Tachupal Tole was the original central square of Bhaktapur and it formed the official seat of Bhaktapur royalty until the late 16th century.

Dattatreya Temple   HINDU TEMPLE

(Map p154; Tachupal Tole) At the east end of Tachupal Tole, the eye-catching Dattatreya Temple was originally built in 1427, supposedly using the timber from a single tree. The slightly mismatched front porch was added later. The temple is dedicated to Dattatreya, a curious hybrid deity, blending elements of Brahma, Vishnu and Shiva. Judging from the Garuda statue and the conch and chakra disc mounted on pillars supported by stone turtles in front of the temple, Vishnu seems to have come out on top.

The three-storey temple is raised above the ground on a brick and terracotta base,

Durbar Square & Taumadhi Tole (Bhaktapur)

which is carved with erotic scenes, including unexpected humour where one bored-looking woman multitasks by washing her hair while being pleasured by her husband. The main steps to the temple are guarded by statues of the same two Malla wrestlers who watch over the first plinth of the Nyatapola Temple (p157).

Bhimsen Temple   HINDU TEMPLE
(Map p154; Tachupal Tole) At the western end of Tachupal Tole, this two-storey, 17th-century temple is sacred to Bhimsen, the god of commerce. The squat rectangular structure has an open ground floor and an inner sanctum on the second level. In front and to the side is a pillar topped by a brass lion with his right paw raised. Steps lead down behind it to the deeply sunken **Bhimsen Pokhari** tank.

Pujari Math   HISTORIC BUILDING
(Map p154) Tachupal Tole is flanked by a series of ornate brick-and-timber build-ings that were originally used as math (Hindu priests' houses). The best known is the Pujari Math, which now serves as the Woodcarving Museum. The building was damaged in the 2015 earthquake, but its most famous feature – the superb 15th-century **Peacock Window** (Map p154), widely regarded as the finest carved window in the Kathmandu Valley – is intact.

The building was first constructed in the 15th century during the reign of King Yaksha Malla, but rebuilt in 1763. German experts renovated the building in 1979 as a wedding gift for the then King Birendra. Many surrounding shops sell miniature wooden copies of the Peacock Window as souvenirs.

Woodcarving Museum   MUSEUM
(Map p154; Tachupal Tole; foreigner/SAARC Rs 150/50, camera/video Rs 100/200; ◷10am-4pm Wed-Sun, to 3pm Mon, to 5pm Wed-Mon mid-Jan–mid-Oct) This museum has some fine examples of Bhaktapur woodcarving displayed in dark, creaky rooms. There isn't enough

WORTH A TRIP

RIVERSIDE GEMS

The impressive collection of chaitya, Shiva statues, Shaivite shrines and lingam in the town's southeast at **Hanuman Ghat** (Map p154) includes what could well be the two largest Shiva lingam (in equally large yoni) in Nepal. The site was damaged in the 2015 quake, but most structures are still standing. Through the archway are more statues beside the stinking confluence of rivers at Hanuman Ghat. Note the exquisitely carved images of Ganesh, Sakyamuni, Ram and Sita, Hanuman and Vishnu/Narayan, reclining on a bed of snakes. Hindu yogis often come here to meditate.

light to justify paying the camera fee, but it's worth a visit, not least for the extravagantly carved windows in the inner courtyard. The same ticket covers entry to the nearby Brass & Bronze Museum, and the National Art Gallery (p155).

Brass & Bronze Museum　　　MUSEUM

(Map p154; Tachupal Tole; foreigner/SAARC Rs 150/50, camera/video Rs 100/200; ⊙10am-4pm Wed-Sun, to 3pm Mon, to 5pm Wed-Mon mid-Jan–mid-Oct) Directly across from the Woodcarving Museum (p159), in another old math (Hindu priest's house) with similar lighting problems, this museum has some excellent examples of traditional metalwork, including ceremonial lamps and ritual vessels from around the valley. Hold on to your ticket to avoid paying entry at the Woodcarving Museum and National Art Gallery (p155).

Salan Ganesh Temple　　　HINDU TEMPLE

(Map p154; Tachupal Tole) On the north side of Tachupal Tole is an open area with a small temple dating from 1654. Backed by a large tank, Ganesh Pokhari, the open temple is ornately decorated, and the image is a natural rock with only the vaguest elephant-head shape.

◉ Potter's Square & Around

Potters' Square　　　SQUARE

(Map p154) Hidden down shop-lined alleyways leading south from the curving road to Taumadhi Tole, Potters' Sq is exactly what you would expect – a public square full of potter's wheels and rows of clay pots drying

in the sun. Nearby buildings were damaged by the 2015 earthquake, but life – and pottery – in the square continues.

This is the centre of Bhaktapur's ceramic industry, and it's a fascinating place to wander around. Several shops sell the finished article, and you can see the firing process at the back of the square, which is lined with mud-covered straw kilns.

On the northern side of the square a small hillock is topped by a shady pipal tree and a **Ganesh shrine**, surrounded by piles of straw for the pottery kilns. In the square itself is a solid-brick **Vishnu Temple**, which was constructed from remnants of temples destroyed in the 1934 quake, and the double-roofed **Jeth Ganesh Temple**, whose priest is chosen from the Kumal (potters') caste. During the harvest in October, every square inch that is not covered by pots is covered by drying rice.

Khalna Tole　　　SQUARE

(Map p154) Southeast of Potters' Sq and above the river is the wide open square of Khalna Tole, the setting for the spectacular Bisket Jatra festival. Many flanking houses were damaged in the 2015 earthquake, but restoration work is under way. In the middle of the square, note the huge stone yoni where the giant lingam is erected during the festival. You may have to pick your way through mountains of drying rice and grain to get here.

Just south of the bridge, past an orange Hanuman statue on the riverbank is the campus of the **Kathmandu University Department of Music** (Map p154; ⊙closed Sat), where the sound of traditional music wafts over the peaceful ornamental gardens.

Across the river are the modern **cremation plinths** (Map p154) at Chuping Ghat.

Nasamana Square　　　SQUARE

(Map p158) This square just northwest of Potters' Sq lost its temples in the 1934 quake, but it still has a large **Garuda statue** praying to a vanished Vishnu shrine. Also here is a tall shikhara housing an important lingam, and two small **Shiva shrines** by a tank filled with alarmingly green algae.

Jaya Varahi Temple　　　HINDU TEMPLE

(Map p154) About 200m west of Potters' Sq, the red-brick Jaya Varahi is dedicated to Parvati as the boar-headed Varahi. Look for two very different depictions of the goddess on the torana above the central doorway and the torana over the window above. The main entrance is actually at the eastern end of the facade, flanked by shiny metal lions and banners.

Ni Bahal
BUDDHIST TEMPLE

(Jetbarna Maha Bihar; Map p154) Signposted next to a hairdresser, look for the tiny, tunnel-like entrance to this small Buddhist temple dedicated to Maitreya Buddha, the future Buddha. The courtyard contains a very old whitewashed chaitya and several Buddhist shrines. Just to the east is a precarious-looking pilgrims' rest house with finely carved timbers.

✦✦ Festivals & Events

Gai Jatra
RELIGIOUS

(☉ Aug or Sep) Bhaktapur is the best place to witness the antics of Gai Jatra, where cows and boys dressed as cows are paraded through the streets. It's not quite the running of the bulls at Pamplona, but it's all good fun. Usually occurs in August or September.

🛏 Sleeping

Ganesh Guest House
GUESTHOUSE $

(Map p154; ☏01-6611550; www.ganeshguest house.com; Sakudhoka; r Rs 600, without bathroom Rs 500, dm Rs 200; @📶) A magnet for shoestring travellers, this laid-back guesthouse gets rave reviews from backpackers for its cheap rates, friendly staff and piping-hot showers. Beds are just a mattress on the floor and the bathrooms are tiny. Its terrace restaurant has the cheapest prices in town and is a good hang-out spot.

Heart of Bhaktapur
Guest House
GUESTHOUSE $

(Map p158; ☏01-6612034; www.heartofbhaktapur. com; Kulmanani; incl breakfast s Rs 1600, d from Rs 2200) This modern 13-room guesthouse supports the Suvadra Foundation (www.sfnepal. org), a local NGO helping children with disabilities. Guests are drawn more by the cause than the rooms, which have hard mattresses and tiny bathrooms, but it's a friendly place with a fine rooftop terrace and the hallways are enlivened by artwork and photos of the children. Rates include tax.

Shiva Guest House
GUESTHOUSE $

(Map p158; ☏01-6613912; www.bhaktapurhotel. com; Durbar Sq; s/d from US$25/30, without bathroom US$7/12; 📶) A well-maintained place on Durbar Sq with comfy rooms (though tiny bathrooms) and a good ground-floor restaurant and coffee shop. Ask for one of the larger corner rooms if you want a view. Otherwise enquire about the larger and quieter rooms for the same price in the annexe on the western side of Durbar Sq.

Golden Gate Guest House
GUESTHOUSE $

(Map p158; ☏01-6610534; www.goldengate guesthouse.com; s/d US$15/20, deluxe US$25/35, without bathroom Rs 600/900; 📶) A peaceful courtyard and attentive staff are the drawcards at this brick-built guesthouse between Durbar Sq and Taumadhi Tole (the rooftop offers views over both squares). Rooms won't win any design awards, but they're clean and some have balconies. Top-floor deluxe rooms are bright and spacious. Look for the 400-year-old carved window separating the restaurant from the kitchen. Tax included.

BISKET JATRA AT KHALNA TOLE

Held annually in the Nepali month of Baisakh (typically in the middle of April), the dramatic Bisket Jatra festival heralds the start of the Nepali New Year. The focal point of the celebrations is the mighty chariot of Bhairab, which is assembled from the timbers scattered beside the Bhairabnath Temple (p157) and Nyatapola Temple (p157) in Taumadhi Tole. As the festival gets under way, the ponderous chariot is hauled through the streets by dozens of devotees to Khalna Tole, with Betal, Bhairab's sidekick, riding out in front like a ship's figurehead. Bhadrakali, the consort of Bhairab, follows behind in her own chariot.

The creaking and swaying chariots lumber around the town, pausing for a huge tug of war between the eastern and western sides of town. The winning side is charged with looking after the images of the gods during their weeklong sojourn in Khalna Tole. The chariots then skid down the steep road leading to Khalna Tole, where a huge 25m-high lingam is erected in a stone base shaped like a yoni.

As night falls on the following day (New Year's Day), the pole is pulled down in another violent tug of war, and as the pole crashes to the ground, the new year officially commences. Bhairab and Betal return to Taumadhi Tole, while Bhadrakali goes back to her shrine by the river. It certainly beats 'Auld Lang Syne'...

City Guest House

HOTEL **$**

(Map p154; 01-6613038; www.cityguesthouse. com.np; Golmadhi Sq; s Rs 1500, d Rs 2200-2500;) If function is more important to you than architectural charm, you might consider this option. The contemporary, clean rooms are devoid of Newari style, but they are bright with modern bathrooms and sit bang in the centre of the old town. Rates include tax.

Khwopa Guest House

GUESTHOUSE **$**

(Map p158; 01-6614661; www.khwopa-guest house.com.np; s/d from Rs 1000/1500;) Just south of Taumadhi Tole, this tiny, creaking family-run guesthouse is a rare budget choice in expensive Bhaktapur. The vibe is easy-going and friendly, and there are nice touches like towels, but the lack of communal areas makes it feel a bit claustrophobic. Mountain bike hire (Rs 1000 per day) can be arranged for guests.

Nyatapola Guest House

GUESTHOUSE **$**

(Map p154; 01-6611344; www.nyatapolaguest house.com; s/d incl breakfast Rs 1200/1600;) Located above a craft shop in a street with plenty of Newari flavour, Nyatapola's rooms are small and low-ceilinged, and its beds have traditional cotton mattresses. Bathrooms have been squeezed in. It's owned by a family of woodcarvers, and they can arrange lessons on the craft.

Peacock Guesthouse

HERITAGE HOTEL **$$**

(Map p154; 01-6611829; www.peacock guesthousenepal.com; Tachupal Tole; incl breakfast s/d US$40/55, deluxe US$70/80;) Right on Tachupal Tole, this wonderful 15th-century building ticks many boxes. It has eight comfortable, traditional and historic character – though anyone over 6ft might struggle with its low ceilings and tiny bathrooms. There's also an attractive front courtyard in which woodworkers beaver away, and a fine courtyard restaurant-cafe (p165) serving pulse-raising Illy coffee. Rates include taxes.

The spacious deluxe room overlooking the square has the best views but also the most street noise. Cheaper back rooms are darker but quieter. Credit cards are accepted.

Milla Guest House

BOUTIQUE HOTEL **$$**

(Map p154; 9851024137; www.millaguesthouse bhaktapur.com; Devli Sq 4; r incl breakfast US$70-85;) Designed by the architect behind the Patan Museum (p141), this place has lots of stylish touches, from the circular showers

🏃 Town Walk
Bhaktapur Backstreets

START DURBAR SQ
END TAUMADHI TOLE
LENGTH 3KM; TWO HOURS

Starting from the northeastern corner of Durbar Sq, walk to the east of the Fasidega Temple, passing a multicoloured ❶ **Ganesh shrine**, where the idol is a rock that naturally resembles an elephant's head. Turn to the right to reach a square with disused buildings and a ruined temple plinth. Walk around the north side of the square and exit at the northeast corner past the hiti, by the strut-roofed ❷ **Tripurasundari Temple**, sacred to one of the Navadurgas. Continue east passing several sweets shops, where the road bends right at a brick Narayan shrine. Past the next alley, a doorway leads into a cramped bahal containing a small ❸ **Bhimsen Temple**, which was created from remains of the Lun Bahal, a 16th-century Buddhist monastery. Note the pots and pans nailed to the roof struts by devotees.

Head back to the Narayan shrine, take a right and head 200m to the unassuming brick facade of a ❹ **Ganesh Temple**, with fine figures of the elephant-headed deity on its torana and an unusual terracotta Ganesh window above the door.

At the next junction take a right, past some carved windows, and then swing left past a small ❺ **Mahakali shrine** with caged windows and buffalo horns, and the Pohalacha Pokhari tank. Continue past a city ticket office to the Bhaktapur–Nagarkot road, take a left and cross the road to climb the steps to a large, slightly damaged ❻ **Mahakali Temple**, which has an eccentric collection of statues inside a gated pavilion. Note the buffalo entrails draped over the guardian statues inside the temple.

Return to the ticket office and take a left until you reach a brick square containing a tiny, yellow-roofed ❼ **Mahalakshmi Temple**, sacred to the goddess of wealth. Turn right (south) and continue straight to a large tank, the ❽ **Naga Pokhari** (p156), where skeins of dyed yarn hang drying on racks beside the lurid green waters. In the middle of the tank is a statue of a cobra.

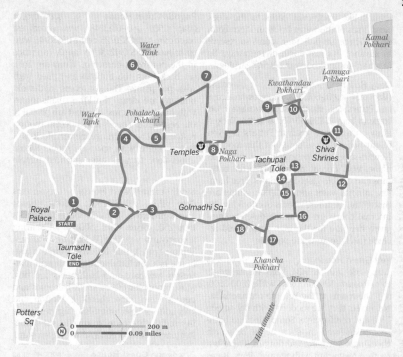

Pass along the north side of the tank, turn left and look for a small opening in a reconstructed wall on your right. A tiny sign above the opening says Dipankar & Prsaannasilar Mahavir. Enter the opening to the second courtyard and continue out the far end past another courtyard. On the left you'll see the white stucco pillars that mark the entrance to the ⑨ **Mul Dipankar Bihar**, enshrining an image of Dipankar, the Past Buddha.

Continue east to the road junction; look left to see a white lotus-roofed Vishnu shrine, behind which is the large Kwathandau Pokhari. Head south at the far end of the tank and you'll pass the ⑩ **Nava Durga Temple**, a Tantric Shaivite temple with a fine gilded torana. Only Hindus are allowed to enter.

Swing southeast through a square, past the gallery occupying the ⑪ **Toni Hagen house**, restored in honour of the famous Swiss geologist. Continue to the junction by a stupa and a dance platform, on the main east–west road. Turn right and immediately on your left you'll see the elaborate entrance to the ⑫ **Wakupati Narayan Temple**, built in 1667. Despite some damage to neighbouring buildings, the ornate, golden mandir survived the 2015 quake; note the entourage of five Garudas supported on pillars on the backs of turtles.

Continue from here past the centuries-old wooden frontage of the ⑬ **Brahmayani Temple**, fronted by two lions and sacred to the patron goddess of Panauti, and then on to ⑭ **Tachupal Tole** (p158). From Tachupal Tole turn left down the side of the Pujari Math, passing the famous ⑮ **Peacock Window** (p159). Follow the lane south and turn right at the small square with a ⑯ **Vishnu Temple** on an octagonal plinth.

Go straight down an atmospheric alley lined with brick houses and follow it around to the left, then to the right into a large square. Detour south from this square down a wide cobbled road to reach a large statue of ⑰ **Sakyamuni**, the historical Buddha. Behind the Buddha are views overlooking the Khancha Pokhari tank and the river below.

Return to the square and take a left and walk west towards the main road linking Taumadhi Tole and Tachupal Tole. Just before the junction turn to the left to enter the unassuming gateway to the ornate Inacho Bahal, containing the narrow ⑱ **Sri Indravarta Mahavihar**, a 17th-century Buddhist temple topped by a lopsided miniature pagoda roof. From here, head back to Taumadhi Tole or visit the Hanuman Ghat at the bottom of the hill.

shaped like traditional baths to the sleek clean lines of the warm brick and terracotta decor. There are only four rooms so reserve in advance. It's just north of Dattatraya Sq in a hard-to-find courtyard. Bring earplugs.

Cosy Hotel
HOTEL $$

(Map p154; ☑01-6616333; www.cosyhotel.com. np; Potters' Sq; standard/superior/deluxe r incl breakfast from US$30/60/65; ❋@❖) Tucked away on a narrow road to Potters' Sq, you might not get views here, but this modern, Newari-style hotel definitely lives up to its name, with decent rooms, big beds, bathtubs and double-glazed windows. Free laundry, mineral water and heaters in winter are thoughtful gestures. Rooms overlooking the internal courtyard are much quieter. Rates given here are for the high season and include tax. Discounts are possible.

Yeti Guest House
HOTEL $$

(Map p158; ☑01-6615434; yetibhaktapur@gmail. com; Taumadhi Tole; r incl breakfast Rs 2500-3500; ❖) The rooms at the Yeti are not abominable, in fact they are modern (with flat-screen TVs) and comfortable. Some have had bathrooms squeezed in, so it might be worth checking a few before settling in. There is a rooftop restaurant with temple views. Rates include taxes.

Pagoda Guest House
GUESTHOUSE $$

(Map p158; ☑01-6613248; www.pagodaguest house.com; s/d US$20/25, deluxe US$35/45, without bathroom US$10/12; ❖) A family-run place in the northwest corner of Taumadhi Tole, set back from the hubbub and piled high with pot plants. The six rooms in the old building are clean, if a little small; rooms with bathroom across the hall are probably the best value. There's also a decent rooftop restaurant.The midrange newer block is a better choice with spacious rooms whose upper-floor terraces offer splendid temple views.

Siddhi Laxmi Guest House
GUESTHOUSE $$

(Map p158; ☑01-6612500; siddhilaxmi.guest house@gmail.com; Taumadhi Tole; s/d from Rs 1500/2500, deluxe AC Rs 3500; ❋❖) Sharing a courtyard with the Til Mahadev Narayan Temple (p158), this Newari-inspired guesthouse has comfortable rooms, though mattresses are hard and bathrooms are tiny. Most rooms have TVs, small balconies and decent views, and there's a rooftop and ground-floor restaurant. Earplugs will come in handy, as there are barking dogs and ringing temple bells to contend with from 4am.

Bhadgaon Guest House
GUESTHOUSE $$

(Map p158; ☑01-6610488; www.bhadgaon.com. np; Taumadhi Tole; s US$50, d US$60-70; ❋❖)

BHAKTAPUR'S PONDS

Around the outskirts of Bhaktapur are a series of enormous tanks, constructed in the medieval period to store water for drinking, bathing and religious rituals. The tanks still play an important role in the social life of Bhaktapur – in the mornings and afternoons, locals gather by the ponds to bathe, socialise, take romantic walks and feed the giant carp and turtles that somehow survive in the murky waters.

The most impressive tank is the ghat-lined **Siddha Pokhari** near the main bus park. This rectangular reservoir is set inside an enormous wall that is broken by rest houses and towers that have been consumed by the roots of giant fig trees. You can buy bags of corn and rice to feed the fish for a few rupees.

During the annual festival of **Naga Panchami** in the Nepali month of Saaun (July to August), residents of Bhaktapur offer a bowl of rice to the nagas (serpent deities who control the rain) who live in the Siddha Pokhari. According to legend, a holy man once attempted to kill an evil naga who lived in the lake by transforming himself into a snake. An attendant waited by with a bowl of magical rice to transform the yogi back into human form, but when the victorious holy man slithered from the water, his terrified assistant fled, taking the holy rice with him and leaving the yogi trapped for eternity in his scaly form. To this day, locals leave a bowl of rice out at Naga Panchami in case the snake-yogi decides to return.

Other significant tanks include the nearby **Bhaiya Pokhari** (across the road to the south), the **Guhya Pokhari** (across the road to the east) and the **Kamal Pokhari** (at the northeast end of Bhaktapur on the road to Nagarkot).

An update of a traditional Newari building, this place has a coffee shop, courtyard restaurant, rooftop bar and a coveted deluxe room (room 505) with a private balcony overlooking Taumadhi Tole. Rooms are modern rather than traditional, with TVs and parquet floors. Its annexe across the square is less appealing, but rates are US$10 cheaper.

Sunny Guest House
GUESTHOUSE $$

(Map p158; ☑01-6616094; www.sunnyguest housenepal.com; Taumadhi Tole; s/d incl breakfast US$33/44; ☎) This long-established place scores points mainly for its atmospheric location at the north end of Taumadhi Tole and attentive staff. Set back from the square, the modern building is relatively quiet, and there's a rooftop for sunny breakfasts. Rooms are decorated with screen-printed bedspreads. Rates include taxes.

Thagu Chhen
APARTMENT $$$

(Map p154; ☑01-6613043; www.thaguchhen. com; Itachhen; apt incl breakfast US$90; ✴@☎) Thagu Chhen offers apartments with sitting areas and kitchenettes livened up with a dash of style through reclaimed brick and carved wood. Each of the rooms takes up an entire floor and all except one have balconies offering views north over the Kathmandu Valley. It's perfect for families and there are low season discounts. Taxes included.

Hotel Heritage
BOUTIQUE HOTEL $$$

(Map p154; ☑01-6611628; www.hotelheritage. com.np; Barahipith; s/d from US$140/150; ✴@☎) Outside the southern boundaries of the old town, this multistorey red-brick Newari building is an eclectic blend of old and new – incorporating reclaimed windows and bricks into its design. While it's well overpriced, it remains the plushest hotel in Bhaktapur with all of the mod cons and nice seating in the garden and rooftop terrace.

🍴 Eating

No-Name Restaurant
NEPALI $

(Map p158; Tadhunchen Bahal; pancakes Rs 100-150; ☺9am-7pm) This nameless hole-in-the-wall consists of little more than a hot plate and a bucket of pancake mix, but it serves up delicious street food. The main item on the menu is *wo* (called *bara* in Nepali), a savoury lentil pancake. It can be served 'plain', two pancakes and a chickpea soup, or 'mixed' with eggs and meat.

KING OF CURDS

While in Bhaktapur, be sure to try the town's great contribution to the world of desserts – *juju dhau*, 'the king of curds'. Just how special can yoghurt be, you might ask? Well, this could just be the richest, creamiest yoghurt in the world! Mind you, it is sweetened and lightly spiced. You'll find this delicacy in many tourist restaurants, but the best places to try it are the hole-in-the-wall restaurants between Durbar Sq and the public bus stand (look for the pictures of bowls of curd outside). King curd comes set in an earthenware bowl for Rs 200, or a single serve costs Rs 40.

Look for the sign advertising 'Nepal barawo available here' and squeeze yourself into the two-table cubby hole adjoining Tadhunchen Bahal (p157).

Mayur Restaurant
INTERNATIONAL $$

(Map p154; ☑01-6611829; Tachupal Tole; mains Rs 350-500; ☺7.30am-8.30pm; ☎) Mayur is an atmospheric place to refuel – dine on tables in a sunken courtyard, surrounded by carved woodwork and, possibly, in the company of woodcarvers. Soup of the day, fresh momos, curries, pad Thai or Nepali set meals are all good, as are the cakes from the Himalayan Bakery and the espresso coffee.

Namaste Restaurant
CAFE $$

(Map p158; Taumadhi Tole; mains Rs 250-300; ☺7.30am-8.30pm; ☎) This tiny, low-ceilinged, upstairs cafe is decked out in attractive decor and offers great views of Taumadhi Tole. The Nepali curries with rice are particularly tasty, breakfasts are good value and there's a ground-floor coffee bar.

Peaceful Restaurant
NEPALI, INTERNATIONAL $$

(Map p154; ☑9840275877; Tachupal Tole; mains Rs 200-500; ☺8am-8pm) This delightful restaurant occupies two courtyards behind the souvenir shops on the south side of Tachupal Tole. Duck your head and wander through to the second shady, peaceful courtyard. The menu covers Italian, Mexican, Indian, Chinese and Nepali dishes, and it is rather well done. Shame the beer is a bit expensive. Taxes included.

**New Watshala
Garden Restaurant**   NEPALI, INTERNATIONAL $$
(Map p158; ☑ 01-6610957; Durbar Sq; mains Rs 300-450, set meals Rs 700; ☺ 8.30am-9.30pm; 🔊) Set in a pot-plant-filled courtyard behind the Shiva Guest House (p161), this place offers a genuine retreat from the Durbar Sq crowds, even if the food is tour-group bland. Sit back with a cold Nepali or Belgian beer and gently exhale...

New Café dé Peacock   NEPALI, INTERNATIONAL $$
(Map p154; Tachupal Tole; mains Rs 350-550; ☺ 7am-9pm) Tachupal Tole's answer to New Café Nyatapola in a wood-fronted former priest's house on the north side of the square is certainly atmospheric, with great views over the square. The food is decent enough and the beer is cold.

Newa Chhen Restaurant   NEPALI $$
(Map p154; Tachupal Tole; mains Rs 250-450; ☺ 9am-7pm) Slightly rundown and dingy, but the food here is cheap and tasty. It gets points for excellent Newari snacks and set meals, and a corner table with views over the square.

New Café Nyatapola   NEPALI, INTERNATIONAL $$$
(Map p158; ☑ 01-6614246; Taumadhi Tole; mains Rs 350-550, set meals Rs 900-1000; ☺ 8.30am-7pm) Occupying prime real estate in Taumadhi Tole, this landmark cafe is touristy and pricey. But what a setting! Tables are arranged on the balconies of a historic pagoda temple – there are even erotic carvings

---

NAVADURGA DANCERS

The colourful masks sold around Bhaktapur and Thimi are not just souvenirs. Every year, as part of the Dasain celebrations in September or October, local residents perform frenetic dances in Bhaktapur's public squares, during which they are said to be possessed by the spirits of the Navadurga, the nine incarnations of the fearsome consort of Shiva. The masks worn by dancers are cremated every year and new masks are made from the ashes, mixed with black clay from the fields around Bhaktapur. Although most of the masks for sale in Bhaktapur are made for the tourist market, they are full of Tantric symbolism. Popular figures include Ganesh, Kali, Bhairab, boar-headed Varahi, red-faced Kumari and roaring Sima and Duma, the eerie harbingers of death.

---

on the roof struts. The menu comprises the usual Nepali, Chinese and continental standards.

**Temple View
Restaurant**   NEPALI, INTERNATIONAL $$$
(Map p158; ☑ 01-6614815; Durbar Sq; mains Rs 300-570, set meals Rs 700-800; ☺ 9am-9pm) Opposite the Royal Palace in a long, historic building, this regal place with one long balcony offers the chance to dine with a view that used to be reserved for the Malla kings.

🍷 Drinking & Nightlife

★**Garuda Bar**   BAR
(Map p158; Taumadhi Tole; cocktails Rs 400-700, beer Rs 550; ☺ 9am-10pm; 🔊) A cosy rooftop bar where you can get a cocktail and order snacks, with stunning views over Taumadhi Tole towards Nyatapola Temple (p157).

Beans Cafe   CAFE
(Map p158; espresso coffee Rs 85-200, cakes Rs 110; ☺ 7am-9pm; 🔊) Good-value, excellent Nepali organic espresso, free wi-fi and baked treats off Durbar Sq make this one of our favourite java stops.

Daily Grind   CAFE
(Map p158; Durbar Sq; espresso Rs 100-180, pizzas Rs 435-600; ☺ 7am-9pm; 🔊) A neat little cafe at the east end of Durbar Sq, where you can grab a quick coffee or sit at the knee-bruising tables for a decent pizza. Also good for cool drinks, smoothies, momos and sandwiches.

Cosmos Coffee Haus   CAFE
(Map p158; Taumadhi Tole; coffee Rs 100-160; ☺ 7am-9pm; 🔊) Sit down to a hot or cold coffee at this tasteful cafe, tucked away from the crowds on the edge of Taumadhi Tole.

☆ Entertainment

Downtown Pub & Grill   LIVE MUSIC
(Map p154; ☑ 01-6613264; Barahipith; mains Rs 300-600; ☺ 10am-10pm, Fri bands 6.30-10pm; 🔊) This plush eating, drinking and entertainment venue sits just outside the southern boundaries of the old town. The food, cocktails and entertainment (Fridays only at this stage) have filled a need in sleepy Bhaktapur.

Dé Ghurkas   LIVE MUSIC
(Map p158; Taumadhi Tole; mains Rs 300-500; ☺ to 9.30pm; 🔊) On Friday evenings this place hosts live bands. It is also a decent spot to head for a rooftop beer or meal in the shadow of the towering Nyatapola Temple (p157).

🛍 Shopping

Bhaktapur is famed for its pottery, which is sold in a staggering number of souvenir shops around the main squares, particularly at Tachupal Tole and Taumadhi Tole. There's also some good metalwork on sale – look out for beaten metal dishes embossed with Buddhist symbols and ornate brass butter lamps in the shape of the Krishna Temple in Patan's Durbar Sq.

Many small factories in Bhaktapur produce handmade paper from the pulp of the *lokta* (daphne) bush, which is sold all over town as cards, notepads, photo albums, envelopes and other stationery items.

Bhaktapur has long been renowned for its woodcarving, and this craft is now used to make objects that fit well into Western homes. Some of the best work is sold from the stalls around Tachupal Tole and the alley beside the Pujari Math (p159). Miniature models of the famous Peacock Window (p159) are always popular souvenirs.

Peacock Shop   ARTS & CRAFTS
(Map p154; ☑ 01-6610820; ⊙ 10am-5pm, workshop closed Sat) This paper emporium is near the Peacock Window (p159), down the side of Pujari Math (p159). Although the paper workshop was badly damaged by the 2015 earthquake it's all up and running again, so you can witness the production process and buy quality Nepali paper products.

ⓘ Information

The **Bhaktapur Money Exchange Centre** (Map p154; Golmadhi; ⊙ 9am-6pm) and the **Money Exchange** (Map p158) are two of several places that change cash, and the **Himalaya Bank** (Map p154; Sukuldhoka) has an ATM.

ⓘ Getting There & Away

Taxis from Kathmandu cost Rs 1000 one way.
Buses (Map p154; Guhya Pokhari) run very frequently from Kathmandu's Bagh Bazar bus stand (Rs 25 to Rs 30, one hour) until around 6pm but stop endlessly, dropping off next to the Guhya Pokhari, a short walk west of Durbar Sq. For Thimi (Rs 15, 20 minutes), take a **local bus** (Map p154; Bharwacho) along the old road to Kathmandu rather than an express bus along the main highway.

Buses for Kathmandu's Gongabu bus station also leave from a stand at the northern edge of Bhaktapur by the Lamuga Pokhari, but the Bagh Bazar buses are much more convenient.

The stand for **buses to Nagarkot** (Map p154; Kamal Pokhari) (Rs 50, 1½ hours, from 7am to 5.30pm) is nearby, beside the Kamal Pokhari tank. A taxi from here takes 45 minutes and costs around Rs 1500.

Buses to Changu Narayan (Map p154; Dekocha) (Rs 15, 30 minutes) leave every 30 minutes or so from the junction with the Changu Narayan road, or take a **taxi** (Map p154) from your hotel for Rs 1000.

For Dhulikhel (Rs 40, one hour) or anywhere further east, you'll have to walk 20 minutes south across the river to the Arniko Hwy to catch a (probably packed) through bus from Kathmandu. Count on Rs 1500 for a **taxi** (Map p158; Durbar Sq) to Dhulikhel.

AROUND BHAKTAPUR

Suriya Binayak Temple

South of Bhaktapur, on the south side of the Arniko Hwy, Suriya Binayak is an important Ganesh temple dating back to the 17th century. The white shikhara-style temple contains some interesting statuary, but the main attractions are the peaceful setting and the walk uphill above the temple to a hillside with sweeping views over Bhaktapur. The temple is flanked by statues of Malla kings and a large statue of Ganesh's vehicle, the rat.

To get here, take the road south from Potters' Sq to Ram Ghat (where there are areas for ritual bathing and cremations) and cross the river to the Arniko Hwy. On the other side, it's a 1km walk along the road to the start of the steps to the temple. Bank on around 30 minutes from Taumadhi Tole.

Thimi

Thimi, known historically as Madhyapur, was once the fourth-largest town in the Kathmandu Valley. Today it's a sleepy backwater, but its winding, brick-paved streets are lined with medieval temples. The town takes its modern name from the Newari phrase for 'capable people', which is fitting as the town is a major centre for the production of pottery and papier-mâché masks. You'll pass a string of mask shops on the road that cuts across the north end of town towards Bhaktapur.

◉ Sights

Thimi's best-known temple is 16th-century **Balkumari Temple**, dedicated to one of Bhairab's shaktis. The goddess' peacock vehicle is depicted on a column in front of the temple, as well as each corner of the temple. It's the focus for the **Balkumari Jatra**, a festival where Thimi welcomes the new year (around mid-April) with riotous scenes as the 32 khats (palanquins) whirl around the temple while red powder is hurled at them.

A passage on the south side of Balkumari Temple's square leads to Thimi's **potters' square**, which is full of kilns made from straw covered with ash.

One kilometre north of Thimi is the village of Bode, with its 17th-century **Mahalakshmi Temple**, which has a small image of Narayan reclining on his snake bed just behind. The village is famous for its annual **tongue-piercing festival**, during which one lucky volunteer pierces their tongue with a 13-inch spike. The festival is believed to protect the village from natural disasters and takes place just after Bisket Jatra in mid-April.

❶ Getting There & Away

Any of the Bhaktapur-bound minibuses from Kathmandu will be able to drop you at Thimi (Rs 15, 40 minutes), either at the southern gateway on the Arniko Hwy or on the back road at the north end of Thimi.

If you are biking to Bhaktapur, the northern (old) road offers a far more pleasant ride. The road branches off the Arniko Hwy to the east of the runway at Tribhuvan Airport.

Changu Narayan Temple

Perched atop a narrow ridge due north of Bhaktapur, the beautiful and historic temple of Changu Narayan is a living museum of carvings from the Licchavi period. The temple is a Unesco World Heritage Site and rightly so, because the statues, and the temple itself, are genuine works of art. However, the site was shaken badly by the 2015 earthquake: several buildings and statues in the temple compound were badly damaged and houses collapsed in the adjacent village. At the time of research, the temple was open and undergoing restoration.

◉ Sights

Changu Narayan Temple   HINDU TEMPLE
(foreigner/SAARC Rs 300/200; ◷6.30am-6pm) This temple is said to be the oldest Hindu temple still in use in the Kathmandu Valley. Built in the two-tiered pagoda style, the main shrine here is guarded on all sides by pairs of real and mythical beasts – elephants, lions, winged lions and ram-horned griffons – and its roof struts feature some amazingly intricate carvings of Tantric deities. Changu Narayan and its associated buildings were badly affected by the 2015 earthquake however; restoration of the complex is under way.

The statue inside shows Vishnu as Narayan, the creator of all life, but the beautifully decorated metal-plate doors are only opened for rituals and only Hindus may enter.

The Garuda figure facing the west door is said to date from the 5th century, and in front of this statue is the oldest stone inscription in the valley, dating from AD 464, which recalls how the king persuaded his mother not to commit *sati* (ritual suicide) after his father's death. Two large pillars carry a conch and chakra disc, the traditional symbols of Vishnu.

Dotted around the courtyard are a series of extraordinary carvings dating from the Licchavi era, showing Vishnu in his various avatars (incarnations). Vishnu appears in the southwest corner of the compound as Narsingha (his man-lion incarnation), disembowelling a demon with his fingers, and as Vikrantha (Vamana), the six-armed dwarf who transformed himself into a giant capable of crossing the universe in three steps to defeat King Bali (look for his outstretched leg).

To the side of these images is a broken slab showing a 10-headed and 10-armed Vishnu, with Ananta reclining on a serpent below. The plaque is divided into three sections – the underworld, the world of man and the heavens. In the northwest corner of the compound is an exquisite 7th-century image of Vishnu astride Garuda, which is illustrated on the Rs 10 banknote.

The squat temple in the southeast corner of the complex is dedicated to the Tantric goddess Chhinnamasta, who beheaded herself to feed the bloodthirsty deities Dakini and Varnini.

Down the steps leading east from the temple complex are the one-storey **Bhimsen Pati**, with its stone guardians, and the remains of a Malla-era royal palace.

Changu Museum   MUSEUM
(foreigner/SAARC/Nepali Rs 300/100/50; ◷9am-5pm) The single brick-paved street

Changu Narayan Temple

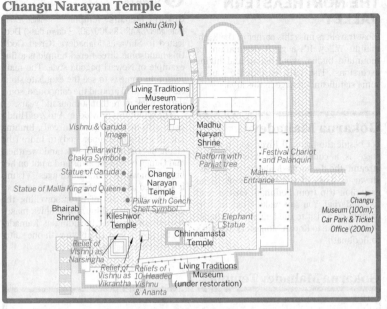

in Changu village climbs from the car park and bus stand past the privately owned Changu Museum, which offers a quirky introduction to traditional village life. The owner will give you a whistle-stop tour of such oddities as a rhino-skin shield, a raincoat made of leaves, a 500-year-old dishwashing rack and some 225-year-old rice. Not to mention a cow's gallstone and the navel of a musk deer.

There's also a fascinating coin collection, including the world's smallest coin, leather coins from the 2nd century and one that equates to one-eighth of a paise – meaning 800 of these are needed to make one rupee!

Living Traditions Museum MUSEUM
(www.livingtraditionsmuseum.org; foreigner/SAARC/Nepali Rs 250/100/60; ☉10am-4pm Tue-Sun) This well-curated museum, housed in a restored building south of Changu Narayan Temple, features over 400 exhibits covering artefacts and displays on ethnic groups from the Kathmandu Valley, the Terai, Middle Hills and the Himalayan Highlands. However, the site was badly damaged in the 2015 earthquake and was still closed for restoration at the time of research.

🛏 Sleeping & Eating

Changu Guest House GUESTHOUSE $
(☎01-5141052, 9841652158; www.changuguesthouse.com; r Rs 2000-3000, without bathroom Rs 1500; 🛜) At the temple entrance, this family owned guesthouse has three sunny rooms with firm mattresses (two rooms have an attached bathroom). There's a rooftop restaurant with stupendous views and an espresso coffee stand. The owners, whose family have been temple priests for 400 years, are passionate about promoting their town and offer tours, including local hikes and thangka painting classes.

❶ Getting There & Away

Regular public buses run the 6km between Changu Narayan and Bhaktapur (Rs 15, 30 minutes), with the last bus around sunset. A taxi from Kathmandu costs around Rs 2000 return, or Rs 1000 from Bhaktapur.

By bike or on foot, it's a steep climb uphill from Bhaktapur (one hour), but an easy downhill trip on the way back. If you're headed to Nagarkot you can take the footpath east to Tharkot and catch a bus for the final uphill stretch. You can also hike west to Bodhnath in about 90 minutes.

THE NORTHEASTERN VALLEY

Most travellers miss this corner of the Kathmandu Valley. It's a great destination for mountain biking, motorbiking and hiking excursions. The 2015 earthquake caused some significant damage in this area.

Gokarna Mahadev

Set beside the Bagmati River, which at this stage is a comparatively clear mountain stream, the Gokarna Mahadev (Gokarneshwar, or Lord of Gokarna) Temple is an easy 5km trip from Bodhnath on the road to Sundarijal. You can make a day of it by combining a visit to the temple with the interesting hike to Kopan Monastery and back to Bodhnath.

⊙ Sights

Gokarna Mahadev Temple HINDU TEMPLE
(foreigner/SAARC Rs 100/50; ⊙ dawn-dusk) Dedicated to Shiva as Mahadeva (Great God), this handsome three-tiered temple is a fine example of Newari pagoda style. The main reason to come is to see the exquisite stone carvings dotted around the compound, some dating back more than a thousand years.

The sculptures provide an A to Z of Hindu deities, from Aditya (the sun god), Brahma and Chandra (the moon god) to Indra (the elephant-borne god of war and weather) and Ganga (with four arms and a pot on her head from which pours the Ganges). Vishnu is depicted as Narsingha, making a particularly thorough job of disembowelling the demon Hiranyakashipu, while Shiva makes several appearances, including as Kamadeva, the god of love, complete with one suitably erect celestial body part.

Gokarna Mahadev Temple

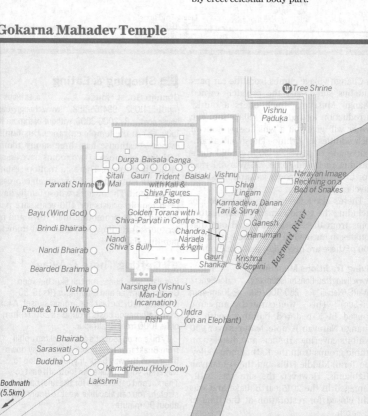

GOKARNA–KOPAN–BODHNATH WALK

There's a pleasant walking or biking route between Gokarna and Bodhnath via the monastery at Kopan. The obvious trail starts just opposite the Gokarna Mahadev Temple, to the right of a series of four roadside statues (signposted 'Sahayogi Multiple College'), and branches left at the college. After five minutes, join the tarmac road as it follows the side of a pine-clad hill. Stay on the paved road as it climbs, offering views of the valley below and the yellow walls of Kopan Monastery ahead atop a hill.

After another 10 minutes, branch left onto a dirt road, which soon becomes a footpath. After another couple of minutes, branch left, passing below Rato Gompa, and follow the hillside to a saddle on the ridge. Where the path forks, take the trail heading uphill to the right, passing another small monastery before reaching the entrance to Kopan (45 minutes).

From Kopan, follow the main road south for 40 minutes to Bodhnath, or jump on one of the frequent minibuses. Travelling on foot, branch off to the left before you hit the built-up area of Bodhnath to reach the stupa.

The god Gauri Shankar is interesting since it contains elements of both Shiva and Parvati. The goddess appears on her own, wearing a dress and standing on a snow lion, in a particularly elegant statue in the northwest corner of the compound. The Brahma figure in the southwest corner appears to have only three heads (he should have four) until you peer around the back and discover the hidden head. Many of the deities have one foot on their *vahana* (spiritual vehicle). Shiva's vehicle Nandi appears as a large statue made of brass laid over a stone base, in front of the main temple, and Shiva is venerated in the form of an enormous lingam inside the main chamber. There's some fine woodcarving on the temple struts.

Behind the temple, just above the river, is the **Vishnu Paduka**, a low pavilion enshrining a metal plate with a footprint of Vishnu. Just in front is an image of Narayan reclining on a bed of snakes, just like the images at Budhanilkantha and Balaju. To the north of the pavilion is an earthquake-damaged **shrine** that has almost been consumed by a fig tree that must have started as a seed on its roof.

Nepalis who have recently lost a father often visit the temple, particularly during Gokarna Aunsi, the Nepali equivalent of Father's Day, which falls in September.

❶ Getting There & Away

To visit Gokarna Mahadev Temple, you can walk (two to three hours from Bodhnath), take a minibus from Kathmandu's Ratna Park station (Rs 30, 45 minutes) or Bodhnath (or Jorpati), or hire a taxi (one way from Kathmandu Rs 800, from Bodhnath Rs 400). The temple is 4km from the Jorpati junction.

Gokarna Forest

The 188-hectare forest at Gokarna was formerly set aside as a hunting reserve for the Nepali royal family, which saved it from the woodcutters. Today the sound of gunshots has been replaced by the thwack of club upon ball. The forest forms part of the Gokarna Forest Resort Golf Course.

🏌 Activities

**Gokarna Forest Resort
Golf Course**   GOLF
(☎ 01-4451212; www.gokarna.com; off Sankhu Rd, Rajnikunj, Thali) This golf course, which was designed by the team behind the famous Gleneagles course in Scotland, is Nepal's best. Green fees for 18 holes are Rs 5000/7000 on weekdays/weekends for nonguests, and you can hire clubs, shoes and caddies for an extra Rs 2700.

🛏 Sleeping

Gokarna Forest Resort   RESORT $$$
(☎ 01-4451212; www.gokarna.com; off Sankhu Rd, Rajnikunj, Thali; s/d incl breakfast from US$180/200) For a top-of-the-line rural retreat this sublimely peaceful property is hard to beat. Wicker furniture on the garden terrace lends a colonial-era feel, and the surrounding forest is alive with deer and monkeys. If golf is not your thing you can pamper yourself with spa treatments, and the resort can arrange guided forest walks, mountain bike hire and horse riding.

The new block is luxurious, but for real character book a room in the Rana-era Hunter's Lodge.

Club rooms are worth the extra expense, but all rooms come with 'advice for preventing monkeys entering the rooms'. After breakfast head to the corner of the resort garden to the 200-year-old pipal tree, where the Buddha (played by Keanu Reeves) in Bertolucci's film *Little Buddha* was tempted by the demon Mara and called the earth to witness his victory.

A taxi from Kathmandu will cost around Rs 1000 one way.

Sankhu

The red-brick town of Sankhu was once an important stop on the old trade route from Kathmandu to Lhasa (Tibet), but this historic settlement was severely damaged by the 2015 earthquake. The damaged, roofless Vajrayogini Temple still stands and receives worshippers on the hillside north of the village, but the winding brick backstreets and traditional squares of the old town were devastated.

◉ Sights

Vajrayogini Temple   HINDU TEMPLE
The main reason for visiting the Vajrayogini Temple is not for the temple itself but rather the off-the-beaten-track hike up through Sankhu. The stately temple was damaged in the 2015 earthquake. It lost its three-tiered roof, but it was not destroyed – note the fine gilded doorway flanked by images of Bhairab, Garuda and other celestial beings. The image of the revered female yogi is only visible when the priest opens the doors for devotees (no photos).

The other temple in the main courtyard enshrines a huge chaitya and its roof struts are decorated with images of Buddhist protector deities. Immediately behind this temple is a chaitya with four Buddha images mounted on a yoni base – a striking fusion of Hindu and Buddhist iconography.

To reach the temple, walk north from the bus stand under a colourful deity-covered archway, veering left at the central Dhunla Tole. As you leave the village, an interesting collection of lingam shrines (one-half destroyed by a tree) and finely crafted statues of Ganesh, Vishnu and Hanuman will show you are on the right path. Shortly afterwards the road forks at a bend; turn left and head downhill to reach the pedestrian steps to the temple, or turn right by bike or car to reach the parking area.

The 40-minute climb from the bus station up the stone steps to the temples is steep and hot, but water spouts along the route offer a chance to cool off. About halfway up is a shelter with carvings of a very thin Kali and an overweight orange Ganesh. A natural stone lingam represents Bhairab, and sacrifices are made at its foot. If you climb the stairway above the Vajrayogini Temple, you will reach a rest house for pilgrims and several small tea stands.

❶ Getting There & Away

Minibuses run to Sankhu from Kathmandu's Ratna Park bus station (Rs 50, one hour). The last bus back to Sankhu leaves Sankhu around 6pm. Some minibuses run to Patan. A one-way taxi from Kathmandu costs Rs 2000.

It's a relatively easy 20km cycle to Sankhu from Kathmandu, or an even easier motorcycle ride. Head to Bodhnath and turn right at Jorpati, then skirt around the Gokarna Forest. If you are walking, you can continue from Sankhu to Changu Narayan by crossing the Manohara River near Bramhakhel.

THE SOUTHERN VALLEY

There are some fascinating temples and Buddhist monasteries in the southern part of the Kathmandu Valley, but it's hard to see too many together in a single day trip, as the villages are strung out on four different roads branching south from the Kathmandu Ring Rd. There's a useful dirt-road shortcut that links the roads to Godavari and Chapagaon, and a walking-only route linking the road to Bungamati and the road to Chobar on the way to Dakshinkali.

Kirtipur

♫ 01 / POP 67,171
Just 5km southwest of Kathmandu, the sleepy town of Kirtipur has a wonderful sense of faded grandeur thanks to the impressive medieval temples dotted around its backstreets. When Prithvi Narayan Shah stormed into the valley in 1768, he made a priority of capturing Kirtipur to provide a base for his crushing attacks on the Malla kingdoms. Kirtipur's resistance was strong, but eventually, after a bitter siege, the town was taken. The inhabitants paid a terrible price for their brave resistance – the king ordered that the nose and lips be cut off every male inhabitant

in the town, sparing only those who could play wind instruments for his entertainment.

As you approach Kirtipur from the Ring Rd, the old town is up the hill straight ahead, best approached by following the main road to the right and climbing the hillside on a wide flight of steps.

◎ Sights

Everything of interest in Kirtipur is at the top of the hill above the road into town.

Bagh Bhairab Temple   HINDU TEMPLE
In a courtyard off the north side of the main square, the imposing Bhairab Temple features an incredible armoury of *tulwars* (swords) and shields belonging to the soldiers defeated by Prithvi Narayan Shah. Befitting the militaristic mood, animal sacrifices are made here early on Tuesday and Saturday mornings.

Main Square   SQUARE
Ringed by the former residences of the royal family of Kirtipur, many showing some signs of earthquake damage, this square is now a popular hang-out for locals. In the middle is a large tank and a whitewashed **Narayan Temple**, guarded by lions and griffons.

Uma Maheshwar Temple   HINDU TEMPLE
From the main square, head west through the village to a Ganesh shrine and a stone stairway that climbs to the triple-roofed Uma Maheshwar Temple. It's flanked by two stone elephants, decked out in spiked saddles to discourage children from sitting on them! The temple was originally built in 1673 with four roofs, but one was lost in the earthquake of 1934. This was the spot where Kirtipur's residents made their last stand during the 1768 siege.

Nagar Mandap
Sri Kirti Vihar   BUDDHIST TEMPLE
At the bottom of the hill, follow the left fork of the main road around the base of the hill to this classic Thai-style *wat* (Buddhist monastery) inaugurated by the Supreme Patriarch of Thailand in 1995.

Lohan Dehar   HINDU TEMPLE
From the main square, take a turn right, exiting at the southeast corner of the square to reach the 16th-century stone shikhara-style Lohan Dehar. Colourful religious ceremonies and low-key blessings are often held here.

Chilanchu Vihara   BUDDHIST STUPA
Built in 1515, this stately stupa crowns the hilltop. The harmika (square tower) above the dome was painted a rich blue, but it was removed for repairs after the 2015 earthquake and had not been reinstated when we last visited. The main stupa is surrounded by a garden of chaitya and fronted by a giant dorje (thunderbolt) symbol. To get here, go behind the Lohan Dehar temple, take a left down the narrow passageway and follow the alleyway down to the stupa.

⮌ Courses

Kagyu Institute of
Buddhist Studies   HEALTH & WELLBEING
(KIBS; ✆ 01-4331679; www.kirtipur.org; Dev Doka) Offers various courses for aspiring scholars of Buddhism, from three-day dharma studies to three-year certificates, at this peaceful hilltop gompa. Personal retreats and thangka painting courses are also offered. Application forms are available online.

AROUND THE KATHMANDU VALLEY KIRTIPUR

ℹ EXPLORING THE SOUTHERN VALLEY

The towns and villages of the southern valley can be explored by using local buses – which are cheap, frequent, overcrowded and slow – or by hiring a taxi for the day from Kathmandu. While most settlements saw some damage in the 2015 earthquake, only a few temples were completely destroyed and there is still much to see.

If you do hire a taxi, set off early and you can probably whizz through Kirtipur, Chobar, Pharping and Dakshinkali in a long day. Expect to pay around Rs 4000 from Kathmandu. In the past, the most enjoyable way of getting from Kathmandu to any of the towns in the southern valley was by rented bicycle. Today, however, ever increasing traffic and a quickly expanding city make this a far less enjoyable prospect, though the stretch between Pharping and Dakshinkali is still a pleasant ride.

For a twist, check out **Vespa Valley's** (www.vespavalley.com; tours US$70; ⊙ 10am) tours of Kirtipur, Bungamati and Khokana from the pillion seat of a Vespa scooter.

🛏 Sleeping & Eating

The Kirtipur Guide Association can organise local homestays (half-board room from Rs 2000), which receive good feedback from travellers looking for a deeper immersion into Newari town life.

Kirtipur Hillside Hotel HOTEL **$$**
(☑ 01-4334010; www.kirtipurhillside.com.np; s/d US$20/30; 🛜) A great option for those wanting to escape Kathmandu's fumes, with large and clean rooms – the best of which look out to the valley, with the Himalaya looming in the distance. Some rooms have balconies and these are offered on a 'first come, first served' basis. There's some lovely artwork (painted by the manager) and a pleasant rooftop restaurant.

Newa Lahani Restaurant NEPALI **$**
(mains Rs 60-180, set meals Rs 250; ⊙10am-7pm) Housed inside the underwhelming Newa Cultural Museum is this authentic Newari cuisine restaurant. Sitting is at ground level on mats, and utensils are provided. Meals consist of seasonal pulses and vegetables and are usually accompanied by beaten rice. Traditional cooking implements grace the walls as part of the museum display.

View Point Restaurant NEPALI, TIBETAN **$**
(☑ 9860429070; mains Rs 90-260; ⊙11am-9pm) Tasty Newari and Tibetan food, cheap beer and fantastic views make this a great stopover. Its rooftop is the prime viewing area, looking out to mountains ahead and Uma Maheshwar Temple (p173) to the side, and its set lunch plates, which come with several different curries, are a crash course in Newari cuisine.

ℹ Information

There's a Rs 100 entry charge to the village payable at the **Kirtipur Guide Association** (☑ 01-4334817; Chhthu; ⊙9am-5pm) office. The community-run guide association maintains a very useful tourist information office on the old town's main street. It can arrange homestays and guided tours of the town (from Rs 500), and hands out free photocopied information pamphlets in English.

ℹ Getting There & Away

Minibuses leave regularly for Kirtipur from Kathmandu's Ratna Park bus station (Rs 20, 30 minutes); the last is at 7pm. Taxis charge around Rs 700.

Pharping

📗 01

About 19km south of Kathmandu, Pharping is a thriving Newari town whose ancient Buddhist pilgrimage sites have been taken over by large numbers of Tibetans. A circuit of its religious sites makes for a compelling day out from Kathmandu. Pharping lies on the road to Dakshinkali and it's easy to visit both villages in a day by taxi, bus or motorbike (and maybe even bicycle if you don't mind the traffic and dust). En route you'll pass the pond at Taudaha, allegedly home to the nagas released from the Kathmandu lake. More Buddhist monasteries are opening up around here every year, some of which accept foreign dharma students.

⊙ Sights

Shesh Narayan Temple HINDU TEMPLE
About 600m downhill from the main junction at Pharping, in the direction of Kathmandu, the Shesh (or Sekh) Narayan Temple is a highly revered Vishnu shrine surrounded by ponds and statues, tucked beneath a rocky cliff wall and a **Tibetan monastery**. The main temple was built in the 17th century, but it's believed that the cave to the right (now dedicated to Padmasambhava, or Guru Rinpoche) has been a place of pilgrimage for far longer.

⊙ The Pilgrimage Route

The best way to visit the sights of Pharping is to join the other pilgrims on an easy, clockwise pilgrimage circuit (a *parikrama* in Nepali, or kora in Tibetan) around the centre of the town taking one to two hours.

Auspicious Pinnacle Dharma Centre of Dzongsar BUDDHIST MONASTERY
As you enter the town from the main road, take the first right and head uphill, passing a **Guru Rinpoche statue** in a glass case. Next to the statue is this dharma centre, a large chörten that contains 16 enormous prayer wheels.

Ralo Gompa BUDDHIST MONASTERY
The large white Ralo Gompa has a brightly painted chörten. It's located up the hill, past the line of Tibetan restaurants, towards the Drölma Lhakhang.

Sakya Tharig Gompa BUDDHIST MONASTERY
This monastery features an enormous and brightly painted chörten – step inside to see

hundreds of miniature chörten and statues of Guru Rinpoche set into alcoves in the walls. If you're lucky dozens of monks will be chanting inside; at such times a visit is utterly magical.

Drölma Lhakhang
BUDDHIST MONASTERY

(Ganesh-Saraswati (Green Tara) Temple) This shrine is sacred to both Hindus and Buddhists, who identify Saraswati as Tara. It's accessed via a set of steps to the west of Sakya Tharig Gompa.

Rigzu Phodrang Gompa
BUDDHIST MONASTERY

Adjacent to the Drölma Lhakhang is the Rigzu Phodrang Gompa, worth visiting for its impressive frieze of statues, with Guru Rinpoche surrounded by his fearsome incarnations as Dorje Drolo (riding a tiger) and Dorje Phurba (with three faces, Garuda-like wings and a coupling consort).

Guru Rinpoche Cave
BUDDHIST SHRINE

(Goraknath Cave) Climb the steps behind the Drölma Lhakhang, passing a rocky fissure jammed full of *tsha tsha* (stupa-shaped clay offerings) and cracks stuffed with little bags of wishes and human hair. Eventually you'll come to the walls of a large white monastery, inside which is this small cave. Take off your shoes and duck between the monastery buildings to reach the soot-darkened cavern, which is illuminated by butter lamps and a row of coloured lights.

Vajra Yogini Temple
BUDDHIST SHRINE

This sacred 17th-century Newari-style temple is devoted to the Tantric goddess Vajrayogini. One of the few female deities in Buddhist mythology, Vajrayogini was a wandering ascetic who achieved a level of enlightenment almost equivalent to the male Buddhas. Sadly, several historic Rana-style buildings that used to flank the courtyard collapsed in the 2015 earthquake.

Architecturally, Vajra Yogini is quite different to any of the other temples in town and is more of a classic Newari design. The temple is accessed down a flight of stairs leading from the Guru Rinpoche Cave.

🛏 Sleeping & Eating

Along the main road uphill from Pharping bazaar are numerous Tibetan restaurants serving momos, *thukpa* (Tibetan noodle soup) and butter tea to hungry pilgrims.

Family Guest House
GUESTHOUSE $

(✆01-4710412; r Rs 1000, without bathroom Rs 600) The only choice in the middle of Pharping, opposite the Guru Rinpoche statue, this well-run guesthouse is right on the pilgrim circuit and has a good rooftop restaurant.

Himalayan Height Resort
RESORT $$$

(✆01-4371537; www.everestlodges.com; Hattiban; r US$90-140; @�🛜) Perched on a ridge high above the valley in a pine forest, this small resort has 28 good-quality rooms, most with balconies that make the most of the stunning Himalayan views. The rooms are huge, with big comfy beds, heaters and modern bathrooms.

From the resort you can make an excellent three-hour (return) hike up to the peak of Champa Devi (2249m). Its main drawback is that it's very inaccessible; to get here you'll need a car to travel 2km on a steep, rutted dirt road that branches off about 3km north of Pharping. The condition of the road varies so ask the hotel about arranging transfers.

❶ Getting There & Away

Buses on route 22 leave throughout the day for Pharping from Kathmandu's Ratna Park bus station (Rs 40, 1½ hours), continuing to Dakshinkali. The last bus back to Kathmandu leaves around 5.30pm.

Around Pharping

Dakshinkali

The road from Pharping continues a few kilometres south to the blood-soaked temple of Dakshinkali, a favourite Hindu pilgrimage destination. Apart from the deep gorge containing the temple and its associated food stalls, there is little more to see here.

◉ Sights

Dakshinkali Temple
HINDU TEMPLE

Set at the confluence of two sacred streams in a rocky cleft in the forest this temple is dedicated to the goddess Kali, the most bloodthirsty incarnation of Parvati. To satisfy the blood-lust of the goddess, pilgrims drag a menagerie of animals down the path to the temple to be beheaded and transformed into cuts of meat by the temple priests, who are also skilled butchers.

PLEASING KALI

The consort of Shiva, Kali, one of the most bloodthirsty of all Hindu gods and goddesses, is the goddess of power and change, time and destruction. Her most famous pose is that of Dakshinkali, where she appears dancing in a destructive frenzy, with her tongue sticking out and drunk on the blood of her victims. The Dakshinkali Temple (p175) is dedicated to her in this form and animal sacrifices are a common occurrence at this and other Kali temples.

The sacrifices are made in order to placate the goddess' desire for blood, and there are strict rules specifying the ritual for how the animals should be sacrificed. It's a gruesome spectacle that some may prefer to avoid. While sacrifices occur frequently in certain Nepalese Hindu temples, it's nowadays somewhat rarer in much of India (it's still common in parts of the south and Bengal though). If you think sacrificing an animal is gruesome, then just be glad you weren't visiting the major Kali temple in Kolkata (India) around 200 years ago, when it's said that a human male child was sacrificed every day...

Once the sacrifice is made, the meat goes in the pot – pilgrims bring all the ingredients for a forest barbecue and spend the rest of the day feasting in the shade of the trees. Saturday is the big sacrificial day, and the blood also flows freely on Tuesday. For the rest of the week Dakshinkali is very quiet. During the annual celebrations of Dasain in October the temple is washed by a crimson tide and the image of Kali is bathed in the gore.

The approach to the temple from the bus stand winds through a religious bazaar, which is often hazy with smoke from barbecue fires. Local farmers sell their produce here to go into the post-sacrifice feasts, along with piles of marigolds, coconuts and other offerings for the goddess. Only Hindus can enter the temple courtyard where the image of Kali resides, but visitors can watch from the surrounding terraces. However, remember that the sacrifices are a religious event, with profound spiritual significance for local people, and not just an excuse to snap gruesome photos.

A pathway leads off from behind the main temple uphill to the small **Mata Temple** on the hilltop, which offers good views over the forest. Several snack stalls at the Dakshinkali bus park serve reviving tea and pappadams.

❶ Getting There & Away

Buses on route 22 run to Dakshinkali regularly from Kathmandu's Shahid Gate (Martyrs' Memorial) and Ratna Park bus station (Rs 50, 2½ hours). There are extra buses on Tuesday and Saturday to accommodate the pilgrimage crowds. From Pharping it's an easy 1km downhill walk or ride, but a steep uphill slog in the other direction.

Dollu

Three kilometres before Pharping on the road from Kathmandu, a side road turns north along a small valley to the village of Dollu, passing several huge Tibetan Buddhist monasteries. These include the **Rigon Tashi Choeling**, which contains some fine murals and statuary, including a fearsome image of Guru Dorje Drolo and his tiger.

Further north, a towering statue of **Guru Rinpoche** overlooks the monasteries and valley of Dollu.

If you walk a few hundred metres along the main road towards Kathmandu from the Dollu junction, you will reach a cluster of houses tucked into a hairpin bend, where a track leads uphill to the enormous **Neydo Tashi Choeling** monastery. This modern gompa looms over the surrounding landscape and the main prayer hall contains some stunning murals and a 15m-high statue of Sakyamuni. There are nearly 200 monks here, so the morning and evening prayer ceremonies are quite an experience.

🛏 Sleeping & Eating

★**Neydo Tashi Choeling**
Monastery Guest House   GUESTHOUSE **$$**
(📞01-6924606; www.neydohotel.com; s/d incl breakfast US$75/87; 🛜) This guesthouse, attached to the Neydo Tashi Choeling Monastery, is something a bit different – and quite wonderful. It offers subtly coloured, calming and highly comfortable rooms, but the best part of a stay is the opportunity to get to know the 200 resident monks: you can eat with them and participate in daily monastic life. Rates include tax.

It's a few kilometres out of Pharping on the road to Kathmandu.

Solid Rock Lodge & Restaurant
GUESTHOUSE $$

(📞 9823233093; https://solidrock.np.com; r Rs 3000; 🛜) Run by a Danish expat, this neat lodge high up in the Dollu valley is an escape from the madding crowds. Surrounded by rural vistas and Buddhist monasteries, your stay is sure to be peaceful. Rooms are in ingenious, earthquake-resistant bamboo cottages and there is a vegetarian restaurant with fabulous valley views.

Bungamati
📍 01 / POP 5720

One of the prettiest villages in the Kathmandu Valley, Bungamati faced the full force of the 2015 earthquake and many buildings and temples collapsed. The scars of the disaster will be a long time healing. Nevertheless, some monuments survived the disaster, while others are being rebuilt.

This historic village is the birthplace of Rato Machhendranath, the patron god of Patan, but the enormous shikhara temple that used to house the deity in the main square in Bungamati was shaken to rubble in the earthquake. Nevertheless, the Rato Machhendranath (p23) festival, which features a famous chariot parade between Bungamati and Patan continues.

Many locals make a living as woodcarvers, and workshops and showrooms surround the main square, which resonates with the tap-tap of chisels. To reach the square from the bus stand, follow the wide road south, then turn right, and then right again at an obvious junction by a Ganesh shrine.

⊙ Sights

With the destruction of the **Rato Machhendranath Temple** and **Bhairab Temple** in the 2015 quake, Bungamati lost part of its soul. These shrines played a hugely important role in the religious life of the valley and their loss is keenly felt by local people. However, their spiritual significance lies in the temple deities; both have been rescued and religious life continues. While the temples are being reconstructed, and this may take quite some time, visitors must make do with the reconstruction work, the temporary shrines for the deities and a handful of smaller temples in the backstreets.

Bungamati Culture Museum
MUSEUM

(Rs 25; ⊙10am-4pm Sat-Thu) On the narrow lane leading from the town's main square is this low-key, dusty museum displaying cultural objects from the area.

Dey Pukha
POND

(Central Pond) If you leave the main square by the northern gate, you'll pass a crumbling Buddhist courtyard monastery and an assortment of chaityas and shrines, then the brick-lined water tank of the Dey Pukha.

Karya Binayak Temple
HINDU TEMPLE

Halfway between Bungamati and Khokana, this temple is dedicated to Ganesh. Local pilgrims flock here on Saturdays for a *bhoj* (feast) and some *bhajan* (devotional music) – the Newari version of a barbecue and sing-along. To reach the temple, turn left when the path from Bungamati meets a larger track by a school.

❶ Getting There & Away

Buses to Bungamati leave frequently from Patan's Lagankhel station (Rs 25, 40 minutes). There are also a few buses direct to Kathmandu's Ratna Park bus station (Rs 35). You can also get here easily by motorcycle (or bike if you're not scared of the crazy traffic), turning off the Kathmandu Ring Rd at Nakhu.

Khokana
📍 01 / POP 12,786

A medieval Newari town, Khokana is smaller and sleepier than Bungamati, but it's still worth a quick look, despite much damage to heritage buildings in the 2015 earthquake. The main road leads through the village, which offers a window back in time, with mattress-makers stuffing cases with cotton, farmers baling straw, tailors stitching, and women spinning wool and winnowing rice. In the main village square is the triple-tiered **Shekala Mai Temple** (Rudrayani) (also known as Rudrayani), damaged but still standing after the disaster, with carved balconies covered by fretwork screens. The five-day **Khokana Jatra festival**, with its masked dancers, is usually held in October and is a good time to visit.

You'll need to pay Rs 100 to visit the town, collected at the tourist information centre. The fee goes to general upkeep of the village's streets.

Chapagaon

Chapagaon saw widespread damage to its tall brick Newari houses in the 2015 earthquake, but its temples were still standing when the dust settled. Beside the main road, which cuts through the central square en route to Tika Bhairab, are a number of shrines, including temples to Bhairab, Krishna and Narayan, but the main attraction here is the Vajra Varahi Temple.

◉ Sights

Vajra Varahi Temple   HINDU TEMPLE
(parking Rs 20) Set in a shady though litter-strewn woodland, this important Tantric temple was built in 1665 and it attracts lots of wedding parties, pilgrims and picnickers who descend en masse on Saturdays. Visitors pour milk and offerings over the statue of Nandi, the bull, in front of the temple and make similar offerings to the image of Vajra Varahi, an incarnation of the 'female Buddha' Vajrayogini.

The Vajra Varahi Temple is about 500m east of the main road on the back route to Godavari (turn left by the Narayan temple).

❶ Getting There & Away

Local minibuses leave from Lagankhel in Patan to Chapagaon (Rs 20, 45 minutes) or direct to the Vajra Varahi Temple (Rs 20).

The road to the temple continues through peaceful countryside to meet the Godavari road just south of Bandegaon. You can walk it in about an hour or cycle it in 20 minutes.

OFF THE BEATEN TRACK

THE LELE VALLEY

For a bit of exploring further afield, you can head towards the Lele Valley, which runs east off the valley of the Nakhu Khola, about 5km south of Chapagaon. Few tourists make it out here and the valley offers a window into a way of life that is fast vanishing in other parts of the Kathmandu Valley.

To get to Lele, follow the trucking road south from Chapagaon to the **Tika Bhairab**, a large rock shrine with a multicoloured painting of Bhairab, set at the confluence of two rivers. Buses run here from Chapagaon, sharing the road with noisy lorries hauling gravel to Kathmandu for construction.

Godavari

🎵 01

Godavari is best known for the green fingers of its inhabitants. The village is home to Nepal's National Botanical Gardens and the approach road is lined with the nurseries that supply Kathmandu with flowers and potted plants.

The 10km road from the Kathmandu Ring Rd forks in the middle of Godavari – the left fork goes to the botanical gardens while the right fork climbs past the Naudhara Kunda temple and turns into a dirt track running up to Pulchowki Mountain.

◉ Sights

If you plan on walking the remote trails in the forests surrounding Godavari, it's a good idea to get a guide, with locals warning of robberies. Hotels or restaurants should be able to help with a guide.

National Botanical Gardens   GARDENS
(foreigner/SAARC/Nepali Rs 226/57/34, camera/video Rs 20/150, child under 10yr half-price; ☺10am-5pm, to 4pm Nov-Jan) The verdant botanical gardens are a quiet and peaceful spot for a walk or picnic, except on Friday and Saturday when the place is overrun with school kids. The visitor centre has exhibits on Nepal's flora, and in the middle is the decorative **Coronation Pond** with its 7m commemorative pillar.

Godavari Kunda   HINDU SITE
If you go straight ahead at the junction before the National Botanical Gardens, you'll reach a cluster of local restaurants, the Godavari Kunda – a sacred spring on the right-hand side of the road – and, on the left, a tank bordered by a neat line of Shaivite shrines. Every 12 years (next in 2027) thousands of pilgrims come to the spring to bathe and gain spiritual merit. Next door is the large **O Sal Choling Godavari** Tibetan monastery.

Naudhara Kunda   HINDU TEMPLE
(Pulchowki Mai Temple) This temple is dedicated to one of the Tantric mother goddesses, and the two large pools before the temple compound are fed by nine spouts (known as the Naudhara Kunda) that represent the nine streams that flow from Pulchowki Mountain. It's located along the road at the junction by St Xavier's School, which veers off to the right.

Although entrance to the temple is free, there's a pretty good chance you'll be asked to pay Rs 100 by the Naudhara Community Forest group, as the temple sits on the edge of the forest.

Naudhara Community Forest   FOREST
(Rs 100, parking Rs 20; ⊘ 7am-4pm) The Naudhara Community Forest is 147 hectares of locally managed woodland, established with support from Bird Conservation Nepal (www.birdlifenepal.org). Guides (who almost certainly won't speak English) can be arranged through the ticket office for Rs 500 for a two- to three-hour tour. Note that some trails have been affected by landslides – check locally to see if tours are currently possible.

Shanti Ban Buddha   BUDDHIST STATUE
On the hillside above Godavari is an enormous golden Buddha image, created by Buddhists who were inspired by the Japanese Peace Pagoda movement. You'll probably need to ask directions to get here, but it's just west of the village proper and quite high above the main road. From the turn-off it's a 20-minute walk along a dirt road. As you get to the very end of the village, look for the green gate with a sign that says 'Shanti'; push through here and clamber up the steps to the statue.

Bishankhu Narayan   HINDU SHRINE
(Godamchowr) If you're looking for an excuse to get off the beaten track, the shrine of Bishankhu Narayan may do nicely. Dedicated to Vishnu, this chain-mail-covered shrine is reached by a steep stairway that climbs to the temple and then drops into a narrow fissure in the rock, where pilgrims test their sin levels by trying to squeeze through the tiny gap. If you get stuck, the sin in question is either gluttony or pride…

The unsealed 3km road to Bishankhu Narayan starts at Bandegaon on the Godavari road, and runs southeast over a small stream. At Godamchowr village, take the left fork at the football ground and climb for about 2km to reach the shrine.

Harisiddhi Bhagwan Temple   HINDU TEMPLE
(Harisiddhi) About 7km northwest of Godavari, on the main road, Harisiddhi is notable for the towering, four-tiered Harisiddhi Bhagwan Temple on its brick-paved market square. Dedicated to one of the fearsome incarnations of Durga, the temple has been painted in bright colours by local devotees and is still imposing, despite some surrounding earthquake damage. Any bus bound for Godavari can drop you here.

OFF THE BEATEN TRACK

PULCHOWKI MOUNTAIN

This 2760m-high mountain is the highest point around the valley and there are magnificent views from the summit, which is also home to the sacred **Pulchowki Mai Temple**. Here you'll find over 570 species of flowering plants and it's a popular spot for **birdwatching**, home to one-third of all the bird species in Nepal. There have been rumours for years that the government will turn this into a national park. The mountain is famous for its springtime (March to April) flowers, in particular its magnificent red and white rhododendrons.

To get here, the only options are a full-day hike along dirt tracks from Naudhara Kunda, or a very rough unsealed road that is only suitable for 4WDs, mountain bikes or trail motorcycles. There are no facilities so bring water, food, a compass and fellow travellers for company (trekkers have been robbed here in the past). It's about a six-hour return hike, but check the status of the trails before you head off.

🛏 Sleeping & Eating

There's nothing in the way of budget hotels here. The upmarket **Godavari Village Resort** (✆ 01-5560675; www.facebook.com/godavarivillageresort; ⟨🖥 ⚞⟩) was damaged in the 2015 earthquake but reopened in early 2018. There are a few cheap restaurants in front of the Godavari Kunda where day-trippers can grab a bite for lunch for not too many rupees.

Hotel View Bhrikuti   HOTEL $$
(✆ 01-5174071; www.hotelviewbhrikuti.com.np; s/d incl breakfast from US$70/90; ❋🖥🕾) A chintzy, well-run, businesslike hotel. Rooms here are large and surprisingly plush, with mod cons such as minibars, modern bathrooms and cable TV. It has an appealing rooftop restaurant too, with postcard-worthy mountain views on clear days.

ℹ Getting There & Away

Local minibuses (No 5) and buses (No 14) run between Lagankhel in Patan and Godavari (Rs 25, 45 minutes). The road is in reasonable condition for cycling or motorcycling, but watch for trucks headed for the mines near Tika Bhairab.

THE VALLEY FRINGE

Beyond Bhaktapur the landscape starts to rise, revealing views (on a clear day) north to the rugged mountain wall of the Himalaya, which is rarely visible from the bottom of the valley. Consequently, the towns at this end of the valley have been traditional weekend escapes for Kathmandu residents, who come not just to enjoy the views, but also the complex of trails that stitches them all together. Travellers have caught on, making the Valley Fringe a strong two- to three-day itinerary, particularly for hikers: the Valley Fringe Hiking Circuit (p183) maximises your time in this area.

Nagarkot

📍 01 / POP 4500 / ELEV 2175M

Nagarkot has a reputation as the top spot for enjoying Himalayan views from the comfort of your hotel balcony. Just 32km from Kathmandu, the village is packed with hotels lining a ridge, affording one of the broadest possible views of the Himalaya, with eight ranges visible (Annapurna, Manaslu, Ganesh Himal, Langtang, Jugal, Rolwaling, Everest and Numbur). However, timing is everything, as the mountains are notorious for disappearing behind cloudy skies. The best viewing seasons are October to December and March to April, when clear skies are likely.

Other than views, the town offers very little, so if you want to get out of your hotel you'll need to head to another resort, or into the outdoors. Note that if you have just arrived at Tribhuvan Airport, it's possible to come directly to Nagarkot and chill out in nature if you wish to avoid the city. Bring warm clothing after mid-October.

⊙ Sights & Activities

Nagarkot only exists because of the views – and what views they are! From any clear point on the ridge, you can take in a Himalayan panorama, from Dhaulagiri (8167m) in the west to Mt Everest (8848m) and Kanchenjunga (8586m) in the east, via Ganesh Himal (7406m), Langtang Lirung (7227m), Shisha Pangma (8012m), Dorje Lakpa (6966m) and Gauri Shankar (7134m).

The best place to enjoy these views is from the hotels that have snapped up all the prime property. The best choices are Hotel Country Villa (p183) or Club Himalaya

Resort (p182), both of which are happy to provide a beer or coffee to complement the vista – or take the edge off the cold. Alternatively, you can visit the Lookout Tower.

Lookout Tower   VIEWPOINT

A popular spot to soak in the Himalayan splendour is this tower, perched at 2164m on a ridge, although the rising vegetation can obscure the vista. It's around an hour's walk (4km) south from the village, and best at sunrise. If you're not up for a dark and chilly walk, taxis and private cars (return Rs 1200) are easily arranged through any hotel or the tourist offices.

**Nagarkot Buddha
Peace Garden**   BUDDHIST STATUE

(road to Nagarkot) FREE If you like climbing Mayan pyramids you will enjoy the steep climb up the stone steps to the garden atop this shrine. The central attraction is a massive gold Buddha, although the views of the adjacent valley, a community forest, aren't bad either. There are plans to build a monastery further up the mountain.

Nature Trail   WALKING

This easy two- to three-hour trekking loop around Nagarkot passes terraced hills, forests, fields of mustard flowers and rustic mudbrick farmhouses belonging to Tamang people. The trail has been further extended from Kartike village to Dhanda Gaun, adding panoramic views. However, signage is non-existent on this extension, so hire a guide if you want to do the full 12km trail.

🛏 Sleeping

Nagarkot has numerous guesthouses and hotels that take advantage of the views on the north side of the ridge, and charge a premium for the privilege. A few hotels still show signs of damage from the 2015 earthquake, although the town has largely recovered from it.

Nagarkot is more popular with domestic and Indian tourists than foreigners and can get very busy (and noisy with parties of young Nepalese playing loud music until late into the night), and hotel prices are much higher, and standards lower, than in areas more popular with foreign tourists. However, most of the hotels offer significant discounts so always ask when you book or check in, particularly in the low seasons (summer/winter).

Sherpa Alpine Cottage GUESTHOUSE $
(☎9841265231; sherpacottage@gmail.com; r Rs 1200, without hot water Rs 800; 🛜) Basic en suite cottages that are about as cheap as you'll find in Nagarkot. Most have memorable views. There's also a pleasant al fresco restaurant, with tables in huts around a terraced garden overlooking the valley.

Nagarkot B&B HOTEL $
(☎01-6680111; s/d incl breakfast US$18/22; 🛜) If you want budget accommodation in the downtown area, these simple rooms above some shops are a good bet if you don't mind some generator noise. The rooftop is your chill-out zone.

⭐**Mystic Mountain** RESORT $$
(☎01-4426646; www.hotelmysticmountain.com; r incl breakfast Rs 7500; P❄🛜☀) The only five-star property in Nagarkot, the newly opened Mystic Mountain is a steal at this upper-midrange price. With the exception of some growing pains in the kitchen, everything is top-notch, especially the staff. Best of all is the dramatic hillside location, which peers into the mists below, a phenomenon best enjoyed from the horizon pool.

⭐**Resort Eco-Home Nagarkot** GUESTHOUSE $$
(☎01-6680180; www.ecohomenagarkot.com; s/d US$28/35; 🛜) 🌿 This German-Nepalese–run guesthouse is the local centre for progressive travel, with a focus on sustainability, local crafts, organic dining and opportunities for women. A portion of profits goes towards local community projects – a rarity in Nepal. At the same time, this is a very well-run operation with consistent attention to detail and a 25% off-season discount. Taxes included.

An open hearth is the focus of the community dining room, and the epitome of this place, which aims to bring people of all kinds together. It does so successfully.

⭐**Nagarkot Farmhouse Resort** RESORT $$
(☎01-6202022; www.nagarkotfarmhouse.com; s/d incl half board Rs 5000/7500; P❄🛜) If you want to disconnect, this peaceful forest hotel is your place. With no TV or phone signal, you'll be forced to sit on your balcony enjoying a sensational sweep of peaks, and lovely valley views as well. Alternatively you can dip into the meditation room for some yoga. A dedicated owner ensures a great stay. Taxes included.

Nagarkot

The best rooms are in the Newari-inspired brick complex on the edge of the garden, with spotless bathrooms, wood stoves, deep mattresses and deckchairs. It's located about 2km past the Hotel Country Villa (p183) down the dirt track to Sankhu – a most difficult road during monsoon.

WORTH A TRIP

THE GIANT SHIVA

Lording it over the small village of Sanga, on the main road between Bhaktapur and Dhulikhel, is **Kailashnath Mahadev** (Sanga; Rs 100) a 43.5m-high Shiva statue said to be the tallest in the world. Completed in 2010, the statue may be on the kitschy side, but its copper paint and twin cobras are still memorable, as many a selfie reveals. Entry is via the Hilltake Health Spa and Resort.

Serene Resort HOTEL $$
(☏01-6680189; www.serene-resort.com; r US$80; P☎) Raising the local bar on style, these attached villas provide modern, nicely appointed rooms with cathedral ceilings in a private gated compound. The adjacent tower, under construction at the time of research, will offer sky box rooms with awesome views and a new restaurant. Rates include tax and service fee.

Peaceful Cottage HOTEL $$
(☏01-6680077; www.peaceful-cottage.com; r incl breakfast with/without view US$60/35, f US$70; ☎) This unique octagonal hotel, run by an irrepressible local entrepreneur, offers a hilltop location on the edge of a cliff, with excellent views, and the pleasant Café du Mont to hang out in. There is a variety of rooms to suit most budgets, all of which come with a free yoga class.

The corner rooms are best, but if you don't mind sacrificing the view, the economy rooms with large private balconies facing the forest are good value. There's also a family room that sleeps eight on top of the octagonal tower, but make sure it's aired out first.

Hotel at the End of the Universe GUESTHOUSE $$
(☏01-6680011; www.endoftheuniverse.com.np; r US$24-40, without bathroom US$15, ste US$60; ☎) ✿ As well as a great name, this resort offers an eclectic selection of accommodation, including rooms, bamboo cabins, 'gingerbread' cottages and A-frame tents, all set in a verdant garden; suites hold up to eight people. Guests enjoy an atmospheric stonewalled restaurant with big windows looking out to mountains and great food.

Best of all is the funky, laid-back vibe, which makes this hilltop hang-out feel like a friendly hostel. This may have something to do with those funny plants in the garden...

Hotel Green Valley HOTEL $$
(☏01-6680078; www.hotelgreenvalley.com.np; d from Rs 3000/3500; P❋☎) Completely renovated following the 2015 earthquake, this new 25-room glass hotel will reopen in April 2018 and offer memorable Himalayan vistas.

★**Club Himalaya Resort** RESORT $$$
(☏01-6680046; www.clubhimalaya.com.np; s/d incl breakfast from US$85/110, economy s/d excl breakfast US$50/80; ⊙restaurant 6.30-10am, 12.30-5pm & 6.30-10pm; P❋☎☀) This well-designed mountain lodge revolves around a huge circular glass room encompassing reception, a nifty heated pool and an able restaurant with an Indian/Chinese/continental menu. There's also an adjoining bar and dance floor with a rock-and-roll theme. But you came for the views, which are some of the best in Nagarkot.

Whether on the public terraces or the balconied rooms, this is an excellent place to hang out as either a guest or a visitor. Ten wheelchair-accessible rooms also offer a rare welcome for travellers with disabilities. Note that the economy rooms have no views, whereas the standard and deluxe do. Otherwise none of them will disappoint.

Nepal Yoga Retreat RESORT $$$
(☏9851092635, 9851037083; www.yogaretreatnepal.com; 1km from Telkot (Tharkot) towards Sankhu; s/d all-inclusive 3-day/2-night US$138/274; ☎) This is one of the best-regarded yoga retreats in Nepal, offering a full complement of expertly guided yoga courses, ayurveda massage, steam baths and more. Accommodation is in fairly simple bamboo cottages and rooms with a nicely elevated view of the valley below. It's more suitable for serious yoga students.

Fort Resort RESORT $$$
(☏01-6680069; www.fortretreat.com; s/d/ste US$90/110/160; @☎) This sprawling Newari brick hotel lives up to its name, with grand entrances, winding corridors and an impeccably trimmed garden terrace looking out over a natural amphitheatre of peaks. While part of the hotel collapsed in the 2015 earthquake, 80% was salvaged and reconstituted as a new wing with classic architectural detail and fine views.

The dignified rooms are split between here and several very cosy cottages nestled in a wooded hillside below, with rustic wood-fire furnaces (make sure yours has been aired out in the off season). These take some legwork to reach so opt for the main building if that's an issue. Everyone will enjoy the atmospheric restaurant rooted in home-grown ingredients.

Eating

The independent restaurants in town are nearly interchangeable, with the same local menu. Most people eat at the lodges; the best choices are the Fort Resort, **Hotel Country Villa** (☑ 01-6680128; www.hotelcountryvilla.com; s/d incl breakfast from US$85/105; P ☀ 🛜) (for breakfast), Club Himalaya Resort, Peaceful Cottage (Café du Mont) and, for a real splash-out, the new five-star Mystic Mountain (p181).

Café du Mont   INTERNATIONAL $$
(☑ 01-6680077; Peaceful Cottage; mains Rs 200-600; ☺ 6am-9.30pm) Open to nonguests, the restaurant at the Peaceful Cottage hotel is housed inside its octagonal tower and has an eclectic menu of local, Chinese, Indian and continental dishes served with a big dollop of mountain-view love. Try the fresh Sagarmatha coffee in the new bakery.

Berg House Café   INTERNATIONAL $$
(dishes Rs 180-400; ☺ 7am-9pm) By the highway's main junction, this colourful and popular local hang-out is packed with fossils, gnarled tree roots and other found bits of bric-a-brac. The traveller-oriented menu runs to pizzas, sandwiches and steaks, although the staff are so laid-back that it can take an age for food to arrive. Pass on the eight guest rooms: hopefully the kitchen is cleaner.

ⓘ Information

There are several **ATMs** near the bus park. Internet is available at NagarkotGuide.com.

Nagarkot Naldum Tourism Development Committee (NNTDC; ☑ 01-6680122; ☺ 10am-5.30pm Sun-Fri) Very helpful, with good information on walks in the area. It can arrange hiking guides for around Rs 3000 per day.

NagarkotGuide.com (☑ 9851016655, 9841412762; www.nagarkotguide.com) Privately run NagarkotGuide.com is a tourist information service that also sells local tours and organises transport to Kathmandu. It's a brilliant resource for information on Nagarkot and its environs.

AROUND THE KATHMANDU VALLEY NAGARKOT

OFF THE BEATEN TRACK

VALLEY FRINGE HIKING CIRCUIT

The Valley Fringe contains a complex web of hiking paths. From any town within it you can hike to another, leaving you wondering what the best route to follow is. All things considered, local guides advise a anticlockwise circuit that begins in Panauti and leads through Balthali and Namobuddha to Dhulikhel. An ideal itinerary is a three-day/two-night excursion from Kathmandu, as follows:

Day One Take an early bus from Kathmandu's Ratna park direct to Panauti (1½ hours). Tour Panauti in the morning, then take a local bus to Khopasi Bridge (you can also walk there in 40 minutes, but the trail follows the dusty road). Cross this scenic suspension bridge and continue on to verdant Balthali (1½ hours), where you can stay in any one of its scenic mountain lodges.

Day Two Pick up a guide from your lodge and head for Namobuddha. This is a great three-hour trek, with a scenic ridge hike and another photo-op suspension bridge. Overnight at the Namobuddha Resort (p191) or even the Thrangu Tashi Yangtse Monastery (p190).

Day Three Hike from Namobuddha to Dhulikhel (three hours). See the sights, have lunch at the Himalayan Restaurant (p188), and then take a bus back to Kathmandu.

It's possible to adapt this basic itinerary to your own needs, of course. You could stay an extra night anywhere along the circuit, or press on and make the entire trek a one-night event. Whichever way you do it, if you use this basic circuit as your template you will maximise the time you dedicate to this area. Since the Valley Fringe is not greatly affected by the monsoon, the circuit is good year-round.

HIKING AND CYCLING TO/FROM NAGARKOT

There are a number of hiking and cycling routes in this area, best walked downhill from Nagarkot. Nepa Maps' 1:25,000 *Nagarkot – Short Trekking on the Kathmandu Valley Rim* is useful, though its 1:50,000 *Around the Kathmandu Valley* is probably good enough.

Mountain bikes can be hired from the Nagarkot Naldum Tourism Development Committee (p183) for Rs 600 per hour.

Bottled water is mostly unavailable on these routes, so be sure to pack plenty of water. Note that some features on these routes may have changed since the earthquake; seek local advice before you set off.

To Dhulikhel (Four to Seven Hours from Nagarkot)

The **Kathmandu Valley Cultural Trekking Trail**, established by NETIF (www.netif-nepal.org), is a direct 20km trail to Dhulikhel. While for the most part it's well signed, there remain some confusing sections, so you'll probably need to ask passing villagers for directions along the way. The trail starts past Club Himalaya Resort (p182), following the road past the army barracks. Keep an eye out for the sign to Dhulikhel, which leads you to the village of Rohini Bhanjyang Sera. From here follow the road straight (don't take the left or right paths) and take the hill up, where you'll need to turn left at the intersection.

After 1km take the small trail on the right that's a steep downhill into the valley, leading you to the village of Tanchok. At Tanchok take the main jeep track and follow it uphill to Tusal. Head right to Opi where you cross the main jeep track and on to the final 5km stretch to Dhulikhel, crossing over the Arniko Hwy to Himalayan Horizon Hotel (p187), 500m from the bus park.

To Changu Narayan (4½ Hours from Nagarkot)

From Nagarkot, it's an easy stroll along the spur to Changu Narayan. The trail runs parallel to the road to Bhaktapur along the ridge, branching off at the sharp hairpin bend at Telkot (marked on some maps as Deurali Bhanjhang). Catching a bus to here from Nagarkot will save you the tedious first half of the walk.

From the bend, follow the middle dirt road up into the Telkot Forest and keep to the left. The track climbs uphill through a pine forest for about 20 minutes to the top of the ridge and then follows the ridge line, dropping gently down to Changu Narayan. On clear days there are good views of the Himalaya. You can follow this track on foot or on a mountain bike or motorcycle.

In the reverse direction, pick up the track near the Changu Narayan Hill Resort, and take the middle road where the track splits. You can also take an onward hike to Bodhnath or Sankhu.

To Sundarijal (One to Two Days from Nagarkot)

It takes two easy days – or one very long day – to skirt around the valley rim to Sundarijal, from where you can travel by road to Gokarna, Bodhnath and Kathmandu, trek for another day along the valley rim to Budhanilkantha, or start the treks to Helambu or Gosainkund. Accommodation is available at Bhotichaur and Sundarijal in local guesthouses, but the trails can be confusing so ask for directions frequently.

Start by following the Sankhu trail as far as Kattike (about one hour), then turn right (north) to Jorsim Pauwa. Walk further down through Bagdhara to Chowki Bhanjyang (about one hour) and on for one more hour through Nagle to Bhotichaur, a good place to stop overnight in a village inn.

On day two, walk back up the trail towards Chowki Bhanjyang and take the fork leading uphill by a chautara (porters' resting place). This path climbs uphill to cross a ridge line before dropping down on the middle of three trails to Chule (or Jhule). Here the path enters the Shivapuri Nagarjun National Park and contours around the edge of the valley for several hours before dropping down to Mulkarkha, on the first stage of the Helambu trek. From Mulkarkha, it's an easy descent beside the water pipeline to Sundarijal.

An alternative route runs northwest from Bhotichaur to Chisopani, the first overnight stop on the Helambu trek, which has several trekking lodges. The next day, you can hike southwest over the ridge through Shivapuri Nagarjun National Park to Sundarijal.

ⓘ Getting There & Away

By the time you read this, NagarkotGuide.com (p183) should have restarted a daily tourist minibus service direct to Kathmandu (Rs 450, two hours). It will depart Nagarkot at 10am from the **bus park**, and collect from local hotels in advance if you organise this through your hotel or the tourist office (p183). From Kathmandu it will depart at 1.30pm from a lot in front of the Hotel Malla in Lainchaur. There is no fixed bus stop, however, so you may need to ask around. Be sure to contact NagarkotGuide.com ahead of time to make sure this service is running.

To reach Nagarkot by public bus from Kathmandu you'll need to transfer at Bhaktapur. From here buses to Nagarkot (Rs 55, 1½ hours) leave every 45 minutes from 5am to 5pm. There are also buses to Sankhu and Bodhnath in the high seasons (autumn/spring).

A one-way taxi from Kathmandu to Nagarkot costs around Rs 4000, or Rs 5500 return.

Dhulikhel

📞 011 / POP 16,000 / ELEV 1550M

Dhulikhel is one of the more popular places from which to observe the high Himalaya. From the edge of the ridge, a stunning panorama of peaks unfolds, from Langtang Lirung (7227m) in the west, through Dorje Lakpa (6966m) to the huge bulk of Gauri Shankar (7134m) and nearby Melungtse (7181m), and as far as Numbur (5945m) in the east. The most common itinerary is two nights with a side trip to the sacred stupa at Namobuddha (p190), a 12km drive or three-hour walk south.

Unlike that other popular viewpoint, Nagarkot, Dhulikhel is also a real Newari town, with a temple-lined village square and a life outside of tourism.

◉ Sights

The old part of the town is interesting to wander around. The main square contains a triple-roofed **Hari Siddhi Temple** and a three-tiered, 16th-century **Vishnu Temple** fronted by two worshipful Garudas in quite different styles and heights. Northwest of the square is a **Ganesh Temple**. Further on lies the modern **Gita Temple** and the adjacent three-tiered, Newari-style **Bhagwati Shiva Temple**.

Shiva Temple　　　　HINDU TEMPLE

If you take the road leading southeast from the bottom of the town square for 2km, you'll pass a playing field and the turn-off to the Kali Temple. Just beyond this junction, a Ganesh shrine marks the path down to a picturesque little Shiva temple at the bottom of a gorge, with a stream trickling by.

The temple enshrines a four-faced lingam topped by a metal dome with four nagas arching down from the pinnacle. You are liable to find holy men dispensing spiritual advice. Note the statues of a Malla royal family in the courtyard.

Kali Temple　　　　HINDU TEMPLE

(Rs 100) If you don't mind a steep 30-minute climb, you can head up a series of switchbacks on concrete steps to reach this modern hilltop temple (also called 'Thousand Steps Temple' for obvious reasons) for excellent mountain views. The viewing tower was being reconstructed at the time of research. On the way you'll pass **Shanti Ban**, a massive golden statue of Buddha.

It's also the way to Namobuddha, so if you plan on heading there, it makes sense to save the walk up here until then.

🏃 Activities

The hike or mountain-bike trip from Dhulikhel to Namobuddha is a fine leg-stretcher, and one of the most popular activities for visitors. It takes about three hours each way.

From Dhulikhel the trail first climbs up to the Kali Temple lookout then drops down to the left after the Deurali Restaurant for half an hour to the village of **Kavre**, by the road to Sindhuli. Cross the road and the walk continues for an hour to the village of **Faskot**. Beyond here you finally crest the ridge and see a Tibetan monastery on a hilltop, with Namobuddha just below it. To reach the stupa, take the right branch where the path forks. The trail is well signed, so you shouldn't need a guide to get here. From here it is possible to reach Panauti via Sunthan (two hours) or Balthali (three hours).

When coming from Namobuddha, you will do this trail in reverse as the last leg of the Valley Fringe Hiking Circuit (p183).

🛏 Sleeping

In general, the quality of accommodation has declined since the 2015 earthquake, due to low visitation. Most of the expensive places with good views are strung out on dirt roads leading off the highway. The cheapies are down the winding back road that leads southeast from the main square.

Dhulikhel & Around

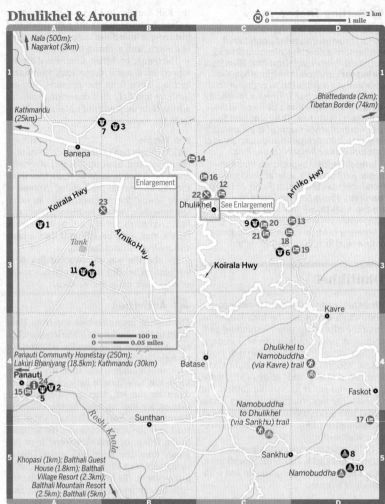

Padma Guesthouse GUESTHOUSE **$**
(☑ 9808992383, 9843567446; r Rs 1200, without bathroom Rs 1000) If you don't mind a 15-minute walk from the bus station, this friendly, family-run guesthouse is your best budget option. Owned by the chef at Dwarika's, located across the street, it offers clean rooms with balconies on several floors and homemade meals (Rs 200 to Rs 500). Some rooms sleep four.

Shiva Guest House GUESTHOUSE **$**
(☑ 9841254988; d Rs 800, without bathroom Rs 700) This family-run farmhouse has four very basic but clean rooms and great views from the upper floors and rooftop. Food comes fresh from the organic garden: you can pick fruit right off the trees. Take the stairs up from Shiva Temple (p185), a 15-minute walk from the bus station, then follow the treacherous cliffside path. Don't try this at night.

Snow View Guest House GUESTHOUSE **$**
(☑ 9841482487; r Rs 1000) While a bit rough, this homestay may be the cheapest place with a proper mountain view, and sits beside a pleasant garden restaurant. Only two rooms look directly onto the mountains, but the rooftop has enough views for everyone.

Dhulikhel & Around

★ Dhulikhel Lodge Resort   HOTEL $$

(☏ 011-490114, Kathmandu 01-4991353; www.dhulik hellodgeresort.com; s/d from US$60/70; ✳️🛜) This wildly popular hotel, which contains the equally popular Himalayan Restaurant (p188), is the go-to destination for Kathmandu weekenders. A modern take on traditional Newari style, it has cracking views (particularly from the top floor) and comfortable rooms. The new spa is underwhelming, however. Make sure to reserve ahead.

Mirabel Resort   HOTEL $$

(☏ 011-490972; www.mirabelresorthotel.com; s/d incl breakfast US$50/70; ✳️🛜) This hotel's attractive layout, with a long colonnade connecting reception to the rooms, forms a peaceful hillside compound with a vague smell of empire about it. Ageing rooms have wooden balconies facing the Himalaya, which can also be seen from the rooftop and gardens. It's a great place to set your period novel, as the eclectic guests would undoubtedly agree.

Panorama Resort & Spa   HOTEL $$

(☏ 011-490887; r Rs 3000; ✳️🛜) An option for those who really want to get away from it all, this remote hotel offers the full 'panorama view' from some rooms plus good food served in an unexpectedly elegant dining room. Just don't expect much company. Located 2km above town on the dirt track to the Kali Temple (p185), it's a real hike without your own transport. Round-trip from the bus stop will cost you Rs 1500.

★ Dwarika's Resort Dhulikhel   LUXURY HOTEL $$$

(☏ 011-490612; www.dwarikas-dhulikhel.com; s/d all-inclusive from US$410/440, Royal Suite US$2000, butler extra; ✳️🛜🏊) One of the finest and most exclusive places to stay in Nepal, this beautifully conceived boutique resort built of red Newari brick sprawls over 22 lush acres. It takes in infinity pools with mountain vistas, meditation suites, massage rooms, several restaurants and bars, and huge but understated terracotta-style rooms, from the entry level junior suite to the two-floor Royal Suite.

Not to be missed is the Crystal House, with walls of back-lit crystals. There is also a spry ayurvedic practitioner who materialises in the garden, discusses the human soul and disappears into the forest. Guests choose between various courses on ceramics, mandala painting, organic cooking, yoga and more. There are also two helipads to whisk you away to the mountains. The only problem is that almost no one in Nepal can afford it. Walk-in guests are limited to lunch and dinner reservations.

Himalayan Horizon Hotel   HOTEL $$$

(☏ 011-490296; www.himalayanhorizon.com; s/d incl breakfast from US$81/103; 🛜) Also known as the Hotel Sun-n-Snow, this huge hillside complex uses traditional brickwork and woodcarving to create a Newari ambience. It's not quite 'old Dhulikhel', but the restaurant and garden terrace exude history. Rooms have sublime views of the snow-covered peaks but are badly in need of renovation.

✗ Eating

There's a very limited choice of places to eat. Most travellers opt to dine at their hotels. If you want to get out, the best option is the popular restaurant at Dhulikhel Lodge Resort (p187).

Chapro   NEPALI $

(daal bhaat Rs 150-200; ⏱7am-8pm) If you haven't overdosed on daal bhaat yet, this local emporium dishes out 500 meals a day at bargain prices, making it a local phenomenon. Look for the Nepali sign with blue Pepsi logos on either side, near the bus stop.

Newa Kitchen   INTERNATIONAL, NEPALI $

(dishes Rs 100-300; ⏱7am-8pm) Cheap and cheerful upstairs eatery by the bus stand with a mixed menu of Nepali, Indian, Chinese and European standards.

★ Himalayan Restaurant   MULTICUISINE $$

(www.dhulikhellodgeresort.com; Dhulikhel Lodge Resort; mains Rs 400-500; ⏱7am-9pm; 🛜) This restaurant at the Dhulikhel Lodge Resort (p187) is the only decent place to eat in downtown Dhulikhel, and it's good enough to attract people all the way from Kathmandu. If the weather allows, grab a seat by the railing and enjoy fantastic mountain views along with the Indian, Chinese and continental menu. Reservations essential on weekends. If the weather doesn't cooperate, you'll find a great circular fireplace inside with an aprés-ski atmosphere.

❶ Getting There & Away

Frequent buses to Dhulikhel leave from Kathmandu's Ratna Park bus station (Rs 55, two hours), passing Bhaktapur (Rs 35, 45 minutes) en route. The last bus goes back to Kathmandu at around 5pm. A taxi to Kathmandu costs Rs 2500.

Buses to Namobuddha (Rs 50) depart every two hours between 8am and 4pm.

The walk to Dhulikhel (p184) from Nagarkot is an interesting alternative.

Panauti

📞 011 / POP 10,000

One of the oldest towns in Nepal, Panauti offers a poignant look at the passage of time. From the crowded bus stand in the sprawling concrete mess of the new town, you slip down a brick street into the Old Bazaar, the remains of an ordered and prosperous medieval city that would have been a wonder to behold in its heyday. Located at the sacred confluence of the Roshi Khola and Pungamati Khola, it is dotted with ancient temples.

Panauti was also once a trading capital, as revealed by several Rana-era mansions restored by the French government. Squint at the merchants lining the street and you can cast your mind back hundreds of years. But when you open your eyes amid today's widespread decay, you'll undoubtedly feel a twinge of melancholy, for while there are some interesting sights in this Newari town, it was clearly much better off centuries ago.

> **WORTH A TRIP**
>
> ### CHANDESHWARI TEMPLE
>
> If you haven't had your fill of Hindu temples in Dhulikhel, there's another famous one in neighbouring Banepa. Legend has it that the people of this valley were once terrorised by a demon known as Chand, who was defeated by one of the fearsome incarnations of Parvati, earning the goddess a new title – Chandeshwari, 'Slayer of Chand'. The **Chandeshwari Temple** has an enormous mural of Bhairab on its wall, and is a popular pilgrimage spot where animals are sacrificed on feast days. The main mandir, built in the stepped Newari style is intact, but the brick shikhara temple in the courtyard collapsed in the 2015 earthquake; only a foundation remains. In front of the temple is a row of columns supporting statues of a menagerie, and the struts supporting the triple-tiered roof show the eight Ashta Matrikas and eight Bhairabs. On the north side of the approach road is a smaller temple dedicated to the **Mother of Chandeshwari**.
>
> Banepa is eight minutes by bus from Dhulikhel. Follow the brick-paved streets heading north from its hellish highway into its old town. Here you'll find a few other temples built between the 14th and 16th centuries, when Banepa was an important stop on the trade route to Tibet.

TRICKERY & REPENTANCE AT PANAUTI

Legend has it that Ahilya, the beautiful wife of a Vedic sage, was seduced by the god Indra, who tricked her by assuming the shape of her husband. When the sage returned and discovered what had happened he took his revenge by causing Indra's body to become covered in yonis – female sexual organs! Naturally, Indra was somewhat put out by this and for many years he and his wife Indrayani repented at the auspicious *sangam* (river confluence) at Panauti.

Parvati, Shiva's consort, took pity upon Indrayani and turned her into the invisible river, Padmabati, but it was some years before Shiva decided to release Indra from his strange affliction. The god appeared in Panauti in the form of a giant lingam and when Indra bathed in the river, his yonis disappeared. Locals maintain that this miraculous Shiva lingam is the one enshrined in the Indreshwar Mahadev Temple.

⊙ Sights

The Old Bazaar is defined by its brick streets. Walk about 200m from the bus station towards the town centre and you'll see the first brick path on the left leading to an arched gateway. Another 100m from here, on the left, is Café Lampati (p190), the best place to lunch. Across the street is a small crafts store specialising in woodcarvings. The street is lined with merchants selling silk and cotton from their shopfronts, which look like large doorways.

Continuing on, turn right just before the Nepal Vocational Academy; there's a souvenir shop on the corner, and one of many homestays above. Walk straight ahead and you'll end up at the famous Indreshwar Mahadev Temple complex. Don't miss the **Panauti Museum** inside, which will give you some historical context on the city.

Behind the Indreshwar Mahadev complex, at the confluence of the two rivers, lies the **Krishna Narayan Temple**. The **Brahmayani Temple** lies across the northern Pungamati River: take one of the twin pedestrian bridges. Having covered the major points of interest, wander, absorb and contemplate.

Indreshwar Mahadev Temple   HINDU TEMPLE
(foreigner/SAARC incl guide & entry to museum Rs 300/100; ⊙7.30am-5pm Oct-Mar, to 5.30pm Apr-Sep) Panauti's most famous temple is set in a vast courtyard full of statuary on the isthmus between the Roshi and Pungamati rivers; some earthquake damage is still visible. Topped by a three-storey pagoda roof, the temple is a magnificent piece of Newari architecture, and one of the tallest pagoda-style temples in Nepal. The first temple here was founded over a lingam in 1294, but the shrine was rebuilt in its present form in the 15th century.

The lingam is said to have been created personally by Shiva. The woodcarvings on the temple's windows, doorways and roof struts are particularly fine, and the erotic carvings here are subtle and romantic rather than pornographic. The upper section of the temple is hung with pots and pans – offerings from young married couples hoping for a prosperous family life.

To the south of the main temple is the rectangular **Unamanta Bhairab Temple**, with three faces peering out of the upstairs windows. Located within is a statue of Bhairab, accompanied by goddesses. A small, double-roofed Shiva temple stands in one corner of the courtyard, and a second shrine containing a huge black image of Vishnu as Narayan faces the temple from the west.

Inside the temple compound is also the well-done **Panauti Museum**, an interesting collection of artefacts from the region – brassware, woodcarvings, statuary – including original sections from the Indreshwar Mahadev Temple.

Panauti Peace Gallery   MUSEUM
(⊙10.30am-5.30pm Sun-Fri) **FREE** Next to the tourism office (p190) in a rickety building, this museum has a rambling collection, including an antique walking-stick sword, straw-brush comb and the gall bladder of an elephant. Turn the wrong way and you will end up in someone's house!

✪ Festivals & Events

Chariot Festival   RELIGIOUS
(⊙May/Jun) Held at the beginning of the monsoon each year (May/June), when images of the gods from the town's various temples are drawn around the streets in wooden chariots, starting from the main square.

Magh Sankranti   RELIGIOUS

Every year during the Nepali month of Magh (usually January), pilgrims come to Panauti to bathe at the two rivers' confluence to celebrate the end of the month of Pus, a dark time when religious ceremonies are forbidden. Every 12 years – next in 2022 – this is accompanied by a huge *mela* (fair) attracting devotees and sadhus from all over Nepal.

🛏 Sleeping

Accommodation options are few and far between, and most visitors come on day trips. Apart from one decent hotel, there are several homestays advertised in the Old Bazaar, but some are only open sporadically, and quality can be a serious problem. If you can't find one to your liking, visit the Panauti Tourism Development Center or Panauti Community Homestay, north of the bus park.

Panauti Community Homestay   ACCOMMODATION SERVICES $

(☏ 11-441015, 9849318778, 9803387171; www.fb.com/panauti.homestay) Local clearing house for homestays. Follow the road leading from the corner of the bus station, next to Janata Bank. The office is 1km away on the right.

Hotel Panauti   HOTEL $

(☏ 011-440055; www.facebook.com/Hotel-Panauti-140104812677698; r Rs 1500, without bathroom Rs 500; 🛜) The only game in town. It's close to the old town and in decent condition.

🍴 Eating

Panauti has two decent restaurants in the Old Bazaar, but only one is open past 6pm. For a truly local experience, enter the purple door across the street from Hotel Panauti ...

Café Lampati   NEPALI $

(mains Rs 100-400; ⊙ 8am-9.30pm) Hidden under the roof of a former temple outbuilding, this restaurant-bar shines like a lighthouse in the fog. It's the perfect stop for lunch while wandering the Old Bazaar. Even better, there is a selection of Nepali whisky, a cultural experience of another kind. Look up to the left about 100m from the main entrance to the Old Bazaar and you'll see the narrow windows perched over the street.

Namaste Café   NEPALI $

(mains Rs 100-300; ⊙ 8am-6pm) Local Nepali resto with outdoor dining near the entrance to the Indreshwar Mahadev Temple (p189).

❶ Information

Panauti Tourism Development Center
(☏ 9841360750, 011-440093; www.welcomepanauti.com; ⊙ 10.30am-4pm Sun-Fri), at the start of the old town, has brochures and can arrange homestays.

❶ Getting There & Away

Panauti is tucked away in a side valley off the Arniko Hwy, about 7km south of Banepa. Buses run every 15 minutes between Panauti and Kathmandu's Ratna Park bus station (Rs 70, 1½ to two hours); the last bus leaves Panauti at 5.30pm. For Dhulikhel you'll have to change in Banepa (Rs 15, 20 minutes). It's also possible to walk to Panauti from Dhulikhel (three to four hours), although the path now leads along a dusty road much of the way.

Namobuddha

With its own enormous Buddhist monastery, a famous stupa and a wonderful, ecologically sensitive resort, all set in a verdant forest, Namobuddha feels like one place where Siddhartha Gautama would feel right at home.

◉ Sights

Thrangu Tashi Yangtse Monastery   BUDDHIST MONASTERY

(☏ 01-1683183; http://namobuddha.org) At the top of Namobuddha hill, the magnificent Thrangu Tashi Yangtse Monastery is a sprawling Tibetan Buddhist monastic complex with gleaming golden arched roofs, officially opened in December 2008. Over 250 monks live here, including many young monks attending its school. Day visitors can sit in the back of the main hall during meditation sessions. Just follow the chanting...

Namobuddha Stupa   BUDDHIST STUPA

Along with Bodhnath and Swayambhunath, the Namobuddha Stupa is one of the three most important Buddhist pilgrimage sites in Nepal, attracting large numbers of Tibetans from Nepal, India and Tibet itself.

The site is sacred due to the inspiring legend about the Buddha, who, when in a previous life as a prince, encountered a tigress that was close to death from starvation and unable to feed her cubs. In an act of compassion he allowed the hungry tigress to consume him, a deed that transported him to the higher realms of existence. A marble tablet depicts the event in a small cave up the forested path to the left of the stupa.

🛏 Sleeping

★ Namobuddha Resort   RESORT $$
(☑ 9851106802; www.namobuddharesort.com;
s/d US$52/72; @ 🛜) 🍃 This delightful eco-
retreat is a 30-minute walk from Namobuddha Stupa. Its charming, upmarket Nepali
cottages feature stone walls with pitched
slate roofs, loft beds, low wooden doorways
and Himalayan views. The sparkling farmhouse kitchen dishes out fresh-baked sour-
dough bread, greens from the garden, cottage cheese and even homemade ice cream
from the all-vegetarian menu. If you ever decide to leave your cosy cottage, there's also a
sauna, floatation tank and yoga/meditation
hall. Reservations highly recommended.

Thrangu Tashi Yangtse
Monastery Guesthouse   MONASTERY $$
(☑ 9808786043; http://namobuddha.org; r incl
meals per person Rs 3000) It's possible to stay
in a single room in the monastic guesthouse,
vegetarian meals included, but it helps to have
a sincere interest in Buddhism, as the monks
appear sensitive to visitor numbers. Looking
uphill, the guesthouse is on the far left. If no
one's present, call the manager on the number
posted at reception. No electronics.

ⓘ Getting There & Away

As befits a pilgrimage, it's best to walk to Namobuddha, either from Dhulikhel (p185) or from
Balthali, as part of the Valley Fringe Hiking Circuit
(p183). There's also a road here from Dhulikhel,
served by unpleasantly crowded buses (Rs 50, 45
minutes, every 90 minutes). They depart from the
bottom of the hill near the stupa.

From the Namobuddha stupa you can hike
directly to Panauti in two hours, although you'll
miss beautiful Balthali. A trail descends from
the right side through forest to the small village of Sankhu (distinct from the other village
called Sankhu in the northeastern valley), with
temples and riverside ghats. Shortly after the
track splits: the right fork leads to Batase and
Dhulikhel, while the left fork winds past terraced
fields to Sunthan and Panauti. As you approach
Panauti, cross the stream over a suspension
bridge to the ghats and then follow the road as it
curves round to the Indreshwar Mahadev Temple
(p189), Panauti's main sight.

Balthali

POP 5000
Balthali is a paradisiacal valley nestled amid
forested hills, its floor coated with golf-
course-green rice paddies whose swirling

contours form a work of art. The village of
the same name has no centre, being strung
out along the road and elsewhere. The misty
mornings here are a particular delight, their
peace broken only by the crowing of roosters
far and wide. This is a largely undiscovered
destination. You'll feel like you have gone
back 50 years.

🛏 Sleeping

There is a surprising concentration of excellent lodges with similar names, one guesthouse and two homestays in the village.

Balthali Guest House   GUESTHOUSE $
(☑ 9841442614, 9851106360; www.facebook.com/
Balthali-Guest-House-1715743521991054; s/d incl
breakfast & dinner Rs 2500/5000, without bathroom Rs 2000/4000) Basic rooms with nice
roof dining in the midst of the village. It's
the salmon-coloured house, but you can ask
directions from anyone.

Balthali Village Resort   LODGE $$
(☑ Kathmandu 01-4108210; www.balthalivillage
resort.com; s/d incl breakfast from US$66/72;
🛜) Just downhill from the Balthali Mountain Resort, and owned by the same family,
this property was the first lodge in Balthali. There is a variety of rooms, some newer
than others, and a nice communal dining
area. Balconies offer superb views of the valley and mountains.

★ Balthali Mountain Resort   LODGE $$$
(☑ 977011691191; www.balthalimountainresort.
com; s/d from US$80/90; 🛜) Beautifully
perched on a hilltop, the tin-roofed red-
brick cottages here are deceptively simple
but perfectly suited for tired trekkers, with
comfy beds and tubs. Two viewing decks,
one with 360-degree views, are a great place
to take your drink from the bar. The great
surprise is the outstanding food; try the special Balthali bread.

You're likely to encounter bands of trekkers on weekends, in which case it is important to appreciate late-night karaoke and
Nepali folk songs.

ⓘ Getting There & Away

Balthali is reached by 4WD from Panauti, or on
foot via the Valley Fringe Hiking Circuit (p183).
The major lodges will also pick you up free of
charge from Khopasi Bridge, a 10-minute bus
ride from Panauti, but it is a beautiful 90-minute
walk from there.

BEYOND THE VALLEY

The roads north to Syabrubesi and Kodari, on the Tibetan border, take travellers to destinations just outside the Kathmandu Valley. Both routes saw severe damage in the 2015 earthquake. At the time of research the road to Syabrubesi and on to Kyrong in Tibet was open, but the border crossing at Kodari was closed. Get the latest road updates before you venture onto these roads. You can only cross into Tibet on an organised tour, but with the state of the roads, more and more travellers are flying in to Lhasa from Kathmandu. This region is also the birthplace of Nepal's adventure-sports industry.

Arniko Highway to Tibet

The Arniko Hwy is one of Nepal's overland links with Tibet and China, but the road has a long history of being blocked by landslides, particularly during the monsoon months (May to August). A major landslide in 2014 created a lake that blocked the highway north of the town of Khadu Chaur for over a month, and repairs were still under way when the 2015 earthquakes brought more devastation.

At the time of research, it was possible to travel as far as the village of Larcha, where an earthquake-damaged bridge over the Bhote Kosi succumbed to a landslide in 2017. The border was subsequently closed and many places along the route are now only accessible by 4WD or walking part of the way. This is a popular road ride for mountain bikers, though bus and truck traffic is heavy – even with the border closed – because of hydro-power construction and sand mining.

🛌 Sleeping

Sunkoshi Beach Camp　　TENTED CAMP **$$**
(📞 01-400023, Kathmandu 01-4381214; http://sunkoshibeach.com; full board per person camping/r Rs 2000/2500) Of the several resorts and camps along the Arniko Hwy, Sunkoshi is one of the closest to Kathmandu. It's geared less at daredevil, thrill-seeking travellers and more at those seeking more laid-back activities, including family-friendly rafting (adult/child US$60/30) and kayaking (US$70 per person). Accommodation is in simple tents and rooms.

Borderlands Resort　　RESORT **$$**
(📞 Kathmandu 01-4700894; www.borderlandresorts.com; 2-day/1-night canyoning/rafting packages per person from US$150/130) Tucked away in a bend of the Bhote Kosi River, 97km from Kathmandu and 15km from Tibet, the superb Borderlands Resort is one of Nepal's top adventure resorts. Adrenaline-charged activities include rafting, trekking and canyoning, and the riverside resort is centred on an attractive bar and dining area, surrounded by safari tents dotted around a lush subtropical garden.

Most people visit on a package that includes activities, accommodation, meals and transport from Kathmandu – drop in to the resort's Kathmandu office next to the Northfield Cafe in Thamel to discuss options, including plenty of combo ones. The resort supports several local schools.

Last Resort　　RESORT **$$**
(📞 Kathmandu 01-470124; www.thelastresort.com.np; bungy jump day trip US$99, accommodation with transport & meals US$55, overnight stay with activities US$60-140; 🕾) Thrill-seekers drop off the Arniko Hwy – quite literally – at the Last Resort. Set in a gorgeous spot on a ridge above the Bhote Kosi River, 12km from the Tibetan border, the resort is reached by a vertiginous suspension bridge that doubles as a bungee-jumper's launch pad. Accommodation is in comfortable two- or four-person safari tents, surrounding a stone-and-slate dining hall-bar.

Most people visit on all-inclusive adventure packages – as well as swinging from a giant elastic band, you can combine rafting, trekking, mountain biking and canyoning.

For less endorphin-motivated travellers, there are solar-heated showers, a plunge pool and a sauna and spa, making it the most luxurious place to stay on this road and a great place to escape the city. Package rates include accommodation, meals and transport to and from Kathmandu – drop into the Kathmandu office in Thamel for more information and to book.

ℹ Getting There & Away

The resorts all offer transport from Kathmandu as part of their packages. This is cheaper and preferable to trying to hire your own 4WD or high-clearance bus.

The border was closed to cross-border traffic at the time of research. Should it reopen, expect restrictions as before, when foreigners could only cross the border into Tibet as part of an organised tour.

ADVENTURE SPORTS ON THE ROAD TO TIBET

The Ultimate Bungee

The bungee at the Last Resort straddles a mighty 160m drop into the gorge of the Bhote Kosi and ranks as one of the world's 10 longest bungee jumps. The roars and squeals of free-falling tourists echo up and down the valley for miles.

As if the tallest bungee in South Asia wasn't enough, the fiendish minds at the resort have devised the 'swing', a stomach-loosening eight-second free fall, followed by a Tarzan-like swing and then three or four pendulum swings back up and then down the length of the gorge. This can be done solo or in tandem. We feel ill just writing about it.

A swing or bungee jump costs US$99 from Kathmandu (including return transport). The price includes whatever lunch your stomach can handle, wisely served up *after* the jump.

Canyoning

This exciting sport is a wild combination of rappelling/abseiling, climbing, sliding and swimming that has been pioneered in the canyons and waterfalls near the Last Resort and Borderlands.

Both operators offer two-day canyoning trips for about US$150. This involves a drive up from Kathmandu, lunch, and some basic abseiling training and practise on nearby cascades on day one. Day two involves a trip out to more exciting falls, with a maximum abseil of up to 90m. Most canyons involve a short hike to get there.

The key bits of kit required are a pair of closed-toe shoes that can get wet (these are better than sandals), hiking shoes for reaching the cascades, a water bottle and a bathing suit. A waterproof camera is a real bonus. Note that canyoning is not possible during the monsoon, and after November wetsuits are a must and are provided.

Kodari

Formerly the main crossing point between Nepal and Tibet, the village of Kodari sustained damage in both the 25 April and 12 May 2015 earthquakes, and the border crossing to Tibet was closed completely after a landslide destroyed a key bridge over the Bhote Kosi. It is unclear whether the border will fully reopen in future. There's little reason to visit if the border remains closed.

The Road to Langtang

A bumpy road heads northwest out of the Kathmandu Valley, offering fantastic views of the Ganesh Himalaya as it crests the ridge at Kakani. Beyond Trisuli Bazaar, the road deteriorates and is travelled mainly by trekkers headed for the Langtang region.

The Langtang region was one of the areas hardest hit by the 2015 earthquake, but lodges have been rebuilt and the region's excellent treks are once again open to trekkers. This area needs your custom more than ever, so now is the perfect time for a trek in this region.

In late 2017, the border crossing with China/Tibet at Rasuwaghadi was finally opened to foreigners, meaning that travellers coming from Tibet via Kyerong can tack on a teahouse trek in the Langtang and Gosainkund regions before continuing to Kathmandu.

ℹ Getting There & Away

Buses run between Kathmandu, Trisuli Bazaar, Dhunche, Syabrubesi (for the Langtang Valley trek) and Rasuwaghadi. With earthquake damage and the rise in truck traffic from the Chinese border, roads are now in a terrible state and progress is painfully slow. Most buses currently travel via Baireni on the Kathmandu–Pokhara Hwy, not via Kakani.

Some travellers band together to hire a comfortable 4WD. A 10-seater jeep from Syabrubesi to Kathmandu costs Rs 13,000.

A new road is nearing completion between Syabrubesi and Trisuli Bazaar, bypassing Dhunche, which should make the drive less of an ordeal.

At Trisuli Bazaar a reasonable road branches southwest to Dhading and Malekhu, on the Kathmandu–Pokhara (Prithvi) Hwy, offering an offbeat shortcut route to Bandipur and Pokhara, and a possible bicycle ride taking in Kakani, Trisuli Bazaar, Dhading and Malekhu.

AROUND THE KATHMANDU VALLEY THE ROAD TO LANGTANG

Kakani

Most of the towns around Kathmandu sit at the bottom of the valley – you have to travel to the valley rim to really get decent views of the Himalaya. Set atop a ridge at 2073m, just off the road to Trisuli Bazaar, Kakani is the quieter, slower cousin of Dhulikhel and Nagarkot. From a series of high points along the ridge, there are magnificent views of the Himalayan skyline stretching all the way from Annapurna to Everest, via Manaslu, Ganesh Himal, Gauri Shankar, Dorje Lekpa and Shishapangma.

Kakani is a major gateway for hiking and mountain biking routes in neighbouring Shivapuri Nagarjun National Park (p135).

◉ Sights

Apart from staring open-mouthed at the view, there's not much to do. The handsome colonial mansion at the start of the village was built as a summer villa for the British embassy, but it's closed to visitors.

🛏 Sleeping & Eating

A couple of hotels take advantage of the views along the ridge, but this is a very low-key place to stay compared to other parts of the Kathmandu Valley.

View Himalaya Resort   HOTEL $
(☏01-6915706; viewhimalaya.resort@gmail.com; r incl breakfast Rs 2000-3000; 🅿) Easily the best option in town, this place has simple but comfortable rooms and the delightful restaurant, garden and rooftop come with views to remember. The large family room with a small balcony offers the best value.

Tara Gaon Resort Hotel   HOTEL $
(☏01-6227750; s/d incl breakfast US$12/16) This old-school government hotel has really seen better days, with paint peeling off the walls and *Fawlty Towers* levels of service, but it still offers a whiff of colonial charm and the views from its lawn are sublime. One of the four tired rooms has mountain views direct from the bed. Come for lunch or a sunset beer instead.

❶ Getting There & Away

Kakani is 1½ hours from Kathmandu by bus or motorcycle. Fit cyclists often make the climb en route to Shivapuri, but you can expect a rough ride until the road-widening work has finished. There are numerous trout restaurants where you can stop for a break. It's a thrilling freewheel back to Kathmandu, but watch for trucks or buses on the corners.

The road to Kakani turns off the Kathmandu–Trisuli Bazaar road just before the Kaulithana police checkpoint, at the crest of the hill. There is one daily bus from Kathmandu's Machha Pokhari stand to Kakani (Rs 60) at 3.30pm, returning from Kakani the next day at 8am. Alternatively take a Ranipauwa-bound bus from just north of Machha Pokhari to Kaulithana junction, from where it's a 3km uphill walk to Kakani centre.

Nuwakot

The small village of Nuwakot (Nine Forts), just southeast of Trisuli Bazaar, has a deserved reputation as one of Nepal's best travel secrets, floating somewhere between the 17th and 21st centuries.

A strategic stopping post on the old trade route with Tibet, the early-Malla-era fort

REBUILDING NUWAKOT

Nuwakot was hit hard by the 2015 earthquake. Of 450 local residences in the village, an estimated 420 were damaged. The owners of the Famous Farm, who played a major role in rescuing the town of Bandipur from dereliction, are spearheading local restoration efforts, trying to convince locals to rebuild in an architecturally cohesive style to maintain the village's traditional character.

Charm costs money, however, and so they have provided a grant to those who clad their houses in expensive traditional brick and have offered free architectural services. It's a long-term view that hopes to protect the town's tourism industry, both for locals and the Famous Farm. It's also a fine example of how tourism entrepreneurs can support their local communities in a country where government support or planning is often sorely missing.

(kot) was captured by Prithvi Narayan Shah, who launched his unifying conquest of the Kathmandu Valley from here in 1768.

Nuwakot was hit badly by the 2015 earthquake, during which many village houses collapsed and the main historic temples were badly damaged. The buildings of Durbar Sq are due to be stabilised and renovated by a Chinese team, with a tentative completion date of 2021.

◎ Sights

Saat Tale Durbar   PALACE
(Durbar Sq) The centrepiece of the village is the Saat Tale Durbar, a seven-storey fortress built in 1762 by Prithvi Narayan Shah as his family palace after taking the town. The town served as Nepal's capital until Shah conquered the Kathmandu Valley six years later. This was also where the great king died in 1775. The building suffered severe cracks in the earthquake and the interior was offlimits to visitors at the time of the writing.

Taleju Temple   HINDU TEMPLE
The Taleju Temple is Durbar Sq's most magnificent temple, but is not open to the public. Even for Hindus admission is restricted; they can only visit it briefly during the annual Dasain and Sinduri Jatra festivals. The 35m-high temple was built in 1564 by Mahendra Malla. The back side of the building partially collapsed during the earthquake.

Taleju Bhawani was originally a goddess from the south of India, but she became the titular deity, or royal goddess, of the Malla kings in the 14th century.

Bhairabi Temple   HINDU TEMPLE
At the far end of the village, and with impressive valley views, is the golden-roofed Bhairabi Temple. It's used for animal sacrifices during the annual Sinduri Jatra festival, when the small statue is carried in a chariot to visit his sister in nearby Devighat. The temple is flanked by two pilgrim rest houses and has been rebuilt since the earthquake.

⚡ Activities

There are several possible walks around Nuwakot, including to the **viewpoint** tower at the Kalika Temple. Another popular destination is the nearby hilltop **Malika Temple**, a simple stone shrine. You can visit both in a three- or four-hour loop.

⌨ Sleeping & Eating

Hotel Nuwakot View   HOTEL $
(☑ 010-413045;   hotelnuwakotview@gmail.com; r Rs 1500; ☎) This concrete building just above Nuwakot centre is pretty charmless, but does offer a decent budget option for backpackers wishing to overnight. The restaurant offers set meals and cold beer. There's no hot water.

★ Famous Farm   BOUTIQUE HOTEL $$$
(☑ Kathmandu   01-4422617,   Nuwakot   010-413044;   www.rural-heritage.com;   s/d incl full board US$130/150; ☎) ✎ It would be hard to imagine a more idyllic après-trek recovery spot than this charming lodge in three artfully converted old village houses. The 13 comfortable rooms are surrounded by a serene and peaceful garden, with views over Nuwakot and the Trisuli Valley. The open kitchen serves up superb Nepali food (cookery lessons are possible).

It's one of Nepal's most serene getaways and it's worth staying at least two nights to soak up the calm and take in local walks. The owners support a local school and home for deaf children and can arrange visits for those wishing to donate school supplies.

ℹ Getting There & Away

There are three direct buses a day from Kathmandu's Machha Pokhari stand (Rs 250, four hours), returning to the capital at 9.30am, 10am and 11am. Ask for Nuwakot Durbar rather than just Nuwakot (the district name). Otherwise, take one of the hourly buses to Trisuli Bazaar (Rs 220) and arrange to be picked up in Bidur.

If you are headed on to the Langtang region by public transport, you can walk downhill along shortcuts to the main highway at Bidur (one hour), which is on the bus route to Trisuli Bazaar, Kathmandu and Syabrubesi.

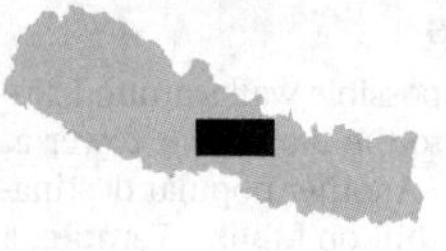

Kathmandu to Pokhara

Best Places to Stay

➡ Old Inn Bandipur (p204)

➡ River Side Springs Resort (p198)

➡ Gorkha Gaun (p201)

➡ Bandipur Adventure Camp (p204)

Best Adventures

➡ Rafting on the Trisuli (p198)

➡ Paragliding in Bandipur (p203)

➡ Caving in Siddha Gufa (p202)

Why Go?

The notorious Prithvi Hwy, which winds through 206km of classic Middle Hills countryside, should be seen as more than just a painful bus ride. While many travellers head directly from Kathmandu to Pokhara, they miss out on some of Nepal's finer attractions. This includes one of the country's architectural gems, the historic town of Bandipur, a lovingly restored, picture-postcard village offering European ambience in the middle of gorgeous Nepalese vistas. As you follow the mighty Trisuli River along the Prithvi Hwy, you also pass its many riverside resorts, with their sandy beaches, laid-back charm and rafting adventures. Add the cultural attractions of Gorkha and Manakamana, and you have more than enough reason to get off the bus.

When to Go

➡ The best time to travel between Kathmandu and Pokhara is during the winter months of November to January. This will maximise your chances of catching sweeping Himalayan views during glorious, mild sunny days.

➡ For those planning to tackle the Trisuli River on a rafting expedition, visiting from October to December or March to May ensures rollicking rapids and sandy beach camps.

➡ Adventurous souls wanting to head up into the skies can arrange tandem paraglide flights in Bandipur between September and June.

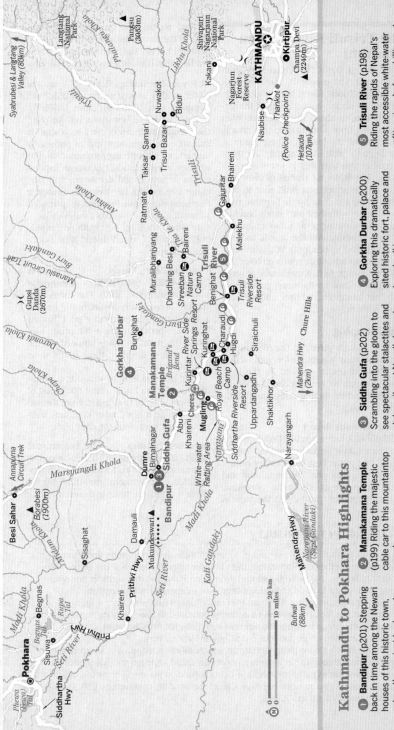

Kathmandu to Pokhara Highlights

1 Bandipur (p201) Stepping back in time among the Newari houses of this historic town, set on the ancient trade route to India.

2 Manakamana Temple (p199) Riding the majestic cable car to this mountaintop pagoda.

3 Siddha Gufa (p202) Scrambling into the gloom to see spectacular stalactites and stalagmites at Nepal's largest cave.

4 Gorkha Durbar (p200) Exploring this dramatically sited historic fort, palace and temple all in one.

5 Trisuli River (p198) Riding the rapids of Nepal's most accessible white-water rafting river, before chilling out at one of its beach camps.

The Trisuli River to Abu Khaireni

When driving down the Prithvi Hwy from Kathmandu, you eventually meet up with the mighty Trisuli River. It runs alongside the road thereafter, having sculpted the serpentine canyon ahead for millennia. With easy access from Kathmandu, this area is the centre of the budget rafting business. The highway will, unfortunately, be there to remind you that this is not wilderness rafting. But this long stretch of river also holds a little secret: you don't have to be a rafter to enjoy it. The hotels here are river resorts, often with their own sandy beaches, and even swimming pools. Cross a romantic suspension bridge over the Trisuli, and it is possible to feel worlds away. With fine scenery, and other adventure sports on offer, this is a great escape from Kathmandu, or some needed downtime for the weary traveller. So grab that hammock and beer, and get busy doing nothing.

🛏 Sleeping

There is enough variety in the riverside resorts to suit any budget. Be forewarned that the cheapest resorts tend to be the truly local ones, which are descended upon by hordes of partiers on weekends. And they do make a mess.

Trisuli Riverside Resort　　　　LODGE $
(☎ 9841534122, Kathmandu 01-4416032; www.trs resort.com; hut per person incl breakfast & dinner US$20) One of the best budget river camps, with a swimming pool, fun restaurant and broad adventure sports menu (kayaking, hiking, canyoning, rafting). At the time of writing, rooms were undergoing renovation; in the meantime, opt for the secluded thatched huts by the river. On Fridays there is a DJ party. Located 4km west of Malekhu.

★**River Side Springs Resort**　　　LODGE $$
(☎ 056-410029; www.rsr.com.np; dm US$12, s/d permanent tents US$50/60, cabins US$70/80; ❄ 🛜 ⚡) With the best views on the river, this colonial-style resort can't be beaten. It manages the impressive feat of remaining upmarket while offering accommodation at all price levels, including Japanese-inspired cabins, a new 12-bed dormitory, and permanent tents. The bar has a jaw-dropping riverbend view, while the massive spring-fed swimming pool below adds a swim-up bar.

In short, this is the best bolthole this side of Kathmandu. Located around 10km before Manakamana.

River Fun Beach Resort　　　RESORT $$
(☎ 01-4443533, 9801035699; www.riverfun beachresort.com; r Rs 3500) The manicured grounds here are very attractive and include a scenic riverside swimming pool. Rooms have nice beds, but are a bit prison-like. While the resort is nicely situated on the north bank of the river, there is still some highway noise.

Note that you have to walk over a pedestrian suspension bridge about 500m east of the resort in order to access it. From the end of the bridge, it is a further 15-minute well-signed walk west along the river bank.

Royal Beach Camp　　HOTEL, CAMPGROUND $$
(☎ 9741010866, Kathmandu 01-6913767; www.royal beachnepal.com; tent incl full board US$25, bungalow US$35, r with/without bathroom US$75/60; ⚡) While it caters primarily to those on rafting

---

RAFTING ON THE TRISULI

The Trisuli has basically two emotions: a raging temper during monsoon, and a smiling face the rest of the year. Rafters love them both for different reasons. If this is your first time rafting, you may wish for a gentle introduction. If not, you may come for one wild ride from August to mid-October. Just choose an established rafting company.

Rafting trips generally set off from the small village of **Bhaireni**. Further along, at **Benighat**, the Trisuli merges with the roaring Buri Gandaki River, creating impressive rapids. Rafting trips break for the night between Benighat and **Charaudi**, about 20km downstream. Some trips continue on to Chitwan National Park.

If you plan on staying along this stretch, your hotel can arrange a trip. Alternatively, you can book through a Kathmandu tour provider (p85), although they will choose your accommodation as part of the package. Costs depend on the length of the trip, which ranges from two hours to several days. A short two-hour trip costs around US$20, while a four-hour trip is around US$35.

or kayaking packages, Royal Beach Camp's soft sandy beach, hammocks and outdoor restaurant-bar also make it a great spot to chill out along the river for a day or two. Guests stay in hotel rooms, permanent tents, or basic bungalows near the water. It's near Charaudi.

Shreeban Nature Camp LODGE $$
(☑ Kathmandu 01-4258427; www.shreeban.com. np; outside Dhading; 2-day/1-night package per person €45) While not on the Trisuli River, this somewhat remote and low-key operation offers an appealing program of trekking, bird-watching and cultural activities for those seeking to get off the beaten track. It's a two- to three-hour walk from the highway – a guide will meet you there. You'll need to make a reservation before visiting.

🛈 Getting There & Away

The Trisuli River resorts are all accessed from the Prithvi Hwy, which parallels the river. The highway-side resorts are within sight of the road. Resorts on the other side of the river require a walk over a suspension bridge and along the opposite bank. Buses stop at all the major settlements along the river.

Manakamana

From the tiny hamlet of **Cheres** (6km before Mugling), an Austrian-engineered cable car soars up a vertiginous hillside to the ancient **Manakamana Temple** (☺ dawn-dusk), the apex of a religious vacation for Hindus far and wide. The temple itself is somewhat disappointing – it's relatively small, and seemingly held together by scaffolding since the 2015 earthquake. But the journey up and the cultural experience at the top make this trip worth doing. Hindus believe that the goddess Bhagwati, who is enshrined here, has the power to grant wishes, and many newlyweds arrive to pray for male children. Tacky, the goddess of bad advertising, also reigns: as the cable car rises, you'll see enormous corporate billboards embedded in the mountainside. Non-Hindus will get many curious glances and endless opportunities to meet fellow travellers, including extended families from India.

◉ Sights

Manakamana Cable Car CABLE CAR
(adult/child return US$20/15, luggage per 1kg Rs 15; ☺ 9am-noon & 1.30-5pm, from 8am Sat) Re-opened after a long earthquake delay, the ever-popular Manakamana cable car rises more than 1000m as it covers the 2.8km from the Prithvi Hwy to the Manakamana ridge. Riders will enjoy panoramic views from their glass gondola. Note that it is best not to return late in the afternoon as there are hour-long lines at this time.

If you are a single traveller, be sure to go to the head of the line as they will squeeze you in to spare seats left open by groups of travellers. This is not jumping the queue but encouraged.

🛏 Sleeping

Manakamana Fulbari Resort HOTEL $$
(☑ 064-460056; r Rs 2500; ☎) The best of the hotels near the temple, this one could use some paint, but the rooms are clean, with balconies and lots of light, and many have fine views – a rarity among the competition. Turn left when you reach the temple; it's the orange building 50m on left.

🛈 Getting There & Away

All buses that run between Kathmandu (Rs 400, three hours, every half hour) and Pokhara (Rs 300, two hours, every half hour) or Chitwan (Rs 200, 1½ hours, every half hour) pass the turn-off to the Manakamana cable car at Cheres. Look for the red-brick archway.

If you want to walk up to the temple (around four hours), get off at Abu Khaireni, which is further on (from Kathmandu). Turn onto the road to Gorkha, then right by the Manakamana Hotel. Cross the suspension bridge and climb through terraced fields and small villages to the top of the ridge.

Gorkha

☑ 064 / POP 32,000 / ELEV 1135M

About 24km north of Abu Khaireni, Gorkha is famous for four things. It is the birthplace of Prithvi Narayan Shah, who unified the rival kingdoms of Nepal in 1769, commencing a dynasty that endured until 2008; it is the location of the Gorkha Durbar, the former palace of the Shahs, which looks over Gorkha from a lofty ridge; it is where the famous Gurkha Battalion in the British Army originated; and it is where the annual Dasain festival officially begins, with a procession to Kathmandu. The town remains an important pilgrimage destination for Newars, who regard the Shahs as living incarnations of Vishnu.

Gorkha

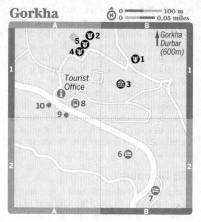

In 2015 Gorkha also became infamous as the epicentre of the worst earthquake to hit Nepal in almost a century, although many buildings avoided damage.

◎ Sights

Gorkha Durbar   PALACE
(Rs 50, camera Rs 200; ☺6am-6pm Feb-Oct, 7am-5pm Nov-Jan) Regarded by many as the crowning glory of Newari architecture, the 16th-century Gorkha Durbar is a fort, palace and temple all in one. Miraculously, the main structure survived the 2015 earthquake, but damage was extensive, and at the time of research, repairs were still under way. The temple-palace perches high above Gorkha on a knife-edge ridge, with superb views over the Trisuli Valley and magnificent panoramas of the soaring peaks of the Annapurna, Manaslu and Ganesh Himalaya.

As the birthplace of Prithvi Narayan Shah, the Durbar has huge significance for Nepalis. The great Shah was born here around 1723, when Gorkha was a minor feudal kingdom. Upon gaining the throne, Prithvi Narayan worked his way around the Kathmandu Valley, subduing rival kingdoms and creating an empire that extended far into India and Tibet.

The Durbar is an important religious site, so leather shoes and belts etc should be removed. Most pilgrims enter through the western gate, emerging on an open terrace in front of the exquisite **Kalika Temple**, a psychedelic 17th-century fantasy of peacocks, demons and serpents, carved into every available inch of timber. Only Brahmin priests and the king can enter the temple, but non-Hindus are permitted to observe from the terrace.

The east wing of the palace complex contains the former palace of Prithvi Narayan Shah, the **Dhuni Pati**, covered in elaborate woodcarvings. This structure was severely damaged in the earthquake, so expect lots of scaffolding. Nearby is the **mausoleum of Guru Gorakhnath**, the reclusive saint who acted as a spiritual guide for the young Prithvi Narayan.

If you leave via the northern gate, you'll pass the former **Royal Guest House** – note the erotic roof struts and the crocodile carvings on the window frames.

Down from here is a vividly painted **Hanuman statue**, and a path leading to a large **chautara** (stone resting platform) on an exposed rocky bluff with awesome views and a set of carved stone footprints, attributed variously to Sita, Rama, Gorakhnath and Guru Padmasambhava.

To reach the Durbar, you can climb an exhausting stairway of 1500 stone steps, snaking up the hillside, or take a taxi (Rs 450 including waiting time) along the road winding up to a car park just below the northern gate.

◉ Old Town

The sights in Gorkha are concentrated in the old town, as revealed by a short circuit. If you follow the road uphill from the bus stand, you'll reach the two-tiered **Vishnu Temple** (☺24hr). Next comes the **Mahadev Temple** (☺24hr), a squat white Shiva temple with a Nandi statue, followed by the **Ganesh Temple** (☺24hr), a small, white *shikhara* (Indian-style temple with tall corn cob–like spire) next to a tank. A little further along, the road opens onto a small square with a miniature pagoda. This **Bhimsen Temple** (⊙24hr) is dedicated to the Newari god of commerce. At this point, the Gorkha Museum lies due south, towards the park.

Gorkha Museum
MUSEUM

(foreigner/SAARC Rs 50/20, camera Rs 200/100; ⊙10.30am-2.30pm Mon, to 3.30pm Wed-Sun Nov-Jan, to 4.30pm Feb-Oct) Housed inside the grand Tallo Durbar, a Newari-style palace built in 1835, this museum's collection is outshone by the building itself, which has a beautiful internal courtyard with carved windows and doors. While the collection is limited, it's a pleasure to wander the old hallways lined with arts and crafts and historical items, and to stroll the 3.5 hectares of garden. This is the natural first stop after the nearby tourist office.

🛏 Sleeping & Eating

The only significant public dining is in hotel restaurants. Your best bet is the outdoor terrace at the Hotel Gorkha Bisauni, particularly at sunset.

Hotel Gorkha Bisauni
HOTEL $

(☑064-420107; www.hotelgorkhabisauni.com; r Rs 800-1500, with AC Rs 2500, without bathroom from Rs 500; 🕾) Set in landscaped grounds about 500m downhill from the bus stand, this hotel and restaurant has a promising facade and lobby, but an uneven collection of rooms, although some improvements are under way. Avoid the dark caves in favour of bright balcony rooms. The highlight is the outdoor terrace, a great spot at sunset and Gorkha's unofficial watering hole.

Gurkha Crown Resort
HOTEL $

(☑9846356011, 064-411132; aryalgokul54@yahoo.com; r incl breakfast US$25) If you don't mind being 6km out of town in rural countryside, this pleasant hotel offers simple but spacious en suite rooms with lots of light in a forest setting. The happy and energetic owner is a pleasure to deal with. Call ahead for directions.

Gurkha Inn
HOTEL $$

(☑064-420206; r US$30; @🕾) While the hallways in this overpriced hotel would make a great dungeon, it does have a nice garden, a patio restaurant, and some surprisingly clean and well-lit rooms (try room 304).

★ Gorkha Gaun
BOUTIQUE HOTEL $$$

(☑9801010557, 9849776022; www.gorkhagaun.com; s/d incl breakfast US$110/150; 🕾) 🖉 Located 6km south of town on a scenic hilltop, this is far and away the best place to stay in this area, and a model of rural tourism. Returning to Nepal after years in the USA, the owners have lovingly crafted their own *gaun* (small village) of guest cottages using local materials and intelligent engineering – and made it earthquake-proof.

Nice touches abound, like the fire pit with views to Manaslu, slate baths, and long beds for Western travellers. The large dining hall offers a wonderful family-style buffet. All activities are included in the price, such as hikes to the hotel from Manakamana (five hours), onwards to the Gorkha Durbar (3½ hours), and explorations of Magar villages in the adjacent valley (four to five hours). Attention to detail extends down to the matching crockery handcrafted in Bandipur. Call ahead for directions.

❶ Information

The **Tourist Office** (Gorkha Tourism Development Center; ☑064-421592; www.visitgorkha.com; ⊙10am-5pm Sun-Fri) has helpful staff members, and lots of them. It's a good source of local maps. Located behind the fence across from the bus stand. There's an ATM located below Hotel Miracle, about 1km southeast of town on the road to Abu Khaireni.

❶ Getting There & Away

On the Prithvi Hwy, unloved Abu Khaireni is the access point for buses to Gorkha (Rs 65, one hour).

Gorkha's noisy **bus stand** is right in the middle of town. The **ticket office** for buses to Kathmandu is at the eastern end; the **ticket office** at the western end sells tickets for buses to Pokhara and Chitwan.

There are daily microbuses to Pokhara (Rs 240, five hours) and numerous buses (Rs 300, five hours) and microbuses (Rs 380, four hours) to Kathmandu from 6.15am until 2.20pm. A single microbus leaves Gorkha at 7am for Bhairawa (Rs 430, six hours) and there are regular buses to Narayangarh (Rs 155, two hours) until midday.

Bandipur

☑065 / POP 16,000 / ELEV 1030M

One of Nepal's most charming towns, Bandipur is a living museum of Newari culture, a beautifully preserved village crowning a lofty ridge, its main street lined with traditional row houses. Time seems to have stood

Bandipur

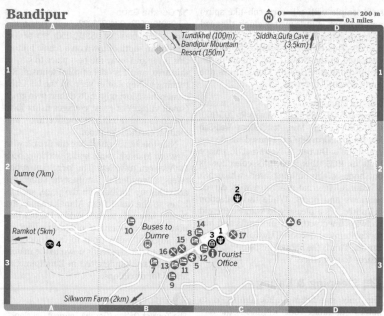

Bandipur

⊙ Sights

⊕ Activities, Courses & Tours

⊜ Sleeping

⊗ Eating

still here, although it has taken a lot of effort to preserve this magic while developing the town as a destination. Derelict buildings have been reborn as cafes and lodges, and temples and civic buildings have been pulled back from the edge of ruin. With its attractive 18th-century architecture, pedestrian zone and outdoor dining, it has a distinctly European feel.

Bandipur was an important stop on the India–Tibet trade route for centuries until it was bypassed by the Prithvi Hwy in the 1960s. While it has since turned to tourism, it remains very much a living community, bustling with farmers and traders going about their business. Pause to savour this unique place.

⊙ Sights

Thani Mai Temple Viewpoint   VIEWPOINT
The main reason to climb up to Thani Mai is for the spectacular sunrise views from **Gurungche Hill**. A clear morning offers some of the most memorable 360-degree vistas in the country, with the Himalaya stretching out along the horizon, and the valley below cloaked in a thick fog that resembles a white lake. The trail starts near the school at the southwest end of the bazaar, and is a steep 30-minute walk.

Siddha Gufa Cave   CAVE
(adult Rs 200; ⊙ dawn-dusk) At 437m deep and 50m high, Siddha Gufa is said to be the largest

cave in Nepal. Its cathedral-like interior is full of stalactites and stalagmites, not to mention hundreds of bats, which whistle overhead. Trekking here and back from Bandipur is a popular (if muddy) half-day trip, including a 1½-hour hike each way. Consider hiring a guide from Bandipur's Tourist Information Centre (p205). Alternatively, you can hike up to the cave from Bimalnagar on the Prithvi Hwy, which only takes 45 minutes.

From Bandipur, follow the signs starting from the north end of the village. These take you along a dirt path running north over the edge of the ridge, turning right at the obvious junction. The stone path is slippery, so mind your step. Compulsory guides (Rs 200) await you at the cave's entrance. Torches (flashlights) are also available for hire.

Tundikhel   VIEWPOINT

In centuries past, traders would gather on this man-made plateau to haggle for goods from India and Tibet before starting the long trek to Lhasa or the Indian plains. It was also a former parade ground for Gurkha soldiers. These days it's a local picnic spot and viewpoint. On a clear day, a stunning panorama of Himalayan peaks is visible, including Dhaulagiri (8167m), Machhapuchhare (6997m), Langtang Lirung (7246m), Manaslu (8162m) and Ganesh Himal (7406m). Try sunrise or sunset.

Bindebasini Temple   HINDU TEMPLE

(⊘24hr) At the northeast end of the bazaar (which is the main shopping strip) this ornate, two-tiered temple is dedicated to Durga. Its ancient walls are covered in carvings. Facing the temple across the square is the **Padma library**, a striking 18th-century building with carved windows and beams.

Khadga Devi Temple   HINDU TEMPLE

(⊘24hr) A wide flight of stone steps leads up the hillside to this barn-like temple, which enshrines the sword of Mukunda Sen, the 16th-century king of Palpa (Tansen). Allegedly a gift from Shiva, the blade is revered as a symbol of shakti (consort or female energy) and once a year during Dasain it gets a taste of sacrificial blood.

Silkworm Farm   FARM

(☑9846453502; admission by donation; ⊘10am-4pm Sun-Fri) An offbeat choice, a visit to Silkworm Farm takes you through the fascinating process of how silk is produced. The farm comprises orchards of mulberry plants, which are grown for worm food – the

worms themselves are reared indoors, usually from August to December and March to May. But you can visit any time, with someone on hand to explain the process using jars of preserved displays.

Getting here involves a trek. Leave town, turning left at Heritage Guest House, follow the slate path all the way to the paved road, then downhill 2.5km. The farm is signed on the left, 50m past where the road turns to dirt.

🏃 Activities

It's easy to pass several peaceful days exploring the countryside around Bandipur. There are dramatic Himalayan backdrops to a gorgeous patchwork of terraced rice and mustard fields and small orchards. Most guesthouses can arrange walking guides for Rs 1000 to Rs 1500 a day.

Along with the Siddha Gufa cave, one of the most popular walks is to the Magar village of **Ramkot**. The scenic four-hour walk takes you to this charming and friendly little village where there are some traditional round houses. There's nowhere to buy food or water here, so pack a lunch, which you can enjoy under the two banyan trees atop the hill, with a great Himalayan panorama. Enquire at the Old Inn Bandipur (p204) about homestays in this village.

Blue Sky Paragliding   PARAGLIDING

(☑9846721920; www.blue-sky-paragliding.com; 30min/1hr Rs 9000/13,000) Blue Sky (based in Pokhara) is the pioneer of paragliding at Bandipur. Make enquiries directly with the company or at the small general store in Bandipur with the Blue Sky paragliding sign. It launches from just above the village and the views are stunning.

Do check to make sure that your pilot has a tandem licence and a logbook to match. Three years of tandem experience seems sensible.

Hardcore Nepal   ROCK CLIMBING, CAVING

(☑9803010011; www.hardcorenepal.com; 2-day all-inclusive rock climbing & caving US$140, 3-day packages from US$200) Keen climbers can tackle the 40m limestone wall along the highway in Bimalnagar, a couple of kilometres east of Dumre. Hardcore Nepal can also arrange caving in Siddha Gufa, involving abseiling 70m through the ceiling entrance, as well as waterfall abseiling in Jalbire Canyon, 10km south of Mugling. Departures from Thamel, Pokhara and Bandipur.

🛌 Sleeping

There's no shortage of accommodation in Bandipur, at all price levels. In particular, the main street contains numerous, well-restored homes that have been converted into hotels. These offer inner courtyards, exposed beams, wooden balconies, and great mountain views – just watch your head! Doorways are much shorter here than normal.

★ Bandipur
Adventure Camp   TENTED CAMP $
(📞 065-520184, 9841235636; www.bandipur adventurecamp.com; 4-person tent Rs 2000, half-board Rs 2500; 📶) This new bargain option is in its own category. A tent camp on a mountain-top, with amazing views of Manaslu towering over the Trisuli River, it's run by a dynamic young management, and makes the perfect backpacking stop. The multi-cuisine restaurant bakes its own bread, pasta and pizza, and the small bar serves beer to match.

On weekends in high season there's live music. All sorts of adventure sports are on offer: hiking, caving, paintball, rock climbing, canyoning and even off-road motocross. The tents are basic, with shared bathrooms, and roofs to keep the sun off. They will hold four people if they all know each other really well. A purpose-built lodge is only a work in progress. It's a 10-minute walk to town, but located next to the highest mobile-phone tower in the area, so you can't get lost coming back.

Hotel Red Rose   HOTEL $
(📞 065-520139; r Rs 1500-2000; 📶) If you'd like to stay in an historic property on a budget, this is your best choice. Located in the centre of the bazaar, it offers simpler rooms with foam beds, but with both street and valley views, cute balconies and a downstairs restaurant.

Newa Guest House   GUESTHOUSE $
(📞 9846117596, 065-520079; kpbandipur@gmail. com; r without bathroom Rs 800; 📶) A great budget option: nice streetside rooms with balconies and shared bathrooms for a bargain price.

Hotel Maya   GUESTHOUSE $
(📞 065-520106; s Rs 400, d Rs 800-900) A cheapie right on the main bazaar with an atmospheric streetside cafe. The rooms in this traditional building are tiny but full of atmosphere, with exposed beams and some

alluring views, not to mention hot water in a bucket.

Heritage Guest House   GUESTHOUSE $
(📞 065-520042; heritageguesthouse60@gmail. com; r with/without bathroom Rs 1500/500; 📶) Housed in a somewhat ramshackle residence at the southwest end of the bazaar, the welcoming Heritage Guest House looks like you are entering a souvenir shop. However, rooms 5 and 6 are some of the best budget rooms in town, with great views and a shared bathroom right outside the door.

The attached restaurant serves some good meals, including Newari specialities such as *jhwai khattee* (warm local wine with millet, ghee, rice and honey).

Bandipur Mountain Resort   HOTEL $$
(📞 065-520125; www.islandjungleresort.com.np; s/d US$50/54, with full board US$84/122; 📶) This hotel has two properties at either end of Tundikhel. The western property is on a forested cliffside. Unlike other hotels in Bandipur, it feels like a jungle lodge. Rooms are freshly painted, with porches offering awesome views. The other property also has sweeping views, but its more modern rooms lack the attractive lodge feel. Reserve ahead in season.

Hotel Depche   LODGE $$
(📞 9841226971; www.hoteldepche.com.np; s/d incl breakfast US$30/60; 📶) A gem on the edge of Bandipur, this attractive mudbrick cottage is tucked away in the fields 300m west of the bazaar. At the time of research, a new restaurant and dining hall were under construction, and room renovations on the way. The location, candlelit courtyard and rooftop have always made this hotel an appealing choice, as has its dedicated entrepreneurial owner.

Bandipur Village Resort   HOTEL $$
(📞 065-520143; bandipurvillageresort@gmail.com; r incl breakfast US$40; 📶) The Village Resort has an attractive historic facade near the jeep stand, but the rooms themselves are in a concrete building out the back. It's a good option if you're looking for modern comfort rather than historic ambience. Room 302 has amazing mountain views, which are also appreciated from the rooftop. Staff are friendly and helpful.

★ Old Inn Bandipur   LODGE $$$
(📞 065-520110; www.theoldinnbandipur.com; all incl breakfast s/d/tr US$105/140/180, without

bathroom US$80/110/145; 🕿) This beautifully restored mansion at the heart of the bazaar offers charming rooms decorated with Buddhist and Newari art, set around a terracotta terrace facing the mountains. Take your pick from views of mountains or captivating streetscapes. Some rooms are on the cosy side (and watch your head!), but newer ones are spacious with private bathrooms and balconies. All have beautiful woodwork.

If the hotel is full, you will probably be referred to Panche Baja, a restored building at the northeast end of the square run by the same owners. It's also long on historic character, but lacks the views of its sibling.

Gaun Ghar　　　　　　　HOTEL **$$$**
(📞065-520129; www.gaunghar.com; s/d incl full board US$225/300; 🕿) A renovated historic home with a lovely central courtyard and internal balconies, Gaun Ghar is also one of the best places to try classic Newari food. Some rooms have balconies overlooking the atmospheric main street. Beds are fitted with electric blankets for chilly winter nights. However, while strongly reminiscent of the adjacent Old Inn, this hotel is significantly more expensive.

✖ Eating

Samay Baji　　　　　　　NEPALI **$**
(📞9841226971; samay baji Rs 350; ⊙7.30am-10pm) This cosy family-run restaurant is named for its signature dish, a sampling of traditional food. And it's a good sample! The dedicated owner doubles as a helpful source of local information. Located at the eastern end of the bazaar.

Himalayan Café　　　　　　　CAFE **$**
(📞9818712232; chocolate brownie Rs 300; ⊙7.30am-9.30pm) A jack of all trades, this new bakery and coffee shop on the main street also has a small bar with occasional live music (Fridays in high season).

Old House Cafe　　　　INTERNATIONAL **$**
(📞9846438274; oldhousecafe01@gmail.com; thali Rs 200-300; ⊙7am-10.30pm; 🕿) A delightful eatery on the bazaar with good momos, pizza and delicious Newari *khaja* (*thali* or set meals). It also has six basic, clean en suite rooms out the back with very nice views (a bargain at single/double Rs 900/1200).

Hill's Heaven　　　　　　　NEPALI **$**
(meals Rs 100-380; ⊙7am-9pm; 🕿) On the main strip, Hill's Heaven is popular for its cheap beer and cheese *pakoda* (think deep-fried cheese balls). There's also four en suite rooms upstairs (Rs 600 to Rs 1000).

❶ Information

The **tourist office** (Bandipur Tourist Information Counter; www.bandipurtourism.com; ⊙10am-5pm Sun-Fri) has brochures and basic information on the area. Guides can be arranged for around Rs 1000 for a half-day. Opening hours are *very* flexible.

There are two somewhat hidden ATMs on the main street, one next to the Old Inn and the other next to Himalayan Cafe.

❶ Getting There & Away

The road to Bandipur branches off the Prithvi Hwy about 2km west of Dumre; buses (Rs 305, 30 minutes, every 45 minutes) and taxis (Rs 500, 30 minutes, every 45 minutes or when full) depart by the highway junction from 7am to 6pm. Hotels can organise a car and driver to Pokhara for Rs 35.

If leaving Bandipur via Dumre, it helps to book a tourist bus a day in advance to ensure that the bus stops in Dumre. Buses to Dumre from Bandipur depart from the western end of the bazaar.

Some people also walk to and from Bandipur via Bimalnagar on the Prithvi Hwy, which allows them to take in the Siddha Gufa cave (p202).

It's an easy walk downhill from Bandipur to Bimalnagar, but a tough uphill walk in the reverse direction, gaining over 1000m in elevation.

Dumre

Located about 17km west of Abu Khaireni, the rough roadside sprawl known as Dumre should be visited only as a transit point, or to use one of several ATMs.

If you should be so unfortunate as to have to spend the night in Dumre, avoid the hotels in the town centre in favour of the Hotel New Star (📞9825107383, 065-580345; r Rs 1500; 🏧🕿). Otherwise travel the 12km to Bandipur, where there are many great accommodation options.

If heading down the Prithvi Hwy, there are regular buses (Rs 350) and microbuses (Rs 400) to Kathmandu (five hours, every 15 minutes), as well as regular buses (Rs 200) and microbuses (Rs 250) to Pokhara (two hours, every 15 minutes).

Local buses (Rs 250) and microbuses (Rs 300) also head north to Besi Sahar (three hours, every 30 minutes), the starting point for the Annapurna Trek.

Pokhara

061 / POP 265,000 / ELEV 884M

Best Places to Eat

➡ Moondance Restaurant (p221)

➡ AoZoRa (p221)

➡ Caffe Concerto (p222)

➡ Krishna's Kitchen (p223)

➡ Metro (p221)

Best Places to Stay

➡ Temple Tree Resort & Spa (p219)

➡ Nanohana Lodge (p218)

➡ Hotel Adam (p215)

➡ Dhaulagiri Lodge (p232)

Why Go?

Pokhara ticks all the right boxes, with spectacular scenery, adventure activities, and accommodation and food choices galore. Whether you've returned from a three-week trek or endured a bus trip from hell, Lakeside Pokhara is the perfect place to recharge your batteries.

The scene is a chilled-out version of Kathmandu's Thamel neighbourhood, stretching along the shore of a tranquil lake with bobbing paddle boats. From the lake, and possibly even from your hotel bed, you can enjoy a clear view of the snow-capped mountains, just 20 or so kilometres away.

There's much more to Pokhara than its laid-back charm. It also boasts a booming adventure-sports industry: it is arguably the best paragliding venue on the globe and is surrounded by white-water rivers. There's a fascinating museum dedicated to the world-famous Gurkha soldier. And last but not least, it's the gateway to the world-famous treks in and around the Annapurna range and beyond.

When to Go
Pokhara

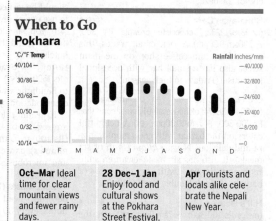

Oct–Mar Ideal time for clear mountain views and fewer rainy days.

28 Dec–1 Jan Enjoy food and cultural shows at the Pokhara Street Festival.

Apr Tourists and locals alike celebrate the Nepali New Year.

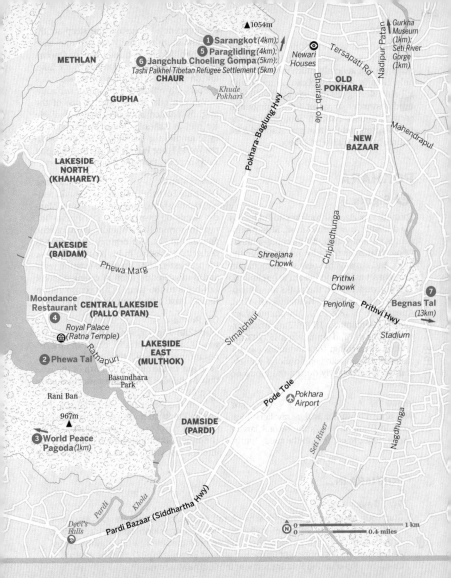

Pokhara Highlights

1 Sarangkot (p227) Waking up to a spectacular panorama as the rising sun illuminates the Himalayas.

2 Phewa Tal (p208) Paddling a colourful boat out to the middle of this lake to reveal a magical reflection of Machhapuchhare and its surrounding peaks.

3 World Peace Pagoda (p210) Climbing a forest trail to this dazzling white pagoda for a bird's-eye view of Pokhara.

4 Moondance Restaurant (p221) Celebrating your trekking triumph with a delicious meal at one of Lakeside's restaurants.

5 Paragliding (p213) Taking to the sky and riding the thermals like an eagle.

6 Jangchub Choeling Gompa (p230) Listening to chanting monks and learning about Tibetan refugees.

7 Begnas Tal (p229) Escaping the crowds and exploring the coffee farms and quiet shores of this serene lake.

Climate

Pokhara sits about 400m lower than Kathmandu, so the autumn and winter temperatures are generally much more comfortable. Even in winter you can get away with a T-shirt during the daytime and you'll only need a sweater or jacket for evenings and early mornings. June to September is the rainy season and the mountains spend a lot of time behind blankets of cloud.

POKHARA

◉ Sights

Forming a spectacular backdrop to Pokhara is the dramatic Annapurna Massif. Most prominent is the emblematic Mt Machhapuchhare, whose triangular mass looms large over the town, and remains the only virgin mountain in Nepal set aside as forbidden to be climbed.

From west to east, the peaks are Annapurna South (7219m), Hiunchuli (6441m), Annapurna I (8091m), Machhapuchhare (6997m), Annapurna III (7555m), Annapurna IV (7525m) and Annapurna II (7937m). A word of warning: the mountains can occasionally disappear behind cloud for several days, particularly during the monsoon season.

Phewa Tal   LAKE
(Map p210) Phewa Tal is the travellers' focal point in Pokhara, and is the second largest lake in Nepal. In contrast to the gaudy tourist development of Lakeside, the steep southwestern shore is densely forested and alive with birdlife. The lush Rani Ban, or Queen's Forest, bestows an emerald hue to the lake, and on a clear day the Annapurna mountains are perfectly reflected on its mirror surface.

You can take to the lake in one of the brightly painted *doongas* (boats) available for rent at Lakeside. Many people walk or cycle around the lakeshore – the trek up to the World Peace Pagoda affords breathtaking views over the tal to the mountains beyond.

Varahi Mandir   HINDU TEMPLE
(Map p216) Pokhara's most famous Hindu temple, the two-tiered pagoda-style Varahi Mandir stands on a small island in Phewa Tal, near the former Ratna Mandir (Royal Palace). Founded in the 18th century, the temple is dedicated to Vishnu in his boar incarnation. It's been extensively renovated over the years and is inhabited by a loft of cooing pigeons. Rowboats to the temple (per person return Rs 100) leave from Varahi Ghat in Lakeside.

Old Pokhara   AREA
(Map p210) For a glimpse of what Pokhara was like before the traffic, chaos and tourist restaurants besieged the erstwhile village, head out to the old town, north of the bustling Mahendra Pul. The best way to explore is on foot.

From the Nepal Telecom building at Mahendra Pul, head northwest along Tersapati, passing a number of **religious shops** selling Hindu and Buddhist paraphernalia. At the intersection with Nala Mukh, check out the

---

POKHARA IN...

Two Days

Start your day browsing through the handicraft shops and cafes of Lakeside before renting a colourful boat for a leisurely paddle on Phewa Tal. After lunch on the strip, climb up to the sublime World Peace Pagoda (p210) for more incredible views. On day two get up early to watch the sunrise light up the Himalaya at Sarangkot (p227). On the return to Lakeside, stop off in Old Pokhara and visit the Gurkha Museum.

Four Days

Hire a bike and ride north around the lake, before visiting a Tibetan refugee settlement. Drop in on Devi's Falls and muster the courage to have a go at tandem paragliding or go on an ultralight flight with a Himalayan backdrop. Get some background research on your trek at the International Mountain Museum and vary it up by wriggling through the Bat Cave (p211).

One Week

Consider a short trek to Poon Hill, Ghandruk or Panchase Danda. Head out to Begnas Tal to spend a peaceful night among the coffee plantations and return to explore the villages on the northern shore of Phewa Tal.

BRAVEST OF THE BRAVE

It might seem like an odd leftover from the days of empire, but the British army maintains a recruiting centre on the outskirts of Pokhara. Every year hundreds of young men from across Nepal come to Pokhara to put themselves through the rigorous selection process to become a Gurkha soldier.

Prospective recruits must perform a series of backbreaking physical tasks, including a 5km uphill run carrying 25kg of rocks in a traditional *doko* (basket). Only the most physically fit and mentally dedicated individuals make it through – it is not unheard of for recruits to keep on running with broken bones in their determination to get selected.

Identified by their curved khukuri knives, Gurkhas are still considered one of the toughest fighting forces in the world. British Gurkhas have carried out peacekeeping missions in Afghanistan, Bosnia and Sierra Leone, and Gurkha soldiers also form elite units of the Indian Army, the Singapore Police Force and the personal bodyguard of the sultan of Brunei.

The primary motivation for most recruits is money. The average daily wage in Nepal is little more than US$3, but Gurkha soldiers earn the equivalent of a Western wage, with a commission lasting up to 16 years and a British Army pension for life, plus the option of settling in Britain on retirement.

Newari houses with decorative brickwork and ornately carved wooden windows.

Continue north on Bhairab Tole to reach the small two-tiered **Bhimsen Temple** (Map p210), a 200-year-old shrine to the Newari god of trade and commerce, decorated with erotic carvings. The surrounding square is full of shops selling baskets and ceramics.

About 200m further north is a small hill, topped by the ancient **Bindhya Basini Temple** (Map p210). Founded in the 17th century, the temple is sacred to Durga, the warlike incarnation of Parvati, worshipped here in the form of a saligram.

International Mountain Museum   MUSEUM
(Map p210; ☎061-460742; www.international mountainmuseum.org; Ghari Patan; foreigner/ SAARC/Nepali Rs 400/200/80; ⊙9am-5pm) This expansive museum is devoted to the mountains of Nepal, the mountaineers who climbed them and the people who call them home. Inside, you can see original gear from many of the first Himalayan ascents, as well as displays on the history, culture, geology, and flora and fauna of the Himalaya.

Once you've been inspired by the climbers of the past, head outside where there's a 21m climbing wall and a 9.5m-high climbable model of Mt Manaslu. A taxi here from Lakeside will cost you around Rs 800 return.

Gurkha Museum   MUSEUM
(Map p210; ☎061-441762; www.gurkhamuseum. org.np; Mahendra Pul; foreigner/SAARC Rs 200/100, camera Rs 20; ⊙8am-4.30pm) Located just north of Mahendra Pul, near the KI Singh Bridge, the Gurkha Museum celebrates the achievements of the renowned Gurkha regiments. Accompanied by sound effects, it covers Gurkha history from the 19th-century Indian Uprising, through two World Wars to current-day disputes and peace-keeping missions, with a fascinating display on Gurkhas who have been awarded the Victoria Cross medal.

Seti River Gorge   PARK
(Map p210; park adult Rs 25; ⊙park 7am-6pm) The roaring Seti River passes right through Pokhara, but you won't see it unless you go looking. The river has carved a deep, narrow chasm through the middle of town, turning the water milky white in the process. The best place to catch a glimpse of the Seti River is the **park** just north of Old Pokhara near the Gurkha Museum.

Devi's Falls   WATERFALL
(Map p210; Pardi Bazaar, Damside; adult Rs 30; ⊙6am-6pm) Also known as Patale Chhango, this waterfall marks the point where the Pardi Khola stream vanishes underground. When the stream is at full bore after monsoon rains, the sound of the water plunging over the falls is deafening. The falls are about 2km southwest of the airport on the road to Butwal, just before the Tashi Ling Tibetan camp.

According to one of the many local legends, the name is a corruption of David's Falls, a reference to a Swiss visitor who tumbled into the sinkhole and drowned, taking his girlfriend with him.

Greater Pokhara

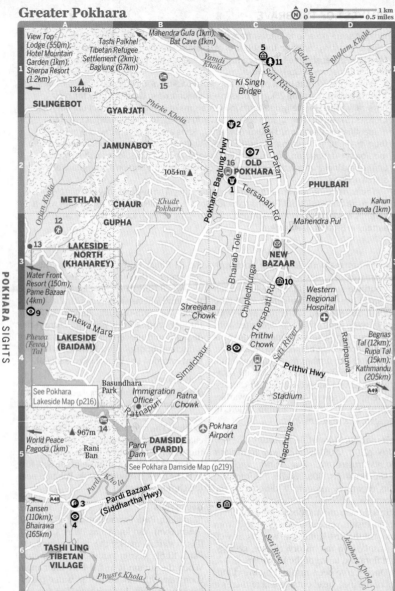

World Peace Pagoda

BUDDHIST PAGODA

(Map p228) Balanced on a narrow ridge high above Phewa Tal, the brilliant-white World Peace Pagoda was constructed by Buddhist monks from the Japanese Nipponzan Myo-hoji organisation. There are three paths up to the pagoda and several small cafes once you arrive. Sadly, there have been muggings on the trails in the past. Check the latest situation before you head off.

Greater Pokhara

Gupteshwor Mahadev Cave CAVE
(Map p210; Pardi Bazaar, Damside; foreigner/SAARC Rs 100/50; ☺6am-7pm) Across the road from Devi's Falls (p209), this venerated cave contains a huge stalagmite worshipped as a Shiva lingam. The ticket allows you to clamber through a tunnel behind the shrine, emerging in a damp cavern adjacent to the thundering waters of Devi's Falls.

Pokhara Regional Museum MUSEUM
(Map p210; ☎061-520413; New Bazaar; foreigner/SAARC Rs 100/50, camera Rs 50/30; ☺10am-5pm, closed Tue) North of the bus station on the road to Mahendra Pul, this little museum is devoted to the history and culture of the Pokhara Valley, including the mystical shamanic beliefs of the original inhabitants of the valley.

Bat Cave CAVE
(Chameri Gufa; adult Rs 100; ☺6am-6pm) You won't find Adam West or Christian Bale lurking in the dark and spooky Bat Cave, but instead thousands of horseshoe bats, clinging to the ceiling of a damp and slippery chamber and occasionally chirruping into the darkness – claustrophobics beware. Daredevils can continue to the back of the vault and wriggle out through a tiny chute to the surface. Torches are supplied, and guides (Rs 300) can show you the narrow exit tunnel. Ask about tours to other caves in the vicinity.

Mahendra Gufa CAVE
(Chameri Gufa; adult Rs 50; ☺6am-6pm) Near Bat Cave is the underwhelming Mahendra Gufa, the first large cave to be discovered in Pokhara. The first 125m of the cave is lit only to reveal dusty vandalised limestone formations, some revered as Shiva lingams. Beyond the electric lights there are bats.

🏃 Activities

There are some fascinating short treks in the lower foothills around Pokhara with epic views of the Annapurna Himalaya.

Zip-Flyer Nepal ADVENTURE SPORTS
(Map p216; ☎061-466399; www.highgroundnepal.com; Central Lakeside; foreigner per bungee or zipline/combo US$82/140, Nepali bungee/zipline/combo Rs 4200/4500/7500) This awesome zipline launches from Sarangkot and drops 600m over 1.8km achieving a speed of 120km/h. It is claimed to be the third highest, longest and fastest zipline in the world. You can also bungee jump from a 70m tower for the same price, which includes pick-up and drop-off from Lakeside, or do both with a 'combo'. Weight and age restrictions apply.

Boating
Heading out onto the calm waters of Phewa Tal is the perfect way to unwind and gain a spectacular reflective mountain view. Colourful wooden *doongas* are available for rent at several boat stations, including Varahi Ghat and Phewa Ghat. Rates vary from ghat to ghat but start at Rs 500 per hour with a boatman, or Rs 450/1000 per hour/day if you paddle yourself. You can also rent aluminium pedalos (small/big Rs 610/810 per hour) and sailboats (Rs 710 per hour, or Rs 910 per hour for lessons). Lifejackets are compulsory at Rs 10, as is the conservation fee per boat, also Rs 10. Another popular way to explore Phewa Tal is by kayak (p212).

Stand Up Paddle Nepal WATER SPORTS
(Map p219; ☎9817105012; Damside; per hour/day Rs 700/3500) One of a few operators providing stand-up paddleboarding on Phewa Tal. Prices include all equipment, including buoyancy vest, and even some personal instructions to get you going. Put in at Damside park, a short stroll from the shop.

POKHARA ACTIVITIES

DON'T MISS

WALKING TO THE WORLD PEACE PAGODA

Balanced on a narrow ridge high above Phewa Tal, the brilliant-white World Peace Pagoda (p210) was constructed by Buddhist monks from the Japanese Nipponzan Myohoji organisation to promote world peace. In addition to the access road, there are three walking paths up to the pagoda and several small cafes for snacks and drinks once you arrive.

The Direct Route (One Hour)

The most obvious route up to the pagoda begins on the south bank of Phewa Tal, behind the Lychee Garden Resort at Anadu. Boatmen charge around Nepali/foreigner Rs 350/420 one way to the trailhead from Varahi Ghat, Lakeside and the path leads straight up the hillside on cut stone steps. Ignore the right-hand fork by the small temple and continue uphill through woodland to reach the pagoda. You can either continue on to Pokhara via the scenic route (described below), catch a bus or taxi, or walk/boat back the way you came.

The Scenic Route (Two Hours)

A more interesting route to the pagoda begins near the footbridge over the Pardi Khola, just south of the Pardi dam. After crossing the bridge, the trail skirts the edge of paddy fields and a tall grey fence, past a small temple, before turning uphill into the forest through a gate in the fence. When you see the poultry farm on your left, you are near the gate. From here the trail climbs for about 2km through gorgeous forest that has repopulated old rice terraces. The main trail continues west in a more or less direct route to the south of the ridge. An alternative trail crosses the main trail about 600m from the gate and takes you up to the main ridge before turning west and skirting the north side of the ridge. This trail provides tree-framed mountain views. Eventually both trails meet up and you reach a restaurant where the trail from Devi's Falls joins. Here there are spectacular views that keep getting better as you approach the pagoda. The approach is now garrisoned by cafes tempting you with cold drinks and espresso coffee.

The Easy Route (20 Minutes)

For views without the fuss, take a taxi (Rs 600) or local bus (Rs 20) from the public bus stand to the car park south of the pagoda. The rough access road to the pagoda leaves the Siddhartha Hwy just south of town. A steep trail of stairs leads up from the car park to the entrance of the pagoda. Instead of returning by car, you can walk down to the lake and catch a boat to Lakeside.

Cycling & Mountain Biking

Cycling is a great way to get around Pokhara, whether you are visiting the museums, braving the bazaar or just cruising Lakeside. Indian mountain bikes are available from dozens of places on the strip in Lakeside and cost around Rs 150/500 per hour/day.

Contact any of the Lakeside travel agents for details of mountain-biking trips in the hills around Pokhara.

Chain 'n' Gear Mountain Bikes CYCLING
(Map p216; ☑061-463696; www.chainngearmtb.
com; Gaurighat Marg, Lakeside East; per day from US$15) To hire quality Trek and Giant mountain bikes, and/or to organise short or extended mountain-bike rides, drop in to see the experts at Chain 'n' Gear in Pokhara's Lakeside.

Pokhara Mountain Bike CYCLING
(Map p216; ☑061-466224; www.nepalmountain
bike.com; Hallan Chowk, Lakeside; per hour/day Rs 200/1000) Mountain-bike rental and mountain-bike tours.

Horse Riding

Travel agents in Pokhara offer pony treks to various viewpoints around town, including Sarangkot, Kahun Danda and the World Peace Pagoda. Half-day trips (Rs 2500) stick to the lakeshore; you'll need a full day (Rs 4000) to reach the viewpoints.

Kayaking & Rafting

Pokhara is a great place to organise rafting trips, particularly down the Kali Gandaki and Seti Rivers. Half-day rafting/kayak trips start at US$60/55 per person. All-inclusive overnight rafting trips start at US$125 per person and trips can be as long as 10 days.

Kayak clinics (from beginner to advanced) are held on the Seti River and scenic drifts down the Narayani River to Chitwan National Park can be arranged.

Paddle Nepal   RAFTING
(Map p216; ☑061-465730; www.paddlenepal.com; Centre Point Complex, Lakeside) As well as several white-water rafting options, there are beginner kayak clinics and combined canyoning/rafting expeditions at this Pokhara-based operation.

Rapidrunner Expeditions   RAFTING
(Map p216; ☑061-462024; www.rapidrunnerexpeditions.com; Central Lakeside; 2-day family rafting adult/child from US$110/90) This Pokhara-based company offers kayak clinics and 'ducky trips' (gentle paddles in small rafts), in addition to serious white-water rafting trips.

Kayak Shack   KAYAKING
(Map p216; ☑061-465730; Central Lakeside; 1hr/half-day/day Rs 300/700/1400; ⊙7am-6pm) The Kayak Shack is a lakeshore branch of Paddle Nepal where you can hire kayaks for one, three or six hours. The price includes a life vest.

Adrenaline Rush Nepal   RAFTING
(Map p216; ☑061-466663; www.adrenalinenepal.com; Hallan Chowk, Lakeside) Big white-water rafting trips are supplemented by river 'tubing' and canyoning; add-on treks can also be organised.

Ganesh Kayak   KAYAKING
(Map p216; ☑061-462657; www.ganeshkayak.com; Central Lakeside; kayaks per hour/half-day/day Rs 300/700/1000, 4-day kayaking & camping safaris US$275) Ganesh Kayak, beside the Moondance Restaurant, rents out kayaks for paddling in Phewa Tal. Fishing safaris (best from March to April and October to November) can also be arranged here.

Massage
Trekkers with aching muscles can get relief from experienced masseurs, including the barbers, in Lakeside. While there are many excellent legitimate practitioners, there are nonetheless a few dodgy operators; females should insist on having a female masseur.

Seeing Hands Nepal   MASSAGE
(Map p216; ☑061-464478; www.seeinghandsnepal.org; Lakeside East; 60/90min massage Rs 1800/2600; ⊙10am-5.30pm) Seeing Hands Nepal has professionally trained blind Nepali therapists who, with a heightened sense

of perception and touch, provide excellent Swedish-style massages. Run by volunteers, Seeing Hands does excellent work in supporting Nepali blind people in a society where they're often marginalised.

Jiva Cafe & Spa   MASSAGE
(Map p216; ☑061-465379; Central Lakeside; massage Rs 2000-3500; ⊙7am-9pm) Jiva does excellent massages, from feet to head, and including a special trekker's massage. You can also get a facial or a body scrub, and the cafe serves snacks and healthy smoothies.

Paragliding
Soaring silently on the thermals against a backdrop of the snow-capped Annapurna is a once-in-a-lifetime experience. However, be forewarned that the popularity of the activity has led to the sky above Sarangkot becoming extremely crowded these days. Operators usually offer both 20-minute and 45-minute flights. Paragliding operates during suitable weather year-round, including during the monsoon. Numerous operators have started up in recent years; the ones we recommend are experienced companies that have stood the test of time.

Frontiers Paragliding   ADVENTURE SPORTS
(Map p216; ☑061-466044; www.himalayan-paragliding.com; Hallan Chowk, Lakeside; 15-20min Rs 8500, 30-45min Rs 11,500) One of the pioneering companies, Frontiers offers pilot courses and multiday tours in addition to the popular tandem flights.

Sunrise Paragliding   ADVENTURE SPORTS
(Map p216; ☑061-463174; www.sunrise-paragliding.com; Central Lakeside; 20-30min Rs 8500, 45-60min Rs 11,500) Sunrise offers courses and tours, and has stood the test of time.

Swimming
The cool waters of Phewa Tal may beckon on a hot day, but there's a fair bit of pollution, so if you do swim it's advisable that you hire a boatman to take you out to the centre of the lake. Keep a watch for currents and don't get too close to the dam in Damside.

A few upmarket hotels let nonguests swim in their pool for a fee, including Mt Kailash Resort (p219; Rs 745), Hotel Barahi (p218; Rs 625), Fish Tail Lodge (p219; Rs 650) and Temple Tree Resort & Spa (p219; Rs 650).

Walking
Even if you don't have the energy or perhaps the inclination to attempt the Annapurna Circuit, there are plenty of short treks in

PHEWA TAL CIRCUIT

If you get an early start, it's possible to walk right around the shore of Phewa Tal, beginning on the path to the World Peace Pagoda. Starting from the pagoda, continue along the ridge to the village of Lukunswara and take the right fork where the path divides. Once you reach Pumdi, ask around for the path down to Margi on the edge of the lake. From Margi, you can either cut across the marshes over a series of log bridges or continue around the edge of the valley to the suspension bridge at Pame Bazaar, where a dirt road continues along the northern shore to Pokhara. If you run out of energy, local buses pass by every hour or so.

the hills around Pokhara. If you just want to stretch your legs and escape the crowds, stroll along the north shore of Phewa Tal. A paved walkway runs west along the shoreline to the village of Pame Bazaar, where you can pick up a bus back to Pokhara or continue on a circuit of Phewa Tal.

Another hike is the three-hour trip to the viewpoint at **Kahun Danda** (1560m) on the east side of the Seti River. There's a viewing tower on the crest of the hill, built over the ruins of an 18th-century fort. The easiest trail to follow begins near the Manipal Teaching Hospital in Phulbari – ask for directions at the base of the hill. One of the most popular walks around Pokhara is the trip to the World Peace Pagoda (p210).

Ultralight & Helicopter Flights

On a clear day you can't miss the buzzing ultralights flying noisily above Pokhara providing their customers with unrivalled mountain views.

Avia Club Nepal   SCENIC FLIGHTS
(Map p216; ☑061-462192; www.aviaclubnepal.com; Hallan Chowk, Lakeside; ultralight flights 15/30/60/90min US$95/170/270/390) Avia Club offers exhilarating ultralight flights around the Pokhara Valley. In 15 minutes you can buzz around the World Peace Pagoda and lakeshore, but you'll need more time to get up above Sarangkot for the full Himalayan panorama. Avia also offers paragliding and ultralight plus paragliding packages.

Pokhara Ultralight   SCENIC FLIGHTS
(Map p216; ☑061-466880; www.flypokhara.com; Central Lakeside; ultralight flights 15/30/60/90 minutes US$100/175/275/395) Pokhara Ultralight offers a range of flights from a quick buzz above Pokhara to more exhilarating flights towards the mountains.

Pokhara Heli Services   SCENIC FLIGHTS
(Map p216; ☑061-467241; www.pokharaheli.com; Central Lakeside; minimum group of 6, per person

US$349; ☺8am-8pm) Why trek when you can helicopter in to Annapurna Base Camp? Nothing demonstrates the changing tourist scene in Pokhara more than this offering. The one-hour tour includes 25 minutes on the ground at ABC; this short stop at altitude is thought to be safe, but the safest way to reach ABC is still the old-fashioned way on foot.

Courses

Pokhara is an ideal setting to contemplate the nature of the universe, and there are several centres offering to help you on your way.

Ganden Yiga Chopen
Meditation Centre   MEDITATION
(Pokhara Buddhist Meditation Centre; Map p216; ☑061-462923; www.pokharabuddhistcentre.com; Lakeside North; 3-day course incl room & meals Rs 6500, daily session Rs 400) This serene retreat holds three-day meditation and yoga courses that start every Friday at 2.30pm. There are also daily sessions from 7.30am to 9am, Monday to Friday.

Sadhana Yoga Retreat   YOGA
(Map p210; ☑061-694041; www.sadhana-asanga-yoga.com; Sedi Bagar; from US$22, incl accommodation from US$83) This retreat is secluded in the village of Sedi Bagar, 2.5km northwest of Lakeside. One- to 21-day courses in Hatha yoga include tuition, steam and mud baths, accommodation and meals. Enquire about yoga treks.

Himalayan Yogini   YOGA
(☑9846185540; www.himalayanyogini.com; Khapaudi-2, Happy Village; from Rs 800; ☺classes 7.30-9.30am & 4.30-6pm) Program includes daily meditation and Hatha yoga classes. One- to five-day courses also available.

Tours

Travel agents in Pokhara can arrange local tours and activities, and it's easy to rent a bike and do things under your own steam.

215

Tibetan Encounter
TOURS

(Map p216; 061-466486; www.tibetan-encounter.com; Lakeside East; half-/full-day tour Rs 4500/6500) This is a great way to experience Pokhara's refugee settlements and learn about Tibetan culture, traditional foods and medicine, and the contemporary life of Tibetan refugees in Nepal.

★ Festivals & Events

Pokhara Street Festival   STREET CARNIVAL
Lakeside comes alive with a festive spirit during this annual event (28 December to 1 January), when the main strip closes to traffic as restaurants set up tables on the road. Visitors cram the street to enjoy food, parades, performances and carnival rides.

Bagh Jatra   CULTURAL
(☉Aug) Every August, Pokhara's Newari community celebrates this three-day festival that recalls the slaying of a deadly marauding tiger.

Phewa Festival   NEW YEAR
(☉Apr) Celebrations for the Nepali New Year, in April, organised by the Pokhara hotel association to promote tourism.

Losar   RELIGIOUS
(Tibetan New Year; ☉Jan/Feb) Tibetan Buddhists hold celebrations and masked dances at gompas around Pokhara in January/February.

🛏 Sleeping

Most people stay in Lakeside, a strip of hotels, travel and trekking agents, restaurants and souvenir shops. As the main traveller centre, Lakeside is packed with hotels, ranging from dirt cheap to three-star luxury. People looking for more peace and quiet can head to the south end of the strip, to Damside. All hotels will hold your luggage if you plan on trekking.

🛏 Central Lakeside

Hotel Travel Inn   HOTEL $
(Map p216; 061-462631; www.hoteltravelin.com; s/d incl breakfast US$10/22, r with AC US$35-50; ❇🛜) Although catering for all budgets, even the cheapest rooms are spotless here. It's worth the step up to deluxe for the comfy beds and bathtubs. The owner here claims tourists want three things: cleanliness, friendliness and quietness, and this modern hotel delivers on all fronts. It's the UN's choice of hotel when it's in town. Rates include taxes.

Lake City Hotel   HOTEL $
(Map p216; 061-464240; www.lakecityhotel.com; dm Rs 300, s/d Rs 1000/1200, without bathroom Rs 660/800, ste Rs 3300; ❇🛜) 🅿 Rooms at Lake City are arranged around a courtyard – much like a motel – and are surprisingly comfortable. Some rooms sport well-appointed, stone-tiled bathrooms. There's also a rooftop restaurant with a fireplace and lake views. Its recycling bins and refillable water supply (Rs 10 per bottle) set an excellent example.

Little Tibetan Guest House   GUESTHOUSE $
(Map p216; 061-461898; littletibgh@yahoo.com; Phewa Marg, Lakeside; s/d from US$10/18; 🛜) This Tibetan-run lodge east of Hallan Chowk is rightly popular for its calm and relaxed atmosphere. Rooms are elegantly decorated with Tibetan wall hangings and bedspreads. Balconies overlook a serene garden and while there's no restaurant, bed and breakfast packages are available.

Mountain Villa   HOTEL $
(Map p216; 061-461954; prabindwa@gmail.com; Phewa Marg, Lakeside; s/d Rs 1200/1500, r with AC Rs 2200; ❇🛜) Mountain Villa's 22 rooms stretch back from busy Phewa Marg on a long block of land with a narrow garden running the length of the property. The rooms at the back are quiet and private. Rooms vary but most have cool and clean stone-tiled or parquet floors and Western-style bathrooms. The recommended Japanese restaurant AoZoRa (p221) is downstairs.

★Hotel Adam   HOTEL $$
(Map p216; 061-462844; www.hoteladamnepal.com; Lakeside; all incl breakfast and taxes s/d US$25/30, s/d with AC US$45/50; ❇🛜) This gem of a hotel is staffed by friendly, calm and informative staff – there's a respected, long-standing travel company (same management) downstairs. Rooms are clean, bathrooms are modern and the beds are comfortable. Some rooms have great views of the lake and mountains. Upstairs is a superb rooftop restaurant with exceptional views.

Butterfly Lodge   HOTEL $$
(Map p216; 061-461892; www.butterfly-lodge.org; Lakeside; all incl breakfast s/d standard US$20/30, deluxe US$30/40, ste US$50/60; ❇🛜) Even the standard rooms at Butterfly Lodge are big and super clean, and all rooms

POKHARA FESTIVALS & EVENTS

Pokhara Lakeside

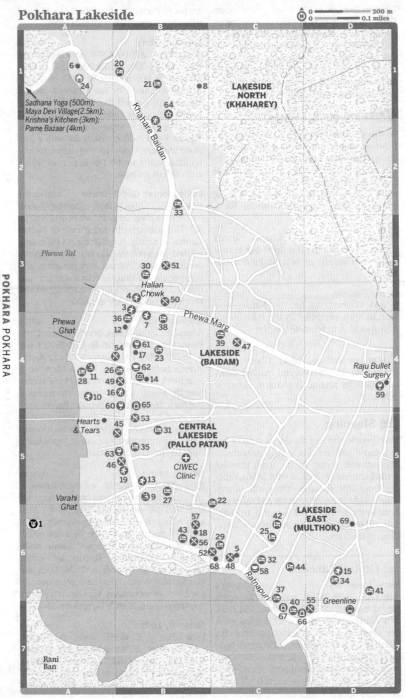

Phewa Tal

Phewa Ghat

Rani Ban

Sadhana Yoga (500m);
Maya Devi Village(2.5km);
Krishna's Kitchen (3km);
Pame Bazaar (4km)

Khahare Baidan

Hallan Chowk

Phewa Marg

LAKESIDE NORTH (KHAHAREY)

LAKESIDE (BAIDAM)

Raju Bullet Surgery

Hearts & Tears

CENTRAL LAKESIDE (PALLO PATAN)

CIWEC Clinic

Varahi Ghat

Ratnapuri

LAKESIDE EAST (MULTHOK)

Greenline

Pokhara Lakeside

POKHARA SLEEPING

are nonsmoking. On the grounds is a lovely lawn with banana lounges and two restaurants, one Chinese, one Indian. Staff are helpful and some of the profits go to the Butterfly Foundation supporting local children.

Hotel Peace Plaza   HOTEL **$$**
(Map p216; ☑ 061-461505; www.hotelpeaceplaza. com; Lakeside; s/d standard US$25/35, with AC US$50/60, ste US$90; ✳🅰🛜) This centrally located, modern four-storey midrange

hotel ticks many boxes. Rooms, several with balconies and lake views, boast soft beds, a desk, a bar fridge and satellite LED TV. Some also have a bathtub. Downstairs is a bright lake-view restaurant plus a street-front bar.

Blue Planet Lodge   HOTEL $$

(Map p216; ☑ 061-465706; www.blueplanetlodge. com; Central Lakeside; r incl breakfast €25-50; ❋ ⚛) Blue Planet Lodge has a range of rooms including seven 'chakra' rooms energised with the colours of the rainbow, special stones and singing bowls. There is also a meditation and yoga hall with a Nepali yoga master. The peaceful garden sports a colourful Ganesh. The rates shown here include all taxes and there are discounts for long stays and singles.

Kotee Home Hotel   HOTEL $$

(Map p216; ☑ 061-464008; www.koteehome hotel.com; Central Lakeside; s/d Rs 1800/2200, d incl breakfast Rs 2500; ❋ ⚛) Centrally located on the Lakeside strip, Kotee is a comfortable midrange choice with a variety of different-sized rooms. All boast LED TVs and quality bathrooms; you should be able to get a discount on one of the smaller rooms when the hotel isn't busy. The in-house Red Tomato restaurant has a bar and international menu.

Hotel Fewa   HOTEL $$

(Map p216; ☑ 061-463151; www.hotelfewa.com; Central Lakeside; s/d US$15/25, s/d cottage US$35/45; ⚛) Hotel Fewa has rustic stone cottages set right on the lake and has a pleasant lakeshore restaurant. The cottages with lofts make for a memorable stay, and include a fireplace and Buddhist motifs. The rooms in the back building, however, lack the same charm.

Hotel Barahi   HOTEL $$$

(Map p216; ☑ 061-460617; www.barahi.com; Central Lakeside; s/d standard US$57/79, deluxe US$115/145; ❋ @ ⚛ ☲) The stone-clad Hotel Barahi features very smart, well-appointed rooms with small balconies. It has 24-hour room service, a sparkling pool and an excellent restaurant. There's also a nightly cultural show. Many rooms boast incredible mountain vistas, but the standard rooms are quite tiny.

🛏 Lakeside East

★ Nanohana Lodge   HOTEL $

(Map p216; ☑ 061-464478; www.nanohanalodge. com; Lakeside East; r US$14-22, with AC US$30-35; ⚛) This renovated hotel is spotless and well managed. Each level has a communal balcony with table and chairs, and many of the rooms have wonderful Annapurna views. The air-con rooms feature plush mattresses, but all rooms are comfortable. It's in a quiet location yet still convenient to the Lakeside restaurants and is associated with the nearby Seeing Hands blind massage clinic (p213).

Sacred Valley Inn   HOTEL $

(Map p216; ☑ 061-461792; www.sacredvalley inn.com; Lakeside East; r with/without bathroom US$15/10, upstairs US$25-30; ⚛) Set in a shady garden, Sacred Valley is a long-established traveller favourite (book early!). All the rooms are well maintained and those upstairs have gleaming marble floors and windows on two sides, allowing in plenty of light. Upstairs is a rooftop garden and, downstairs, the pleasant Sacred Valley Café.

Hotel Nirvana   HOTEL $

(Map p216; ☑ 061-463332; hotelnirvana@hotmail. com; Lakeside East; r ground/1st/2nd fl Rs 1200/2000/2500; ⚛) Almost invisible behind its lush garden, Hotel Nirvana is a much-loved, fastidiously clean place with a prim garden and spacious rooms with colourful bedspreads and curtains. Hotel management are welcoming and helpful. Rooms get pricier as you climb the stairs.

Peace Eye Guest House   HOTEL $

(Map p216; ☑ 061-461699; www.peaceeye-guest house.com; Lakeside East; s/d Rs 800/1000, without bathroom Rs 500/600, deluxe r Rs 1200; ⚛) Established in 1977, the chilled-out Peace Eye retains all the qualities that attracted the original visitors to Pokhara 40 years ago. Inexpensive, laid-back and friendly, its brightly decorated rooms are well kept and clean. Budget rooms are smallish but the others are spacious. It also has a vegetarian restaurant and small German bakery.

Gauri Shankar Guest House   HOTEL $

(Map p216; ☑ 061-462422; www.gaurishankar.com; Lakeside East; dm/s/d Rs 300/700-1350/850-1800; ⚛) Calm, quiet and reasonably priced, Gauri Shankar has cosy, bright rooms set in a secluded garden of pebbles and plants. The better and pricier rooms are upstairs. It has a garden cafe for breakfasts, a rooftop terrace, a TV common room and library; its atmosphere is social and friendly.

Hotel Trekkers Inn   HOTEL $

(Map p216; ☑ 061-463244; Gaurighat, Lakeside East; r with/without AC Rs 4000/2000; ❋ ⚛) Having undergone recent renovations, the Trekkers Inn features spacious rooms, comfortable mattresses and flat-screen TVs. Most rooms have lake or mountain views (the higher up, the better the view). The other furnishings are a bit plain, but the bathrooms have been updated. The more expensive air-con rooms come with free breakfast.

Hotel Yeti HOTEL **$**
(Map p216; ☏061-462768; www.hotelyeti.com.np; Lakeside East; r US$13-30; ☏) Draped in vines that flower bright red or yellow (depending on the time of year), Hotel Yeti's striking facade makes an excellent first impression. Rooms vary in size and price but all are clean and bright. There's a small garden and the manager here is very helpful with onward travel arrangements.

Lake View Resort HOTEL **$$**
(Map p216; ☏061-461477; www.pokharahotels.com; Lakeside East; s/d deluxe US$50/60, super deluxe US$60/70, huts US$90/100; P✱@☎) Lake View Resort is one of Lakeside's oldest establishments, and as such it offers old-fashioned spacious rooms set in a neat garden. The air-con deluxe rooms and huts are great value considering the quality of the beds and other furnishings. The respected restaurant with lake views and a nightly culture show are a bonus. Big discounts available in summer. It also runs a budget option (Hotel Lakeside) nearby (single/double US$15/20).

★Temple Tree
Resort & Spa LUXURY HOTEL **$$$**
(Map p216; ☏061-465819; www.templetree nepal.com; Lakeside East; s/d from US$160/180; ✱@☎✈) Tricked-out Temple Tree raises the bar in Lakeside. Plenty of timber and slate and straw-coloured render add delightful earthy tones. The standard rooms aren't huge but are exceptionally comfortable and most sport a bathtub and private balcony. The super deluxe rooms are spacious. There are two restaurants, a health spa, and a bar beside the lovely pool.

Fish Tail Lodge LUXURY HOTEL **$$$**
(Map p210; ☏061-465071; www.fishtail-lodge.com; r from US$170; ✱@☎✈) Reached by a rope-drawn pontoon from Basundhara Park, Fish Tail is charmingly understated, with heritage rooms housed in low slate-roofed bungalows in a lush garden. Rooms 16, 17 and 18 have excellent lake and mountain views but you'll need to book well in advance. Discounts are usually available. Profits are donated to a trust that helps cardiac patients in Nepal.

Pokhara Damside

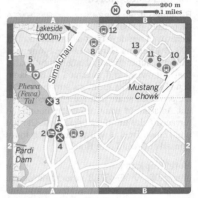

Mt Kailash Resort HOTEL **$$$**
(Map p216; ☏061-465703; www.mountkailash resort.com; Lakeside East; s/d from US$150/180; ✱@☎✈) This is a comfortable and professionally managed choice aimed at tour groups but with discounts available for longer stays. The modern, well-appointed rooms have a double and a single bed with very decent mattresses. The bright and airy upper-floor rooms have mountain views, and there is a health spa, large pool and a restaurant.

Lakeside North

Banana Garden Lodge
GUESTHOUSE $

(Map p216; 061-464901; www.bananagarden lodge.com; Lakeside North; r without bathroom Rs 400;) Banana Garden Lodge is one of a cluster of super friendly, budget guesthouses that are owned and managed by the same genial family. The clean guestrooms at Banana Garden share four solar-heated showers. Adjacent to Banana Garden among the terraced fields are the similar Palm Garden and Lemon Tree, as well as the slightly more upmarket Green Peace Hotel.

Hotel Tropicana
HOTEL $

(Map p216; 061-462118; www.hoteltropicana. com.np; Lakeside North; r US$11-22;) This time-honoured hotel of more than 20 years has large, spotless rooms with great lake and mountain views from the upper floors. Rooms on the 3rd floor (US$17) are the best value. The swing chair upstairs is a lovely spot to read a book, looking out to the lake.

Freedom Café & Bar
HUT $

(Map p216; 061-464135; freedomcafe@hotmail. com; Lakeside North; r without bathroom Rs 800;) The huts here are very basic and tiny – one bed, one window, one desk – with no attached bathrooms. The lakefront huts sport a hammock; however, here it's all about the communal areas, chilled-out alcoves where folks strum a guitar, curl up with a book and cool down with a drink. There's a pool table and live music most weekends.

3 Sisters Guest House
HOTEL $$

(Map p216; 061-466883; www.3sistersadven turetrek.com; Lakeside North; s/d incl breakfast US$20/30;) Much smarter than the surrounding hotels, this tidy pink-brick lodge is owned by the same folk as 3 Sisters Adventure Trekking (p384). Rooms are tastefully decorated and the location is peaceful, but the hotel is very popular, so booking well ahead is advised. Pick-up from the airport or bus station is offered with prior notice.

Maya Devi Village
HUT $$

(Map p228; 9814125635; www.mayadevivillage. com; Khapaudi, Happy Village; r from US$40;) This ultra-relaxed spot at the north end of the lake is on the road to Pame village. Accommodation is in tricked-out, thatched, round huts with a balcony, bathroom and second storey.

Water Front Resort
RESORT $$$

(Map p228; 061-466304; www.ktmgh.com/ waterfront-resort; Lakeside North; r from US$110;) Part of the Kathmandu Guest House chain, the Water Front nestles in the northern shore of Phewa Tal, not far from where the paragliders return to earth. The spacious rooms have lake and mountain views, and there is a glorious swimming pool to cool off in. There are a couple restaurants; one is designed to capture lake views and cooling breezes.

Damside & Elsewhere

Park Anadu Restaurant & Lodge
HOTEL $

(Map p228; 9846025557; Anandu; r incl boat trip Rs 1000;) Perched high on Phewa Tal's western shore, the secluded Park Anadu has unbeatable views with rooms opening up to a perfect lake vista framed by a Himalayan backdrop. Situated a 20-minute boat trip from Lakeside (free transit back and forth), the rooms boast balconies and there's an inexpensive restaurant.

Hotel Mona Lisa
HOTEL $$

(Map p219; 061-463863; www.hotelmona lisa.com.np; Damside; s/d US$20/30, with AC US$40/50;) The best and brightest of several similar places in this peaceful area, Hotel Mona Lisa tempts Japanese visitors with brightly coloured rooms and lounges with low *kotatsu* tables and cushions. Rooms are spotless and the best have balconies with mountain, Rani Ban and lake views.

Tiger Mountain Pokhara Lodge
HOTEL $$$

(Map p228; 061-691887, in Kathmandu 01-4720580; www.tigermountainpokhara.com; cottages US$470;) This lodge is set on a lofty ridge about 10km east of Pokhara, and the owners have made a real effort to make it blend into the surroundings. Rooms are contained in stylish stone bungalows and there's an amazing mountain-view swimming pool. Rates include meals and transfers to/from Pokhara. Tiger Mountain prides itself on its independently audited sustainable tourism initiatives.

🍴 Eating

Lakeside has numerous restaurants, bars and cafes serving up Western, Nepali, Indian and Chinese food to hungry travellers and trekkers.

✕ Central Lakeside

★ Metro
CRÊPES $

(Map p216; Lakeside; crepes Rs 185-375; ⏲7am-9pm; 🛜) At Metro it's all about the crepes that are deliriously delicious: lemon sugar, cinnamon sugar, apple and caramel cream and so on. Also on the menu are savoury crepes, espresso coffee, ice cream and slushies.

Saleways
SUPERMARKET $

(Map p216; Centre Point Complex, Lakeside; ⏲8am-10pm) Excellent supermarket (it expands downstairs) with most of what you need plus a bottle shop.

Desi Tadka
INDIAN $

(Map p216; ☑9856033809; Phewa Marg, Lakeside; mains Rs 140-490; ⏲7am-11pm; 🛜) In a neighbourhood of similar tandoori restaurants, Desi Tadka gets our vote for succulent tandoori chicken, brilliant biryanis and delicious curries. There is also a very good South Indian menu.

China Town
CHINESE $

(Map p216; Central Lakeside; mains Rs 200-650; ⏲11am-10pm; 🛜) With red-tassled lanterns and paintings of goldfish, this is a bona fide Chinatown experience. The Chinese chef creates authentic Cantonese and spicy Sichuan classics with a delicious selection of duck and pork dishes. We recommend the spicy *mapo dofu* (tofu) and *gong bao* chicken (chicken, chilli and peanuts).

Boomerang Restaurant & German Bakery
INTERNATIONAL $

(Map p216; Central Lakeside; mains Rs 195-795; ⏲7am-10pm; 🛜) The best of the 'garden and dinner show' places, Boomerang has a large, shady garden with fresh flowers on each table. The international menu is very good, as is its Lakeside setting. There's a cultural show nightly from 7pm. The roadside German bakery, featuring buttery pastries and donuts, is also recommended for a post-trek energy boost.

Tibetan Pema Restaurant
TIBETAN $

(Map p216; Tibetan Mini Market, Central Lakeside; mains Rs 180-200; ⏲7.30am-10pm) This cosy little restaurant at the very rear of the Tibetan Mini Market is painted in bright colours and does delicious, cheap momos (potato and cheese, veg, chicken and buffalo) and other Tibetan classics.

★ Moondance Restaurant
INTERNATIONAL $$

(Map p216; www.moondancepokhara.com; Central Lakeside; mains Rs 240-1400; ⏲7am-10.30pm; 🛜) The much-loved Moondance is a Lakeside institution and deservedly so. Quality food, good service and a roaring open fire all contribute to the popularity of this tastefully decorated restaurant. Its menu features salads, pizzas, imported steaks and excellent Indian and Thai curries. For dessert, the lemon meringue pie is legendary.

★ AoZoRa
JAPANESE $$

(Map p216; ☑061-461707; Phewa Marg, Lakeside; mains Rs 250-490; ⏲8am-9pm; 🛜) AoZoRa is a bamboo-lined 'hole-in-the-wall' with a classic Japanese menu featuring donburi, ramen, sushi and several set menus, such as chicken teriyaki served with rice, miso and pickle. The Japanese-speaking staff welcome you with a glass of *mugi* (roasted barley tea), and point out the seasonal specials board. There's seating out the back if the front tables are full.

OR2K Restaurant
VEGETARIAN $$

(Map p216; ☑061-467114; www.or2k.net; Centre Point Complex, Lakeside; mains Rs 325-595; ⏲8am-11pm; 🛜) A branch of the popular Thamel restaurant occupies the top floor of the Centre Point Complex. Enjoy the Middle Eastern dishes, pasta, pizza and sizzlers with serene lake and mountain views. Beer, cocktails and wine by the glass are available; and there's even outdoor seating where you *don't* have to remove your shoes.

Pokhara Thakali Kitchen
NEPALI $$

(Map p216; Gaurighat, Lakeside East; thali veg Rs 290-350, nonveg Rs 340-600; ⏲11am-10pm; 🛜) This cosy, atmospheric restaurant specialises in regional Thakali cuisine presented as *thalis*, each with three curries – choose veg or non-veg, standard or special. Snacks include exotic offerings such as Mustang potatoes, buckwheat finger chips and fried strips of goat meat.

Byanjan
INTERNATIONAL $$

(Map p216; Central Lakeside; mains Rs 325-495; ⏲8am-10pm; 🛜) This eatery, associated with the upmarket Hotel Barahi, uses chilled white-and-blue decor, raw rocks and subtle lighting to achieve a modern-global air of sophistication. The menu is wide-ranging with Chinese, Thai, Indian and Nepalese dishes. If the low tables look uncomfortable, head upstairs or out the back into the garden.

POKHARA EATING

Old Mike's Kitchen INTERNATIONAL $$

(Map p216; 061-463151; Lakeside; mains Rs 280-550; 7am-9pm;) With a Lakeside setting under the spreading boughs of a pipal tree, Old Mike's makes a delightful spot for a hearty breakfast, lunch or dinner. Among the wide range of dishes are several Mexican options, such as quesadillas and tostadas. The lakeside tables are a great place to settle in with an evening drink.

Café in the Garden INTERNATIONAL $$

(Map p216; www.annapurnaactivities.com; Phewa Marg, Lakeside; mains Rs 280-650; 8.30am-9pm;) At this delightful garden restaurant you can watch as the meals are cooked before you. There are separate breakfast, snacks, lunch and dinner menus, and every day there is an international special, such as American buff burger (Tuesday) or British bangers and mash (Saturday). The Nepali Dal Bhat features eight items. Simple accommodation in just three rooms is also available.

Maya Pub & Restaurant INTERNATIONAL $$

(Map p216; Central Lakeside; mains Rs 275-430; 7am-11pm;) Serving up travellers' fare since 1989, the atmospheric Maya is still going strong, with an almost identical sister restaurant nearby. The walls are decorated with colourful images of Hindu deities, and the comfortable wicker furniture makes this a great spot to people-watch with a pizza, pasta, momos or Nepali *thali* and a cold beer.

Everest Steak House STEAK $$$

(Map p216; 061-466828; Phewa Marg, Lakeside; mains Rs 400-1400; 9am-10pm;) Carnivores flock to this old-fashioned steakhouse for 5cm-thick hunks of freshly grilled beef flown in from West Bengal. Take your pick from an impressive selection of 31 versions of steak sauces, including the popular 'Trekkers steak with veges and chips' and the 'Really red wine sauce'. Other meats such as fish, pork and chicken are available.

Lakeside East

Marwadi Restaurant INDIAN $

(Map p216; 9856027322; Lakeside East; mains Rs 160-300; 7.30am-10pm;) Marwadi is a skinny, technicolour, pure-veg restaurant with inexpensive North and South Indian cuisine. Generous spice and chilli levels make the food here a bit more authentic than the multicuisine eateries that dominate Lakeside. We like the chequered tablecloths

and attentive staff, and the tawa and tandoori breads to mop up the curries.

Potala Tibetan Restaurant TIBETAN $

(Map p216; Tibetan Mini Market, Lakeside East; momos Rs 100-270, mains Rs 190-450; 8am-9pm) The family-run Potala Tibetan has some of the best momos in town (veg, buffalo, chicken, cheese) and is located upstairs at the front of the Tibetan Mini Market. You can also slurp your way through *thukpa, tingmo* and *sha bak ley* and other noodley offerings along with *tongba* (Tibetan millet beer).

Natssul KOREAN $$

(Map p216; 98066743394; www.natssul.com; Lakeside East; mains Rs 450-700; noon-10pm;) After a welcoming drink of *bonicha* (tea), Natssul serves up lip-smacking Korean barbecue, kimchi, and plenty of pork and chicken dishes. Try the *samgyeopsal* – sliced pork belly, pan-fried at the table to be dipped in sesame or red soy paste and wrapped in fresh lettuce. Vegetarians can feast on *bibimbap* (rice coated in sesame oil with mixed vegetables and fried egg).

★ Caffe Concerto ITALIAN $$$

(Map p216; 061-463529; Lakeside East; mains Rs 500-680; 7am-10.30pm;) Rustic ambience, an open fireplace and jazz on the stereo add to the bistro atmosphere of this cosy Italian pizzeria. The breakfasts are big and tasty, while the thin-crust pizzas come in 24 varieties (or compile your own) and are the best in town. The pasta dishes and salads are authentic, wine is available by the glass or bottle, and the espresso and gelato are superb. *Bellissimo!*

Lakeside North

Things get decidedly simpler as you go north of Camping (Hallan) Chowk, but there are plenty of cosy and rustic restaurants with a sleepy charm, and an unexpected gem of a Thai restaurant.

Godfather's Pizzeria ITALIAN $$

(Map p216; 061-466501; Lakeside; pizzas Rs 350-790; 8am-11pm;) The aromas from the open kitchen and wood-fired oven entice many passers-by to drop in for cheesy veg and non-veg pizzas. Many locals vote these offerings as the best pizza in town – and there's a lot of competition these days. Pastas and salads also grace the menu. Their success has led to a second branch in Central Lakeside.

★ **Krishna's Kitchen** THAI $$$
(Map p228; ☑9846232501; www.krishnaskitchen.
com; Khapaudi; mains Rs 510-630; ☺10am-11pm;
☎) Krishna's is a superb Thai garden restaurant nestling at the north end of Phewa Tal. Homemade tofu, organic herbs and vegetables, and professional presentation mean this would be a great Thai restaurant anywhere. To match the excellence of the food there are gourmet teas and a quality wine list. Walk, cycle or taxi the 3km from Lakeside. The restaurant can organise a taxi back to your hotel.

✗ Damside

In Damside there are a cluster of *sekuwa* or *jhir* restaurants where succulent morsels of chicken, pork or buffalo are barbecued before your eyes and served up with a fiery sauce. The dish goes down a treat with a cold beer on a warm afternoon. Look for the smoky barbecues and the throng of locals' motorbikes parked out front (afternoons only).

German Bakery BAKERY $
(Map p219; Damside; cakes Rs 40-210; ☺7am-9pm) This is one of the original 'German bakeries', which supplies cafes from Pokhara to Jomsom. Come here for breakfasts, sweet cheesecake, Danish pastries, and apple pie or crumble. Unfortunately, they only supply instant coffee nowadays.

Don't Pass Me By INTERNATIONAL $
(Map p219; Damside; mains Rs 120-300; ☺8am-9pm) The pick of the Damside eateries is this cosy restaurant that sits smack on the edge of the lake. It has decent if not exciting travellers' fare of Italian, Indian and continental dishes, made all the better for the outdoor seating among colourful flowers by the lake. A peaceful and delightful spot.

🍷 **Drinking & Nightlife**

Pokhara nightlife generally winds down around 11pm, but a handful of bars flout the rules and rock till around midnight. Local bands move from bar to bar on a nightly rotation, playing covers of Western rock hits.

Busy Bee Café BAR
(Map p216; www.cafebusybee.com; Central Lakeside; ☺9am-late; ☎) The Busy Bee has live bands rocking every night from 8pm, though Friday and Saturday are usually the best nights when locals and travellers converge en masse. There's a restaurant and bar plus a courtyard with a fire pit, which is a great spot to meet other travellers, and there's also a smoky pool room down in the den.

Olive Café CAFE
(Map p216; Central Lakeside; espressos from Rs 80, mains Rs 350-1390; ☎) This sophisticated yet relaxing cafe is brought to you by the folks from Moondance Restaurant (p221). With Italian or local espresso, Baskin Robbins ice cream and their very own mischievously sweet Machhapuchhare ice-cream cake, it makes a great place to break a shopping spree. At night it becomes a romantic restaurant.

Paradiso Sports Bar & Grill BAR
(Map p216; Central Lakeside; ☺10am-late; ☎) The occasionally boisterous Paradiso is a revamp of the venerable Club Amsterdam on the Lakeside strip. With live music (from 7.45pm), pool tables, cocktails and mocktails, and football on the big screen, it's got it all covered. Head for the fire pit out back if you want a conversation.

Am/Pm Organic Café CAFE
(Map p216; Lakeside East; espressos from Rs 100; ☺6am-10pm; ☎) This cosy cafe, up a side street, is run by a Nepali who trained as a barista in London and boasts organic Himalayan coffee from Palpa (Tansen) plus tasty pastries from its German bakery. Also recommended for breakfasts, smoothies and light lunches.

Old Blues Bar BAR
(Map p216; Lakeside; ☺4-11.30pm) A super-relaxed option, the Blues Bar is popular with stoners, and large banners of Jimi Hendrix and John Lennon add to its appeal. There's often a local covers band (from 7.30pm).

Bullet Basecamp BAR
(Map p216; Jarebar; ☺4-11.30pm; ☎) Away from the Lakeside glitz and adjacent to a motorcycle repair workshop, Bullet Basecamp has an unmistakable storyline. Sprockets, driveshafts and Tata truck grills have been turned into light fittings and bar furniture. If you are travelling on an Enfield, this place is a must-do pit-stop. It's located about a kilometre east of Camping (Hallan) Chowk on Phewa Marg.

☆ **Entertainment**

Several restaurants located along the strip have nightly Nepali cultural song-and-dance shows that are enthusiastic, if not entirely authentic, and usually there is no additional charge.

Movie Garden CINEMA
(Map p216; Lakeside North; Rs 350) This makeshift outdoor 'cinema' is a lot of fun. Built into an old rice terrace but surrounded by budget hotels, it's a good example of Nepali enterprise and resourcefulness. Movies start at 7pm, so get here at 6.30pm to find a seat and settle in with a drink and popcorn (or pizza). It's a bit of an epic journey going to and from the cinema via a rough stone staircase with low overhanging corrugated roofing – be careful.

Hotel Barahi DANCE
(Map p216; Central Lakeside; ⊙ shows 7-9pm) Bookings are required for the buffet dinner and cultural show from 6.30pm (Rs 1240).

**Boomerang Restaurant &
German Bakery** DANCE
(Map p216; Central Lakeside; ⊙ shows at 7pm) A long-standing and popular restaurant with an evening cultural show.

Fewa Paradise Garden Restaurant DANCE
(Map p216; Central Lakeside; ⊙ shows at 7pm) An all-day restaurant with a traveller menu and an evening song-and-dance show at 7pm.

🛍 Shopping

Boutiques in Lakeside sell Hindu and Buddhist paraphernalia, prayer flags, counterfeit trekking gear, wall hangings, khukuri knives and antiques of dubious antiquity. Pokhara is also a good place to pick up saligram fossils.

There are numerous supermarkets in Lakeside where you can stock up on chocolate, biscuits, toiletries and other goods before heading out on your trek.

As well as the shops in Lakeside, Tibetan refugee women set out their wares under the shade of trees offering Tibetan jewellery for sale. For an even greater selection of Tibetan arts and crafts, including handmade carpets, head either to the Tashi Palkhel and Tashi Ling Tibetan communities, respectively north and south of Pokhara, or to the Tibetan Mini Market in Lakeside East.

Helping Hands ARTS & CRAFTS
(Map p216; www.yeshelpinghands.com; Central Lakeside; ⊙ 8am-8pm) Over 80% of the woven products on sale here have been made locally by deaf and blind men and women in an initiative to empower local people with disabilities.

**Women's Skills Development
Organisation** ARTS & CRAFTS
(Map p216; www.womensskillsdevelopment.org; Lakeside East; ⊙ 8am-8pm) The woven and stitched bags, belts and toys display real skill and care, and make a great souvenir. Sales help generate income for disadvantaged women across rural Nepal. There's another branch in Lakeside Central.

Tibetan Mini Market ARTS & CRAFTS
(Map p216; Lakeside East; ⊙ 8am-8pm) The people's cooperative society of Tashi Palkhel run this arcade in Lakeside East where you can shop for Tibetan crafts, organise a tour of the refugee camps, and grab a plate of steaming hot momos.

North Face SPORTS & OUTDOORS
(Map p216; Central Lakeside; ⊙ 10am-8pm) The only outlet selling the real thing at prices similar to home.

Sherpa Adventure SPORTS & OUTDOORS
(Map p216; Lakeside East; ⊙ 10am-8pm) Sherpa Adventure is the place to find outdoor gear

---

ℹ TREKKING PERMITS

If you plan to trek anywhere inside the Annapurna Conservation Area, you'll need a permit from the Annapurna Conservation Area Project in Damside.

The admission fee to the conservation area is Rs 2000/200 (foreigner/SAARC) and permits are issued on the spot (bring two passport-sized photos). There are ACAP checkpoints throughout the reserve and if you get caught without a permit, the fee rises to Rs 4000/400 (foreigner/SAARC).

Independent trekkers without a guide will need to register with the **Trekkers Information Management System** (TIMS; www.timsnepal.com), which can be purchased from the Nepal Tourism Board tourist office or the office of the **Trekking Agencies Association of Nepal** (TAAN; Map p216; ☑ in Kathmandu 01-463033; Central Lakeside; ⊙ 10am-5pm Sun-Fri, to 4pm Sat). Another two passport-sized photos are necessary for TIMS, which costs the equivalent of Rs 1000 in Nepali currency, if booking through a local registered travel agent, or Rs 2000 for independent trekkers.

that is of a better quality than most of the counterfeit stuff that dominates the bazaar. They also sell genuine gear from Osprey, Keen, Ice Breaker and Exped.

Nepal Mandala Bookshop BOOKS
(Map p216; Central Lakeside; ☉8am-8pm) There is no dearth of bookshops in Lakeside but Nepal Mandala probably has the best selection of books and maps in town.

ℹ Information

DANGERS & ANNOYANCES
Pokhara is generally a very safe place for travellers, but the usual precautions apply.
➜ There have been infrequent reports of solo walkers being mugged trekking up to the World Peace Pagoda and around Sarangkot.
➜ There have also been reports of attacks on solo women near trance parties.
➜ Safety in numbers appears to be the key message.

EMERGENCY
Tourist police (Map p219; ☑ 061-462761; Damside) are located in Damside at the same site as the tourist office. They also operate a small booth opposite Moondance Restaurant.

MEDICAL SERVICES
There are several pharmacies in Lakeside selling everyday medicines, antibiotics and first-aid supplies. For anything serious, head to CIWEC Clinic.
CIWEC Clinic (Map p216; ☑ 061-463082; www. ciwec-clinic.com; Mansarovar Path, Central Lakeside; ☉24hr) Provides emergency treatment and travel medicine advice, and should be your first choice for medical treatment in Pokhara. Payments can be made by credit card and the clinic is used to liaising with insurance companies.
Western Regional Hospital (Gandaki Hospital; Map p210; ☑ 061-520066; Ram Ghat) Pokhara's large Western Regional Hospital is on the east bank of the Seti River.

MONEY
There are plenty of foreign-exchange offices in Lakeside that change cash in major currencies. All are open daily. There are several ATMs along the main strip in Lakeside, including a 24-hour **ATM 'lounge** (Map p216; Centre Point Complex, Lakeside)', that accept foreign cards.

POST
The main **post office** (Map p210; New Bazaar; ☉10am-5pm Sun-Thu, to 3pm Fri) is a hike from Lakeside at Mahendra Pul. There's a much smaller branch in Lakeside East, though alternatively, most bookstores in Lakeside sell stamps and have a post box for letters and postcards.

POKHARA WITH CHILDREN
Pokhara is a child-friendly destination, notable for its lack of chaotic traffic and choking pollution that beleaguer Kathmandu.

The footpaths are usually level enough for strollers and restaurants are accommodating to families, many having highchairs and smaller portions plus familiar international dishes.

If you want to send anything valuable, **UPS** (Map p216; ☑ 061-463209; Central Lakeside; ☉9am-8pm) in Lakeside is reliable.

TOURIST INFORMATION
The Nepal Tourism Board runs a helpful **tourist office** (Map p219; ☑ 061-465292; Damside; ☉10am-1pm & 2-5pm Sun-Fri) in Damside, sharing a building with the **Annapurna Conservation Area Project** (ACAP; Map p219; ☑ 061-463376; Damside; ☉10am-5pm Sun-Fri, to 4pm Sat, to 4pm winter). Here you can get your TIMS card (www.timsnepal.com) if you are an independent trekker.

TRAVEL AGENCIES
Most of the travel agents in Lakeside can book tours, flights and bus tickets. The businesses listed below are all reputable travel agents.
Adam Tours & Travels (Map p216; ☑ 061-461806; www.adamnepal.com; Central Lakeside; ☉9am-9pm) IATA-accredited agency for international flights.
Blue Sky Travel & Tours (Map p216; ☑ 061-462199; www.blue-sky-tours.com; Central Lakeside; ☉9am-8pm) In addition to ticketing, Blue Sky run their own Kathmandu–Pokhara coach service.
Wayfarers (Map p216; ☑ 061-463774; shankhara@hotmail.com; Lakeside East; ☉9am-8pm) For all ticketing and trekking.

VISA EXTENSIONS
The **immigration office** (Map p210; ☑ 061-465167; www.nepalimmigration.gov.np; Sahid Chowk, Damside; ☉10am-3pm Sun-Thu, to 1pm Fri) is in Damside. Visa extensions need to be applied for online at www.nepalimmigration.gov. np. Click 'Online Application' and 'Tourist Visa', upload a photo (by clicking on the photo box) and note down your Submission ID number. You have 15 days to take this number to the Immigration Office. Fees are US$30 for 15 days, and US$2 per extra day (up to 15 extra days). There's an additional US$20 for multiple-entry visas. Bring your passport and the visa fee in Nepali rupees.

ⓘ Getting There & Away

AIR

Pokhara's **airport** (Map p210) is in Damside. A new international airport is due to open in 2020.

There are numerous flights to/from Kathmandu (US$121, 25 minutes) all day, weather permitting, with **Buddha Air** (Map p219; ☎ 061-465998; www.buddhaair.com; Mustang Chowk, Damside; ☺ 8am-5.30pm), **Yeti Airlines** (Map p219; ☎ 061-464888, airport 061-465888; www.yetiairlines.com; Mustang Chowk, Damside; ☺ 9am-6pm), **Nepal Airlines** (Map p219; ☎ 061-465021, airport 061-465040; www.nepalairlines.com.np; Mustang Chowk, Damside) and **Simrik Airlines** (Map p219; ☎ 061-465887; www.simrikairlines.com; Mustang Chowk, Damside; ☺ 8.30am-5pm) sharing the load. There are great Himalayan views if you sit on the right-hand side of the plane heading into Pokhara (or the left on the way to Kathmandu).

Buddha Air (Map p219; ☎ 061-465998; www.buddhaair.com; Mustang Chowk, Damside; ☺ 8am-5.30pm) also has daily flights to/from Bharatpur (for Chitwan, US$92, 20 mins) and Siddharthanagar (Bhairawa; for Lumbini, US$97, 40 mins).

At the time of writing only **Tara Air** (p235; a division of Yeti Airlines) had daily flights (five) to Jomsom (US$124, 20 minutes). Simrik Airlines and Nepal Airlines have flown the route in the past and may do so again. Nepal Airlines has flown to Manang (25 minutes) in the past, but again there were no scheduled flights at the time of writing.

All the airlines have offices near the airport and Mustang Chowk, but it's often easier to use the services of one of the travel agents in Lakeside.

BUS

There are three bus stations in Pokhara. Tourist buses to Kathmandu and Royal Chitwan National Park leave from the **tourist bus park** (Map p219; Damside) near Mustang Chowk. The dusty and chaotic **main Pokhara bus park** (Map p210) at the northeast end of the Pokhara airstrip has buses to Kathmandu and towns in the Terai. You will find the main ticket office at the back and the night buses office at the top of the steps near the main highway. Buses going to the trailheads for the Annapurna Conservation Area leave from the **Baglung bus park** (Map p210; Baglung), about 2km north of the centre on the main highway.

To/From Kathmandu

The bus trip between Kathmandu and Pokhara takes six to eight hours, depending on the condition of the road. Tourist buses (Rs 700 to Rs 1000) are the most hassle-free option and leave from the tourist bus park at 7.30am. Taxis meet the tourist buses on arrival but brace yourself for Pokhara's notorious hotel touts.

Greenline (Map p216; ☎ 061-464472; www.greenline.com.np; Lakeside East) has a daily air-con bus to Thamel (US$25 with lunch, six to seven hours) departing at 7.30am from its Lakeside East office. **Golden Travels** (Map p219; ☎ 061-460120; Damside; ☺ 6.30am-5pm) has a similar service to Durbar Marg (US$15 with lunch) in central Kathmandu, leaving from the tourist bus park. Other reputable tourist buses include: **Mountain Overland** (Map p219; ☎ 061-466703; Damside; ☺ 7am-6pm), which costs US$17 with lunch, and Blue Sky Travel (p225), which costs Rs 700, and stops for breakfast and lunch.

Public buses to Kathmandu (day/night Rs 600/650) leave from the main public bus station. Faster microbuses run to Kathmandu (Kalanki) for Rs 650, leaving from the highway in front of the public bus stand.

Stops along the road to Kathmandu include Dumre (for Bandipur, Rs 150, two hours), Abu Khaireni (Rs 250, three hours) and Mugling/Manakamana (Rs 350, four hours). There are also four daily direct buses going to Gorkha (Rs 400, five hours) leaving from the main bus park.

To/From Chitwan National Park

The best way to get to Chitwan is by tourist bus (seven hours). Buses leave the tourist bus park daily at 7am for Sauraha (air-con from Rs 600), arriving at Bachhauli, a 15-minute walk from town, or there are taxis waiting to transfer travellers to their hotel.

Greenline has a daily air-con bus to Sauraha (US$25 including lunch, 5½ hours) departing at 7.30am from its Lakeside East office (the return journey drops off at the tourist bus park). Mountain Overland charge Rs 750 and leave from the tourist bus park at 7am.

POKHARA TO BENI BUS STOPS

STOP	FARE (RS)	DURATION (HR)	ROUTE
Hyangja	65	1	Ghachok trek
Phedi	90	1½	Annapurna Sanctuary Trek
Naya Pul	240	2	Ghorepani (Poon Hill) to Ghandruk trek, Annapurna Sanctuary Trek, Annapurna Circuit Trek; bus route to Jomsom
Baglung	350	3	bus route to Jomsom
Beni	400	4	bus route to Jomsom

To/From the Indian Border

The closest border crossing to Pokhara is Belahiya/Sunauli, which is just south of the town of Siddharthanagar (Bhairawa).

You must change buses at the border for most tickets to India. However, there is an air-con bus that departs the tourist bus park every Monday, Thursday and Saturday at noon bound for New Delhi (Rs 3700, 31 hours).

There are two (sometimes three) buses to Siddharthanagar (Bhaiwara; Rs 800, seven to nine hours), via Narayangarh (departing 7.15am) or the Siddhartha Hwy (the speedier option, departing at 8.30am), from the tourist bus park. From the main Pokhara bus park there are nearly 20 day and night buses daily for Siddharthanagar (Bhaiwara; day/night Rs 450/500, eight hours), where you can pick up a local bus to the border post at Sunauli.

There are buses heading to Birganj (Rs 650, nine hours), Nepalganj (Rs 1300, 12 hours), Bhimdatta (Mahendranagar; Rs 1500, 16 hours) and Kakarbhitta (Rs 1650, 17 hours).

To/From the Terai

As well as the buses to the Indian border, there are regular day/night services to Narayangarh (Rs 450, five hours), where you can change to buses heading east and west along the Mahendra Hwy. All buses leave from the main Pokhara bus park. Most buses go via Mugling, but there are also buses along the dramatic Siddhartha Hwy to Butwal (Rs 650, six hours) via Tansen (Rs 550, five hours).

To/From Trekking Routes

Buses to the trailheads for most treks in the Annapurna Conservation Area leave from the Baglung bus park. Buses leave Baglung about every half-hour from 5.30am to 3.30pm.

One important exception is the start of the Annapurna Circuit Trek; in this case you head east for Besi Sahar. For Besi Sahar (Rs 450, five hours), there is a tourist bus leaving at 6.30am from the tourist bus park, or you can take any bus bound for Kathmandu and change at Dumre.

A daily direct bus to Jomsom (Rs 1300, eight to nine hours) departs from Hallan Chowk at 7am. In the other direction the departure time is the same and the bus leaves from near the airport. Book through one of the Lakeside travel agencies.

TAXI

Getting a group together and taking a taxi to the trail heads is worth considering. Costs from Lakeside are roughly: Hyangja (Rs 800), Phedi (Rs 1400), Naya Pul/Birethanti (Rs 2500), Baglung (Rs 3500), Beni (Rs 4200).

🛈 Getting Around

TO/FROM THE AIRPORT

Taxis charge Rs 300 to take you to hotels in Lakeside from Pokhara Airport.

BICYCLE

There are lots of bicycle rental places at Lakeside charging Rs 150/500 per hour/day. Pay more (up to Rs 1500 per day) for better quality bikes.

BUS

Local buses shuttle between Lakeside, the airport, the public bus stand and Mahendra Pul but routes (like the driving) are erratic and there isn't much space for baggage. Fares start at Rs 15.

Local buses to Pame Bazaar (Rs 20) and other places on the north shore of Phewa Tal leave Hallan Chowk every hour or so until midafternoon. **Buses** (Map p219) to Begnas Tal (Rs 40) leave from the main bus stand and Mustang Chowk (Rs 50) in Damside.

MOTORCYCLE

Several places in Lakeside rent out bikes (scooters/motorcycles/Royal Enfields Rs 1200/1400/3000 per day, not including fuel). A helmet will be provided, and if you don't wear it, the police are likely to fine you and impound the bike. Check the bikes out first to make sure they start easily, brake smoothly and the lights work.

Hearts & Tears (Map p216; ☏ 061-464846; www.heartsandtears.com; Central Lakeside) is a great place to learn to ride (it rents bikes from Rs 5000 per day) or to join a motorcycle tour around Nepal. **Raju Bullet Surgery** (Map p216; ☏ 9804164839; Phewa Mard) is, as the name implies, a motorcycle workshop specialising in Royal Enfield Bullets.

TAXI

Taxis meet tourist buses at the tourist bus park (Mustang Chowk), but you can expect a hotel tout to come along for the ride. The fare to Lakeside is Rs 200 whether you take the tout's advice or not, so insist on being taken where you want to go. Heading out from Lakeside, you'll pay Rs 300 to the main Pokhara bus park and the airport, and Rs 400 to the Baglung bus park. Taxis from the airport charge at least Rs 300 to Lakeside.

POKHARA SARANGKOT

AROUND POKHARA

Trekking in the Annapurna Conservation Area Project is easily the biggest attraction around Pokhara, but you don't have to be a seasoned trekker to appreciate the glory of the peaks. There are several dramatic viewpoints on the rim of the Pokhara Valley that can be reached by foot, taxi, mountain bike or rented motorcycle from Pokhara.

Sarangkot

The view of the Annapurna Himalaya from Sarangkot (foreigner/Nepali Rs 50/20) is

Around Pokhara

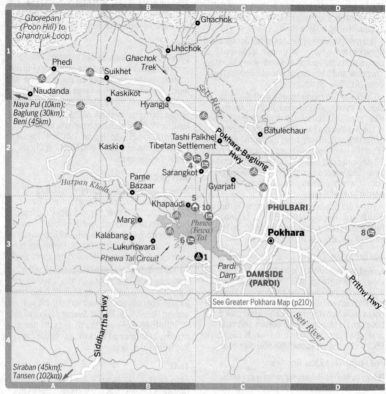

See Greater Pokhara Map (p210)

almost a religious experience. From here, you can see a panoramic sweep of Himalayan peaks, from Dhaulagiri (8167m) in the west to the perfect pyramid of Machhapuchhare (6997m), the tent-like peak of Annapurna II (7937m) to Lamjung (6983m) in the east. Most people come here at dawn or dusk, when the sun picks out the peaks, transforming them from a purple-pink to a celestial gold. If you feel noisy teenagers are ruining the peace at the viewing tower, try walking further along to the secluded grassy helicopter pad.

The main village is just below the ridge, but a set of steps leads uphill to a dramatic viewpoint, the site of an ancient kot (fort). There's a ruined fort at Kaskikot (1788m), a one-hour walk west of Sarangkot along the ridge road, with similarly jaw-dropping views.

🛏 Sleeping & Eating

There are several places to stay and eat in Sarangkot. The cheapest options are along

the concrete steps to the viewpoint, the better places are beyond the viewpoint. The massive construction site is a new Japanese-funded hotel that will boast a cable car!

View Top Lodge HOTEL $
(Map p228; ☎ 9846292257; bikithapa@gmail.com; r with/without bathroom Rs 1500/800; 🛜) Just below the viewing tower, this inviting hotel has a bright lobby and cosy, basic, carpeted rooms. The best feature is the wonderful sunny verandah, with mountain and lake views; it's a wonderful spot for breakfast.

Sherpa Resort HOTEL $
(Map p228; ☎ 061-691171, in Kathmandu 01-4259769; www.sherparesort.com; r with/without view Rs 1700/1300; 🛜) A few hundred metres west of the viewing tower is this venerable, light-filled hotel with wide corridors and simple, old-fashioned rooms. The rooms vary in size, as do bathrooms, and some beds are on the hard side, though it's a small sacrifice

0 — 5 km
0 — 2.5 miles

Kalikathan
Chitepani
Thulokot
Naudanda
Lipini
Shaklung
Begnas
Chisopani
Dipang Tal
Begnas Tal
Sisuwa
Begnas Bazaar
Pachabhaiya
Rupa Tal
Madi Khola
Skyline Trek
Annapurna
3
2
7

There is a large sparkling pool and all of Sarangkot's adventure activities can be organised here. Rates include taxes.

ⓘ Getting There & Away

Taxi drivers in Lakeside offer dawn rides up to the ridge to catch the sunrise for around Rs 2000. The taxi fare is the same whether the driver waits to drive you back or you walk down. Be prepared for a guide to jump in your taxi and do his best to convince you of the need for his services, though a guide is unnecessary as it is easy to get to the top via the path.

By motorcycle or mountain bike, follow the road that branches off the Pokhara–Baglung Hwy near the Bindhya Basini Temple. When the road levels out below the ridge, look for the Sarangkot turn-off on the right, opposite a large group of tin-roofed school buildings.

A more challenging option is the three- to four-hour (steep) walk from Pokhara. The most popular path begins on the highway opposite the Baglung bus park. The obvious trail runs west across the fields and up the side of Gyarjati Hill, meeting the dirt road at Silangabot, about 1km east of the Sarangkot turn-off.

There's also a scenic route from Phewa Tal but the trail is hard to follow and there have been muggings along this path (don't attempt it alone). The trail begins near the village of Khapaudi on the road to Pame Bazaar (look for the signpost about 50m after the Green Peace Lodge), meeting the road just west of the turn-off to Sarangkot. It's easier to follow this trail on the way down.

Begnas Tal & Rupa Tal

About 10km southeast of Pokhara, a road leaves the Prithvi Hwy heading north for

to wake up with the Himalaya outside your window. Rooms 201 and 202 are good picks.

Hotel Mountain Garden   HOTEL **$**
(Map p228; 📱9806748684; sh.rajkumar25@hotmail.com; Bhumare Gaira; s/d Rs 1200/1500; 🛜) Just west of the viewing tower, this friendly hotel has a garden with exceptional views. Rooms are clean and bright, some with their own balcony, and you can dine on the roof for more of the great views.

★ Himalayan Front Resort   RESORT **$$**
(Map p210; www.ktmgh.com/himalayanfront; r incl breakfast US$115; ❄@🛜🏊) On the road to Sarangkot, the Himalayan Front is a sister resort to the group's Water Front Resort (p220) on Phewa Tal. The spacious deluxe rooms are very comfortable with soft beds and LED TVs, but it's the Himalayan views through panoramic windows that are the selling point, which are made even better with a drink in your hand at the Earth Watch Lounge.

Begnas Tal and Rupa Tal, two gloriously serene lakes that receive few foreign visitors, despite their proximity to Pokhara.

After leaving the highway, a narrow road runs through flat terrain of rice fields towards the hills that nestle around the lakes. Begnas is the larger of the twin lakes. As well as the scruffy Begnas Bazaar there is a large fish farm and paddle boats are available for a leisurely paddle. The village of Begnas lies across the waters to the north among the terraces.

Pachabhaiya village is spread out along the ridge between the two lakes and the guesthouses look down on either lake depending upon their orientation. There are also views across the lakes to the snowy Himalaya peaks.

🛏 Sleeping & Eating

There are hotels near Begnas Bazaar, but if you are after tranquillity you are much better off heading up along the narrow ridge that separates the lakes. Here, in the village of Pachabhaiya, you will find a top-end lodge and several budget guesthouses. It's more isolated than staying near the bazaar, but the surrounding countryside, friendly guesthouses and stunning views make it all worthwhile.

★ Begnas Coffee House & Hotel   GUESTHOUSE $
(Map p228; ✆9846046028, 0919101056; www.
nepaliorganiccoffee.com; Pachabhaiya; deluxe r

incl breakfast Rs 2000, r with/without bathroom Rs 800/500; ☎) This delightful family home sits in an idyllic setting and features a dozen guestrooms – all spotless and comfortable with solar hot showers. There are wonderful views, wonderful food and wonderful coffee – this is the home of Machhapuchhare Flying Bird coffee. Coffee beans from the surrounding hills are processed and roasted on-site. There are discounts for long-term stays.

The family also have honey bees and make several flavours, depending on the blossoms in season, including coffee honey!

Rupa View Point   GUESTHOUSE $
(Map p228; ✆9856023828; rupaview@hotmail.
com; Pachabhaiya; r/cottage Rs 1000/800; ☎) This family-run place, situated on a ridge overlooking Rupa Tal, features a red-brick building with decent rooms and solar hot water. There's another two older rooms in a separate cottage. All rooms have attached bathrooms. In the evening home-cooked meals are prepared using vegetables from the garden.

Begnas Lake Resort & Villas   HOTEL $$$
(Map p228; ✆061-560030; www.begnaslake
resort.com; Sundari Danda; s/d incl breakfast from US$120/130, ste US$220; ❋☎❉) A delightful, luxury resort on the sloping shores of Begnas Tal. All rooms – set in stone and wood cottages and surrounded by gardens – have

---

TIBETAN REFUGEE SETTLEMENTS

Many of the Tibetan refugees who hawk souvenirs in Lakeside live in the Tibetan refugee settlements within and around Pokhara. The largest settlement close to Pokhara is **Tashi Palkhel**, about 5km northwest of town at Hyangja, on the road to Baglung. With prayer flags flapping in the breeze in the rocky valley, it genuinely feels like you're in Tibet. The colourful **Jangchub Choeling Gompa** in the middle of the village is home to around 200 monks. Try to time your visit in the afternoon to experience the rumbling of monks chanting and horns blowing during the prayer session (held 3.30pm to 5pm).

Masked dances are held here in January/February as part of the annual Losar (Tibetan New Year) celebrations. To reach the gompa you have to run the gauntlet past an arcade of very persistent handicraft vendors. A 'tashi delek' (a greeting in Tibetan) will win many smiles here. Nearby is a chörten (Tibetan-style stupa), piled with carved mani stones bearing Buddhist mantras, and a carpet-weaving centre, where you can see all stages of the process and buy the finished article. There are a few hole-in-the-wall restaurants, such as **Rita's** (no English sign), serving excellent thukpa (Tibetan noodle soup) and momos (dumplings). You can reach Tashi Palkhel by bike (30 minutes), bus (Rs 30), taxi (Rs 500) or foot (one hour) from Lakeside. The folks from Tashi Palkhel have a Tibetan Mini Market (p224) in Lakeside with craft shops and restaurants.

About 3km south of Lakeside, on the road to Butwal and near Devi's Falls, is the smaller settlement of **Tashi Ling**. Near the entrance of the camp is a small open space where handicraft purveyors set up stalls and entice visitors to part with cash. There's also a small carpet factory and showroom. A smaller settlement, **Paljorling** (Map p210; Prithvi Hwy), resides in the city centre near Prithvi Chowk.

lake and mountain views. The balconied restaurant, barbecue area and bar are the focal point at mealtimes, and in between you can relax at the pool and Ayurvedic spa. Pick-up and drop-off services to the airport (US$20) are provided.

ℹ Getting There & Away

Buses to Begnas Tal (Rs 40, one hour) stop on the highway opposite the main public bus stand in Pokhara and **Mustang Chowk** (p227) (Rs 50) in Damside. A few start from Varahi Chowk (Rs 60) in Lakeside.

By bike or motorcycle, take the Prithvi Hwy towards Mugling and turn left at the obvious junction in Tal Chowk. A taxi will cost Rs 1300 to Begnas Bazaar and Rs 1800 to Pachabhaiya one way.

Pachabhaiya village is reached via a 3km hike or drive along a road that winds uphill directly from the bus stand in Begnas Bazaar.

POKHARA TO JOMSOM

With the upgrading of the path to Jomsom (Dzongsam) into a road, growing numbers of travellers are heading north into the mountains to savour the views and clean mountain air. As well as offering a shortcut to explore mountain villages such as Tatopani and Muktinath, which used to take days of trekking to reach, the road opens up opportunities to several trailheads.

For much of the year, landslides are a constant risk because of the steep terrain, destabilising effect of road building and heavy rains. The Kali Gandaki River was briefly blocked by a landslide in May 2015, triggering widespread evacuations downstream.

Pokhara to Beni

The journey from Pokhara to Beni is along mostly blacktop road, but nonetheless the 80km drive to Beni will take three to four hours by taxi and longer by bus. It's a scenic mountain drive that weaves you past the Annapurna trailheads of Phedi, Kande and Naya Pul. The valley of the Kali Gandaki is reached at Kusum, and the next major town is Baglung, where you may have to change vehicles to continue north.

Beni (830m) is a short drive from Baglung along the Kali Gandaki valley. It's a scruffy settlement, from which trails and roads from Dolpo, Mustang and Pokhara converge. It's a key transport hub, but no destination for

sightseeing. If you must spend a night, there are several hotels opposite the bus park or a short stroll away.

Beni has several ATMs that accept foreign cards and banks for foreign exchange, including **Machhapuchchhre Bank**.

🛏 Sleeping & Eating

There are numerous hotels of the inexpensive, local variety in Beni; most are strung out west of and above the bus park. It is better to push on to Pokhara or Tatopani depending on the direction you're headed.

Hotel Yeti   HOTEL **$**
(☑069-520142; www.hotelyeti.com; r Rs 1000; [P] 🛜) One of Beni's best hotels, the Yeti has clean and tolerably comfortable rooms, a welcoming host and good food in its Thakali Restaurant. It's a short stroll from the bus park and close to the Machhapuchchhre Bank.

Hotel Yak   HOTEL **$$**
(☑9857640009; www.hotelyak.com.np; s/d from US$10/30; 🛜) A reliable place to find a decent meal and bed not far from the bus stand in chaotic Beni.

ℹ Getting There & Away

From Pokhara to Beni, there are regular buses (Rs 400, four hours) leaving the Baglung bus park in Pokhara and just as many returning. However, if you intend to head to Jomsom you are better off catching the direct bus from Pokhara (Hallan Chowk) to/from Jomsom. There are buses and share jeeps departing Beni towards Jomsom via Ghasa (Rs 800), where you may have to change vehicles.

Beni to Tatopani

From Beni the road deteriorates, and depending on recent rainfall it can be quite a challenging and exciting drive – when it's raining, it can be downright scary. Often the 'road' is just a bulldozer scrape into the side of a mountain, and you get the feeling that mother nature would like to heal the scar at every opportunity. During the monsoon season, landslides, rivers and waterfalls periodically cut the road, delaying rather than preventing your journey. Onward travel requires relay teams of vehicles on either side of the blockage. Nonplussed passengers simply hoist their luggage onto their shoulders and walk through the stream or across a hastily constructed footbridge to the waiting vehicles on the other side. It's not unheard of to do this several times during the rainy season.

The 25km drive from Beni to Tatopani could take two to three hours depending on the conditions. The views of the river and the steep gorge are spectacular as the forested valley walls close in and the terraced hills disappear.

Tatopani

Tatopani (1190m) means 'hot water' in Nepali and the village gets its name from the hot springs that emanate from the rocks beside the Kali Gandaki River. Tatopani has long been a favourite stop with weary trekkers, and while the road has lured away some of these visitors, it now also brings folks up from Pokhara on short overnight trips. After crossing the river at Tatopani, the **Annapurna Circuit trail** heads up to **Ghorepani** (2750m) on the greatest ascent of the entire trail. In the other direction, the road and the trail – often the latter is on the opposite bank of the river to the former – continue north towards Jomsom. Tatopani is a great place to break the journey no matter which direction you are headed. There is a TIMS checkpoint at the southern end of town beside the road.

At Tatopani's **hot springs** (Rs 150), there are two stone-lined pools that are used on alternate days, so that each can be cleaned

---

① TIMS CARD

To journey beyond Tatopani you must be able to present an Annapurna Conservation Area Project (ACAP) permit and a Trekkers' Information Management System (TIMS) card at the respective ACAP and TIMS checkpoints. If you don't have an ACAP permit when you reach the checkpoint at Ghasa you will have to pay double (Rs 4000) for the ACAP permit.

At the time of writing you could purchase a TIMS card at the TIMS checkpoints at Tatopani and Jomsom for the same cost as getting one in Pokhara or Kathmandu. As with all regulations, these rules are subject to change and it is worth making enquiries at the ACAP office (p225) and the tourist office (p225), both in Damside in Pokhara. Pokhara (p224) is a good place to purchase the ACAP permit and TIMS card before you leave for Jomsom.

---

regularly. There is a snack bar (happy hour in the afternoon brings beer and popcorn for Rs 500) on-site. Don't forget your bathing costume, and be prepared to take some time acclimatising to the astonishingly hot water – 37°C may not sound hot, but you'll get a good idea of what it feels like to be a lobster cooking in a pot!

🛏 Sleeping & Eating

⭐**Dhaulagiri Lodge**   HOTEL $
(☑9741194872; r Rs 1000, r without bathroom Rs 200-500; ☎) The delightful Dhaulagiri Lodge sits just above Tatopani's hot springs, which are a short walk from its back gate. The comfortable rooms are arranged around a sunny garden of orange and banana trees. The restaurant here gets good reviews for its travellers' fare, including Mexican, Italian, Continental, Indian and Nepali dishes. Wi-fi access costs Rs 100.

Hotel Himalaya   HOTEL $
(☑9936950006; r with/without bathroom Rs 1000/300) Hotel Himalaya is in the old bazaar above the new road and the hot springs, which are only a short walk away. Along with its clean and comfortable rooms, it has a bakery, a restaurant, laundry services and moneychanging – a one-stop shop.

Hotel Annapurna   HOTEL $
(☑9847611928; Tatopani; r with/without bathroom Rs 600/300; ☎) This hotel has been built beside the road on the north edge of the village. It is a concrete tower and lacks the charm of the hotels in the old bazaar, but it is a comfortable, if predictable option. There is a decent restaurant, and of course it is convenient to the road for parking.

① Getting There & Away

Buses and share 4WDs run north from Beni to Tatopani (Rs 500). If you are moving on to Jomsom, you may need to change buses in Ghasa (a district border); the fare from Tatopani to Jomsom is Rs 800 to Rs 900. These are fares for foreigners, as opposed to the much lower local fares, which you may be able to get.

If your destination is Tatopani and you are not travelling further north or trekking towards Ghorepani, you do not need an ACAP permit.

Tatopani to Marpha

From Tatopani the road enters the 'deepest valley in the world'. The rationale for this claim is that between the top of Annapurna I and the top of Dhaulagiri I (both above 8000m and only 38km apart), the terrain drops to below 2200m. The road sticks to the west bank of the Kali Gandaki, passing the villages of Guithe and Dana before reaching the spectacular and notorious **Rupse Chhahara** (Beautiful Waterfall).

Man's attempts at traversing this natural wonder often get swept away each monsoon season. So if you are here any time before October, don't be surprised if you have to alight from your bus, cross the footbridge below the thunderous falls, and find a bus on the other side. There is a colourful little teahouse below the road right by the Rupse Khola (stream). The new bridge completed in 2017 should finally put an end to the successive 'seasonal' bridges. The next stretch of road is through the steepest and narrowest part of the Kali Gandaki Valley; much of the road is cut through solid rock and subject to frequent landslides.

Here, in its upper reaches, people call the Kali Gandaki the Thak Khola, thus the name Thakali for those who live in this region. **Ghasa** (2010m) is the first Thakali village on the road north and the southernmost limit of Tibetan Buddhism in the valley. At Ghasa there is an ACAP checkpost where you will need to show your permit. Also, because you are moving from one jurisdiction to another, the bus companies can make you change vehicles here. This was not the case at the time of writing, but it could be reintroduced.

The best of the overnight options can be found at the towns of Tukuche and Marpha, just south of Jomsom. **Tukuche** (2580m) was the main meeting point along the trade route, where traders coming with salt and wool from Tibet and the upper Thak valley bartered with traders carrying grain from the south. The hotels of Tukuche are in beautiful old Thakali homes with carved wooden windows, doorways and balconies. It's worth spending some time here to visit the **Tukuche Distillery** or the village's four Buddhist gompas.

From Tukuche you'll notice a dramatic change in the scenery; gone are the verdant conifer forests, and instead you'll travel through dry, wind-swept desert-like country. A feature of the dramatic topography is the fierce anabatic wind that howls up the valley throughout the late morning and afternoon. From here to Jomsom (and beyond into Mustang), this daily strong wind will be blowing dust and sand into every crack and crevice of your vehicle if not your body.

CHHAIRO

Between Tukuche and Marpha a footbridge leads across the Kali Gandaki to the Tibetan refugee settlement of Chhairo. The 300-year-old **Chhairo Gompa** here is under restoration. See www.chhairogompa.org for how you can be part of this. The Guru Rinpoche Lhakhang in particular has some fine old statues, thangkas (Tibetan religious paintings) and murals.

As the road proceeds north, it passes the apple orchards of a successful agricultural project that started in 1966. As well as the fruit, most shops around here stock bottles of apple, apricot and peach brandy from the distillery.

🛏 Sleeping

There is no dearth of accommodation options in the spread-out village of Ghasa, or further on at Lete, Kalopani, Larjung, Kobang, Tukuche or Marpha – all erstwhile halts on the great trading route of the Kali Gandaki, and subsequently teahouse stops on the Annapurna Circuit.

High Plains Inn
HOTEL **$**

(☑ 9756703091; www.highplainsinn.com; Tukuche; r with/without bathroom Rs 700/300; 🛜) This Nepali-Dutch enterprise at the northern end of the village is a delight. It has super-clean rooms and bathrooms, a fireplace, a Dutch bakery and a fine restaurant with great food featuring international and Nepali dishes.

Tukuche Guest House
GUESTHOUSE **$**

(☑ 9741170035; Tukuche; r with/without bathroom Rs 700/500; 🛜) Within the stone-walled and flagstoned village is this charming whitewashed building that features spotless, comfortable rooms surrounding a central courtyard and a cosy Tibetan-style dining room. There's a fascinating explanation of local history on the wall of the entranceway.

Eagle Nest Guest House
HOTEL **$**

(☑ 9857650101; Ghasa; dm Rs 150, r with/without bathroom Rs 1000/400) At the southern end of the village, Eagle Nest has the best location in Ghasa. The hotel has clean and comfortable rooms, and there is a pleasant garden and a good restaurant and bakery. Ask the owner about birdwatching opportunities in the area.

Lodge Thasang Village HOTEL $$$
(☑ 019-446514; www.lodgethasangvillage.com;
Larjung; s/d US$215/250; 🖤) High on a ridge
above Larjung, with exceptional views of
Dhaulagiri, Nilgiri and the Thak Khola, is
this luxury lodge. This is not your average
teahouse – as you no doubt guessed from the
tariff. As well as the luxurious beds and the
fire-warmed lobby, you can organise short
walks and jeep rides to surrounding villages
and viewpoints.

🟦 Getting There & Away

Buses and share jeeps run north and south with
similar fares. The fare from Tatopani to Jomsom
is Rs 800 to Rs 900. The fare from Ghasa to
Jomsom is Rs 700 to Rs 900. These are fares for
foreigners, as opposed to the much lower local
fares that you may be able to get.

Marpha

The historic town of Marpha (2680m) hud-
dles behind a ridge for protection from the
up-valley wind, and exhibits typical Thak
Khola architecture of flat roofs and nar-
row paved alleys. The low rainfall in this
region makes these flat roofs practical; they
also serve as a drying place for grains and
vegetables. Fortunately, the dusty road by-
passes the old flagstoned main street and
so has not destroyed the town's traditional
atmosphere.

Most travellers move quickly through
Marpha, but it is worth spending some
time in this pleasant town. There are lots
of things to do here, including climbing
the ridge to the west of town to the original
settlement of **Old Marpha**. Marpha's large
Samtenling Gompa (Tashi Lhakang) was
renovated in 1996. This is a Nyingma Bud-
dhist gompa, and the Mani Rimdu festival
is celebrated here in autumn. Like all the
buildings in Marpha, the gompa is painted
in whitewash produced from a local stone.
If you have time, take in the views of the
town from the ochre-painted, natural stone
chörten on the mountainside north of town.

🛏 Sleeping & Eating

Neeru Guest House HOTEL $
(☑ 069-400029; r with/without bathroom Rs
500/1000; 🖤🖳) The excellent and atmos-
pheric Neeru Guest House has a good res-
taurant and decent rooms with hot showers
and free wi-fi.

Jomsom

☑ 069 / POP 1755
Straddling the Kali Gandaki, Jomsom
(2760m), or more correctly Dzongsam (New
Fort), is the region's administrative head-
quarters and the main hub for onward
travel to Upper Mustang and Muktinath.
At the southwestern end of town is the air-
port, where you'll also find the bus station
and ticket office, tourist hotels, restaurants,
shops and airline offices.

Also at the southern end of town, a con-
crete stairway leads to the **Mustang Eco Mu-
seum** (Rs 100; ☉ 10am-5pm Tue-Thu, Sat & Sun, to
3pm Fri, to 4pm in winter), which is worth a visit
for its displays on Tibetan herbal medicine
(*amchi*) and its re-created Buddhist chapel.

Taking the bus or flying here brings you
very close to the peaks. With a few days to
spare, you could walk south to Marpha or
go northeast to Kagbeni and Muktinath.
Hotels can arrange porters for around Rs
1500 per day.

🛏 Sleeping & Eating

There many hotels in the southwestern part
of Jomsom alongside the airfield. Alterna-
tively, you could cross the river to old Jom-
som and stay in one of the smaller hotels
there. Keeping warm at night can be a real
issue in the cheaper places during winter, so
consider bringing a sleeping bag.

All the hotels feature decent restaurants
and you can get good coffee and cakes at the
cafes at Xanadu Guesthouse and Om's Home.

Alka Marco Polo Hotel HOTEL $
(☑ 069-440007; r with/without bathroom from Rs
1500/800; @🖤) The Alka Marco Polo has a
range of comfortable rooms. The hotel boasts
a sauna, and an internet cafe in the lobby,
which is faster than the free wi-fi on offer.

Xanadu Guesthouse HOTEL $
(☑ 069-440060; r with/without bathroom from
Rs 800/500; 🖤) This friendly guesthouse
is popular for its clean rooms, excellent
restaurant (yak steaks and hot chocolate
apple pie!) and laundry service. The down-
stairs shop and cafe sells books, espresso
coffee, cake and good nak cheese. It also has
a 4WD for hire.

Hotel Majesty HOTEL $
(☑ 069-440057, 9843509222; r Rs 800-2000;
🖤) The Majesty is a sprawling complex of
32 rooms spread over two buildings. The

cheaper rooms are in the old wing, the better rooms and restaurant in the new wing. It's not majestic or palatial, but is a good choice with clean rooms and friendly staff.

Thak Khola Lodge
HOTEL $

(☑ 069-440003; r Rs 300) The very basic Thak Khola is found over the bridge towards the northeastern end of town. Rooms are drab and share a shower.

This lodge's claim to fame is the graffiti message – behind the TV in the dining room and almost obscured by overzealous splashes of whitewash – allegedly left behind by Jimi Hendrix in 1967: 'If I don't see you in this world I'll see you in the next one; don't be late.'

★ Om's Home
HOTEL $$

(☑ 069-440042; www.omshomejomsom.com; s/d from Rs 2600/3000; ☎) The extensive Om's Home comprises 26 comfortable rooms all with TVs and tiled hot-water bathrooms. There's also a sunny courtyard with an espresso cafe, a decent restaurant, bike hire and a table-tennis table.

ⓘ Information

The **Machhapuchchhre Bank** (⊘ 9am-2.30pm Sun-Thu, to 12.30pm Fri) changes cash and has an ATM (Visa only) that works when there is electricity, but it's not reliable. The Nepal Bank also changes cash.

The **ACAP Tourist Information Centre & Checkpost** (⊘ 6am-6pm, winter 7am-5pm) is across the road from Om's Home hotel and a **TIMS Checkpost**. You will need to have both your ACAP and TIMS cards recorded and stamped. You can buy water from the Safe Drinking Water station beside the ACAP office (Rs 40/L).

ⓘ Getting There & Away

Tara Air (☑ 069-440069; www.taraair.com) operates flights between Pokhara and Jomsom (US$124, 20 minutes), and has offices where you can book and confirm tickets. All flights depart between 7am and 10am, and there are up to five flights a day. In the recent past both **Simrik Airlines** (☑ 069-440167; www.simrikairlines.com) and **Nepal Airlines** (☑ 069-440081; www.nepalairlines.com.np) have flown the route and may do so again. However, they were not flying to Jomsom at the time of writing.

A daily direct bus to Jomsom (Rs 1300, eight hours) departs at 7am. In the other direction, the departure is from Pokhara's Hallan Chowk and also at 7am. Buses and share-4WDs head south to Marpha (Rs 150 to Rs 200), Tukuche (Rs 300 to Rs 350), Larjung (Rs 400 to Rs 500), Kalopani (Rs 600 to Rs 700) and Ghasa (Rs 800 to Rs

900). Buses depart at 7am, 8am, noon and 4pm from outside the ticket office beside the Alka Marco Polo Hotel.

At Ghasa you may need to change buses to continue on to Beni (Rs 800). Beni is about 80km by road west of Pokhara, and where you can board a bus to Pokhara (Rs 400, four hours). Road blockages (where you may need to carry your gear over a landslide to find waiting vehicles) are fairly common, especially after heavy rain.

Around Jomsom

Muktinath

The temple and religious shrines of Muktinath (3800m) are the most important pilgrimage sites for Hindus and Buddhists in the Himalaya. Pilgrims have worn a path to here for centuries. You'll see Tibetan traders and sadhus (wandering Hindu holy men) from as far away as South India. The township serving Muktinath is the adjacent village of **Ranipauwa**: dusty, overdeveloped and always busy with pilgrims coming and going.

The shrines, in a grove of trees, include a Buddhist gompa, a Vishnu temple and the **Jwalamai (Goddess of Fire) Temple**, which shelters a spring and natural gas jets that provide Muktinath's famous eternal flame. It's the combination of earth, water and fire in such proximity that accounts for Muktinath's great religious significance. You can find more information at www.muktinath.org.

In the middle of nearby Ranipauwa is a police checkpost where you'll need to register, and an ACAP visitor centre with safe drinking water.

🛏 Sleeping & Eating

Hotel Bob Marley
HOTEL $

(☑ 9857650097; Ranipauwa; r without bathroom Rs 200-400; ☎) This funky hotel has 25 clean rooms and each floor has a solar-heated bathroom featuring a pebble-floor shower. Bob Marley receives raves for it delicious food, particularly pasta, cooked by an experienced chef who also grows his own herbs. Room rates vary according to occupancy.

Hotel North Pole
HOTEL $

(☑ 9847670336; Ranipauwa; r with/without bath Rs 450/300; ☎) The North Pole is a good choice with comfortable rooms, a friendly hostess and very good food in the restaurant.

THINI

The small village of Thini, or Thinigaon (2860m), is visible across the valley from Jomsom and makes for an excellent short hike; if you are still feeling energetic, there is a small lake and a wonderful gompa to explore. From the bridge dividing old and new Jomsom, take the signed trail southwest, a half-hour walk through terraced fields.

Thini is the oldest village in the valley and features an old Gompa (once Bon now Buddhist). From the village an obvious trail leads uphill to **Tilicho Tal**, but this is certainly not for day-trippers. Instead, if you want to continue exploring, turn south and drop down to cross the Lungpuhyun Khola, climb the other side and pass by the hilltop ruins of **Gharab Dzong**, a fortress built by king Thing Migchen. Beyond is the pretty, prayer-flag-festooned **Dhumba Tal** (2830m).

From the ridge above the lake you can head towards the Katsapterenga Gompa (2920m) for its spectacular 360-degree views of Nilgiri peak, Tilicho Pass, Syang village and Thini and Jomsom below you.

❶ Getting There & Away

Muktinath is a feasible overnight excursion from Jomsom. Vehicles heading up to Muktinath leave from Old Jomsom, near the large monastery at the north of town. When the road is open, 4WDs depart from 7am to 6pm when full (12 passengers). The journey takes one to 1½ hours and costs Rs 400.

Kagbeni

One more excursion from Jomsom, which could easily be appended to a visit to Muktinath, is the fascinating and beautiful village of Kagbeni (2840m). Kagbeni (or Kag) is found upstream on the Kali Gandaki, on the road/trail to Lo Manthang. You could walk along the river or catch a share 4WD the roughly 10km from Jomsom. You can't venture north of Kagbeni without an Upper Mustang permit, but you can explore the village and even trek back to Jomsom via the high west-bank route that takes you through the village of Phalyak (seven to eight hours).

Kagbeni retains its medieval feel with its narrow, covered flagstone alleys, antique chörtens, and large, ochre monastery perched above the town. As you wander through town, look for the clay effigies of the village protectors. 'Evi' (Grandmother) is a small figure attached to a wall, while 'Meme' (Grandfather) is a huge, knife-weilding figure in a permanent state of arousal. Pay a visit to **Kagchode Thubten Sampheling Gompa** (Kagbeni; Rs 200; ⊙6am-6pm), a Sakyapa monastery founded in 1429. The main hall holds some fine festival masks and *kangling* (trumpets), as well as a 500-year-old text written in gold.

For a taste of forbidden Mustang, cross the Kali Gandaki on the bridge below the gompa and hike an hour north out to the village of Tiri on the west bank of the valley. No restricted-area permits are required on this side of the river as far as Tiri. Above Tiri is the **Sumdu Choeden Gompa**, whose entrance is guarded by fine slate carvings of the Four Guardian Kings.

Kagbeni is about 10km from Jomsom and share jeeps ply the route (Rs 20).

🛏 Sleeping & Eating

New Asia Trekkers Home HOTEL $
(☑9847680504; r with/without bathroom Rs 800/500; ☎) This comfortable option has solar hot showers and great valley views from the upstairs rear rooms. Wi-fi available only in the dining room.

Hotel Shangri-La HOTEL $
(☑9841163727; r with/without bathroom Rs 500/300; ☎) The venerable Shangri-La has warm hosts, solar hot water and a heated dining table. Rooms are cosy and comfortable with plenty of warm blankets. If you can, join the porters and family in the cosy kitchen for a chat and a feed. The 'potatoes fried in sesame seeds with sauce and veg' is recommended.

Red House Lodge HOTEL $$
(☑9851038325; www.redhouselodge.com; r without bathroom US$25, s/d from US$40/45; ☎) With its private 350-year-old Tibetan-style chapel and Buddhist murals in the dining room, the rambling Red House Lodge is probably the most interesting option in town. Rooms vary in size and airiness, but all are well kept and comfortable.

The Terai & Mahabharat Range

Includes ➜

Best Places to Eat

➜ KC's Restaurant (p253)

➜ Nanglo West (p267)

➜ Candy's Place (p271)

➜ Ghaari (p289)

Best Places to Stay

➜ Tiger Tops Tharu Lodge (p252)

➜ Sapana Village Lodge (p251)

➜ Kasara Resort (p252)

Why Go?

When you think of Nepal, it's usually the northern half that comes to mind, the extraordinary, world-famous Himalaya. But what about the southern half of the country? Most of it is the very opposite, a hot, subtropical plain known as the Terai, which stretches north from the border with India. The Mahabharat Range and Chure Hills stand in the middle, as if mediating between snow-capped peaks and a flat horizon.

For the traveller, this area has a bipolar personality. From west to east, the Terai offers a succession of beautiful and relatively well-managed national parks: Sukla Phanta, Bardia, Chitwan and Koshi Tappu. Meanwhile, the major population centres look like victims of aerial bombardment, with broken, trash-strewn streets, haphazard construction and an omnipresent cloud of dust. The people are as cheery as ever, but mountain villages aside, the cities of the Terai are mainly transit points to the national parks, India or somewhere else.

When to Go
Bhairawa

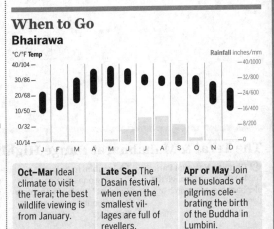

Oct–Mar Ideal climate to visit the Terai; the best wildlife viewing is from January.

Late Sep The Dasain festival, when even the smallest villages are full of revellers.

Apr or May Join the busloads of pilgrims celebrating the birth of the Buddha in Lumbini.

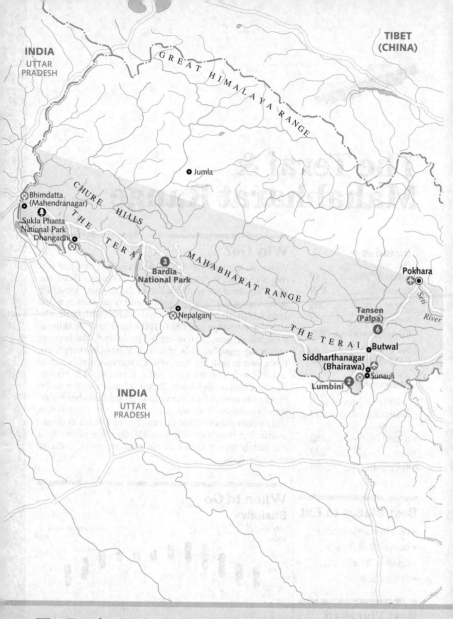

The Terai & Mahabharat Range Highlights

1 Chitwan National Park
(p243) Roaming through the elephant grass in search of tigers and rhinos.

2 Lumbini (p258)
Exploring one amazing Buddhist temple after another in the Buddha's very own birthplace.

3 Bardia National Park
(p272) Rafting through the extraordinary natural beauty of this vast wilderness, looking out for those marsh muggers!

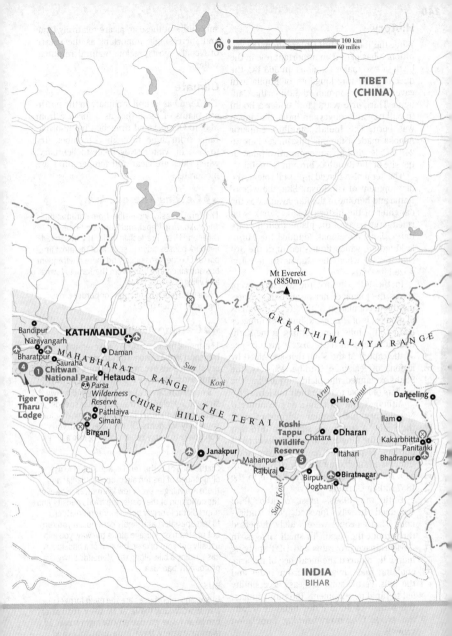

4 **Tiger Tops Tharu Lodge** (p252) Enjoying a sundowner with a pair of elephants.

5 **Koshi Tappu Wildlife Reserve** (p283) Grabbing your binoculars and walking the reserve's extraordinary birdwatching trail.

6 **Tansen** (p265) Day hiking and off-track exploring to the Magar villages and temples surrounding this historic mountain town.

History

While the Terai has little international recognition, it has played an important role in the birth of two major religions. In 563 BC, the queen of the tiny kingdom of Kapilavastu gave birth to a son named Siddhartha Gautama. Thirty-five years later, under a Bodhi (pipal) tree at Bodhgaya in India, Buddhism was born. The Indian Buddhist emperor Ashoka made a famous pilgrimage here in 249 BC, leaving a commemorative pillar at the site of the Buddha's birth in Lumbini.

The Terai also played a pivotal role in the development of Hinduism. Sita, the wife of Rama and heroine of the Ramayana, was the daughter of the historical king Janak, who ruled large parts of the plains from his capital at Janakpur. Janak founded the Mithila kingdom, which flourished until the 3rd century AD when the Guptas from Patna seized its lands.

In the 14th century, the Mughals swept across the plains of northern India, triggering the depopulation of the Terai. Hundreds of thousands of Hindu and Buddhist refugees fled into the hills, many settling in the Kathmandu Valley, which later rose to prominence as the capital of the Shah dynasty. Aided by legions of fearsome Gurkha warriors, the Shahs reclaimed the plains, expanding the borders of Nepal to twice their modern size.

Although the British never conquered Nepal, they had regular skirmishes with the Shahs. A treaty was signed in 1816 that trimmed the kingdom to roughly its current borders. Nepal later regained some additional land (including the city of Nepalganj) as a reward for assisting the British in the 1857 Indian Uprising.

Until the 1950s, most of the Terai remained heavily forested. The indigenous Tharu people were widely dispersed throughout the region in small villages. In 1954 drainage programs and DDT spraying markedly reduced the incidence of malaria, enabling mass migration from India and the hills. Fertile soils and easy accessibility led to rapid development. Too rapid, in fact: the nature of Terai cities today is largely the product of overwhelming population growth.

Today, the Tharu are one of the most disadvantaged groups in Nepal, and huge areas of the forest have been cleared for farmland. Only patches of this once magnificent wilderness remain, conserved in a series of national parks and community forests. For the subcontinent these areas are relatively large and increasingly important as the source of Nepal's most precious natural resource: water.

Climate

The Terai has a similar climate to the northern plains of India: hot as a furnace from May to October and drenched by monsoon rains from June through September. Try to visit in winter (November to February) when skies are clear and temperatures are moderate.

ⓘ Getting There & Away

The Terai is easily accessible from Kathmandu and Pokhara in Nepal, and from West Bengal, Bihar and Uttar Pradesh in India. The Indian rail network passes close to several of the most important border crossings, and there are frequent bus and air connections from the Terai to towns and villages across Nepal.

See the Transport chapter for border crossings information (p387).

ⓘ Getting Around

The annual monsoon rains can severely affect transport in the region – dirt roads turn to mud, dry streambeds become raging torrents, and roads and bridges are routinely washed away.

Since the Terai is flat and the Mahendra Hwy straight, vehicles also travel at faster speeds on the plains than in the mountains, making for some ugly accidents. On the other hand, you don't have to worry about plunging into a gorge.

BICYCLE

On the face of it, the Terai is well suited to cycling: much of the terrain is pool-table flat and there are villages every few kilometres. However, the condition of the roads, the traffic density and unpredictable driver behaviour require riders to be super-alert and highly cautious. If you run out of steam or courage along the way, you can usually put your bike on the roof of a bus. In any case, riding a bike along the Mahendra Hwy is a profoundly bad idea.

BUS

Buses and microbuses are the main form of transport around the Terai. However, road safety can be an issue, particularly for night travel. To maximise safety, travel in daylight hours and avoid the front seats.

Roof riding is prohibited in the Kathmandu Valley, but there is no such restriction in the Terai. Riding on the luggage rack with the wind in your hair can be an exhilarating experience, but in no sense of the word is it safe.

CENTRAL TERAI

The central Terai is the most visited part of the plains. The highway from Mugling to Narayangarh is the principal route south from Kathmandu and Pokhara, while the border crossing at Sunauli is the most popular border crossing between Nepal and India. Its two principal attractions are world-famous Chitwan National Park and Lumbini, the birthplace of the Buddha.

Narayangarh & Bharatpur

🌙 056 / POP 280,000

Narayangarh (also Narayangadh and Narayanghat) sits on the banks of the Narayani River where the Narayangarh–Mugling Hwy, the main route over the hills to Kathmandu and Pokhara, meets the Mahendra Hwy, the main artery between eastern and western Nepal. Hardly a sacred confluence, but a very practical one. Along with its twin city Bharatpur, which adds an airport, Narayangarh is a key transport hub, redirecting visitors on their way to or from Chitwan National Park, India and Kathmandu. Unlike other Terai cities, Bharatpur and Narayangarh also have some singular standout options for accommodation and refreshments, as well as nearby sights, meaning that you can have at least one rewarding overnight here if you plan well.

👁 Sights

★ Shashwat Dham   HINDU TEMPLE
(Map p244; www.cgshashwatdham.org; entrance Rs 100, museum Rs 100; ⊘8am-8pm) Burned out on ancient sites? Here's a contemporary

take on the temple compound, and it's very impressive. The centrepiece is a Shiva temple that resembles an enormous sandcastle, with every square centimetre intricately carved. In the basement is a religious museum with an interesting visual summary of the top Hindu sites in Nepal, signed in English. A gift shop and a veggie restaurant round out this 5-hectare site. Located on the Mahendra Hwy 23km west of Narayangarh, and unmissable.

🛏 Sleeping & Eating

Hotel Image Palace   HOTEL $
(📞056-530731, 9807200474; www.imagepalace. com.np; Narayangarh; r with/without AC Rs 1500/1000; 🅿) This new hotel offers clean rooms in different buildings on either side of the quiet street behind the bus station. Start with the tall mustard and salmon-coloured building, which offers river views. You may be one of the first foreign guests.

★ Hotel Global   HOTEL $$
(📞056-525513; www.hotel-global.com.np; Chaubiskoti Chowk, Bharatpur; s US$20-40, d US$25-50; ❄@🅿🛜🏊) This surprisingly pleasant hotel boasts manicured gardens, a gym, a sauna and a sparkling palm-fringed swimming pool only a short walk from the airport. The standard rooms are a little undersized, while the deluxe rooms, while mildly more expensive, are superb, with tiled floors and porches on the leafy courtyard. Go for room 40 (US$40).

★ New Kitchen Cafe   INTERNATIONAL $
(📞056-520453; mains Rs 200-425, thali Rs 300-4000; ⊘8am-9.30pm; ❄) Just south of the bridge over the Narayani, this bustling restaurant serves the best food in town in

Central Terai

DEVGHAT

Hidden away in the forest 6km northeast of Narayangarh, Devghat marks the confluence of the Kali Gandaki and Trisuli Rivers, forming the Naryani, an important tributary of the Ganges. Hindus regard the point where the rivers meet as especially sacred and many elderly high-caste Nepalis come here to live out their final years and eventually die on the banks. Far from being gloomy, the calm, contemplative atmosphere is wonderfully soothing after the hectic pace of the plains.

The village is reached via a suspension footbridge high over the rushing waters of the Trisuli. The best way to experience Devghat is to wander the streets, which are lined with ashrams and temples that hum and ring with chants and clashing cymbals. On the first day of the Nepali month of Magh (mid-January), thousands of pilgrims flock to Devghat to immerse themselves in the river to celebrate the Hindu festival of Magh Sankranti.

Local buses to Devghat (Rs 20, 20 minutes) leave from the Pokhara bus stand in Narayangarh.

either the air-con dining room or the outdoor porch. The menu is extensive, though the set meals (Indian and Nepali *thalis*) are probably the best choice.

🍷 Drinking & Nightlife

⭐ **Chulho** ROOFTOP BAR
(📞 056-570151; www.chulhorestaurant.com.np; Sangam Chowk, Narayangarh; bamboo biryani Rs 350-600; ⊙ noon-11pm) Without a doubt the place to be in Narayangarh, this crowded bar and restaurant hums with unleashed activity. Perched on the top floor of a building overlooking bustling Sangam Chowk (look for the glass walls), it offers a full bar with a long drinks list and a multicuisine restaurant with creative fare unavailable elsewhere in the Terai.

The house speciality is bamboo biryani, which comes in a long bamboo tube. The pizza is a blessing. There are also live bands from Friday to Sunday playing contemporary music. Walk out on the long balcony and watch the darkness fall on the street below: the bulbs in the streetlights haven't been replaced in years.

ℹ️ Information

Nabil Bank (⊙ 10am-5pm Sun-Thu, to 3pm Fri) has both foreign exchange and an ATM accepting foreign cards.

ℹ️ Getting There & Away

AIR
Bharatpur airport (2km south of Narayangarh) is the closest airport to Chitwan National Park. There are several flights every day to/from Kath-mandu (US$109, 30 minutes) with **Buddha Air** (📞 Bharatpur 056-528790; www.buddhaair.com), **Yeti Airlines** (📞 Bharatpur 056-523136; www.yetiairlines.com) and **Nepal Airlines** (📞 Bharatpur 056-530470; www.nepalairlines.com.np).

BUS
The main bus stand in Narayangarh is called the **Pokhara bus stand**, located at the east end of Narayangarh on the highway to Mugling. Buses run regularly to Pokhara (Rs 350, four to five hours, every 30 minutes), as do microbuses (Rs 600, four to five hours, every 20 minutes). Likewise, buses run regularly to Kathmandu (Rs 350, five hours, every 30 minutes) and so do microbuses (Rs 600, five hours, hourly). A few buses also run to Gorkha (Rs 250, three hours, two to three times per day) and local buses head to Devghat (Rs 20, 20 minutes). Buses to Kathmandu can also be caught at the busy Pulchowk intersection.

The **Bharatpur bus park** is about 1km south of the airport. From here there are buses to Kathmandu (Rs 350, five hours, hourly), Butwal (Rs 300, three hours, every 30 minutes), Suna-uli/Siddharthanagar (Bhairawa; Rs 350, three hours, every 30 minutes), Birganj (Rs 300, three hours, every 30 minutes), Janakpur (Rs 600, six hours, hourly), Biratnagar (Rs 1000, nine hours), Nepalganj (Rs 1200, 10 hours), Kakarbhitta (Rs 1500, 12 hours) and Bhimdatta (Mahendrana-gar; Rs 1500, 12 hours).

To reach Sauraha, you can take a local bus from the side of the Mahendra Hwy south of Pulchowk (just before you reach the next inter-section) to Tandi Bazaar/Sauraha Chowk (Rs 30, 20 minutes). From there you can take a share jeep (Rs 60) to Bachhauli bus park (p254), which serves Sauraha. It's much quicker to take a taxi (Rs 1800 to Rs 2000) all the way to Sauraha from Pulchowk or Bharatpur airport.

Chitwan National Park

♪ 056

Chitwan National Park is one of the premier drawcards in Nepal. This World Heritage–listed reserve protects more than 932 sq km of forests, marshland and grassland containing sizeable animal populations, making it one of the best national parks for viewing wildlife in Asia. You'll have an excellent chance of spotting one-horned rhinos, deer, monkeys and some of the more than 500 species of birds. If you're extremely lucky, you may spot a leopard, wild elephant or sloth bear – though it's the once-in-a-lifetime chance to spot a majestic royal Bengal tiger that is the premier attraction. You'll also have the chance to experience domesticated elephants, although how that interaction takes place is now undergoing a paradigm shift driven by animal rights concerns. There is a daily admission fee that is normally bundled into the overall cost of a tour.

There are no longer any lodges within the park itself, as the Nepali government ejected them all in 2012. Rumours persist that this policy may change at some later date, but no one is holding their breath.

Many people visit Chitwan on package tours arranged through travel agents in Kathmandu, Pokhara or overseas. This is by far the easiest approach if you plan to stay at one of the lodges outside of Sauraha, where transport to and from the lodge is not straightforward. However, if you're planning to stay in Sauraha, packages are unnecessary and expensive. It's easy enough to arrange accommodation and activities independently. Discounts of 20% to 50% are available in the low season, particularly from May to September. Be aware that you'll need at least two days here; the popular four-day, three-night packages out of Kathmandu and Pokhara include a day of travel at either end.

History

Ironically, the history of Chitwan National Park begins with its organisation as a hunting reserve in the 19th century. Britain's King George V and his son, the young future Edward VIII, managed to shoot a staggering 39 tigers and 18 rhinos during just one blood-soaked safari in 1911. Despite such occasional slaughter, the reserve status probably protected more animals than were killed.

Population growth proved to be a more potent threat. Until the late 1950s, the only inhabitants of the Chitwan Valley were small communities of Tharu villagers, who were blessed with a degree of resistance to malaria. After a massive malaria eradication program in 1954, land-hungry peasants from the hills swarmed into the region and huge tracts of forest were cleared to make space for farmland. As natural habitat dwindled, many animals disappeared with it. By the mid-1960s there were fewer than 100 rhinos and 20 tigers left. When news of the dramatic decline reached the ears of King Mahendra, the area was declared a royal reserve. In 1973 it became a national park. Some 22,000 peasants were relocated, but it was only when army patrols were introduced to stop poaching that animal numbers began to rise. In 1984 Chitwan was added to the Unesco World Heritage list, and in 2012 the six lodges within the park boundaries were forced to relocate.

In the meantime the park went through a dark period. While Chitwan means 'Heart of the Jungle', it suffered a cardiac arrest during the decade-long Maoist insurgency (1996 to 2006). Preoccupied with the conflict, the army was unable to provide adequate protection from poachers, who sold animal parts on to middlemen in China. Rhino and tiger numbers fell by 25%. With regular army patrols and several significant arrests, protection was restored and wildlife numbers once again began to rise. By 2017 rhino numbers had substantially recovered, with over 600 individuals counted, and it was estimated that tiger numbers had increased to around 140 individuals, a 15% rise since the 2013 census.

Geography

Chitwan National Park covers an impressive 932 sq km. A further 499 sq km is set aside as the Parsa Wildlife Reserve. Multiuse conservation areas have also been created in the community forests of Baghmara, Chitrasen, Jankauli and Kumrose, which have been replanted with trees to provide villages with a source of firewood and fodder. Because of the topography, most tourist activities are restricted to the floodplain of the Rapti River.

As well as the river, there are numerous tal (small lakes) dotted around the forest. The most interesting of these, particularly for viewing birds, are **Devi Tal** near Tiger Tops Jungle Lodge and **Lami Tal** near Kasara. There's another group of lakes and pools just outside the park boundary, known collectively as **Bis Hajaar Tal** (literally '20,000 lakes').

THE TERAI & MAHABHARAT RANGE CHITWAN NATIONAL PARK

Chitwan National Park

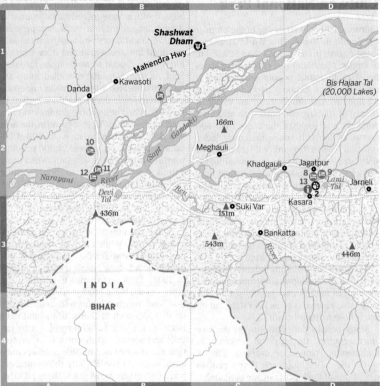

Chitwan National Park

⦿ Top Sights
1 Shashwat Dham C1

⦿ Sights
2 Crocodile Breeding Project D2
3 Tharu Cultural Museum F2
4 Tharu Cultural Museum &
  Research Centre F2

✺ Activities, Courses & Tours
5 Bird Education Society E2

🛏 Sleeping
6 Green Park E2
7 Island Jungle Resort B1
8 Jagatpur Lodge D2
9 Kasara Resort D2
10 Machan Country Villa A2
   Sapana Village Lodge .... (see 5)
11 Temple Tiger Green Jungle Resort B2
12 Tiger Tops Tharu Lodge A2

ℹ Information
13 Park Headquarters (Kasara) D2

Plants

Around 70% of the national park is covered in sal forest; sal is a large-leaved hardwood tree, whose heavy timber is favoured for furniture and boat building. There are also large swathes of *phanta* (grassland), particularly along the banks of the Rapti and Narayani Rivers. Growing up to 8m in height, the local elephant grass provides excellent cover for rhinos and tigers, and food for elephants. When travelling through the forest, you'll see shisham (a valuable timber species), towering kapok (silk cotton tree), strangler figs and the pungent curry leaf tree, among many others.

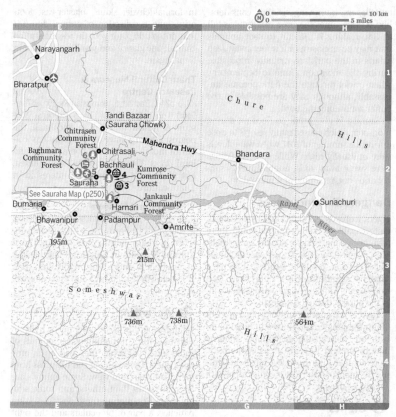

Animals

Chitwan boasts 68 different species of mammals, including rhinos, tigers, deer, monkeys, elephants, leopards, sloth bears, wild boar and hyenas. Birdwatchers can tick off 544 different species of birds, while butterfly-spotters have identified at least 67 species, some as large as your hand.

The one-horned Indian rhinoceros is the most famous animal at Chitwan and you stand a good chance of seeing one on a safari. Chitwan also has significant populations of gharial crocodiles.

As well as these high-profile animals, you may spot barking deer, spotted deer, hog deer, sambar and massive gaurs (Indian wild oxen). The most commonly seen monkey at Chitwan is the stocky rhesus macaque, but you also have a very good chance of spotting the larger and more elegant grey langur. Spotted deer are often seen follow-ing the langurs around, taking advantage of their profligate feeding habits. They also cooperate to alert each other when predators are in the area: the hoots of monkeys or deer serve as a good indicator to keep your eyes peeled for a lurking tiger.

Birds seen in Chitwan include bulbuls, mynahs, egrets, parakeets, jungle fowl, peacocks, kingfishers, orioles and various species of drongos. Keen birders should keep an eye out for rare species, such as ruby-cheeked sunbirds, emerald doves, jungle owlets and crested hornbills.

When to Visit

The most comfortable time to visit Chitwan is from October to March, when skies are relatively clear and the average daily temperature is a balmy 25°C. However, the best time to see animals is late January to March when the towering *phanta* grass is slashed by villagers, improving visibility considerably. At other times the grass can grow as tall as 8m, making it difficult to spot animals that may be as close as a few feet away. Jeep safaris in the park are virtually impossible during the monsoon (June to September), when tracks through the park become impassable, although they are possible in the buffer zone along the border.

Sauraha is also prone to flooding during monsoon, which caused many resorts to close during the summer of 2017, when water levels were unusually high. While some buildings were swept away, most establishments simply dried out, repainted and pressed on.

Dangers & Annoyances

Tigers, leopards, elephants and rhinos are all quite capable of killing humans, and there have been some serious attacks on tourists. Most people have a good experience on jungle walks, but you should be aware that there's a small but significant risk – being chased by a rhino seems a lot less funny when you consider the phrase 'trampled to death'.

Insects are another unwelcome aspect of life in the jungle. Mosquitoes in large numbers are inescapable year-round. Malaria may be present in some areas of the park, so remember to bring insect repellent. During the monsoon the forest comes alive with *jukha* (leeches).

◉ Sights

Safaris take centre stage in Sauraha, but there are a handful of things to see in the village, plus an underwhelming elephant breeding centre 3km west of the village, beyond the Bhude Rapti River; animals are kept in poor conditions so it's not a rewarding or recommended detour.

Crocodile Breeding Project   ZOO
(Map p244; ☎056-521932; Kasara; gharial breeding project admission Rs 100; ⊙6am-6pm) A few hundred metres past the park headquarters in Kasara is a crocodile breeding project, where you can see both gharials and marsh muggers up close. The decade-long program has been a great success in releasing both endangered species back into the wild.

Wildlife Display & Information Centre   MUSEUM
(Map p250; Sauraha; Rs 100; ⊙7am-5pm) Aimed more at school groups than tourists, this educational centre has displays on wildlife, including a rather macabre display of animals

in formaldehyde, skulls, plaster-cast footprints and a collection of animal dung. If that doesn't do it for you, there's the stuffed gharial: one glance and you'll never swim in Nepal again.

Tharu Cultural Museum & Research Centre   MUSEUM
(Map p244; Bachhauli; admission Rs 25; ⊙7am-5pm) The informative Tharu Cultural Museum & Research Centre in Bachhauli, the nearest Tharu village to Sauraha, has colourful murals and exhibits on artefacts and local dress. The collection is fairly limited, but it's a must-see for those interested in Tharu culture.

Tharu Cultural Museum   MUSEUM
(Map p244; Harnari; admission by donation; ⊙hours variable) For those with a serious interest in Tharu culture, there's a tiny Tharu Cultural Museum in Harnari. It has displays of ornaments and a *rakshi* distillery pot. If it's closed, ask around and someone will open it up.

🏃 Activities

Wildlife spotting is the premier activity in Chitwan. You will definitely see animals of some kind, but what they will be is anyone's guess. Dense jungle and tall grass keep many animals from view. Some animals are far more wary than others, and some simply rarer. Conquering these obstacles takes patience, a pair of binoculars and the right attitude. A good approach is to treat wildlife viewing like fishing: some days you'll get plenty of bites, others not a nibble. In any case, it's all about the thrill of the chase in tiger and rhino country.

For some activities there is a minimum group size necessary to achieve the stated per-person costs. You'll also need to add another Rs 1695 for the daily park permit to prices.

Bird Education Society   BIRDWATCHING
(Map p244; ☎056-580113, 9745003399; www.besnepal.org; binocular rental per hour/day Rs 50/100) Run by local volunteers and funded by donations, the friendly Bird Education Society should be the first port of call for twitchers seeking local knowledge, binocular rentals or guided excursions. The society's building (on the road to the elephant breeding centre) has a small library, but the lower floor was wiped out by the 2017 flood. Call ahead to assess the current state of affairs.

Elephant Safaris

Lumbering through the jungle on the back of a five-tonne elephant spotting wildlife has long been the defining Chitwan experience. But times are changing, and fast, due to mounting animal-rights concerns. While elephant rides were traditionally offered by both the government and private contractors, the government now no longer offers them at all. At the time of research, private elephant safaris were restricted to the park buffer zones or community forests, while some major lodges (such as Tiger Tops; p252) and guide services (such as United Jungle Guide Service; p249) have stopped offering these tours altogether.

There is now overwhelming evidence to support claims by animal-welfare experts that elephant rides are harmful for elephants. We recommend avoiding elephant riding in favour of the many other animal-friendly activities available in the park.

Jungle Walks

Exploring the park on foot when accompanied by a guide is a fantastic way to get close to the wildlife. Most walks start with a gentle canoe drift downstream followed by the walk. Be aware that you enter the park with the real risk of encountering bad-tempered mother rhinos, tigers or sloth bears protecting their young. Generally, the bigger the group, the safer the walk, but the experience of your guide counts for a lot. Levels of experience vary and some of the guides have a worryingly devil-may-care attitude to creeping up on rhinos. Therefore, jungle walks are not recommended for the faint-hearted. Rules stipulate that two guides are required even if there is only one customer. Before you opt for a whole-day jungle walk, consider the very real risks associated with venturing deep into the park and being far from rescue and medical facilities, possibly without communication.

Jungle walks can be arranged through any of the lodges or travel agents in Sauraha. Independent guides hang around the National Park Visitors Centre (p254). Don't worry, they'll find you! Although they can be irritating when they are spruiking for business, they are, as a rule, well intentioned, licensed, informed and local Tharu. Another option is to use one of the cooperatives such as United Jungle Guide Service (p249) and **Nepal Dynamic Eco Tours** (Map p250; ☑ 9845107720; half-day jungle walk excl park fees Rs 1300-1500), organised groups of local guides providing numerous options for jungle walks. Ask them about the more adventurous multiday

ELEPHANT WELLBEING

Many visitors to Chitwan are upset by the sight of shackled elephants at the breeding centre, and there is a growing backlash against the use of elephants for safaris. Animal welfare groups warn that elephants are often maltreated as part of their training, while carrying too many passengers can cause spinal damage and leave them crippled in later life.

The commercial model for elephant tourism in Nepal's national parks is also controversial. Despite local breeding centres, elephants are still captured in India and smuggled into Nepal to satisfy tourist demand. Animal welfare organisations have released distressing reports about traditional desensitisation methods in training and the ongoing treatment of domesticated elephants.

The WWF has launched an initiative to introduce less harmful training methods. Elephant Aid International (www.elephantaidinternational.org) is further working with the Nepali government to introduce compassionate elephant care and chain-free corrals in Chitwan. With public awareness rising, many tourists are now refraining from riding elephants and tour the park by jeep, canoe or on foot instead.

As these changes take hold, another emerging concern is human safety. If mahouts cannot use traditional means of disciplining elephants, how are they going to calm them in a dangerous situation? When wild elephants and domesticated elephants interact, it can further undo previous conditioning. In 2017 a near-fatal attack on a mahout in Suklha Phanta was attributed to this.

Elephant welfare is thus a multidimensional issue, but one thing is clear: the way that human beings experience these magnificent animals is evolving in a new direction. It may be that the new model (p255) put forth by Tiger Tops – in which the emphasis is on ethical human-elephant interactions that seek to respect and observe (rather than control) natural behaviours – is the wave of the future.

jungle walks where you exit the park each night to stay in a Tharu village. For jungle walks, the cost per person based on three walkers for a half-day is Rs 1300.

Canoeing

A relaxing way to explore the park is on a canoeing trip on the Rapti or Narayani Rivers. You have an excellent chance of spotting waterbirds and crocodiles. The typical canoe trips (from Rs 1500 per person) start from Sauraha and include a one-hour trip downriver followed by a two-hour guided walk back to Sauraha, with a stop at the elephant breeding centre. Canoe trips can be easily arranged either through your hotel or a booking agency in Sauraha.

Longer excursions are ideal for those not on a package as they get you away from the crowds. One recommended option is a two-hour canoe ride followed by a 16km walk to Kasara (park HQ) and a jeep ride home. This will cost around Rs 4000 per person for a group of three or more (Rs 5000 per person for a couple).

4WD Safari

As an alternative to elephant safaris, 4WD safaris are a popular way to explore the park. Animals are less concerned by the rumble of engines than you might suspect and you'll have the opportunity to go further into the jungle. Safaris can be booked either through your hotel or an agency in Sauraha. Costs are typically Rs 11,000/13,000 for a half-/full day for up to seven passengers per jeep.

Cycling

You can't cycle inside the park, but the surrounding countryside is ideal for bicycle touring, with dozens of small Tharu farming communities to visit.

JUNGLE SAFETY

Chitwan and Bardia national parks are among the few wildlife parks in the world that you can explore on foot (when accompanied by a guide). It's an exhilarating and humbling experience being on a level playing field within the animal hierarchy, where your only protection is the bamboo stick carried by your guide (which can be surprisingly effective in beating off advancing animals). The sound of a twig snapping in the forest or the warning cry of deer and monkeys alerting each other of nearby predators will make your heart race.

Jungle walks are a real risk. While dangerous run-ins are not overly common, you'll hear enough stories of tourists experiencing terrifying encounters with animals to make you devise a plan of retreat if an angry rhino charges at 40km/h in your direction. Nearly all incidents involve protective mothers in the company of their young. The most crucial piece of advice is: never venture into the park without a guide, nor outside the park visiting hours.

Rhinos

Being charged by rhinos is the most common dangerous encounter tourists have in the park. With poor eyesight, rhinos rely on a keen sense of smell that enables them to sniff out threats, which includes humans. If you are charged, the best evasive action is to climb a tree. Alternatively, hiding behind a tree can be effective, though be prepared for several repeated charges from the rhino. If trees are in short supply, run away in a zigzag pattern while dropping something (such as an item of clothing or a camera) as a decoy.

Sloth Bears

Due to their unpredictable temperament, sloth bears are one of the most-feared animals in Chitwan. Their nocturnal hours make sightings rare, though mothers and cubs sometimes move about during the day. The best response is to huddle together as a group and stay perfectly still while your guide bangs on the ground to scare the bear off.

Tigers

Tigers are known to be extremely shy. In the unlikely event that you cross paths with a tiger, the best advice is to maintain eye contact and back away – easier said than done!

Elephants

Due to numerous deaths of villagers each year, locals rightfully fear wild elephants. Anyone in a tent at night is especially vulnerable. If you are in a threatening situation, the most effective means of escape is to simply run for dear life!

☞ Tours

United Jungle Guide Service
SAFARI

(Map p250; ☎056-693691; www.unitedjungle guide.com; half-day jungle walk Rs 2500) This is a clearinghouse for all forms of guided tours. Jungle walks for a half-/full day are Rs 2500/4000. Jeep safaris for four/eight hours are Rs 1800/4000. Overnights in the jungle are Rs 3000 to Rs 5000. Other tours include birdwatching, Tharu villages and more. They no longer offer elephant safaris. Note that quoted prices depend on the size of the party.

🛏 Sleeping

Chitwan has some great accommodation, including everything from Tharu village homestays and riverfront resorts to luxury jungle lodges. Budget travellers favour Sauraha and its lively backpacker scene, but it also has some excellent midrange options. The luxury lodges well west of Sauraha not only have the best quality but provide a better sense of adventure, less crowding and access to remote areas, making them the best option for experiencing the park.

🛏 Sauraha

★ Hotel Shiva's Dream
HOTEL $

(Map p250; ☎056-580488; www.hotelshivas dream.com.np; r Rs 800, with AC Rs 1500-2000; ✳) Sparkling from an impressive 2016 renovation, Shiva's Dream sports renovated rooms and an entirely new building with a winning design that pumps lots of light into the rooms via corner windows. This is a budget hotel that hits all the right notes: fresh paint, large and spotless bathrooms, great mattresses, an elevated open-air restaurant, deep local knowledge and all the tours you need. Run by the same family as Bardia's top-rated Forest Hideaway (p274).

★ Chitwan Gaida Lodge
LODGE $

(Map p250; ☎056-580083, in Kathmandu 01-4444527; www.chitwangaidalodge.com; r Rs 500-800, with AC Rs 1200-2000; ☎) Run by one of Nepal's leading ornithologists, Tika Ram Giri, Gaida Lodge has a range of rooms including some original bungalows plus newer modern rooms in a four-floor building facing the forest; all hold at least three people and are attractively priced. The rooms on the 4th floor have treetop views and catch a cool breeze.

The cool green garden has a bird pond and numerous hammocks to lounge in. This is the place for birdwatchers; some proceeds go to bird conservation programs.

Travellers Jungle Camp
HOTEL $

(Map p250; ☎9855055845, 056-580013; www. nepaljunglecamp.com; r Rs 1000, deluxe Rs 1500-2000; ✳☎) At this family-owned courtyard hotel you'll receive a warm welcome, enjoy a relaxing garden and even meet the resident pachyderm, Chanchal Kali. Rooms are comfortable and tidy. The owner is well attuned to travellers' needs and offers packages for independent travellers on the website.

Sauraha Resort
HOTEL $

(Map p250; ☎056-580114, 9855066114; www. sauraharesort.com; r Rs 1000-2000; ✳☎) This family-run hotel is close to town but tucked back from the street. The well-kept rooms range from simple twins and larger doubles (with an extra single bed and TV) to air-con doubles. All feature mosquito nets and fans. Although low-key, all jungle activities can be arranged. The restaurant has a nice pavilion in the centre of the courtyard.

Hotel Nature Heritage
HOTEL $

(Map p250; ☎9855062899, 056-580432; www. hotelnatureheritage.com.np; r Rs 1800-2200; ✳☎) This rather imposing cement tower has a range of clean and comfortable rooms, all appointed with TVs, air-con and running hot water. The mattresses are on the thin side, however. The room tariff increases as you climb the stairs and gain river views. Nevertheless, the Rs 1800 rooms on the top floor are a good deal.

Jungle Adventure World
HOTEL $

(Map p250; ☎056-580064, 9845065985; www. jungleadventureworld.com; r Rs 1500, with AC Rs 2000) This rustic lodge has a laid-back tropical-island feel. It consists of numerous bungalows with small porches, of a similar design, scattered in a shady garden. The bungalows are a bit tight inside, but hold three people. The garden makes for a great place to escape the heat.

Hotel River Side
HOTEL $

(Map p250; ☎056-580009, in Kathmandu 01-4249416; www.hotelriversidenepal.com; r Rs 1500-4500; ☎) With its broad porches, this hotel has a lovely neo-colonial feel. Take your choice between delightful terracotta-tiled huts or modern wood-panelled rooms with balconies delivering unbeatable river views. The cheapest rooms on the bottom floor are decent but unremarkable. There's a riverside restaurant and helpful staff.

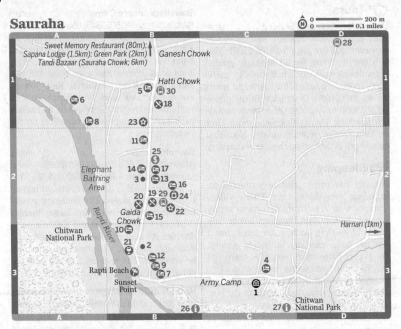

Sauraha

Chitwan Rest House
HOTEL **$**

(Map p250; ☏ 056-580261; ro.chaudhary@yahoo. com; r Rs 600-1000) Located 500m north of Gaida Chowk, this is a friendly, uber-budget option with basic rooms (no piped hot water) in adobe cottages, a small but verdant garden and a cheap restaurant. The grounds are a mess but the new addition has some clean and well-lit rooms with balconies.

★ Sapana Village Lodge
LODGE **$$**

(Map p244; ☏ 056-580308, 9855056498; www. sapanalodge.com; all incl breakfast, s US$35, d US$45-60; ❄ ⑆) Situated 1.5km north of Sauraha, this serene lodge is an excellent option for anyone, but especially those with an interest in Tharu culture. Set up by its dedicated owner with the aim of supporting the local Tharu community, particularly a local school, it promotes various activities that bring Tharu and tourists together, in addition to the usual wildlife activities. This includes village walking tours, planting rice in the fields, fishing trips and classes in cooking and art.

The rooms are decked out in charming village-style designs with vibrant paintings and rugs. The outstanding al-fresco lounge and restaurant overlooking the Budhi Rapti River and rice paddies is one of the best spots to eat or drink in Sauraha. Accommodation plus activity packages are detailed on the website.

★ River View Jungle Camp
HOTEL **$$**

(Map p250; ☏ 056-580096, 9855080096; www. rvjcnepal.com; B&B cottage US$15-35, B&B deluxe r US$30-65; ❄ ⑆) It's hard to beat this hotel's riverside location, with superb views across a broad floodplain. Rooms are divided between tidy khaki brick cottages set along a long garden, with fans, air-con and mosquito nets; and more deluxe rooms overlooking the river, with modern bathrooms, flat-screen TVs, plush mattresses and private balconies. If you're lucky, you'll spot a rhino at dusk.

Royal Park Hotel
HOTEL **$$**

(Map p250; ☏ 056-580061, in Kathmandu 01-4412987; www.royalparkhotel.com.np; r incl breakfast US$46; ❄ ⑆ ❖) Set in extensive park-like gardens, the attractive adobe-and-thatch bungalows boast huge rooms and gorgeous stone- or marble-tiled bathrooms. Upstairs rooms are best, with soaring ceilings and inviting balconies. There's a restaurant and cultural shows when a group is being hosted.

Chitwan Riverside Resort
HOTEL **$$**

(Map p250; ☏ 056-580297, in Kathmandu 01-4256696; www.chitwanriverside.com; r US$25-30;

❄ ⑆) Here it's all about the idyllic riverside location away from bustling Sauraha bazaar. There's a choice between lovely cottages without views or rooms in the newer building with excellent river views. The shaded viewing platform atop the riverbank is a magnificent spot to sit back during sunset with a beer and, if you're lucky, you'll spot some thirsty wildlife.

Jungle Safari Lodge
HOTEL **$$**

(Map p250; ☏ 056-580500; www.junglesafari lodge.com; r incl breakfast Rs 2500, ste Rs 5000; ❄ @ ⑆) A long-standing, central hotel that has experienced staff and a warm welcome. There have been some recent renovations, so rooms vary depending on age. The new deluxe rooms are the best choice: clean and bright, with comfy beds, modern bathrooms and upper-storey views to the courtyard. There is a nice terrace for outside dining. Avoid the musty older rooms.

Hotel Hermitage
HOTEL **$$**

(Map p250; ☏ 056-580090, in Kathmandu 01-4424390; www.nepalhotelhermitage.com; cottage Rs 2500, boathouse Rs 3500; ❄ @ ❖) Although apparently geared towards travellers on a package, this lodge nonetheless boasts very experienced guides and commands one of the better elevated riverside positions, while still being an easy stroll from town. Rooms in the moat-surrounded 'boathouse' are spacious and cool, while the restaurant and 'drinks' area are perfectly positioned on the riverbank.

Chitwan Tiger Camp
HOTEL **$$**

(Map p250; ☏ 056-580060, in Kathmandu 01-4441572; www.chitwantigercamp.com; s/d US$25/40, deluxe US$40/60; ⑆) Located near Sunset Point, the quiet end of Sauraha, this hotel has a nice elevated view of the river from its restaurant; a beach and a cold beer are just across the street. There are standard budget rooms downstairs, while the upstairs rooms with tubs (that need cleaning) and bamboo decor are much better but somewhat overpriced.

★ Green Park
RESORT **$$$**

(Map p244; ☏ 9801207111, 056-580510, in Kathmandu 01-4256612; www.greenparkchitwan.com; Baghmara; r incl breakfast US$140; ❄ ⑆ ❖) If you want a more traditional hotel, this is the best choice in the Sauraha area. The peaceful Green Park consists of several buildings of four rooms, each set in beautiful grounds to the north of town. The spacious rooms

THARU VILLAGES

Chitwan is surrounded by small agricultural villages populated by the Tharu, the dominant ethnic group in the Terai. The villages are noted for their mud-walled houses, sometimes decorated with Mithila paintings (p284) and adobe bas-reliefs of animals. Resist the urge to hand out sweets, pens and money; if you want to help the local people, patronising local businesses is the best way, including hiring local guides.

The nearest Tharu village is Bachhauli, a pleasant cycle or 20-minute walk from Sauraha through the rice or bright-yellow mustard fields. Here you will find the informative Tharu Cultural Museum & Research Centre (p246).

Harnari is one of the best villages to get a taste of Tharu culture. Bordering the Kumrose Community Forest, it's less visited than Bachhauli and feels more authentic. There's a tiny Tharu Cultural Museum (p246) here, a 20-minute bike ride from Sauraha.

Sapana Village Lodge (p251) runs excellent tours of these and other Tharu villages. There are also Tharu cultural shows in Sauraha.

---

have large balconies, nice woodwork, tile floors and to-die-for mattresses.

The large pool has a bar and is also good for kids, if a bit stark. The air-conditioned dining room is the front end of a spotless kitchen. Steep discounts of up to 40% make this a bargain (ask). Located 2km north of Sauraha.

Elsewhere

★ **Tiger Tops Tharu Lodge** LODGE $$$
(Map p244; in Kathmandu 01-4411225; www.tiger tops.com; Amaltari; inclusive packages per person per night safari tent US$150, r US$200; @ 📶 🌊) Chitwan's leading lodge is still on Top. Tiger Tops was the very first lodge in the park, before it even was one, and later helped lobby for the park's creation. When lodges were banned from the park in 2012, it constructed this new lodge, which is hard to beat. Accommodation is atmospheric, service is impeccable and the vintage Land Rovers pitch perfect.

Built with local material in the traditional Tharu style, rooms are arranged in two long houses; end room 1 is particularly nice. As well as wildlife activities with expert guides, there are village tours and cultural shows. Most notably, Tiger Tops is taking the lead again by redefining the nature of the elephant experience (p255) at the heart of Chitwan tourism. This includes six safari tents with attached baths by the new Elephant Camp.

The lodge is located near the Narayani River on the western border of the park (specifically Amaltari, Nawalparashi, 7km off the Mahendra Hwy at Danda, a small town just past Kawasoti) but guests are usually picked up and dropped off at Bharatpur airport. The expansive grounds contain the lodge's own organic farm and well-kept elephants in expansive new corrals. Tiger Tops also supports the local community with a medical clinic and school.

★ **Kasara Resort** LODGE $$$
(Map p244; 056-411001, in Kathmandu 01-443757; www.kasararesort.com; Patihani; packages per person per night US$180; 🌊 📶 🌊) A minimalist palace set in lush grounds, Kasara Resort easily wins the best design award among Chitwan lodges. Where else does the entryway to your villa have its own private bridge? The bathrooms with large open-air showers are another nice touch, while the huge dining pavilion cannot fail to impress. Package prices include food and certain activities, including safaris. When you consider all this the price is great value. Located along the western boundary of the park.

Temple Tiger
Green Jungle Resort LODGE $$$
(Map p244; 9845089992, in Kathmandu 01-4263480; www.greenjungleresort.com; Amaltari Ghat; packages per person per night US$225; 🌊 @ 📶) While its landscaping needs some attention, this eco-friendly lodge offers beautiful elevated villas with thatched roofs and rural vistas. Hardwood floors, big baths and super mattresses are just some of their comforts. Tiger footprints pressed into bathroom floors are a cute touch. Wildlife lectures as well as meals are taken in the central restaurant and bar. Water-based safaris are a plus.

Jagatpur Lodge LODGE $$$
(Map p244; in Kathmandu 01-4223602; www.jagatpurlodge.com; Jagatpur; all incl breakfast r s/d US$220/300, tent s/d US$730/850; 🌊 📶 🌊) Accommodation here is rather oddly split between five blocks of modern and spa-

cious rooms, which feel a bit like a high-end motel, and some very nice luxury safari tents from South Africa, with big decks and internal baths, arrayed along the river. All the usual activities are catered for including excursions to nearby lakes. Be sure to negotiate your rate. The lodge is located along the western border of the park, near the village of Jagatpur, and has enough security for the most paranoid billionaire.

Machan Country Villa   LODGE **$$$**
(Map p244; ☑9855055293, Kathmandu 01-4225001; www.machanwildliferesort.com; Gauchhada; 1-/2-night package per person US$190/380, additional night US$135; ❋@🛜🛝) You've got luxury lodge prices here but management pitches a notch lower. Modern and spacious accommodation is divided between longhouse rooms and cute concrete cottages with porches but is let down by foam mattresses. The atmospheric dining hall features Mithila paintings (p284). Situated on the northern bank of the Narayani River in the village of Gauchhada, towards the park's western end.

Island Jungle Resort   LODGE **$$$**
(Map p244; ☑9847073718, Kathmandu 01-4220162; www.islandjungleresort.com.np; Kawaswati; 3-day/2-night package per person US$250, additional night US$90; ❋🛜) Located on the Narayani River at the western end of the park, this lodge offers simple but comfortable cottages arranged to face the main dining hall. There are great riverside views from the observation tower. You are a long way from anywhere here, which is why people come.

🍴 Eating

Most lodges and hotels in Sauraha have restaurants, of which the best is Sapana Village Lodge (p251); all are open to the public. For those not on all-inclusive packages, there are also several independent restaurants on the main street. Most tourist restaurants offer a multicuisine menu from 6am to around 10pm.

Sweet Memory Restaurant   NEPALI **$**
(Ganesh Chowk, Sauraha; mains Rs 170-500; ☉7am-9pm) An expanding family-run shack restaurant with plenty of flowers and pot plants, Sweet Memory prides itself on its home-style cooking. The momos and the chicken curry are recommended, and it also serves up good filtered coffee, coffee cocktails and sweet lime (*mausambi*) juice.

It's tucked down a side alley with two floors of open-air dining. Lodgings on the way.

★Friends Café   ITALIAN, MEXICAN **$$**
(Map p250; ☑056-580403; Sauraha; mains Rs 300-550; ☉7am-10pm) This rooftop restaurant is easy to miss, but don't! It's the best place to hang out in downtown Sauraha, at any time of day, with a cool vibe and tunes to match. The handmade menus on beer-carton cardboard reflect the personal touch of the creative owners, who have put new spins on mainly Mexican and Italian dishes. Also a great spot for coffee and cocktails.

★KC's Restaurant   MULTICUISINE **$$**
(Map p250; Gaida Chowk, Sauraha; mains Rs 350-550; ☉6.30am-10.30pm) A Sauraha classic, KC's is set in a cool, thatch-roofed bungalow with an open terrace overlooking a manicured garden, with a fire pit for winter dinners. The chefs here look the part and the well-executed menu runs from Nepali and Indian curries to pizzas and pasta. We recommend the top-up-able *thalis* and authentic tandoori dishes, washed down with a lassi. Ever popular, this is a great place to meet people, including the friendly owner, who promises that Sherpa craft beer from Kathmandu will be on the menu soon.

Jungle View Restaurant   INTERNATIONAL **$$**
(Map p250; Gaida Chowk, Sauraha; mains Rs 250-550; ☉6.30am-10pm; 🛜) A pleasant rooftop restaurant overlooking Gaida Chowk, Jungle View has good curries and barbecue, plus all your cheesy traveller favourites including pizzas and enchiladas. Happy hour (5pm to 10pm) brings popcorn with your cocktail.

🍷 Drinking & Nightlife

Sunset View Restaurant & Bar   BAR
(Map p250; Sauraha; ☉7am-11pm) This riverside tiki hut at Sunset Point was one of the first establishments to be rebuilt after monsoonal flooding in the area in 2017. As the name suggests, it's the perfect spot for an early coffee or sunset beer.

☆ Entertainment

In Sauraha most of the larger lodges put on shows of traditional Tharu songs and dances for guests, including the popular stick dance, where a great circle of running men whack sticks together in time. It's very much a tourist experience, but fun. There are nightly performances at the Sauraha Tharu Culture House and the Tharu Culture Program.

Gig House
LIVE MUSIC

(Map p250; Sauraha; ⊘ music 7-10pm) Follow the early-evening sound of live music in downtown Sauraha and you're likely to end up at Gig House. It's definitely not the club scene you are used to, but it beats another night at the hotel. There's also a multicuisine menu (Rs 350 to Rs 450).

Accoustica
LIVE MUSIC

(Map p250; ☑ 9855046238; Sauraha; ⊘ 7am-11pm, live music from 7pm) This funky restaurant is defined by its live music, complemented by veggie, chicken or buffalo burgers. They also set up elephant walks similar to those pioneered by Tiger Tops.

Sauraha Tharu Culture House
LIVE PERFORMANCE

(Map p250; Sauraha; Rs 100; ⊘ show 7.30pm) Nightly shows of traditional Tharu songs and dances for guests, including the popular stick dance.

Tharu Culture Program
LIVE PERFORMANCE

(Map p250; ☑ 9845024469; Rs 100; ⊘ show 7pm Oct-May, 8pm Jun-Sep) Offers nightly performances of the Tharu stick dance.

🏠 Shopping

While it's no Thamel, Sauraha definitely has the best shopping in the Terai. Simply stroll down the main steet from one end to the other, with side trips to its tributaries, and you'll find a wide range of Tibetan and Nepali arts and crafts. Highlights include Tharu jewellery, batik prints, Mithila paintings, el-ephant-dung paper products, woodcarvings and some beautiful brightly coloured textiles.

Happy House
ARTS & CRAFTS

(Map p250; ☑ 056-580026; Gaida Chowk, Sauraha; ⊘ 7am-9pm) With a good selection of souvenirs, this small, family-run business produces its own honey in various delectable flavours and sells batik art and colourful Mithila paintings (p284) on handmade paper produced by women's craft cooperatives near Janakpur.

Women Art & Handicrafts Shop
ARTS & CRAFTS

(Map p250; Sauraha; ⊘ 7am-10am) For batik clothing, jewellery, hand-painted T-shirts and elephant-dung paper, which is a lot nicer than it sounds. No sign: located directly beneath Gig House.

ⓘ Information

Park Headquarters (Map p244; ☑ 056-521932; foreigner/SAARC/child under 10yr per day Rs 1500/1000/free plus 13% tax; ⊘ 6am-6pm) is located in Kasara, about 13km west of Sauraha. There is a separate **Park Office** (Map p250; ☑ 056-521932; foreigner/SAARC/child under 10yr per day Rs 1500/1000/free plus 13% tax; ⊘ ticket office 6-9am & noon-4pm) in Sauraha, which handles the eastern sector of the park. Both sell daily entry tickets, but most visitors will have no need to go to either facility to procure them, as this is typically handled by your tour provider. At the time of research, the **National Park Visitors Centre** (Map p250) was closed for renovations following extensive flood damage during the monsoon of 2017.

There are numerous ATMs in town, though not all accept foreign cards. The following were

---

A NEW ELEPHANT EXPERIENCE

In response to rising concerns about elephant welfare, pioneering Tiger Tops Tharu Lodge (p252) has once again led the way through the development of an entirely new elephant experience for guests, along with new captivity and treatment standards. The lodge has developed an Elephant Camp with large corrals where their dozen elephants are free to roam. The elephants are still 'working elephants', providing an interactive encounter for guests, but instead of riding on the back of an elephant in a lurching howdah (which risks causing injury to these gentle giants), visitors now walk alongside them on jungle walks. Elephants are, after all, the ultimate security detail, and they can clear the way very efficiently when necessary.

The most charming new program is Sundowners with Elephants, a fresh take on elephant bathing in which visitors are served a classy happy hour on the riverbank while the elephants bathe before them at sunset. This is a truly affecting experience, for the elephants are enormously affectionate creatures, wrapping their trunks around each other with great pachyderm hugs. Mahouts are an essential part of these new experiences, so the program still provides a living for local people. Tiger Tops is rolling out a similar program at their Bardia lodge (p275).

accepting foreign cards at the time of research, though they frequently run out of money. The Prabhu Bank has an ATM near Travellers Jungle Camp and one south of Gaida Chowk, where there is also a Himalaya Bank ATM. The Kumari Bank ATM is directly north of Hotel Shiva's Dream, while the Nabil Bank ATM is next door.

There are also several private moneychangers accepting foreign currency and travellers cheques. **Chitwan Money Changer** (Map p250; Sauraha; ⊘7am-8pm) changes cash.

❶ Getting There & Away

AIR

If you're bound for Chitwan, the best option is to fly into Bharatpur and take a taxi (Rs 1800 to Rs 2000 to Sauraha). Both Buddha Air and Yeti Airlines offer daily flights to Bharatpur from Kathmandu (US$109, 30 minutes). Travel agents and hotels can make bookings.

BUS

Chitwan's main bus terminal is the **Bachhauli Bus Park** (Map p250), located northeast of town. By far the easiest way to reach Chitwan is by tourist bus/AC bus from Kathmandu (Rs 500/Rs 650, five to seven hours). Buses leave the Thamel end of Kantipath in Kathmandu at around 7am.

From Pokhara, tourist buses (Rs 400 to Rs 450, five to seven hours) depart from the tourist bus stand at 7.30am. The final stop is Bachhauli tourist bus park, a 15-minute walk from Sauraha. Jeeps, and the dreaded hotel touts, wait to transfer new arrivals to hotels for Rs 50. There's no obligation to commit to staying at any particular resort, regardless of what the touts say.

There is one tourist bus (Rs 600) that heads for the Indian border at Sunauli/Belahiya. When leaving Sauraha, all the tourist buses leave Bachhauli at 9.30am. Any hotel or travel agent can make bookings.

A more comfortable option is the daily AC bus operated by **Greenline** (Map p250; ✍ 056-560267; www.greenline.com.np), which runs to/from Kathmandu or Pokhara for US$20 including brunch. From Kathmandu or Pokhara it leaves at 7.30am; from Greenline's stop in Sauraha, it leaves at 9.15am. Service is intermittent or suspended during monsoon. **Rose Cosmetics** (Map p250; ✍ 9845024203; Hathi Chowk, Sauraha) in Sauraha runs a daily microbus (Rs 500) to Kathmandu (Kalanki) departing at 5am and arriving before noon. The return journey departs Kathmandu at 1pm.

You can also pick up public buses at Tandi Bazaar (also known as Sauraha Chowk) on the Mahendra Hwy, about 6km north of Sauraha. Destinations include Kathmandu, Pokhara and Siddharthanagar (Bhairawa)/Sunauli (Rs 300, five to six hours, every 30 minutes). For the airport in Bharatpur you can get a local bus from Tandi Bazaar to Narayangarh (Rs 40).

CAR

Travel agents and hotels can arrange a private car from Pokhara or Kathmandu to Chitwan for around US$100. The journey takes about five hours either way.

RAFT

A more interesting way to arrive at Chitwan is by river raft. Most of the big Kathmandu rafting operators offer trips down the Trisuli and Narayani Rivers, culminating at the national park, usually as part of a package tour. The rafting experience is more of a leisurely drift – but there are some fine views and the sandy beaches along the riverside offer great camping spots.

Mugling is the main embarkation point on the Prithvi Hwy, about halfway between Kathmandu and Pokhara. It takes a day to raft from there to Chitwan. Most people combine rafting with a safari package in the national park – expect to pay around US$90 per person for the rafting section of the trip. Rafting companies can usually make arrangements.

FOOT

From tiny Hugdi, halfway between Benighat and Mugling, it is possible to trek south to Sauraha in five days, passing through the homeland of the Chepang tribe. En route, you can visit forts and mountain viewpoints, go birdwatching and get involved in a variety of cultural activities. Numerous trekking operators in Kathmandu and Pokhara promote this route.

❶ Getting Around

BICYCLE

Several shops in Sauraha, particularly around Gaida Chowk, rent out bicycles for exploring the surrounding villages; the going rate is Rs 250 to Rs 300 per day.

JEEP & PONY CART

From Sauraha, a reserved jeep (ie a nonshared vehicle) to the Bachauli bus stand costs Rs 300. By shared *tonga* (pony cart) it will cost Rs 100. A taxi to Tandi Bazaar on the Mahendra Hwy is Rs 700, while one to Bharatpur airport costs Rs 1800 to Rs 2000.

Siddharthanagar (Bhairawa) & Sunauli

✍ 071 / POP 165,000

The border crossing at Sunauli is the most touristed route between Nepal and India, seeing scores of people on the way south to Varanasi or Delhi, or northwards to Lumbini,

Pokhara and Kathmandu. Most people refer to both sides of the border as Sunauli, though officially the Nepali border town is called Belahiya.

Typical of many border towns, it is dusty and chaotic. Most people just get their passports stamped and continue on their way. If you do need to spend a night here there are hotels along the unattractive strip, but it makes more sense to stay in the more relaxed town of Siddharthanagar, also known as Bhairawa, 4km north.

Buses run directly from the border to most major towns in Nepal, so unless you plan to stay overnight or are heading to Lumbini, there's no real need to go into Siddharthanagar (Bhairawa), which has no sights of interest.

🛏 Sleeping & Eating

🛏 Sunauli

Hotel Mamata
HOTEL $

(☑ 071-418011; www.hotelmamata.com; Siddhartha Hwy, Belahiya; r Rs 1200, with AC Rs 2000) Hotel Mamata is probably the best hotel close to the border, with decent rooms and professional management, but don't expect luxury. There is a good restaurant and two ATMs in front of the building that accept foreign cards. The owner knows everything about local travel.

Hotel Aakash
HOTEL $

(☑ 071-418072; aakashshahi@hotmail.com; Siddhartha Hwy, Belahiya; s/d Rs 800/1000, with AC Rs 1400/1600; ❄🐾) Although the lobby, aircon and room tariff suggest a quantum leap above Belahiya's typical dives, this hotel's rather gloomy and grubby rooms are really only a marginal step up. It's close to immigration, has a good travel desk out front for booking onward buses and there's a State Bank of India ATM.

🛏 Siddharthanagar (Bhairawa)

Hotel Glasgow
HOTEL $

(☑ 071-523737; www.theglasgowhotel; Bank Rd, Siddharthanagar; s/d Rs 1200/1400, with AC Rs 1600/1800; ❄🐾) The best-value place in the centre of town, Hotel Glasgow has comfortable if variable-sized rooms, piping-hot showers, attentive staff and a decent restaurant and bar. It suffers less from road noise than similar nearby options.

Hotel Nirvana
HOTEL $$

(☑ 071-520516; www.nirvana.com.np; Paklihawa Rd, Siddharthanagar; s/d incl breakfast US$50/60; ❄@🐾) This is easily the highest quality hotel in town. It boasts deep mattresses, tubs, professional staff and an elegant restaurant facing a garden. There's also airport pick-up (Rs 500), a bar and (best of all) a quiet location, so sleep on those wonderful beds is guaranteed. Car travel to/from Lumbini can be arranged. Ask for a discount.

White Lotus
HOTEL $$

(☑ 071-520276; www.hotelwhitelotus.com; Siddhartha Hwy, Siddharthanagar; s/d Rs 2000/2500; ❄🐾) Very sharp, surprisingly comfy rooms make this a bargain. The air-con restaurant offers a multicuisine menu.

🍷 Drinking & Nightlife

⭐ TNT Rock Bar
BAR

(☑ 9857022021; Bank Rd, Siddharthanagar; beer Rs 350; ⏱7-10pm) A rock bar in the Terai? Yes it's true, thanks to the heroic efforts of its dynamic young owners. There's always live music, no cover and a very young crowd, at least until the police shut it down (around 11pm). On Bank Rd 100m west of Devkot Chowk. Look for top-floor sign.

ℹ Information

Siddharthanagar (Bharaiwa) has several banks but it's usually easier to change money at the border. The State Bank of India ATM beside the Hotel Aakash, Belahiya, accepts only Visa credit cards, while the Nabil Bank and Siddhartha Bank ATMs at the Hotel Mamata accept most foreign cards. There are lots of ATMs in Siddharthanagar; the Nabil and Standard Chartered bank ATMs accept most foreign cards.

The government of Nepal runs a small **tourist information office** (☑ 071-520304; Belahiya; ⏱10am-5pm Sun-Fri) on the Nepal side of the border.

ℹ Getting There & Away

AIR

Gautam Buddha International Airport, about 1km west of town, is due to open in early 2019. For the time being, **Buddha Air** (☑ 071-526893; www.buddhaair.com), **Yeti Airlines** (☑ 071-527527; www.yetiairlines.com) and **Nepal Airlines** (www.nepalairlines.com.np) offer daily flights (US$135, 35 minutes) between Kathmandu and Siddharthanagar (Bharaiwa), as do the smaller carriers Saurya Airlines (www.saurya airlines.com), Shree Airlines (www.shreeair lines.com) and Simrik Airlines (simrikairlines.

CROSSING THE BORDER: BELAHIYA TO SUNAULI

Border Hours

The immigration offices on both sides of the border are open to walk-ins 24 hours, but the Indian border post is closed to vehicles from 10pm to 6am. After 7pm and before 7am, you may need to go searching for the immigration officials on either side.

Foreign Exchange

There are no moneychangers on the Indian side of Sunauli. Several moneychangers on the Nepali side of the border exchange Nepali and Indian rupees, as well as cash and travellers cheques in US dollars, UK pounds and euros. Shops and hotels on both sides of the border accept Indian and Nepali rupees at a fixed rate of 1.6 Nepali rupees to one Indian rupee.

Onward to India

Regular buses run from Sunauli to Gorakhpur (₹94, three hours, every 15 minutes from 4am to 7pm), from where you can catch trains to Varanasi. A few morning (4.30am, 5.30am, 6.30am and 7.30am) and afternoon (4.30pm, 5.30pm and 6.30pm) buses run direct to Varanasi (₹271, 11 hours), but it's a long, bumpy ride. There's an AC bus (Rs 400) at 8am and 9am. Faster collective cars and jeeps to Gorakhpur hang out alongside the road after Indian immigration and leave when full (₹150 to ₹300, two hours).

Be wary of buying 'through' tickets from Kathmandu or Pokhara to Varanasi. Some travellers report being intimidated into buying another ticket once over the border. Travelling in either direction, it's better to take a local bus to the border, walk across and take another onward bus (pay the conductor on board). Travellers have also complained about being pressured into paying extra luggage charges for buses out of Sunauli. You shouldn't have to, so politely decline.

com). Airline offices and agents are found around the junction of Bank Rd and Siddhartha Hwy near Hotel Yeti in Siddharthanagar. You can also book tickets through hotels.

A taxi to/from Siddharthanagar (Bharaiwa) and Sunauli costs Rs 400/500.

BUS

Buses for Kathmandu and Pokhara leave from both Sunauli/Belahiya and Siddharthanagar (Bharaiwa). From Sunauli, Kathmandu-bound buses (Rs 550, eight hours) leave around 5.30am. Tourist class air-con buses cost Rs 800 to Rs 1200. Buses to Pokhara (Rs 500, eight hours) leave hourly starting at 5am. After these times and for all other destinations, you will need to head to Siddharthanagar (Bharaiwa). Be suspicious of travel agents in India or Nepal who claim to offer 'through tickets' between the two countries: everyone has to change buses at the border.

The most comfortable option is the Salina AC bus to Kathmandu (Rs 800 to Rs 1200, six to seven hours). There's one at 7am and four buses from 6pm to 8pm. Buses leave Kathmandu's Kalanki junction by the southeastern ring road at 7am and 7.30am and Sunauli at 7am. Services run daily in conjunction with the Baba Bhairav Travels and Buddha Darshan travel companies,

so don't be worried if you end up on a bus with one of these names.

From the bus stand in Siddharthanagar (Bharaiwa) there are frequent microbuses to Kathmandu (Rs 700, eight hours, hourly) via Narayangarh (Rs 350, three hours). For Pokhara, there are buses (Rs 500, nine hours) departing hourly from 6am to noon, and from 4pm to 8pm. They travel via Tansen (Rs 250, five hours) along the Siddhartha Hwy, as well as via Mugling (Rs 650, eight hours).

Also from Siddharthanagar (Bharaiwa) there are services every 15 minutes to Butwal (Rs 80, 45 minutes), from where you can connect with many more services heading west and up the Siddhartha Hwy. Heading east from Siddharthanagar (Bharaiwa), there is one bus to Janakpur (Rs 900, eight hours) leaving at 6.10am.

Local buses for Lumbini (Rs 50, one hour) and Taulihawa (Rs 100, three hours) leave hourly from the junction of the Siddhartha Hwy and the road to Lumbini, about 1km north of Bank Rd.

ⓘ Getting Around

Crowded share jeeps and local buses shuttle between the border and Siddharthanagar (Bharaiwa) for Rs 15. A rickshaw will cost at least Rs 100 to Rs 150.

Lumbini

♪ 071

Located 22km west of Siddharthanagar (Bhairawa), Lumbini is a unique religious site with much to say, whether intentionally or not, making for a very thought-provoking visit. It was here, around the year 563 BC, that one of history's most revered figures, Siddhartha Gautama – better known as the Buddha – was born. The actual location is marked by the poignant Maya Devi Temple, named after the Buddha's mother. Its origins date back over two millennia.

Today the Maya Devi Temple is part of a huge 3km by 2km park jarringly known as the Lumbini Development Zone. Designed by Japanese architect Kenzo Tange in 1978, it consists of a long central canal flanked by streets of monastic temples contributed by Buddhist communities around the world, and thus reflecting various regional architectural styles. It's still a work in progress, but the odd feeling you get is of entering the Epcot Centre of Buddhism, and one that could absorb far more visitors than it gets, were it not so far out of the way. Some of the temples are absolutely amazing, led by those from Southeast Asia. Tange's own brutal modernist buildings, which resemble stacked barrels, do not fit in at all. Maintenance levels vary from compound to compound, and construction is still ongoing, but you can spend an entire day visiting one temple after another.

When you finally end up at the humble Maya Devi Temple, it is time to reflect on what the Buddha might think of all this. As originally conceived, Buddhism is not a religion, but a psychological approach to liberating oneself from the suffering of the world. There is no God in Buddhism, nor any indication that the Buddha wished to be deified. And yet the latter process is everywhere on display. One can see, in the nativity story of the baby Gautama, and the sanctification of his mother, strong parallels to Christian theology. And that is what is most fascinating about Lumbini: walk from one end of the Development Zone to the other, and you can feel Buddhism developing into a true religion.

History

After many years of work at Lumbini, archaeologists are fairly certain that Siddhartha Gautama, the historical Buddha, was indeed born here. A huge complex of monasteries and stupas was erected on the site by his followers, and the Indian emperor Ashoka made a pilgrimage here in 249 BC, erecting one of his famous pillars. Shortly after this, an unknown cataclysm affected Lumbini. When the Chinese pilgrim Fa Hsien (Fa Xian) visited in AD 403, he found the monasteries abandoned and the city of Kapilavastu in ruins. Two hundred years later, Hsuan Tang (Xuan Zang), another Chinese pilgrim, described 1000 derelict monasteries and Ashoka's pillar shattered by lightning and lying on the ground.

However, the site was not entirely forgotten. The Nepali King Ripu Malla made a pilgrimage here in 1312, possibly leaving the nativity statue that is still worshipped in the Maya Devi Temple.

Mughal invaders arrived in the region at the end of the 14th century and destroyed the remaining 'pagan' monuments at both Kapilavastu and Lumbini. The whole region then returned to wilderness and the sites were lost to humanity, until the governor of Palpa, Khadga Shumsher Rana, began the excavation of Ashoka's pillar in late 1896.

◉ Sights

★ **Maya Devi Temple**   BUDDHIST TEMPLE
(foreigner/SAARC Rs 200/100; ⊘ 6am-6pm) The spiritual heart of Lumbini, Maya Devi Temple marks the spot where Queen Maya Devi gave birth to Siddhartha Gautama in around 563BC. In the adjoining sacred garden you'll find the pillar of Ashoka, ancient ruins of stupas, and maroon- and saffron-robed monks congregating under a sprawling Bodhi (pipal) tree decorated with prayer flags. Buy your entrance ticket 50m north of the gate to the Sacred Garden, and remove your shoes at the gate.

Excavations carried out in 1992 revealed a succession of ruins dating back at least 2200 years, including a commemorative stone on a brick plinth, matching the description of a stone laid down by Emperor Ashoka in the 3rd century BC. There are plans to raise a grand monument on the site, but for now a sturdy brick pavilion protects the temple ruins.

You can walk around the ruins on a raised boardwalk. The focal point for pilgrims is a sandstone carving of the birth of the Buddha, reputedly left here by the Malla king, Ripu Malla, in the 14th century, when Maya Devi was worshipped as an incarnation of the Hindu mother goddess. The carving has been worn almost flat by centuries of veneration, but you can just discern the shape of Maya Devi grasping a tree branch and giving birth to the Buddha, with Indra and Brahma looking on. Directly beneath this is a marker stone encased within bulletproof glass, which pinpoints the spot where the Buddha was born.

The sacred pond beside the temple is believed to be where Maya Devi bathed before giving birth to the Buddha. Dotted around the grounds are the ruined foundations of a number of brick stupas and monasteries dating from the 2nd century BC to the 9th century AD.

Ashokan Pillar
MONUMENT

The Indian emperor Ashoka visited Lumbini in 249 BC, leaving behind an inscribed sandstone pillar to commemorate the occasion. After being lost for centuries, Ashoka's pillar was rediscovered by the governor of Palpa, Khadga Shumsher Rana, in 1896. The 6m-high pink sandstone pillar has now been returned to its original site in front of the Maya Devi Temple.

Lumbini Museum
MUSEUM

(☑071-404053; foreigner/SAARC Rs 50/20; ⊙10am-4pm Wed-Mon) Tucked away at the northern end of the compound, this museum is devoted to the life of the Buddha, with a nice collection of artefacts and photos from Buddhist sites around the world. There's also an excellent model of the Master Plan for Lumbini's Development Zone.

★ World Peace Pagoda
BUDDHIST TEMPLE

(⊙dawn-dusk) Located outside the main compound, but easily accessible by bike, the impressive gleaming-white World Peace Pagoda, one of the world's greatest stupas, was constructed by Japanese Buddhists at a cost of US$1 million. The shining golden statue depicts the Buddha in the posture he assumed when he was born. Near the base of the stupa is the grave of a Japanese monk murdered by anti-Buddhist extremists during the construction of the monument.

THE BIRTH OF THE BUDDHA

The historical Buddha, Siddhartha Gautama, was the son of Suddhodana, ruler of Kapilavastu, and Maya Devi, a princess from the neighbouring kingdom of Devdaha. According to legend, the pregnant Maya Devi was travelling between the two states when she came upon a tranquil pond surrounded by flowering sal trees. After bathing in the cool water, she suddenly went into labour, and just had enough time to walk 25 steps and grab the branch of a Bodhi tree for support before the baby was born. The year was around 563 BC and the location has been positively identified as Lumbini.

After the birth, a seer predicted that the boy would become a great teacher or a great king. Eager to ensure the latter, King Suddhodana shielded him from all knowledge of the world outside the palace. At the age of 29, Siddhartha left the city for the first time and came face to face with an old man, a sick man, a hermit and a corpse. Shocked by this sudden exposure to human suffering, the prince abandoned his luxurious life to become a mendicant holy man, fasting and meditating on the nature of existence. After some severe austerities, the former prince realised that life as a starving pauper was no more conducive to wisdom than life as a pampered prince. Thus was born the 'Middle Way'.

Finally, after 49 days meditating under a Bodhi tree on the site of modern-day Bodhgaya in India, Siddhartha attained enlightenment – a fundamental grasp of the nature of human existence. He travelled to Sarnath, near Varanasi, to preach his first sermon and Buddhism was born. Renamed Buddha ('the enlightened one'), Siddhartha spent the next 46 years teaching the Middle Way – a path of moderation and self-knowledge through which human beings could escape the cycle of birth and rebirth and achieve nirvana, a state of eternal bliss.

The Buddha died at the age of 80 at Kushinagar, near Gorakhpur in India. Despite his rejection of divinity and materialism, all the sites associated with the Buddha's life have become centres for pilgrimage, and he is now worshipped as a deity across the Buddhist world. Devotees still cross continents to visit Lumbini, Bodhgaya, Sarnath and Kushinagar.

The ruins of Kapilavastu were unearthed close to Lumbini at Tilaurakot, and more recently the site of Devdaha, the home of Maya Devi, was identified on the outskirts of the Nepali town of Butwal.

Lumbini

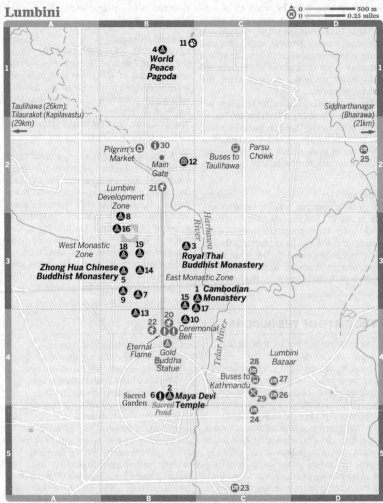

THE TERAI & MAHABHARAT RANGE LUMBINI

Lumbini Crane Sanctuary WILDLIFE RESERVE

The wetlands surrounding the World Peace Pagoda are protected as a crane sanctuary and you stand a good chance of seeing rare sarus cranes stalking through the fields, as well as the large, antelope-like blue bull. The entrance is on the right just before the gate of the pagoda. Follow the path to the watchtower for excellent views over the wetlands.

Buddhist Monasteries

Tange's Master Plan divides the Development Zone into four main parts. The Maya Devi Temple (p258) anchors the southern Sacred Garden. The brilliant white World Peace Pagoda (p259) lies at the northern end, along with administrative, residential and research facilities. In the middle, divided north–south by the 1.6km central canal, lies the Monastic Zone. The West Monastic Zone is set aside for monasteries from the Mahayana school, distinguished by monks in maroon robes and a more clamorous style of prayer involving blowing horns and clashing cymbals. The East Monastic Zone is set aside for monasteries from the Theravada school, common throughout Southeast Asia and Sri Lanka, and recognisable by

Lumbini

the monks' saffron-coloured robes. Together they create a fascinating map of world Buddhist philosophy, and a living one, with many monks resident full-time. A model of the Master Plan is displayed at the Lumbini Museum (p259).

Unless otherwise stated, monasteries are open daily from 8am to noon, and from 1pm to 5pm. You have to take your shoes off to enter one, so make sure you bring a pair of socks, or you may find yourself sprinting across hot courtyard tiles in the broiling sun.

WEST MONASTIC ZONE

★**Zhong Hua Chinese Buddhist Monastery**   BUDDHIST MONASTERY
(☺8am-12pm & 1-5pm) This elegant monastery is one of the most impressive structures at Lumbini. Reached through a gateway flanked by dogs of Fo, the elegant pagoda-style monastery looks like a small Forbidden City. Its perfectly manicured internal courtyard is an oasis of peace.

Korean Buddhist Temple   BUDDHIST TEMPLE
(☺8am-12pm & 1-5pm) At the time of research, the government of South Korea was finishing up this massive temple. The interior is magnificent; you might find workers still painting its intricate ceiling, which will take over a year to complete.

Manang Samaj Stupa   BUDDHIST TEMPLE
(☺8am-12pm & 1-5pm) This grand yet tasteful chörten (Tibetan reliquary stupa) was constructed by Buddhists from Manang in northern Nepal, but needs some work. There's a golden buddha statue inside surrounded by colourful murals.

Drubgyud Chöling Gompa   BUDDHIST MONASTERY
(☺8am-12pm & 1-5pm) This classic Tibetan-style gompa (Buddhist monastery) was built in 2001 by Buddhists from Singapore and Nepal. The mural work inside is quite refined. There is also a gigantic, spiralling golden stupa next door.

Mother Temple of the Graduated Path to Enlightenment   BUDDHIST TEMPLE
(☺8am-12pm & 1-5pm) The Austrian Geden International Foundation constructed this complex of stupas and monastery buildings, the latter in classical Greek style.

Vietnam Phat Quoc Tu Temple   BUDDHIST TEMPLE
(☺8am-12pm & 1-5pm) Vietnam's contribution has a grand roof but one kitschy lawn: its fake mountains resemble a minigolf hole. The faded grandeur is also a reminder that complicated designs require consistent maintenance.

Nepal Vajrayana Mahavihara Temple   BUDDHIST TEMPLE

This beautiful Newari temple with central courtyard was nearing completion at time of research.

Thrangu Vajra Vidhya Monastery   BUDDHIST MONASTERY

(⊙8am-12pm & 1-5pm) This monastic temple funded by Canadians opened in 2014; 80% of the residents are nuns. The temple is noted for the nearly three thousand Buddha statues lining the interior walls, each one representing a different donor.

Great Drigung Kagyud Lotus Stupa   BUDDHIST TEMPLE

(⊙8am-noon & 1-5pm) This truly extravagant stupa, constructed by the German Tara Foundation, contains a hollow crown partly covered in glass, revealing a small Buddha within. The domed ceiling of the main prayer room is covered in Buddhist murals.

EAST MONASTIC ZONE

★Royal Thai Buddhist Monastery   BUDDHIST MONASTERY

(⊙8am-noon & 1-5pm) Close to the north end of the pond, this stunning and imposing *wat* (Thai-style monastery) is built from gleaming white marble. The blue-roofed meditation centre next door is another fine piece of architecture. Arguably the greatest compound in the monastic zone.

Myanmar Golden Temple   BUDDHIST TEMPLE

(⊙8am-12pm & 1-5pm) The Myanmar Golden Temple is one of the oldest structures in the compound. There are three prayer halls – the most impressive is topped by a corn-cob-shaped shikhara (tower), styled after the temples of Bagan.

Lokamani Pula Pagoda   BUDDHIST SITE

Located on the grounds of the Myanmar Golden Temple is this huge gilded stupa in the southern Burmese style, inspired by the Shwedagon Paya in Yangon.

Sri Lankan Monastery   BUDDHIST MONASTERY

(⊙8am-12pm & 1-5pm) The grand and moated Sri Lankan Monastery contains elaborate and colourful murals depicting the life of Buddha.

★Cambodian Monastery   BUDDHIST MONASTERY

With strong touches of Angkor Wat, this colourful fantasy due for completion in 2018 is already one of the most fascinating temples in Lumbini. The temple is surrounded by a square railing topped off by four 50m green snakes whose tails entwine at the corners. The compound itself has a vast outer wall decorated with intricate designs.

🏃 Activities

Panditarama International Vipassana Meditation Centre   MEDITATION

(☎071-580118; www.panditarama-lumbini.info) A meditation centre, where practitioners can study for a nominal donation. To reach it, start at the Eternal Flame (just north of the Maya Devi Temple), and follow the dirt road along the west bank of the pond.

Anapana Meditation   MEDITATION

FREE The attractive Lumbini World Peace and Harmony Visitor Center, sponsored out of Thailand, offers regular 30-minute anapana meditation sessions for visitors between 9.30am and 5.30pm. It also has the nicest bathrooms in Lumbini (Rs 10), something to remember on your long walk.

Canal Boat Trips   BOATING

(per person Rs 70) Classic Southeast Asian longtails (ie, think propeller on a long stalk) offer mild rides up and down the central, all-too-green canal. Board at the north end of the canal, near the main gate.

👉 Tours

Hiring a guide to explain the various sights within the Development Zone is a good way to see the area. The going rate is around Rs 2000 to Rs 3000 per day; a rickshaw is extra. Otherwise, many hotels and travel agents rent out bicycles for Rs 150 per day.

Holiday Pilgrims Care Tour & Travels   TOURS

(☎071-580432; www.pilgrimsnepal.com; Lumbini Bazaar) Attached to Lumbini Village Lodge, this company arranges tours that really get under the surface of life in the Terai. Village tours (Rs 500, plus Rs 150 for breakfast) are available by bicycle, and they provide a free map so you can make your own way around by bike. They also run a birdwatching tour that includes visiting a 'vulture restaurant', where clean, diclofenac-free meat is served up to endangered vultures.

🎊 Festivals & Events

Buddha Jayanti   RELIGIOUS

(⊙Apr/May) The most important Buddhist celebration at Lumbini is this annual festival

TILAURAKOT

About 29km west of Lumbini, Tilaurakot has been identified as the historical site of Kapilavastu, where Siddhartha Gautama spent the first 29 years of his life. The site sits in a peaceful meadow on the banks of the Banganga River. Although you can still see the foundations of a large residential compound, it takes a certain amount of imagination to visualise the city of extravagant luxury that drove the Buddha to question the nature of existence. The showy shrine nearby with several carved pachyderms is dedicated to Maya Devi.

There's a small **museum** (foreigner/SAARC Rs 100/50; ☉10am-5pm Wed-Sun, to 3pm Mon) at the final turn-off to Tilaurakot that displays some of the artefacts found at the site. A new and larger museum building, under construction at time of research, is due by 2020.

To get to Tilaurakot from Lumbini, catch a local bus from the Lumbini bus stand to the junction at Parsu Chowk (Rs 15, 10 minutes, every 30 minutes) and change to a bus bound for Tilaurakot (Rs 50, 1½ hours, every 30 minutes), 3km north of Taulihawa. You can take a rickshaw to the site from Tilaurakot for Rs 100/175 one way/return. The best way to get here, though, is through Lumbini Village Lodge, which can organise a vehicle for Rs 800 with a day's notice. Otherwise a taxi can make the return trip from Lumbini for around Rs 3000.

held in April or May, when busloads of Buddhists from India and Nepal come here to celebrate the birth of the Buddha. Pilgrims also come here to worship each *purnima* (the night of the full moon) and *astami* (the eighth night after the full moon).

Rupa Devi RELIGIOUS
(☉Apr-May) Many Hindus regard the Buddha as an incarnation of Vishnu and thousands of Hindu pilgrims come here on the full moon of the Nepali month of Baisakh to worship Maya Devi as Rupa Devi, the mother goddess of Lumbini.

🛏 Sleeping & Eating

Most of the budget options are in Lumbini Bazaar (also known as Buddhanagar), the small village opposite the eastern entrance to the Lumbini Development Zone. The upmarket hotels are either in the Development Zone north of the Bhairawa–Taulihawa Rd or on the periphery road around the eastern side of the Development Zone.

★Lumbini Village Lodge HOTEL $
(☎071-580432; lumbinivillagelodge@yahoo.com; Lumbini Bazaar; dm Rs 400, s Rs 550-750, d Rs 850-950; ☎) This charming and welcoming budget lodge has a cool central courtyard shaded by a mango tree, big spotless rooms with fans and insect-screened windows (corner room 306 is a winner), and a small rooftop cafe. It's all kept bright with a fresh paint job every year. The owners run tours of the surrounding villages.

Lumbini Guest House HOTEL $
(☎071-580142; www.lumbiniguesthouse.com; Lumbini Bazaar; s/d Rs 500/600, deluxe r with/without AC Rs 2000/1200; ☀@☎) The Lumbini Guest House is a comfortable budget option in the bazaar, with a decent multicuisine restaurant. All rooms are spacious and clean, with attached bathrooms and LCD TVs, plus there are several air-con rooms to shelter from the heat.

Lumbini Buddha Garden HOTEL $$
(☎9851100566, 071-4442016; www.lumbinibuddhagarden.com; Telar River; s/d incl breakfast US$70/80; ☀☎) Spread over 4 hectares, this hotel offers a mix of rooms and thatched cottages with cathedral ceilings. Both are well-equipped with air-con, ceiling fans, nets and comfy beds, and share a similar style, but the cottages are a bit dated. En suite tents are forthcoming for single/double US$20/25. Also offers nature itineraries in the region.

**Hotel Lumbini Garden
New Crystal** HOTEL $$
(☎071-580145; www.newcrystalhotels.com; Lumbini Bazaar; s/d US$62/70; ☀@☎) Aimed at well-heeled pilgrims, usually in tour groups, this is a comfortable three-star hotel and rooms boast all the amenities you could ask for. There's a multicuisine restaurant and bar, and plenty of religious paraphernalia available in the lobby. There are 72 mostly Western-style rooms, plus a handful in Japanese-style.

Sunflower Travellers Lodge HOTEL $$
(☎071-580004; www.sunflower-tl.com; Lumbini Bazaar; r Rs 2400, with AC Rs 2700; ☀☎) On the

eastern periphery road, this bright guesthouse has cheerful rooms and efficient Chinese management. Rooms are on the small side, but spotless. There are no TVs. There's a small upstairs restaurant with excellent Chinese food (mains Rs 160 to Rs 380), a downstairs souvenir shop and after a rough day of sightseeing, an hour of acupressure massage for US$20.

Buddha Maya Garden Hotel   HOTEL $$$
(☑ 071-580220, in Kathmandu 01-4434705; www.ktmgh.com; s/d from US$120/140; ✴🛜🌀) Set in large grounds in the southeast corner of the Development Zone, this well-run resort offers elegant, tasteful and spacious rooms in a tranquil village setting. There's an excellent restaurant (though avoid the buffet at dinner) and staff who are keen to help. Ask about discounts.

Lumbini Invitation 365   INTERNATIONAL $
(Fusian Garden; ☑ 071-580211; Lumbini Bazaar; mains Rs 150-250; 🛜) You have to love this popular little restaurant, with its outdoor umbrellas and far-flung menu, ranging from burgers and pancakes to momos and the usual *thali*. The entrepreneurial owners are branching into budget accommodation with a new guesthouse coming around the corner (rooms Rs 1000 to Rs 1200).

❶ Information

There is a **tourist information centre** (⊘ 6am-6pm) located next to the ticket office, just inside the main gate.

There are five ATMs in Lumbini Bazaar, with the Everest Bank being the most reliable for foreign cards. For cash moneychangers, try your hotel.

❶ Getting There & Away

Local buses run regularly between Lumbini and the local bus stand in Siddharthanagar (Bhairawa) (Rs 50, one hour, hourly). Taxis from Lumbini Bazaar charge Rs 1000 to the main Siddharthanagar (Bhairawa) bus stand and Rs 1500 to the border at Sunauli (Belahiya). Lumbini Village Lodge helps arrange share taxis so a group of travellers can share the cost.

To reach Taulihawa from Lumbini, take a local bus to the junction with the Siddharthanagar (Bhairawa) road (Rs 20) and change to a bus bound for Taulihawa (Rs 130, 1½ hours, every half-hour).

A public bus bound for Kathmandu (Rs 550, nine to 10 hours) departs Lumbini Bazaar between 6am and 7am. Sakura Travels runs a semi-tourist bus (ie no air-con) to Kathmandu's Kakani bus stand (Rs 750, nine hours). Salina's

air-con tourist bus to Kathmandu costs Rs 850. Buy tickets at any travel agency or have your hotel organise it for a small fee.

❶ Getting Around

The best way to get around the compound is by bicycle. Lumbini Village Lodge (p263) in Lumbini Bazaar charges Rs 150 per day for reliable Hero-brand bikes.

Hiring an electric rickshaw is a good alternative. Loads of rickshaw-wallahs loiter near the main (north) gate to the Development Zone, charging around Rs 200 per hour.

THE SIDDHARTHA HIGHWAY

Most travellers heading from Sunauli to Pokhara follow the Mahendra Hwy to Narayangarh and then the Prithvi Hwy from Mugling to Pokhara. A more interesting route is the Siddhartha Hwy, which weaves its way north through the dramatic Tinau Gorge towards Pokhara via the scenic mountain village of Tansen (Palpa). It's a spectacular road clinging to near-vertical canyon walls with views of peaks, valleys and waterfalls, making it one of the finest drives in Nepal. It takes around five hours by car from beginning to end.

Butwal
☑ 071 / POP 121,000

Crowded, dry and dusty, Butwal has all the hallmarks of a typical Terai city, its bustling streets dominated by bell-ringing rickshaws. Sitting on an ancient trade route from the Indian plains towards the Himalaya, it remains an important trade and transport hub at the crossroads of the north–south Siddhartha Hwy and east–west Mahendra Hwy. Nevertheless, Butwal is a dry well when it comes to tourism, so most pass right through.

Archaeologists have identified a village 15km east of Butwal as the site of the kingdom of **Devdaha**, home to Maya Devi, the mother of Siddhartha Gautama, otherwise known as the Buddha. There's a small memorial park on the site, signposted off the Mahendra Hwy towards Narayangarh.

🍴 Sleeping & Eating

Hotel Kandara   HOTEL $
(☑ 071-540175; Traffic Chowk; s/d Rs 600/800, r with AC Rs 1600; ✴🛜) Situated on the busy

highway near Traffic Chowk, Kandara is a reasonable budget choice with a breezy, open feel assisted by high ceilings. You can take your pick between simple rooms with attached bathrooms and deluxe rooms with bathtubs and air-con. There's a decent restaurant and safe off-street parking.

De Novo
HOTEL **$$**

(🖊 071-438885; www.clubdenovo.com; s/d US$42/48; ▣ 🔊 ▤) This modern hotel, the best in Butwal, has a business feel but also a fun side, with a pool and karaoke bar. The rooms are nicely furnished, too.

★ Olive Garden Family Restaurant
MULTICUISINE **$**

(🖊 071-544455; Siddhartha Hwy; Rs 150-300; ⊙ 8am-10pm; ▣ 🔊) Butwal's most popular restaurant offers a multicuisine menu, sprawling rooms, outdoor dining and live music Fridays at 6pm. Located immediately on the right as you enter Butwal from the north.

ℹ️ Information

There are several ATMs around Traffic Chowk; the one opposite the Hotel Royal takes international cards.

ℹ️ Getting There & Away

All long-distance buses leave from the main bus park just south of Traffic Chowk. There are buses to Kathmandu (Rs 510, eight to 10 hours, every half-hour) and Pokhara (Rs 490, nine hours, every two to three hours) via Mugling and the Prithvi Hwy. There are also one or two morning buses on the scenic route to Pokhara (Rs 450, six hours) via Tansen (Rs 100, 2½ hours). Local buses leave for Sunauli/Siddharthanagar (Bhairawa; Rs 80, 45 minutes) every 10 minutes.

Along the Mahendra Hwy, there are regular buses east to Narayangarh (Rs 250, three hours, every 15 minutes), and west to Dhangadhi (Rs 845, 10 hours, three to five times per day) and Bhimdatta (Mahendranagar; Rs 955, 12 hours, two to three times per day) for connections to Nepalganj (get off at Kohalpur) and Bardia National Park (alight at Ambassa – blink and you'll miss it).

Tansen (Palpa)

🖊 075 / ELEV 1372M

Perched high above the Kali Gandaki River, Tansen is an untouristed town whose reward is precisely that. There is a sense of discovery here as you unearth the evidence of a rich history, all the while experiencing daily life in this mountain village. Here you'll notice some intricately carved Newari windows; there you'll hear the clacking of looms. While it doesn't have the pretty face of Bandipur, these deeper charms emerge over time. If you're lucky, one will be the mist that often carpets the Madi Valley in the morning, locally known as the 'White Lake'. Just be sure to bring your walking shoes: the steep streets will provide all the exercise you need.

The people of Tansen are fiercely proud of their home town, which no doubt stems from its glory years as the capital of the Magar kingdom of Tanahun. Until the rise of the Shahs, Tanahun was one of the most powerful kingdoms in Nepal. In the 16th century, under the leadership of King Mukunda Sen, its troops even came close to conquering Kathmandu. The power of the Magars waned in the 18th century, however, and Tansen was ultimately reinvented as a Newari trading post on the route between India and Tibet. Today it is the administrative headquarters of Palpa district. Some Nepalis refer to it as Palpa.

⦿ Sights

Sitalpati
PLAZA

The main square in Tansen is dominated by (and named after) a curious octagonal pavilion, used for public functions in the days when Tansen was ruled by the governors of the Shah regime. Today it's a popular meeting spot for locals to have a chat. At the northwest corner of the square, the small, two-tiered **Bhimsen Mandir** is sacred to the Newari god of trade and commerce. To the south lies the great gate **Baggi (Mul) Dhoka**.

Tansen Durbar
PALACE

At the southern end of Sitalpati is the striking red Tansen Durbar, which has been nicely restored after being razed during one of the Maoist insurgency's most violent battles. The original building was built for the provincial governor in 1927.

In more recent times the building served as district administration headquarters, which explains why the Maoists targeted it. It now includes a museum of local culture and history; they were just starting to populate the collection at time of research.

Amar Narayan Mandir
HINDU TEMPLE

(⊙ 24hr) At the bottom of Asan Tole (the steep road running east from Sitalpati), the Amar Narayan Mandir is a classic three-tiered, pagoda-style wooden temple. The mandir was built in 1807 by Amar Singh Thapa, the

Tansen (Palpa)

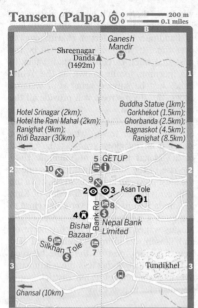

Tansen (Palpa)

⊙ Sights
1 Amar Narayan Mandir B2
2 Baggi (Mul) Dhoka A2
3 Sitalpati B2
4 Tansen Durbar A2

🛏 Sleeping
5 City View Homestay A2
6 Hotel Gauri Shankar Guest House A3
7 Hotel the White Lake A3
8 Palpali Chhen B2

⊗ Eating
9 Nanglo West A2
10 Royal Inn A2

first governor of Tansen, and it's considered to be one of the most beautiful temples outside Kathmandu Valley. The carved wooden deities are exquisite; note the erotic scenes on the roof struts, and the alternating skulls and animal heads on the lintel.

Devotees come here every evening to light butter lamps in honour of the patron deity, Lord Vishnu.

At the start of the steps to the Amar Narayan Temple is the similar but smaller **Mahadev Mandir**, a Shiva temple.

🛏 Sleeping

★ City View Homestay   HOMESTAY $
(☑ 075-520563, 9847028885; shrestha.manmohan @gmail.com; r Rs 500-700) The best budget option in town is the four rooms within the home of Mohan Shrestha, the energetic man behind GETUP, the volunteer tourist information service. The roof affords great views of the city and beyond. The rooms are simple, but spacious and spotless. If they are full, Mohan can find similar homestays nearby. Located a block north of Sitalpati.

Hotel Gauri Shankar Guest House   HOTEL $
(☑ 9847043540; Silkhan Tole; old rooms Rs 800-1000, without bathroom Rs 400, new rooms Rs 1500-3500) This hotel is split between its old just-bearable budget rooms, and a new addition with a spotless restaurant, including a rare glass-walled kitchen, and a spread of greatly improved rooms with lots of light. The rough neighbourhood hasn't changed.

★ Hotel Srinagar   HOTEL $$
(☑ 075-520045; www.hotelsrinagar.com; Asan Tole; s/d US$44/58; ☎) This upmarket option is about 2km from town on the ridge, a 20-minute walk west of the summit of Shreenagar Danda. Although rather isolated, the views of Dhaulagiri and the Annapurna range are simply sensational, particularly from corner room 503. The wood-panelled rooms are comfortable with renovated bathrooms, and the restaurant terrace has views to the mountains on one side and the 'White Lake' on the other.

Hotel the White Lake   HOTEL $$
(☑ 075-520291; Silkhan Tole; s/d US$15/18, deluxe US$30/35; ☎) The sprawling White Lake has a variety of rooms – the standard ones are pretty ordinary and overpriced, but the new wing boasts more comfortable deluxe rooms with lots of light and cosy balconies; request a corner room. The restaurant and terrace, as well as some of the rooms, have vertigo-inducing views of the 'White Lake'.

Palpali Chhen   B&B $$
(☑ 075-521845; www.palpalichhen.com.np; Bank Rd; incl breakfast s/d Rs 2400/2800, deluxe Rs 3000/3400; ☎) This is a new enterprise by the folks from Nanglo West. It is a bright, spotless hotel with standard rooms that are rather pokey, and those we looked at lacked windows. Superior rooms have bouncier mattresses and flat-screen TVs. Beware of musty rooms not used in awhile.

✕ Eating

Royal Inn NEPALI **$**
(☑075-522780; mains Rs 170-350; ◷10am-9pm; 🛜) Housed in a delightfully restored Newari house (duck your head through the doorways!) is this atmospheric restaurant run by young enterprising locals, located about 300m northwest of town. In addition to the recommended Nepali *thali,* there are pizzas, burgers, *thukpa* (Tibetan noodle soup) and superb momos. Both floor and chair seating.

★ Nanglo West NEPALI **$$**
(☑075-520184; mains Rs 175-425, Newari set Rs 315-415; ◷10am-7pm; 🛜) You can't go without sampling the Nepali delights at this atmospheric oasis in the centre of Tansen. In addition to a great Newari set *thali* with veg, chicken or mutton, they serve local dishes like *choela* (dried buffalo or duck meat with chilli and ginger), served with *chiura* (flattened rice) and spiced potatoes in curd. There's also an international menu.

Out front you'll find Nanglo West's bakery (open from 7am to 7pm) with delicious buttery biscuits, cream cakes and pastries. Freshly baked goods arrive on the shelves around 10am.

❶ Information

The most excellent **GETUP** (Group for Environmental & Tourism Upgrading Palpa; ☑075-520563, 9847028885; shrestha.manmohan@gmail.com; ◷9am-5pm Sun-Fri) is your first stop for tourist information.

For foreign exchange there are moneychangers and several banks near the south end of Bank Rd, including **Nepal Bank Limited** (◷10am-3pm Sun-Fri) and **Himalayan Bank**.

❶ Getting There & Away

The bus station is at the bottom of town at the southern entrance to Tansen, and the ticket office is at the east end of the stand. Buses to Pokhara (Rs 350, five hours) leave at 6am and 10am; there are also buses/microbuses to Kathmandu (Rs 620/850, 11 hours) at 6am and 6.45pm.

There are regular services south to Butwal (Rs 100, 2½ hours, every 30 minutes) from 6.30am to 5pm. There're also buses to Bhairawa (Rs 140, 2½ hours, mornings) where you can change for Lumbini. One tourist bus from Pokhara heading to Lumbini (Rs 300) passes through Bartung (on the highway) around midday, but check timings. Local buses for Ridi Bazaar (Rs 120, two hours, every 20 minutes) leave fairly regularly during the same hours – get an early-morning start if you want to be back the same day.

If you get dropped off by any bus at Bartung on the highway, rather than the bus park, either take a taxi up to Tansen or ask directions for the foot-trail or shortcut up to Tundikhel. Walking to town along the winding road will take forever.

Around Tansen

As well as the popular walks around Tansen, there are two other interesting places that you can reach on foot or by bus, Ranighat Durbar and Ridi Bazaar.

Ranighat Durbar

The most famous sight near Tansen is the eerie Ranighat Durbar on the east bank of the Kali Gandaki. Fancifully referred to as Nepal's Taj Mahal, this crumbling baroque palace was built in 1896 by Khadga Shamsher Rana in memory of his beloved wife, Tej Kumari. Khadga was an ambitious politician who was exiled from Kathmandu for plotting against the prime minister. He followed up with another abortive attempt to seize power in 1921 and was exiled again, this time to India. After his departure, the Durbar was stripped of its valuable fittings, but the building still stands, slowly fading on the banks of the Kali Gandaki, prompting recent renovation efforts.

Outside of monsoon, when conditions are awful, you can walk to Ranighat in three to four hours (return trip eight hours) along an easy-to-follow trail, beginning in Gorkhekot at the east end of Shreenagar Danda. GETUP in Tansen sells a guide and map (Rs 50). The route down to the river is mainly downhill, through rice paddies and forest from which the ruined palace materialises. The return leg is fairly tough going, following a steeply ascending trail on the next ridge, emerging near Hotel Srinagar. Aim to leave before 8am and turn back before 1.30pm. Take a torch (flashlight) to look around the darkened palace, and in case you get caught on the trail after sunset. There's also basic accommodation in Ranighat if you choose to stay the night.

Some rafting trips on the Kali Gandaki also make it as far as the palace.

Ridi Bazaar

About 28km northwest of Tansen by road (or 13km on foot), the Newari village of Ridi Bazaar sits at the sacred confluence of the Kali Gandaki and Ridi Khola rivers. Ridi

WORTH A TRIP

WALKS AROUND TANSEN

Tansen is surrounded by excellent walking country. The tourist office **GETUP** (p267) can recommend walks, provide maps and brochures at cost, and help organise local guides. You would be smart to check your itinerary with them prior to setting off.

One of the nicest short walks is the one-hour stroll up **Shreenagar Danda**, the 1492m-high hill directly north of town. The trail starts near the small **Ganesh Mandir** (temple) above Tansen and climbs steeply through open woodland to the crest of the hill. When you reach the ridge, turn right: a 35-minute stroll will take you to a modern **Buddha statue** and a viewpoint with fabulous views over the gorge of the Kali Gandaki River to the Himalaya.

Another short and easy walk is the two-hour stroll to the **Bhairab Sthan Temple**, 9km west of Tansen. The courtyard in front of the temple contains a gigantic brass trident. Inside is a silver mask of Bhairab, allegedly plundered from Kathmandu by Mukunda Sen. The walk follows the road from Tansen to Ridi Bazaar.

If you fancy something more challenging, the three-hour walk to the village of **Ghansal** passes several hilltop viewpoints, emerging on the highway about 3km south of Tansen. The walk is mainly downhill with spectacular valley views from Bhut Dada, about halfway along the route.

A full-day walk begins at **Bagnaskot**, on the ridge east of **Gorkhekot**, a wonderfully exposed hilltop viewpoint with a small Devi temple. From here you can continue to **Aryabhanjyang** on the Siddhartha Hwy. To return you can hop on a south-bound bus coming from Pokhara. A good option between December and March is to get dropped off at the Organic Coffee plantation near Bartung, the highway turn-off to Tansen.

All these walks can be completed in a day if you get an early start, or there's simple homestay lodging along the way if you're not in a hurry.

If you are keen to go on longer walks and experience Magar village homestays, there's an overnight walk to **Baugha Gumha** and a four-day trek to **Kaudelake** and **Remigha** (Rimgha). You can also follow the old trade route from Tansen to Butwal – GETUP has maps (Rs 50) with a detailed description of all these trails and can provide advice and local guides.

is a popular destination for pilgrimages, and is further sanctified by the presence of saligrams (p270) – ammonite fossils revered as symbols of Vishnu. Accordingly, the principal religious monument is the **Rishikesh Mandir**, which was founded by Mukunda Sen in the 16th century. By legend, the Vishnu idol inside was discovered fully formed in the river and miraculously aged from boy to man. The temple is on the south bank of the Ridi Khola, near the bus stand, and contains a room full of saligrams.

To reach Ridi on foot, take the trail leading northwest from the Tansen–Tamghas road near Hotel Srinagar. Buses to Ridi (Rs 100, two hours) leave from the public bus stand in Tansen every half-hour. Either way it is a significant investment of time. What you get in return is a sense of isolation in a beautiful spot, and a friendly, working village where a foreigner will turn many heads, making meeting people a breeze. If you wish to stay overnight, your best bet is the **Ho-**

tel Sunrise & Guest House (☑079-400009, 9857068454; Ridi Bazaar; s/d Rs 700/900), just around the corner from the bus stand. Choose a streetside room for light.

THE TRIBHUVAN HIGHWAY

From Birganj, the easiest and quickest route to Kathmandu or Pokhara is along the Mahendra Hwy to Narayangarh and then north to Mugling, but when were the best travel experiences ever easy? If you don't mind the incessant potholes, it's much more fun to take the winding and dramatic Tribhuvan Hwy, which leaves the Mahendra Hwy at Hetauda, east of Chitwan National Park. The route is prone to landslides in the monsoon but the scenery is breathtaking. Furthermore, you can stop on the way at Daman to stretch your legs and take in some of the best Himalayan views in Nepal.

Hetauda

📞 057 / POP 153,000

The bustling town of Hetauda marks the junction between the flat Mahendra Hwy and the steep, spectacular Tribhuvan Hwy. There isn't any great reason to stop here except to change buses or prepare your bike and legs for the steep climb to Daman.

🛏 Sleeping & Eating

Motel Avocado & Orchid Resort   HOTEL $

(📞057-520429; www.orchidresort.com; Tribhuvan Hwy; Nissen hut s/d Rs 1000/1300, s/d from Rs 1500/2000, deluxe from Rs 2000/2500; ❄) This local institution rests among a garden of orchids, rhododendron and avocado trees, and is a great choice for travellers on all budgets. The budget rooms are in converted Nissen huts with attached bathrooms, cold showers and bucket hot water, while the 'motel' rooms are well appointed and comfortable. The multicuisine restaurant offer excellent curries, tandoori, and garden BBQs.

Decades of passing cyclists and motorcyclists have contributed to the journals housed in the restaurant and make for good reading (ask at counter). Orchid and birding enthusiasts can arrange local tours here.

❶ Getting There & Away

Buddha Air (www.buddhaair.com) has two to four flights a day to Kathmandu (US$101, 10 minutes) from Simara airport, a 35-minute drive south of Hetauda.

The main bus stand is just west of Buddha Chowk. There are regular morning and afternoon buses to Pokhara (Rs 450, six hours, every 45 minutes) and Kathmandu (Rs 400, six hours) via Narayangarh (Rs 120, one hour). You can also pick up services to destinations east and west along the Mahendra Hwy. Local buses and minibuses run regularly to Birganj (Rs 80, two hours).

Buses along the Tribhuvan Hwy leave from a smaller bus stand just north of Motel Avocado's gate. There are buses every hour or so to Kathmandu (Rs 400, eight hours) via Daman (Rs 150, four hours) until around 2pm. Microbuses destined for Palung cost Rs 240 to Daman. Autorickshaws can ferry you from town to the bus stand for Rs 500.

There is also a jeep service to Kathmandu (Rs 400, four hours, every fifteen minutes) via Bimphedi and Pharping, but the mountain road is narrow and prone to delays.

Daman

📞 057 / POP 8500

Perched 2322m above sea level, with clear views to the north, east and west, the tiny village of Daman boasts what is arguably *the* most spectacular outlook on the Himalaya in the whole of Nepal. There are unimpeded views of the entire range from Dhaulagiri to Mt Everest. Unfortunately, the town itself appears largely forgotten. But it makes a great break to stretch your legs after a long drive on the Tribhuvan Hwy, or potentially to find Shangri La, in the form of its one remarkable resort.

◉ Sights

**Daman Mountain Resort
View Tower**   VIEWPOINT

(Rs 30) Some of the best views of the Himalaya in Nepal can be had from the concrete viewing tower inside the Daman Mountain Resort. Unfortunately, the resort has closed and is seeking a new owner, but the viewing tower is still open. If no one is present at the small ticket office, which will likely be the case, just walk up.

**Shree Rikheshwar
Mahadev Mandir**   HINDU TEMPLE

About 1km south of the village, a narrow trail leads west through the forest to this tiny Shiva temple. On the way, you can drop into a gorgeous little gompa in a glade of trees draped with thousands of prayer flags. From the highway, it's 1km to the gompa and 1.5km to the temple.

Mountain Botanical Gardens   PARK

(🕙10am-5pm; 🅿) The Mountain Botanical Gardens span 15 hectares of forest. To the nonbotanist this is more of a woodland walk than anything else, and guides are available. February to March is the best time to visit, when the rhododendrons (the national flower of Nepal) are in full bloom, forming a nice contrast with the Himalaya backdrop. It's just up the hill from the Daman Mountain Resort Viewing Tower, on the left.

🛏 Sleeping

There are a couple of rustic guesthouses right on the highway in the middle of the village that have very basic rooms (from Rs 300) and daal bhaat.

SALIGRAMS

Saligrams are black stones that, when broken open, reveal the fossilised remains of ammonites, a mollusc that lived in the Tethys Sea 140 million years ago. During the geological collision that gave birth to the Himalaya, the sea dried up and the fossils ascended with the mountains. Today the Himalaya continues to rise and the Kali Gandaki and her tributaries wash through the ancient sediment to reveal these fossils. Hindus venerate saligrams as manifestations of the god Vishnu, who was turned to stone by the beautiful and virtuous Vrinda after he tried to seduce her.

★**Everest Panorama Resort** HOTEL $$$
(☑ 057-621480, Kathmandu 01-4412864; www.face book.com/Everestpanoramaresort; s/d US$96/120; ☎) This is one mountain resort that actually deserves to be called Shangri La. The long way in resembles the movie version of *Lost Horizon*, the book that gave birth to the enduring image of the lost Himalayan valley. After the road ends, a 200m path runs alongside a steep hill, finally reaching a cleft in a rock wall: the hotel's entrance.

Pass through, and a valley opens up before you, with the wall of the Himalaya beyond. The hotel is built along the hillside, with individual cottages arrayed lengthwise along a stone platform, facing the mountains. The highlight is the two-storey restaurant and bar (mains Rs 200 to Rs 550), which is thrust out into the sky: a little-known classic. Do not come expecting polish: there are no hot towels to greet you upon arrival. In fact, in the off-season you might even have the place to yourself. But there is Western food, a mildly attentive staff, and those views to keep you company. Guided walks and mountain biking can also be arranged. Or you might just kick back and read *Lost Horizon*.

ℹ Getting There & Away

There are three daily buses to Kathmandu: a microbus (Rs 200, four hours) and three buses (Rs 220) departing at 7.30am (best), 9am, noon and 3pm; late buses have a habit of not showing up. There are also buses to Hetauda (Rs 250, four hours) leaving at 7am, 9am, 10.30am and 1pm. Alternatively, this is one of the most spectacular (and gruelling) mountain-bike routes in Nepal.

WESTERN TERAI

The Mahendra Hwy runs west from Butwal to meet the Indian border at Bhimdatta (Mahendranagar). The centrepiece of this area is the spectacular Bardia National Park, which is attracting increasing numbers of visitors. Above lies the far west, Nepal's last frontier, including Jumla and Khaptad National Park. Access is typically via the Nepalganj airport. Adventurers will be rewarded by natural beauty and solitude.

Nepalganj

☑ 081 / POP 138,950

Home to Nepal's largest Muslim community, Nepalganj is a gritty border town with a hectic Indian (in particular, Uttar Pradesh) flavour. You'll hear more Hindi spoken than Nepali. The city is also an important air transport hub, serving Bardia National Park as well as many remote mountain airstrips in northwestern Nepal. With its oppressive heat and dust, many see it as a necessary evil on the way to somewhere else. And they are quite right. As you enter the city along the main road, it presents itself as a long tunnel of haphazard construction viewed through a white haze, with vehicles swerving in all directions. It doesn't improve upon close inspection.

While Nepalganj sprawls in all directions, finding something to do here is not easy. There are half a dozen small temples strung out along the main road through the bazaar, with the garish **Bageshwari Mandir**, devoted to Kali, being the most interesting. You might find some local clothing or silver Tharu jewellery here as well.

🛏 Sleeping & Eating

★**Galaxy Durbar** HOTEL $
(☑ 081-523213; www.thegalaxydurbar.com; Surkhet Rd 1; s/d Rs 2100/2300; ❀☎) It's especially nice to find a design-conscious hotel like this in a dust cloud like Nepalganj. Rooms have super-cosy layouts, with deep mattresses and many four-poster beds. There's two restaurants to choose from, with nice decor to match; the glass street-level restaurant offers a prix fixe menu for Rs 350. And the price can't be beaten. Look for the wavy glass front.

Hotel Maruti Nandan HOTEL $
(☑ 081-527551; www.hotelmarutinandan.com; New Rd; s/d Rs 1000/1200) This colourful family-run hotel has spacious, well-lit rooms with

rock-hard mattresses at a bargain price. A busy restaurant is attached. Located 400m east of Dhamboji Chowk.

Traveller's Village GUESTHOUSE **$$**
(☎081-550329; travil2000@gmail.com; Surkhet Rd; s/d US$25/35; ❄@📶) The first choice for UN and NGO workers, this charming hotel is located about 2km northeast of Birendra Chowk, almost opposite the Unicef compound. It's owned by Candy, a friendly American lady who's lived here 40 years. Rooms are cosy and spotless, with air-con, hot water and TV. The unique in-house restaurant, Candy's Place, is first-rate. Reservations are essential.

Kitchen Hut HOTEL **$$**
(☎081-551231; www.kitchenhut.com.np; Surkhet Rd; s/d Rs 2000/2500; ❄@📶) This modern business hotel, situated about 3km northeast of Birendra Chowk, started as one of Nepalganj's best restaurants. Rooms vary in quality, but were undergoing renovation along with some new construction at the time of research. Very good multicuisine dishes are served in the Tripti restaurant.

★**Candy's Place** INTERNATIONAL **$$**
(☎081-550329; Surkhet Rd; mains Rs 300-600; ⌚6.30am-9.30pm) A stack of blueberry pancakes for breakfast? Real cheeseburgers with bacon? Oven-roasted chicken with stuffing – and tenderloin steak? Who would've thought you'd find American home cooking in Nepalganj?! And yet here you are, in the cosy six-table cafe atop the Traveller's Village. If you've OD'd on daal bhaat, this is heaven. Just don't miss Candy's famous lemon meringue pie.

ℹ Information

Nabil Bank (Ratna Rajmarg; ⌚10am-4.30pm Sun-Thu, to 2.30pm Fri) has foreign-exchange services and a 24-hour ATM located just south of Karkado Chowk.

ℹ Getting There & Away

AIR

There is regular daily service between Nepalganj and Kathmandu (US$149, 45 minutes to an hour, nine times per day) through **Yeti Airlines** (☎081-526556; www.yetiairlines.com) and **Buddha Air** (☎081-525745; www.buddhaair.com). You might also try smaller carriers Saurya Airlines (www.sauryaairlines.com) and Shree Airlines (www.shreeairlines.com).

Nepalganj is the main air hub for western Nepal. **Nepal Airlines** (☎081-520727; www.nepalairlines.com.np) and **Tara Air** (☎081-526556) both serve Jumla (US$131, 45 minutes), with the former departing Monday at 11am and the latter on Wednesday and Friday at 11.45am. They also serve Dolpo (US$110, 35 minutes, seven to eight times per day) and Simikot (US$140, 50 minutes, seven to eight times per day), though delays and cancellations are common due to poor weather. Tara Air offers Friday flights to Rara (US$185, 40 minutes) at 11.45am.

BUS

The bus stand is about 1km northeast of Birendra Chowk. Buses to Kathmandu (Rs 1180 to Rs 1230, 12 hours, 10 times per day) and Pokhara (Rs 1100, 12 hours, three times per day) leave early in the morning or early in the afternoon. Kathmandu buses run via Narayangarh (Rs 920, 10 hours). Buses for Bhimdatta (Mahendranagar; Rs 600, five hours) leave hourly from 5.30am until 1pm. Buses to Butwal (Rs 500, seven hours) leave hourly.

CROSSING THE BORDER: NEPALGANGJ TO JAMUNAHA/ RUPAIDHA BAZAAR

Border Hours

The border is open from 6am to 10pm. The immigration office is about 1km beyond the border.

Foreign Exchange

There are several moneychangers on the Nepali side of the border, but they only exchange Indian and Nepali rupees. The Nabil and Standard Chartered banks in Nepalganj can exchange other currencies.

Onward to India

For Rs 200 to Rs 300 you can take a rickshaw from the Nepalganj bus stand to the border at Jamunaha and on to the bus stand in Rupaidha Bazaar. From here, buses and share taxis run regularly to Lucknow (five hours). The nearest point on the Indian rail network is Nanpara, 17km from the border.

Western Terai

Local buses to Thakurdwara (for Bardia National Park) leave at 11.20am and 1.30pm (Rs 350, three hours). There are also frequent buses to Jumla, Surkhet, Dang, Biratnagar and Bhatrapur.

ⓘ Getting Around

Shared tempos (three-wheelers) run between the bus stand and the border for Rs 25; *tongas* (horse carriages) are being phased out.

An e-rickshaw costs Rs 70 per person to the airport and about the same to Rupaidha Bazaar in India. A taxi to the airport costs Rs 200.

Bardia National Park

☑ 084

Bardia National Park (☑ 084-429719; www.bardianationalpark.gov.np; permits foreigner/SAARC/child under 10yr Rs 1130/500/free; ☉ dawn-dusk Sun-Fri) is the largest national park in the Terai, a beautiful, unspoiled wilderness of sal forest, grassland and alluvial washes cut by the many fingers of the Karnali River. Largely unpopulated, it is often described as what Chitwan National Park was like 30 years ago, before its commercial development. One can raft through the park for hours on end and not encounter another person.

The park suffered greatly during the Maoist insurgency of the 1990s. Tourism dried up, lodges were mothballed and wildlife was hit hard by poaching, particularly the rhino population. The good news is that this damage is now being reversed, with 31 rhino being counted in 2014, and five more transferred from Chitwan in 2017.

For the patient wildlife spotter, the park affords excellent opportunities. Bengal tigers, one-horned rhinos, leopards and wild elephants are among the 30 species of mammals living here. Gangetic dolphins are occasionally seen on rafting and canoe trips along the Geruwa River, the eastern channel of the Karnali River, but numbers have declined to dangerously low levels. Unlike in Chitwan, the gharial crocodile is plentiful, as is the wonderfully named marsh mugger. Bardia also has more than 250 species of birds, including the endangered Bengal florican and sarus crane.

The park may be inaccessible from May to September due to flooding.

ⓞ Sights

The headquarters of Bardia National Park is located about 13km south of the Mahendra Hwy in the village of Thakurdwara. The bumpy access road leaves the highway at Ambassa, about 500m before the Amreni army checkpost. It leads to a walled compound, which contains a number of attractions. Just past the gate is a simple **visitor centre** (☉ 10am-4pm) consisting of two large rooms with placards on the park's species. Opposite lies the **Tharu Cultural Museum** (adult Rs 50; ☉ 10am-4pm Tue-Sun), which holds various artefacts of Tharu life, including some interesting jewellery. If this piques your interest you can arrange cultural tours of Tharu villages through most hotels; otherwise you can rent a bike and explore by yourself. Further on lies a small **breeding centre** (adult Rs 125; ☉ dawn-dusk Sun-Fri) for marsh mugger and

gharial crocodiles, as well as turtles. An adjacent enclosure contains Shivaram, a rhino who was injured as a baby in Chitwan. Blind in one eye, he used to wander freely around the park headquarters until he killed a man. Best not to pet this one.

Note that if you bring your park permit, the admission fee to visit the animal exhibits is waived. Otherwise you can use your animal exhibit ticket to get into the cultural museum, too.

There's also an **elephant breeding centre** (adult Rs 50; ⏰ dawn-dusk) about 2km southwest of park headquarters. The best time to visit is morning and afternoon when the elephants have returned from grazing in the park (10am to 4pm). The mothers and calves are occasionally visited by free-ranging wild males – if this happens keep well clear of the male!

🏃 Activities

For some activities there is a minimum group size to achieve the stated per-person costs.

Wild Planet Tour & Guide Office   SAFARI
(📞 9848070831, 084-402082; e.westnepal@gmail.com) This entrepreneurial effort by some long-standing local guides is aimed at creating a free-standing tour agency beyond the lodges – and may well be less expensive because of it. The park entrance fee, breakfast, lunch and guide for an entire day is Rs 3000 per person, with a reduction after three people.

In addition to jeep and rafting safaris, they also organise 12-day long-distance treks to Jumla and Rara Lake. They also rent scooters (Rs 800 per day), bicycles (Rs 300 per day) and motorcycles (Rs 1000 per day). Located on the left just prior to reaching park headquarters.

Birdwatching
Three-hour birdwatching tours venture into the buffer zone (Rs 1500). Full-day birding trips enter the park and come with a packed lunch (Rs 7000).

Elephant Safari
One way to explore the park is on the back of an elephant. However, the tide has turned against this practice due to the animal-welfare issues involved – elephants typically undergo harsh training regimes in order to 'learn' how to accept riders, and can suffer injuries from carrying too many people on their backs. Leading lodges like Tiger Tops and Forest Hideaway are no longer promoting it. We recommend pursuing one of the many other animal-friendly activities available here instead.

Fishing
The Karnali and Babai rivers are famous for *mahseer*, the giant South Asian river carp that can reach 80kg in weight. Anglers can obtain **fishing permits** (Rs 2000) at the park headquarters, but a guide would certainly help unless you know the local waters. You will also need a park permit. Due to their endangered status, any fish you catch will need to be released back into the water.

Guided Walks
A great way to spot wildlife in the park, and potentially the most thrilling, is on a guided walk. Venturing into the park on foot with your guide, however, is obviously done at your own risk. The cost including park permit, packed lunch and guide is Rs 3500 for a half-day, Rs 5500 for a full day.

4WD Safari
4WD safaris (half-/full day Rs 5000/6000 per person, minimum four people) can be arranged directly through the lodges. These include the park permit and a guide, as well as lunch on the full-day safari. An alternative half-day trip takes you to see the black-buck that reside outside the park. These safaris are best March through May.

Rafting
A downstream drift in an inflatable raft (Rs 5000 to Rs 8000 per person, two to four passengers) is a relaxing way of experiencing the park, as well as giving you a chance

FAR-WESTERN NEPAL

Nepal's far west is still an off-the-beaten-track destination, but that could change as entrepreneurs move to promote the area, opening it up to mainstream tourism. One such group is the **Tourism Development Society** (www.farwestnepal.org) based in Dhangadhi. As well as promoting local accommodation, this not-for-profit organisation can help arrange cultural tours to Hindu pilgrimage sites and Tharu villages, where you can stay with a local family in traditional homestays. They also offer more adventurous multiday treks into the region. If you wish to hike to the far west from Bardia, contact the Wild Planet Tour & Guide Office (p273) there.

Remote **Khaptad National Park** is one of the best trekking destinations in the far west, with oak and pine forests, rolling meadows filled with wildflowers and several lakes. There is also a variety of animals, including ghoral (a goat-antelope), Himalayan black bear, yellow-throated marten, barking deer, wild boar, and both rhesus and langur monkeys. Treks typically start from the town of Silghadi, an eight-hour drive from Dhangadhi airport, and take a week or more. Inside the park, visitors stay at **Bichpani Camp** and **Khaptad Camp**, which are connected by a beautiful 15km trail. Named after Khaptad Baba, a Hindu holy man, the park also contains **Khaptad Baba Ashram** near its headquarters, which attracts Shiva-worshipping pilgrims. In addition to Wild Planet, there are numerous Kathmandu-based trekking companies now offering Khaptad itineraries, which run around US$1500 all included. The best time to visit is September to December and March to May.

at spotting wildlife. A typical drift starts on the Karnali River, just above the Chisapani Bridge, and turns left into one of its branches, the Geruwa River, which marks the park's westernmost edge. Stopping for lunch, you get to walk around the sandy riverbank where you can observe the heavy traffic of animal footprints, or make deeper forays into the jungle, including tiger hotspots. Crater marks of elephants and rhinos are criss-crossed with perfectly imprinted tiger pugmarks and delicate monkey and deer prints. Even if you don't spot anything, the journey is so peaceful and picturesque that it is its own reward. This is not white-water rafting, although there are some gentle dips. Given the crocodiles in the river, swimming is not advised, as several locals have unfortunately discovered.

🛏 Sleeping & Eating

Most of the lodges are in close vicinity to each other near the village of Thakurdwara, on the border of the park buffer zone, about 13km from the Mahendra Hwy. Room quality is fairly uniform, so price comparison pays off.

★**Forest Hideaway**　　　　LODGE **$**
(📞 9758001414, 084-402016, in Kathmandu 01-4225973; www.foresthideaway.com; safari tents Rs 400, dm Rs 600, r Rs 1000-1200, deluxe r incl breakfast Rs 1800; @ 🛜) Run by the super-

dedicated Mohan Aryal, this resort combines a charming atmosphere with deep local knowledge. The peaceful grounds contain spacious, spic-and-span Tharu mud-walled cottages with fans, nets, hot water, bathrooms and endearing porches. You can also hang out in the lovely outdoor dining cabanas or numerous hammocks. Meals are served buffet-style in a dining hall that is movie-set perfect.

Transport can be arranged with Mohan. Pick-up and drop-off at Ambassa is free if you stay at least two nights.

Bardia Jungle Cottage　　　LODGE **$**
(📞 084-402014; www.bardiajunglecottage.com.np; r Rs 400-2500; 🛜) Right opposite the army camp entrance, this low-key, long-standing lodge offers a great range of rooms from simple mud-walled singles to cement cottages with tiled bathrooms. Cross a tiny bamboo bridge to the central dining hall to hear stories from the owner Premi, a former park warden, who offers numerous activities from fishing to volunteering. At the time of research, a new building was under way.

Tharu Home　　　　　LODGE **$**
(📞 084-402035; www.tharuhomeresort.com.np; r Rs 1200-2200) With a roaring campfire and youthful owners who've been working as guides since they were 11, this is one of the more social places in town, and also one of the best run, with everything in excellent

condition. The Rs 1200 rooms have attached bathrooms but a shared hot-water shower. The more expensive rooms have their own hot-water heater and nice stone baths. All rooms boast rather quaint curtains, bed covers and thick rugs.

Bardia Wildlife Resort LODGE $
(☑084-402041; https://bardiawildliferesort.com; r Rs 500-1200; ☎) Peacefully situated along a branch of the Karnali River 1.5km south of park headquarters, this friendly family-run lodge offers great value for money. The en suite rooms with solar hot water are priced half as much as equivalent accommodation elsewhere. There's a campfire and a lovely garden with papaya trees, too. Kudos to the hostess, Bardia's first female safari guide.

Bardia Adventure Resort LODGE $
(☑084-402023; www.bardia-adventure.com; r Rs 800-1500) With a prime location looking out to the jungle, this resort has simple Tharu-style, thatched mud-floor huts as well as more comfortable carpeted cottages with tiled bathrooms. The highlight here is the resort's own watchtower, where you can enjoy a cold beer while keeping your eyes peeled for a leopard lurking on the park's perimeter.

Samsara Safari Camp LODGE $
(☑084-402064; www.samsarasafari.com; s/d Rs 1000/1500) This lodge specialises in bird tours, although anyone is welcome. Accommodation is in neat and tidy cottages with flowered beds, nets and porches (with neighbours). There's also a cosy little restaurant cottage.

Racy Shade Resort LODGE $
(☑084-402020; www.racyshaderesort.com; r Rs 1000-1500; ☎) This lodge is nicely polished, with neatly trimmed lawn paths leading from the lovely open-sided restaurant-bar through leafy grounds to the thatched-roof rooms. The cheaper rooms are perfectly comfortable, while the deluxe rooms boast verandahs and big bathrooms, some with tubs.

Mango Tree Lodge LODGE $$
(☑084-402008; www.mangotreelodge.com; r Rs 1000-3000; ☎) ☝ With a biogas plant, organic garden and solar water heaters, Mango Tree Lodge leads the eco-friendly trend in Bardia. The open-sided communal dining area is one of the best around. From the spacious suites down to the thatch-roofed stone-walled cottages, the Tharu rooms are a delight. There's even a wood-fired pizza oven, a most acceptable break from tradition.

⭐Tiger Tops Karnali Lodge LODGE $$$
(☑in Kathmandu 01-4361500; www.tigertops.com; inclusive packages per person per night US$250, signature room US$350; ☎) ☝ Run by the same pioneering team as Tiger Tops in Chitwan, this top-end lodge is set on the southern edge of the buffer zone near Thakurdwara and offers the most experienced wildlife guides in Bardia. Accommodation is in stylish Tharu-style cottages; the signature rooms could be used for a safari fashion shoot. And the food! Every course is consistently above par.

Package rates include all meals and activities (park fees and local transfers are extra), including jeep drives, rafting and jungle walks. Thank them for boldly leading the charge for elephant welfare (p255).

🍷 Drinking & Nightlife

⭐Sunset View Café & Jungle Bar BAR
(☺10am-late) Can it be true? In that desert known as Terai nightlife, here's a noteworthy exception...in the middle of the jungle! Offering a different kind of wildlife, this

---

ON THE TIGER TRAIL

Together with the adjacent 550 sq km Banke National Park, Bardia's 968 sq km now forms one of the largest protected tiger habitats in the world, with an estimated 50-plus tigers in Bardia alone. While this is less than Chitwan, you probably stand a much better chance of seeing one here if you put in the hours at one of the 'hotspots' for tiger sightings: **Tinkuni** (three corners), **Kingfisher** and the **Balcony**. All the guides know these places well and you will certainly be taken to them on a safari. Don't be surprised to find a large troop of tiger-spotters already in position when you arrive. Some people spend the entire day sitting and waiting (and whispering) with a packed lunch for that elusive glimpse. The best time of the year to see tigers is February to May and the best tactic is to sit and wait at one of the hotspots. Don't forget to bring binoculars or a telephoto lens for your camera, and maybe a book to while away the hours. Raft trips may also stop at one or more hotspots en route, although this limits your time at them.

well-stocked thatched hut does coffee in the morning, Irish coffee in the afternoon and whisky shots beyond. There's also a small library to amuse yourself if necessary. Located opposite the elephant breeding centre.

ⓘ Information

The ticket office (p272) is just inside the gate of the Park Headquarters. Entry fees for the park are generally paid here on your behalf by your tour provider and added to your bill, so most visitors have no reason to come here.

ⓘ Getting There & Away

Most of the lodges are close to Thakurdwara, but because of the poor condition of the roads, visitors are usually transferred to the lodges by 4WD. If you intend to make your own way to the park, call ahead to make sure your lodge is open and able to arrange a pick-up from Ambassa (Rs 1200 one way). The nearest airport is at Nepalganj and your lodge will charge about Rs 6000 (Rs 7000 for air-con) to pick you up or drop you off. If you're on a package, ensure the transfer is included.

To reach Bardia by public transport, buses leave Pokhara (Rs 1500, 14 to 16 hours) at 1pm and 1.30pm; from Kathmandu (Rs 1500, 14 to 18 hours) there are five buses departing between 1pm and 5pm. There are two buses leaving from Narayangarh heading to Bardia (Rs 750, nine hours) at midnight and 4pm.

In the other direction, buses depart Ambassa for Pokhara at 3pm and 4.30pm. Several buses originating in Bhimdatta (Mahendranagar) and Danghadi bound for Kathmandu pass through Ambassa and your lodge should be able to help you make a connection. These buses are usually better than the public bus (Rs 1500), which leaves Ambassa at 4pm.

Painfully slow local buses depart Thakurdwara at 7am, 8am and 9am bound for Nepalganj (Rs 400, five hours) via Ambassa (Rs 70). Change at Ambassa for buses to Bhimdatta (Mahendranagar; Rs 400, four hours, every half-hour).

Sukla Phanta National Park

Tucked against the Indian border, Sukla Phanta National Park covers 305 sq km of sal forest and *phanta* along the banks of the Bahini River. While facilities are more basic than Bardia National Park, the reserve has around 20 tigers, a handful of rhinos, crocodiles, wild elephants, Nepal's largest population of swamp deer and large numbers of migratory birds.

The best time to visit is from November to February; the main vehicle track within the park is impassable from June to September because of monsoonal flooding. In September 2017 the entire park was closed for an indefinite period due to an aggressive herd of over 50 wild elephants that had entered the park from India.

🛏 Sleeping & Eating

Shuklaphanta Jungle Cottage　　LODGE $
(☏099-414223; shuklaphantajc@gmail.com; r US$15, with AC US$25; ❉ ❧) Located in the buffer zone close to the reserve's headquarters, this new lodge sports comfortable rooms in concrete buildings set in a garden. They grow their own organic vegetables for the warehouse-like restaurant and organise safaris, birdwatching and even excursions to Nainital in India.

Suklaphanta Wildlife Camp　　LODGE $$
(2-night & 3-day packages from US$175) Located about 500m from the reserve's headquarters, this permanent camp of basic safari tents with shared bathrooms is run by the **Suklaphanta Nature Guides Association** (☏9741060150). Rates include meals, accommodation, park fees and jeep transfer to/from Bhimdatta (Mahendranagar). Transfer to/from Dhangadhi airport and New Delhi can be arranged.

CROSSING THE BORDER: DHANGADHI TO GAURIPHANTA

The little-used border crossing from Dhangadhi to Gauriphanta, Uttar Pradesh, is useful for moving on to Lucknow, New Delhi or Dudhwa National Park. The Gauriphanta railway station is permanently closed. Ongoing travel is via the bus terminal.

Nepali immigration is open from 7am to 8pm. For ATM and foreign exchange use the Nabil Bank near the bus station, about 4km from the border. If heading east into Nepal, there is hourly bus service to Ambassa, the entry point to Bardia National Park (Rs 300, 3½ hours) and onward to Nepalganj (Rs 350, four hours). If heading west to Bhimdatta (Mahendranagar) there are also hourly buses (Rs 200, two hours). If you need to stay overnight, choose the central **Hotel Flora** (☏091-417544, single/double Rs 3200/4200) right off the main road.

ℹ️ Information

The **ticket office** (☎ 099-521309; foreigner/ SAARC per day Rs 1000/500) is located at the main building at park headquarters. However, there is generally no need to buy a ticket, as your hotel/tour provider will simply add the entrance fee to your bill.

ℹ️ Getting There & Away

The few visitors who make it to the park generally come on package tours with the accommodation providers listed here or on day trips from Bhimdatta (Mahendranagar) with a hired car and driver (Rs 5000 per jeep).

Bhimdatta (Mahendranagar)

☎ 099 / POP 105,000

Bhimdatta – formerly Mahendranagar, and still widely known by that name – is the most westerly border crossing into India and offers an interesting back route to Delhi and the hill towns of Uttaranchal. While it's not somewhere you'll want to spend any length of time (ie only until your bus is ready to depart), it's somewhat less chaotic than other India–Nepal border crossings. If you have time here, the town provides a useful base to visit Sukla Phanta National Park, although staying there would be vastly preferable.

Bhimdatta (Mahendranagar) is just south of the Mahendra Hwy, about 5km east of the Indian border. From the Nepali border post at Gaddachauki, it's about 1km to the Indian border post at Banbassa.

🛏️ Sleeping & Eating

Hotel Sweet Dream　　　　　　HOTEL $
(☎ 099-522313; Mahendra Hwy; r Rs 850, with AC Rs 1700; ❄️🛜) This hotel is conveniently located about 100m east of the bus station. Spacious en suite rooms are carpeted but in need of fresh paint. The restaurant has an Indian and Chinese menu and pleasant courtyard seating. A location set back from the road limits noise.

Hotel Opera　　　　　　　　HOTEL $$
(☎ 099-522101; www.hoteloperanepal.com; r Rs 1500, deluxe Rs 2500-3500; ❄️🛜🏊) Pavarotti wouldn't sing about it, but this is probably the best hotel in town, with a pool, a health club, a casino and a decent restaurant serving hearty Nepali and Indian dishes. You have to be careful to choose the renovated

GHODAGHODI TAL

This picturesque grouping of oxbow lakes is renowned for its birdwatching. Located about 40km west of Chisopani, the scene is straight out of an Impressionist painting, with lotus flowers, water lilies and dappled light. The lakes are home to 142 different species of birds, including the grey-headed fishing eagle. Through your hotel you can organise an air-con 4WD and guide for Rs 16,000 (for up to five people), or you can catch a bus (Rs 700 return) from Ambassa.

---

rooms, particularly as the old rooms have plumbing issues.

ℹ️ Information

The **immigration office** (☎ 099-523773; ⊙10am-5pm) doubles as an informal tourist information centre, although there's no sign to indicate this. They are happy to help out.

Foreign exchange and an ATM is found at **Nabil Bank** (☎ 099-525450; ⊙10am-5pm Sun-Thu, to 3pm Fri), a 15-minute autorickshaw ride (Rs 120) from the border.

ℹ️ Getting There & Away

AIR

The Bhimdatta (Mahendranagar) airport is closed. The closest airport is at Dhangadhi, 60km east. Flights to Kathmandu (US$215, one hour) depart daily at 9am, 1pm, 3pm, and 5pm. Providers include **Buddha Air** (☎ Dhangadhi 091-417445; www.buddhaair.com), **Yeti Airlines** (☎ Dhangadhi 091-520004; www.yetiairlines. com), **Nepal Airlines** (☎ Dhangadhi 091-575314; www.nepalairlines.com), Tara Air (www.taraair. com), and Saurya Airlines (www.sauryaairlines. com). A taxi from Bhimdatta to the Dhangadhi airport will cost Rs 3500 to Rs 4000 depending on the vehicle. Alternatively, buses to Dhangadhi (Rs 120) depart every 10 minutes, but this may entail a connection to the airport.

BUS

The bus station is about 1km from the centre on the Mahendra Hwy. Long-haul buses leave for Kathmandu (Rs 1200, 15 hours) at 5am, 1.30pm, 2.30pm, 2.45pm and 3.45pm. An AC bus is Rs 1680. There's a single Pokhara service (Rs 1100, 16 hours) at 2.20pm; AC is Rs 1400.

Local buses run every 30 minutes to Nepalganj (Rs 600, five hours), passing the turn-off for Bardia National Park at Ambassa (Rs 350, four hours).

CROSSING THE BORDER: BHIMDATTA (MAHENDRANAGAR) TO BANBASSA

Border Hours

The Nepali side of the border (Gaddachauki) is open to tourists 24 hours, but before 5am and after 10pm you may need to go searching for immigration officials. The Indian side of the border (Banbassa) is open 24 hours, but is only open to vehicles from 6am to 8am, 10am to noon, 2pm to 4pm and 6pm to 7pm.

Foreign Exchange

There's a small bank counter near the Nepali customs post, but it only exchanges Indian and Nepali rupees. In Bhimdatta (Mahendranagar), Nabil Bank (p277) has foreign exchange and an ATM.

Onward to India

From the Bhimdatta (Mahendranagar) bus station an AC bus (₹600) departs for Delhi at 5.30pm. Alternatively, take a rickshaw from the Indian border post to the bus station in Banbassa, where you can pick up regular long-distance buses to Delhi (₹300, 10 hours). Local buses and shared jeeps serve Almora, Nainital and other towns in Uttaranchal from here.

There's also a train station in Banbassa with service to Bareilly, from where you can pick up trains to other destinations in India. The new Banbassa station, due to open in November 2018, will expand service to Delhi and Dehradun.

For further information, head to shop.lonelyplanet.com to purchase a downloadable PDF of the Delhi chapter from Lonely Planet's *India* guidebook.

ⓘ Getting Around

Buses and autorickshaws run regularly between the bus station and the border for Rs 100. From the border into the main town a rickshaw costs around Rs 100, and a motorbike Rs 200.

Taxis can be hired for trips to Sukla Phanta National Park for around Rs 6000 to Rs 7000 per day.

EASTERN TERAI

Bound by the Indian states of Bihar, Sikkim and West Bengal, the eastern Terai is broadly a mirror image of the west. The rolling hills of the Mahabharat Range are squeezed between the dry eastern plains and the Himalaya. The Mahendra Hwy cuts east to meet the Indian border at Kakarbhitta, providing easy access to Sikkim and Darjeeling. There is less English spoken here, and life is generally sleepier. It often feels like a throwback to another time.

Birganj

♨ 051 / POP 140,000

There's very little in the hectic border town of Birganj to suggest that you're not in India. As the main transit point for freight between India and Nepal, the town is mobbed by trucks, deafened by car horns and jostled by rickshaws. It is most commonly visited by travellers crossing to/from Kolkata. Nevertheless, it is cleaner and friendlier than one might expect.

The amazing, multitiered and beautifully restored clock tower on the main road, so at odds with everything around it, serves as a useful landmark. From here it is east to the bus station, and south to the town centre and Indian border. A lively bazaar extends along the main road near Mahabirsthan Chowk and offers good shopping for local clothing.

🛏 Sleeping & Eating

⭐ **Hotel Makalu** HOTEL $

(☎ 051-523054; hmakalu@gmail.com; Alakhiya Rd; r from Rs 2200; ❇ 🛜) After long travel in the Terai, this place is a surprising godsend. The old rooms are so-so, but the renovated rooms are top-notch, with modern furnishings, nice baths and satellite TV: you will stand there blinking. It feels calm and relaxed – just what you need in hectic Birganj – and there's a good Indian restaurant. Book ahead.

Hotel Vishuwa HOTEL $$

(☎ 051-417003; www.vishuwa.com; Bypass Rd; s/d Rs 4000/5000; ❇ 🛜 ⊠) On the outskirts of town, the three-star Vishuwa is a good choice for those wanting comfort. It also has the best restaurant in town, a small bar, and a rare pool in which you will want to keep your eyes closed.

ℹ Information

There are several banks in town with ATMs, including the Nabil Bank ATM at Hotel Vishuwa.

ℹ Getting There & Away

Birganj is served by Simara Airport, 22km north of the city. A taxi costs around Rs 1500.

Buddha Air (☎ Kathmandu 01-5542494) has up to five daily flights between Simara and Kathmandu (US$100, 20 minutes). Nepal Airlines (www.nepalairlines.com) adds one flight per day at 10.15am for US$80 to US$100.

Buses leave from the large, sprawling, ear-splittingly noisy bus stand at the end of Ghantaghar Rd (New Rd). There are plenty of buses to Kathmandu (ordinary/deluxe/air-con Rs 600/725/900, six to seven hours) from 5am until 8.30pm. However, the most comfortable and quickest option is to get a Tata Sumo '4WD' (Rs 550 to Rs 800, four to five hours), which depart every 20 minutes, finishing up around 5pm. There are also morning buses to Pokhara (Rs 600, eight hours) via Narayangarh (Rs 250, four hours) at 5am, 6.30am and 7.30am, as well as two to three evening buses from 5pm to 7pm. Regular buses head to Janakpur (Rs 300 to Rs 400, five hours) every 20 minutes until 4pm.

ℹ Getting Around

Rickshaws charge around Rs 300 to go from town to the Nepali border post and on to Raxaul Bazaar. Alternatively, you can take a rickshaw from the bus station to the Nepali border post for Rs 25 and then walk 500m to the Indian side, but it's likely they'll charge more for your bag.

Janakpur

📞 041 / POP 170,000

Open sewers in the heart of the city, garbage burning in the streets, filthy green ponds, omnipresent broken roads – we hate to say it, but Janakpur is a cesspool. It's too bad, because under its repellent surface lie some otherwise interesting sights.

Janakpur is best known as an important pilgrimage site for Hindus, due to its connection with the Hindu epic, the Ramayana. Legend has it that it's where Sita was born and married Rama. This gives the city a heady religious atmosphere, in which the residents often speak of the characters in the Ramayana as if they were walking the streets today.

While Janakpur's culture is primarily Indian, it was also once the capital of the ancient kingdom of Mithila, a territory now divided between Nepal and India. More than two million people here still speak Maithili. The

---

CROSSING THE BORDER: BIRGANJ TO RAXAUL BAZAAR

Border Hours

The Nepali side of the border is officially open from 5am to 10pm, but the staff sometimes clock off early and you'll need to find someone to stamp you in or out of Nepal. Similarly, the Indian side is staffed from 5am to 10pm, but you can find someone at other times. Nepali visas are available on arrival from the Nepal immigration office, but payment must be in US dollars.

Foreign Exchange

There are no facilities at the border, but there are banks and one moneychanger, Lakshmi, near the Ganeshman Chowk. The Indian rupee is widely accepted in Birganj.

Onward to India

The border is 3km south of Birganj, from where it's a further 2km to the bus station in Raxaul Bazaar. Most people take a rickshaw straight through from Birganj (Rs 300).

From Raxaul, there are regular buses to Patna (non-AC/AC ₹180/230, six hours) or you can take the daily Mithila Express train to Kolkata's Howrah train station, departing Raxaul at 10am. Seats cost sleeper/3AC/2AC ₹365/990/1425 (note that sleeper and two-tier class prices include air-con) and the trip takes 18 hours. There is also an evening train from Raxaul to Kolkata departing Thursday and Saturday at 8.30pm. The Satyagrah Express runs daily to New Delhi (sleeper/3AC/2AC ₹455/1215/1765, 24 hours, departing at 9.05am). There is also a new luxury bus from Raxaul to New Delhi, which departs at 12.30pm (sleeper ₹1300, 18½ hours).

Eastern Terai

Maithili people are famous for their wildly colourful paintings (p284).

Janakpur is actually the third city on this site. The city mythologised in the Ramayana existed around 700 BC, but it was later abandoned and sank back into the forest. Simaraungarh grew up in its place, but this city was also destroyed, this time by Muslim invaders in the 14th century. Construction of the modern city began in the late 18th century.

◉ Sights

The sugar-cane fields and Maithili villages around Janakpur form a lush and magical mosaic. Many of the villages are built in the traditional Mithila style, with mud walls decorated with colourful paintings and raised wall engravings of people and animals. People are very friendly, as long as you aren't too intrusive with your camera.

The easiest village to reach is **Kuwa**, about 1km south of Murali Chowk, where you can drop in on the Janakpur Women's Development Centre (p284). If you feel like roaming further afield, **Dhanushadham**, 15km northeast of Janakpur, marks the spot where Rama allegedly drew Shiva's magic bow. Worshippers believe a fossilised fragment of the broken bow lies here. Further rural adventures and wall art await in the village of **Phulgama**, a 30-minute bus ride (Rs 20) south of Janakpur.

★ Janaki Mandir   HINDU TEMPLE
(⊙ 4.30am-11pm) At the heart of Janakpur lies the marble Janaki Mandir, one of the grander pieces of architecture in Nepal, and

the city's must-see sight. Built in extravagant baroque Mughal style, the temple is dedicated to Sita, the wife of Rama and heroine of the Ramayana. It's believed to stand on the spot where King Janak found the infant Sita lying in the furrow of a ploughed field.

A steady stream of pilgrims file in through the gatehouse to worship the Sita statue in the inner sanctum. The temple is particularly popular with women, who wear their best and most colourful saris for the occasion. Early evening is the most atmospheric time to visit, as the temple is draped with colourful lights and pilgrims arrive en masse. You never know what you might see here!

The temple only dates from 1910, but with its white marble arches, domes, turrets and screens, it feels much older.

At the back of the complex is a small **museum** (admission Rs 15) with some amusingly retro moving statues telling the story of Rama and Sita.

Ram Sita Bibaha Mandap   HINDU TEMPLE
(admission Rs 5, camera/video Rs 5/21; ⊙ 4.30am-11pm) This rather bizarre temple next to the Janaki Mandir marks the spot where Rama and Sita were married. The temple is topped by a modernist interpretation of a tiered pagoda roof, and the walls are glass so you can peer in at the kitschy life-sized models of Sita and Rama.

Ram Mandir & Danush Sagar   HINDU TEMPLE
(⊙ 4.30am-11pm) Hidden away in a stone courtyard southeast of the Janaki Mandir, the Ram Mandir is the oldest temple in Janakpur (1782) and built in the classic tiered pagoda style of the hills. The main

temple is dedicated to Rama but there are several smaller shrines to Shiva, Hanuman and Durga dotted around the compound. It's busiest in the early evening, when the courtyard is filled with incense smoke and music.

Opposite the entrance are a series of ghats (steps for ritual bathing) leading down into the **Danush Sagar**, the largest ceremonial tank at Janakpur. There are small shrines all around the perimeter, and vendors in front sell flower garlands, tika powder, sacred threads and other ritual objects for pujas (prayers).

✱ Festivals & Events

Maha Ganga Aarati   CULTURAL
(Ganga Sagar; ⊙7pm Mar-Sep, 6pm Oct-Feb) Every evening at the large, central bathing tank of **Ganga Sagar**, a small puja ceremony involving a lot of crashing of cymbals, ringing of bells and waving of candles takes place. Anyone is welcome to join in.

Sita Bibaha Panchami   RELIGIOUS
(⊙Nov/Dec) By far the most interesting time to visit Janakpur is during the fifth day of the waxing moon in November/December, when tens of thousands of pilgrims descend on the town to celebrate the re-enactment of Sita's marriage to Rama (also known as Vivaha Panchami). There are processions and performances of scenes from the Ramayana in the streets.

Rama Navami   RELIGIOUS
(⊙Mar/Apr) Celebrations for Rama's birthday in March/April are accompanied by a huge procession, which attracts many sadhus (wandering Hindu holy men).

Dasain   RELIGIOUS
(⊙Sep/Oct) If you visit during the end of the Dasain festival (late September to early October), you and the rest of an enormous crowd will have the chance to see the ritual nighttime burning of an enormous paper Rama on Danush Sagar.

Holi   RELIGIOUS
(⊙Mar) In March, Janakpur gets boisterous during this riotously colourful affair, but be warned: foreigners are not exempt from a ritual splattering with coloured powder and water.

Tihar   RELIGIOUS
(⊙Oct/Nov) If you visit during October/November, you'll see Maithili women repainting the murals on their houses.

🛏 Sleeping & Eating

Rama Hotel   HOTEL $
(📞041-520059; arunc581@gmail.com; r with/without AC Rs 1600/800; 🅿@📶) Whoever washes the linens here hasn't heard of bleach, but given the street beyond this courtyard hotel you will be deliriously happy with its relative peace and order, even if the mattresses are paper thin and reception stone cold. The City Pride restaurant is your best choice in town, and very popular, perhaps due to the absence of other options.

Hotel City Star   HOTEL $
(📞041-530327; hotelcitystarjnp@gmail.com; Shiv Chowk; r with AC/fan only Rs 2000/1000; ❄📶) A solid budget choice in the centre of town, with a good restaurant. The City Star has small, luridly painted rooms that are kept spotless and have hot-water bathrooms. Interior rooms lack windows but are much quieter. There are also some overpriced suites at Rs 6000.

★Hotel Welcome   HOTEL $$
(📞9801620064, 041-520646; www.nepalhotelwelcome.com; Station Rd; r Rs 2500, tr Rs 3500; ❄📶) The hotel 'where welcome never ends' has spent the past couple of years receiving a serious facelift, which makes its 60 or so rooms the best in town: spacious, bright and decorated with art. Other pluses are the helpful management and in-house restaurant.

Rooftop Family Restaurant   INDIAN $$
(Station Rd; mains Rs 300-500; ⊙10am-9.30pm) This upstairs restaurant is the best, and really only, pleasant restaurant option in

THE TERAI & MAHABHARAT RANGE JANAKPUR

Janakpur

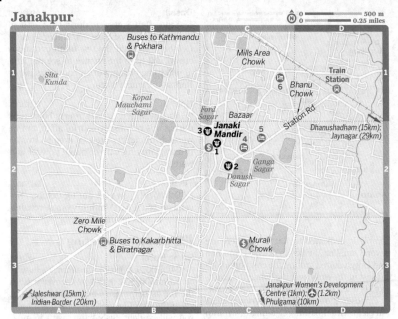

Janakpur outside the hotels. There's an excellent selection of vegetarian curries to wash down with cold beer, but it's really known for its handful of outdoor tables facing the northern end of Danush Sagar.

❶ Information

Everest Bank has an **ATM** tucked away inside the eastern entry of Janaki Mandir. There's also an ATM just inside Hotel Welcome (p281), and another **ATM** near the police station.

❶ Getting There & Away

AIR

Buddha Air (☎ 041-420522; www.buddhaair. com) and **Yeti Airlines** (☎ 041-520047; www. yetiairlines.com) have three daily flights between them from Janakpur to Kathmandu (US$117, 20 minutes). The airport is a Rs 175 rickshaw ride south of the centre. If arriving at Janakpur airport, rickshaws are considerably cheaper if you make the short walk outside the airport. It will cost Rs 800 to Rs 2000 for an air-con taxi to your hotel.

BUS

Regular daily buses to **Kathmandu** (deluxe/ air-con Rs 700/1000, 10 hours) via Narayangarh (Rs 450 to Rs 700, five hours) depart from the highway at Ramanand Chowk every 15 minutes. The first bus is at 5.30am and last at 5.30pm. Microbuses and jeeps travel to Kathmandu via the Sindhuli road (Rs 800, seven hours, hourly) from 7am to 3pm. There is one bus to Pokhara (Rs 700, 12 hours) at 5pm. Local buses run hourly to Birganj (Rs 250 to Rs 340, four hours) until about 3pm.

Four buses head east to **Kakarbhitta** (Rs 525, seven hours) from the dusty bus park near Zero Mile Chowk from 6am to 4pm. You'll also find several morning buses for Biratnagar (Rs 350, five hours) until 10.30am. Either of these buses can also be picked up at Ramanand Chowk, the preferred terminal, which is a Rs 50 rickshaw ride from central Janakpur.

TRAIN

A very slow metre-gauge railway leads across the border to India and the dusty plains town of Jaynagar. However, at the time of research the line was closed for a long-term upgrade. No trains will puff out of Janakpur until 2018 at the earliest. Train buffs might still enjoy the stroll down to the station to check out the pair of rusty old trains slowly dissolving into the vegetation.

Koshi Tappu Wildlife Reserve

📍 025

The smallest of the Terai's national parks, Koshi Tappu Wildlife Reserve is a birdwatcher's paradise. But you don't need to be a serious twitcher to enjoy it. Here you'll find a captivating walk that anyone will appreciate.

The park contains an ideal mix of river, ponds, wetlands and paddies, all of it cut by a long straight and paved trail, making navigation a breeze. Thin foliage further allows for long-distance viewing. In a single 90min, 6km walk you will see scores of different bird species. It's the terrestrial equivalent of spotting tropical fish on a coral reef.

An added bonus is branching off to the nearby Sapt Kosi River, where the endangered arna roam their last habitat. A kind of water buffalo, these black beasts are renowned for the enormous breadth of their horns, and move in herds.

Koshi Tappu ('river islands') was founded in 1976 to protect a small triangle of phanta and tappu (small islands) in the floodplain of the Sapt Kosi River – one of the three main tributaries of the Ganges. Consisting of 175 sq km of wet and grassland habitat, it is home to at least 527 species of birds, including rare species such as the swamp francolin and Bengal florican. Migratory species from Siberia and Tibet take up residence from November to February.

While it lacks heavy hitters like tigers and rhinos, the park is also home to many mammal and reptile species, including blue bulls, deer, golden jackals, marsh muggers, fishing cats, mongooses, civet cats and porcupines. Gangetic dolphins have been spotted from the bridge at Koshi Barrage, but sadly, their numbers are now so low no one is even sure how many are left. The park is also home to 12 wild elephants, some of whom have taken the lives of local villagers.

⊙ Sights

The park headquarters is located in Kusaha, near Koshi Tappu Birdwatching Camp, and contains a number of sights. Following the path from the main gate, you come first to the **Information Centre** (Kusaha; ⊙ 6am-6pm), actually a small museum, with displays of elephant, deer and arna skulls, along with a desiccated gharial.

As elsewhere in the Terai, park rangers use elephants to patrol the park. Continue on and you will eventually reach an **elephant camp**. Unfortunately, the sight of the five resident elephants here chained to posts is a depressing spectacle. If any wild elephants are present, be careful. Males come out of the forest to mate with the park elephants and in the process can be very hostile to visitors (one further assumes they like their privacy).

From here head to the **observation tower**. Apart from being the safest place of all if male elephants are around, it provides broad and pleasant views over the fields and forests near the park headquarters.

Coming soon to park headquarters: an animal rescue centre for eastern Nepal.

🏃 Activities

A popular way to explore Koshi is by elephant. Consider exploring the park on one of the many other animal-friendly ways, such as by river boat or jeep, however, as there is now overwhelming evidence to support claims by animal-welfare experts that elephant safaris are harmful to elephants.

Birdwatching

Every lodge has a resident ornithologist who leads bird-spotting walks around the park (usually included in package rates). Early morning, when the air is cool and the mist is lifting, and late afternoon as the sun varnishes the waters pink, are the prime birdwatching times and, birder or not, it's hard not to enjoy the experience.

Some of the lodges also have bird hides that can be a good spot to tick a few species off your list.

Jeep Safaris

Many lodges offer morning or late-afternoon jeep safaris as part of their package.

MITHILA ART

The vibrant artwork produced by Maithili women can be traced back as far as the 7th century and has been passed from generation to generation since. As the former capital of the kingdom of Mithila, Janakpur (p281) has emerged as the centre for both preserving and promoting this ancient art.

Mithila painting is part decoration and part social commentary, recording the lives of rural women in a society where reading and writing are reserved for high-caste men. Scenes in Mithila paintings colourfully record the female experience of life in the Terai – work, childbirth, marriage and the social network among village women. Today you will also see more modern subject matter, such as aeroplanes and buses, blended with traditional themes like Hindu mythology and village life.

Traditionally, Mithila paintings were used as a transient form of decoration during festivals when the mud walls of village huts were painted in white and ochre with abstract patterns or complex scenes of everyday village life. You can still see houses in the villages surrounding Janakpur with painted walls and raised patterns. More recently, Mithila painting has taken off as a more contemporary and collectable art form, with women artists painting on canvases of rough handmade paper that is similar in texture to the mud hut walls. Not only are Mithila paintings now exhibited in galleries across the world, but more importantly the art has also opened up a new industry for women in impoverished rural communities.

One of the best-known social projects is the **Janakpur Women's Development Centre** (JWDC, Nare Bekas Kendra; ☑ 041-620932, 9808205576; ◷ 10am-5pm Sun-Thu, to 4pm Fri Apr-Sep, 10am-4pm Sun-Fri Oct-Mar), just south of the city in the village of Kuwa. Around 40 Maithili women are employed at the centre, producing paper paintings, papier-mâché boxes and mirrors, screen-printed fabrics and hand-thrown ceramics. Money raised goes directly towards improving the lives of rural women. A rickshaw from Janakpur to the centre will cost around Rs 150 to Rs 200.

Although you're unlikely to see a huge amount of wildlife, it's a good way of getting a feel for the park and its habitat, and jeep safaris are normally combined with a birdwatching walk.

River Trips

Exploring the park on the river via a gentle paddle in a rubber dinghy, canoe or *dhunga* (wooden boat) is a great way to see larger wildlife, particularly arna, but isn't quite so good for birdwatching. Rates are usually included in the lodges' package rates; otherwise the going rate for a wooden boat and driver is Rs 1500 per hour or the lodges can supply a rubber dingy for US$50 per hour.

🛏 Sleeping & Eating

Prebooking for accommodation in the reserve is essential. While rates may appear exorbitant, keep in mind that they include all meals and activities. Lodges close during the monsoon (June to September).

There are two homestays near the park headquarters, one in Prakashpur and another in Madhuban; enquire at the park office.

Aquabirds Unlimited　　　　TENTED CAMP $
(☑ 9741370325, 9852830280; www.facebook.com/Aquabirds.Unlimited; full board incl birdwatching Rs 3500) This could be your budget approach to the park. Located on the edge of a rice paddie, this seasonal camp offers 10 basic tents (apart from their AC units!), with shared bathrooms some distance away. At the time of research local management was offering full board and activities for only Rs 3500 per person, a huge discount. How long this will last is anyone's guess. Located 1.5km from the national highway, just behind the reserve.

★ **Koshi Camp**　　　　TENTED CAMP $$$
(☑ 9851003677; www.koshicamp.co.uk; half-board s/d US$95/135, package per person per night US$155) Located in the delightful village of Madhuban, 7km from the highway, Koshi Camp has an attractive setting on the edge of the park, with its own pond and bird hide. Lodging is in tents with firm beds and huge ensuite bathrooms, making for a pleasant stay. The guides are superb. Open September to May.

The bird guides here are first-rate and the restaurant has a safari feel, with plenty of ornithological reading material on hand.

Koshi Tappu
Birdwatching Camp TENTED CAMP $$$
(📞9804020868, 9800930709; www.koshitappu.
net; full board incl birdwatching per person US$150)
Right next to the park offices and informa-
tion centre, this camp has five small and
immaculate tents with separate, shared
bathrooms on an island in a small artificial
pond, plus a couple of rooms in mud-walled
houses (same price as tents). All accommo-
dation options and grounds are nicely kept.
Open November to April.

Koshi Tappu
Wildlife Camp TENTED CAMP $$$
(📞01-4226130; www.koshitappu.com; half-board
s/d US$125/140, all-inclusive with activities s/d
US$225/340) The longest established of the
park's camps, this one has pleasingly landscaped gardens, a ramshackle bird hide
overlooking a swamp, and tents that don't
quite justify the high prices. Bathrooms are
in shared, separate blocks. It's in the village
of Prakashpur. Opens in November.

ⓘ Information

The **ticket office** (📞9852055405; per day for-
eigner/SAARC/child under 10yr Rs 1000/500/
free; ⊙7am-5pm) is located just inside the gate
to the park headquarters, but you will probably
not have to use it, as the price is added to the
cost of organised tours. Just be sure to bring
your ticket with you if you want to see the sights
at park headquarters.

ⓘ Getting There & Away

Most visitors come on a package tour with a
prearranged pick-up from Biratnagar airport,
but it's easy enough to travel here as an independent traveller. The best way is to fly from
Kathmandu to Biratnagar, then take a taxi (Rs
500 to Rs 600, 1½ hours) to the park.

By public transport, you can catch a bus along
the Mahendra Hwy to Laukahi (Rs 150 from
Biratnagar), 15km east of the Koshi Barrage. Get
off at the police station, from where rickshaws
serve both the Koshi Camp and Koshi Tappu
Wildlife Camp. Otherwise, call ahead for one of
the lodges to pick you up for around Rs 1000. For
the park headquarters and Koshi Tappu Birdwatching Camp, get off at Jamuha, from where
it's a further 2.5km walk.

Buses from Kathmandu (12 to 14 hours) are Rs
1000 for an ordinary bus and Rs 1200 for a deluxe bus (which, let's be honest, is only deluxe in
name), while from the east you can jump on any
bus heading along the Mahendra Hwy.

Biratnagar
📞021 / POP 210,000

Competing with Nepalganj and Janakpur
for the Terai's ultimate sprawling dusty
mess, Biratnagar looks like ground zero after a second strike. Worsening the unregu-
lated growth and lack of basic services was
the mass influx of people after 2015 due to
the city's reputation as a safe haven from
earthquakes. In any case, this is a pure transit point: there is nothing of interest to the
traveller apart from the bus station and the
airport.

🛏 Sleeping

Hotel Panchali HOTEL $
(📞021-472520; www.hotelpanchali.com.np; Nawa
Jyoti Marg; s/d with fan Rs 1200/1500, s/d Rs
2200/2500; ❊🛜) This garishly painted business hotel is one of three similar offerings
in this neighbourhood. Rooms are fairly
no-frills, but everything is kept ship-shape
smart and the bathrooms are, for once, fairly pleasant. The other choices are the Xenial
and Everest hotels down the street. It's close
to the bus park.

Hotel Eastern Star HOTEL $$
(📞021-471626; www.hoteleasternstar.com; Road-
cess Chowk; s/d with fan Rs 1500/1900, s/d with
AC from Rs 2400/2800; P❊🛜) This hotel
has a quiet location south of the bus park,
some English-speaking staff and a dose of
faded grandeur. The massive, well-furnished
rooms have comfortable beds, satellite TV
and clean bathrooms. There's a colourful In-
dian restaurant and well-stocked bar.

Ratna Hotel HOTEL $$
(📞021-470399; www.ratnahotel.com.np; Mahen-
dra Chowk; s/d with fan Rs 1800/2200, s/d with AC
2500/2800; P❊🛜) In a land where hotels
may go decades without a fresh coat of paint,
the new Ratna stands out. Relocated to a
new building from across the main street, it
now offers greatly improved rooms –
clean, bright and priced right. A major additional complex of 52 rooms, a pool and two
restaurants is set to open in 2019.

The outdoor Evening Round-Up Bar and
Grill adds hope of buffalo steak.

Hotel Swagatam HOTEL $$
(📞021-472450; www.hotelswagatam.com; Road-
cess Chowk; s/d with AC Rs 3000/3500, without AC
Rs 1500/2000) This old business hotel manag-
es an iota of charm, helped along by friendly

staff. There is a wide assortment of rooms, including some surprisingly good ones with tubs and wood floors. High-quality room 311 (Rs 4000) is great value. The best feature is a peaceful location off the highway. Located 50m south of Roadcess Chowk.

✕ Eating

Angan INDIAN **$**
(Main Rd; mains Rs 200-400; ☺8am-9pm) Part of an Indian chain, this restaurant and sweet shop offers cool, air-conditioned comfort and cleanliness. There's an array of veggie curries and tandoori dishes, but it's best known for its *dosa* and gulab jamun.

★Unique
Sweet & Snack VEGETARIAN, INDIAN **$$**
(Main Rd; mains Rs 320-380; ☺9am-9pm) This two-floor establishment is the perfect lunch stop. Fans of *dosa* will want to head upstairs to its popular South Indian vegetarian eatery, which offers an impressive array of *dosa* – the 'unique special *dosa*' is superb! Afterwards, pop down to the ground floor for dessert from the sweet shop. On Traffic Chowk.

❶ Information

There are several banks with ATMs along or just off Main Rd.

❶ Getting There & Away

AIR
Buddha Air (☑021-526901; www.buddhaair. com), **Yeti Airlines** (☑021-536612; www.yeti airlines.com), Saurya Airlines (www.saurya airlines.com) and Tara Air (www.taraair.com) all have numerous daily flights between Birat-nagar and Kathmandu (US$150 to US$190, 35 minutes). **Nepal Airlines** (☑021-470675; www. nepalairlines.com) serves Bhojpur on Tuesday, Thursday and Saturday at 10.30am, and Kha-nidanda on Monday and Saturday at 8.30am. A rickshaw to the airport costs Rs 400 to Rs 500.

BUS
The bus stand is a Rs 30 rickshaw ride south-west from Traffic Chowk in the city centre. There are hourly buses to Kathmandu (normal/deluxe/ air-con Rs 1050/1200/1500, 15 hours) via Narayangarh from 6am to 4pm, and two buses to Pokhara (Rs 1500, 15 hours) at 6am and 4pm. Several buses leave between 7am and 11am for Janakpur (Rs 800 to Rs 1000, six hours). There are also regular services to Kakarbhitta (Rs 200 to Rs 250, three hours, every 30 minutes) from the Mahendra Hwy.

Local buses run to Dharan (Rs 80, 1½ hours, every 10 minutes) throughout the day. There are also hourly buses to Dhankuta (Rs 300 to Rs 400, three hours) from 5am to 2pm, and to Hile (Rs 300 to Rs 500, 3½ hours).

Dharan to Hile

About 17km north of the busy and uneventful roadside town of Itahari, Dharan marks the start of yet another dramatic route into the hills. A decent paved road runs north from here into the foothills of the Himalaya, providing access to a series of attractive hill towns and trekking trailheads.

Dharan

☑025 / POP 125,000
The sprawling town of Dharan has three distinct characters. The far western perimeter feels like an affluent suburb, with quiet streets lined with well-maintained bungalows, neatly paved pavements, rubbish bins and a golf club. Until 1990 Dharan was the Gurkha recruiting area, and the relative wealth here is largely due to money repatriated by these world-famous Nepali–British soldiers. In contrast, the eastern side of town has steep streets and a relaxed village feel with banana plants, bamboo-forested hills and rustic shacks. Dividing the two areas is the lively Dharan Bazaar, which has a more typical Terai flavour, with its flat and dusty market.

Dharan is one of the *shakti peeths* marking the spot where part of the body of Shiva's first wife, Sati, fell after she was consumed by flames. There are several important Shaivite temples northeast of the centre in the village of Bijayapur. A short walk from here is the **Budha Subba Mandir**, set among dense bamboo thickets down the path, with a curious collection of rocks covered in mud – said to represent the reclining body of Mahadev (Shiva). You're likely to encounter chickens being sacrificed.

To reach Bijayapur, take a right at Chata Chowk (a 10-minute walk from Dharan Bazaar), which leads to steps at the bottom of the hill; from here it's a 20-minute walk. An autorickshaw costs Rs 300 return.

🛌 Sleeping & Eating

★ **New Dreamland Hotel & Lodge** HOTEL **$**
(☑025-525024; Dhankute Rd; r with/without bathroom Rs 1200/700, with AC Rs 2300; P ✳ ☎)

With two floors of wraparound verandah, spacious halls and well-kept gardens, this extraordinary bargain wins you over with its charming tropical colonial ambience. One can imagine Maugham characters sipping gin at sunset. Located in the best section of Dharan, its only drawback is foam mattresses. Head west three blocks from Bhanu Chowk, the clock tower square in the town centre.

Hotel Nava Yug GUESTHOUSE $
(☑025-524797; www.facebook.com/hotelnavayug; Dhesi Line; r with/without AC Rs 2400/1800; ❄ 🛜) This newly renovated hotel has a hilarious entrance: having removed the entire previous hotel from a city block, as if with a drunken backhoe, they simply put the new front door in the rear of the remains. It is like entering a tooth through a cavity. Nevertheless, the fan rooms are very nice, with large baths and new furnishings, if hard mattresses.

And the new location is certainly quieter than previously. Only the in-house restaurant suffers: it's now like a cave.

★**Olive Cafe & Restaurant** PIZZERIA, INTERNATIONAL $$
(Putali Line; pizzas Rs 295-330; mains Rs 300; ⏲10am-10pm) This place must have got lost on its way to Thamel, the tourist central of Kathmandu, but we're sure glad it did. It offers very acceptable wood-fired pizzas, as well as some local dishes and pasta creations, all served up in a setting, adorned with wooden masks, that invites you to linger over dinner.

🍷 Drinking & Nightlife

Nectar Juice Bar JUICE BAR
(Putali Line; juices Rs 150-250; ⏲9am-9pm; 🛜) This splash of flavour is just the type of contemporary spin Dharan needs – and after a hard day of travel, you'll appreciate it too. Choose from a wild assortment of juices and smoothies from the Kiwi Mint Punch to the Cocoa Banana smoothie. Along the Putali Line, across from Baskin Robbins. You do have to be patient with the juicemakers.

ℹ️ Getting There & Away

Two buses a day leave from Bhanu Chowk for Kathmandu (normal/deluxe Rs 800/1000, 14 hours), with the first at 4am and the last at 5pm. There is also a 7am microbus that travels via the Sindhuli road (Rs 1250, seven to eight hours).

Heading south, there are buses to Biratnagar (Rs 80, 1½ hours). Local buses run north regularly from 5am to 4pm to Bhedetar (Rs 55, 45 minutes, every 15 minutes), Dhankuta (Rs 150, three hours) and Hile (Rs 250, four hours). There are also buses heading east to the Indian border at Kakarbhitta (Rs 350, four to five hours).

Bhedetar
☑026 / POP 2750
Arriving from the hot dusty plains of the Terai, the cool climate of tiny, laid-back Bhedetar makes for a refreshing change. Perched at 1420m, the soaring views over Everest and Makalu are spectacular on a clear day. The village basically exists as a mountain viewpoint for local tourists. Unfortunately the main viewpoint, **Charles Tower**, has been closed since the 2015 earthquake, and is not expected to reopen until 2019 at the earliest. The town's fortunes appear to have waned accordingly.

The frequent buses plying the hills between Dharan and Hile all stop in Bhedetar.

🛏️ Sleeping & Eating

Hotel Arun Valley GUESTHOUSE $
(☑9842450740; r Rs 1200-1600, without bathroom Rs 600; 🛜) Hotel Arun Valley is a pleasant place to spend the night. Set among a garden of bright flowers, its rooms are delightfully decorated with thick carpets, wicker furniture and comfortable beds with warm blankets. The restaurant here is also the best place to eat in Bhedetar. Follow the upper road that splits off the highway towards Hile.

Hile
☑026 / POP 2500
Hile was once the starting point for the camping trek to Makalu and the end point for the lodge trek from Lukla, but the road has advanced along the valley, now reaching as far as Basantapur. As a result, Hile is no longer the busy trekking hub it once was, and its hotels feel mildly abandoned because of it. Nevertheless, the village has a bustling bazaar feel, particularly during the weekly Thursday market, and there's a good mountain viewpoint about 30 minutes' walk above town (follow the Basantapur road to the army post and then turn north along the trail to Hattikharka). If neither of those appeal, it's simply a fine place to get off the beaten track.

🛏 Sleeping & Eating

Most hotels serve filling Tibetan food and warming wooden pots of *tongba* (hot millet beer).

Kanjirowa Makalu Hotel   HOTEL $
(☑ 026-540509; r with/without AC Rs 1500/2500; 📶) This smart red-brick hotel has the best rooms in Hile, but that doesn't imply soft mattresses or functioning hot-water heaters. Thankfully 12 new rooms are on the way. The restaurant/bar has a good international menu and an impressive cocktail list, but food is glacial in both serving time and temperature.

Located on the left side of the main road about 500m before entering town. The hotel has two gates, but only the second one is used.

Hotel Mountain   HOTEL $
(☑ 026-540403; r with/without bathroom Rs 700/500) This lodge is marginally better than the other rough accommodation options in the town centre. There are valley views from the rear-facing balconies and a reasonable restaurant serving the basics (mains Rs 120 to Rs 200). Choose your room carefully. Located on the main road just south of town centre, across the street from Rastriya Banijya Bank and near the bus park.

ℹ Getting There & Away

Frequent local buses run from Dharan to Hile (Rs 250, two hours, every 20 minutes), with the last bus at 4.30pm. A few continue up the Arun Valley as far as Leguwa (Rs 120, three hours, every three to four hours). Some buses from Dharan continue to Basantapur (Rs 100 from Hile, 1½ hours).

Ilam

☑ 027 / POP 20,000

Situated in the far east of Nepal, 90km from the border at Kakarbhitta, Ilam ('ee-lam') is reached via the Mechi Hwy, one of the Terai's great mountain roads, with plenty of switchbacks, vertiginous drops and valley views. It's also in excellent condition. Upon entering the mountain village you'll notice its charming wooden buildings, their balconies thrust out over the bustling street – unusual in the Terai.

Like its neighbour Darjeeling across the border, Ilam is synonymous with one thing – tea. The two share an almost identical climate and topography, although Darjeeling tea is by far the better known. The tea fields that carpet the surrounding hills make for a very peaceful walk in refreshing mountain air.

⊙ Sights

Ilam View Tower   VIEWPOINT
(Rs 150) This tower offers captivating views of the Ilam Bazaar and the remote villages of surrounding valleys. There's also a daal bhaat restaurant (meals Rs 250 to Rs 300) where you can buy a drink.

🛏 Sleeping

Chiyabari Cottage Ilam   GUESTHOUSE $
(☑ 027-520149, 9842636512; www.ilamchiyabari.com; r Rs 1700; 📶) Perched on the hill overlooking magical views of the tea plantations and surrounding hills, this cheery guesthouse has spacious rooms enlivened by small aquariums. Now that's new! It's also a top spot for a meal or drink at sunset. Call to arrange free transport pick-up to avoid the sweaty climb up. Located just a few hundred metres south of the view tower.

Green View Guest House   HOTEL $
(☑ 9842627063, 027-520616; www.greenviewilam.com; Campus Rd; old building r with/without bathroom Rs 1000/500, new building r Rs 1500-3000; 📶) An interior designer's nightmare, Green View has basic rooms where everything clashes, but it's otherwise well run, friendly and has a prime location at the edge of a tea garden. Several rooms out the back do indeed have a green view (your best choice). Cheaper rooms, which share bathrooms, are across the road in a separate building; room 502 has a prime balcony.

Summit Hotel   HOTEL $$
(☑ 027-520972; www.summithotelilam.com; Narayansthan Marg; r with/without AC Rs 4000/1500) The nicest hotel in Ilam, the Summit has a glass front allowing for rooms with glass sitting areas and nice views (Rs 4000), some of which sleep four. Others in the Rs 2000 range are quite cosy, too; Rs 5000 gets you the honeymoon suite.

🔒 Shopping

★ **Ilam Tea House**   TEA
(☑ 9842646121; www.ilamteahouse.com; ⊙ 7am-7pm) This superb little shop has every tea product that you could possibly want to buy, and some charming old ladies to sell it to you. Located near the Green View Guest House, its counter opens directly onto the street.

❶ Information

There are several ATMs in the bazaar, while Bank of Asia up the road also has an ATM and can exchange foreign currency.

❶ Getting There & Away

The dusty bus/jeep stand is to the west of town, while the taxi stand is just off the main square.

The road to Ilam branches off at two points along the Mahendra Hwy. Buses and jeeps depart at either Charali (if arriving from Kakarbhitta) or Birtamod (if you're coming from Kathmandu). Jeeps do the journey in a little more than three hours (Rs 250) from either place. There is one daily bus direct to Kathmandu (Rs 1700, 16 hours) at 2pm.

If you're heading high to conquer the Kanchenjunga trails, jeeps go fairly frequently throughout the morning to Taplejung (Rs 1200, six to seven hours).

Around Ilam

A pleasant half-day trip from Ilam is the attractive lake at **Mai Pokhari**. The 1½-hour jeep trip along a rocky track leads you to this peaceful spot, which was declared a heritage site in 2008. An important pilgrimage site for Hindus and Buddhists, the lake is a striking emerald colour and is covered in water lilies and teeming with goldfish. Surrounded by cone trees and rhododendrons (which bloom in March), it makes for a beautiful stroll, and is home to 300 species of birds.

Your best bet to get here is to catch a jeep or taxi to Biblate (Rs 50), from where you can arrange onward transport to Mai Pokhari. Otherwise it makes for an excellent eight-hour round-trip walk from Ilam.

Some other trips possible from Ilam include the **Kanyam Tea Gardens**, located 46km from Ilam (taxi Rs 200), where you can visit the tea factory. If you're getting the bus here, it's about a 15-minute walk down the hill to the factory. Here you'll also find a picnic spot popular with groups of merry Nepali teenagers.

Another excellent option is a visit to **Sandakpur**, on the border with India, where you can watch an incredible sunrise over four of the world's five highest peaks; it's also a habitat for red pandas. However, it's not the easiest place to get to: it involves getting a taxi from Ilam Bazaar to Biblate (Rs 35, 15 minutes), then another taxi for 2½ hours to Khorsanitar (Rs 250 if you're lucky enough to find a shared taxi; otherwise a privately hired jeep from Ilam to Khorsanitar will cost around Rs 6000 for a special hire). Once you finally get to Khorsanitar it's a six-hour walk to Sandakpur. There are several basic lodges here, and you'll need to ensure you bring warm clothing.

Kakarbhitta

📞 023 / POP 22,000

Kakarbhitta (Kakarvitta) is the easternmost crossing between India and Nepal, and just a few hours' drive from Siliguri and Darjeeling in West Bengal and Gangtok in Sikkim. Nevertheless, this is not just another dusty Terai border town. Perhaps it is due to the tea and rice fields that surround it, or its peaceful riverfront location, but it feels more contained, and more intimate. It's definitely cleaner. So regardless of its bustling centre, you don't feel as stressed, and won't mind hanging around for awhile, if you want to get to know the place. With hardly any tourism, you will be steeped in authentic tea country.

🛏 Sleeping & Eating

Hotel Rajat HOTEL $
(📞 09851089479; tw Rs 2000-2500, r with AC Rs 1600; ❄ 🛜) The welcome here is friendly and the rooms are simple but well lit. The pricier rooms are worth the difference. But cheap or expensive, all rooms are very pink. There's a bistro-like restaurant with gingham tablecloths downstairs. It's just behind the bus stand, and may get a bit noisy.

Hotel Darbar HOTEL $$
(📞 023-562384; www.facebook.com/hoteldarbar. nepal; s/d Rs 2500/3500; ❄ 🛜) The Darbar offers large, carpeted and well-furnished rooms with fans and air-con and hot-water bathrooms. There's a generator to keep you lit up during the town's frequent blackouts. The sophisticated owner speaks superb English and is well travelled in the Terai. Located in the centre of town, on the main street.

★ Ghaari Restaurant NEPALI $$
(mains Rs 150-600; ⊙ 9am-9pm) Easily the best place to eat and drink in Kakarbhitta, this hugely popular riverside restaurant comes as a bit of a shock it's so nice. Located 1km north of the border, it has a great elevated position overlooking the water towards India. Individual dining pavilions set amidst stands of bamboo ensure privacy. Extensive bar menu.

CROSSING THE BORDER: KAKARBHITTA TO PANITANKI

Border Hours
Both sides of the border are staffed from around 7am to 10pm, however, when it's cold/ wet the border hours can be more flexible and sometimes close as early as 7pm. At such times you can often still cross but you'll need to go searching for immigration officials.

Foreign Exchange
There are numerous foreign-exchange services on either side of the border, including Nepal Bank, which also has an ATM.

Onward to India
It's about 100m from the Kakarbhitta bus stand to the border, and a little under 1km to the Indian border post at Panitanki (aka Raniganj) – around Rs 100 by rickshaw from Kakarbhitta bus stand to the Indian border including waiting time at the Nepali immigration. Otherwise you can catch a shared taxi or jeep from outside the Nepali immigration office to Siliguri for ₹200 (or ₹1200 for a special hire). From Siliguri you can head to Darjeeling by shared jeep (₹200 to ₹300, three hours). You can also catch a train to Kolkata, the Kanchanjunga Express (sleeper/3A 350/950, 11½ hours), which departs at 7.50am, and the Darjeeling Mail (sleeper/3A 400/1200, 10 hours) departing at 8pm.

ⓘ Information

Tourist Information Centre (⊙ 6am-7pm Sun-Fri) The government of Nepal runs a small tourist information centre just before the border. It's more country-wide than local information, but staff is friendly.

Nepal Bank (⊙ 10am-5pm) has an ATM close to the border. There are several money exchange offices.

ⓘ Getting There & Away

AIR
The nearest airport is at Bhadrapur, 10km southeast of Birtamod, which in turn is 13km west of Kakarbhitta. A taxi from Kakarbhitta bus stand to the airport costs Rs 1500, or you can take a local bus to Birtamod, then a second bus to Bhadrapur followed by a rickshaw to the airport. **Yeti Airlines** (☏ Bhadrapur 023-455232; www.yetiairlines.com) and **Buddha Air** (☏ Bhadrapur 023-455218; www.buddhaair.com) have daily flights to Kathmandu (around US$135, 50 minutes). **Nepal Airlines** (☏ Bhadrapur

023-456638; www.nepalairlines.com) also has similar flights on Sunday, Wednesday, and Friday in the afternoon. Any of the travel agents around the bus stand can issue tickets, including **Jhapa Travels** (☏ 023-562820, 023-562020; www.jhapatravel.com.np).

BUS
Travel agents in Kathmandu and Pokhara offer 'through-tickets' to Darjeeling, but you must change buses at Kakarbhitta. It is just as easy, and cheaper, to do the trip in stages. A jeep or bus from Karkarbhitta to Darjeeling is Rs 110.

There is one bus to Kathmandu (standard/deluxe Rs 1145/1375, 14 to 16 hours) at 4am, then every half-hour from 4pm to 6pm. There are also buses to Pokhara (Rs 1140, 15 hours), which depart at the same times.

To get to Ilam, there are plenty of buses to Birtamod (Rs 50, 25 minutes, every 15 minutes until 6pm), from where you can take a bus or jeep. There are 4am buses to Janakpur (Rs 750, seven hours), Biratnagar (Rs 300, 3½ hours) and Birganj (Rs 1200, 10 hours).

Trekking Routes

Best Everest Detours

➡ Gokyo Lakes (p299)

➡ Chhukung (p298)

➡ Kunde & Khumjung (p297)

Best Annapurna Detours

➡ Milarepa's Cave (p304)

➡ Upper Pisang (p304)

➡ Jhong & Purang (p305)

➡ Praken Gompa (p304)

Why Go?

Easily the best way to see Nepal is on foot, following a network of trails trodden for centuries by porters, traders, pilgrims, mountaineers and locals travelling from village to village, plains to hills, Nepal to Tibet. Nothing beats walking under your own steam under a crystal-clear Himalayan sky, passing Sherpa, Gurung and Thakali villages, Tibetan monasteries and sacred lakes, while staring at a range of 8000m peaks.

Treks in the Langtang, Annapurna and Everest regions are ideal for travellers who want to trek without too much forward planning – permits are easy to organise and trekking lodges line the trails, offering meals and accommodation.

Our best advice is not to rush your walk. Adding on a few days to your itinerary allows you to take in side trips, detours and monasteries, or just take a day off every now and then. These just might end up being the highlights of your trip.

When to Go

➡ For the clearest skies and most pleasant temperatures, but also high-season crowds, visit during October and November.

➡ March through to early May rhododendron blooms in the mountains but there are high temperatures in the lowlands.

➡ A good time for visiting upper Mustang and Dolpo is July through to September, however you'll encounter monsoon clouds and leeches elsewhere.

CHOOSING A TREK

Teahouse treks account for the bulk of trekking trips in Nepal, largely because of the convenience of being able to get food and accommodation every few hours along the trail. Easily the most popular options are the Annapurna Circuit Trek and Everest Base Camp Trek. Both treks offer spectacular scenery, cultural depth and plenty of scope for detours, as well as plenty of crowds.

Over the last few years Everest has become very busy in high season, while the Annapurna region has been affected at both beginning and end by road construction. The Annapurna Circuit has the advantage of being a loop route, while Everest is an out-and-back trek, returning to Lukla via the same route unless you add on the excellent side trips to the Gokyo Lakes or over the Three Passes. Everest requires a return flight (or weeklong approach walk), which makes it a more expensive option than Annapurna.

An excellent alternative to these big two treks is the Langtang region to the north of Kathmandu. The Langtang Valley, Gosainkund and Helambu treks were all hit hard by the 2015 earthquake but lodges have been rebuilt and the treks are once again firmly open for business. Trek in this region and you'll be contributing directly to the area's economic regeneration, while enjoying some of Nepal's finest and most varied mountain scenery.

If that's not enough for you, it is also possible to combine treks. The Annapurna Sanctuary Trek is easily pinned onto the end of the Annapurna Circuit to create a full month

of superb trekking. Join the Langtang and Gosainkund treks together and you'll get two weeks of walking that brings you all the way back into the Kathmandu Valley.

For full information on these routes, as well as camping and teahouse treks in more remote regions, see Lonely Planet's *Trekking in the Nepal Himalaya*.

Shorter Treks

If you don't have time for a big trek, several shorter treks from Pokhara in the southern foothills of the Annapurnas can give you a delightful taste of life on Nepal's trails. The Ghandruk Loop (three days) and Ghorepani and Ghandruk loop (six days) both offer fine mountain views, villages and trekking lodges, while trips to Ghachok or Panchase offer quieter trails away from the main Annapurna routes. All are excellent low-altitude or winter choices.

It's also possible to cobble together a mini-trek of several days around the rim of the Kathmandu Valley via Chisopani, Nagarkot and Dhulikhel, linking medieval towns, Himalayan viewpoints and the Tibetan pilgrimage site of Namobuddha.

You can also throw in a couple of flights here and there to speed up the trekking process. As an example, fly in to Jomsom, overnight in Marpha (to aid acclimatisation) and take a few days to hike to the surrounding villages of Kagbeni, Thini and Muktinath before flying back to Pokhara for a four- or five-day trip.

A weeklong Everest taster from Lukla could take you on a delightful loop through Namche Bazaar, Thame, Khunde, Khumjung and Tengboche Monastery. This is a particularly good option in winter (December to February) or if you want to avoid high altitude.

LIFE ON THE TRAIL

Routes & Conditions

Most teahouse trails are clear, signposted and easy to follow, though they are often steep and taxing, with long stretches of switchbacks or knee-jarring stone staircases. A typical day's walk lasts from between five to seven hours and rarely spends much time on level ground. You'll soon realise that distances on the map are largely irrelevant

---

EARTHQUAKE DAMAGE IN TREKKING AREAS

With most trekking lodges around Nepal built using traditional methods, it would have been impossible for trekking to not be affected by the 2015 earthquake. The Annapurna region and eastern and western Nepal were mostly unaffected. The Everest region also escaped the worst, though many died in an avalanche at Everest Base Camp, and houses and lodges were damaged around Namche Bazaar and Thame. Hundreds of trekkers and local people lost their lives in Langtang, Helambu and Manaslu but most lodges have been rebuilt and these trekking routes are once again open for business.

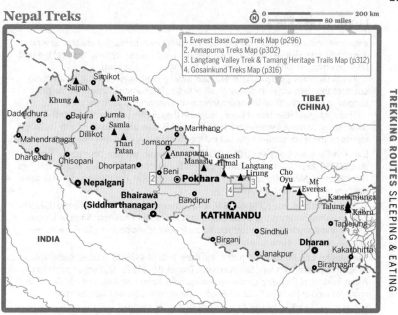

0 ⟶ 200 km
0 ⟶ 80 miles

1. Everest Base Camp Trek Map (p296)
2. Annapurna Treks Map (p302)
3. Langtang Valley Trek & Tamang Heritage Trails Map (p312)
4. Gosainkund Treks Map (p316)

given the many ups and downs and twists and turns of Nepal's trails.

A rudimentary knowledge of the Nepali language will help to make your trek easier and more interesting, although finding your way is rarely difficult on the major trekking routes and English is widely spoken.

Sleeping & Eating

On the Everest and Annapurna treks it's unlikely that you will walk more than an hour or two without coming across some kind of teahouse offering food and lodging, giving you great flexibility to walk as far as you wish and avoid the crowds. These lodges range from plywood barracks-style extensions of a traditional family home to quite luxurious places with private rooms, multipage menus, attached toilets and wi-fi.

Most mattresses are foam and some bedding is always supplied. Nevertheless, it's still a good idea to carry a sleeping bag, especially at higher elevations and during peak season.

Solar-heated hot showers or a bucket of hot water are often available for between Rs 100 and Rs 400, and most places can recharge your batteries for around Rs 250. Solar lighting is the norm at higher altitudes.

When choosing a room always consider:
➡ the thickness of the foam mattress
➡ proximity to the smoky, noisy kitchen or the fragrant, noisy bathroom
➡ a corner room offers more light but is generally colder at high altitudes

Food in teahouses centres on endless carb combinations of pasta, noodles, potato, rice and vegetables, plus momos (dumplings), spring rolls and a half-dozen types of tea, by the cup or pot. Breakfast is normally eggs, porridge or muesli with hot milk. The local staple of daal bhaat (rice, lentils and vegetables) is nutritious, available everywhere and requires minimum fuel for preparation. With most places offering a free refill of rice and daal, it's also the only meal that will truly fill you up after a day's trekking.

Lodges on the main trails stock expensive Snickers bars, toilet paper etc but it's wise to carry your own emergency food supplies such as muesli bars, dried fruit or chocolate. You can save some money by bringing your own instant coffee, though most places charge a fee for a cup of boiling water.

The lodges and cafes around Jomsom, Namche Bazaar and even Kyanjin Ri specialise in delicious apple pie, a trekkers' staple these days, along with local versions

LUXURY TREKKING

If you demand a bit of luxury on your trek and don't want to rough it in a tent, several companies offer deluxe lodges in the Annapurna and Everest regions. You'll get the best rates on an organised trek (as opposed to turning up on your own).

Ker & Downey (Map p70; ☎01-4435686; www.keranddowneynepal.com; Bhatbhateni) operates treks staying in its deluxe chain of lodges in Dhampus, Ghandruk, Majgaun, Landruk and Birethanti on the approaches to the Annapurna Sanctuary.

There is a good selection of luxury lodges in the lower reaches of the Everest region, allowing you to make a weeklong trek to Namche Bazaar and around. Priority is given to guests on these company's treks but independent trekkers can also make bookings.

Everest Summit Lodges (☎01-4371537; www.everestlodges.com; Dhumbarahi, Kathmandu; r US$130-200) Operates the luxury Everest Summit Lodges in Lukla, Monjo, Tashinga (near Photse), Mende (near Thame) and Pangboche, as well as the Annapurna Lodge in Kagbeni on the Annapurna Circuit.

Yeti Mountain Home (☎01-4413847; www.yetimountainhome.com; r half-board US$250-270) A chain of six attractive stone lodges in Lukla, Monjo, Phakding, Namche Bazaar, Thame and Kongde, the latter on a particularly remote and spectacular ridge. A new lodge is planned for Debuche in 2019.

Himalayan Eco Resorts (Map p90; ☎in Kathmandu 01-4424249, in Lobuche 9841984132; www.himalayanecoresort.com; Bhagwan Bahal, Thamel; d US$15-25) Midrange resorts run by Asian Trekking at Phakding (under reconstruction), Khumjung, Lobuche and Gokyo, with more planned at Namche Bazaar, Debuche, Dingboche, Dole and Macchermo.

Hotel Everest View (☎038-540118, in Kathmandu 01-5180047; www.hoteleverestview.com; Shyangboche; s/d US$140/194, incl meals US$256/405) Said to be the highest hotel in the world, on a ridge above Namche Bazaar.

Beyul Hermitage & Farm (☎9813766450; www.thebeyul.com; Chhuserma; r per person with three meals US$100) A stylish and secluded luxe option, off the main Everest trekking trail between Ghat and Phakding, with six rooms and occasional 10-day Vipassana retreats.

of pizza. After a week or more on the trail you might find yourself succumbing to the charms of a Snickers roll (Snickers wrapped in a chapati and fried) or a Mustang coffee (fortified with a shot of *rakshi*).

It's surprising how many places even have cold beer available as well; before you complain about the price (up to Rs 700), consider that somebody had to carry that bottle of beer all the way up there and will probably have to carry the empty bottle back again!

You should bring your own form of water purification, either chemical tablets, a filter or a Steripen.

EVEREST BASE CAMP TREK

Duration 14 to 20 days

Maximum elevation 5545m

Best season October to December

Start Lukla

Finish Lukla

Permits Sagarmatha National Park ticket, local admission permit

Summary Spectacular high mountain scenery, Sherpa culture, excellent lodges and views of beautiful Mt Ama Dablam are the highlights of this busy and popular trek.

Everybody wants a glimpse of the world's highest mountain and that's the reason why the Everest Base Camp Trek is so popular. The trek has a number of stunning attractions, not least of these is being able to say you've visited the highest mountain in the world. The trek gets you right into the high-altitude heart of the high Himalaya, more so than any other teahouse trek. There are some lovely villages and gompas (monasteries), and the friendly Sherpa people of the Solu Khumbu region make trekking through the area a joy.

Most of the trek is through the **Sagarmatha National Park** (Monjo; adult Rs 3000; ⊙6am-6pm), a Unesco World Heritage Site

(Sagarmatha is the Nepali name for Everest) and a refuge for musk deer, snow leopard, Himalayan tahr, black bear and many spectacular types of iridescent pheasant.

A return trek to Everest Base Camp from the airstrip at Lukla takes at least 14 days but you are better off budgeting a further week to take in some of the stunning and less-visited side valleys. If you have the time, one way to beat the crowds and acclimatise slowly is to walk in from Shivalaya (six days). If you fly straight to Lukla, be sure to schedule acclimatisation days at Namche and Pheriche to avoid altitude sickness.

The trek reaches a high point of 5545m at Kala Pattar, a small peak offering views of Mt Everest and the Khumbu Icefall. Ironically, the Everest views from base camp are actually quite unimpressive (in the words of mountain writer Ed Douglas, 'Everest is like a grossly fat man in a room full of beautiful women'). Far more stirring are the graceful lines of surrounding peaks, such as Ama Dablam, Pumori and Nuptse. Perhaps the best scenery of the trek is found in the neighbouring Gokyo Valley, off the main trail.

In the last decade the tourist crowds in the Khumbu region have swollen to record numbers, with 36,000 attempting the trek each year. This is one trek you might consider tackling outside of October or November, when you won't face such a scramble for bed space and aeroplane seats.

Facilities on the Everest trek are excellent. The upper reaches of the trek are through essentially uninhabited areas but lodges operate throughout the trekking season. These days trekking and mountaineering are the backbone of the Sherpa economy. More than half of the population in the region is now involved with tourism, and the bookstore, trek-gear shops, bakeries and internet cafes in Namche Bazaar make it look more like an alpine resort than a Sherpa village.

The villages of Khumjung, Pheriche and Thame were badly affected by the 2015 earthquake but most lodges have been rebuilt and there is accommodation in all the key overnight stops.

The walking on this trek is (surprisingly) not all that strenuous, mainly because new arrivals can only walk a few hours each day before they have to stop for the night to acclimatise. If trekkers fail to reach their goal it is usually because they failed to devote enough time to acclimatisation. It may be tempting to keep walking at the end of a three-hour day, but it's essential to take it slowly on the first 10 days of this trek.

The introduction by local Sherpa authorities of a Rs 2000 entry fee to the Everest region has effectively replaced the TIMS card here, so there's no need to get a TIMS card (p38) in Kathmandu if you are just headed to the Everest region.

Emergency Facilities

There are small hospitals in Jiri, Phaplu and Khunde (just north of Namche Bazaar); the Himalayan Rescue Association (HRA) has a medical facility in Pherichen and at Everest Base Camp. In the Gokyo Valley the International Porters Protection Group runs clinics in Machhermo and Gokyo. All three have foreign doctors and offer a recommended free daily talk on acute mountain sickness (AMS) at 3pm.

Access

Most Everest trekkers opt to fly to Lukla (US$177) from Kathmandu to maximise their time in the high mountains, and up to 75 flights land here each day during the high season. Tara Air has the most flights and is the best option. Backlogs of hundreds of trekkers (7000 in October 2011!) can build up during spates of bad weather, so give yourself a buffer of a day or two to get back to Kathmandu.

Flight safety at Lukla is not good. In 2008 a Yeti Airlines plane crashed here due to bad visibility, killing all 18 passengers. In 2010 an Agni Air plane crashed between Lukla and Kathmandu, killing 14. In 2012 a Sita Air flight to Lukla crashed near Kathmandu, killing all on board. In May 2017 a Goma Air (now Summit Air) freight plane crashed at Lukla, killing two.

As an alternative, consider the weeklong trek in from Shivalaya near Jiri.

Shivalaya Trek

While most people fly in and out of Lukla these days, it's possible to trek in or out from the trailhead at Shivalaya, just past Jiri. The trek from Shivalaya to Lukla is a hard slog and pretty sparse in the breathtaking-views department, but you will have the trails to yourself. The trek doesn't follow valleys, it cuts across them, so day after day it is a tiring process of dropping down one side of a steep valley and climbing up the other.

Everest Base Camp Trek

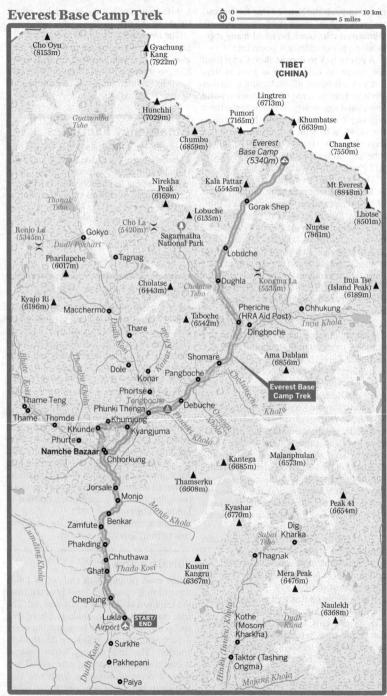

N

0 ————— 10 km
0 ————— 5 miles

Cho Oyu
(8153m)

Gyachung
Kang
(7922m)

**TIBET
(CHINA)**

Hunchhi
(7029m)

Lingtren
(6713m)

Gyazumtha
Tsho

Pumori
(7165m)

Khumbatse
(6639m)

Chumbu
(6859m)

*Everest
Base Camp
(5340m)*

Changtse
(7550m)

Thonak
Tsho

Nirekha
Peak
(6169m)

Kala Pattar
(5545m)

Mt Everest
(8848m)

Renjo La
(5345m)

Gokyo

Cho La
(5420m)

Lobuche
(6135m)

Gorak Shep

Lhotse
(8501m)

Dudh Pokhari

Sagarmatha
National Park

Nuptse
(7861m)

Pharilapche
(6017m)

Tagnag

Lobuche

Kyajo Ri
(6186m)

Macchermo

Cholatse
(6443m)

Cholatse
Tsho

Dughla

Kongma La
(5535m)

Imja Tse
(Island Peak)
(6189m)

Thare

Taboche
(6542m)

Pheriche
(HRA Aid Post)

Chhukung

Dudh Kosi

Imja Khola

Dole

Konar

Pangboche

Dingboche

Ama Dablam
(6856m)

Konar Khola

Shomare

**Everest Base
Camp Trek**

Phortse

Bhote Kosi

Thesbu Khola

Thame Teng

Thame

Thomde

Phunki Thenga

Tengboche

Debuche

Khumjung

Khunde

Kyangjuma

Phunki Khola

Imja Khola

Phurte

Namche Bazaar

Chhorkung

Kanteng
(6685m)

Malanphulan
(6573m)

Jorsale

Thamserku
(6608m)

Monjo

Zamfute

Benkar

Monjo Khola

Kyashar
(6770m)

Peak 41
(6654m)

Phakding

Lunding Khola

Chhuthawa

Thado Kosi

Dig
Kharka

Ghat

Sabai
Tsho

Thagnak

Cheplung

Kusum
Kangru
(6367m)

Mera Peak
(6476m)

Lukla
Airport

**START/
END**

Surkhe

Kothe
(Mosom
Kharkha)

Dudh
Kund

Naulekh
(6368m)

Pakhepani

Dudh Kosi

Hinku (Inuku) Khola

Paiya

Taktor (Tashing
Ongma)

Mojang Khola

By the time you reach the base camp, your ascents will total almost 9000m – the full height of Everest from sea level!

Note that villages along this route were damaged in the 2015 earthquake, and buildings were destroyed in Jiri and Shivalaya. Lodges are apparently back up and running but it's a good idea to check locally to make sure that accommodation is available at all your planned stops before embarking on this route.

Kathmandu's Ratna Park (City) bus station has buses at 6am and 8am to Jiri (Rs 580, six hours) and Shivalaya (Rs 690, eight hours), and you may also find a direct bus to Bhandar. Buy tickets in the station the day before. Keep a close eye on your luggage.

Proposed road construction from Jiri to Surkhe (just before Lukla) will likely change this trek over the coming years. Dirt roads currently run to Bhandar and Kinja.

The trek stages generally work out as follows:

Day 1: Shivalaya to Bhandar

Day 2: Bhandar to Sete

Day 3: Sete to Junbesi

Day 4: Junbesi to Nunthala

Day 5: Nunthala to Bupsa

Day 6: Bupsa to Lukla

The Trek

Day One: Lukla to Phakding

After flying to Lukla, arranging your packs and maybe a porter, trek downhill to lodges at Cheplung (Chablung). From here the trail contours along the side of the Dudh Kosi Valley before ascending to Ghat (Lhawa; 2530m). The trail climbs again to Phakding, a boisterous collection of 25 lodges and several bars at 2610m. Alternatively, you could continue to Zamfute or Benkar.

Day Two: Phakding to Namche Bazaar

The trail crosses the river on a long, swaying bridge and then leads you along the river to climb to Benkar (2700m); a decent alternative overnight stop. A short distance beyond Benkar the trail crosses the Dudh Kosi on a suspension bridge to its east bank, and then climbs to Chumoa.

From Chumoa, it's a short climb through forests to Monjo (2800m), where there are some good places to stay, despite a fair bit of earthquake damage. Show your park ticket or buy one for Rs 3390 at the Sagarmatha National Park entrance station (you will probably also have to pay a Rs 2000 local entry fee introduced in late 2017), then descend to cross the Dudh Kosi. On the other side it's a short distance to Jorsale (Thumbug; 2830m), the last settlement before Namche Bazaar. This is a good lunch stop, though several places were damaged by the quake. The trail then crosses back to the east side of the river before climbing to the high suspension bridge over the Dudh Kosi.

It's a tough two-hour climb from here to Namche Bazaar (3420m). As this is the first climb to an altitude where acute mountain sickness (AMS), also known as altitude sickness, may be a problem, take it easy and avoid rushing. Halfway up is a public toilet marking the first views of Everest. There is another national park entrance station just below Namche where permits are again checked.

Day Three: Acclimatisation Day in Namche Bazaar

Namche Bazaar is the main trade and administrative centre for the entire Solu Khumbu region and has outdoor gear shops, restaurants, bakeries, pharmacies, hotels with hot showers, bars, massage, a post office, a moneychanger, a bank, an ATM and wi-fi everywhere. Pay a visit to the **Sherpa Culture Museum** (☎038-540005; www.sherpa-culture.com.np; Chhorkhung; admission Rs 100; ⊙6am-sunset), on the ridge east above town, and the nearby **Sagarmatha National Park Visitor Centre** (Chhorkhung; ⊙8am-4pm Sun-Fri) FREE for its visitor displays and Himalayan views. There is a colourful market each Saturday.

There is plenty to do around Namche Bazaar and you should spend a day here acclimatising. Remember that victims of AMS are often the fittest, healthiest people who foolishly overextend themselves. It's helpful to do a strenuous day walk to a higher altitude as part of your acclimatisation, coming back down to Namche to sleep. One popular day trip is the seven-hour return walk west to Thame village and its earthquake-damaged monastery. Alternatively try the strenuous but scenic six-hour loop hike north to charming Khunde and Khumjung villages.

Day Four: Namche Bazaar to Tengboche

The slightly longer route from Namche Bazaar to Tengboche via Khumjung and Khunde is more interesting than the direct one. The route starts by climbing up to the Syangboche airstrip. Above the airstrip is the Hotel Everest View, listed in the Guinness Book of Records as the highest hotel on earth.

From the hotel or the airstrip you climb to Khunde (3840m), then Khumjung (3790m), which lost a number of houses in the earthquake. From here you drop down to rejoin the direct trail to Tengboche. The trail descends to the Dudh Kosi (3250m) where there are several small lodges and a series of picturesque water-driven prayer wheels. A steep 400m ascent brings you to Tengboche (3870m). The famous gompa, with its background of Ama Dablam, Everest and other peaks, burnt down in 1989 but rose phoenix-like from the ashes. There are several busy lodges, or you can carry on 30 minutes downhill to quieter Debuche.

During the October/November full moon, the colourful Mani Rimdu festival is held here with masked dancing and Tibetan opera in the monastery courtyard – accommodation becomes extremely difficult to find.

Day Five: Tengboche to Pheriche/Dingboche

Beyond Tengboche, the altitude really starts to show. The trail drops down to Debuche, crosses the Imja Khola and climbs through rhododendron forest past superb mani stones (carved with the Tibetan Buddhist mantra *om mani padme hum*) to Pangboche (3860m). The gompa in the upper village above the main trail is the oldest in the Khumbu and houses the skull of a yeti. The village is a good place for a lunch stop.

The trail then climbs past Shomare and Orsho to Pheriche (4240m), where there is an HRA trekkers' aid post and possible medical assistance. Accommodation is available, but you can also continue to Dingboche (4410m), 30 minutes over the hill.

Day Six: Acclimatisation Day in Pheriche/Dingboche

Another acclimatisation day should be spent at Pheriche or Dingboche. As at Namche, a solid day walk to a higher altitude is better than just resting. Nangkartshang Gompa, an hour's climb up the ridge above Dingboche, offers good views east to Makalu (8462m), the world's fifth-highest mountain.

Chhukung (4730m) is a six-hour return hike up the Imja Khola Valley, which offers stunning views. There is food and accommodation at Chhukung and some great full-day side trips to Chhukung Ri and Island Peak Base Camp but don't overnight here before spending a night first at Dingboche.

Day Seven: Pheriche/Dingboche to Duglha

From Pheriche, the trail climbs to Phulang Kala (4340m) then Duglha (4620m). It's only a two-hour trek to Duglha and many trekkers are tempted to push on but the HRA doctors at Pheriche urge everyone to stay a night in Duglha in order to aid acclimatisation. There are two lodges here.

Day Eight: Duglha to Lobuche

From Duglha the trail goes directly up the gravely terminal moraine of the Khumbu Glacier for about an hour, then bears left to a group of memorials to lost climbers and Sherpas, including Scott Fischer who died in the 1996 Everest disaster. It's a short climb past views of Pumori to the summer village of Lobuche (4930m). The altitude, cold and crummy beds will combine to ensure a fitful night's sleep.

Day Nine: Lobuche to Gorak Shep

The return trip from Lobuche to Gorak Shep (5160m) takes just a couple of hours, leaving enough time to continue to the peak of Kala Pattar (three hours return) – or you can overnight in Gorak Shep and reach Kala Pattar early the next morning for the best chance of good weather. At 5545m, this small peak offers the best view you'll get of Everest on this trek.

Gorak Shep was the base camp for the 1952 Swiss expedition to Everest. There is good accommodation here but the altitude makes life uncomfortable. If the altitude is getting to you, descending to Lobuche or, better, Pheriche or Dingboche makes a real difference.

EVEREST NUTS

The world's highest peak has attracted many commendable achievements: the first ascent without oxygen (1978), first summit with an artificial leg (1998), the first ski descent (2000), the first blind ascent (2001), most ascents (21), youngest ascent (aged 13), oldest ascent (aged 78) and fastest ascent (eight hours). Sherpa Babu Chiru spent a particularly amazing 21 hours on top of Everest without oxygen in 1999.

But there have also been some admirably silly achievements. Perhaps most ambitious was the Briton Maurice Wilson, who planned to crash his Gypsy Moth airplane halfway up the mountain and then climb from there to the top, not letting his almost total lack of mountaineering or flying experience get in the way of an obviously flawed plan. He eventually froze to death at Camp III dressed in a light sweater (and, it is rumoured, women's clothing).

Maybe it's something in the national psyche (this is after all the nation that gave us *Monty Python*), for it was also a team of Brits who trekked all the way to Everest Base Camp to play the 'world's highest game of rugby' at 5140m. They lost.

Our personal Everest heroes are the (inevitably) British pair who carried an ironing board up Everest to 5440m to do some extreme ironing ('part domestic chore, part extreme sport'). For anyone contemplating a repeat expedition, the duo have revealed that expedition preparation can be limited to three important factors: 'a few beers, a drunken bet and a stolen ironing board'.

Day 10: Gorak Shep to Everest Base Camp & Lobuche

If you want to visit Everest Base Camp (5360m), it's a six-hour round trip from Gorak Shep. EBC is dotted with tents in the April/May climbing season but outside of those months, there's not a great deal to see except for views of the Khumbu Icefall; Everest itself is hidden from view by the surrounding peaks. During the 2015 earthquake an avalanche killed 18 climbers and guides, making it the mountain's worst disaster to date. If you only have the energy for one side trip, make it Kala Pattar.

The two-hour trek back down to Lobuche seems easy after all the climbing, and some trekkers continue for another three hours down to Dingboche or Pheriche the same day.

Day 11: Lobuche to Dingboche

Descend to spend the night at Pheriche or Dingboche, which boasts Nepal's highest internet cafe and fine views of Island Peak (Imja Tse; 6189m) and Lhotse (8516m).

Days 12 to 14: Dingboche to Lukla

The next three days retrace your steps down to Lukla via Tengboche and Namche Bazaar. If you are flying out of Lukla, get to the airline office between 3pm and 4pm the day before your flight to reconfirm your seat. Your lodge owner will often do this for you. If the weather has been bad, you might be vying for a flight with hundreds of other trekkers, but generally you shouldn't have a problem.

Alternative Routes & Side Trips

The side trips off the Everest Base Camp Trek rank as some of the region's highlights, so it makes sense to add an extra week or so to your itinerary to explore the region more fully.

A particularly scenic side trip is the six-day detour from Namche Bazaar to the multiple blue lakes of the **Gokyo Valley**, culminating in the Everest region's most spectacular glacier and lake viewpoint at Gokyo Ri (5360m). It's important to ascend the valley slowly, overnighting in Phortse Thenga, Dole, Machhermo and Gokyo to aid acclimatisation. From Gokyo you can rejoin the main Everest Base Camp trail near Khumjung or upper Pangboche.

You can combine both the Gokyo Valley and Everest Base Camp by crossing the Cho La (5420m) via Dzonglha, for a total duration of 17 days, but you need to take this route seriously and enquire about the conditions before setting out. Some months the pass is clear of snow; at other times you'll need crampons for this high crossing. You can hire a guide (Rs 2000) at most lodges to guide you across the glacier and pass.

TREKKING PEAKS

If you want to take the first step from trekking to mountaineering, consider a short mountaineering course that takes in one of Nepal's 'trekking peaks'. Several companies organise basic training and ascents in the Solu Khumbu region and can add these on to an organised trek to Everest Base Camp or elsewhere. All are physically demanding but not too technically demanding.

Most popular is a four-day ascent of **Island Peak**, properly known as Imja Tse (6189m), from a base in Chhukung. After acclimatisation, briefing, training and a half-day hike to base camp, the peak is generally climbed in a single six- to eight-hour day, departing early in the morning. There may be some crevasses to cross, though guides report that retreating glaciers mean some rock climbing is increasingly required. Trips run weekly in season (mid-October to mid-November, end March to May) and cost US$750 to US$900 from Chhukung to Chhukung.

The second most popular option is to the false summit of **Lobuche East** (6119m), a more technically difficult ascent that requires two days of training. The three- or four-day round trip from Dzongla costs around US$650 (including boots and equipment) through **Astrek Climbing Wall** (p86), which operates a fixed high camp here and accepts walk-ins. Trips operate from mid-September to mid-November and from mid-April to end May.

Also in the Everest region, **Mera Peak** (6476m) involves more trekking than climbing, though it is the highest of the trekking peaks and has perhaps the widest Himalayan views. It's a minimum 15-day trip from Lukla and involves trekking up to the 5415m Mera La, from where the climbing begins, with an overnight at base camp and a night-time summit bid. Teahouse treks from Kathmandu cost around US$1500 and some agencies now offer independent trekkers a four-day return climb from Khare for around US$1000. Plastic climbing boots are now available for hire in Khare. Trips run in October, November, April and May.

For most of these trips you will need to hire your own plastic climbing boots and gaiters, available either from Kathmandu or Namche Bazaar, and you will need a down jacket, sleeping bag and gloves, as well as travel insurance that covers you for climbing above 6000m. Prices include permits, equipment, guides, tent accommodation and food. Expect a group size of around six to eight climbers.

In the Annapurna region, Pisang Peak (6091m), Chulu Far East (6059m) and Chulu East (6584m) are all four-day excursions from Manang and can be neatly slotted into an Annapurna Circuit Trek, though you need to bring all equipment from Kathmandu or Pokhara.

Himalayan Ecstasy (Map p90; ☑ 01-4700001; www.himalayanecstasynepal.com; Chaksibari Marg) is one of the best options for well-run tuition and peak climbing. Add US$200 to the above prices for a recommended extra two days of instruction in glacier travel and rope work. Contact Anil Bhattarai.

The following companies in Kathmandu also organise ascents.

Climb High Himalaya (Map p90; ☑ 01-4701398; www.climbhighhimalaya.com; Mandala St)

Equator Expeditions (p48)

Mountain Monarch (☑ 01-4373881; www.mountainmonarch.com; Hattigauda)

Throw in the high crossings of the Renjo La (5345m), between Thame and Gokyo, and the Kongma La (5535m), between Lobuche and Chhukung, and you get the **Three Passes Trek**, a 20-day trek for experienced connoisseurs.

Another recommended three-day side trip is up the Imja Khola Valley to **Chhukung**, for awesome mountain views. Chhukung is also the staging post for climbers heading to Island Peak and the valley is well worth exploring.

As an alternative to flying back to Kathmandu, you can escape the crowds on the nine-day teahouse trek southeast from **Lukla to Tumlingtar**, from where you can fly or bus back to Kathmandu. For full details see Lonely Planet's *Trekking in the Nepal Himalaya* guide.

ANNAPURNA CIRCUIT TREK

Duration 10 to 17 days

Maximum elevation 5416m

Best season October to November

Start Dharapani or Chame

Finish Jomsom or Naya Pul

Permits TIMS card, ACAP permit

Summary The sense of journey, the challenging crossing of a high pass, and the possibility of excellent day trips to monasteries and mountain lakes make this a Himalayan classic, despite some road traffic.

For scenery and cultural diversity, this has long been considered the best trek in Nepal and one of the world's classic walks. It follows the Marsyangdi Valley to the north of the main Himalayan range and crosses a 5416m pass to descend into the dramatic desert-like, Tibetan-style scenery of the upper Kali Gandaki Valley.

The walk passes picturesque villages home to Gurungs, Manangis and Thakalis, offers spectacular mountain views of the numerous 7000m-plus Annapurna peaks and boasts some of the best trekking lodges in Nepal.

Our best tip for this trek is to remember that the side trips and excursions from places like Manang, Muktinath and Jomsom rank as the highlights of the trek. It's well worth adding a couple of days to explore some of these trails. You'll be better acclimatised for the pass and you'll manage to shake some of the crowds. This is not scenery to rush through.

The circuit is usually walked counter-clockwise because the climb to the Thorung La (5416m) from the western side is too strenuous and has too much elevation gain to consider in one day. The Thorung La is often closed due to snow from mid-December to March, and bad weather can move in at any time. Now that roads reach Manang it is tempting to start from there straight away but it is essential to take your time between Manang and the pass to acclimatise properly.

There was only minor damage to this route from the 2015 earthquake; of far more consequence to trekkers is the spread of roads. The bumpy dirt road road on the Marsyangdi side has now reached as far as Manang, while on the Kali Gandaki side, a seasonal road runs all the way to Jomsom and Muktinath.

The start point of the trek has changed repeatedly over recent years. The lower section of the old trail from Besi Sahar to Ngadi is worth avoiding due to road and dam construction. Most people take a bus to Besi Sahar and then change to a 4WD to either Dharapani or Chame.

It's also possible to start walking at the stone village of Jagat or Tal. Where exactly you start the trek depends on the state of the road and transport options. It's possible to avoid the road in sections (look for the red-and-white trail markers) but you will still notice its presence. If you start walking in Chame, your trek will be one day less than our route.

If you did not get your Annapurna Conservation Area Project (ACAP) permit in Kathmandu or Pokhara, you can purchase one (Rs 2000) in Besi Sahar at the ACAP entry fee office. If you get all the way to the Dharapani ACAP checkpoint without a permit you will have to pay Rs 4000 for one.

Access: Kathmandu or Pokhara to Besi Sahar

Buses run to Besi Sahar (Rs 400, six hours) between 6.30am and 10am from Kathmandu's Gongabu bus station, with tourist buses (Rs 450) at 7am, 8am and 10am. Buses also run to Bhulbule (Rs 475) at 6.45am and 8.30am.

From Pokhara (Rs 450, five hours), there is a tourist bus leaving at 6.30am from the tourist bus park, or you can take any bus or microbus bound for Kathmandu and change at Dumre.

From Besi Sahar, cramped 4WDs run to Chame (Rs 1500) and on to Manang (Rs 3000), when the dirt road isn't blocked by monsoon landslides. Drivers seem to particularly enjoy overcharging foreigners on this route so negotiate your fare. Transport options are bound to change as road conditions improve, so you'll have to check the situation on arrival.

The Trek

Day One: Dharapani to Chame

Many people start their trek at Dharapani (1960m), which is marked by a stone entrance chörten (Tibetan Buddhist stupa) typical of the Tibetan-influenced villages from here northward. That said, much of today's walk will be on or near the new dirt

Annapurna Treks

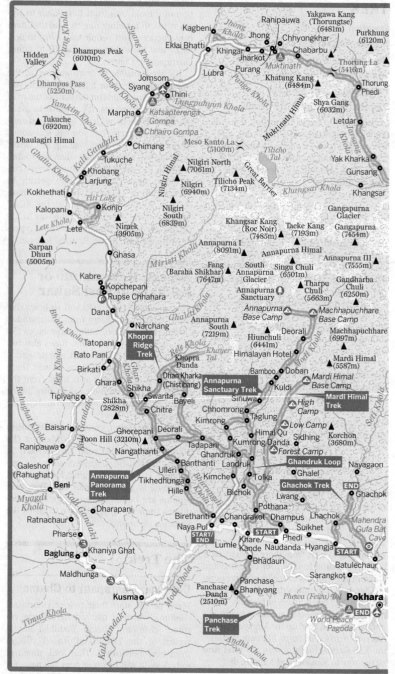

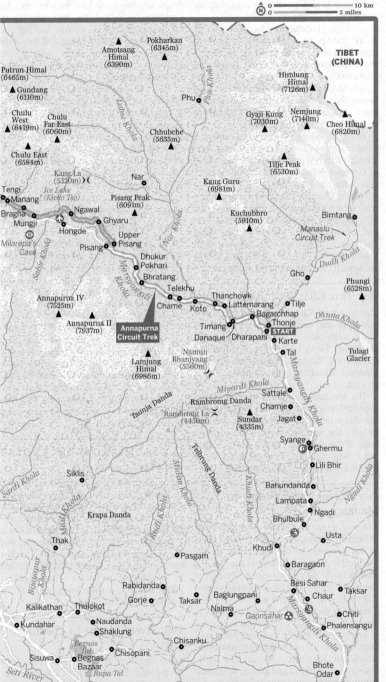

road, so it is also possible to start walking further on in Chame.

In upper (northern) Dharapani is an ACAP checkpoint where you will need to register. Just beyond here at Thoche is the confluence with the Dudh Khola and Manaslu Circuit trail.

A landslide roared through the centre of Bagarchhap (2160m) in late 1995, wiping out much of it, including two lodges. There are more lodges at nearby Danaque.

The trail climbs steeply from Danaque, gaining 500m to Timang and then continues through a forest, past the traditional village of Thanchowk to Koto (2640m), at the junction of the Nar-Phu Valley.

Nearby Chame (2710m) is the headquarters of the Manang district and it has lodges, internet cafes, trek-gear shops, a health post and a bank. At the entrance to the village you pass a large mani wall adorned with prayer wheels. There are fine views of Annapurna II (7937m) as you approach Chame.

Day Two: Chame to Upper Pisang

The trail from Chame runs through forest in a steep and narrow valley and recrosses to the south bank of the Marsyangdi Khola at 3080m. Views include the first sight of the soaring Paungda Danda rock face, an awesome testament to the power of glacial erosion.

The trail/road continues to climb to the popular lunch spot at Dhukur Pokhari. After the village follow the red-and-white markers to leave the road and cross to the northern bank of the river. This trail leads up to Upper Pisang (3310m), where you'll get amazing views and decent accommodation.

Day Three: Upper Pisang to Manang

The walk is now through the drier upper part of Manang district, cut off from the full effect of the monsoon by the Annapurna Range. The people of the upper part of the Manang district herd yaks and raise crops for part of the year, but they also continue to enjoy special trading rights gained way back in 1784. Today they use these rights to buy goods in Bangkok and Hong Kong to resell in Nepal.

From Upper Pisang there are two trails, north and south of the Marsyangdi Khola, which meet up again at Mungji. The southern route via the road and airstrip at Hongde (3420m) involves dropping to Lower Pisang.

It also involves much less climbing than the northern route, but the mountain views on the upper trail via Ghyaru and Ngawal (3660m) are infinitely better and this walk will aid your acclimatisation. Both Ghyaru and Ngawal have good lodges and offer overnight alternatives.

The trail continues from Mungji (3500m) past the picturesque village and gompa of Bragha (3470m) to nearby Manang (3540m), where there are numerous lodges, shops, a museum and an HRA post (it's worth attending the free daily lecture on altitude sickness). Bragha also has good lodges plus some excellent side trips, and is a quieter place to base yourself than Manang village.

Days Four & Five: Acclimatisation Days in Manang

It's important to spend at least one day acclimatising in Manang before pushing on to Thorung La (5416m). We'd actually recommend two as there are many fine day walks and magnificent viewpoints around Manang.

The view of Gangapurna Glacier is terrific, either from the viewpoint above the lake or from the Praken Gompa, an hour's walk above Manang. More strenuous day hikes include to Milarepa's cave on the south side of the valley and the Ice Lake, high above the valley floor on the north side at 4600m.

Manang is a major trading centre and you can buy batteries, sunscreen, chocolate and just about anything else a trekker could break, lose or crave.

Day Six: Manang to Yak Kharkha or Letdar

From Manang it's an ascent of nearly 2000m to Thorung La, spread over three days. The trail (no road!) climbs steadily through Tengi and Gunsang, leaving the Marsyangdi Valley and continuing along the Jarsang Khola Valley. The vegetation becomes shorter and sparser as you reach lodges in Yak Kharkha (4020m) and then Letdar (4230m). A night in Yak Kharkha or Letdar is important for acclimatisation, despite being only three or four hours from Manang.

Day Seven: Letdar to Thorung Phedi

Cross the river at 4310m and then climb up through desolate scenery and avalanche zones to Thorung Phedi (4540m). There are

SAFETY ON THE THORUNG LA

The 5416m Thorung La is one of Nepal's highest passes and crossing it is potentially dangerous. In terms of altitude acclimatisation it is safest to cross it from east to west. The trek up to the pass from Manang is not difficult but it is a long way at high elevation, which can cause problems. Be sure to read up on acute mountain sickness (AMS) before you go, so that you can be aware of the symptoms. Be prepared to return all the way to Besi Sahar if it is impossible or dangerous to cross the Thorung La. Trekkers have died on the Thorung La because of altitude sickness, exposure, cold and avalanches. All trekkers, including porters, must be adequately equipped for severe cold and snow.

It is impossible to give exact dates, but the Thorung La is usually snowbound and closed from mid-December to March. The trail to the pass can be extremely hard to find in fresh snow and you should be prepared to turn back or stay put in a lodge in bad weather. At any time local storms or cyclones generated in the Arabian Sea or Bay of Bengal can close it with sudden and massive snowfalls. In such conditions and at these altitudes, simply sitting out bad weather in a lodge can be life saving.

Tragically this was made all too clear in October 2014 when almost 1.8m of snow fell in 12 hours. In the ensuing days over 500 people were rescued in the vicinity of Thorung La and Muktinath, and 43 lives were lost. Those who lost their lives were caught outdoors by avalanches, extreme cold and white-out conditions.

two lodges here – at the height of the season as many as 200 trekkers a day may cross over Thorung La and beds can be in short supply. Some trekkers find themselves suffering from AMS at Phedi. If you are one of these, you must retreat downhill; even the descent to Letdar can make a difference. Be sure to boil or treat water here; the sanitation in Letdar and Thorung Phedi is poor. There is a phone in Thorung Phedi that you can use in an emergency.

There is another lodge, Thorung High View Camp, an hour above Thorung Phedi at 4850m, but it is uncomfortable and potentially dangerous to spend a night at this altitude.

Day Eight: Thorung Phedi to Muktinath

Phedi means 'foot of the hill' and that's exactly where it is, at the foot of the 5416m Thorung La. The trail climbs steeply but is well used and easy to follow. The altitude will have you gasping and snow can cause problems; when the pass is covered in fresh snow it is often impossible to cross – don't try it. Wait until it stops snowing and a mule team has been through cutting a trail.

It takes about four to six hours to reach the pass, marked by chörtens and prayer flags, and en route you'll pass a couple of teahouses, plus one on the pass itself. The effort is worthwhile as the view from the top – from the Annapurnas, along the Great Barrier to the barren Kali Gandaki Valley – is magnificent. From the pass you have a knee-busting and sometimes slippery 1600m descent to Muktinath (3800m).

Some people start out for the pass at 3am but this is not only unnecessary but also potentially dangerous due to the risk of frostbite and accidents in the darkness. A better starting time is 5am to 6am.

Muktinath (p235), a pilgrimage site for Hindus and Buddhists, has accommodation 10 minutes away at Ranipauwa, where there is also an ACAP checkpoint.

Day Nine: Muktinath to Kagbeni

From Ranipauwa, the road descends through a desert-like trans-Himalayan landscape to the dramatic village of Jharkot (3500m), with its large chörten, gompa and atmospheric animist totems. The trail continues to Khingar (3400m) and then follows the road down steeply to the medieval-looking village of Kagbeni (2840m).

If you have half a day to spare, it's worth making the short detour across the valley to the traditional villages of Chhyongkhar, Jhong and Purang, all culturally part of Mustang but visitable without the need for extra permits.

There's an interesting alternative route (trail-marked in blue-and-white stripes) to Jomsom that bypasses the road and goes via the Lubra village. Check first in Ranipauwa as the route isn't passable when river levels are high.

DAMS, ROADS & AUTOMOBILES

Road construction is having an effect on the Annapurna Circuit but it is certainly not the disaster made out by some. You are still guaranteed to cross raging torrents on giddying suspension bridges, meet friendly locals, lose your breath on ridiculously steep trails and be gobsmacked by the mountain views.

The first half of the circuit on the Manang side is less affected by traffic than the Kali Gandaki Valley on the west side, but the construction activity (including roads) associated with hydro projects is certainly making a visual impact. While some trekkers now end their trek in Jomsom by driving or flying back to Pokhara, they are missing out on some excellent trekking.

As you trek, look for the network of alternative trails marked with red-and-white trail markers that take you off the road and into the countryside. Furthermore, the trails marked with blue-and-white markers take you on some fabulous detours and side trips. The scenery on the new trails is equally if not more spectacular than the old route, and the lodges are excellent. The nature of the trail has changed; however, in reality this trek was never a 'wilderness' experience, and it can still be walked the entire way and augmented with numerous day hikes from overnight bases.

Day 10: Kagbeni to Jomsom

The Tibetan-influenced settlement of Kagbeni (p236) has a number of good lodges and is as close as you can get to Lo Manthang, the capital of the legendary kingdom of Mustang further to the north; Mustang permits cost US$500 for 10 days.

From Kagbeni it is a dusty but mostly flat stroll along the road or riverbed to Jomsom (2760m). Jomsom (p234) is the major centre in the region and it has facilities such as a hospital, an ACAP visitor centre and a police checkpost (where you must register and get your ACAP permit stamped). Jomsom has regular morning flights to Pokhara (US$124) and a direct bus to Pokhara, with other transport running to Ghasa, Beni and beyond, so this is where some travellers end their trek.

If you have the time, it's worth continuing south to the traditional whitewashed stone village of Marpha (p234) (2680m), which has a gompa and several smaller shrines. The town boasts some of the best accommodation to be found along the trail, which makes it a good alternative to staying in Jomsom.

If walking, try to be on the trail early in the morning in the Kali Gandaki Valley, as strong winds tend to pick up after 11am.

Days 11 to 17: Jomsom to Naya Pul

The Annapurna Circuit south of Jomsom follows the new road south through the Kali Gandaki Valley to Naya Pul. This section of the trek has become less popular since the road was constructed but it's still a rewarding walk if you take the detours on the east bank that avoid the road as much as possible. Furthermore, the trail leaves the road altogether at Tatopani to cross the ridge at Ghorepani and descend to Naya Pul. ACAP's progress in building trails and bridges on the east bank to enable trekkers to avoid the road is very successful. Figure on three days to Tatopani or four to five days to Ghorepani. There are excellent lodges at Marpha, Tukuche, Larjung, Lete, Kalopani, Ghasa and Tatopani.

South of Jomsom it's worth detouring down the east bank via Dhumba Lake to Katsapterenga Gompa, before returning to the road at Syang and continuing to Marpha.

Just south of Marpha another detour heads down the eastern bank from the Tibetan settlement around Chhairo Gompa (p233) to Chimang, which offers superb views of Dhaulagiri, the world's sixth largest mountain.

Back on the west bank, Tukuche (p233) at 2580m is one of the valley's most important Thakali villages and once was a depot and customs spot for salt traders from Tibet. Several grand houses and gompas hark back to a more prosperous past.

The road continues to Khobang and Larjung (2560m), past good views of Dhaulagiri (8167m) and Nilgiri North (7061m). Larjung is the base for a tough full-day excursion up to the Dhaulagiri Icefall.

Another excursion branches off the road at Kokhethati, leading to Titi Lake (2670m) for views of the eastern flank of Dhaulagiri and then down to the villages of Konjo and Taglung, with their spectacular views of Nilgiri peak. The trails eventually rejoin the road just south of Lete (2480m).

The road continues south to Ghasa (2000m), the last Thakali village in the valley, and then a foot trail branches down the east side of the narrowing gorge, rejoining the road after a couple of hours at the waterfall of Rupse Chhahara (1560m). The road continues down to Dana and Tatopani at 1190m, noted for its hot springs.

From Tatopani you branch off the road and head up the steep side valley from Ghar Khola, gaining an epic 1600m to Ghorepani in the Annapurna foothills. This is one of the hardest days on the circuit but it's possible to break the day in Shikha or Chitre en route. A side trail near Chitre branches left for the Khopra Ridge trek.

An hour's climb from the ridge at upper Ghorepani (also known as Deorali) will take you to Poon Hill (3210m), one of the best (but most popular!) Himalayan viewpoints in the lower hills.

From Ghorepani you can descend the long, stone staircases to Nangathanti (2460m), Banthanti (2250m) and Ulleri, which is a large Magar village at 1960m, before continuing steeply to Tikhedhunga, Birethanti (1000m) and the nearby roadhead at Naya Pul.

A two-day trail also runs from Ghorepani to Ghandruk, where you can join up with the Annapurna Sanctuary Trek.

ANNAPURNA SANCTUARY TREK

Duration 10 to 14 days

Maximum elevation 4095m

Best season October to November

Start Phedi

Finish Naya Pul

Permits TIMS card, ACAP permit

Summary Classic walk through Gurung villages climbing to an amphitheatre surrounded by stunning peaks and glaciers.

The Annapurna Sanctuary Trek leads you right into the frozen heart of the Annapurna Range, a magnificent arena of rock and ice

on a staggering scale. The trail starts in rice paddies and leads through a gorge of bamboo and forests to end among glaciers and soaring peaks – an unparalleled mountain adventure. It's an amazing experience to have an open-air breakfast surrounded by 7000m or 8000m peaks in every direction.

Other highlights include sublime views of fish-tailed Machhapuchhare (6997m) and one of Nepal's largest and prettiest Gurung villages at Ghandruk, which is a short detour off the main trail.

The return trek can take as little as 10 days but 14 days will give you more time to soak up the scenery. You can tack a walk to the sanctuary on to the Annapurna Circuit for an epic 25- to 30-day walk, or combine the Annapurna Sanctuary with the Mardi Himal teahouse trek.

There are several possible routes to the sanctuary, all meeting at Chhomrong. One alternative is to start in Naya Pul and take a jeep as far as Kimche. The diversion from the Annapurna Circuit Trek branches off from Ghorepani to reach Chhomrong via Tadapani. This route was not affected by the 2015 earthquake.

Access: Pokhara to Phedi

Buses leave every 40 minutes or so from Pokhara's Baglung bus stand to Phedi (Rs 90, 1½ hours), a cluster of shacks, from where the trail starts up a series of stone steps. Alternatively, catch a bus to Naya Pul (Rs 240, two hours) and a 4WD to Kimche (Rs 500) before walking to Ghandruk.

The Trek

Day One: Phedi to Tolka

From Phedi (1130m) the trail climbs steeply to Dhampus (1750m), which stretches for several kilometres from 1580m to 1700m. The views are stupendous. Dhampus has a number of hotels strung along the ridge and is connected by a road.

The trail climbs to lodges at pretty Pothana (1990m) and descends steeply through a forest towards Bichok. It emerges in the Modi Khola Valley and continues to drop to Tolka (1810m). If you have the energy, continue 45 minutes to the better accommodation at Landruk.

AVALANCHES ON THE SANCTUARY TRAIL

There is significant danger of avalanches along the route to the Annapurna Sanctuary between Doban and Machhapuchhare Base Camp. Trekkers have died and trekking parties have been stranded in the sanctuary for days, the trail blocked by tonnes of ice and snow. Always check with the ACAP office in Chhomrong and lodges in Deorali for a report on current trail conditions, and do not proceed into the sanctuary if there has been recent heavy rain or snow.

Day Two: Tolka to Chhomrong

From Tolka the trail descends a long stone staircase and then follows a ridge to the Gurung village of Landruk (1620m). Ten minutes from here the path splits – north takes you to Chhomrong and the sanctuary.

The sanctuary trail turns up the Modi Khola Valley to Himal Qu (also known as Naya Pul; 1340m). It then continues up to Jhinu Danda (1750m), and its nearby hot springs, before a steep climb to Taglung (2190m), where it joins the Ghandruk to Chhomrong trail.

Chhomrong (2210m) is the last permanent settlement in the valley. This large and sprawling Gurung village has excellent lodges, fine views and an ACAP office where you can enquire about trail conditions in the sanctuary.

Day Three: Chhomrong to Bamboo

The trail drops down a set of stone steps to the Chhomrong Khola, and then climbs to Sinuwa and on through rhododendron forests to Kuldi (2470m). The trek now enters the upper Modi Khola Valley, where ACAP controls the location and number of lodges and limits their size. This section of the trail is a bottleneck and you may find the lodges in Bamboo (2310m) are full during the high season, in which case you may have to continue for an hour to the next accommodation in Doban or sleep in the dining room. In winter it is common to find snow from this point on.

Day Four: Bamboo to Himalayan Hotel

The trail climbs through rhododendron forests to Doban (2540m) and on to the two lodges at Himalayan Hotel at 2840m. This stretch of the trail passes several avalanche chutes. If you arrive early, it's possible to continue on to Deorali to make the following day easier.

Day Five: Himalayan Hotel to Machhapuchhare Base Camp

From Himalayan Hotel it's on to Hinko (3100m) then to lodges at Deorali (3140m), at the gateway to the sanctuary. The next stretch of trail is the most subject to avalanches and you detour temporarily to the east side of the valley to avoid a dangerous chute.

At Machhapuchhare Base Camp (which isn't really a base camp since climbing the mountain is not permitted), at 3700m, there is decent accommodation available. Be alert to signs of altitude sickness before heading off to Annapurna Base Camp.

Day Six: Machhapuchhare Base Camp to Annapurna Base Camp

The climb to the Annapurna Base Camp at 4130m takes about two hours and is best done early in the day before clouds roll in. If there is snow, the trail may be difficult to follow. The lodges here can get very crowded at the height of the season. The frozen dawn is best observed from the glacial moraine a short stroll from your cosy lodge.

Days Seven to 14: Annapurna Base Camp to Naya Pul

On the return trip, head south to Chhomrong (two days) and on to Ghandruk (one day) via the deep valley of the Khumnu Khola. From Ghandruk you can follow the valley directly down to Kimche, Birethanti and Naya Pul in a day. Transport is available from Kimche to Naya Pul (Rs 500).

Alternatively, detour west to Ghorepani to visit Poon Hill, before descending to Birethanti (four days) and Naya Pul. Buses to Pokhara stop in Naya Pul (Rs 240, two hours).

OTHER ANNAPURNA TREKS

Ghachok Trek (Two Days)

This interesting two-day trek ascends the hills north of Pokhara to the traditional Gurung villages around Ghachok (1260m). It starts from Hyangja, near the Tashi Palkhel Tibetan settlement, and crosses the Mardi Khola to Lhachok before ascending to the stone-walled village of Ghachok, where you can stop overnight in a teahouse before turning south and returning to Pokhara via Batulechaur. With more time, you can extend this walk to visit some even more remote villages in the valley leading north from Ghachok.

Ghandruk Loop (Three Days)

A short but steep three-day trek offering mountain views and Gurung villages, with numerous quality lodges with excellent mountain views at Ghandruk. The trail starts at Phedi and follows Day One of the Annapurna Sanctuary trail to overnight at Tolka (1810m). From Tolka, trek 45 minutes to Landruk (an alternative first-night halt) and then drop steeply down a stone staircase to the Modi Khola at 1315m. It's then a very steep climb up more stone stairs, thankfully via several refreshment stops, to Ghandruk (1970m).

On day three descend to the road at Kimche, where you can catch transport or continue walking back to Birethanti and Naya Pul.

Panchase Trek (Three to Four Days)

Panchase is a region close to Pokhara boasting some great mountain views of Annapurna South and Machhapuchhare peaks, with the added benefits that it is easily accessed from Lakeside and no ACAP or TIMS cards are required. There are several variations of the route focussed around the highpoint of Panchase Danda (2500m) and it can be done in any direction. There are five trekking lodges at Panchase Bhanjyang. Figure on three or four days at a leisurely pace. A guide is useful to follow the trail between Panchase Bhanjyang and Bhumdi.

Trails to Panchase start west of Pokhara, either at Naudanda or Khare on the Baglung Hwy or west of Phewa Tal at Ghatichhina. The trails climb through traditional villages to Panchase Bhanjyang (2030m), where most people overnight. Start early the next morning to trek up to the peak and Hindu temple of Panchase Danda for a sunrise vista of the Himalaya. The trek can then conclude along any of several daylong routes back to Pokhara, including one that routes via a teahouse at Palyam Chauteri (west of Bhumdi) to the Peace Pagoda (hotel accommodation) and Pokhara's Lakeside via a boat ride on Phewa Tal.

Annapurna Panorama (Six Days)

This loop walk features Gurung villages and marvellous views from the popular Poon Hill (3210m) viewpoint and is a good choice in winter. It can also be done in either direction. The overnight stops on this trek are shared with the Annapurna Circuit and Sanctuary treks and therefore teahouse accommodation is plentiful.

The trail starts at Naya Pul, on the road from Pokhara to Baglung, and follows the Annapurna Circuit trail in reverse for the first two days, with overnight stops in Tikhedhunga and Ghorepani. On day three, most people leave before dawn for the short 1.5km hike to Poon Hill and its fine vista of snowy peaks, including Annapurna South (7273m) and Machhapuchhare (6997m). Relax in Ghorepani for the rest of the day.

Day four involves a gentle descent to Tadapani, and day five continues downhill to Ghandruk, a scenic Gurung village of stone and slate houses with a colourful Buddhist monastery. The final day is an easy descent back to Kimche, Birethanti or Naya Pul, all of which offer jeeps or buses back to Pokhara. Alternatively, head east across the valley to Landruk and stop overnight at Tolka, before continuing to Phedi on the Baglung Hwy.

Mardi Himal Trek (Seven to Eight Days)

This relatively new weeklong teahouse trek is another fine option from Pokhara. The trail starts at Khare/Kande (1770m), or possibly Dhampus (1650m), and climbs past Australian Camp to lodges at Pothana

(1890m) or Deurali (2100m). Day two takes you up the ridgeline of the Gorujure Danda to Forest Camp (2520m) at Kokar. From there are two relatively short days to Low Camp (2970m) and High Camp (3540m).

From High Camp get an early start for the day-return hike to Mardi Himal Base Camp West (4250m), offering wonderful close-up views of Machhapuchhare, Himchuli and the Annapurnas.

You can return the way you came, or descend into the Mardi Khola to roadheads at Sidhing, Ghalel and Lwang, all of which have homestay accommodation. Alternatively head southwest from Forest Camp to Landruk and link up with trails to Ghandruk and the Annapurna Sanctuary trail.

Khopra Ridge (Eight to Nine Days)

This trek detours from the more frequented Annapurna trails to take you to several outstanding viewpoints. It can be done in either direction, and via a number of different routes, and be appended to either the Annapurna Circuit or Annapurna Sanctuary treks. Formerly frequented only by camping groups, there are now community-owned lodges and private guesthouses allowing teahouse trekking.

Start trekking from Naya Pul or Kimche (or Phedi) to take one or two days to reach Ghandruk. Day two takes you to Tadapani, with day three detouring north to overnight in Bayeli (3450m); strong acclimatised hikers can do this in one day. From here it's a worthwhile 30-minute detour to Muldai viewpoint. A hard-to-follow direct upper trail runs from Bayeli to the high point of the trek at Khopra Danda (3660m). From Khopra Danda (*danda* means ridge) here there is an ambitious optional full-day side trek up to the sacred lake Khayer Tal (4830m).

The return route is via the village of Dhan Kharka (Chistibang; 2990m) to Swanta (day six) before the trail joins the Annapurna Circuit near Chitre. Head east to Ulleri (day seven) via Ghorepani, and then to Birethanti or Naya Pul the following day.

A more interesting alternative ending climbs from Swanta to the fabulous lodge and viewpoint at Mohare Danda, before descending over the next two days to Nangi, Banskharka and the roadhead at Galeshwar, not far from Beni. There are community homestays or guesthouses along this route.

LANGTANG VALLEY TREK

Duration Seven to eight days

Maximum elevation 3870m

Best season September to May

Start Syabrubesi

Finish Syabrubesi

Permits TIMS card, Langtang National Park ticket

Summary A wonderful variety of scenery and accessible high alpine landscapes, though the bus trip to the trailhead is hard work.

The Langtang Valley is a superb short trek that packs a lot of scenic punch into a small amount of time. The trail ascends the Langtang Valley from just 1470m at Syabrubesi to hit 3870m at Kyanjin Gompa, following the rushing Langtang Khola river past lush forests and bamboo groves to a collection of high alpine pastures, glaciers and peaks on the border with Tibet.

The superb day hikes from Kyanjin Gompa in particular offer spectacular close-up views of the surrounding peaks and glaciers of Langtang Lirung (7246m), Kimshung (6781m) and Langshisha Ri (6370m). It's worth budgeting a couple of days here to take advantage of the fabulous scenic side trips.

After suffering greatly in the 2015 earthquake, the valley is now fully open for business. Choose to trek here and you'll be directly contributing to the recovery of communities who lost much on that dark day.

Potential add-ons to a Langtang trek include a visit to the Gosainkund lakes, after which you can either return to Dhunche (12 days total) or continue over Laurebina La back to Kathmandu along the Helambu trekking route (14 days total).

Another potential add-on is the six-day trek along the Tamang Heritage Trail, which also starts in Syabrubesi.

The treks all enter the Langtang National Park (entry Rs 3390).

Emergency Facilities

Mobile phone facilities are available in most of the stops along the trail, mostly through the Sky Phone network, so summoning a helicopter in an emergency shouldn't be too hard. The Yak Guest House in Kyanjin Gompa has a Gamow bag for emergency cases of mountain sickness and there is a simple clinic in nearby Munji.

Access: Kathmandu to Syabrubesi

The bus ride from Kathmandu to Syabrubesi is probably the worst thing about the Langtang trek.

Buses leave from Kathmandu's Machha Pokhari stand. There are daily tourist buses (Rs 600) at 6.30am and 8am, and and local services (Rs 450) at 6.20am and 7am to Syabrubesi via Dhunche.

For the return to Kathmandu, buses leave at 7am, 7.15am, 8am and 11am, and you should book at least the afternoon before. Cramped 4WDs (Rs 700) also depart at 7am and 7.30am. A chartered 4WD costs Rs 13,000.

Syabrubesi has several good roadside lodges. The **Peaceful Guest House** (☑ 010-541009; Syabrubesi; r with/without bathroom Rs 600/300; ☎) is set back from the main road and therefore is indeed a little more peaceful than others. There's a beer garden and warmish showers. **Hotel Namaste** (☑ 9843534282, 010-541012; getmechheten@yahoo.co.in; Syabrubesi; r Rs 500-800; ☎) across the road has good rooms with private bathrooms and the lady who owns the hotel, Chheten Lama, is a good source of trail information. There are several other good places.

The Trek

Day One: Syabrubesi to Lama Hotel

After registering at the police post at the top of town, continue along the main road for about 1km and branch off right to cross a suspension bridge over the Bhote Kosi. Turn left and then immediately right at the eastern end of the bridge to pass through the village of Old Syabru and continue up the trail on the north side of the Langtang Khola (don't take the first bridge after the village). After around 30 minutes, near Tibetan Camp, you cross to the southern bank of the river on a metal suspension bridge and follow the trail up the valley.

The trek becomes a pleasant walk through trees where langur monkeys frolic, passing a bridge, a small waterfall and *bhattis* (village inns) beside the stream at Doman (1680m). The trail then makes a steep climb over a rocky ridge to the junction where the route from Thulo Syabru joins from above (if coming from Gosainkund you would join the Langtang trek here).

It's then a long climb in forest past the waterfalls and two simple lodges of Pairo (meaning 'landslide'; 1800m) to Bamboo, a cluster of lodges at 1930m. Beyond the lodges of Bamboo (which make for a perfect lunch stop) the trail crosses the Dangdung

---

THE EARTHQUAKE IN LANGTANG

Seconds after the 25 April 2015 earthquake hit Nepal, a huge wall of snow, rock and ice broke off Langtang Lirung peak and hurtled unseen towards Langtang village, burying within seconds the large village and everyone in it. Around 155 villagers were killed instantly, along with around 40 international trekkers and many Nepali porters and guides. Villagers from nearby Kyanjin Gompa rushed to the village to find their houses and families vanished without warning under 20m of rubble. Most bodies were never recovered.

A memorial chörten in new Langtang village records the names of the dead: villagers from Langtang, Gumba and Sindum; seven trekkers from Spain and four French walkers from the same family. Individual memorials to lost trekkers are visible along other parts of the trail.

It's a sobering experience talking to lodge owners about the day. Almost everyone in the upper valley lost several family members. The good news is that after weathering two years with almost no trekking trade, the self-reliant survivors have rebuilt most of the lodges and the trek is once again fully open for business. The trail has been rerouted to avoid one section of landslides but is in good shape.

Come trekking here and you'll know that every cup of tea and daal bhaat you order is helping a community recover from the worst disaster in living memory.

Langtang Valley Trek

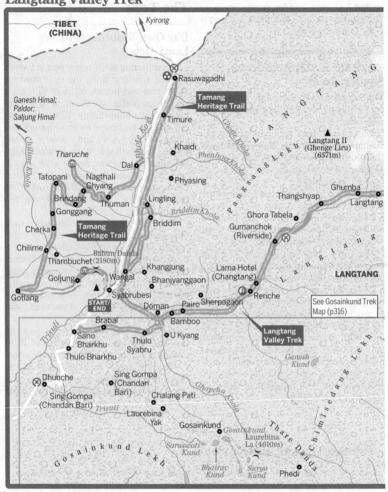

Khola, then climbs to a steel suspension bridge over the Langtang Khola at 2000m.

On the north bank of the Langtang Khola, the route climbs alongside a series of waterfalls formed by a jumble of house-sized boulders. Climb steeply to a landslide and the Ganesh View Lodge at Renche (2400m), by the junction with an alternative return trail to Syabrubesi via Sherpagaon. The main trail climbs gently to a collection of half-a-dozen lodges at Changtang, popularly known as Lama Hotel, at 2480m.

Day Two: Lama Hotel to Langtang

The trail continues to follow the Langtang Khola, climbing steeply through a forest of hemlocks, maples and rhododendrons, past isolated lodges at Gumanchok (Riverside) and Ghunama. Ten minutes (a few hundred metres) after the Hotel Woodland the new trail crosses a bridge to the south side, climbing past fine views of Langtang Lirung to recross the river and rejoin the main trail at the lodges of Ghora Tabela (2970m).

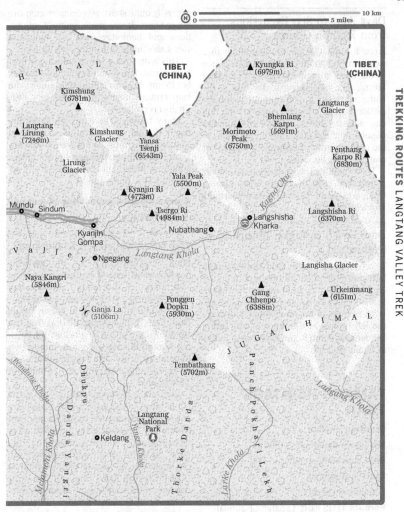

From Ghora Tabela the trail climbs more gradually through a U-shaped glacial valley to the villages of Thangshyap (three good lodges) and Ghumba, whose half-dozen newly rebuilt lodges make a much nicer night rest spot than nearby Langtang, a further 20 minutes (1km) on.

Langtang village (3430m) was completely wiped out in the 2015 earthquake and walking over the landslide area where the village once stood is an eerie experience. Since then, locals have built a dozen or more new lodges in the new village past the landslide area.

Day Three: Langtang to Kyanjin Gompa

It only takes a couple of hours to climb past lodges at Mundu to Kyanjin Gompa (3860m) where there is a monastery, over a dozen new lodges and a cheese factory (per kg Rs 1800). It's worth spending two to three full days here to really appreciate the scenery on a series of side trips. The Dorje Bakery Cafe here serves a fine apple pie.

Days Four to Six: Excursions from Kyanjin Gompa

From Kyanjin Gompa you can climb to a viewpoint at 4300m on the glacial moraine to the north for superb views of Langtang Lirung. The most popular day hike is the half-day trip to the Kyanjin Ri viewpoint (4600m), while a tougher option is the full-day climb to Tsergo Ri (4984m). Another popular long day hike leads up the valley to the pastures around Langshisha Kharka for more spectacular views.

For something less exhausting but equally picturesque, cross the bridge below Kyanjin Gompa to picnic beside the five charming Tsona lakes.

Days Seven to Eight: Return to Syabrubesi

To return to Syabrubesi, take the same path back down the valley for two days, or detour along the high trail from Renche via the village of Sherpagaon, which has good lodges.

To connect to the Gosainkund trek, take the left branch at the junction just before Doman and climb to the dozen or so lodges at Thulo Syabru.

TAMANG HERITAGE TRAIL

Duration Six days

Maximum elevation 3700m

Best season September to May

Start Syabrubesi

Finish Syabrubesi

Permits TIMS card, Langtang National Park ticket

Summary Traditional Tamang villages and fine views into Tibet make this little-trod cultural trek a fine add-on to the Langtang trek.

This relatively new trail is an excellent walk, either on its own or in conjunction with a Langtang Valley trek. It attracts far fewer trekkers and is less commercialised than most other trails, leading many people to compare it to trekking through Nepal 30 years ago.

It's not an easy trek by any means, with plenty of steep ups and downs, but days are generally quite short, averaging around five to six hours. If you prefer cultural interactions and homestays over big mountain views, this might be just the trek for you.

This is one trek where a guide is particularly useful, not so much for route finding but to smooth along cultural encounters and help arrange homestays, where very little English is spoken.

Many travellers have written to recommend Gotlang resident and guide Durga Tamang, who runs **Himalayan Unforgettable Adventure** (www.nepalmountaintrekking.com). Figure on around US$20/25 per day for a local porter/guide.

The Trek

Day One: Syabrubesi to Gotlang

From Syabrubesi look for the shortcuts heading west that avoid the huge looping switchbacks of the road. The steep trail gains 720m to two teahouses and a viewpoint (a 15-minute detour) at Bahun Danda Pass (Rongga Bhanjyang; 2180m). You can see the village of Goljung below. It's possible to avoid this steep climb by jumping on the afternoon bus that passes through Syabrubesi around 3pm en route to Chilime or Thambuchet.

Walk along the upper dirt road for a couple of hours to the lovely traditional village of Gotlang (2240m), the largest Tamang settlement in the area. Many buildings were damaged in the 2015 earthquake and reconstruction is still continuing. From here you can make the 45-minute detour uphill to peaceful Parvati Kund Lake and its nearby damaged gompa and cheese factory. Accommodation in Gotlang includes the private Paldor Peak and Gotlang guesthouses (r with/without bathroom Rs 800/400) and half a dozen homestays. The rebuilt village community lodge is currently being turned into a local museum.

Day Two: Gotlang to Tatopani

After a morning in Gotlang, follow the delightful line of 108 stone chörtens (some damaged in the earthquake) down the valley, branching left after an hour (4km or so) to drop down and eventually cross the river before Chilime village (1760m). At the far end of Chilime, cross the river on a suspension bridge and climb steeply past teahouses at Cherka and Gonggang (2230m; lodges available) to the half-dozen lodges at Tatopani (2600m), an ascent of 840m. Tatopani's eponymous hot springs lost their heat during the 2015 earthquake.

Day Three: Tatopani to Nagthali Ghyang

Keep an eye on the trail (trail-finding can be tricky on this initial section) as you climb 560m via the settlement and gompa of Brimdang to the ridgetop meadow and lodges of Nagthali Ghyang (Five Houses; three hours; 3165m). In clear weather there are fine views of Langtang Lirung, Ganesh Himal, Paldor peak, Saljung Himal and over into Tibet. It's well worth getting up early to make the three-hour return walk along the rhododendron-cloaked ridge to the lovely viewpoint at Tharuche (3700m). The best lodges are probably the Great Wall or Mountain View.

Day Four: Nagthali Ghyang to Thuman

If you didn't do it yesterday, start off with an early-morning hike to Tharuche viewpoint for the clearest views. From Nagthali descend steeply for 820m through forest to the pleasant Tamang village of Thuman (take a right 10 minutes after leaving Nagthali). Thuman (2240m) has a small gompa, half a dozen pleasant lodges and a couple of hard-to-find homestays, and is a fine place to spend an afternoon exploring.

Day Five: Thuman to Briddim

In the past most people used to walk from Thuman to Timure (1760m) and from there to the Tibetan border (a further 45 minutes), but today a series of huge hydroelectric projects and busy truck traffic with the new China border crossing at Rasuwagadhi make this a far less enjoyable experience.

Instead, it's now better to descend steeply from Thuman directly to the Bhote Khosi, which you cross on a suspension bridge, and then go up to the village of Lingling where food and charming lodging are available at the traditional Lingling Homestay. From Lingling it's a two-hour, 400m ascent via the Pelko View Restaurant to Briddim (2230m), a scenic Tamang village, which has a gompa above the town. The Lhasa Guest House, Tibet Homestay and Family Homestay at the top of the village are excellent.

With buses and jeeps now plying the route on a frequent basis between Syabrubesi and Timure, it would be easy to finish the trek on the road below Briddim or Lingling.

Day Six: Briddim to Syabrubesi

It's all downhill through pine forest to Syabrubesi (2½ hours, approximately 4km, 770m descent), short-cutting past the dirt road during the last section. Alternatively link up with the Langtang trek by taking the high northern route via Khangjim and Sherpagaon.

GOSAINKUND TREK

Duration Seven to eight days

Maximum elevation 4610m

Best season October to November, March to April

Start Dhunche or Thulo Syabru

Finish Sundarijal

Permits TIMS card, Langtang National Park and Shivapuri Nagarjun National Park tickets

Summary High alpine lakes and Himalayan panoramas are the highlights, as is the chance to continue walking all the way back to Kathmandu.

The Gosainkund lakes are a collection of scenic high-altitude holy lakes set in a mountain bowl at around 4400m. The lakes are a major pilgrimage site for Hindus and attract up to 20,000 pilgrims during the August full-moon festival of Janai Purnima. The Himalayan views from just above Laurebina Yak stretch from Manaslu and the peaks of Ganesh Himal into Tibet and rank as some of the best in central Nepal.

One distinct advantage of walking the route through Helambu all the way to Kathmandu is that you don't have to suffer the bus ride from Dhunche back to the capital. The sense of journey is also very satisfying.

There are lots of route options for visiting the sacred lake at Gosainkund. The most popular option is to link the Langtang, Gosainkund and Helambu treks into one 16-day trek.

It's also possible to hike the route as a trek by itself (as described here) or as a return visit from Dhunche to the lakes (seven

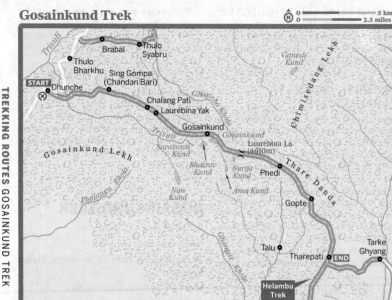

Gosainkund Trek

days), though the rate of ascent in both these cases can cause acclimatisation problems (if you've already done the Langtang Valley trek, you'll be well acclimatised). Take particular care to acclimatise if attempting this trek in the opposite direction.

If you are combining the Langtang and Gosainkund treks, you turn off the Langtang trek just before Doman and climb from there to the lodges at Thulo Syabru.

There are lodges all along the route, so finding food and accommodation is not a problem. Lodge facilities are good in Thulo Syabru, Sing Gompa and Tharepati, but rooms in Phedi and Gopte are basic.

This route over the Laurebina La becomes impassable during winter and isn't recommended if there's been fresh snowfall.

Access: Kathmandu to Dhunche

Buses from Kathmandu to Syabrubesi pass through Dhunche (Rs 500, 10 hours). Returning to Kathmandu buses leave Dhunche at 7am, 7.30am and 8am, and there are also a few 4WD (Rs 600). A private 4WD to Kathmandu costs Rs 12,000.

Dhunche has a few simple hotels. The Hotel Langtang View (☏010-540191; Dhunche;

s/d Rs 800/1000; ☏) claims to be 'probably the best hotel in town', which is true but not really a great claim. Jimmy Carter apparently stayed in room 107 during election monitoring.

Room rates in trekking lodges along the trail range from Rs 200 to Rs 500.

The Trek

Day One: Dhunche to Sing Gompa

The first day is a strenuous one, climbing from Dhunche at 1950m to Sing Gompa (Chandan Bari) at 3330m, via lodges at Deorali. There are half a dozen good lodges at Sing Gompa.

If you are coming from the Langtang trek, the climb from Thulo Syabru (2260m) to Sing Gompa, via Phobrang Danda, is easier to follow than the direct route to Chalang Pati.

Day Two: Sing Gompa to Laurebina Yak

The walk climbs steeply, quickly offering fine views of the Ganesh Himal range, then emerging onto a saddle at the teahouses of

Chalang Pati (3550m). The trail continues to climb to the four simple lodges at Laurebina Yak (3920m). The magnificent dawn views include the Annapurnas, Manaslu (8156m), the four peaks of the Ganesh Himal and Langtang Lirung. You should overnight in Laurebina Yak to help acclimatisation. You are now above the tree line.

Day Three: Laurebina Yak to Gosainkund Lakes

The trail climbs to a pass (say goodbye to the epic mountain views) and then continues on an exposed trail, offering views of Saraswati Kund at 4100m, the first of the Gosainkund lakes. The second lake is Bhairav (or Bhairab) Kund and the third is Gosainkund itself, at an altitude of 4380m. There are half a dozen lodges, a shrine and numerous pilgrim shelters on the northwestern side of the lake. You can walk around the lake in an hour, or climb the ridge above the lodges (20 minutes) for fabulous mountain and lake views.

Day Four: Gosainkund Lakes to Gopte

The trail climbs from the Gosainkund lakes to four more lakes near the Laurebina La (4610m), including Surya Lake beside the pass. It then drops steeply past a disused lodge at Bera Goth to two simple lodges at Phedi (3740m), near the site of a 1992 Thai Airways plane crash. Continue in and out of side valleys (not down the main valley) to ascend Kasturee Danda (Musk Deer Ridge) before dropping to two simple lodges at Gopte (3440m).

Day Five: Gopte to Tharepati

Today's walk descends to a stream and then climbs to three lodges at Tharepati (3640m), where the trail meets up with the Helambu trek. Tharepati is only a couple of hours' walk from Gopte but the early-morning mountain panoramas are superb. If the views aren't visible it's easy to continue to lodges at Mangengoth, 90 minutes downhill.

Days Six to Eight: Tharepati to Sundarijal

From Tharepati, the Helambu trail descends the ridgeline south to Mangengoth, Khutumsang, Gul Bhanjyang, Chipling, Thankhune Bhanjhang, Pati Bhanjhang, Chisopani, Mulkharha and Sundarijal (two to three days). There's teahouse accommodation at all places, with the nicest options at Mangengoth, Khutumsang and Chipling. The section from Gul Bhanjyang to Chipling mostly follows a dirt road, except for the final descent.

If you want to finish the trek early, a somewhat unreliable bus now runs from Thagani near Thankhune Bhanjyang to Kathmandu (Rs 130, five hours), departing at 8am. It's also possible to descend on village trails from Khutumsang to Chunaute (three hours) in the Melamchi Valley, from where buses run to Kathmandu every 30 minutes until 2pm. Buses might drop you at Jorpatti, near Bodhnath, so check.

The final day is spent crossing Shivapuri Nagarjun National Park (admission Rs 565) from either Chisopani or Pati Bhanjhang.

You can bus back to Kathmandu from Sundarijal in less than an hour (last bus 6.30pm).

RESTRICTED AREA & OTHER TREKS

The teahouse treks are the ones walked by the vast majority of trekkers in Nepal. If you want to head off the beaten track, it's possible to explore remote areas like Makalu and Kanchenjunga in the east or Humla and Dolpo in the west, but you must be self-sufficient and will likely have to make camping arrangements through a trekking company. In these relatively untouched areas there is little surplus food for sale and the practice of catering to trekkers has not yet developed.

There are trekking lodges during high season along the Manaslu, Tsum, Nar-Phu, Mustang and Makalu treks but lodges at the latter in particular are quite simple.

Most of these regions require a trekking permit fee that can only be arranged through a trekking agency. Throw in flights for you and your porters and it's easy to see that the remoter the trek, the more expensive it becomes.

See Lonely Planet's *Trekking in the Nepal Himalaya* for the complete story on trekking in Nepal. It has comprehensive advice on equipment selection, a dedicated health and safety section, and comprehensive route descriptions for both the popular treks and interesting, less heavily used routes. The following are currently the most popular restricted-area treks.

THE GREAT HIMALAYAN TRAIL

If you are up for a challenge, you might want to consider the Great Himalayan Trail, a 2500km walk across the entire spine of the Nepal Himalaya, from Kanchenjunga in the east to Humla in the west. There are several logistical hurdles to overcome, not least coordinating a whole fistful of timed trekking permits, but at least one trekking company (World Expeditions) offers the trail as a commercial trip, lasting for 157 days and costing a cool US$30,000. Several extreme athletes have completed the route (self-supported) in as little as 49 days.

The trail is partly a pre-existing network of trekking routes and partly a slick marketing campaign aimed at getting trekkers into regions currently not benefiting economically from tourism. Perhaps the best way to attempt the trail is to do it in segments, biting off chunks such as the Annapurna–Manaslu route or Jiri–Everest section, and doing it over several years.

For more information, see the excellent The Great Himalaya Trail website (www. thegreathimalayatrail.org). And good luck.

Nar-Phu A seven-day add-on to the Annapurna Circuit trail that takes you to the photogenic traditional villages of Nar and Phu near the Tibetan border, crossing the 5320m Kang-La pass on the way back. Trekking lodges available.

Mustang The most popular of the restricted-area treks leads to this long-forbidden Tibetan kingdom in a remote and arid land of spectacular Tibetan monasteries, canyons and cave complexes that border Tibet. The new road from Jomsom to the Chinese border is changing the region quickly. Possible as an organised teahouse or camping trek.

Manaslu Circuit This 16-day teahouse trek is often regarded by those in the know as Nepal's best overall trek. The half loop leads from Arughat in the Gorkha district up the Buri Gandaki Valley to the culturally Tibetan village of Sama, crossing the 5100m Larkya La to end at Dharapani on the Annapurna Circuit. There are fine views of Manaslu, the world's eighth-tallest mountain, and some great side trips to lakes and glaciers. The early stages of the trek were badly hit by the earthquake but lodges have reopened and some sections of trail have been rerouted.

Tsum Valley This remote and culturally Tibetan valley is reached off the Manaslu Circuit trail and can be done as an add-on to the Manaslu Circuit or as a two-week trek in itself. The valley was badly hit by the 2015 earthquake but lodges and monasteries are being rebuilt.

Tarap Valley Loop Popular 12-day loop in remote Dolpo that follows the Tarap Valley to the Tibetan-style villages and monasteries around Do Tarap, then crosses the breathtaking 5000m-plus passes of the Numa La and Baga La to arrive at the turquoise Phoksumdo Lake, probably the most beautiful lake in Nepal. Camping only.

Beni to Dolpo Excellent 12-day traverse from Beni, northwest of Pokhara, to Tarakot in outer Dolpo, crossing six passes and a huge swathe of midwestern Nepal in the footsteps of the book *The Snow Leopard*. Camping only.

Kanchenjunga Least visited of all is the far east, where two long routes lead to the north and south bases of the world's third-highest mountain. Figure on three weeks for the spectacular northern route, two weeks for the southern, or a month to combine both. Camping only, though simple teahouses are available along much of the trail.

Makalu Base Camp Another trek that gets you right into the heart of the mountains, following the Barun Valley up to base camp at around 5000m, offering fine views of Everest and Lhotse. The 15-day trek involves a flight to Tumlingtar and then a drive to Num, or you can trek in from Lukla in 11 days. It's just about doable as a simple teahouse trek but only in high season and you'd be wise to carry a tent as a backup.

Biking, Rafting & Kayaking

Best Places to be a Beginner

➡ Trisuli River (p325)

➡ Pokhara to Sarangkot & Naudanda (p325)

➡ Upper Sun Kosi (p326)

Best Places to be an Adrenaline Junkie

➡ Upper Mustang – Jomsom to Lo Manthang (p322)

➡ Marsyangdi (p327)

➡ Karnali (p327)

Why Go

While Nepal may be synonymous with trekking, its world-class rapids and exhilarating mountain descents are made for white-water rafting and mountain biking. Many of the bike trails are best suited to more experienced riders with a good level of fitness. And while most can be done on your own, you'll often need to rely on locals for directions, so hiring a guide or signing up for an organised tour will make life considerably easier. Nepal boasts rafting and kayaking routes suitable for beginners and pros alike, and your choice is dependent on how much of a buzz you can handle.

With the nature of mountain biking and rafting, these physical pursuits were not adversely affected by the 2015 earthquakes, but check before you set off for a route to make sure the trails are clear and rivers are flowing freely.

When to Go

➡ For cyclists October to November is a good time to go as it offers generally clear skies, warm daytime temperatures and it's not too cold at night.

➡ Mid- to late October through to the end of November is the best time for rafting and kayaking as it offers the warmest waters and rapids that are exciting without being life threatening. March to May is good for families.

Biking, Rafting & Kayaking in Nepal

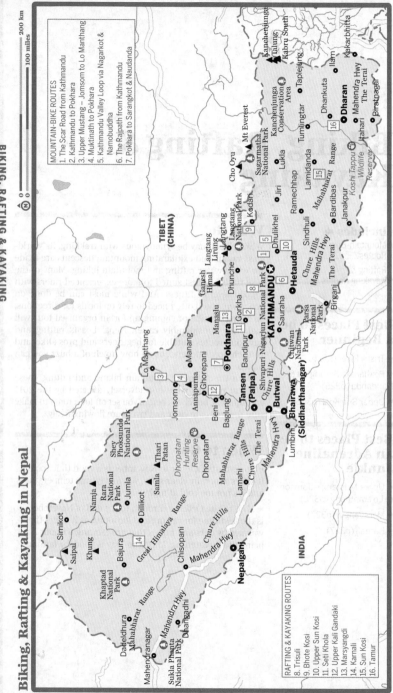

MOUNTAIN-BIKE ROUTES
1. The Scar Road from Kathmandu
2. Kathmandu to Pokhara
3. Upper Mustang – Jomsom to Lo Manthang
4. Muktinath to Pokhara
5. Kathmandu Valley Loop via Nagarkot & Namobuddha
6. The Rajpath from Kathmandu
7. Pokhara to Sarangkot & Naudanda

RAFTING & KAYAKING ROUTES
8. Trisuli
9. Bhote Kosi
10. Upper Sun Kosi
11. Seti Khola
12. Upper Kali Gandaki
13. Marsyangdi
14. Karnali
15. Sun Kosi
16. Tamur

TIBET (CHINA)

INDIA

MOUNTAIN-BIKE ROUTES

The Scar Road from Kathmandu

Distance 65km

Duration Seven hours, or two days with overnight in Kakani

Start Kathmandu

Finish Kathmandu

Summary Fine views and a challenging descent through a national park, after a tough initial climb of around 700m.

This trip northwest of Kathmandu can be a fairly demanding ride, and is suited to more experienced riders; having a guide is highly recommended.

Leaving Kathmandu (elevation 1337m), head towards Balaju on the Ring Rd 2km north of Thamel, and follow the sealed Trisuli Bazaar road towards Kakani, 23km away at an altitude of 2073m. You start to climb out of the valley as the track twists and turns past Nagarjun Hill, which provides the road with a leafy canopy. Once you're through the initial pass and out of the valley, the road continues northwest and offers a view of endless terraced fields to your left. (If you don't fancy the climb, you can avoid cycling on the road by putting your bike on the roof of the early-morning bus to Dhunche and getting off there.) On reaching the summit of the ridge, take a turn right (at a clearly marked T-junction), instead of continuing down to Trisuli Bazaar. (If you go too far, you reach a checkpoint just 100m beyond.) At this point magnificent views of the Ganesh Himal (*himal* means a range with permanent snow) provide the inspiration required to complete the remaining 4km of steep and deteriorating blacktop to the crown of the hill at Kakani for a well-deserved rest. It's an excellent idea to overnight here at the Tara Gaon (p194), or another such guesthouse, and savour the dawn views over the Himalaya.

After admiring the view, descend for just 30m beyond the gate and take the first left onto a 4WD track. This track will take you through the popular picnic grounds frequented on Saturday by Kathmandu locals. Continue in an easterly direction towards Shivapuri. The track narrows after a few kilometres near a metal gate on your left.

Through the gate, you are faced with some rough stone steps and then a 10-minute push/carry up and over the hilltop to an army checkpoint. Here it's necessary for foreigners to pay a Rs 556 entry fee to the Shivapuri Nagarjun National Park (p135), plus a Rs 1000 fee for their bike. Exit the army camp, turning right where the Scar Rd is clearly visible in front of you. You are now positioned at the day's highest point – approximately 2200m.

Taking the right-hand track you will start to descend dramatically along an extremely steep, rutted single trail with several water crossings. The trail is literally cut into the side of the hill, with sharp drops on the right that challenge a rider's skill and nerve. As you hurtle along, take time to admire the view of the sprawling Kathmandu Valley below – it's one of the best. In recent years the trail has become quite overgrown so you may have to carry your bike for several stretches and seek out the correct path. A guide would be useful for this section.

The trail widens, after one long gnarly climb before the saddle, then it's relatively flat through the protected Shivapuri watershed area. This beautiful mountain-biking section lasts for nearly 25km before the trail descends into the valley down a 7km spiral on a gravel road. This joins a sealed road, to the relief of jarred wrists, at **Budhanilkantha**, where you can buy refreshments. Take a moment to see the Sleeping Vishnu just up on your left at the main intersection. From here the sealed road descends gently for the remaining 15km back into the bustle of Kathmandu, although this part of the ride is generally through busy city traffic and not much fun.

Kathmandu to Pokhara

Distance 263km

Duration Five days

Start Kathmandu

Finish Pokhara

Summary Fine views and challenging trails that take you off the beaten track and through historic Newari towns.

It's possible to ride from Kathmandu to Pokhara in 12 to 14 hours along the busy Prithvi Hwy, but unless you're in a hurry the back roads are much better suited to mountain biking. Different companies offer different routes, some up to eight days' duration. This route will take you along some fairly rural trails that see few foreigners, so a guide or an organised tour is a good idea. Otherwise you'll need to rely on villagers to point you in the right direction. Hotels and places to eat can be a little thin on the ground in places and many tour companies recommend doing this ride as a full camping trip.

Day one sees you leaving Thamel in a northerly direction along the busy tarmac road, taking a left at the Kantipath exit. Continue along this road for 3km, past the American embassy and cross the Ring Rd at Maharajganj. From here it's a steady 6km uphill to **Budhanilkantha**, taking a break to see the Sleeping Vishnu. Continuing on, you leave the tarmac behind in a cloud of dust. The trail begins with a 3.5km climb to the army checkpoint where you pay the entry fees (Rs 560 for you, Rs 1000 for the bike) to Shivapuri Nagarjun National Park (p135). Follow the rocky trail through the forest for 4km until you reach a clearing. Ignore the first small road on your right, and instead take the next right after it, leading you downhill for 18km. Ignore the crossroads and head straight. If unsure, ask locals the way to Bidur, or better yet, get a guide.

After the descent you head along a mostly flat road with the Likhu Khola on your right. After 8km you'll cross the river and then go on to a paved road where the river will be on your left for about 5km before meeting the Trisuli River. Cross the bridge on your right and take a left through the village, riding through town before taking another left at the small paved road. On reaching the main road, head right and ride 3km to **Bidur**, from where you need to look out for a small turn on your right. Ask the locals for the way to Nuwakot Durbar, a steep 1½-hour climb from Bidur.

Day two is an up-and-down affair that covers a distance of 65km, starting with a gradual climb along a tarmac road from Trisuli Bazaar 12km uphill to Samari. From here it's a rough trail that passes through Taksar, finishing up on a sealed road leading to **Dhadhing Besi** (via Ratmate), where you spend the night.

The next day starts along tarmac, taking you up to Muralibhanjyang, from where it's a dirt road past Nepal's second-largest tar (flatland river valley) at Tallo Rampur. Continue along the Budhi Gandaki River, which you cross, and then pass through Bunkghat. The last stretch is a gradual ascent to the Newari town of **Gorkha**, famous for its Shah palace at Gorkha Durbar (p200).

Day four starts with a 10km descent, crossing Daraudi River at Chhepetar. From here it's a relatively easy 35km cross-country ride passing more tars and jungle, finishing up the day at **Sundarbazar**.

This brings you to the final day, saving the best views till last, as you whiz past towering Himalayan vistas. It's an undulating day of riding that covers around 63km, finishing up with a night out in **Pokhara** to celebrate the completion of your ride.

Upper Mustang: Jomsom to Lo Manthang

Distance 210km

Duration 12 days, including a rest day

Maximum elevation 5545m

Start Jomsom

Finish Jomsom

Summary An epic journey through remote and stunning stretches of the country. It's a challenging and technical ride, suitable for experienced riders only. There are teahouses on this route.

The first obstacle is forking out the US$500 permit to visit the restricted region of Upper Mustang (applicable for 10 days). Furthermore, you'll need to be part of an organised tour – but this can be as simple as employing a guide, which in the long run is a good idea to make sure you're on the right path. With the amount of hills you're about to tackle, a porter is highly recommended too.

Flying into **Jomsom** (unless you're nuts and want to ride there from Pokhara, an increasingly popular uphill assault), the journey begins with a gentle two-hour ride that'll take you to the first night's stop at the Buddhist village of **Kagbeni** (2801m). Day two is a mostly uphill ride along the jeep track to **Muktinath**, taking things slowly to get acclimatised to the altitude, while allowing you to take in stunning mountain views. The next day takes you into the restricted region of Upper Mustang, starting with an uphill climb to Gyu La (4077m). This involves carrying your bike at times, but you are rewarded with a 1000m descent along a single track. The final stage is a slight climb and river crossing to reach **Chele** (3050m), where you spend the night.

The next day is shorter but no less taxing, as you head up into the hills taking on no less than four passes, all exceeding 3600m. You'll be following jeep and single tracks, with a mix of steep climbs and descents, and once again you'll have to lug your bike uphill at times. Stop for the night below Syangboche La (3800m) on the **Syangboche River**.

While day five begins with more climbing (sigh), once you've cleared Syangboche La and Nyi La (4010m), rest assured the remainder of the day has mostly flat tracks. It also has some of the best scenery you'll see on the trip, with great views of the Himalaya, valleys and bright-yellow mustard fields. Overnight in **Charang** (Tsarang), with its 400-year-old Gulpa Sect Monastery.

Day six sets out to the crowning jewel of the journey, the walled kingdom city of **Lo Manthang**. You'll catch your first glimpse of it as you cross the 'Windy Pass' of Lo La (3950m). Today is a bit of a climb, but riding is mostly easy along a jeep track, with a 25km total riding distance. Arrive in Lo Manthang at lunchtime, and take a well-earned break. Spend a day or two here taking in the atmosphere of this amazing medieval kingdom. An option for your 'rest day' is a side trip up to Garphu following the Kali Gandaki River to Ghom cave.

After giving your legs a day off, it's time to leave Lo Manthang, starting with a challenging climb over Pangga (Samduling) at 4090m, a 75% rideable single track. From here it's a thrilling downhill road to Dhakmar, with dramatic landscapes. Head on to **Ghemi** (Ghami) for the night; it's your last stop in Mustang.

Heading back, on day nine you retrace the same trail with a single-track climb followed by a downhill to Syangboche, spending the night in **Samar**. Day 10 takes you over Dajori La (3735m) and Taklam La (3624m), passing sky burials en route. Next you cycle downhill to spend the night in **Chhusang**. From here you leave Upper Mustang and head back into the Annapurna region, a steady ride along the river taking you back to Kagbeni. You have the option to overnight or continue on down the valley to Jomsom, where you either fly to Pokhara or Kathmandu, or otherwise complete the ride through to Pokhara.

Muktinath to Pokhara

Distance 164km

Duration Six days

Maximum elevation 3710m

Start Jomsom

Finish Pokhara

Summary Mostly downhill journey that follows half the Annapurna Circuit, often along the jeep track from Jomsom.

While the construction of the road from Jomsom has trekkers mourning the death of the old Annapurna trekking route, mountain bikers are salivating at this new trail opening up to them. Most people start this increasingly popular route by flying into Jomsom.

From Jomsom enjoy a mostly flat two-hour ride to **Kagbeni**, where you could stay the night. Day two is a 1000m climb from Kagbeni up to **Muktinath**, with arid desert landscape and spectacular views to Dhaulagiri and other 8000m peaks. The next day is an undulating trail taking you to **Marpha** via Lupra, with 30% of the day involving pushing or carrying your bike. Day four sees another downhill leg heading to **Tatopani**, where you can soothe those aching leg muscles in natural hot-water springs. Getting back on the bike for day five, a descent leads you along the Kali Gandaki River to **Beni**. From here it's a highway ride to **Naudanda** and then a jeep track to **Sarangkot**. Hang around for the night to see spectacular sunrise views of the Himalaya and finish the journey on day six via the steep narrow trail to **Pokhara**.

Kathmandu Valley Loop via Nagarkot & Namobuddha

Distance 110km

Duration Three days

Start Kathmandu

Finish Kathmandu

Summary A circular route past a classic selection of the valley's cultural sights. There are numerous routes on offer, so you can tailor your trip according to tastes. Another popular option goes via Bhaktapur and Changu Narayan.

This route passes through areas that were badly affected by the 2015 earthquake, but the biking trails themselves are mostly unaffected. From Thamel head east past the Royal Palace, follow the road straight through Naxal and cross over the Ring Rd to visit the Pashupatinath Temple (p124). Continue along a hectic road to **Bodhnath**, stopping to explore this fascinating Tibetan Buddhist town. Ride on to Jorpati, where you take a right, passing along the edge of Gokarna Forest. Continue on to Sankhu, along the old trade route from Kathmandu to Lhasa, for another temple stop and refreshments. From here it's a jeep trail that heads mostly uphill past the Vajrayogini Temple (p172) and Lapsiphedi village en route to Jarsingpauwa. Trails from here are mostly flat until you reach Kattike, from where you'll need to suck it up for the 10km uphill to **Nagarkot**, where you'll spend the night.

Follow the trekking trail linking Nagarkot to Dhulikhel; the rough track is a one- to two-hour ride. To access it, you'll need to follow the tarmac road heading to the viewing tower, pass by the army camp and head down to the village of Rohini Bhanjyang. From here you choose the trail on the left side; look out for the signs. After 1km, take a right down a small trail that'll lead you through to the villages of Kankre and Tanchok. From here the trail continues to Opi, passing farmhouses, from where it's a further 5km to **Dhulikhel**. Stop here for lunch, refreshments and mesmerising mountain views. The final leg is a two-hour up-and-down journey through gorgeous scenery to **Namobuddha**, home to a monumental Tibetan Buddhist monastery up on a hill.

Get an early start to explore Namobuddha Monastery, before jumping on your bike for a downhill section followed by a cross-country trail to the Newari town of **Panauti**. Leave at least an hour to explore the old town before heading off. Don't let the heavenly first 4.5km of tarmac lull you into a false sense of security. The road soon deteriorates into 3km of dirt road to the village of Kushadevi, followed by 2.5km of bone-jarring stony track to Riyale. From here the valley starts to close in and gets increasingly remote – this is definitely not the place to blow a tyre! It's amazing how remote the route is, considering how close it is to Kathmandu. If you're not an experienced mountain biker, you're probably better off considering this as a motorbike route.

The next 8.5km is on a smooth dirt road that switchbacks up the hillsides to **Lakuri Bhanjyang** (1960m). You may find some basic food stalls but the actual summit is currently occupied by the army. In the past, travel companies have set up tented camp accommodation near here but this depends on tourism numbers and the level of army presence. Figure on spending two to three hours to get to here.

From this point on it's all downhill. The first section drops down the back side of the hill, blocking the views, but you soon get great views of the Annapurna and Ganesh Himal massifs – particularly spectacular in sunset's pink glow.

A further 5km of descent, rough at times, brings you to the turn-off left to Sisneri and the first village on this side of the pass. Soon the asphalt kicks in again, shortly followed by the pleasant village of **Lubbhu**, with its impressive central three-tiered Mahalakshmi Mahadev Temple. Traffic levels pick up for the final 5km to the Kathmandu ring road near Patan; be prepared for 'civilisation' to come as a bit of a shock after such a beautiful, peaceful ride.

The Rajpath from Kathmandu

Distance 150km

Duration Two days

Start Kathmandu

Finish Hetauda

Summary Classic but gruelling and dangerous (because of traffic) on-road ride over a 2488m pass, culminating with incomparable Himalayan views at Daman.

The ride begins on the Kathmandu–Pokhara (Prithvi) Hwy, which gives the only access to the valley. After leaving the valley, the highway descends to Naubise, at the base of the Mahesh Khola Valley, 27km from Kathmandu, where the Rajpath intersects with the Prithvi Hwy. Take the Rajpath, which forks to the left and is well signposted, for Hetauda. Start a 35km climb to Tistung (2030m) past terraced fields carved into steep hillsides. On reaching the pass at Tistung you descend for 7km into the beautiful Palung Valley before the final steep 9km climb to **Daman**, at a height of 2322m.

This day's ride (almost all climbing) takes between six and nine hours in the saddle. With an early start it is possible to stay in Daman, which will give you the thrill of waking up to the broadest Himalayan panorama Nepal has to offer. The following day the road climbs a further 3km to the top of the pass, at 2488m. At this point you can savour the very real prospect of an exhilarating 2300m descent in 60km!

As you descend towards Nepal's Terai plains, laid out before you to the south, notice the contrast with the side you climbed, as the south side is lush and semitropical. With innumerable switchbacks and a bit of speed you should watch out for the numerous buses and trucks looming around blind corners. The road eventually flattens out after the right turn to cross a newly constructed bridge and the first main river crossing. The rest of the journey is a gently undulating route alongside a river; a further 10km brings you to **Hetauda**. (Note that there are useful cyclists' notebooks in the Motel Avocado (p269). After a night's rest you can continue along the Rajpath towards India or turn right at the statue of the king in the centre of town and head towards Chitwan National Park.

Pokhara to Sarangkot & Naudanda

Distance 54km

Duration Seven hours, or an overnight trip

Start Pokhara

Finish Pokhara

Summary Work up a sweat to two of Pokhara's best Himalayan viewpoints, followed by a great downhill coast.

Leave early and ride along Lakeside (towards the mountains) to the last main intersection and sealed road. Turn right; this is the road that returns to central Pokhara. After 2km you turn left and continue straight (north). This intersection is the zero kilometre road marker. After a further 2km there is a smaller sealed road to the left, signposted as the road to Sarangkot.

This road winds its way along a ridge into Sarangkot, providing outstanding views of the Himalaya, which seems close enough to reach out and touch. After 6km a few teahouses make a welcome refreshment stop just where the stone steps mark the walking trail to the summit. From here your path is a 4WD track that closely hugs the edge of the mountain overlooking Phewa Tal. Continue until you join a Y-intersection that doubles back sharply to the right and marks the final climb to **Sarangkot**. You can turn this ride into a relaxed overnight trip by staying in lodges here.

From Sarangkot continue straight ahead, riding the narrower motorcycle trails leading to Kaski and Naudanda. After the Sarangkot turn-off the trail soon begins to climb to Kaski, towards the hill immediately in front of you. The section to Kaski takes around 30 to 60 minutes, and you may need to push your bicycle on the steeper section near the crown of the hill. Over the top you follow the trail through to **Naudanda**. You are now at around 1590m, having gained

around 840m of altitude from Pokhara. The trail is rocky in parts and will test your equipment to the extreme, so do not consider riding this trail on a cheap hired bicycle.

From Naudanda it's a 32km downhill run to Pokhara along the smooth asphalt highway. The route starts with a twisting 6km descent into the Mardi Khola Valley then descends gently following the river, allowing an enjoyable coast almost all the way to Pokhara.

RAFTING & KAYAKING ROUTES

Trisuli

Distance 40km

Duration One to two days

Start Baireni or Charaudi

Finish Multiple locations

Summary Popular introduction to rafting, and a wild ride during the monsoon.

With easy access just out of Kathmandu, the Trisuli is where many budget river trips operate, and is the obvious choice if you are looking for a short introduction to rafting at the cheapest possible price.

After diving into the valley west of Kathmandu, the Prithvi Hwy follows the Trisuli River. Most of the rapids along this route are class II to class III, but the water can build up to class IV in the monsoon.

The Trisuli has some good scenery but with the main busy road to Kathmandu beside the river it is not wilderness rafting. Some operators have their own fixed campsites or lodges, ranging from safari-style resorts to windblown village beaches complete with begging kids and scavenging dogs.

When booking, ask where the put-in point is: anything starting at Kuringhat or Mugling will mainly be a relaxing float. During the mid-monsoon months (August to early October) the Trisuli changes character completely as huge runoffs make the river swell like an immense ribbon of churning ocean, especially after its confluence with the Bhodi Gandaki. At these flows it provides a classic big-volume Himalayan river so make sure you choose a reputable company to go with.

Multiday trips continue downriver towards Narayangarh and Chitwan National Park, but the rapids below Kurintar are much more gentle.

Bhote Kosi

Distance 9km

Duration One day

Start 95km from Kathmandu, near the Tibetan border

Finish Barabise

Summary Just three hours from Kathmandu, the Bhote Kosi is one of the best short raft trips to be found anywhere in the world.

The Bhote Kosi is the steepest river rafted in Nepal – technical and totally committing. With that said, beginners can still give it a go. With a gradient of 16m per kilometre, it's a full eight times as steep as the Sun Kosi, which it feeds further downstream. The rapids are steep and continuous class IV, with a lot of continuous class III in between.

This river is one of the most fun things you can do right out of Kathmandu and a great way to get an adrenaline fix during the low-water months, but it should only be attempted with a company that has a lot of experience and has the absolute best guides, safety equipment and safety kayakers.

Sadly, a huge landslide and the subsequent build up of a natural dam in mid-2014 has, for the moment at least, rather taken the shine off this river and currently few people are rafting it. Enquire with Kathmandu agencies for the latest news.

Upper Sun Kosi

Distance 20km

Duration One day

Start Khadichour

Finish Dolalghat or Sukute Beach

Summary A great place for a short family trip or learner kayak clinics. Can be combined over two days with the Bhote Kosi.

The top section of the Upper Sun Kosi from below the dam to near Sukute Beach is a class III white-water run offering a good opportunity to get a feel for rafting.

The lower section is a mellow scenic float, with forest down to the river, and it is a popular river for kayak clinics. At high flows during and just after the monsoon rains, the Upper Sun Kosi is a full-on class III to IV high-adrenaline day trip.

Seti Khola

Distance 32km

Duration Two days

Start Damauli

Finish Gaighat

Summary A quieter river that is perfect for beginners, birdwatchers, families and learner kayakers.

The Seti is an excellent two-day trip in an isolated area, with beautiful jungle, white sandy beaches and plenty of class II to III rapids. The warm water also makes it a popular place for winter trips and kayak clinics. During the monsoon the river changes radically as monsoon runoff creates class III to IV rapids.

The logical starting point is Damauli on the Prithvi Hwy between Mugling and Pokhara. This would give you 32km of rafting to the confluence with the Trisuli River. From the take-out at Gaighat it's just a one-hour drive to Chitwan National Park.

Upper Kali Gandaki

Distance 60km

Duration Three days (two days rafting)

Start Beni or Baglung

Finish Andhi Khola

Summary Diverse trip down the holy river, through deep gorges and past waterfalls.

The Upper Kali Gandaki is an excellent alternative to the Trisuli (p325), as there is no road alongside, and the scenery, villages and temples all combine to make it a great trip.

The rapids on the Kali Gandaki are technical and continuous (at class III to IV, sometimes even V depending on the flows), and in high water it's no place to be unless you are an accomplished kayaker experienced in avoiding big holes. At medium and lower flows it's a fun and challenging river with rapids that will keep you busy.

The Kali Gandaki is one of the holiest rivers in Nepal, and every river junction is dotted with cremation sites and burial mounds. If you're wondering what's under that pile of rocks, we recommend against exploring! Because of the recent construction of a dam at the confluence with the Andhi Khola, what was once a four- to five-day trip has now become a three-day trip, starting at either Beni or Baglung (depending on the operator) and taking out at the dam site, Marmi. At very high flows it will probably be possible to run the full five-day trip to Ramdhighat by just portaging the dam site. This option would add some great white water and you could visit the fantastic derelict palace at **Ranighat**.

If you can raft to Ramdhighat beside the Siddhartha Hwy between Pokhara and Sunauli, you could continue on to the confluence with the Trisuli at Devghat along the **Lower Kali Gandaki**. This adds another 130km and three or four more days. The lower section below Ramdhighat doesn't have much white water, but it is seldom rafted and offers a very isolated area with lots of wildlife.

Marsyangdi

Distance 27km

Duration Four days (two days rafting)

Start Ngadi

Finish Phaliya Sanghu (Phalesangu)

Summary A magnificent blue white-water river with a spectacular mountain backdrop. Best suited to experienced rafters.

The Marsyangdi is steeper and offers more continuous white water than most other rivers in Nepal; it's not called the 'Raging River' for nothing! You can go by bus to Khudi or Bhulbule, from where it's a short walk up to the village of Ngadi, with great views of Manaslu ahead all the way the whole time.

From Ngadi downstream to the dam side above Phaliya Sanghu, it's pretty much solid white water. Rapids are steep, technical and consecutive, making the Marsyangdi a serious undertaking. Successful navigation of the Marsyangdi requires companies to have previous experience on the river and to use the best guides and equipment. Rafts must be self-bailing, and should be running with a minimum of weight and gear on board. Professional safety kayakers should be considered a standard safety measure on this river.

A hydro project has severely affected this world-class rafting and kayaking river but it is still possible to have a two-day run on the rapids before reaching the dam. You could divert around the dam and continue on the lower section for another two days but at this stage it is hard to tell how much water will be released and whether it will be worth doing. Future dams are planned for the river so you might want to raft this one soon.

Karnali

Distance 180km

Duration 10 days (seven days rafting)

Start Dungeshwar

Finish Chisopani

Summary A classic trip in far western Nepal down its largest and longest river.

The Karnali is a gem, combining a short (two-hour) trek with some of the prettiest canyons and jungle scenery in Nepal. Most experienced river people who have paddled the Karnali find it one of the best all-round river trips they've ever done. In high water it is a serious commitment, combining huge, though fairly straightforward, rapids with a seriously remote location. The river flows through some steep and constricted canyons where the rapids are close together, giving little opportunity to correct for potential mistakes. Pick your company carefully.

At low water the Karnali is still a fantastic trip. The rapids become smaller when the river drops, but the steeper gradient and constricted channel keep it interesting.

The trip starts with a long, but interesting, two-day bus ride to the remote far west of Nepal. If you're allergic to bus rides, it's possible to fly to Nepalganj and cut the bus transport down to about four hours on the way over, and two hours on the way back. The new road now runs from Surkhet to Dungeshwar on the river. Once you start on the Karnali it's 180km to the next road access at Chisopani, on the northern border of the Bardia National Park (p272).

The river section takes about seven days, giving plenty of time to explore some of the side canyons and waterfalls that come into the river valley. Better-run trips also include a layover day, where the expedition stays at the same campsite for two nights. The combination of long bus rides and trekking puts some people off, but anyone who has ever done the trip raves about it. Finish with a visit to the Bardia National Park for an unbeatable combination.

Adventurers can raft the even more remote **Seti Karnali**, a rarely run scenic stretch of river that starts at Gopghat and takes around seven days to get to Chisopani.

Sun Kosi

Distance 270km

Duration Eight to nine days (six to seven days rafting)

Start Dolalghat

Finish Chatara

Summary A self-sufficient expedition through central Nepal from the Himalaya to the Gangetic plain.

This is the longest river trip offered in Nepal, traversing 270km through the beautiful Mahabharat Range on its meandering way from the put-in at Dolalghat to the take-out at Chatara in the far east of the country. It's quite an experience to begin a river trip just three hours out of Kathmandu, barely 60km from the Tibetan border, and end the trip looking down the hot, dusty gun barrel of the north Indian plain just eight or nine days later. Because it's one of the easiest trips logistically, it's also one of the least expensive for the days you spend on a river.

The Sun Kosi (River of Gold) starts off fairly relaxed, with only class II and small class III rapids to warm up on during the first couple of days. Savvy guides will take this opportunity to get teams working together with precision.

The river volume increases with the air temperature as several major tributaries join the river, and from the third day the rapids become more powerful and frequent. During high-water trips you may well find yourselves astonished at just how big a river wave can get. While the lower sections of large-volume rivers are usually rather flat, the Sun Kosi reserves some of its biggest and best rapids for the last days, and the last section is nonstop class IV before a final quiet float down the Sapt Kosi. Some companies add an extra day's rafting on the lower section of the Tamur, from Mulghat down. At the right flow it's an incredible combination of white water, scenery, villages and quiet, introspective evenings.

Note that a new road runs alongside the river for the first 40km of rafting, until the large rapid at Harkapur. It's therefore possible to start here and make a six-day trip on the river.

Tamur

Distance 131km

Duration 12 days

Start Dobhan

Finish Chatara

Summary Remote expedition in the foothills of Kanchenjunga in the far east of the country; combines a four-day trek with great rapid running.

Way out in the far east, this river combines one of the best short treks in Nepal with some really challenging white-water action. The logistics of this trip make it a real expedition, and while it is a little more complicated to run than many rivers in Nepal, the rewards are worth the effort.

First you have to get to Basantapur, a 16-hour drive from Kathmandu or a one-hour flight to Biratnagar and then a six-hour drive. Most expeditions begin with a stunning three- or four-day trek from Basantapur up over the Milke Danda Range, past the alpine lake of Gupha Pokhari to Dobhan. At Dobhan three tributaries of the Tamur join forces, combining the waters of the mountains to the north (including Kanchenjunga, the world's third-largest mountain). The first 16km of rapids is intense, with rapid after rapid, and the white water just keeps coming through towering canyons until the big finale. The best time to raft is at medium flows between mid-October and mid-November.

Other Rivers

The **Upper Seti River**, just outside Pokhara, makes an excellent half-day trip when it is at high flows. Trips operate in mid-September and November (class III+).

The **Balephi Khola** (above the Bhote Kosi) is run by a few companies from Jalbire to its confluence with the Upper Sun Kosi. Trips normally run only when the river is high from mid-September to early November and in May; it's a two-day trip that combines this river with the Upper Sun Kosi.

The **Bheri River**, which is in the west, is a great float trip with incredible jungle scenery and lots of wildlife, making it a possible family trip. This is also one of Nepal's best fishing rivers and can be combined with a visit to the Bardia National Park (p272).

The powerful **Arun River** from Tumlingtar makes an excellent three-day wilderness trip with good class III rapids and pristine canyons, although the logistics of flying to the start of the river and getting gear there makes it an expensive trip.

Understand Nepal

Nepal Today

Over the last few decades, Nepal has endured a Maoist uprising that turned into a civil war, the collapse of a centuries-old monarchy and the creation of a democratic federal republic. Its greatest crisis of modern times, however, was the devastating earthquakes that struck in 2015, killing more than 8500 people. Rebuilding has been slow and local livelihoods remain severely impacted, but tourism is bouncing back, injecting badly needed foreign funds and business optimism.

Best in Film

Himalaya (1999) Stunningly shot by Eric Valli in Dolpo; also released as *Caravan*.

Everest (1998) David Breashears' Imax film shot during the disastrous 1997 climbing season.

Best in Print

The Snow Leopard (Peter Matthiessen; 1978) Classic and profound account of a trek to Dolpo.

Arresting God in Kathmandu (Samrat Upadhyay; 2001) Nine short stories from the first Nepali writer to be published in English.

Snake Lake (Jeff Greenwald; 2010) Memoir of family loss set against Nepal's political revolution.

Little Princes (Conor Grennan; 2011) Inspiring account of volunteering in a Nepali orphanage.

While the Gods Were Sleeping (Elizabeth Enslin; 2014) Part memoir, part-anthropological account of life in a Brahman family in western Nepal.

Kathmandu (Thomas Bell; 2016) Impressionistic historical portrait of Kathmandu.

Destruction & Reconstruction

The tremors that shook the Kathmandu Valley in April and May 2015 saw destruction on a level that had not been seen for almost a century. Temples and palaces crumbled to dust, houses toppled, roads buckled, and landslides and avalanches destroyed whole villages. The economic cost of the disaster is estimated at US$10 billion, nearly half of Nepal's gross domestic product, but the human cost is even more tragic; thousands of families lost loved ones and hundreds of thousands were left homeless.

Nepal's greatest challenge over the coming years will be to rebuild infrastructure, houses and livelihoods. Visitor numbers dropped dramatically after the earthquake but are now back to pre-earthquake levels, contributing almost 10% of GDP.

Money has flooded into Nepal from international donors, but the country has a long way to go to raise the estimated US$6.7 billion needed for reconstruction. Nepal's recovery will depend on the resilience of its people, as well as the goodwill of foreign governments and the willingness of foreign travellers to look beyond the tragedy and return to Nepal's hotels, restaurants and trekking lodges.

Economic Ups & Downs

Despite the political disarray there are signs of life in Nepal's economy. A spate of multibillion-dollar contracts with both China and India will see several hydroelectric and road-building projects come to fruition over coming years. India's role in harnessing Nepal's rivers and China's influence on Nepal's Tibetan refugee community remain hot topics as Nepal juggles influences from its giant neighbours.

China's presence in Nepal in particular is becoming pronounced. As road, air and eventually perhaps even rail links bridge the Himalaya, Chinese tourists are now a significant part of the Nepali economy. Tourism remains essential to Nepal's economy, employing around one million people directly or indirectly. Funds are being poured into new hotel construction in anticipation of further growth.

However, more tourism brings the added problem of growing infrastructure to match. Tourists heading to remote areas are placing an increasing burden on local resources, and on the porters and guides leading travellers around the mountains. In April 2014, 16 Sherpas were killed on the Khumbu icefall, shutting down Everest climbing for a season as Sherpa families sought compensation in a labour dispute with the government. Just six months later a blizzard in central Nepal killed 43 trekkers and guides in the Annapurna region, turning a spotlight on mountain safety and renewing calls for tighter controls on Nepal's trekking industry.

A feature of the Nepal economy is the large numbers of Nepalis heading abroad for employment opportunities. Remittances remain the number one source of foreign currency for Nepal, dwarfing tourism, but halting the skill and brain drain will be essential to the country's future.

From War to Elections

Against the backdrop of the 2015 earthquakes, the ordinary struggles of day-to-day politics seem somehow less important, but Nepal is still struggling with the legacy of a decade of armed conflict. Inflation is rampant, and crumbling infrastructure, held back by years of under-investment, makes daily life a struggle for most Nepalis. Kathmandu's population, in particular, boomed during the civil war and the city is now close to breaking point, with gridlocked traffic, choking pollution levels and daily electricity shortages.

Since the end of the civil war, the Maoists have seen a spectacular fall from grace, from winning the national election in 2008 to coming third in 2013. As former fighters start to lose political influence and contentious issues such as immunity from crimes committed during the civil war come to a head, there is always the danger that Nepali politics will return to the days of strikes and political violence.

Disappointingly little has been achieved since the end of the war. Years of deadlock and wrangling between Communist and Congress parties has resulted in the rise and fall of nine governments in 10 years.

The 2015 constitution recently established Nepal as a 'federal democratic republic'. It accepts several electoral systems for different tiers of representation, right from the presidential election to the lowest level of ward members. Nepal democracy has evolved into a complicated system of local, district and provincial (state) elections and a combination of first-past-the-post and proportional voting that is sure to keep the pundits guessing.

The election to the House of Representatives and State Assemblies in December 2017 saw a resounding win for the CPN Communist-Maoist alliance, returning the Maoists to power once again.

POPULATION: **29 MILLION (2016 ESTIMATE)**

AREA: **147,181 SQ KM**

ADULT LITERACY RATE: **64% MALE/FEMALE LITERACY 76/53%**

LIFE EXPECTANCY: **71 YEARS**

UN HUMAN DEVELOPMENT INDEX: **144, OUT OF 188 COUNTRIES (2016)**

if Nepal were 100 people

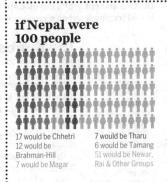

17 would be Chhetri
12 would be Brahman-Hill
7 would be Magar
7 would be Tharu
6 would be Tamang
51 would be Newar, Rai & Other Groups

belief systems
(% of population)

81 Hindu
9 Buddhist
4 Muslim
3 Kirant
3 Other

population per sq km

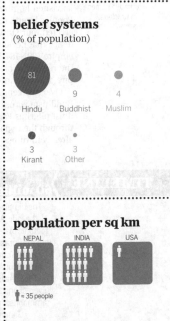

NEPAL   INDIA   USA

👤 ≈ 35 people

History

Squeezed between the Tibetan plateau and the plains of the subcontinent – the modern-day giants of China and India – Nepal has long prospered from its location as a resting place for mountain traders, travellers and pilgrims. An ethnic melting pot, it has bridged cultures and absorbed elements of its neighbours, yet has retained a unique character. Despite ancient roots, the modern state of Nepal emerged only in the 18th century and is still forging itself as a modern nation state.

The Kiratis & Buddhist Beginnings

Nepal's recorded history emerges from the fog of antiquity with the Hindu Kiratis. Arriving from the east around the 7th or 8th century BC, these Mongoloid people are the earliest known rulers of the Kathmandu Valley. King Yalambar, the first of their 29 kings, is mentioned in the Mahabharata, the Hindu epic, but little more is known about the Kiratis.

In the 6th century BC, Prince Siddhartha Gautama was born into the Sakya royal family of Kapilavastu, near Lumbini, later embarking on a path of meditation and thought that led him to enlightenment as the Buddha, or 'Enlightened One'. The religion that grew up around him continues to shape the face of Asia.

Around the 3rd century BC, the great Indian Buddhist emperor Ashoka visited Lumbini and erected a pillar at the birthplace of the Buddha. Popular legend recounts how he then visited the Kathmandu Valley and erected four stupas around Patan (these still exist), but there is no evidence that he actually made it there in person. Either way, his Mauryan empire (321–184 BC) played a major role in popularising Buddhism in the region, a role continued by the north Indian Buddhist Kushan empire, which spanned the 1st to 3rd centuries AD.

Over the centuries the resurgent faith of Hinduism came to eclipse Buddhism across the entire subcontinent. By the time the Chinese Buddhist pilgrims Fa Xian (Fa Hsien) and Xuan Zang (Hsuan Tsang) passed through the region in the 5th and 7th centuries, the site of Lumbini was already in ruins.

References for most things in Nepal are notoriously inconsistent. Spellings, statistics, historical dates and temple names always have several variants. We use the most commonly agreed options, with alternative names in brackets.

TIMELINE

60 million BC	100,000 BC	c 563 BC
The Himalaya rise as the Indo-Australian tectonic plate crashes into the Eurasian plate. The Tethys Sea is pushed up, resulting in sea shells atop Mt Everest and fossilised ammonites in the Kali Gandaki Valley.	Kathmandu Valley is created as a former lake bed dries. Legend relates how the Buddhist bodhisattva Manjushri created the valley by cutting the Chobar Gorge and draining the lake's waters.	Siddhartha Gautama is born in Lumbini into royalty and lives as both prince and ascetic in Nepal before gaining enlightenment, as the Buddha, under a Bodhi (pipal) tree.

Licchavis, Thakuris, then Darkness

Hinduism reasserted itself in Nepal with the arrival from northern India of the Licchavis. In AD 300 they overthrew the Kiratis, who resettled in the east to become the ancestors of today's Rai and Limbu people.

Between the 4th and 9th centuries the Licchavis ushered in a golden age of cultural brilliance. Their strategic position allowed them to prosper from trade between India and China. The chaitya (a style of stupa) and monuments of this era can still be seen at the Changu Narayan Temple (p168), north of Bhaktapur, and in the backstreets of Kathmandu's old town. It's believed that the original stupas at Chabahil, Bodhnath and Swayambhunath date from the Licchavi era.

Amsuvarman, the first Thakuri king, came to power in 602, succeeding his Licchavi father-in-law. He consolidated his power to the north and south by marrying his sister to an Indian prince and his daughter Bhrikuti to the great Tibetan king Songsten Gampo. Together with the Tibetan king's Chinese wife Wencheng, Bhrikuti managed to convert the Tibetan king to Buddhism around 640, profoundly changing the face of both Tibet and the Himalaya. As Buddhism lost ground in India, Buddhism's key texts and concepts would eventually return to Nepal from Tibet across the high Himalayan passes.

From the late 7th century until the 13th century, Nepal slipped into its 'dark ages', of which little is known. Tibet invaded in 705 and Kashmir invaded in 782. The Kathmandu Valley's strategic location and fertile soil, however, ensured the kingdom's growth and survival. King Gunakamadeva is credited with founding Kantipur, today's Kathmandu, around the 10th century.

The Golden Age of the Mallas

The first of the Malla (literally 'wrestlers' in Sanskrit) kings came to power in the Kathmandu Valley around 1200, after being exiled from India. This period was a golden one that stretched over 550 years, though it was peppered with fighting over the valuable trade routes to Tibet.

The first Malla rulers had to cope with several disasters. A huge earthquake in 1255 killed around one-third of Nepal's population. A devastating Muslim invasion by Sultan Shams-ud-din of Bengal less than a century later left hundreds of smouldering and plundered Hindu and Buddhist shrines in its wake, though the invasion did not leave a lasting cultural effect (unlike the invasion of the Kashmir Valley, which remains Muslim to this day). In India the damage was more widespread and many Hindus were driven into the hills and mountains of Nepal, where they established small Rajput principalities.

Travellers can visit the archaeological site of Kapilavastu, at Tilaurakot, where Siddhartha Gautama (the Buddha) lived for the first 29 years of his life.

HISTORY LICCHAVIS, THAKURIS, THEN DARKNESS

A History of Nepal by John Whelpton is one of the few available titles on the subject. It focuses on the last 250 years and explains not only political events but also the changes in people's lives. It's for sale in Nepal at a discounted local price.

c 250 BC	57 BC	AD 464	629
Mauryan Emperor Ashoka (r 268–231 BC) visits Lumbini, embraces Buddhism and reputedly builds four stupas on the outskirts of Patan, ushering in a golden age for Buddhism.	Nepal's official Vikram (Bikram) Samwat calendar starts, in spring. Thus to Nepalis the year 2018 is 2075.	Nepal's earliest surviving inscription is carved into the beautiful Changu Narayan Temple in the Kathmandu Valley on the orders of King Manadeva.	The Chinese Buddhist pilgrim Xuan Zang (Hsuan Tsang) visits Lumbini and describes the Ashoka pillar marking the Buddha's birthplace. His text helps archaeologists relocate and excavate the lost site in 1895.

Apart from this, the earlier Malla years (1220–1482) were largely stable, reaching a high point under the third Malla dynasty of Jayasthithi Malla (r 1382–95), who united the valley and codified its laws, including the caste system.

After the death of Jayasthithi Malla's grandson Yaksha Malla in 1482, the Kathmandu Valley was divided up among his sons into the three kingdoms of Bhaktapur (Bhadgaon), Kathmandu (Kantipur) and Patan (Lalitpur). The rest of what we today call Nepal consisted of a fragmented patchwork of almost 50 independent states, stretching from Palpa and Jumla in the west to the semi-independent states of Banepa and Pharping, most of them minting their own coins and maintaining standing armies.

The rivalry between the three kingdoms of the Kathmandu Valley expressed itself not only through warfare but also through the patronage of architecture and culture, which flourished in the climate of jealous one-upmanship. The outstanding collections of exquisite temples and buildings in each city's Durbar Sq are testament to the fortunes spent by the kings in their attempts to outdo each other.

The building boom was financed by trade in everything from musk and wool to salt and Chinese silk. The Kathmandu Valley stood at the departure point for two separate routes into Tibet, via Banepa to the northeast and via Rasuwa and the Kyirong Valley near Langtang to the northwest. Traders would cross the jungle-infested Terai during winter to avoid the virulent malaria and then wait in Kathmandu for the mountain passes to open later that summer. Kathmandu grew rich, and its rulers converted their wealth into gilded pagodas and ornately carved royal palaces. In the mid-17th century Nepal gained the right to mint Tibet's coins using Tibetan silver, further enriching the kingdom's coffers.

In Kathmandu, King Pratap Malla (r 1641–74) oversaw that city's cultural high point with the construction of the Hanuman Dhoka (p75) palace and the Rani Pokhari (p83) pond. He also built the first of several subsequent pillars that featured a statue of the king facing the protective temple of Taleju, who the Mallas had by that point adopted as their protective deity. The mid-17th century also saw a high point of building in Patan.

The Malla era shaped the religious as well as the artistic landscape, introducing the dramatic annual chariot festivals of Indra Jatra and Machhendranath. The Malla kings shored up their divine right to rule by claiming to be reincarnations of the Hindu god Vishnu and by establishing the cult of the Kumari, a living goddess whose role it was to bless the Malla's rule during an annual celebration.

The cosmopolitan Mallas also absorbed foreign influences. The Indian Mughal court influenced Malla dress and painting, introduced the Nepalis to firearms and exported the system of land grants in return

In 2013 archaeologists unearthed a 6th-century BC shrine underneath Lumbini's Maya Devi shrine, making this the earliest Buddhist shrine ever uncovered. Within the shrine were the remains of a tree, possibly the tree that Maya held onto when giving birth to Siddhartha (the Buddha).

The mid-14th century saw the de facto rule of Malla Queen Maya Devi, the most powerful woman in Nepal's history.

c 1260	13th to 15th centuries	1349	1380
Nepali architect Arniko travels to Lhasa and Kublai Khan's capital Dadu (Beijing), bringing with him the design of the pagoda and changing the face of religious temples across Asia.	The Khasa empire of the western Mallas reaches its peak in the far western Karnali basin around Jumla. Its lasting contribution is Nepali – the national language spoken today.	The Muslim armies of Sultan Shams-ud-din plunder the Kathmandu Valley, destroying the stupa at Swayambhunath and carrying off cartloads of booty.	Ame Pal founds the kingdom of Lo (Mustang). The last king of Mustang, Jigme Palbar Bista, who died in 2016, could trace his family back 25 generations to this king. Mustang remains independent until 1951.

for military service, a system that would have a profound effect in later years. But change didn't only come from abroad. A storm was brewing inside Nepal, just 100km to the east of Kathmandu.

Unification under the Shahs

In 1768 Prithvi Narayan Shah, ruler of the tiny hilltop kingdom of Gorkha (halfway between Pokhara and Kathmandu), stood poised on the edge of the Kathmandu Valley, ready to realise his dream of a unified Nepal. It had taken more than a quarter of a century of conquest and consolidation to get here, but Shah was about to redraw the political landscape of the Himalaya.

Shah had taken the strategic hilltop fort of Nuwakot in 1744, after fighting off reinforcements from the British East India Company, but it took him another 24 years to take Kathmandu, finally sneaking in while everyone was drunk during the Indra Jatra festival. A year later he eventually took Kirtipur, after three lengthy failed attempts. In terrible retribution his troops hacked over 50kg of noses and lips off Kirtipur's residents; unsurprisingly, resistance melted away in the wake of the atrocity. In 1769 he advanced on the three cowering Malla kings and ended the Malla rule, thus unifying Nepal.

Shah moved his capital from Gorkha to Kathmandu, establishing the Shah dynasty, whose line continued right up until 2008. Shah himself, however, did not live long after his conquest; he died in Nuwakot in 1775, just six years after unification, but is still revered as the founder of the nation.

Shah had built his empire on conquest, and his insatiable army needed ever more booty and land to keep it satisfied. Within six years the Gurkhas had conquered eastern Nepal and Sikkim. The expansion then turned westwards into Kumaon and Garhwal, only halted on the borders of the Punjab by the armies of the powerful one-eyed ruler Ranjit Singh.

The expanding boundaries of 'Greater Nepal' by this time stretched from Kashmir to Sikkim, eventually putting it on a collision course with the world's most powerful empire, the British Raj. Despite early treaties with the British, disputes over the Terai led to the first Anglo-Nepali War, which the British won after a two-year fight. The British were so impressed by their enemy that they decided to incorporate Gurkha mercenaries into their own army, a practice that continues to this day.

The 1816 Sugauli treaty called a screeching halt to Nepal's expansion and laid down its modern boundaries. Nepal lost Sikkim, Kumaon, Garhwal and much of the Terai, though some of this land was restored to Nepal in 1858 in return for support given to the British during the Indian Mutiny (Indian War of Independence). A British resident was sent to Kathmandu to keep an eye on things, but the British knew that it would

Nepal is said to get its name from Nepa, the name given to the Newari kingdom of the Kathmandu Valley; the word Nepa is derived from the name of a mythological Hindu sage, Ne, who once lived in the valley.

1428–82	1531–34	1641–74	18th century
The rule of Yaksha Malla, the high point of the Malla reign, ends in the fracture of the Kathmandu Valley into the three rival kingdoms of Kathmandu, Patan and Bhaktapur.	Sherpas (literally 'easterners') settle in the Solu-Khumbu region near Mt Everest. The Nangpa La remains the most important Sherpa trade route with Tibet.	Rule of Malla king Pratap Malla, a dancer, poet and great supporter of arts, who shapes the face of Kathmandu, building large parts of Hanuman Dhoka palace.	Capuchin missionaries pass through Nepal to Tibet, later supplying the West with its first descriptions of exotic Kathmandu.

be too difficult to colonise the impossible hill terrain and were content to keep Nepal as a buffer state. Nepalis to this day are proud that their country was never colonised by the British, unlike the neighbouring hill states of India.

Following its humiliating defeat, Nepal cut itself off from all foreign contact from 1816 until 1951. The British residents in Kathmandu were the only Westerners to set eyes on Nepal for more than a century.

On the cultural front, temple construction continued apace, though perhaps of more import to ordinary people was the revolutionary introduction, via India, of chillies, potatoes, tobacco and other New World crops.

The Shah rulers, meanwhile, swung from ineffectual to sadistic. At one point the kingdom was governed by a 12-year-old female regent, in charge of a nine-year-old king, while Crown Prince Surendra (r 1847–81) expanded the horizons of human suffering by ordering subjects to jump down wells or ride off cliffs, just to see whether they would survive.

The Ranocracy

The death of Prithvi Narayan Shah in 1775 set in motion a string of succession struggles, infighting, assassinations, backstabbing and intrigue that culminated in the Kot Massacre in 1846. This blood-stained night was engineered by the young Chhetri noble Jung Bahadur and it catapulted his family into power, just as it sidelined the Shah dynasty.

Ambitious and ruthless, Jung Bahadur organised (with the queen's consent) for his soldiers to massacre 55 of the most important noblemen in the kingdom in one night, while they were assembled in the Kot courtyard adjoining Kathmandu's Durbar Sq. He then exiled 6000 members of their families to prevent revenge attacks.

Jung Bahadur took the title of prime minister and changed his family name to the more prestigious 'Rana'. He later extended his title to *maharajah* (king) and decreed it hereditary. The Ranas became a parallel 'royal family' within the kingdom and held the reins of power, as the Shah kings were relegated to listless, irrelevant figureheads, requiring permission even to leave their palace.

The family line of Rana prime ministers held power for more than a century, eventually intermarrying with the Shahs. Development in Nepal stagnated, although the country did at least manage to preserve its independence.

Jung Bahadur Rana travelled to Europe in 1850, attending the opera and the races at Epsom, and brought back a taste for neoclassical architecture that can be seen in Kathmandu today. Under the Ranas, *sati* (the Hindu practice of casting a widow on her husband's funeral pyre) was abolished, 60,000 slaves were released from bondage, and a school and college were established in the capital. Despite the advances, the

Nepal's founding father, Prithvi Narayan Shah, referred to Nepal as 'a yam between two boulders' – namely China and India – a metaphor that is as true geologically as it is historically.

1750	1768–69	1790–92	1814–16
King Jaya Prakash Malla builds Kathmandu's Kumari Temple, followed by the Nyatapola Temple in Bhaktapur, the literal high point of stupa-style architecture in Nepal.	Nepal is unified under Prithvi Narayan Shah (1723–75), known as the father of the Nepali nation, to form the Shah dynasty. Kathmandu becomes the capital.	Nepal invades Tibet and sacks Shigatse. Avenging Chinese troops advance down the Kyirong Valley as far as Nuwakot. As part of the ensuing treaty the Nepalis pay tribute to the Chinese emperor until 1912.	The Anglo-Nepali War ends in victory for Britain. The ensuing Treaty of Sugauli establishes Nepal's boundaries and gives Britain the right to recruit Gurkha soldiers and maintain a residency in Kathmandu.

peasants in the hills were locked in a medieval existence, while the Ranas and their relatives lived lives of opulent luxury.

Modernisation began to dawn on Kathmandu with the opening of the Bir Hospital, Nepal's first, in 1889. Over the next 15 years Kathmandu saw its first piped water system, the introduction of limited electricity and the construction of the Singh Durbar, considered at one time the largest palace in Asia. The 29-year reign (1901–29) of Prime Minister Chandra Shumsher in particular brought sweeping changes, including the introduction of electricity and the outlawing of slavery. In 1923 Britain formally acknowledged Nepal's independence and in 1930 the kingdom of Gorkha was renamed the kingdom of Nepal, reflecting a growing sense of national consciousness.

Elsewhere in the region dramatic changes were taking place. The Nepalis supplied logistical help during Britain's invasion of Tibet in 1903, and over 300,000 Nepalis fought in WWI and WWII, garnering a total of 13 Victoria Crosses – Britain's highest military honour – for their efforts.

After WWII, India gained its independence and the communist revolution took place in China. Tibetan refugees fled into Nepal in the first of several waves when the new People's Republic of China tightened its grip on Tibet, and Nepal became a buffer zone between the two rival Asian giants. Meanwhile King Tribhuvan, forgotten in his palace, was being primed to overthrow the Ranas.

> You can visit the birthplace and launching pad of Nepal's unifier, Prithvi Narayan Shah, at Gorkha, and see his second royal palace at Nuwakot.

HISTORY THE RANOCRACY

TRANS-HIMALAYAN TRADE

For centuries, hardy caravans of yaks and goats criss-crossed the high Himalaya, bringing salt harvested from Tibet's great inland lakes to exchange for rice and barley carried up from the Middle Hills of Nepal. Wool, livestock and butter from Tibet were exchanged for sugar, tea, spices, tobacco and Indian manufactured goods. Twelve major passes linked Nepal and Tibet, the easiest of which were in Mustang, ensuring that the Kali Gandaki Valley became the main entrepôt for transferring, storing and taxing the trade.

Over the last half century much of the traditional border trade has dried up. The arrival of the Indian railway line at the Nepali border greatly aided the transportation of cheap Indian salt, sounding a death knell for the caravan trade. The real nail in the coffin came in the 1960s, when the Chinese closed the borders to local trade.

Ironically the Chinese are currently leading a resurgence of trade and road construction. Chinese truckers now drive over the passes to Lo Manthang in Mustang and in 2012 another road border crossing opened at Rasuwaghadi, linking the Tibetan Kyirong Valley with Nepal's Langtang region along a route long used for trade and invasion. You'll see the occasional yak caravan headed for the Tibetan border laden with timber and the medicinal fungus *yartse gumba*, as well as telltale cans of Lhasa Beer littering trekking routes in the Manaslu, Everest and Mustang regions.

1815	1846	1854	1856
Five thousand Nepali soldiers begin serving as troops in the East India Company after impressing the British with their valour and loyalty.	The Kot Massacre ends in the killing of the cream of the court aristocracy, ushering in the Rana era (1846–1951) and sidelining the Shah kings to puppet status.	The Muluki Ain legal code formalises the Nepali caste system, defining diet, legal and sexual codes and enshrining state discrimination against lower castes. The law is revised only in 1963.	Peak XV is declared the world's highest peak. It is later renamed Everest after the head of Trigonometric Survey, George Everest (who actually pronounced his name *eve*-rest).

Restoration of the Shahs

In late 1950 King Tribhuvan was driving himself to a hunting trip at Nagarjun when he suddenly swerved James Bond–style into the Indian embassy, where he then claimed political immunity and jumped into an Indian Air Force jet to Delhi. At the same time, the recently formed Nepali Congress Party, led by BP Koirala, managed to take most of the Terai by force from the Ranas and established a provisional government that ruled from the border town of Birganj. India exerted its considerable influence and negotiated a solution to Nepal's turmoil, and King Tribhuvan returned in glory to Nepal in 1951 to set up a new government composed of demoted Ranas and members of the Nepali Congress Party.

Although Nepal gradually reopened its long-closed doors and established relations with other nations, dreams of a new democratic system never quite got off the ground. Tribhuvan died in 1955 and was succeeded by his cautious son Mahendra. A new constitution provided for a parliamentary system of government, resulting in Nepal's first ever general election in 1959. The Nepali Congress Party won a clear victory and BP Koirala became the new prime minister. In late 1960, however, the king decided the government wasn't to his taste after all, had the cabinet arrested and swapped his ceremonial role for direct control (much as King Gyanendra would do 46 years later).

In 1962 Mahendra decided that a partyless, indirect *panchayat* (council) system of government was more appropriate to Nepal. The real power remained with the king, who chose 16 members out of the 35-member National Panchayat, and appointed both the prime minister and his cabinet. Political parties were banned.

Mahendra died in 1972 and was succeeded by his 27-year-old British-educated son Birendra. Nepal's hippie community was unceremoniously booted out of the country when visa laws were tightened in the run-up to Birendra's spectacular coronation in 1975. Simmering discontent with corruption, the slow rate of development and the rising cost of living erupted into violent riots in Kathmandu in 1979. King Birendra announced a referendum to choose between the *panchayat* system and one that would permit political parties to operate. The result was 55% to 45% in favour of the *panchayat* system; democracy had been outvoted.

Nepal's military and police apparatus were among the least publicly accountable in the world and strict censorship was enforced. Mass arrests, torture and beatings of suspected activists were well documented, and the leaders of the main opposition, the Nepali Congress, spent the years between 1960 and 1990 in and out of prison.

The first cars were transported to the Kathmandu Valley in parts, on the backs of porters, before there were even any roads or petrol in the kingdom. You can see one of these, an early Hudson, at Kathmandu's National Museum.

Confusingly, three Koirala brothers have all served as prime ministers of Nepal; BP Koirala in 1959, MP Koirala in 1951 and 1953 and GP Koirala, four times, most recently in 2006. Their cousin Sushil Koirala was prime minister in 2015.

1914–18	1934	1949	1951
Around 100,000 Nepalis fight and 10,000 lose their lives in WWI. Thirty years later 200,000 Gurkhas and army forces serve in WWII, mostly in Myanmar (Burma).	A massive earthquake destroys much of the Kathmandu Valley, killing over 8000 people in under a minute, injuring 16,000 and destroying a quarter of all homes in Nepal.	Bill Tilman gets permission from King Tribhuvan to trek in Nepal, including around the Kali Gandaki, Helambu and Solu Khumbu regions. He is the first foreigner to trek to Everest Base Camp.	King Tribhuvan and the Nepali Congress Party, with Indian support, overthrow the Rana regime and establish a new coalition government. Nepal opens its doors to the outside world.

During this time over one million hill people moved to the Terai in search of land and several million crossed the border to seek work in India (Nepalis are able to cross the border and work freely in India), creating a major demographic shift in favour of the now malaria-free Terai.

People Power

In 1989, as communist states across Europe crumbled and pro-democracy demonstrations occupied China's Tiananmen Sq, Nepali opposition parties formed a coalition to fight for a multiparty democracy with the king as constitutional head; the upsurge of protest was called the Jana Andolan, or People's Movement.

In early 1990 the government responded to a nonviolent gathering of over 200,000 people with bullets, tear gas and arrests. After several months of intermittent rioting and pressure from foreign-aid donors, the government was forced to back down. On 9 April King Birendra announced he was lifting the ban on political parties and was ready to accept the role of constitutional monarch. Nepal was to become a democracy.

In May 1991 the Nepali Congress Party won the general election and two years later a midterm election resulted in a coalition government led by the Communist Party. This was one of the few times in the world that a communist government had come to power by popular vote.

Political stability did not last long, and the late 1990s were littered with dozens of broken coalitions, dissolved governments and sacked politicians.

In 1996 the Maoists, a Communist-party splinter group, angered by government corruption, the dissolution of the communist government and the failure of democracy to deliver improvements to the people, declared a 'people's war'.

The insurgency began in midwestern Nepal and gathered momentum, but it was initially ignored by Kathmandu's politicians. The repercussions of this nonchalance came to a head in November 2001 when the Maoists broke their ceasefire and attacked an army barracks west of Kathmandu. The initial Maoist forces were armed with little more than ancient muskets and khukuris (Ghurkha knives), but they quickly obtained guns looted from police stations. They were bankrolled by robbery and extortion and aided by the open border with India.

Initial police heavy-handedness fuelled a cycle of violence and retribution that only succeeded in alienating the local people. Political disenfranchisement, rural poverty, resentment against the caste system, issues of land reform and a lack of faith in the squabbling, self-interested politicians of distant Kathmandu swelled the ranks of the Maoists. Attacks spread to almost every one of Nepal's 75 districts, including Kathmandu. At their peak Maoists effectively controlled around 40% of the country.

Nepal's flag is like no other, consisting of two overlapping red triangles, bearing a white moon and a white 12-pointed sun (the first mythological kings of Nepal are said to be descendants of the sun and moon).

1953	1955–72	1959	1960
Everest is summited for the first time by New Zealander Edmund Hillary and Tibetan Sherpa Tenzing Norgay on 29 May, just in time for the coronation of Queen Elizabeth II.	The rule of King Mahendra sees the introduction of elections, which are then voided as the king seizes direct power, introducing the *panchayat* system of government.	Nepal's first general election is held. The Dalai Lama flees Tibet and China closes the Tibet–Nepal border, seriously affecting the trade of salt for grain and creating great social change in the Himalaya.	The eradication of malaria opens the Terai to rapid population growth. Today the Terai contains around half of Nepal's population and most of its industry and agricultural land.

The political temperature reached boiling point when the king brought in the army and armed militias loyal to the government in 2001. The USA labelled Nepal's Maoists a terrorist group and handed over millions of dollars to help fight Nepal's own 'war on terror'. Ironically the 'people's' armed struggle was led by two high-caste intellectuals: Pushpa Kamal Dahal (known by his nom de guerre Prachanda, which means 'the fierce') and Baburam Bhattarai, both of whom would later serve as Nepal's prime minister.

Several Maoist truces, notably in 2003 and 2005, offered some respite, though these reflected as much a need to regroup and rearm as they did any move towards a lasting peace. By 2005 nearly 13,000 people, including many civilians, had been killed in the insurgency. Amnesty International accused both sides of horrific human-rights abuses, including summary executions, abductions, torture and child conscription. Dark days had come to Nepal.

Stalled Development & the Failure of Aid

During the second half of the 20th century Nepal saw impressive movements towards development, particularly in education and road construction, with the number of schools increasing from 300 in 1950 to over 40,000 by 2000. Since then relentless population growth (Nepal's population grew from 8.4 million in 1954 to 26 million in 2004) has simply cancelled out many of these advances, turning Nepal from a food exporter to a net importer within a generation.

The Maoist insurgency only worsened the plight of the rural poor by bombing bridges and telephone lines, halting road construction, diverting much-needed government funds away from development and causing aid programs to suspend activity due to security concerns. It is estimated that during the decade-long conflict the Maoists destroyed Rs 30 billion of government infrastructure, while the government blew US$108 billion on military spending. Caught in the middle, an entire generation of rural Nepali children missed out on their education.

After a half-century of outside assistance and over US$4 billion in aid (60% of its development budget), Nepal remains one of the world's poorest countries, with the highest income disparity in Asia and one of its lowest health-spending levels. Seven million Nepalis lack adequate food or basic health care and education.

Royal Troubles & Political Change

On 1 June 2001 the Nepali psyche was dealt a huge blow when Crown Prince Dipendra gunned down almost every member of the royal family during a get-together in Kathmandu. Ironically Dipendra did not die straight away and was pronounced the king of Nepal, despite being in

Forget Kathmandu: An Elegy for Democracy, by Manjushree Thapa, starts with Nepal's royal massacre, moves to a political history of the last 200 years, then ends with a description of a trek through Maoist-held areas in 2003.

For background on the Maoist rebellion read *Himalayan People's War: Nepal's Maoist Rebellion*, edited by Michael Hutt.

1965	1975	1990	1996–2006
Colonel James 'Jimmy' Roberts founds Mountain Travel, Nepal's first trekking company, and leads a group of women up the Kali Gandaki Valley, laying the path for Nepal's trekking industry.	Birendra is crowned king in Kathmandu's Hanuman Dhoka, three years after the death of his father Mahendra. The king wears the traditional jewel-encrusted and feathered headdress of the Shah kings.	The mass demonstrations of the People's Movement force King Birendra to accept a new constitution, restoring democracy and relegating the king to the role of constitutional Hindu monarch.	A decade-long Maoist insurgency brings the country to its knees and results in the death of 13,000 Nepalis. Development projects stall and tourism levels plummet.

THE ROYAL MASSACRE

The night of 1 June 2001 has entered the annals of history as one of Nepal's greatest tragedies, a bloodbath that could have been lifted straight from the pages of Shakespeare.

That night, in a hail of bullets, 10 members of Nepal's royal family, including King Birendra and Queen Aishwarya, were gunned down during a gathering at the Narayanhiti Palace by a deranged, drunken Crown Prince Dipendra, who eventually turned a weapon on himself. The real motive behind the massacre will never be known, but many believe Dipendra's rage was prompted by his parents' disapproval of the woman he wanted to marry.

The initial disbelief and shock gave way to suspicion and a host of conspiracy theories, many concerning the new king, Gyanendra (who was in Pokhara at the time of the massacre), and his son Paras (who emerged unscathed from the attack). None of this was helped by an official inquiry that initially suggested the automatic weapon had been discharged by accident, or the fact that the victims were quickly cremated without full post-mortems and the palace building then razed to the ground. Other theories included that old chestnut – a CIA or Indian secret-service plot.

A surreal royal exorcism followed on the 11th day of mourning, as a high-caste priest, dressed in the gold suit, shoes and black-rimmed glasses of King Birendra and donning a paper crown, climbed onto an elephant and slowly lumbered out of the valley, taking with him the ghost of the dead king. The same scapegoat ritual (known as a *katto* ceremony) was performed for Dipendra, except that a pregnant woman dashed underneath his elephant en route, believing this would ensure she give birth to a boy. She was trampled by the elephant and died, adding a further twist to the tragedy.

Doubtless, the truth of what really happened that night will never be known.

---

a coma. His rule ended two days later, when he too was declared dead. King Birendra's brother Gyanendra was then crowned in what may for him have been a moment of déjà vu – he had already been crowned once before, aged three, and ruled as king for three months, after his grandfather Tribhuvan fled to India in 1950.

In the days that followed the massacre, a tide of emotions washed over the Nepali people – shock, grief, horror, disbelief and denial. A 13-day period of mourning was declared and in Kathmandu impromptu shrines were set up for people to pray for their king and queen. About 400 shaven-headed men roamed the streets around the palace on motorbikes, carrying pictures of the monarch. Half a million stunned Nepalis lined the streets during the funeral procession. When the shock of this loss subsided the uncertainty of what lay ahead hit home.

For an impressionistic historical portrait of Kathmandu, check out journalist Thomas Bell's kaleidoscopic *Kathmandu*, published in India and available in Kathmandu.

May 1996	1999	June 2001	February 2005
Eight climbers die on a single day, 11 May, on Everest. An Imax film and Jon Krakauer's book *Into Thin Air* chronicle the disaster.	The body of British climber George Mallory is discovered near the summit of Everest, reigniting conjecture that he made it to the top of the world a good 30 years before Hillary.	Prince Dipendra massacres 10 members of the royal family in the Narayanhiti Palace, including his father, King Birendra, before shooting himself. The king's brother, Gyanendra, is crowned king of Nepal.	King Gyanendra dismisses the government and assumes direct control of the country in a state of emergency, citing the need to crush the Maoist rebels.

The beginning of the 21st century saw the political situation in the country turn from bad to worse. Prime ministers were sacked and replaced six times between 2000 and 2005, marking a total of nine governments in 10 years. The fragile position of Nepali politicians is well illustrated by Sher Bahadur Deuba, who was appointed prime minister for the second time in 2001, before being dismissed in 2002, reinstated in 2004, sacked again in 2005, thrown in jail on corruption charges and then released. In 2017 he found himself in the role of prime minister yet again.

Nepal's disappointing experiment with democracy faced a major setback in February 2005 when King Gyanendra dissolved the government amid a state of emergency, promising a return to democracy within three years. Freedom of the press was curtailed and telephone lines were cut periodically to prevent demonstrations. Tourism levels slumped and a mood of pessimism descended over the country.

Everything changed in April 2006, when days of mass demonstrations and curfews, and the deaths of 16 protesters forced the king to restore parliamentary democracy. The following month the newly restored parliament voted to reduce the king to a figurehead, ending powers that the royal Shah lineage had enjoyed for over 200 years. The removal of the king was the price required to bring the Maoists to the negotiating table, and a peace accord was signed later that year, drawing a close to the bloody decade-long insurgency.

The ensuing pace of political change in Nepal was head-spinning. One month after the Maoists achieved a majority in the April 2008 elections parliament abolished the monarchy completely by a margin of 560 votes to four, ending 240 years of royal rule. The new government saw former guerrilla leader Pushpa Kamal Dahal as prime minister and Dr Baburam Bhattarai as finance minister. In 2009 Pushpa Kamal Dahal resigned due to infighting, hinting at political turmoil to come.

Following the 2008 abolition of the monarchy, the king's face was removed from the Rs 10 note, the prefix 'Royal' disappeared from the name of the national airline as well as national parks, and the king's birthday was dumped as a national holiday.

Former Maoist 'terrorists' became cabinet ministers, members of the People's Liberation Army joined the national army and a new constitution was commissioned (it was eventually adopted in 2015), all as part of a process to bind the former guerrillas into the political mainstream. After a decade of darkness, violence and social upheaval, a renewed optimism in the political process was palpable throughout Nepal. It remains to be seen whether this spirit of optimism can survive ongoing political wrangles and the economic uncertainty that Nepal continues to face.

2006 〉	May 2008 〉	2014 〉	2015 〉
After weeks of protests, King Gyanendra reinstates parliament, which votes to curtail his emergency powers. Maoists and government officials sign a peace agreement and the Maoist rebels enter an interim government.	Parliament abolishes the Nepali monarchy, ending 240 years of royal rule.	Twin disasters hit Nepal's mountains. In April, 16 Sherpa guides are killed on the Khumbu icefall in one of Nepal's deadliest disasters. In October, 43 trekkers and porters die after heavy snowfall in the Annapurna region.	A 7.8 magnitude earthquake strikes central Nepal on 25 April, killing 8500 and causing devastation across the Kathmandu Valley. A few weeks later a 7.3 magnitude quake strikes near Everest Base Camp, with more casualties.

People & Culture

Nepal's spectacular and physically challenging geography has most assuredly influenced the culture and outlook of its hardy and resourceful people. And yet it is hard to generalise about a 'Nepali people' when one considers the diversity of its 60 or more ethnic and caste groups, and myriad (up to 123) languages. From the lowlands bordering India to the Himalayan heights bordering Tibet, Nepal boasts a complex mosaic of customs and beliefs that will baffle, fascinate and charm travellers.

The National Psyche

Perhaps the dominant Nepali cultural concepts are those of caste and status, both of which contribute to a strictly defined system of social hierarchy and deference. Caste determines not only a person's status, but also their career and marriage partner, how that person interacts with other Nepalis and how others react back. This system of hierarchy extends even to the family, where everyone has a clearly defined rank. The Nepali language has half a dozen words for 'you', each of which conveys varying shades of respect.

When it comes to their religious beliefs, Nepalis are admirably flexible, pragmatic and, above all, tolerant – there is almost no religious or ethnic tension in Nepal. Nepalis are generally good humoured and patient, quick to smile and slow to anger, though they also have a reputation as fierce fighters.

The Nepali view of the world is dominated by prayer and ritual, and a knowledge that the gods are not remote, abstract concepts but living, present beings who can influence human affairs in very direct ways. Nepalis perceive the divine everywhere, from the greeting *namaste,* which literally means 'I greet the divine inside of you', to the spirits and gods present in trees, passes, sacred river confluences and mountain peaks.

The notions of karma and caste, when combined with a tangled bureaucracy and deep-rooted corruption, tend to create an endemic sense of fatalism in Nepal. Confronted with problems, many Nepalis will simply respond with a shrug of the shoulders and the phrase *khe garne?,* or 'what is there to do?', which Westerners often find frustrating yet oddly addictive.

Tourism generates around US$500 million each year in foreign earnings for Nepal and it is estimated that the money spent by each tourist supports 10 or 11 Nepalis.

MOVING TIGERS

Nepal's national board game is *bagh chal,* which literally means 'move the tigers'. The game is played on a lined board with 25 intersecting points. One player has four tigers, the other has 20 goats, and the aim is for the tiger player to 'eat' five goats by jumping over them before the goat player can encircle the tigers and prevent them moving. You can buy attractive brass *bagh chal* sets in Kathmandu and Patan, where they are made.

Nepal's other popular game is *carom,* which looks like finger snooker. Players use discs that glide over a chalked-up board to pot other discs into the corner pockets.

Traditional Lifestyle

The cornerstones of Nepali life are the demands (as well as the rewards) of one's family, ethnic group and caste. To break these time-honoured traditions is to risk being ostracised from family and community. While young Nepali people, especially in urban areas, are increasingly influenced by Western values and lifestyle, the majority of people still live by traditional customs and principles.

In most ethnic groups, joint and extended families live in the same house. In some smaller villages extended clans make up the entire community. Traditional family life has been dislocated by the large number of Nepali men forced to seek work away from home, whether in Kathmandu or the Terai, or abroad in India, Malaysia or the Gulf States.

Arranged marriages remain the norm in Nepali Hindu society and are generally between members of the same caste or ethnic group, although there is a growing number of 'love marriages'. Child marriages have been illegal since 1963 and today the average age of marriage for girls with an education is just under 19. It is just under 17 for girls without formal education. The family connections generated by a marriage are as much a social contract as a personal affair, and most families consult matchmakers and astrologers when making such an important decision.

To decide not to have children is almost unheard of and Nepali women will often pity you if you are childless. Having a son is important, especially for Hindu families, as some religious rites (such as lighting the funeral pyre to ensure a peaceful passage into the next life) can only be performed by the eldest son. Girls are regarded by many groups as financial burdens whose honour needs to be protected until they are married.

Children stay at school for up to 12 years; 70% of children will begin school but only 15% will reach their 10th school year, when they sit their School Leaving Certificate (SLC) board examination. Many villages only have a primary school, which means children either have to walk long distances each day or board in a bigger town to attend secondary school. The ratio of boys to girls at secondary schools can be almost 2:1 in favour of boys.

Despite the rapid increase in urbanisation – over 40% of Nepalis now live in urban centres – there are still considerable numbers that are rural and poor. Farming continues to be a major occupation and debt is a factor in most people's lives. Large areas of land are still owned by *zamindar*s (absent landlords) and up to 50% of a landless farmer's production may go to the landowner as rent.

Most rural Nepali families are remarkably self-sufficient in their food supply, selling any excess in the nearest town, where they'll stock up on things such as sugar, soap, cigarettes, tea, salt, cloth and jewellery. Throughout Nepal this exchange of goods has created a dense network of trails trodden by everyone from traders and porters to mule caravans and trekking groups.

The rhythms of village life are determined by the seasons and marked by festivals – New Year, harvest and religious festivals being the most important. Dasain remains the biggest event of the calendar in the Middle Hills and is a time when most Nepali families get together.

Older people are respected members of the community and are cared for by their children. Old age is a time for relaxation, prayer and meditation. The dead are generally cremated and the deceased's sons will shave their heads and wear white for an entire year following the death.

Changes in trading patterns and traditional culture among Nepal's Himalayan people are examined in *Himalayan Traders*, by Christoph von Fürer-Haimendorf.

Up to three million Nepalis work overseas – over 40% in India, 38% in the Gulf States, and smaller numbers in Malaysia and elsewhere. In the 2015–16 fiscal year, overseas workers sent home over US$6 billion, or about 29% of Nepal's GDP, making this Nepal's largest single source of foreign currency.

Population

Nepal currently has a population of around 30 million (2017 estimate), a number that is increasing at the rate of 1.35% annually. Over 2.5 million people live in the Kathmandu Valley and around one million in Kathmandu. Four million Nepalis reside in India. Around half of Nepal's population lives in the flat fertile lands of the Terai, which also acts as the nation's industrial base, and the population here is increasing rapidly.

The website www. mountainvoices. org/nepal.asp. html has an interesting collection of interviews with Nepali mountain folk on a wide variety of topics.

People

The human geography of Nepal is a remarkable cultural mosaic of peoples who have not so much assimilated as learned to coexist. The ethnic divisions are complex and numerous; you'll have to do your homework to be able to differentiate between a Limbu, Lepcha, Lhopa and Lhomi – and that's just the Ls!

Nepal is the meeting place of the Indo-Aryan people of India and the Mongoloid peoples of the Himalaya. There are three main physical and cultural zones running east to west: the north, including the Himalaya; the Middle Hills; and the Terai. People living in these zones have adapted lifestyles and farming practices to suit their environment but, thanks largely to Nepal's tortured topography, each has retained its own traditions. Social taboos, especially among caste Hindus, have limited further assimilation between groups.

Nepal's diverse ethnic groups speak somewhere between 24 and 123 different languages and dialects, depending on how finely the distinctions are made. Nepali functions as the unifying language, though less than half of Nepal's people speak Nepali as their first language.

People of the Himalaya

The hardy Tibetan peoples who inhabit the high Himalaya are known in Nepal as Bhotias (Bhotiyas), a slightly derogatory term among caste Hindus. Each group remains distinct but their languages are all Tibetan-based and, with a few exceptions, they are Tibetan Buddhists.

The Bhotiyas' names combine the region they came from with the suffix 'pa' and include the Sherpas (literally 'easterners') of the Everest region, the Dolpopas of the west and the Lopas, or Lobas (literally 'southerners'), of the Mustang region.

The withering of Trans-Himalayan trade routes and the difficulty of farming and herding at high altitude drive these people to lower elevations during winter, either to graze their animals or to trade in India and the Terai. Apart from tourism, yak herding and the barley harvest remain the economic bedrocks of the high Himalaya.

NEPALI NAMES

You can tell a lot about a Nepali person from their name, including often their caste, profession, ethnic group and where they live. Gurung and Sherpa are ethnic groups as well as surnames. The surname Bista or Pant indicates that the person is a Brahman, originally from western Nepal; Devkota indicates an eastern origin. Thapa, Pande and Bhasnet are names related to the former Rana ruling family. Shrestha is a high-caste Newari name. The initials KC often stand for Khatri Chhetri, a mixed-caste name. The surname Kami is the Nepali equivalent of Smith.

Sherpa names even reveal which day of the week the person was born: Dawa (Monday), Mingmar (Tuesday), Lhakpa (Wednesday), Phurba (Thursday), Pasang (Friday), Pemba (Saturday) and Nyima (Sunday). The one thing you can't tell from a Sherpa name is their sex – Lhakpa Sherpa could be a man or a woman!

Thakalis

Originating along the Kali Gandaki Valley in central Nepal, the Thakalis have emerged as the entrepreneurs of Nepal. They once played an important part in the salt trade between the subcontinent and Tibet, and travellers will meet them most frequently in their adopted roles as hoteliers and lodge owners, especially on the Annapurna Circuit. Originally Buddhist, many pragmatic Thakalis have now adopted Hinduism.

Tamangs

The Tamangs make up one of the largest groups in the country. They live mainly in the hills north of Kathmandu and have a noticeably strong Tibetan influence, from their monasteries, known as *ghyang,* to the mani walls that mark the entrance to their villages. You can stay in traditional Tamang villages along the Tamang Heritage Trail.

According to some accounts, ancestors of the Tamang were horse traders and cavalrymen from an invading Tibetan army who settled in Nepal. They are well known for their independence and suspicion of authority, probably caused by the fact that in the 19th century they were relegated to a low status, with much of their land distributed to Bahuns and Chhetris. As bonded labourers they were dependent upon menial work such as portering. Many of the 'Tibetan' souvenirs, carpets and thangkas (religious paintings) you see in Kathmandu are made by Tamangs.

Tibetans

About 20,000 of the 130,000 Tibetans in exile around the world live in Nepal. Most were born here and are officially stateless. Although their numbers are small, Tibetans have a high profile, partly because of the important roles they play in tourism and the Tibetan carpet industry.

Tibetans are devout Buddhists and their arrival in the valley has rejuvenated a number of important religious sites, most notably the stupas at Swayambhunath (p117) and Bodhnath (p128). These two places are constantly humming with Tibetans praying, spinning prayer wheels and slowly circumambulating the great stupas.

For decades Tibetan refugees in Nepal have marked the anniversary of the failed 1959 uprising against Chinese rule in Tibet with annual protests. However, in recent years, with the increasing influence of Chinese investment and political power, the Nepalese authorities have started to clamp down on the protestors. Police now quickly silence protests in notable areas such as near the Chinese Embassy and Bodhnath, further straining the relationship between the Tibetan community and the Nepalese government.

Sherpas

The Sherpas who live high in the mountains of eastern and central Nepal are probably the best-known Nepali ethnic group. These nomadic Tibetan herders moved to the Solu Khumbu region of Nepal 500 years ago from eastern Tibet, bringing with them their Tibetan Buddhist religion and building the beautiful gompas (monasteries) that dot the steep hillsides. Traditionally Sherpas would be recognised by their Tibetan clothing, but modern Sherpas have developed Western tastes in clothes matching their relatively strong earnings. They are associated with the Khumbu region around Mt Everest, although only a small percentage of Sherpas actually live in the Khumbu; the rest live in the lower valleys of the Solu region. Potatoes were introduced to the region in the late 19th century and are now the main Sherpa crop.

Tourism stepped in after the collapse of trade over the Nangpa La in 1959, when the Chinese sent thousands of troops to enforce their claim

Sherpas: Reflections on Change in Himalayan Nepal, by James F Fisher, offers an anthropological snapshot of how tourism and modernisation have affected Sherpa religious and cultural life. Fisher worked with Edmund Hillary in the Khumbu in the 1960s, bringing the first schools and airstrip to the region.

on Tibet. These days the Sherpa name is synonymous with mountaineering and trekking, and Sherpas can be found working as high-altitude mountain guides as well as owners of travel agencies and trekking lodges.

People of the Middle Hills

The Middle Hills of Nepal are the best places to witness village life at its most traditional. In the east are the Kirati, who are divided into the Rai and Limbu groups. The Newari people dominate the central hills around the Kathmandu Valley, while the Magars and Gurungs inhabit the hills of the Kali Gandaki northwest of Pokhara.

Moving west, the Bahun and Chhetri are the dominant groups, although the lines between castes have become blurred over time.

Rais & Limbus

The Rais and Limbus are thought to have ruled the Kathmandu Valley in the 7th century BC until they were defeated around AD 300. They then moved into the steep hill country of eastern Nepal, from the Arun Valley to the Sikkim border, where many remain today. Others have moved to the Terai or India as economic migrants. Many Rai work as porters in the Middle Hills.

Describing themselves as Kirati, these tribes are easily distinguishable by their Mongolian features. They are of Tibeto-Burmese descent and their traditional religion is distinct from Buddhism and Hinduism, although the latter is exerting a growing influence. Himalayan hunter-warriors, they are still excellent soldiers and are well represented in the Gurkha regiments.

Many of the men still carry a large khukuri (traditional curved knife) tucked into their belt and wear a *topi* (traditional Nepali cap). Some communities in upper Arun live in bamboo houses.

Newars

The Newars of the Kathmandu Valley number about 1.3 million and make up 5% of the population. Their language, Newari, is distinct from Tibetan, Nepali or Hindi, and is reputed to be one of the world's most difficult languages to learn. The Newars are excellent farmers and merchants, as well as skilled artists, famed across Asia. The Kathmandu Valley is filled with spectacular examples of their artistic work, and their aesthetic influence was felt as far away as Lhasa.

Their origins are shrouded in mystery: most Newars have both Mongoloid and Caucasian physical characteristics. It's generally accepted that their ancestors were migrants of varied ethnicity who settled in the Kathmandu Valley over centuries – possibly originating with the Kiratis, or an even earlier group.

Newars lead a communal way of life and have developed several unique customs, including the worship of the Kumari, a girl believed to be a living goddess, and the annual chariot festivals that provide the high point of the valley's cultural life. Living so close to the centre of power has also meant there are many Newars in the bureaucracies of Kathmandu.

Traditionally, Newari men wear *surwal* (trousers with a baggy seat that are tighter around the calves, like jodhpurs), a *daura* (thigh-length double-breasted shirt), a vest or coat and the traditional *topi* hat. Newari castes include the Sakyas (priests), Tamrakar (metal casters) and the Jyapu (farmers). Jyapu women wear a black sari with a red border, while the men often wear the traditional trousers and shirt with a long piece of cotton wrapped around the waist.

Despite clichéd Western-held beliefs, Sherpas actually do very little portering, focusing mostly on high-altitude expedition work. Most of the porters you meet on the trails are Tamang or Rai, or from other groups.

PEOPLE & CULTURE PEOPLE

Gurungs

The Gurungs, a Tibeto-Burmese people, live mainly in the central midlands, from Gorkha and Baglung up to Manang and the southern slopes of the Annapurnas, around Pokhara. One of the biggest Gurung settlements is Ghandruk, with its sweeping views of the Annapurnas and Machhapuchhare. Gurung women wear nose rings, known as *phuli,* and coral necklaces.

The Gurungs (who call themselves Tamu, or highlanders) originally migrated from western Tibet, bringing with them their animist Bön faith. One distinctive aspect of village life is the *rodi,* a cross between a town hall and a youth centre, where teenagers hang out and cooperative village tasks are planned. In the 1970s photographs portraying the alarmingly brave honey-collecting antics of Gurung men became world famous. The harvesting of hives continues, but increasing demands from tourists have led to questions about its sustainability.

> Traditional prejudice against daughters is reflected in the bitter Nepali proverb: 'Raising a girl is like watering your neighbour's garden.'

Magars

The Magars, a large group (around 8% of the total population), are a Tibeto-Burmese people who live in many parts of the midlands zone of western and central Nepal. With such a large physical spread there are considerable regional variations.

The Magars are excellent soldiers and fought with Prithvi Narayan Shah to help unify Nepal. Their kingdom of Palpa (based at Tansen) was one of the last to be incorporated into a unified Nepal.

The Magars generally live in two-storey, rectangular or square thatched houses washed in red clay. They have been heavily influenced by Hinduism, and in terms of religion, farming practices, housing and dress, they are hard to distinguish from Chhetris.

Bahuns & Chhetris

The Hindu caste groups of Bahuns and Chhetris are dominant in the Middle Hills, making up 30% of the country's population.

Even though the caste system was formally abolished in 1963, these two groups remain the top cats of the caste hierarchy. Although there is no formal relationship in Hinduism between caste and ethnicity, Nepal's Bahuns and Chhetris (Brahmin priests and Kshatriya warriors, respectively) are considered ethnic groups as well as the two highest castes.

> Both Magars and Gurungs have made up large numbers of Gurkha regiments, and army incomes have contributed greatly to the economy of their regions.

Bahuns and Chhetris played an important role in the court and armies of Prithvi Narayan Shah and after unification they were rewarded with tracts of land. Their language, Khas Kura, then became the national language of Nepal and their high-caste position was religiously, culturally and legally enforced. Ever since, Bahuns and Chhetris have dominated the government in Kathmandu, making up over 80% of the civil service.

THE GURKHAS: BRAVEST OF THE BRAVE

Gurkhas are renowned soldiers associated with unrivalled bravery, tenacity and loyalty, and a very big, very sharp knife – the khukuri. Nepalis who joined the British East India army after the Anglo-Nepalese War and who later enlisted with the British and Indian armies became known as Gurkhas. The British coined the name, derived from the town of Gorkha between Kathmandu and Pokhara, which was the home of Prithvi Narayan Shah, the founder king of Nepal.

The UK still maintains Gurkha recruiting centres in Nepal, most notably in Pokhara, where there is a Gurkha Museum (p209). Most Gurkhas are Rais, Limbus, Gurungs and Magars in roughly equal number, although Gurkha regiments do accept recruits from other ethnic groups.

MAHADESI

Who are the Madhesi? Generally the term refers to several identifiable groups (based on language and religion) that originated in India and settled in the Terai. It includes Muslims and Abadhi-speaking people in the western Terai, Maithili speakers of the eastern Terai, and Bhojpuri-speaking people of the central Terai. Tharus and migrants from the hills generally do not identify as Madhesi.

Migration from India to the Terai was encouraged by Nepal's rulers as early as the late 18th century and yet these citizens of Nepal have long felt that they were not accorded full equality with their hill-inhabiting or hill-originating peers. Therefore, the term is more political than racial or cultural. This was amply demonstrated when Madhesi activists blockaded landlocked Nepal's vital fuel imports from India in 2015. Madhesi groups have since won concessions in Nepal's constitution, potentially enabling more political representation in the 2017 elections.

A number of Bahuns and Chhetris had roles as tax collectors under the Shah and Rana regimes and to this day many are moneylenders with a great deal of power. Outside the Kathmandu Valley, the majority of these groups are simple farmers, indistinguishable in most respects from their neighbours.

The Bahuns tend to be more caste-conscious and orthodox than other Nepali Hindus, which sometimes leads to difficulties in relationships with 'untouchable' Westerners. Many are vegetarians and do not drink alcohol; marriages are arranged within the caste.

People of the Terai

Until the eradication of malaria in the 1950s, the only people to live in the valleys of the inner Terai and along much of the Terai proper were Tharus and a few small associated groups, who enjoyed a natural immunity to the disease. After the Terai opened for development, large numbers of people from the midlands settled here – every group is represented and around 50% of Nepali people live in the region.

A number of large groups straddle another part of the Terai – the India–Nepal border. In the eastern Terai, Maithili people dominate; in the central Terai, there are many Bhojpuri-speaking people; and in the western Terai, Abadhi-speaking people are significant. All are basically cultures of the Gangetic plain and Hindu caste structure is strictly upheld.

Tharus

One of the most visible groups is the Tharus, who are thought to be the earliest inhabitants of the Terai and descended from either Rajasthani Rajputs or the royal clan of Sakya, the Buddha's family. More than 1.5 million Tharu speakers inhabit the length of the Terai, including the inner Terai around Chitwan, although they mainly live in the west.

Tharu clans have traditionally lived in thatched huts with wattle and daub walls or in traditional long houses. Their beliefs are largely animistic, involving the worship of forest spirits and ancestral deities, but they are increasingly influenced by Hinduism.

Over generations many Tharus have been exploited by *zamindars* and fallen into debt or entered into bonded labour. In 2000 the *kamaiyas* (bonded labourers) were freed by government legislation, but little has been done to help these people who are now without land and work. Consequently, in most Terai towns in western Nepal you will see squatter settlements of former *kamaiyas*. Visitors to Chitwan or Bardia national parks can tour Tharu villages, stay in village homestays and be entertained by traditional dances. Many Tharus work as wildlife guides in the tourism industry.

Bahun and Chhetri men can be recognised by their sacred thread – the *janai*, worn over the left shoulder and under the right arm – which is changed once a year during the Janai Purnima festival.

HUMAN TRAFFICKING IN NEPAL

Trafficking of girls is a major problem in Nepal's most impoverished rural areas. As many as 10,000 to 15,000 girls are believed to be tricked or sold every year into servitude as domestic, factory or sex workers. It is also believed that over 100,000 Nepali women work in Indian brothels, often in conditions resembling slavery, and around half of these women are thought to be HIV positive. When obvious AIDS symptoms force these women out of work, some manage to return to Nepal. However, they are shunned by their families and there is virtually no assistance available for them or their children.

Once common in the Tharu areas of Dang and Bardia is the tradition of selling young daughters, aged seven to 10, to work as *kamlaris,* or indentured slaves, in the families of wealthy high-caste households. This practice was made illegal in 2000 and was re-affirmed in a 2006 proclamation.

Maithili

Mithila was an ancient kingdom, also known as Videha, that was centred on what is now the city of Janakpur in eastern Nepal. The inhabitants of the Mithila region, the Maithili, speak their own language and their erstwhile kingdom is now divided between India and Nepal. Maithili are orthodox Hindus worshipping chiefly Shiva, Shakti and Vishnu with some ancient animist influences. Today they are best known for the enigmatic naive art (p284) produced by the women of the community.

The lives and roles of Nepali women are examined in the insightful *The Violet Shyness of their Eyes: Notes from Nepal,* by Barbara J Scot, and *Nepali Aama,* by Broughton Coburn, which details the life of a remarkable Gurung woman.

Women in Nepal

Women have a hard time of it in Nepal. Female mortality rates are higher than men's, literacy rates are lower and women generally work harder and longer than men, for less reward. Women only truly gain status in traditional society when they bear their husband a son. Bearing children is so important that a man can legally take a second wife if the first has not had a child after 10 years.

Nepal has a strongly patriarchal society, though this is less the case among Himalayan communities such as the Sherpa, where women often run the show (and the lodge). Boys are strongly favoured over girls, who are often the last to eat and the first to be pulled from school during financial difficulties. Nepal has a national literacy rate of 64%, with the rate among women at 53%.

Even in cosmopolitan Kathmandu, conservative Nepali society still places taboos on topics such as menstruation. Upon their first period girls are considered 'untouchable', and women can be isolated from male family members during menstruation as they are considered 'impure'. In 2017 a women's rights activist was assaulted and accused of witchcraft by her conservative neighbours. Her attackers included other women.

The annual festival of Teej is the biggest festival for women, though ironically it honours their husbands. The activities include feasting, fasting, ritual bathing (in the red and gold saris they were married in) and ritual offerings.

Religion

Religion permeates most aspects of life in Nepal. From the simple, early-morning offerings of a Kathmandu shopkeeper to the rhythmic chants of Buddhist monks in a mountaintop monastery, religious ritual punctuates daily routines and reinforces centuries of tradition. Indian and Tibetan influences merge seamlessly in the Nepali religious sphere, where Hinduism and Buddhism share temples and deities, and where ancient elements of animism and mysterious Tantric practices persist in a fabulous, flamboyant and, above all, tolerant amalgam.

Hinduism

Hinduism is a polytheistic religion that has its origins in the Aryan tribes of central India dating back about 3500 years ago. Hindus believe in a cycle of life, death and rebirth with the aim being to achieve *moksha* (release) from this cycle. With each rebirth you can move closer to, or further from, eventual *moksha;* the deciding factor is karma, which is literally a law of cause and effect. Buddhism later adapted this concept into one of its core principles.

The life of a Nepali Hindu is defined by 16 major rites (*sanskar* or *samskara*), from a baby's first haircut or meal of rice all the way through marriage to death rites. The core concepts of ritual bathing, purification and sacrifice date from the religion's earliest roots.

Despite common misconceptions, it is possible to become a Hindu, although Hinduism itself is not a proselytising religion. Once you are a Hindu you cannot change your caste – you're born into it and are stuck with your lot in life for the rest of that lifetime.

> The kings of Nepal long enjoyed added legitimacy to their rule because they were considered to be incarnations of Vishnu.

PUJA & SACRIFICE

Every morning, Hindu women all over Nepal can be seen walking through the streets carrying a plate, usually copper, filled with an assortment of goodies. These women are not delivering breakfast but are taking part in an important daily ritual called puja. The plate might contain flower petals, rice, yoghurt, fruit or sweets, and is an offering to the gods made at the local temple. Each of the items is sprinkled onto a temple deity in a set order and a bell is rung to let the gods know an offering is being made. Once an offering is made it is transformed into a sacred object and a small portion (referred to as *prasad*) is returned to the giver as a blessing from the deity. Upon returning home from her morning trip, the woman will give a small part of the blessed offerings to each member of the household.

Marigolds and sweets don't cut it with Nepal's more terrifying gods, notably Kali and Bhairab, who require a little extra appeasement in the form of bloody animal sacrifices. You might witness the gory executions, from chickens to water buffalo, at Dakshinkali (p175) in the Kathmandu Valley, Manakamana Temple (p199) and the Kalika Temple at Gorkha, or during the annual Dasain (p281) festival in October, when these temples are literally awash with blood offerings.

The controversial five-yearly Gadhimai Festival traditionally involved the slaughter of tens of thousands of buffalo, goats, chickens and even rats over the course of a few hours, but in July 2015 it was announced that the festival will be free from bloodshed from 2019.

Hinduism in Practice

The Hindu religion has three basic practices: puja (religious offering or prayer), the cremation of the dead, and the highly stratified rules and regulations of the caste system.

You'll see cremation ghats at many rivers in Nepal, but none are holier than those at Pashupatinath. Before a cremation the dead body is washed, laid on a bier and covered with a shroud. Afterwards the ashes are swept into the Bagmati River. Before the burning of the body the chief mourner (normally the eldest son) takes a ritual purification bath; 10 days later the entire family bathes and the house is ritually purified.

Hindu temples are where the spiritual and mundane worlds intersect. Nepalis visit a temple for many reasons – to show devotion, perform a puja, pray for a boon or to gain *darshan,* a word that means viewing a deity but also has the connotation of being viewed by it. The central image in a temple is treated like a royal guest: awakened, washed, dressed, fed and put back to bed by the priest. Devotees make offerings to the deity, from coconuts and garlands of marigolds to milk, vermillion powder and incense.

There are four main Hindu castes: Brahmin (Brahman ethnic group; priest caste); Kshatriya (Chhetri in Nepali; soldiers and governors); Vaisya (tradespeople and farmers); and Sudra (menial workers and craftspeople). These castes are then subdivided, although this is not taken to the same extreme in Nepal as it is in India. Beneath all the castes are the Harijans, or 'untouchables' – the lowest, casteless class for whom the most menial and degrading tasks are reserved.

Sita is believed to have been born in Janakpur, and a temple there marks the site where she and Rama married. A great festival takes place on the site in November/December.

Hindu Gods

Westerners often have trouble coming to grips with Hinduism, principally because of its vast pantheon of gods. The best way to look upon the dozens of different Hindu gods is simply as pictorial representations of the many attributes of the divine. The one omnipresent god usually has three physical representations: Shiva the destroyer and reproducer, Vishnu the preserver and Brahma the creator. Most temples are dedicated to one of these gods, but most Hindus profess to be either Vaishnavites (followers of Vishnu) or Shaivites (followers of Shiva).

The oldest deities are the elemental Indo-European Vedic gods, such as Indra (the god of war, storms and rain), Suriya (the sun), Chandra (the moon) and Agni (fire). Added to this is a range of ancient local mountain spirits, which Hinduism quickly co-opted. The Annapurna and the Ganesh Himal massifs are named after Hindu deities, and Gauri Shankar and Mt Kailash in Tibet are said to be the residences of Shiva and his Parvati.

The pipal tree, under which the Buddha gained enlightenment, is also known by its highly appropriate Latin name, *Ficus religious.*

Shiva

As reproducer and destroyer, Shiva is probably the most important god in Nepal – so it's important to keep on his good side! You can spot Shiva through his *vahana* (vehicle), the bull Nandi, which you'll often see outside Shiva temples, and also by the trident in his hand.

Shiva also appears as Nataraja, whose dance shook the cosmos and created the world, and as the terrible manifestation Bhairab who can appear in 64 different forms, none of them pretty.

LINGAM & YONI

Apart from being a potentially great name for a Nepali crime-fighting duo, the lingam and yoni are the most common religious symbols in Nepal and you'll see thousands of them across the country. The phallic lingam represents male energy and Shiva in particular, while the vaginal yoni symbolises female energy and Parvati. Together they symbolise light and dark, passive and active, the union of the male and female and the totality of existence.

TIKA

A visit to Nepal is not complete without being offered a *tika* by one of the country's many sadhus (wandering Hindu holy men) or *pujari* (Hindu priests). The ubiquitous *tika* is a symbol of blessing from the gods and is worn by both women and men. It can range from a small dot to a full-on mixture of yoghurt, rice and *sindur* (a red powder and mustard-oil mixture) smeared on the forehead. The *tika* represents the all-seeing, all-knowing third eye, placed on an important *chakra* (energy point), and receiving this blessing is a common part of most Hindu ceremonies. It is an acknowledgment of a divine presence at the occasion and a sign of protection for those receiving it. Shops these days carry a huge range of tiny plastic *tikas*, known as *bindi*, that Nepali women have turned into an iconic fashion statement.

Shiva's home is Mt Kailash in Tibet. In the Kathmandu Valley, Shiva is most popularly worshipped as Pashupati, the lord of the beasts. The temple of Pashupatinath (p124), outside Kathmandu, is the most important Hindu temple in the country. Outside of the Kathmandu Valley, Shiva is most commonly worshipped as Mahadeva (Great God), the supreme deity.

Vishnu

Vishnu is the preserver in Hindu belief. In Nepal he often appears as Narayan, asleep on the cosmic ocean, from whose navel appears Brahma, who creates the universe.

Vishnu has four arms and can often be identified by the symbols he holds: the *sankha* (conch shell); the disc-like weapon known as a *chakra;* the stick-like weapon known as a *gada;* and a *padma* (lotus flower). Vishnu's vehicle is the faithful man-bird Garuda; a winged Garuda will often be seen kneeling reverently in front of a Vishnu temple. Garuda has an intense hatred of snakes and is often seen destroying them. Vishnu's *shakti* (female energy) is Lakshmi, the goddess of wealth and prosperity.

Vishnu has 10 incarnations, including Narsingha (half-man and half-lion), Krishna, the fun-loving, gentle and much-loved cowherd, and Rama, the hero of the Ramayana, who married the goddess Sita at Janakpur in the eastern Terai.

Brahma

Despite his supreme position, Brahma appears much less often than Shiva or Vishnu. Like those gods, Brahma has four arms, but he also has four heads, to represent his all-seeing presence. The four Vedas are supposed to have emanated from his mouths.

Parvati

Shiva's shakti is Parvati the beautiful. Just as Shiva is also known as Mahadeva (the Great God), Parvati is Mahadevi (or just Devi), the Great Goddess. Their relationship is a sexual one and it is often Parvati who is the energetic and dominant partner.

Shiva's shakti has as many forms as Shiva himself. She may be peaceful Parvati, Uma or Gauri, but she may also be fearsome Kali, the black goddess, or Durga, the terrible. In these fearsome forms she holds a variety of weapons in her hands, struggles with demons and rides a lion or tiger. As skeletal Kali, she demands blood sacrifices and wears a garland of skulls.

Ganesh

Ganesh, with his elephant head, is probably the most easily recognised and popular of the gods. He is the god of prosperity and wisdom, and there are thousands of Ganesh shrines and temples across Nepal. His

Actor Uma Thurman gets her name from the beautiful Hindu goddess Uma, a manifestation of Parvati. Uma forms half of the Uma-Maheshwar image, a common representation of Shiva and Parvati.

parents are Shiva and Parvati and he has his father's temper to thank for his elephant head. Returning from a long trip, Shiva discovered Parvati in bed with a young man. Not pausing to think that their son might have grown up a little during his absence, Shiva lopped his head off. Parvati then forced Shiva to bring their son back to life, but he could only do so by giving him the head of the first living thing he saw – which happened to be an elephant.

Chubby Ganesh has a super-sweet tooth and is often depicted with his trunk in a mound of sweets and with one broken tusk; one story tells how he broke it off and threw it at the moon for making fun of his weight. Another tale states that Ganesh used the tusk to write the Mahabharata.

Hanuman

The monkey god Hanuman is an important character from the Ramayana. Hanuman's trustworthy and alert nature is commemorated by the many statues of the god that guard palace entrances, most famously the Hanuman Dhoka (p75) in Kathmandu's Durbar Sq.

Machhendranath

A strictly Nepali Hindu god, Machhendranath (also known as Bunga Dyo) has power over the rains and the monsoon and is regarded as protector of the Kathmandu Valley. Typical of the intermingling of Hindu and Buddhist beliefs in Nepal, in the Kathmandu Valley at least, Machhendranath has come to be thought of as an incarnation of Avalokiteshvara, the Buddhist's Bodhisattva of Compassion. Among Tibetan Buddhists, the Dalai Lama is regarded as an incarnation on earth of Avalokiteshvara.

Saraswati

The goddess of learning and the consort of Brahma, Saraswati rides upon a white swan and holds the stringed musical instrument known as a *veena*. Students, in particular, honour Saraswati during the spring festival of Basant Panchami, when locals flock to her shrine at Swayambhunath (p117), outside Kathmandu.

Buddhism

Strictly speaking, Buddhism is a philosophy rather than a religion, as it is centred not on a god but on a system of thought and a code of morality. Buddhism was founded in northern India in the 6th century BC when prince Siddhartha Gautama achieved enlightenment.

The Buddha ('awakened one') was born in Lumbini in Nepal over 25 centuries ago, but the Buddhist religion first arrived in the country later,

Both Hindus and Buddhist see the land in terms of a sacred landscape. River confluences and sources, mountain lakes, and high passes and peaks are all considered particularly sacred, while water sources teem with holy naga (serpent deities).

TIBETAN BUDDHIST SYMBOLS

Prayer flags These multicoloured squares of cloth are printed with Buddhist sutras and an image of the wind horse *(lungta)*, which carries the prayers to the heavens. Rooted in pre-Buddhist beliefs, they are strung on passes and houses to sanctify the air and pacify the gods. The five colours represent the elements of fire, water, air, wood and earth (some say ether).

Mani stones These stones are carved with Tibetan mantras and placed in walls several hundred metres long as an act of merit. The most common mantra is *om mani padme hum,* which roughly means 'Hail to the jewel in the lotus'.

Prayer wheels Containing up to one million rolled up printed prayers, prayer wheels are turned as an act of devotion and to gain merit. The wheels vary from the size of a fist to that of a small building (known as a *mani lhakhang*).

around 250 BC, thanks to the great Indian-Buddhist emperor Ashoka. Buddhism eventually lost ground to Hinduism, although the Tantric form of Tibetan Buddhism eventually made its way back into Nepal in the 8th century AD. Today, Tibetan Buddhism is practised mainly by the people of the high Himalaya, such as the Sherpas, Tamangs and Manangi, and by Tibetan refugees who have revitalised religious practice in the region over the last 50 years.

The Buddha was born a prince but renounced his privileged life to search for enlightenment. His insight was that severe asceticism did not lead to enlightenment any more than material comfort, and that the best course of action was to follow the Middle Way (moderation in all things). The Buddha taught that all life is suffering, and that suffering comes from our desires and the illusion of their importance.

By following the 'eightfold path' these desires can be extinguished and a state of nirvana, where we are free from their delusions, can be attained. Buddhists believe that life entails a series of reincarnations until nirvana is reached and no more rebirths into the world of suffering are necessary. The path that takes you through this cycle of births is karma, but this is not simply fate. Karma is a law of cause and effect; your actions in one life determine what you will experience in your next life. Only you are the master of your own fate.

Buddhist Deities

The first images of the Buddha date from the 5th century AD, 1000 years after his death (stupas were the main symbol of Buddhism before this). The Buddha didn't want idols made of himself, but a pantheon of Buddhist gods grew up regardless, with strong iconographical influence from Hinduism. As in Hinduism, the many Buddhist deities reflect various aspects of the divine, or 'Buddha-nature'. Multiple heads convey multiple personalities, *mudra* (hand positions) convey coded messages, and everything from eyebrows to stances indicate the nature of the deity.

There are many different types of Buddha images, though the most common are those of the past (Dipamkara), present (Sakyamuni) and future (Maitreya) Buddhas. The Buddha is recognised by 32 physical marks, including a bump on the top of his head, his third eye and the images of the Wheel of Law on the soles of his feet. In his left hand he holds a begging bowl and his right hand touches the earth in the witness *mudra*. He is often flanked by his two disciples.

Bodhisattvas are beings who have achieved enlightenment but decide to help everyone else gain enlightenment before entering nirvana. The Bodhisattva of Wisdom Manjushri has strong connections to the Kathmandu Valley. The Dalai Lama is considered a reincarnation of Avalokiteshvara (Chenresig in Tibetan), the Bodhisattva of Compassion.

Tibetan Buddhism also has a host of fierce protector gods, called *dharmapala,* who on one level at least symbolise the demons of the ego. Typical of Tantric deities (and with roots deep in Hindu iconography), these bloodcurdling deities have multiple arms and weapons, dance on a corpse and wear a headdress of skulls.

Tibetan Buddhism

The Buddha never wrote down his *dharma* (teachings) and a schism that developed later means that today there are two major Buddhist schools: Hinayana and Mahayana. One offshoot of Mahayana is Vajrayana, or Tibetan Buddhism, and it is this that you will see mostly in Nepal.

There are four major schools of Tibetan (Vajrayana) Buddhism, all represented in the Kathmandu Valley: Nyingmapa, Kagyupa, Sakyapa and Gelugpa. The Nyingmapa order is the oldest and most dominant in the Nepal Himalaya. Its origins come from the Indian sage Padmasambhava

Bön is Tibet's pre-Buddhist animist faith, now largely considered a fifth school of Tibetan Buddhism. Nepal has small pockets of Bön followers.

RELIGION BUDDHISM

Padmasambhava (Guru Rinpoche) is a common image in Nyingmapa monasteries and is recognisable by his *khatvanga* staff of human heads and his fabulously curly moustache.

SADHUS & SADHVIS

Sadhus are Hindu ascetics who have left their homes, jobs and families and embarked upon a spiritual search. Most are male, but there are a small number of women *sadhvis*. They're an easily recognised group, often wandering around half-naked, smeared in dust with their hair matted, and carrying nothing except a *trisul* (trident) and a begging bowl.

Sadhus/*sadhvis* wander all over the subcontinent, occasionally coming together at great religious gatherings such as the Maha Shivaratri Festival (p127) at Pashupatinath in Kathmandu and the Janai Purnima Festival (p146) at the sacred Hindu lakes of Gosainkund. You may also see them wandering around Thamel and posing for photos in Kathmandu's Durbar Sq.

A few are simply beggars using a more sophisticated approach to gathering donations, but most are genuine in their search. Remember that if you take a picture of a sadhu or *sadhvi*, or accept a *tika* blessing, you will be expected to pay some *baksheesh* (tip), so negotiate your photo fee in advance to avoid any unpleasantness.

(Guru Rinpoche), sometimes called the 'second Buddha' and who is credited with the establishment of Buddhism in Tibet and the Himalaya in the 8th century.

The Dalai Lama is the head of the Gelugpa school and the spiritual leader of Tibetan Buddhists. In some texts the Gelugpa are known as the Yellow Hats, while the other schools are sometimes collectively referred to as Red Hats.

> Thanks to the tendency towards assimilation and synthesis there is little religious tension in Nepal and religion has long played little part in the country's politics. In Kathmandu Tibetan Buddhists and Nepali Hindus often worship at the same temples.

Islam

Nepal's small population of Muslims (about 4% of the total population) is mainly found close to the border with India, with a large population in Nepalganj. The first Muslims, who were mostly Kashmiri traders, arrived in the Kathmandu Valley in the 15th century. A second group arrived in the 17th century from northern India and they primarily manufactured armaments for the small hill states. Nepal's Muslims have strong ties with Muslim communities in the Indian states of Bihar and Uttar Pradesh.

Shamanism

Shamanism is practised by many mountain peoples throughout the Himalaya and dates back some 50,000 years. Its ancient healing traditions are based on a cosmology that divides the world into three main levels: the Upper World where the sun, moon, stars, planets, deities and spirits important to the shaman's healing work abide; the Middle World of human life; and the Lower World, where more malevolent deities and spirits exist.

Faith healers protect against a wide range of spirits, including headless *mulkattas*, who have eyes in their chest and signify imminent death; *pret*, the ghosts of the recently deceased that loiter at crossroads; and *kichikinni*, the ghost of a beautiful and sexually insatiable siren who is recognisable by her sagging breasts and the fact that her feet are on backwards.

> The humble cow is the most holy animal of Hinduism, and killing a cow in Nepal brings a jail term.

During ceremonies, the *dhami* or *jhankri* (shaman or faith healer) uses techniques of drumming, divination, trances and sacrifices to invoke deities and spirits that he or she wishes to assist in the ritual. The shaman essentially acts as a broker between the human and spirit worlds.

Arts & Architecture

Despite the devastating effects of the 2015 earthquakes, Nepal is still blessed with an astonishing array of ancient temples and palaces, and countless intricate woodcarvings and stone sculptures are dotted around its backstreets. Walking through the historic towns of the Kathmandu Valley, you will still discover magnificent medieval architecture at every turn. Nepal's artistic masterpieces are not hidden away in dusty museums but are part of a living culture, to be touched, worshipped, feared – or simply paid no heed.

Architecture & Sculpture

Architecture and the sculpting arts in Nepal are inextricably intermingled. The finest woodcarvings and stone sculptures are often part of a building. Indeed a temple is simply not a temple without its deity statue and finely carved adornments.

The earliest architecture in the Kathmandu Valley has faded with history. Grassy mounds are all that remain where Patan's four Ashoka stupas once stood, and the impressive stupas of Swayambhunath (p117) and Bodhnath (p128) have been rebuilt many times over the centuries.

The Licchavi period from the 4th to 9th centuries AD was a golden age for Nepal, and while the temples may have disappeared, magnificent stone sculptures have withstood the ravages of time and can still be found. Beautiful pieces lie scattered around temples of the Kathmandu Valley. The Licchavi sculptures at the temple of Changu Narayan (p168) near Bhaktapur are particularly good examples, as is the statue of Vishnu asleep on a bed of serpents at Budhanilkantha.

No wooden buildings and carvings are known to have survived in Nepal from that period, or indeed before the 12th century. However, within Lhasa's Jokhang Temple there are carved wooden beams and columns dating from before the 9th century that are clearly the work of Newari artisans.

It was in the Malla period that Nepali artistry with wood really came into its own, as the famed skills of the valley's Newari people reached their zenith, particularly between the 15th and 17th centuries. Squabbling and one-upmanship between the city states of Kathmandu, Patan and Bhaktapur fuelled a competitive building boom as each tried to outdo the other with ever-more magnificent palaces and temples.

The great age of Nepali architecture came to a dramatic end when Prithvi Narayan Shah invaded the valley in 1769. These days traditional building skills are still evidenced in the ongoing restoration projects in Kathmandu, Patan and Bhaktapur. Moreover, today's architects will often incorporate traditional features into their buildings, particularly hotels.

Newari Pagoda Temples

The Nepali architect Arniko can be said to be the father of the Asian pagoda. He kick-started the introduction and reinterpretation of the pagoda in China and eastern Asia when he brought the multiroofed Nepali pagoda design to the court of Kublai Khan in the late 13th century.

Kathmandu Valley's Unesco World Heritage Sites

Durbar Sq (Kathmandu)

Durbar Sq (Patan)

Durbar Sq (Bhaktapur)

Swayambhunath Stupa

Bodhnath Stupa

Pashupatinath

Changu Narayan

Get a great overview of Buddhist and Nepali art at the Patan Museum and at Kathmandu's National Museum, both of which explain the concepts behind Buddhist and Hindu art and iconography in an accessible way.

The distinctive Newari pagoda temples are a major feature of the Kathmandu Valley skyline, echoing, and possibly inspired by, the horizon's pyramid-shaped mountain peaks. While strictly speaking they are neither wholly Newari nor pagodas, the term has been widely adopted to describe the temples of the valley.

The temples are generally square in design, and may be either Hindu or Buddhist (or both, as is the nature of Nepali religion). On occasion, temples are rectangular or octagonal; Krishna can occupy an octagonal temple, but Ganesh, Shiva and Vishnu can only inhabit square temples.

The major feature of the temples is the tiered roof, which may have one to five tiers, with two or three being the most common. In the Kathmandu Valley there are two temples with four roofs and the Nyatapola Temple (p157) at Bhaktapur and the Kumbeshwar Temple (p143) at Patan have five, though the latter saw severe damage to its upper tier in the 2015 quake. The sloping roofs are usually covered with distinctive *jhingati* (baked clay tiles), although richer temples will often have one roof of gilded copper. The bell-shaped *gajur* (pinnacle) is made of baked clay or gilded copper.

The temples are usually built on a stepped plinth, which may be as high as or even higher than the temple itself. In many cases the number of steps on the plinth corresponds with the number of roofs on the temple.

The temple building itself has a small sanctum, known as a *garbhagriha* (literally 'womb room'), housing the deity. Worshippers practise individually, with devotees standing outside the door to make their supplications. The only people permitted to actually enter the sanctum are *pujari* (temple priests).

Perhaps the most interesting feature of the temples is the detailed decoration, which is only evident close up. Under each roof there are of-

RESTORING THE PAST

Visitors to Kathmandu Valley's major architectural sites – the three major Durbar squares and numerous outlying temples – will notice that much is being done to restore these wonderful structures. But there is much, much more still to be done.

The government routinely gets criticised in the press for failing to release sufficient funds for earthquake relief – notably housing for displaced persons and important infrastructure. And it is the same with temple restoration. Thankfully foreign governments, private residents, charities and NGOs have stepped up where the government has stalled.

Numerous temples and monuments have been restored and many are in the process of restoration. Notable examples include the stupa at Bodhnath, where cash, gold bullion and labour were quickly contributed by locals and Buddhist organisations from across the world. The world-renowned stupa was one of the first of the country's more than 700 quake-damaged heritage structures to have been restored to its pre-quake glory.

The independent charity Kathmandu Valley Preservation Trust (KVPT; www.kvptearth quakeresponse.org) has been responsible for restoring sites in the valley since 1991 and is the major source of funds and expertise for the restoration works. It has secured experts, traditional craftspeople and foreign funds, and already has scores on the board in terms of completed restorations, particularly in Patan's Durbar Sq.

Among the structures in Patan flattened by the quake was the 16th-century Jagganarayan (Char Narayan). KVPT expects this temple to be restored by 2019. Thanks to the trust and hordes of local volunteers, many of the carvings in this temple (as well as other temples) were quickly rescued, catalogued and safely stored. All this, despite the tragic and tumultuous times that immediately followed the quake – such is the respect of Nepalis for their cultural heritage. The trust employs traditional craftspeople who have turned from making tourist replicas to restoring the real thing. However, there is currently a shortfall of funds, with more than 50% of Kathmandu's monuments still requiring funding as this book went to print.

ten brass or other metal decorations, such as *kinkinimala* (rows of small bells) or embossed metal banners. The metal streamer that often hangs from above the uppermost roof to below the level of the lowest roof (such as on the Golden Temple (p143) in Patan) is called a *pataka*. Its function is to give the deity a way to descend to earth.

The other major decorative elements are the wooden *tunala* (struts) that support the roofs. The intricate carvings are usually of deities associated with the temple or of the *vahana* (deity's vehicle), but quite a few depict explicit sexual acts.

Numerous temples, both large and small, dotted throughout the Kathmandu Valley and beyond succumbed to the 2015 earthquakes. Some will be rebuilt, many will carry on as places of worship despite remaining damaged, and a few will undoubtably fall further into ruin.

Shikhara Temples

The second-most common temples are the shikhara temples, which have a heavy Indian influence. The temples are so named because their tapering towers resemble a *shikhara* (mountain peak, in Sanskrit). Although the style developed in India in the 6th century, it first appeared in Nepal in the late Licchavi period.

The tapering, pyramidal tower is the main feature, and is often surrounded by four similar but smaller towers. These may be located on porches over the shrine's entrances.

The spire of the Mahabouddha Temple (p145) in Patan, and the Krishna Mandir (p139) and the octagonal Krishna Temple (p140), both in Patan's Durbar Sq, are all excellent examples of this style.

Several striking shikhara temples were destroyed in the 2015 earthquakes, including the ones that used to flank the main stupa at Swayambhunath and the Vatsala Durga temple that once graced Bhaktapur's Durbar Sq.

The Buddhist Gompa

The monastery of Tibetan Buddhists is called a gompa, and across the mountains of Nepal there are gompas that hum with prayers and clash with cymbals. Most historic gompas are located on a hill with a fine view, demonstrating their strategic importance and reflecting the desires of the monks for peace and solitude. Newer, more lavish gompas, such as the one at Jomsom, reflect the increasing wealth of Tibetan Buddhists in Nepal, and are often sited close to town. Conspicuous on the roof of most gompas is the golden dharma wheel flanked by two deer. The wheel is a representation of Buddha's teachings and the deer symbolise the Buddha's first sermon at Sarnath after reaching enlightenment – in a deer park.

You enter a gompa through an entrance vestibule decorated with colourful paintings of *Bhavachakra,* the Wheel of Life clutched by the fearsome Yama, and the Four Guardian Kings, watching over the four cardinal points of the world. Most small gompas have only one room, the *dukhang,* or assembly hall, decorated with bright murals and thangkas (religious paintings on cloth). The main altar will be dominated by a central statue flanked by two or more others – the statues could include Sakyamuni, the historical Buddha; Jampa, the future Buddha; or the lotus-born saint Guru Rinpoche. Another common figure is the 11th-century poet Milerapa, who is said to have travelled widely throughout the Himalaya, including to Shey Gompa and the Manang valley.

The altar will usually have photos of important lineage holders, such as the Dalai Lama, plus bowls of water, flickering butter lamps and colourful *torma,* constructions of flour-and-butter dough. Hanging off to the side are demonic festival masks and ceremonial trumpets.

Nepal, by Michael Hutt, is an excellent guide to the art and architecture of the Kathmandu Valley. It outlines the main forms of art and architecture and describes specific sites within the valley, often with layout plans. It has great colour plates and black-and-white photos.

The Art of God Making

Newari art and craft skills extend far beyond the woodwork for which they are so well known and include ceramics, brickwork, stone sculptures and intricate metalwork. The finest metalwork includes the stunning images of the two Tara goddesses at Swayambhunath (p117) and the Golden Gate (p156) in Bhaktapur.

Statues are created through two main techniques – the repoussé method of hammering thin sheets of metal and the 'lost wax' method. In the latter, the statue is carved in wax, which is then encased in clay and left to dry. The wax is then melted, metal is poured into the clay mould and the mould is then broken, revealing the statue. Finishing touches include grinding, polishing and painting before the statue is ready to be sanctified.

The website www.mountain musicproject.com has links to radio and video clips of several Nepali musicians, including Rubin Gandharba – the 'Nepali Bob Dylan'.

Repoussé Metalwork

Many of the richly decorated objects used for religious rituals in Nepal make use of the ancient technique of repoussé – where a design is hammered into the metal from the back using hammers and punches. First the metal shape is set into a bed of *jhau* (a mixture of resin and brick dust), then the design is painstakingly applied and the resin is melted away, allowing finishing touches to be added from the front using engraving tools. This style of metalwork has been produced since at least the 2nd millennium BC and the technique is still practised today in alleyways across the Kathmandu Valley.

Painting

Chinese, Tibetan, Indian and Mughal influences can all be seen in Nepali painting styles. The earliest Newari paintings were illuminated manuscripts dating from the 11th century. Newari *paubha* paintings are iconic religious paintings similar to Tibetan thangkas. Notable to both is a lack of perspective, symbolic use of colour and strict iconographic rules.

Modern Nepali artists struggle to make a living, although there are a few galleries in Kathmandu that feature local artists. Some artists are fortunate enough to get a sponsored overseas exhibition or a posting at an art college outside the country to teach their skills. Commissioning a painting by a local artist is a way to support the arts and take home a unique souvenir of your trip.

The eastern Terai has its own distinct form of colourful mural painting called Mithila art (p284).

NEPAL'S STOLEN HERITAGE

In recent decades Nepal has had a staggering amount of its artistic heritage spirited out of the country by art thieves, and this problem is only likely to grow following the destruction of so many monuments in the 2015 earthquakes. Virtually all the Nepalese antique art that has come on to the international market in the last three to four decades has been stolen. Much of the stolen art languishes in museums or private collections in Europe and in the USA, while in Nepal remaining temple statues are increasingly kept under lock and key.

One of the reasons photography is banned in some temples is that thieves often put photos of temple artefacts in their underground 'shopping catalogues'. Pieces are then stolen to order, often with the aid of corrupt officials, to fetch high prices in the lucrative international art market. UN conventions against the trade exist, but are weakly enforced.

Catalogues of stolen Nepali art have been produced in an attempt to locate these treasures, and several pieces have been given back to Kathmandu's National Museum, including a Buddha statue stolen from Patan that was returned after a dealer tried to sell it to a museum in Austria for a cool US$200,000.

Music & Dance

Recent decades have seen a revival in Nepali music and songs, both folk and 'Nepali modern'. The ever-present Hindi film songs have been partly supplanted by a vibrant local music scene.

In the countryside most villagers supply their own entertainment. Dancing and traditional music enliven festivals and family celebrations, when villages erupt with the energetic sounds of *bansari* (flutes), *madal* (drums) and cymbals, or sway to the moving soulful sounds of devotional singing and the gentle twang of the four-stringed *sarang*. Singing is one important way that girls and boys in the hills can interact and flirt, showing their grace and wit through dances and improvised songs.

There are several musician castes, including the *gaine*, a dwindling caste of travelling minstrels, the *ghandarba*, whose music you can hear in Kathmandu, and the *damai*, who often perform in wedding bands. Women generally do not perform music in public.

Nepali dance styles are as numerous and varied as Nepal's ethnic groups. They range from the stick dances of the Tharu in the Terai to the line-dancing style of the mountain Sherpas. Joining in with an enthusiastic group of porters at the end of a trek is a great way to learn some of the moves. Masked dances are also common, from the Cham dances performed by Tibetan Buddhist monks to the masked Hindu dances of Nava Durga in Bhaktapur.

Providing a good introduction to Nepali folk music is the group Sur Sudha (www.sursudha.com), Nepal's de facto musical ambassadors, whose evocative recordings will take you back to the region long after you've tasted your last daal bhaat. Try their *Festivals of Nepal* and *Images of Nepal* recordings.

One of Nepal's most famous singers is the Tibetan nun Choying Drolma (www.choying.com). Her CDs *Cho* and *Selwa*, recorded with guitarist Steve Tibbetts, are transcendentally beautiful and highly recommended.

The folk song that you hear everywhere in Nepal (you'll know which one we mean when you get there) is 'Resham Pheeree Ree' ('My Heart is Fluttering Like Silk in the Wind').

Film

The Nepali film industry has come a long way since the 1980s and early '90s, when only four or five films were produced annually. According to John Whelpton in his *History of Nepal*, the first film shown in Kathmandu depicted the wedding of the Hindu god Ram. The audience threw petals and offerings at the screen as they would do at a temple or if the god himself were present.

The Oscar-nominated Nepali-French film *Caravan*, directed by Eric Valli, is the most famous 'Nepali' film and played to packed houses in Kathmandu. It features magnificent footage of the Upper Dolpo district of western Nepal as it tells the tale of yak caravaners during a change of generations. It was renamed for distribution abroad as *Himalaya*. Perhaps the best-known film shot in Nepal is Bernardo Bertolucci's *Little Buddha*, which was partly filmed at Bhaktapur's Durbar Sq and the Gokarna Forest.

The 2016 film *White Sun*, written and directed by Deepak Rauniyar, depicts the aftermath of the Nepali civil war on a family where two brothers campaigned for opposing sides. The film received several international awards and was entered for nomination for the Best Foreign Language Film in the 2017 Academy Awards.

The Kathmandu International Mountain Film Festival (www.kimff.org) screens over 60 Nepali and international films every December. Film South Asia (www.filmsouthasia.org) is a biennial (odd years) festival of South Asian documentaries.

Kagbeni, by Bhusan Dahal, is Nepal's first ever high-definition movie. A creepy supernatural tale adapted from the short story *The Monkey's Paw*, by WW Jacobs, it is set in the foothills around Annapurna.

ARTS & ARCHITECTURE MUSIC & DANCE

TIBETAN CARPETS

One of the most amazing success stories of the last few decades is the local Tibetan carpet industry. Although carpet production has long been a cottage industry inside Tibet, in 1960 the Nepal International Tibetan Refugee Relief Committee, with the support of renowned Swiss geologist Toni Hagen and the Swiss government, began encouraging Tibetan refugees in Patan to make and sell carpets.

Tibetan and New Zealand wool is used to make the carpets. The exuberant colours and lively designs of traditional carpets have been toned down for the international market, but the old ways of producing carpets remain the same. The intricacies of the senna loop method are hard to pick out in the blur of hands that is usually seen at a carpet workshop; each thread is looped around a gauge rod that will determine the height of the carpet pile, then each row is hammered down and the loops of thread split to release the rod. To finish it off the pile is clipped to bring out the design.

Literature

Nepal's literary history is brief, dating back to just the 19th century. The written language was little used before then, although religious verse, folklore, songs and translations of Sanskrit and Urdu dating back to the 13th century have been found.

One of the first authors to establish Nepali as a literary language was Bhanubhakta Acharya (1814–68), who broke away from the influence of Indian literature and recorded the Ramayana in Nepali; this was not simply a translation but a Nepali-ised version of the Hindu epic. Motiram Bhatta (1866–96) also played a major role in 19th-century literature, as did Lakshmi Prasad Devkota (1909–59) in the 20th century.

In a country where literacy levels are low, Nepal's literary community has always struggled. However, today a vibrant and enthusiastic literary community exists, meeting in teashops and at bookstalls in Kathmandu and other urban centres.

Nepali Novels

Recent years have seen a bounty of novels written by Nepali writers. Pack one of them in your backpack for added insights into the country.

Arresting God in Kathmandu, by Samrat Upadhyay, is an engaging and readable series of short stories set in Kathmandu by an author billed as the first Nepali writer writing in English (he is now living in the USA). His follow-ups include the novel *Guru of Love* and *The Royal Ghosts,* a series of short stories set against the backdrop of the Maoist uprising.

Mountains Painted with Turmeric, by Lil Bahadur Chettri, is a classic 1958 short novel, translated into English by Michael Hutt. The novel realistically portrays the struggles of a farming family trapped in a cycle of poverty and social conservatism in eastern Nepal.

Several novels have tried to make sense of the political chaos in Nepal's recent history. *Palpasa Café,* by Narayan Wagle, tells the story of an artist, an expat Nepali and a guerrilla, set against the backdrop of the war, revolution and political violence that has dominated life in rural Nepal in the recent past. The author is a former editor of the *Kantipur* newspaper.

Seasons of Flight, by Manjushree Thapa, is a novel about a young Nepali woman Prema who escapes from her village in Nepal to Los Angeles, California, in search of fortune. Thapa is also the author of *The Tutor of History,* a portrait of a rural Nepali village in western Nepal during the run-up to elections. It's worth a read for its insights into modern Nepal.

Himalayan Voices: an Introduction to Modern Nepali Literature, by Michael Hutt, includes work by contemporary poets and short-story writers.

Environment & Wildlife

Nepal is both blessed and burdened by its incredible environment. Its economy, history, resources and culture are all intrinsically tied to the string of magnificent mountains that represent a continental collision zone. This often-daunting landscape has played a role in setting back development because of the logistical problems of bringing roads, electricity, health care and education to remote communities in mountainous areas. However, as technology aids development of once-remote ecosystems, the Himalaya and plains are faced with enormous environmental threats.

The Lay of the Land

Nepal is a small, landlocked strip of land, 800km long and 200km wide. However, it fits a lot of terrain into just 147,181 sq km. Heading north from the Indian border, the landscape rises from just 70m above sea level to 8848m at the tip of Mt Everest. This dramatic landscape provides an unparalleled variety of habitats to support an incredible array of plants and animals.

Nepalis divide the year into six, not four, seasons: Basanta (spring), Grisma (premonsoon heat), Barkha (monsoon), Sharad (postmonsoon), Hemanta (autumn) and Sheet (winter).

Colliding Continents

Imagine the space currently occupied by Nepal as an open expanse of water, and the Tibetan plateau as the coast. This was the situation until 60 million years ago when the Indo-Australian plate collided with the Eurasian continent, bucking the earth's crust up into mighty ridges and forming the mountains we now call the Himalaya.

The upheaval of mountains caused the temporary obstruction of rivers that once flowed unimped from Eurasia to the sea. Simultaneously, new rivers arose on the southern slopes of these young mountains as moist winds from the tropical seas to the south rose and precipitated. For the next 60 million years, the mountains moved up, and rivers and glaciers cut downwards, creating the peaks and valleys seen across Nepal today.

EARTHQUAKE-PRONE NEPAL

The massive tremors that ravaged central Nepal on 25 April and 12 May 2015 were not the first major earthquakes to hit the former Himalayan kingdom. The phenomenal pressure created by the collision of the Indo-Australian and Eurasian plates has caused a series of catastrophic earthquakes over the centuries.

The 1934 Bihar-Nepal earthquake, which occurred on the same fault line as the 2015 tremors, killed an estimated 10,000 people, while a third of the population of Kathmandu are thought to have died in the deadly quake that struck in 1255. In all these cases, the damage was amplified by the geology of the Kathmandu Valley – a deep base of soft clay makes the area highly vulnerable to soil liquefaction in earthquake conditions.

Scientists believe that the 2015 quakes have relieved a considerable amount of pressure along the fault line, but with the Indo-Australian plate still sliding under the Eurasian plate at a rate of 27mm per year, further tremors and quakes are inevitable.

The modern landscape of Nepal – a grid of four major mountain systems, incised by the north–south gorges of rivers – is not the final story. The Indo-Australian plate is still sliding under the Eurasian Himalaya at a rate of 27mm per year and pushing the Himalaya even higher. As fast as the mountains rise, they are being eroded by glaciers, rivers and landslides, and chipped away by earthquakes and the effects of cold and heat.

Nepal is still an active seismic zone, as demonstrated by the massive earthquakes that struck central Nepal in April and May 2015.

> The Terai makes up only 17% of Nepal's area but holds around 50% of its population and 70% of its agricultural land.

Valley Low & Mountain High

Nepal's concertina topography consists of several physiographic regions, or natural zones: the southern plains, the four mountain ranges, and the valleys and hills in between. Most people live in the fertile lowlands or on the sunny southern slopes of mountains. Above 4000m the only residents are yak herders, who retreat into the valleys with the onset of winter.

The Terai & Chure Hills

The only truly flat land in Nepal is the Terai (or Tarai), a patchwork of paddy fields, sal and riverine forests, tiny thatched villages and sprawling industrial cities. The vast expanse of the Gangetic plain extends for 40km into Nepal before the land rises to create the Chure Hills. With an average height of 1000m, this minor ridge runs the length of the country, separating the Terai from a second low-lying area called the inner Terai, or the Dun.

Mahabharat Range

North of the inner Terai, the land rises again to form the Mahabharat Range, or the 'Middle Hills'. These vary between 1500m and 2700m in height and form the heartland of the inhabited highlands of Nepal. Locals cultivate rice, barley, millet, wheat, maize and other crops on spectacular terraced fields set among patches of subtropical and temperate forest. These hills are cut by three major river systems: the Karnali, the Narayani and the Sapt Kosi.

> The Sanskrit word Himalaya means abode (alaya) of the snows (himal). There is no such thing as the 'Himalayas'. To pronounce it correctly, as they do in the corridors of the Royal Geographical Society, emphasise the second syllable – him-aaar-liya, old chap...

Pahar Zone

Between the Mahabharat Range and the Himalaya lies a broad, extensively cultivated belt called the Pahar zone. This includes the fertile valleys of Kathmandu, Banepa and Pokhara, which were once the beds of lakes, formed by trapped rivers. After the Terai this is the most inhabited part of Nepal, and the expanding human population is putting a massive strain on natural resources.

The Himalaya

One-third of the total length of the Himalaya lies inside Nepal's borders, and the country claims 10 of the world's 14 tallest mountains. Because of the southerly latitude (similar to that of Florida), along with the reliable rainfall, the mountains are cloaked in vegetation to a height of 3500m to 4000m. People mainly inhabit the areas below 2700m.

HUMANS VS WILDLIFE

Human–wildlife conflict is a fact of life for what's left of the wildlife surviving in Nepal's protected areas and the expanding population of local human inhabitants. In 2016–17, 19 people lost their life from encounters with wildlife in or near Chitwan and Bardia national parks. The incidents involved tigers, elephants and rhinos. The parks paid out almost Rs 15 million in compensation, although most of these tragic interactions resulted from humans trespassing in the parks.

MT EVEREST

Everest has gone by a number of different names over the years. The Survey of India christened the mountain 'Peak XV', but it was renamed Everest after Sir George Everest (pronounced eve-rest), the surveyor general of India in 1865. It was later discovered that the mountain already had a name – Sherpas call the peak Chomolungma, after the female guardian deity of the mountain, who rides a red tiger and is one of the five sisters of long life. There was no Nepali name for the mountain until 1956 when the historian Babu Ram Acharya created the name Sagarmatha, meaning 'head of the sky'.

Using triangulation from the plains of India, the Survey of India established the elevation of the summit of Everest at 8839m. In 1954 this was revised to 8848m using data from 12 different survey stations around the mountain. In 1999 a team sponsored by National Geographic used GPS data to produce a new elevation of 8850m, but in 2002 a Chinese team made measurements from the summit using ice radar and GPS systems and produced a height of 8844.43m.

So is Everest shrinking? No; the Chinese calculated the height of the bedrock of the mountain, without the accumulated snow and ice. In fact, Everest is still growing at a rate of 6mm a year as plate tectonics drive the Indian subcontinent underneath Eurasia. In 2011 the Chinese agreed with the Nepalis that the official height is 8848m.

A Chinese study after the 2015 earthquake concluded that the entire bulk of Mt Everest shifted southwest by 3cm but remained the same height! In 2017 Nepal reinstigated a project to measure the mountain, as did the Survey of India; celebrating its 250th anniversary, it proposed a joint investigation with the Nepalis. What will it mean? With all the latest technology, the accuracy range is about plus or minus 30cm. So the new numbers will help improve accuracy, but may not confirm any changes in the mountain due to the 2015 quake.

Also in 2017, mountaineers confirmed that a famous rocky outcrop near the peak of Mt Everest, the Hillary Step, had partially collapsed, potentially making the climb more dangerous. The 12m-high rocky outcrop was a nearly vertical climb on the southeast ridge of the mountain.

The Trans-Himalaya

North of the first ridge of the Himalaya is a high-altitude desert, similar to the Tibetan plateau. This area encompasses the arid valleys of Mustang, Manang and Dolpo. The moisture-laden clouds of the monsoon drop all their rain on the south side of the mountains, leaving the Trans-Himalaya in permanent rain shadow. Surreal crags, spires and badlands eroded by the scouring action of the wind are characteristic of this starkly beautiful landscape.

The Kali Gandaki Valley between the Annapurna and Dhaulagiri massifs is considered the world's deepest, with a vertical gain of 7km.

Wildlife

Nepal is a region of exceptional biodiversity, with a rare concentration of varied landscapes and climatic conditions. If you're a nature buff, it's worth carrying a spotters' guide.

Mammals & Birds

The diverse environments of the Himalaya and the Middle Hills provide a home for a remarkable array of birds, reptiles, amphibians and mammals. However, poaching and hunting threaten many mammal and bird species. Your best chances for spotting wildlife are in national parks and conservation areas, or high in the mountains far away from human habitation.

Signature Species

Nepal has a number of 'signature species' that every visitor wants to see. Unfortunately, these also tend to be the species most threatened by poaching and habitat loss. Opportunities to view the following animals

CROCODILES

Nepal is home to two species of crocodile. The endangered and striking-looking gharial inhabits rivers, hunting for fish with its elongated snout lined with sharp teeth. Fossils of similar crocodiles have been found that date back 100 million years, attesting to the effectiveness of its odd-looking design. The gharial was hunted to the brink of extinction, but populations have recovered since the establishment of hatcheries.

The stocky marsh mugger prefers stagnant water and is omnivorous, feeding on anything within reach, including people. In fact, the Western word 'mugger' comes from the Hindi/Nepali name for this skulking predator.

are usually restricted to national parks, reserves and sparsely populated areas of western Nepal. Chitwan National Park is home to most of the signature species, including tigers, leopards, rhinos and sloth bears.

At the top of the jungle food chain is the royal Bengal tiger (*bagh* in Nepali), which is solitary and territorial. Chitwan, Bardia and Banke national parks and Sukla Phanta National Park in the Terai protect sufficient habitat to sustain viable breeding populations. In addition to loss of habitat, a major threat to tigers is poaching to supply body parts for Tibetan and Chinese traditional medicine and clothing.

The spotted leopard (*chituwa*) is more common than the tiger and is a significant threat to livestock. Like the tiger, this nocturnal creature has been known to target humans when it is unable, through old age or illness, to hunt its usual prey. The endangered snow leopard (*heung chituwa*) is so rare and shy that it is seldom seen, but there are thought to be 350 to 500 snow leopards surviving in the high Himalaya, particularly around Dolpo. Snow leopards are so elusive that many locals believe the animals have the power to vanish at will.

Found in the grass plains (*phanta*) of the Terai region, the one-horned rhinoceros (*gaida*) is the largest of the three Asian rhino species. Rhino populations plummeted due to poaching during the Maoist insurgency, but they have gradually recovered since 2005 – today there are around 600 rhinos in Chitwan and smaller populations in Bardia National Park and Sukla Phanta National Park.

The lumbering and shaggy-coated sloth bear (*bhalu*) boasts a formidable set of front claws for tearing into termite mounds. The bear's poor eyesight and its tendency to swipe away with those claws when startled has earned it a gnarly reputation.

The only wild Asian elephants (*hathi*) in Nepal are in the western part of the Terai and Chure Hills. However, herds of domesticated elephants are found at all the national parks in the Terai, where they are used for antipoaching patrols and carrying tourists on safaris. However, as more information is revealed about the cruelty involved in the conditioning of these intelligent animals to facilitate domestication, the latter activity is losing appeal and we recommend against supporting the practice.

Perhaps the rarest animal of all is the endangered Ganges River dolphin (*susu*). This mammalian predator lacks lenses in its eyes and is almost blind. It hunts its way through the silty waters of lowland rivers using sonar. There are thought to be fewer than 50 dolphins left in Nepal, with most living in the Karnali River.

Smaller Mammals

Deer are abundant in the lowland national parks, providing a vital food source for tigers and leopards. Prominent species include the sambar and the spotted deer. In forests up to 2400m, you may hear the uncannily dog-like call of the barking deer (*muntjac*). At higher altitudes, look

Saligrams (fossilised ammonites) are found throughout the Himalaya and are regarded as symbols of Vishnu – they also provide proof that the Himalaya used to lie beneath the ancient Tethys Sea.

Nepal covers only 0.1% of the world's surface area but is home to nearly 10% of the world's species of birds, including 72 critically endangered species.

for the pocked-sized musk deer, which stands just 50cm high at the shoulder. Unfortunately these animals have been severely depleted by hunting to obtain the musk gland found in the abdomen of male deer.

At high altitudes, look out for the Himalayan tahr, a shaggy mountain goat, and the blue sheep (*naur* in Tibetan, *bharal* in Nepali), which is genetically positioned somewhere between goats and sheep. The boulder fields and stunted forests of the high Himalaya also provide shelter for several small rodents. The mouse-hare *(pika)* is commonly spotted scurrying nervously between rocks on trekking trails. You must climb even higher to the Trans-Himalayan zone in western Nepal to see the Himalayan marmot, related to the American groundhog.

Birds

More than 850 bird species are known in Nepal and almost half of these can be spotted in the Kathmandu Valley. The main breeding season and the best time to spot birds is March to May. Resident bird numbers are augmented by migratory species, which arrive in the Terai from November to March from Tibet and Siberia. The best places in Nepal for birdwatching are Koshi Tappu Wildlife Reserve and Chitwan National Park. The best spots in the Kathmandu Valley are Pulchowki Mountain, Nagarjun Hill and Shivapuri Nagarjun National Park.

Eight species of stork have been identified along the watercourses of the Terai, and demoiselle cranes fly down the Kali Gandaki and Dudh Kosi for the winter, before returning in spring to their Tibetan nesting grounds. The endangered sarus crane can be spotted in Bardia National Park and the Lumbini Crane Sanctuary.

Raptors and birds of prey of all sizes are found in Nepal. In the Kathmandu Valley and Terai, keep an eye out for the sweeping silhouettes of vultures and fork-tailed pariah kites circling ominously in the haze. In the mountains, watch for golden eagles and the huge Himalayan griffon and lammergeier.

There are six species of pheasant in Nepal, including the national bird, the *danphe,* also known as the Himalayan monal or Impeyan pheasant. Females are a dull brown, while males are an iridescent rainbow of colours. In areas frequented by trekkers, these birds are often quite tame, though they will launch themselves downhill in a falling, erratic flight if disturbed.

Nepal hosts 17 species of cuckoo, which arrive in March, heralding the coming of spring. The call of the Indian cuckoo is likened to the Nepali phrase *kaphal pakyo,* meaning 'the fruit of the box myrtle is ripe'. The call of the common hawk cuckoo sounds like the words 'brain fever' – or so it was described by British *sahibs* (gentlemen) as they lay sweating with malarial fevers.

While trekking through forests, keep an eye out for members of the timalid family. The spiny babbler is Nepal's only endemic species, and the black-capped sibia, with its constant prattle and ringing song, is

Birds of Nepal, by Robert Fleming Sr, Robert Fleming Jr and Lain Singh Bangdel, is a field guide to Nepal's many hundreds of bird species. Birds of Nepal, by Richard Grimmett and Carol Inskipp, is a comprehensive paperback with line drawings.

Bis Hajaar Tal (literally '20,000 lakes') in Chitwan National Park and the Koshi Tappu Wildlife Reserve are both Ramsar sites (www.ramsar. org), designated as wetlands of international importance.

ENVIRONMENT & WILDLIFE WILDLIFE

MONKEY MAYHEM

Because of Hanuman, the monkey god from the Ramayana, monkeys are considered holy and are well protected, if not pampered, in Nepal. You will often see troops of muscular red-rumped rhesus macaques harassing tourists and pilgrims for food scraps at Kathmandu's monuments and temples. These monkeys can be openly aggressive and they carry rabies, so appreciate them from a distance (and if that doesn't work, carry a stick).

You may also spot the slender common langur, with its short grey fur and black face, in forested areas up to 3700m. This species is more gentle than the thuggish macaque but again, keep your bananas out of sight and out of reach.

DINNER AT THE ROTTING CARCASS

Three of Nepal's nine species of vultures are critically endangered, with thousands of vultures dying every year after scavenging dead cows that have been treated with the anti-inflammatory drug diclofenac. When the problem was recognised the drug was soon banned (2006) and a replacement found. Unfortunately, however, there is still illegal use of similar drugs in Nepal and India.

Nevertheless, a scheme to feed vultures with uncontaminated meat has yielded remarkable results. Nicknamed the 'vulture restaurant', the project doubled the vulture population of Nawalparasi district (near Tiger Tops Tharu Lodge) in the western Terai in just two years. Old cattle, being sacred to Hindus, are not killed and can become a burden to farmers. Now they can be sold to the vulture restaurant where they are tested for contamination, allowed to live out their full life, and only fed to vultures after a natural death. Five other vulture restaurants have been established across Nepal, including one near Lumbini and one near Pokhara.

frequently heard in wet temperate forests. In the Pokhara region, the Indian roller is conspicuous when it takes flight, flashing iridescent turquoise on its wings. Local superstition has it that if someone about to embark on a journey sees a roller going their way it is a good omen.

Himalayan Flowers & Trees, by Dorothy Mierow and Tirtha Bahadur Shrestha, is the best available field guide to the plants of Nepal.

Another colourful character is the hoopoe, which has a retractable crest, a long curved bill, eye-catching orange plumage, and black-and-white stripes on its wings. Nepal is also home to 30 species of flycatchers and 60 species of warblers, as well as bee-eaters, drongos, minivets, parakeets and sunbirds.

Around watercourses, look out for thrushes, such as the handsome white-capped river chat and the delightfully named plumbeous redstart. Scan the surrounding trees for the black-and-white pied kingfisher and the white-breasted kingfisher with its iridescent turquoise jacket.

Different species of crows have adapted to different altitudes. The yellow-billed blue magpie and Himalayan tree pie are commonly seen in the temperate zone. Above the tree line, red- and yellow-billed choughs gather in flocks, particularly in areas frequented by humans. In the Trans-Himalaya region you will also see the menacing black raven, which scours the valleys looking for scavenging opportunities.

Plants

There are about 6500 known species of trees, shrubs and wildflowers in Nepal, but perhaps the most famous is *Rhododendron arboreum* (*lali gurans* in Nepali), the national flower of Nepal. It might better be described as a tree, reaching heights of 18m and forming whole forests in the Himalaya region. More than 30 other species of rhododendrons are found in the foothills of the Himalaya. The rhododendron forests burst into flower in March and April, painting the landscape in swaths of white, pink and red.

Bird Conservation Nepal (www.birdlifenepal.org) is an excellent Nepali organisation based in Kathmandu that organises birdwatching trips and publishes books, birding checklists and a good quarterly newsletter.

The best time to see the other wildflowers of the Himalaya in bloom is during the monsoon. The mountain views may be often obscured, but the ground underfoot will be a carpet of colour. Many of the alpine species found above the tree line bear flowers in autumn, including irises, gentians, anemones and the downy-petalled edelweiss.

In the foothills of the Himalaya, as well as in the plains, look for the magnificent mushrooming canopies of banyan and pipal trees, which often form the focal point of villages. The pipal tree has a special religious significance in Nepal – the Buddha gained enlightenment under a pipal tree and Hindus revere various species of pipal as symbols of Vishnu and Hanuman.

Sal, a broad-leaved, semideciduous hardwood, dominates the low-lying forests of the Terai. Sal leaves are used as disposable plates and the heavy wood is used for construction and boat building. On the flat plains, many areas are covered by *phanta* – this grass can grow to 2.5m high and is used by villagers for thatching and by elephants for a snack on the run.

National Parks & Reserves

Nepal's first national park, Chitwan, was established in 1973 in the Terai. There are now 12 national parks, one wildlife reserve, six conservation areas and, somewhat incongruously, one hunting reserve, protecting 18% of the land in Nepal. Entry fees apply for all the national parks and reserves, including conserved areas on trekking routes in the mountains.

The main agency overseeing national parks and conservation areas is the Department of National Parks & Wildlife Conservation (www.dnpwc.gov.np). However, the last few years have seen a shift in the management to international nongovernmental organisations (NGOs) and not-for-profit organisations with a degree of autonomy from the government of Nepal. The National Trust for Nature Conservation (www.ntnc.org.np) runs the Annapurna Conservation Area Project and Manaslu Conservation Area. The Mountain Institute (www.mountain.org) runs a number of conservation projects in the Himalaya.

The government imposed the first protected areas with little partnership with locals and initially without their cooperation. More recent initiatives have concentrated on educating local people and accommodating their needs, rather than evicting them completely from the land.

The community forest model has been particularly successful in Nepal – many protected areas are surrounded by buffer zones of community-owned forests, whose owners harvest natural resources and thus have a stake in their continued existence. See the website of the Federation of Community Forestry Users Nepal (www.fecofun.org.np) for more information.

Environmental Challenges

The environment of Nepal is fragile and a rapidly growing population is constantly adding to environmental pressures. Much of the land between the Himalaya and the Terai has been vigorously modified to provide space for crops, animals and houses. Forests have been cleared and wildlife populations depleted, and roads have eaten into valleys that were previously accessible only on foot. As a result, Shangri La is not immune to the environmental challenges that confront a shrinking planet.

Population growth is the biggest issue facing the environment in Nepal. More people need more land for agriculture and more natural resources for building, heating and cooking. The population of Nepal is increasing at a rate of 1.2% every year (as of 2017), and food security and growth is providing the economic incentive for the settlement of

Nepal's celebrated and less well-known national parks and conservation areas are described in detail at www.welcomenepal.com/places-to-see/must-see-national-parks-of-nepal.html.

ENVIRONMENT & WILDLIFE NATIONAL PARKS & RESERVES

BANKE NATIONAL PARK

With the creation of the 550-sq-km Banke National Park in 2010, Nepal gained its 10th national park and was able to boast one of the largest stretches of tiger habitat in Asia. Banke adjoins Suhelwa Wildlife Sanctuary in India and is connected to Bardia National Park through community forests and buffer zones. Along with India's Katerniaghat Wildlife Sanctuary, these reserves provide an important corridor for wild elephants and rhinos, and, it is hoped, a significant boost to tiger conservation. This increase in officially protected tiger habitat was part of Nepal's 2010 pledge to double the country's tiger population by 2022 (the next Chinese zodiac Year of the Tiger).

previously uninhabited areas. In 2017 Kathmandu earned the dubious distinction of being the seventh most polluted city in the world.

However, there have also been some environmental successes in Nepal. Foreign and Nepali NGOs have provided solar panels, biogas and kerosene-powered stoves, and parabolic solar cookers for thousands of farms, trekking lodges, schools and monasteries across Nepal.

A number of organisations can provide more information on environmental issues in Nepal.

Bird Conservation Nepal (www.birdlifenepal.org)
Himalayan Nature (www.himalayannature.org)
International Centre for Integrated Mountain Development (www.icimod.org)
International Union for Conservation of Nature (www.iucn.org)
National Trust for Nature Conservation (www.ntnc.org.np)
Resources Himalaya (www.resourceshimalaya.org)
Wildlife Conservation Nepal (www.wcn.org.np)
World Wildlife Fund Nepal (www.wwfnepal.org)

> For information on alternative energy projects in Nepal, visit the websites of the Centre for Rural Technology (www.crtnepal.org), the Foundation for Sustainable Technologies (www.fostnepal.org) and Drokpa (www.drokpa.org).

Deforestation

Over 80% of Nepali citizens rely on firewood for heating and cooking, particularly in the mountains, leading to massive problems with deforestation. Nepal has lost more than 70% of its forest cover in modern times and travellers contribute to the problem by increasing the demand for firewood in trekking areas.

As well as robbing native species of their natural habitat, deforestation drives animals directly into conflict with human beings. The loss of tree cover is a major contributing factor to the landslides that scar the valleys of the Himalaya after every monsoon.

It's not all doom and gloom though – in recent years, a number of community forests have been established on the boundaries of national

NATIONAL PARKS & CONSERVATION AREAS

CA = Conservation Area, HR = Hunting Reserve, NP = National Park, WR = Wildlife Reserve

NAME	LOCATION	FEATURES	BEST TIME TO VISIT	FOREIGNER ENTRY FEE (RS)
Annapurna CA (p12)	north of Pokhara	most popular trekking area in Nepal, high peaks, diverse landscapes, varied culture	Oct-Apr, May	2000
Banke NP (p369)	far western Terai	sal forest, tigers, one-horned rhinoceros	Oct-early Apr	500
Bardia NP (p272)	far western Terai	Geruwa River, tigers, rhinoceros, over 250 bird species	Oct-early Apr	1000
Chitwan NP (p243)	central Terai	sal forest, rhinoceros, tigers, gharials, 450 bird species, World Heritage site	Oct-Feb	1500
Dhorpatan HR	west-central Nepal	Nepal's only hunting reserve (access is difficult), blue sheep	Mar-Apr	3000
Kanchenjunga CA (p317)	far eastern Nepal	third-highest mountain in the world, blue sheep, snow leopards	Mar-Apr, Oct-Nov	2000
Khaptad NP (p274)	far western Nepal	core area is important religious site	Mar-Apr	3000
Koshi Tappu WR (p283)	eastern Nepal	Sapt Kosi River, grasslands, 439 bird species	Mar-Apr, Oct-Nov	1000

parks. The forests are communally owned and the sustainable harvest of timber and other natural resources provides an economic alternative to poaching and resource gathering inside the parks. See the website of the Federation of Community Forestry Users (www.fecofun.org.np) for more information.

Wildlife Poaching

Nepal's 10-year Maoist insurgency did not only affect human beings. Soldiers were withdrawn from national-park checkpoints, leading to a massive upsurge in poaching. Nepal's rhino population fell by 30% between 2000 and 2005; elephants, tigers, leopards and other endangered species were also targeted.

The main engines driving poaching are the trade in animal parts for Chinese and Tibetan traditional medicine and to a lesser extent the trade in animal pelts to Tibet for traditional costumes known as *chubas*. Travellers can avoid contributing to the problem by rejecting souvenirs made from animal products.

Hydroelectricity

On the face of things, harnessing the power of Nepal's rivers to create electricity sounds like a win-win situation, but the environmental impact of building new hydroelectric plants can be devastating. Entire valleys may be flooded to create reservoirs and most of the energy may be diverted to the overpopulated Kathmandu Valley or exported to China and India.

As well as displacing local people and damaging the environment, large hydro schemes affect the flow of water downstream, disrupting the passage of nutrient-rich silt to agricultural land in the plains.

Nepal's Terai national parks are under threat from an alien invader – the South American creeper *Mikania micrantha*, which is dubbed 'mile a minute' owing to its prodigious growth rate.

ENVIRONMENT & WILDLIFE ENVIRONMENTAL CHALLENGES

NAME	LOCATION	FEATURES	BEST TIME TO VISIT	FOREIGNER ENTRY FEE (RS)
Langtang NP	northeast of Kathmandu	varied topography, culture, migratory birds	Mar-Apr	3390
Makalu-Barun NP (p317)	eastern Nepal	bordering Sagarmatha NP, protecting diverse mountain landscapes	Oct-May	3390
Manaslu CA	west-central Nepal	rugged terrain, 11 types of forest, bordering Annapurna CA	Mar-Apr, Oct-Nov	2000
Parsa NP	central Terai	bordering Chitwan NP, sal forests, wild elephants, 300 bird species	Oct-Apr	1000
Rara NP	northwestern Nepal	Nepal's biggest lake, little visited, migratory birds	Mar-May, Oct-Dec	3000
Sagarmatha NP (p294)	Everest region	highest mountains on the planet, World Heritage site, monasteries, Sherpa culture	Oct-May	3390
Shey Phoksumdo NP	Dolpo, western Nepal	Trans-Himalaya ecosystem, alpine flowers, snow leopards, blue sheep	Jun-Sep	3390
Shivapuri Nagarjun NP (p135)	northeast of Kathmandu	close to Kathmandu, many bird & butterfly species, good hiking & cycling	Oct-May	565
Sukla Phanta NP (p276)	southwestern Nepal	riverine flood plain, grasslands, endangered swamp deer, wild elephants	Oct-Apr	1000

CLIMATE CHANGE IN THE HIMALAYA

Every year, during the monsoon, the Terai faces severe flooding problems exacerbated by deforestation on the mountain slopes and the plains themselves.

In the mountains, the flood risk comes from a different source. Rising global temperatures are melting the glaciers that snake down from the Himalaya, swelling glacial lakes to dangerous levels.

In 1985 a natural dam collapsed in the Thame Valley, releasing the trapped waters of the Dig Tsho lake and sending devastating floods roaring along the Dudh Kosi Valley.

Scientists are now watching the Imja Tsho in the Chhukung Valley with alarm. Since 1960 the lake has grown by over 34 million cu metres – if it ruptured, experts are predicting a 'vertical tsunami' raging through one of the most heavily populated and trekked parts of the Himalaya. In 2016 the Nepalese Army constructed an outlet and drained over 4 million cu metres of water from the lake. Funding was provided by the UN.

Although there is no such thing as a 'normal' monsoon, the recent devastating monsoons of 2013, 2014 and 2017 also raise concerns about climate change. In these years massive rain events inundated large areas of Nepal's Terai, as well as India, and led to massive landslides and loss of life and property.

Currently there are large-scale hydroelectric power plants on the Babai, Bhote Kosi, Kali Gandaki, Marsyangdi, Rapti, Roshi, Trisuli and West Seti rivers. In 2017 there were five hydroelectricity projects under construction and over 30 new projects were being actively considered.

Tourism

Tourism has brought health care, education, electricity and wealth to some of the most remote, isolated communities on earth, but it has also had a massive impact on the local environment.

Forests are cleared to provide timber for the construction of lodges and fuel for cooking and heating, and trekkers contribute massively to the build-up of litter and the erosion of mountain trails.

Even the apparent benefits of tourism can have environmental implications – the wealth that tourism has brought to villages in the Himalaya has allowed many farmers to increase the size of their herds of goats, cows and yaks, leading to yet more deforestation as woodland is cleared to provide temporary pastures.

Nature Treks (www.nature-treks.com) offers organised walks with expert naturalists at Shivapuri Nagarjun National Park, Chitwan National Park, Bardia National Park and in the Langtang area.

Water Supplies

Despite the natural abundance of water, water shortages are another chronic problem in Nepal, particularly in the Kathmandu Valley. Where water is available, it is often contaminated with heavy metals, industrial chemicals, bacteria and human waste. In Kathmandu, the holy Bagmati River has become one of the most polluted rivers on earth, although there have been concerted efforts to clean the river of visible litter.

In the Terai, one of the biggest problems is arsenic poisoning from contaminated drinking water. Up to 1.4 million people are thought to be at risk from this deadly toxin, which is drawn into wells and reservoirs from contaminated aquifers.

Survival
Guide

Directory A-Z

Accommodation

In Kathmandu and Pokhara there's a wide variety of accommodation, from rock-bottom fleapits to five-star international hotels. Some of Nepal's best deals are to be found in its stylish midrange and top-end accommodation. Only in high season (October to December) does accommodation need to be booked (well) in advance.

Homestays Becoming popular; immerse yourself in local communities.

Teahouses Along the major trekking routes are these basic hotels where you can get a bed and meals.

Hotels The most common form of accommodation in Nepal, from simple, even grotty affairs, to luxury pads. Most commonly, however, they are inexpensive, comfortable and clean.

Most hotels have a wide range of rooms under one roof, including larger (often top-floor) deluxe rooms that are good for families and small groups.

Budget rooms are often on the darker, lower floors and have solar-heated hot-water showers, which won't be hot in the mornings or on cloudy days. Midrange rooms have better mattresses, satellite TV and a tub. Almost all hotels offer wi-fi these days.

Most hotels have different rates for single and double occupancy, but the 'single room' may be much smaller than the double. The best deal for a solo traveller is to get a double room for a single price.

Discounts

Nepal's hotel prices are highly seasonal, with peak season running from October to November and March to April, but even beyond this room rates fluctuate according to tourist demand. You will find that rates drop even lower during the monsoon season (June to September).

The exact room rate you will be quoted depends on the season and current numbers of tourists. At many hotels the printed tariffs are pure fiction, published to fulfil government star-rating requirements and

in the hope that you might be silly enough to pay them. Some midrange hotels offer discounts for booking online (and a free airport transfer), but you'll get at least this much on the spot, if not more.

If business is slow you can often negotiate a deluxe room for a standard-room rate or inclusive of tax. When business picks up, you may just have to take what's on offer.

You can also negotiate cheaper rates for longer stays. In the cool of autumn and spring you can get a further discount on rooms that are air-conditioned simply by agreeing to turn off the air-con.

Activities

Nepal is renowned as the world's greatest trekking destination, but there are also plenty of fine day hikes, particularly in the Kathmandu Valley and around Bandipur, Tansen and Pokhara. Then there is the world-class rafting, kayaking, canyoning and climbing. Nepal is a great place to learn a new adventure sport.

For more information see Outdoor Activities (p42) and Planning Your Trek (p30).

Children

Increasing numbers of people are travelling with their children in Nepal, and

---

SLEEPING PRICE RANGES

The following price indicators refer to a double room with bathroom in high season. Rates generally do not include taxes, unless otherwise noted.

$ less than US$25 (Rs 2500)

$$ US$25–US$80 (Rs 2500–Rs 8000)

$$$ more than US$80 (Rs 8000)

with a bit of planning it can be remarkably hassle-free. Many people trek with older children, but heading out on the trail with smaller children for any length of time or on any higher routes with children of any age is generally not to be advised.

Check out Lonely Planet's *Travel with Children* for handy hints and advice about the pros and cons of travelling with kids.

Practicalities

➡ In the main tourist centres (Kathmandu and Pokhara), most hotels have triple rooms and quite often a suite with four beds, which are ideal for families with young children. Finding a room with a bathtub can be a problem at the bottom end of the market.

➡ Many Kathmandu hotels have a garden or roof garden, which can be good play areas. Check them thoroughly, however, as some are definitely not safe for young children.

➡ Walking the crowded, narrow and pavement-less streets of Kathmandu and other towns can be a hassle with young kids unless you can get them up off the ground – a backpack or sling is ideal. A pusher or stroller is more trouble than it's worth unless you bring one with oversized wheels, suitable for rough pavements.

➡ Keep mealtimes stress-free by eating breakfast at your hotel, having lunch at a place with a garden (there are plenty of these) and going to restaurants armed with colouring books, stories and other distractions.

➡ Disposable nappies (diapers) are available in Kathmandu and Pokhara, but for a price – it's better to bring them with you if possible.

➡ Cots are generally not available in budget or midrange hotels; similarly, nappy-changing facilities and high chairs are a rarity.

PRACTICALITIES

Newspapers Nepal's main English-language papers are the daily *Kathmandu Post* (www.kathmandupost.ekantipur.com), *Himalayan Times* (www.thehimalayantimes.com) and *Republica* (www.myrepublica.com). The *Nepali Times* (www.nepalitimes.com) comes out weekly.

Magazines *ECS* (www.ecs.com.np) is a glossy, expat-oriented monthly magazine with interesting articles on travel and culture, plus apartment listings. *Himal* magazine (www.himalmag.com) is also good.

TV Most hotel rooms offer satellite TV, which generally includes Star TV, BBC World and CNN.

Weights & Measures Nepal uses the metric system, alongside some traditional measures.

➡ Trekking is possible with children, but it pays to limit the altitude; consider hiring a porter to carry younger children in a *doko* basket.

Customs Regulations

All baggage is X-rayed on arrival and departure, though it's a pretty haphazard process. In addition to the import and export of drugs, customs is concerned with the illegal export of antiques.

➡ You may not import Nepali rupees, and only nationals of Nepal and India may import Indian currency.

➡ There are no other restrictions on bringing in either cash or travellers cheques, but the amount taken out at departure should not exceed the amount brought in.

➡ Officially you should declare cash or travellers cheques in excess of US$2000, or the equivalent, but no one seems to bother with this, and it is laxly enforced.

Antiques

Customs' main concern is preventing the export of antique works of art, and with good reason: Nepal has been a particular victim of international art theft over the last 20 years.

It is very unlikely that souvenirs sold to travellers will be antique (despite the claims of the vendors), but if there is any doubt, they should be cleared and a certificate obtained from the **Department of Archaeology** (Map p70; ☎01-4250683; www.doa.gov.np; Ramshah Path, Kathmandu; ◷10am-2pm Sat, to 3pm Sun-Thu) in central Kathmandu's National Archives building. If you visit the department between 10am and 1pm, you should be able to pick up a certificate by 5pm the same day. These controls also apply to the export of precious and semiprecious stones.

BOOK YOUR STAY ONLINE

For more accommodation reviews by Lonely Planet authors, check out http://lonelyplanet.com/hotels/. You'll find independent reviews, as well as recommendations on the best places to stay. Best of all, you can book online.

Electricity

Electricity is 230V/50 cycles; 120V appliances from the USA will need a transformer. Sockets usually take plugs with three round pins: sometimes the small variety, sometimes the large. Some sockets take plugs with two round pins. Local electrical shops sell cheap adapters.

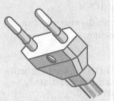

Type C
230V/50Hz

Type D
230V/50Hz

Embassies & Consulates

Travellers continuing beyond Nepal may need visas for Bangladesh, China, India, Myanmar (Burma) and Thailand.

The only visas available in Kathmandu for Tibet (actually there's no such thing as a 'visa for Tibet'; it's just a Chinese group visa and a travel permit for Tibet) are for organised groups. Individuals wishing to travel directly to China (not Tibet) will need to show an air ticket to Chengdu, Beijing, Shanghai or Guangzhou to prove that they aren't going to Tibet.

To find Nepali embassies and consulates in other countries, check out the websites of Nepal's **Ministry of Foreign Affairs** (www. mofa.gov.np) or **Department of Immigration** (www.nepal immigration.gov.np). Major embassies and consulates in Nepal include the following:

Australian Embassy (☎01-4371678; www.nepal.embassy. gov.au; Bansbari, Kathmandu)

Canadian Consulate (Map p70; ☎01-4441976; canadaconsul@ mail.com.np; 47 Lal Durbar Marg, Kathmandu; ☺9am-noon Mon-Fri)

Chinese Embassy (Map p70; ☎01-4440286; http://np.chi na-embassy.org/eng; Hattisar, Kathmandu; ☺9.45-11am Mon-Fri) Visa applications are accepted on Monday to Friday from 9.45am to 11am; visas normally take three working days to be issued but can be done in just one day if you pay extra. The visa section is located in Hattisar; the main **embassy** (Map p70; ☎01-4411740; www.np.chi na-embassy.org; Baluwatar; ☺9am-noon & 2-5pm Mon-Fri) is in Baluwatar.

French Embassy (Map p70; ☎01-4412332; www.amba france-np.org; Lazimpat, Kathmandu; ☺9am-11.30am Mon, Tue, Thu & Fri)

German Embassy (Map p70; ☎01-4217200; www.kath mandu.diplo.de; Gyaneshwar Marg 690, Kathmandu; ☺9am-11.30am)

Indian Embassy (Map p70; ☎01-4410900; www.indianem bassy.org.np; 336 Kapurdhara Marg, Lainchaur; ☺9.30am-noon & 1.30-5pm Mon-Fri) Most tourists can now get an e-visa for up to 60 days if they apply in advance. Getting an Indian tourist visa in Nepal is a more expensive and time-consuming process.

Israeli Embassy (Map p70; ☎01-4441310; http://kath mandu.mfa.gov.il; Lazimpat, Kathmandu; ☺9am-5pm Mon-Thu, to 2pm Fri)

UK Embassy (Map p70; ☎01-4237100; www.ukinnepal.fco. gov.uk; Lainchaur, Kathmandu; ☺8.30am-noon Mon, Tue, Thu & Fri)

US Embassy (☎01-4234000; http://np.usembassy.gov; Maharajganj, Kathmandu; ☺8am-5pm Mon-Fri)

Food

You can eat like a king in Kathmandu and Pokhara, where restaurants offer a world map of cuisines, with dishes from Tibet, China, India, Japan, Thailand, Mexico, Italy, France and the Middle East. Take advantage of these offerings – once you start trekking the choice is more limited.

The staple meal of Nepal is *daal bhaat tarkari* – literally lentil soup, rice and curried vegetables. It's a tried and true fuel to keep you trekking, all day, every day.

For more on Nepali food see p58.

LGBT Travellers

Nepal is the only country in South Asia that does not criminalise same-sex relations. A landmark Supreme Court hearing in December 2007 ordered the government to end discrimination against sexual minorities and to ensure equal rights. That said, there's not a big open gay scene in Nepal and gay Nepalis are vulnerable to police harassment and blackmail.

Gay couples holding hands in public will experience no difficulties, as this is socially acceptable, but public displays of intimacy by anyone are frowned upon.

Nepal recognises a third gender in its official documents, including passports. Kathmandu has a long tradition of *hijra* (transsexuals), though many report police harassment.

Pink Mountain Travels (☏9851018660; www.gaytourinnepal.com) is a LGBT-friendly agency in Kathmandu that can arrange treks and tours.

Insurance

A travel-insurance policy to cover theft, loss and medical problems is an excellent idea for travel in Nepal. There are a wide variety of policies available, so check the small print carefully. Some policies exclude 'dangerous activities', which may include riding a motorbike and trekking (and definitely bungee jumping and rafting).

Choose a policy that covers medical and emergency repatriation, including helicopter evacuation for trekkers and general medical evacuation to Bangkok or Delhi, which alone can cost a cool US$40,000.

You may prefer a policy that pays doctors or hospitals directly rather than you having to pay on the spot and claim later. In Nepal, most medical treatment must be paid for at the point of delivery. If your insurance company does not provide upfront payment, be sure to obtain receipts so you can reclaim later.

Worldwide traveller insurance is available at http://www.lonelyplanet.com/travel-insurance. You can buy, extend and claim online anytime – even if you are already on the road.

Internet Access

Almost every hotel, restaurant and cafe in Kathmandu, Pokhara and larger towns offer free wi-fi and connections are pretty good. You can even get (paid) wi-fi in places like Namche Bazaar along the Everest Base Camp trek.

Internet cafes are available in smaller towns and generally cost around Rs 50 per hour.

Language Courses

Nepali is not a difficult language to learn, and you will see notices around Kathmandu advertising language courses. Most schools offer courses or individual tuition. Expect to pay about US$50 for a two-week course or around US$3 to US$5 per hour for private tuition.

There are often flyers around Bodhnath advertising Tibetan-language tuition as well as opportunities to volunteer teaching English to Tibetan refugees.

There are a number of language centres in Kathmandu and Pokhara.

Rangjung Yeshe Institute (Map p129;☏01-4483575; www.ryi.org) This affiliate of Kathmandu University offers a variety of long-term courses on Buddhist studies and Tibetan language.

Cosmic Brontosaurus Language School (Map p216;☏9846069834; www.cosmicbrontosaurus.com; Lakeside North; per hour Rs 500; ⊙7am-7pm) Offering individual or group lessons from beginner to advanced, the rather primitive

classroom in a wooden shack along the lake is surrounded by banana plants and is the perfect spot to learn Nepali. Prem, who runs the school, is a lovely guy, and has several years' experience working with the UN as a translator.

Intercultural Training & Research Centre (ITC; Map p90; ☏01-4414493; Kathmandu) This well-respected language centre works with many NGOs, including the UK's Voluntary Service Overseas (VSO). It offers crash courses (three hours), 60-hour beginner courses and six-week intermediate courses. Tuition is one-on-one and costs around Rs 400 per hour.

Kathmandu Environmental Education Project (KEEP; Map p90;☏01-4267471; www.keepnepal.org; Jyatha, Thamel; ⊙10am-5pm Sun-Fri; ☏) Offers six-day Nepali-language classes over the last week of each month. Cost is US$50 per person.

Legal Matters

Hashish has been illegal since 1973, but it's still readily available in Nepal. Thamel is

BARGAINING

Haggling is an integral part of most commercial transactions in Nepal, especially when dealing with souvenir shops, hotels and guides. Ideally, it should be an enjoyable social exchange, rather than a conflict of egos. A good deal is reached when both parties are happy; Rs 10 might make quite a difference to the seller, but to a foreign traveller it amounts to less than US$0.10.

full of shifty, whispering dealers. In practice, Nepali police aren't very interested in people with a small amount of marijuana on them (they're more focused on smuggling), but the technical penalty for drug possession is around five years in prison, so potential smokers should keep the less-than-salubrious condition of Nepali jails firmly in mind. Don't try taking any out of the country, either – travellers have been arrested at the airport on departure.

If you get caught smuggling something serious – drugs or gold – the chances are you'll end up in jail, without trial, and will remain there until someone pays for you to get out. Jail conditions in Nepal are reportedly horrific. Bribery is sometimes used to avoid jail. This is illegal and can land the perpetrator in deeper strife. Deniability that a bribe was offered – where the accused believed it was a legitimate fee – is the only defence.

Killing a cow is illegal in Nepal and carries a punishment of two years in prison.

Money

The Nepali rupee (Rs) is divided into 100 paisa. There are coins for denominations of one, two, five and 10 rupees, and banknotes in denominations of one, two, five, 10, 20, 50, 100, 500 and 1000 rupees. Since the abolition of the monarchy in 2008, images of Mt Everest have replaced the king on all banknotes.

Away from major centres, changing a Rs 1000 note can be difficult, so it is always a good idea to keep a stash of small denomination notes.

ATMs

Standard Chartered Bank has 24-hour ATMs in Kathmandu and Pokhara. Other banks, such as Himalaya Bank and Nabil Bank, have ATMs and are present in most reasonable sized towns, but some don't accept foreign bank cards (despite Visa signs indicating that they do). Quite a lot of machines seem to have a per-transaction withdrawal limit of Rs 15,000, but there doesn't appear to be any rhyme or reason as to which machines do and don't. Fees are around Rs 500 per withdrawal.

Frequent power outages can limit the machines' working hours, so use one when you see it's working. Using an ATM attached to a bank during business hours will minimise hassle in the rare event that the machine eats your card.

Inform your bank that you'll be using your card in Nepal, otherwise they might suspect fraud and freeze your card.

Changing Money

Official exchange rates are set by the government's Nepal Rastra Bank and listed in the daily newspapers. Rates at the private banks vary, but are generally not far from the official rate.

There are exchange counters at the international terminal at Kathmandu's

Tribhuvan Airport and banks and/or moneychangers at the various border crossings. Pokhara and the major border towns also have official money-changing facilities, but changing travellers cheques can be time consuming elsewhere in the country, even in some quite large towns. If you are trekking, take enough cash in small-denomination rupees to last the whole trek.

The best private banks are Himalaya Bank, Nepal Bank and Standard Chartered Bank. Some hotels and resorts are licensed to change money, but their rates are lower. Travellers cheques from the main companies can be exchanged in banks in Kathmandu and Pokhara for a 2% surcharge. Euro travellers cheques are also charged a flat US$10 fee per cheque. With each passing year it gets harder to change cheques.

When you change money officially, you are required to show your passport, and you are issued with a foreign exchange encashment receipt showing your identity and the amount of currency you have changed. Hang onto the receipts as you need them to change excess rupees back into foreign currency at banks. You can change rupees back into foreign currency at most moneychangers without a receipt.

Many upmarket hotels and businesses are obliged by the government to demand payment in hard currency (euros or US dollars); they will also accept rupees, but only if you can show a foreign exchange encashment receipt that covers the amount you owe them. In practice this regulation seems to be widely disregarded. Airlines are also required to charge tourists in hard currency, either in cash US dollars, travellers cheques or credit cards, and this rule is generally followed.

In addition to the banks, there are licensed moneychangers in Kathmandu, Pokhara, Birganj, Kakarbhitta and Sunauli/Bhairawa. The rates are often marginally lower than the banks, but there are no commissions; they have much longer opening hours (typically from 9am to 7pm daily) and they are also much quicker, the whole process often taking no more than a few minutes.

Most licensed money-changers will provide an exchange receipt; if they don't you may be able to negotiate better rates than those posted on their boards.

Credit Cards

Major credit cards are widely accepted at midrange and better hotels, restaurants and fancy shops in the Kathmandu Valley and Pokhara only. Most places levy a 3% to 4% surcharge to cover the credit card company's fees to the vendor.

Branches of Standard Chartered Bank and some other banks such as Nabil Bank and Himalaya Bank give cash advances against Visa and MasterCard in Nepali rupees only (no commission is charged), and will also sell you foreign-currency travellers cheques against the cards with a 2% commission.

International Transfers

In general, it's easiest to send money through companies such as Western Union (www.westernunion.com) or Moneygram (www.visitnepal. com/moneygram), which can arrange transfers within minutes. To pick up funds at a Western Union branch, you'll need your passport and 10-digit transfer code.

Note that money can often only be received in Nepali rupees, rather than US dollars.

Tipping

Taxis Round up the fare for taxi drivers; rickshaw drivers will also appreciate a modest tip.

Restaurants Tipping waiting staff is uncommon, but tips are invariably appreciated.

Guides & Porters Trekking guides and porters generally expect a tip of 10% to 15% for a job well done.

Opening Hours

Standard opening hours are as follows.

BUSINESS	OPENING HOURS
Airline offices	9am-1pm & 2-6pm Sun-Fri, 9am-1pm Sat
Banks	9am-noon, 2-4pm Sun-Fri, 10am-noon Sat
Bars & clubs	generally closed by midnight (1am in Kathmandu)
Embassies	9am-1pm & 2-5pm Mon-Fri
Government offices	10am-1pm & 2-5pm (to 4pm in winter) Mon-Thu, 10am-1pm Fri (also 10am-5pm Sun outside the Kathmandu Valley)
Museums	generally 10.30am-4.30pm, often closed Tue
Restaurants	8am-10pm
Shops	10am-8pm (some shops closed on Sat)

Photography

Bringing a video camera to Nepal poses no real problem and there are no video fees to worry about. The exception to this is in the upper Mustang region, where there is technically an astonishing US$1000 fee to take video footage, though unless you're obviously a professional film crew it's highly unlikely anyone will ask you for this.

Courses

Budding bloggers, photo-journalists and citizen journalists might be interested in the annual eight-day photography course run by **Kathmandu Inside Out** (www.kathmanduinsideout. com), which focuses on storytelling through photos. The US$1600 fee includes the course and funding for two aspiring Nepali journalists. The course usually takes place in November or December.

Memory Cards & Equipment

Almost all flavours of memory stick, flash card etc and batteries are available in Kathmandu. Note that travellers have reported buying cheap cards in Kathmandu that do not have as much memory as the packet claims.

Photographing People

Most Nepalis are content to have their photograph taken, but always ask permission

TAXING TAXES

Most midrange and top-end hotels and restaurants add a 13% value added tax (VAT), as well as a 10% service charge. The service charge is craftily calculated from the total *after* VAT, resulting in a whopping 24.3% surcharge to your bill. You'll have to mentally figure in the taxes to avoid a nasty shock when your bill comes, though on the plus side it does away with the dilemma of how much to tip! Some budget places charge only VAT or service, especially restaurants.

DASAIN STOPPAGES

Dasain (15 days in September or October) is the most important of all Nepali celebrations. Tens of thousands of Nepalis hit the road to return home to celebrate with their families. This means that while villages are full of life if you are trekking, buses and planes are fully booked and overflowing, porters may be hard to find (or more expensive than usual) and cars are difficult to hire. Many hotels and restaurants in regional towns close down completely, and doing business in Kathmandu (outside Thamel) becomes almost impossible. Most restaurants run a limited menu at this time.

The most important days, when everything comes to a total halt, are the ninth day (when thousands of animals are sacrificed) and the 10th day (when blessings are received from elder relatives and superiors). Banks and government offices are generally closed from the eighth day of the festival to the 12th day.

first. Sherpa people are an exception and can be very camera-shy.

➡ Bear in mind that if a sadhu (holy man) poses for you, they will probably insist on being given *baksheesh* (a tip).

Restrictions

➡ It is not uncommon for temple guardians to not allow photos of their temple, and these wishes should be respected.

➡ Don't photograph army camps, checkpoints or bridges.

Post

The postal service to and from Nepal is, at best, erratic but can occasionally be amazingly efficient. Most articles do arrive at their destination...eventually.

Couriers

To send 500g of documents from Kathmandu, **FedEx** (Map p70; ☏01-4269248; www.fedex.com/np; Kantipath; ◷9am-7pm Sun-Fri, to 1pm Sat) and **DHL** (Map p70; ☏01-2298124; www.dhl.com.np; Kamaladi; ◷9.30am-6pm Sun-Fri) charge around US$40 to the USA/UK, and slightly less to Australia. Packages take about a week.

Parcel Post

Having stocked up on gifts and souvenirs in Nepal, many people send them home from Kathmandu. Parcel post is not cheap or quick, but the service is reliable. Sea mail is much cheaper than airmail, but it is also much slower (packages take about 3½ months) and less reliable.

As an indication, a 2kg package to the UK/USA costs Rs 1645/2045 via airmail, or 25% less at 'book post' rate (a special rate for books only).

The contents of a parcel must be inspected by officials *before* it is wrapped. There are packers at the Kathmandu foreign post office who will wrap it for a small fee. The maximum weight for sea mail is 20kg; for airmail it's 10kg, or 5kg for book post.

If an object is shipped out to you in Nepal, you may find that customs' charges for clearance and collection at your end add up to more than the initial cost of sending it. Often it's worth paying extra to take it with you on the plane in the first place.

Postal Rates

Airmail rates for a 20g letter/postcard within Nepal are Rs 5/2; to India and surrounding countries Rs 25/20; to Europe and the UK Rs 40/30; and to the USA and Australia Rs 50/35.

Public Holidays

A remarkable number of holidays and festivals affect the working hours of Nepal's government offices and banks, which seem to close every other day and certainly for public holidays and some or all festival days. Exact festival timings (and thus their public holiday dates) change annually according to Nepal's lunar calendar. The following are just the major holidays.

Prithvi Narayan Shah's Birthday 10 January

Basanta Panchami (start of Spring) January/February

Maha Shivaratri (Shiva's Birthday) February/March

Bisket Jatra (Nepali New Year) 14 April

Janai Purnima July/August

Teej (Festival of Women) August/September

Constitution Day 19 September

Indra Jatra (Indra Festival) September

Dasain September/October

Tihar (Divali) October/November

Safe Travel

In political terms, Nepal is more stable than it has been in years, and crime is not a major risk for travellers. It makes sense to consult local and international news sources before you travel to Nepal so you are aware of any issues.

➡ Be aware that damage from the earthquake has affected travel in many areas. Some roads are still damaged and experts warn of an increased risk of landslides and avalanches following the disaster.

➡ Statistically speaking, the most dangerous thing you'll

do in Nepal is simply taking public transport along the country's busy highways.

You should heed the following general advice for travelling in Nepal:

➧ Register with your embassy in Kathmandu, especially if you plan to go trekking.

➧ Don't trek alone. Solo women should avoid travelling alone with a male guide.

➧ Be familiar with the symptoms of altitude sickness when trekking and follow the guidelines for safe acclimatisation.

➧ Avoid travelling on night buses as these are prone to accidents.

➧ Take copies of your passport, visa, air ticket and trekking permits and keep these separate from the originals.

Demonstrations & Strikes

Nepal has a long history of demonstrations and strikes – some by politicians, some by students, some by Maoists, and some by all three! The political situation has greatly improved, but occasionally demonstrations still occur and they can turn violent.

A normal demonstration is a *julus*. If things escalate there may be a *chakka jam* ('jam the wheels'), when all vehicles stay off the street, or a *bandh,* when all shops, schools and offices are closed. In the event of a strike, the best thing to do is hole up in your hotel with a good book. In this case you'll likely have to dine at your hotel.

If political instability returns, it pays to heed the following points:

➧ Keep an eye on the local press and news websites to find out about impending strikes, demonstrations and curfews – follow websites such as www.kathmandupost.

ekantipur.com, www.thehimalayantimes.com and www.nepalitimes.com.

➧ Don't ever break curfews and avoid travelling by road during *bandhs* or blockades, particularly in a rented vehicle, as vehicles flouting travel bans are often vandalised. Be nervous if you notice that your car is the only one on the streets of Kathmandu!

➧ When roads are closed, the government generally runs buses with armed police from the airport to major hotels, returning to the airport from Tridevi Marg at the east end of Thamel.

Scams

Whilst the overwhelming majority of Nepalis couldn't be any nicer, there are some who are impressively inventive in their range of imaginative scams. Watch out for the following:

➧ Deals offered by gem dealers that involve you buying stones to sell for a 'vast profit' at home. The dealers normally claim they are not able to export the stones without paying heavy taxes, so you take them and meet another dealer when you get home, who will sell them to a local contact and you both share the profit. Except they don't. And you don't.

➧ Children or young mothers asking for milk. You buy the milk at a designated store at an inflated price, the child then returns the milk and pockets some of the mark-up.

➧ Kids who seem to know the capital of any country you can think of; they are charming but a request for money will arrive at some point.

➧ 'Holy men' who do their best to plant a *tika* (a red paste denoting a blessing) on your forehead, only to then demand significant payment.

➧ Credit card scams; travellers have bought souvenirs and then found thousands of dollars worth of internet porn subscriptions chalked up on their bill.

Theft

While petty theft is not on the scale that exists in many countries, reports of theft from hotel rooms in tourist areas (including along trekking routes) do occasionally reach us, and theft with violence is not unheard of. Never store valuables or money in your hotel room.

NEPALI CALENDARS

Nepali holidays and festivals are principally dated by the lunar calendar, falling on days relating to new or full moons. The lunar calendar is divided into bright and dark fortnights. The bright fortnight is the two weeks of the waxing moon, as it grows to become *purnima* (the full moon). The dark fortnight is the two weeks of the waning moon, as the full moon shrinks to become *aunsi* (the new moon).

The Nepali New Year starts on 14 April with the month of Baisakh. The Nepali calendar is 57 years ahead of the Gregorian calendar used in the West, thus the year 2018 in the West is 2075 in Nepal.

The Newars of the Kathmandu Valley, on the other hand, start their New Year from the day after Deepawali (the third day of Tihar), which falls on the night of the new moon in late October or early November. Their calendar is 880 years behind the Gregorian calendar, so 2018 in the West is 1138 to the Newars.

GOVERNMENT TRAVEL ADVICE

The folllowing government websites offer travel advisories and information on current hotspots. Some of this official travel advice can sound a little alarmist, but if your government issues a travel warning advising against 'all travel' or 'all but essential travel' to a specific area, then your travel insurance may be invalid if you ignore this advice.

Australian Department of Foreign Affairs (www.smartraveller.gov.au)

Government of Canada (www.voyage.gc.ca)

New Zealand Depaqrtment of Foreign Affairs & Trade (www.safetravel.govt.nz)

UK Foreign & Commonwealth Office (www.gov.uk/foreign-travel-advice)

US Department of State (www.state.gov/travel)

One of the most common forms of theft is when backpacks are rifled through when they're left on the roof of a bus. Try to make your pack as theft-proof as possible – small padlocks and cover bags are a good deterrent.

There's little chance of ever retrieving your gear if it is stolen, and even getting a police report for an insurance claim can be difficult. Try the tourist police, or, if there aren't any, the local police station. If you're not getting anywhere, go to **Interpol** (Map p70; ☎01-4412836; www. nepalpolice.gov.np; Naxal) at the Police Headquarters in Naxal, Kathmandu.

Telephone

The phone system in Nepal works pretty well and making local, STD and international calls is easy. Reverse-charge (collect) calls can only be made to the UK, USA, Canada and Japan.

To make a call, look for signs advertising STD/ISD services. Many hotels offer international direct-dial facilities, but always check their charges before making a call. Out in rural areas you may find yourself using someone's mobile phone

at a public call centre. Most people in rural areas use mobile phones rather than fixed lines to communicate.

Mobile Phones

You will need an unlocked GSM 900–compatible phone to use local Nepali networks.

Unlike using a landline, you need to dial the local area code when making a local call on a mobile.

Ncell (www.ncell.com.np) is the most popular and convenient provider for tourists, but in mountain areas Ncell reception is often nonexistent. To get a SIM card take a copy of your passport and one photo to an Ncell office. Ncell offer a 'traveller package' for Rs 1000 that gets you Rs 600 worth of local calls, Rs 500 of international calls and 500MB of data, for 15 days. Otherwise, local calls cost around Rs 2 to Rs 3 per minute and incoming calls are free. International calls cost around Rs 5 to Rs 15 per minute depending on the destination. It's easy to buy a scratch card to top up your balance, in denominations from Rs 50 to 1000.

If you are staying longer than 15 days you can buy a SIM card for Rs 150 and then top up your balance with scratch cards. Call *101#

to check your balance and *102# to add balance with a scratch card.

For data use you are better off adding a pre-paid data package; a 2.5GB package costs Rs 800 for 30 days.

With a 3G connection you can even get internet access on the Everest Base Camp Trek! (The first tweet from the summit of Everest was sent in May 2011...)

Nepal Telecom (www. ntc.net.np) operates the Namaste Mobile network, but signing up for a SIM card is a more laborious process than for Ncell. However, Namaste has much wider reception in the mountains so is the one to go for if you're spending a lot of time hiking and contact with the world beyond is important to you.

Time

Nepal is 5¾ hours ahead of GMT/UTC; this curious time differential is intended to make it very clear that Nepal is a separate place to India, where the time is 5½ hours ahead of GMT/UTC. There is no daylight-saving time in Nepal.

When it's noon in Nepal it's 1.15am in New York, 6.15am in London, 1.15pm in Bangkok, 2.15pm in Tibet, 4.15pm in Sydney and 10.15pm the previous day in Los Angeles, not allowing for daylight saving or other local variations.

Toilets

➡ Outside of Kathmandu and Pokhara, the 'squat toilet' is the norm, except in hotels and guesthouses geared towards tourists.

➡ Next to a squat toilet (*charpi* in Nepali) is a bucket and/or tap, which has a twofold function: flushing the toilet and cleaning the nether regions (with the left hand only) while still squatting over the toilet.

➡ In tourist areas you'll find Western toilets and probably toilet paper (depending on how classy the place is). In general, put used toilet paper in the separate bin; don't flush it down the toilet.

➡ Most rural places don't supply toilet paper, so always carry an emergency stash.

➡ More rustic toilets in rural areas may consist of a few planks precariously positioned over a pit in the ground.

Tourist Information

The **Nepal Tourism Board** (www.welcomenepal.com) operates a booth in Kathmandu's Tribhuvan Airport and a more substantial office at the **Tourist Service Centre** (Map p70; ☏01-4256909 ext 223; www.welcomenepal.com; Bhrikuti Mandap; ⊙10am-1pm & 2-5pm Sun-Fri, TIMS card 10am-5.30pm, national park tickets 9am-2pm Sun-Fri) in central Kathmandu, both of which have simple brochures and maps but not much else.

The other tourist offices in Pokhara, Bhairawa, Birganj, Janakpur and Kakarbhitta are virtually useless unless you have a specific question.

Travellers with Disabilities

Wheelchair facilities, ramps and lifts (and even pavements!) are virtually nonexistent throughout Nepal and getting around the packed, twisting streets of traditional towns can be a real challenge if you are in a wheelchair. It is common for hotels to be multilevel, with most rooms on the upper floors. Many places – even midrange establishments – do not have lifts. Bathrooms equipped with grips and railings are not found anywhere, except perhaps in some of the top-end hotels.

There is no reason why a visit and even a trek could not be customised through a reliable agent for those with reasonable mobility. As an inspiration, consider Erik Weihenmayer, who became the first blind climber to summit Everest in 2001 (and wrote a book called *Touch the Top of the World*), or Thomas Whittaker, who summited in 1998 with an artificial leg, at the age of 50.

Download Lonely Planet's free Accessible Travel guide from https://lptravel.to/AccessibleTravel.

Other useful online resources include Access-Able Travel Source (www.access-able) and Accessible Journeys (www.disabilitytravel.com).

Visas

All foreigners, except Indians, must have a visa. Nepali embassies and consulates overseas issue visas with no fuss. You can also get one on the spot when you arrive in Nepal, either at Kathmandu's Tribhuvan Airport or at road borders at Nepalganj, Birganj/Raxaul Bazaar, Sunauli, Kakarbhitta, Mahendranagar, Dhangadhi and even the Rasuwagadhi checkpoint at the China/Tibetan border.

A Nepali visa is valid for entry for three to six months from the date of issue.

INDIAN VISAS IN NEPAL

Many travellers now get their Indian visa online and fly to New Delhi. However, if you want to travel overland to India and don't already have a visa, you'll need to get one in Nepal and it's not a straightforward process.

Visa applications must be made at the **India Visa Service Centre** (Map p70; ☏01-4001516; www.nepalsbi.com.np/content/indian-visa-service-center-ivsc.cfm; Kapurdhara Marg, Lainchaur; ⊙9.30am-noon Mon-Fri), at the State Bank of India to the right of the embassy, not at the embassy itself. Applications are accepted only between 9.30am and midday, but it pays to get there earlier than 9.30am so as to be one of the first people in line. You will need a printed copy of the completed online visa form (https://indianvisaonline.gov.in), your passport, a copy of your passport info pages and a copy of your Nepalese visa. You will also need two 51mm x 51mm passport photos (this is larger than a standard passport photo, but most passport photo places in Kathmandu know about Indian visa regulations) and the visa fee. Five working days later you will need to return to the embassy between 9.30am and 1pm with your passport and visa payment receipt. At this point you will leave your passport with the embassy. The following working day you can collect your passport between 5pm and 5.30pm – hopefully with a shiny, new Indian tourist visa in it.

Visa fees for a six-month tourist visa vary depending on nationality, but for most nationalities it's Rs 4350. However, for Japanese passport holders it's a mere Rs 1050, for US passport holders the fee is Rs 6450 and for UK passport holders it's a whopping Rs 13,600.

Transit visas (Rs 2300 for most nationalities) are issued the same day, but start from the date of issue and are non-extendable.

Children under 10 require a visa but are not charged a visa fee. Citizens of South Asian countries (except India) and China need visas, but if you're only entering once in a calendar year then these are free.

To obtain a visa upon arrival by air in Nepal you must fill in an application form at one of the automatic registration machines, which will also take your digital photo. You can save some time by filling in the form beforehand online at http://online.nepalimmigration.gov.np/tourist-visa and uploading a digital photo, but you must do this less than 15 days before your arrival date.

A single-entry visa valid for 15/30/90 days costs US$25/40/100. At Kathmandu's Tribhuvan Airport the fee is payable in any major currency, but at land borders officials require payment in cash US dollars; bring small bills.

SAARC countries can get a 30-day visa for free on arrival. Indian passport holders do not need a visa to enter Nepal.

Multiple-entry visas are useful if you are planning a side trip to Tibet, Bhutan or India and cost US$20 extra. You can change your single-entry visa to a multiple-entry visa at Kathmandu's Central Immigration Office for the same US$20 fee.

Don't overstay your visa. You can pay a fine of US$3 per day at the airport if you have overstayed less than 30 days (plus a US$2 per day visa extension fee), but it's far better to get it all sorted out in advance at Kathmandu's **Central Immigration Office** (Map p70; ☏01-4429659; www.nepalimmigration.gov.np; Kalikasthan, Dilli Bazaar; ☺10am-4pm Sun-Thu,

10am-3pm Fri, 11am-1pm Sat), as a delay could cause you to miss your flight.

It's a good idea to keep a number of passport photos with your passport so they are immediately handy for trekking permits, visa applications and other official documents.

Visa Extensions

Visa extensions are available from immigration offices in Kathmandu and Pokhara only and cost a minimum US$30 (payable in rupees only) for a 15-day extension, plus US$2 per day after that. To extend for 30 days is US$50 and to extend a multiple-entry visa add on US$20. If you'll be in Nepal for more than 60 days, you are better off getting a 90-day visa on arrival, rather than a 60-day visa plus an extension.

Every visa extension requires your passport, the fee, one photo and an application form that must be completed online first. One of the questions on this online application form asks for your Nepalese street address with house/building number. Hardly any street addresses have a building number so feel free to just make this up. Collect all these documents together before you join the queue; plenty of photo shops in Kathmandu and Pokhara can make a set of eight digital passport photos for around Rs 250.

Visa extensions are available the same day, normally within two hours, though some travellers have paid an extra Rs 300 fee to get their extensions within 10 minutes. For a fee, trekking and travel agencies can assist with the visa-extension process and save you the time and tedium of queuing.

You can extend a tourist visa up to a total stay of 150 days within a calendar year, though as you get close to that maximum you'll have to provide an air ticket to show you're leaving the country.

You can get up-to-date visa information at the website of the Department of Immigration (www.nepalimmigration.gov.np).

Women Travellers

Generally speaking, Nepal is a safe country for women travellers. However, women should still be cautious. Some Nepali men may have peculiar ideas about the morality of Western women, given their exposure to Western films portraying women wearing 'immodest' clothing. Dress modestly, which means wearing clothes that cover the shoulders and thighs – take your cue from the locals to gauge what's acceptable in the area. Several women have written to say that a long skirt is very useful for impromptu toilet trips, especially when trekking.

Sexual harassment is low-key but does exist. Trekking guides have been known to take advantage of their position of trust and responsibility and some lone women trekkers who hire a guide have had to put up with repeated sexual pestering. The best advice is to never trek alone with a local male guide. **3 Sisters Adventure Trekking** (Map p216; ☏061-462066; www.3sistersadventuretrek.com; Lakeside North) in Pokhara is run by women and specialises in providing female staff for treks.

Transport

GETTING THERE & AWAY

Considering the enduring popularity of Nepal as a travel destination, there are surprisingly few direct international flight connections into Kathmandu and fares are normally much higher than they are to nearby Indian cities such as Delhi. Most long-distance routes come in via South Asia, Southeast Asia or the Middle East. If you are coming during the prime travel and trekking months of October and November, book your long-haul and domestic flights well in advance.

However, overland and air-travel connections to India are extensive, so it's easy to combine a dream trip to both Nepal and India, with possible add-ons to Bhutan and Tibet. Note that you can only buy tickets from Kathmandu to Lhasa as part of a tour-group package. You must also join an organised tour of Bhutan to fly to Paro. For onward travel in India, good online agencies include Cleartrip (www.cleartrip.com), Make My Trip (www.makemytrip.com) and Yatra (www.yatra.com).

Flights, tours and even treks can be booked online at lonelyplanet.com/bookings.

Entering the Country

Nepal makes things easy for foreign travellers. Visas are available on arrival at the international airport in Kathmandu and at all land border crossings that are open to foreigners, as long as you have passport photos on hand (not necessary at Kathmandu airport) and can pay the visa fee in foreign currency (some crossings insist on payment in US dollars). Your passport must be valid for at least six months and you will need a whole free page for your visa.

Air

During the autumn trekking season, from October to November, every flight into and out of Kathmandu can be booked solid, and travellers sometimes have to resort to travelling overland to India to get a flight out of the region. To beat the rush, book well in advance and give yourself plenty of time between the end of your trek and your international flight home. If you are booking a flight in Kathmandu, book at the start of your trip, not at the end.

If you are connecting through Delhi on two separate tickets, you will likely need to collect your luggage and check in separately for the connecting flight, for which you will need to have arranged a transit or tourist visa in advance. Sometimes an airline representative can collect and check in the bags on your behalf, but you should check this. Some

---

CLIMATE CHANGE & TRAVEL

Every form of transport that relies on carbon-based fuel generates CO_2, the main cause of human-induced climate change. Modern travel is dependent on aeroplanes, which might use less fuel per kilometre per person than most cars but travel much greater distances. The altitude at which aircraft emit gases (including CO_2) and particles also contributes to their climate change impact. Many websites offer 'carbon calculators' that allow people to estimate the carbon emissions generated by their journey and, for those who wish to do so, to offset the impact of the greenhouse gases emitted with contributions to portfolios of climate-friendly initiatives throughout the world. Lonely Planet offsets the carbon footprint of all staff and author travel.

DEPARTURE TAX

When flying out of Kathmandu, there is no international departure tax to pay, but you do have to pay a small departure tax of Rs 200 for domestic flights.

airlines have refused to fly passengers to Delhi to connect with other flights if they don't have an Indian visa.

Airports & Airlines

Nepal has one international airport, **Tribhuvan International Airport** (☑01-4472256; www.tiairport.com.np), just east of Kathmandu. There are few direct long-distance flights to Nepal – getting here from Europe, the Americas or Australasia will almost always involve a stop in the Middle East or Asia.

In 2014 Tribhuvan was voted the third worst airport in the world. This is actually more than a little unfair as there are lots of worse international airports but they're just not ones visited by many international tourists. A new international airport is under construction in Pokhara and due to open in July 2020. Work is also under way to transform Bhairawa airport into an international airport by 2019. An even larger airport, capable of handling the A380, is planned for Hetauda. All three of these projects have experienced significant delays.

Facilities at Tribhuvan are limited – there are foreign-exchange booths before and after immigration, and there is a dusty tourist information counter by the terminal exit. Fill out the forms for your visa on arrival before you go to the immigration counter, as queues can be long here. A small stand provides instant passport photos, but bring some from home to be safe.

On departure, all baggage must go through the X-ray machine as you enter the terminal. Make sure that customs officials stamp all the baggage labels for your carry-on luggage. There are a couple of cafes in departures once you pass through security.

AIRLINES

Because Nepal does not lie on any major transit routes, flights to Kathmandu are expensive, particularly during the peak trekking season (October to November). Budget travellers fly to India first, and then pick up a cheap transfer to Kathmandu, though this incurs its own visa hassles and the added expense often adds up to the same as the flight price difference.

Nepal's flagship carrier **Nepal Airlines** (☑081-520727; www.nepalairlines.com.np) is a shoestring operation; amazingly, you cannot even book through its website. Delays and cancellations are common: Hong Kong–Kathmandu passengers were delayed for two full days in 2011 when a rogue mouse was spotted on board, and in 2007, after a fault with one of their planes, two goats were sacrificed in order to appease Akash Bhairav, the Hindu god of safety and protection. Goats or not, the airline has had a number of serious incidents and is, like all Nepalese airlines, banned from EU airspace. There are flights to Delhi, Dubai, Doha, Hong Kong, Bangkok, Kuala Lumpur, Mumbai and Bangalore.

A number of other airlines serve Nepal from abroad, although this list changes frequently:

Air Arabia (www.airarabia.com) Serves the Gulf states and Russia.

Air Asia (www.airasia.com) Budget flights throughout Asia via Kuala Lumpur.

Air China (www.airchina.com) Daily routes to Lhasa, Chengdu and around China.

Air India (www.airindia.in) Serves the subcontinent, including Kolkata and Delhi.

Bhutan Airlines (www.bhutanairlines.bt) Serves Paro several times daily.

Biman Bangladesh Airlines (www.biman-airlines.com) Daily flights to Dhaka.

Cathay Dragon (www.cathaypacific.com) Four to five flights to Beijing per week.

China Eastern Airlines (en.ceair.com) Serves Lhasa, Kunming and Shanghai.

China Southern Airlines (www.flychinasouthern.com) Serves Guangzhou and Lhasa.

Drukair (www.drukair.com.bt) Serves Paro daily.

Etihad Airways (www.etihad.com) Daily connections via Abu Dhabi to the rest of the world.

Fly Dubai (www.flydubai.com) Several flights per day.

Himalaya Airlines (www.himalaya-airlines.com) Reaches the Gulf and Malaysia.

IndiGo (www.goindigo.in) The budget choice for Delhi.

Jet Airways (www.jetairways.com). Daily connections to Bangalore, Delhi, Mumbai and Kolkata.

Malaysia Airlines (www.malaysiaairlines.com) For Kuala Lumpur.

Malindo Air (www.malindoair.com) For Kuala Lumpur.

Oman Air (www.omanair.com) For Muscat.

Qatar Airways (www.qatarairways.com) Daily connections through Doha, with excellent onward flights to the USA and Europe.

Sichuan Airlines (www.sichuanair.com) For Chengdu and Lhasa.

Thai Airways (www.thaiairways.com) Provides the most popular Southeast Asian route to Nepal via Bangkok.

Turkish Airlines (www.turkishairlines.com) Daily connections via Istanbul.

Land

You can enter Nepal overland at seven border crossings – six from India and one from Tibet.

Border Crossings

INDIA

All of the land borders between India and Nepal are in the Terai, and were unaffected by the earthquake. The most popular crossing point is Sunauli, near Bhairawa, which provides easy access to Delhi and Varanasi in India.

There are direct buses between Kathmandu and Delhi run by the Delhi Transport Corporation. They leave Delhi at 10am and Kathmandu (Swayambhu) at 9am. Tickets cost ₹ 2300. The journey takes 27 to 28 hours if there are no road delays.

Indian domestic train tickets can be booked in advance online at **Cleartrip** (www.cleartrip.com) or **IRCTC** (www.irctc.co.in). Get timetables and fares using Indian Railways' **National Train Enquiry System** (www.trainenquiry.com). The Man in Seat 61 (www.seat61.com/India.htm) is a good general resource.

Belahiya to Sunauli

The crossing from Belahiya to Sunauli (p257) is by far the most popular route between India and Nepal. Regular buses run from Sunauli to Gorakhpur, from where you can catch trains to Varanasi and Delhi.

Upon entering Nepal, you can visit the Buddhist pilgrimage centre of Lumbini before you continue your journey. From the nearby town of Siddharthanagar (Bhairawa), buses run regularly to Kathmandu and Pokhara, usually passing through Narayangarh, where you can change for Chitwan National Park. There are regular daily flights from Siddharthanagar (Bhairawa) to Kathmandu.

Bhimdatta (Mahendranagar) to Banbasa

The western border crossing at Bhimdatta (Mahendranagar; p278) is also reasonably convenient for Delhi. There are daily buses from Delhi's Anand Vihar bus stand to Banbasa (10 hours), the nearest Indian village to the border. Banbasa is also connected by bus with most towns in Uttarakhand.

From Bhimdatta (Mahendranagar) there are slow overnight bus services to Kathmandu (15 hours), but it's better to do the trip in daylight and break the journey at Bardia National Park, Nepalganj or Narayangarh. Check that the road is open because it sometimes gets blocked during the monsoon.

Kakarbhitta to Panitanki

The eastern border crossing at Kakarbhitta offers easy onward connections to Darjeeling, Sikkim, Kolkata and India's northeast states.

From Darjeeling, take a morning shared jeep to Siliguri (three hours), then another shared jeep or a taxi (one hour) to Panitanki on the Indian side of the border. Jeeps also run to the border from Kalimpong and Gangtok in Sikkim. Coming from Kolkata, you can take the overnight Darjeeling Mail or Kanchankaya Express from Sealdah station to New Jalpaiguri (NJP) near Siliguri, then a bus to the border.

From Kakarbhitta there are both day and overnight buses to Kathmandu (14 to 16 hours) or Pokhara (15 hours), but it's more interesting to break the journey at Chitwan National Park (accessible from Sauraha Chowk on the Mahendra Hwy). Yeti Airlines and Buddha Air have daily flights to Kathmandu from nearby Bhadrapur airport (around US$135, 50 minutes).

Birganj to Raxaul Bazaar

The border crossing from Birganj to Raxaul Bazaar (p279) is handy for Patna and Kolkata. Buses run from the bus station in Patna straight to Raxaul Bazaar (six hours). From Kolkata, take the daily Mithila Express train.

From Birganj, there are regular day/night buses to Kathmandu (six to seven hours) as well as faster Tata Sumo jeeps (four to five hours). There are also morning buses to Pokhara (eight hours), via Narayangarh (four hours). Buddha Air has up to five daily flights between nearby Simara Airport and Kathmandu (US$100, 20 minutes).

NEPAL–INDIA BORDER CROSSINGS

BORDER CROSSING (NEPAL TO INDIA)	NEAREST INDIAN TOWNS
Belahiya to Sunauli	Gorakhpur, Varanasi, Agra & Delhi
Bhimdatta (Mahendranagar) to Banbasa	Delhi & hill towns in Uttarakhand
Kakarbhitta to Panitanki	Darjeeling, Sikkim & Kolkata
Birganj to Raxaul Bazaar	Patna & Kolkata
Nepalganj to Jamunaha/Rupaidha Bazaar	Lucknow
Dhanghadi to Gauriphanta	Lucknow, Delhi & Dudhwa National Park

Nepalganj to Jamunaha

Few people use the crossing at Nepalganj (p271) in western Nepal as it's not particularly convenient for anywhere else. The nearest town in India is Lucknow, where you can pick up slow buses to Rupaidha Bazaar (seven hours), near the border post at Jamunaha. You might also consider taking a train to Nanpara, 17km from the border.

Over the border in Nepalganj, there are regular day/night buses to Kathmandu (12 hours) and buses to Pokhara (12 hours), passing through Narayangarh (10 hours). Yeti Airlines and Buddha Air have flights from Nepalganj to Kathmandu (US$187).

Dhangadhi to Gauriphanta

The little-used border crossing from Dhangadhi to Gauriphanta (p276), Uttar Pradesh, is useful for moving on to Lucknow and New Delhi or visiting Dudhwa National Park. Nepal immigration is open from 7am to 8pm. From Dhangadhi there are daily flights to Kathmandu and buses to the Mahendra Hwy that continue west to Mahendranagar and east towards Ambassa (for Bardia National Park), Nepalganj and beyond.

TIBET

Officially only organised 'groups' are allowed into Tibet from Nepal. The good news is that travel agencies in Kathmandu are experts in assembling overland groups to get around this restriction. In general, travellers face fewer restrictions entering Tibet through China, so it makes more sense to visit Nepal after a trip through Tibet, not before. The rules are in constant flux, so allow three working days for your agency or tour operator to arrange the necessary travel permit.

Travelling overland to Tibet from Nepal is not an easy option. Altitude sickness is a real danger: the maximum altitude along the road is 5140m and tours do not always allow sufficient time to acclimatise safely. Adding to the problems, the road to the main border at Kodari was severely damaged by the 2015 earthquake, and is closed indefinitely. The new border point is at Rasuwagadhi, due north of Kathmandu on the Langtang road, which only opened to foreigners in August 2017; the Tibetan side is Kyirung. The border is open 10am to 5pm Tibet time (Nepal time plus 2¼ hours).

Landslides are highly likely on this route during the monsoon months (May to August) and there are often additional restrictions on travel at times of political tension. Other road connections, including the road from Tibet to Mustang, are not open to foreigners, although organised groups can trek from Simikot through far-western Nepal to Mt Kailash.

Travel Restrictions

At the time of research, it was only possible to cross into Tibet with a Tibet Tourism Permit, which can only be arranged through a travel agency when you book a package tour to Lhasa. If you turn up at the border at Rasuwagadhi with just a Chinese visa you'll be turned away, and Air China won't sell you an air ticket to Lhasa without this permit. Permits are valid for 21 days (although it's sometimes possible to get a 28-day permit) and can be issued for one or more people.

In order to get a Tibet Tourism Permit, you must supply a ticket out of Tibet – either a flight ticket or train ticket to elsewhere in mainland China or a tour back to Nepal. Kathmandu-based tour companies can supply these. To get a permit takes around 15 days, although it's possible to pay extra and get one in three days. Splitting from your group-visa members in Lhasa is almost impossible, but it is apparently possible (although a headache) to fly out of Tibet to Chengdu and then continue through China on a standard Chinese tourist visa.

Note that Tibet travel permits are not issued between late February and late March, and travel in Tibet is not allowed for foreign tourists during this period. Also, the Chinese Embassy in Kathmandu closes from 1 to 8 October, so no visas can be obtained during this time, even though Tibet remains open for tourists.

Tour Options

The easiest way to visit Tibet from Nepal is to join a drive-in, fly-out overland jeep tour from Kathmandu to Lhasa, overnighting in Nyalam, Dingri/Lhatse, Shigatse, Gyantse and Lhasa. Several agencies offer eight-day trips for around US$800, including permit fees, transport by cramped Land Cruiser or minibus, accommodation in dorms and shared twin rooms, and sightseeing (but not meals). Trips normally leave on Tuesday and Saturday from April to October and weekly at other times. Don't expect too much from these budget tours. A private trip for four people in a Land Cruiser costs around US$900 to US$1200 per person. Add on to this the cost of a group visa, which depends on nationality: US$177 for US citizens, US$121 for Canadians and US$89 for other nationals. Transport out of Tibet currently costs around US$415 to US$450 for a flight back to Kathmandu.

Some agencies also offer pricey trips that include a detour to Mt Everest Base Camp (on the Tibetan side). There are also very expensive trekking trips from Simikot in far-western Nepal to Purang in far-western Tibet, and then on to Mt Kailash. Land Cruiser trips to Mt Kailash are also possible. Rates increase from July to September, and there are fewer tours from December to February.

The agency will need one to two weeks to get your visa and permits. If you are headed on to China, your agency will need to get you your own separate 'group' visa. For more details see Lonely Planet's *Tibet* and *China* guides.

Most of the companies advertising Tibet trips in Kathmandu are agencies for other companies. **Explore Nepal** (Map p70; ☑01-4226130; www.xplorenepal. com), **Royal Mount Trekking** (Map p70; ☑01-4241452; www.royalmountaintrekking. com; Durbar Marg) and **Tibet Tashi Delek Treks** (Map p90; ☑01-4410746; www.tibettour. travel; Thamel) run their own trips, so you can be confident that staff know what they're talking about.

Car & Motorcycle

A steady trickle of people drive their own motorbikes or vehicles overland from Europe, for which an international carnet is required. If you want to abandon your transport in Nepal, you must either pay a prohibitive import duty or surrender it to customs. It is not possible to import cars more than five years old. Make sure you bring an international driving permit.

GETTING AROUND

Getting around in Nepal can be a challenging business. Because of the terrain, the weather conditions and the condition of vehicles, few trips go exactly according to plan. Damage to roads from the 2015 earthquake has only exacerbated these problems. Nepali ingenuity will usually get you to your destination in the end, but build plenty of time into your itinerary and treat the delays and mishaps as part of the rich tapestry that is Nepal.

The wise traveller avoids going anywhere during major festivals, when buses, flights and hotels are booked solid.

Air

Considering the nature of the landscape, Nepal has an excellent network of domestic flights. Engineers have created runways deep in the jungle and high in the mountains, clinging to the sides of Himalayan peaks. However, pilots must still find their way to these airstrips using visual navigation and few years pass without some kind of air disaster in the mountains. All of Nepal's domestic airports are functioning after the 2015 earthquake.

Because flights are dependent on clear weather, services rarely leave on time and many flights are cancelled at the last minute because of poor visibility. It is essential to build extra time into your itinerary. Even if you take off on time, you may not be able to land at your intended destination because of fog. It would be unwise to book a flight back to Kathmandu within three days of your international flight out of the country.

In the event of a cancellation, airlines will try to find you a seat on the next available flight (some airlines run extra flights to clear the backlog once the weather clears). If you decide not to wait, you should be able to cancel the ticket without penalty, though it can take a long time to arrange a refund.

Airlines in Nepal

There are three major domestic airlines: **Nepal Airlines,** (Map p70; ☑01-4227133; www.nepalairlines. com.np; Kantipath; ☺10am-5pm) **Buddha Air** (Map p70; ☑01-5542494; www. buddhaair.com; Hattisar) and **Yeti Airlines** (Map p90; ☑01-4213012; www.yetiairlines.com; Thamel Chowk). There are also smaller operators who tend to come and go. These include Saurya Airlines (www. sauryaairlines.com), Shree

Domestic Air Routes

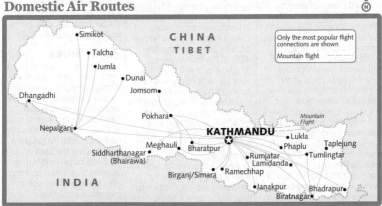

AIR SAFETY IN NEPAL

Air safety is something you should bear in mind when deciding to fly internally in Nepal, but this has to be weighed up against the risks of travelling by road and the time that is saved by flying. Given the choice between a 45-minute flight and a 17-hour bus ride on poorly maintained mountain roads, most people prefer to fly.

However, it's worth being aware of the potential dangers. There have been eight fatal accidents involving domestic airlines in Nepal since 2008, an average of one disaster per year. In the most recent incident in 2016, a Tara Air flight from Pokhara to Jomsom crashed near Myagdi killing three crew and 20 passengers, while 18 people were killed in 2014 when a Nepal Airlines flight from Kathmandu crashed into a hillside en route to Jumla. As a result of these incidents, at the time of writing, no Nepalese airline is permitted to fly within EU airspace.

Subsequent investigations have blamed 'loss of situational awareness' as a primary factor in many accidents, with pilots flying too close to terrain in poor visibility, a danger that will always be present when flying in mountainous areas. If you prefer not to fly, it's worth noting that many trailheads can be reached by bus or by walking from lower elevations, which will also improve your acclimatisation to altitude.

Airlines (www.shreeairlines.com), Simrik Airlines (www.simrikairlines.com), Tara Air (www.taraair.com) and Summit Air (www.summitair.com.np).

Nepal Airlines is the national carrier, and is notoriously unreliable. All things considered, it has a comparable safety record to the rest, but if your destination is served by a private airline, the latter will generally be the better option. Nepal Airlines currently has services to Biratnagar, Pokhara, Lukla, Phaplu, Bhojpur, Lamidanda, Tumlingtar, Dolpo and Jumla, among other airstrips.

While services are more reliable on Nepal's private airlines, fares are slightly higher. Most flights operate out of Kathmandu, but there are minor air hubs at Pokhara, Nepalganj in the southwest and Biratnagar in the southeast. In addition to these, common destinations include Dhangadi, Bhairawa, Janakpur, Bhadrapur, Jumla, Jomsom, Juphal and Lukla, among others. Most airlines also offer scenic 'mountain flights' in the morning – if you're flying from Kathmandu you will probably have to wait until the airline finishes its morning quota before domestic services begin.

Domestic Nepali airlines all have offices in Kathmandu.

Tickets

Airlines come and go and schedules change, so it's best to make reservations through a travel agent, a trekking agency or your hotel. Foreign visitors must pay for airfares in hard currency, typically US dollars. Residents and Nepali citizens pay approximately 40% of the tourist price, which helps if you are flying your guide or porter out to Lukla for the Everest trek.

All travellers are charged an insurance surcharge of US$2 per leg, as well as a fuel surcharge. Fares quoted generally include all these surcharges.

Note that domestic airlines have a 15kg allowance for hold baggage – and on some flights you cannot pay to carry excess baggage. There is a reduced limit of 10kg for hold baggage and 5kg for hand luggage for certain mountain airstrips like Lukla, Jomsom and Juphal. Knives, cigarette lighters, gas cylinders and trekking poles are not permitted in carry-on luggage.

Bicycle

There are plenty of bicycle-rental shops in Kathmandu and Pokhara, and this is a cheap and convenient way of getting around. Generic Indian- and Chinese-made bicycles cost around Rs 350 to Rs 450 per day to rent, but the clunky gears make even a downhill stretch seem like hard work. Several cycling agencies in Kathmandu rent out imported mountain bikes for around US$12 per day. Cycling around Kathmandu and much of the Kathmandu Valley was once a popular activity, but increased traffic and urban sprawl make this far less appealing today.

Bus

Buses are the main form of public transport in Nepal and they're incredibly cheap. Often they're also incredibly uncomfortable. Buses run pretty much everywhere and will stop for anyone, but you'll find it much easier to get a seat if you catch a bus at its source rather than mid-run. For longer-distance buses, it's best to book a couple of days in advance.

Public Buses

Most towns in lowland Nepal are accessible by bus from Kathmandu or Pokhara, but Nepali buses are slow, noisy and uncomfortable, and breakdowns are almost guaranteed, even on the so-called 'deluxe' buses. Fortunately, services are frequent enough that you can always hop onto another bus if your first bus dies on a lonely stretch of highway.

On longer journeys, buses stop regularly for refreshments, but travel after dark is not recommended – drivers take advantage of the quiet roads to do some crazy speeding, and accidents and fatalities are depressingly common. In fact, you are 30 times more likely to die in a road accident in Nepal than in any developed country. Some night buses stop for a few hours' sleep en route, but others keep blazing through the night with the music blaring at full volume. The single best thing you can do to stay safe is to avoid travelling by road at night.

Myriad private companies run 'ordinary buses' and faster, more expensive 'express buses' that offer seats with more padding and luxuries such as curtains to keep out the sun. Tickets can be purchased in advance at the relevant counter (ask locals where to go as signs are often in Nepali) or on board from the driver. 'Deluxe' buses often come with air-conditioning, and some claim to offer nonstop services between two centres (but rarely does this happen).

Large pieces of baggage go on the roof – the conductor will take your bag up for a tip or you can do it yourself. Theft from luggage is not uncommon so padlock your bags shut and tie the straps to the railings. Always keep an eye on your belongings at rest stops – backpacks are extremely easy for thieves to walk off with.

The fast, frequent and phenomenally crowded 'local buses' that run between smaller towns are handy for day trips, but you'll have your work cut out getting on board with a backpack. Prices for foreigners are often bumped up by unscrupulous conductors on these buses.

Note that road travel in the far east and west of Nepal can be impossible after the monsoon. Every year the rains lead to floods that destroy stretches of road and wash away bridges.

Tourist Buses

Travel agencies run a number of useful bus services to popular tourist destinations, leaving from the Tourist Bus Park in Pokhara and the Thamel end of Kantipath in Kathmandu. These are more comfortable and less crowded than local buses but cost a little more.

Greenline (Map p90; ☑01-4417199; www.greenline.com. np; Tridevi Marg; ◷6am-6pm) has deluxe buses between Kathmandu, Pokhara and Sauraha (for Chitwan National Park).

Car & Motorcycle

Hire

There are no drive-yourself rental cars available in Nepal, but you can easily hire a car or jeep with a driver through a travel agency. Expect to pay between US$60 and US$100 per day, including fuel. Taxis are cheaper but less comfortable and you must negotiate a fare directly with the driver. Remember that you'll have to pay for the driver's return trip whether or not you return, as well as their food and accommodation for overnight trips.

Motorcycles can be rented in Kathmandu and Pokhara for around Rs 600 to Rs 1500 per day depending on the type of bike. You'll need an international driving permit or a licence from your own country that shows you are licensed to ride a motorcycle – a car drivers' licence won't cut it. You must also leave your passport as a deposit. It's not a bad idea to take some digital photographs of the bike in case operators complain about damages that existed before you ever set foot on the bike.

Note that there are major fuel shortages in Nepal. Petrol stations can be dry for days at a time and the only option for motorists is to queue for hours at the few stations that have fuel or to buy fuel in reused bottles from local shops.

Insurance

If you are planning to drive a motorbike in Nepal you should double-check to see if you are covered by your travel insurance. Rental companies rarely offer insurance and you will be fully liable for the vehicle and damage to other vehicles in the event of an accident. Also make sure that you have a *motorcycle* driver's licence as your travel

THE E-RICKSHAW

Forget Tesla – the e-rickshaw (electronic rickshaw) is taking over the globe! Or at least Nepal.

The humble rickshaw began its life as a two-wheel cart pulled by a man. The first advance was pedal power, in the form of the bicycle rickshaw. Then came the auto-rickshaw, with its petrol engine. Now, finally, we have the battery-powered e-rickshaw, the perfect choice for a more sustainable age.

Since 2012, when they were first introduced to Nepal, the e-rickshaw has taken over the country. Apart from the environmental gains, it has revolutionised the lives of thousands of rickshaw drivers, who can now go up to 20km in a single trip – and thereby make a lot more money – without the significant cost of petrol. Taxi drivers aren't so happy with this new competition. But as with all technological advances, there are winners and losers.

AIR-CONDITIONING OF THE GODS

With the cramped conditions inside Nepal's buses, many locals and foreigners prefer to ride up on the roof. For legal reasons, we are required to say this is probably not a good idea – but the truth is that it is probably not significantly more dangerous than riding inside. You'll also get the sense of being surrounded by the environment you are passing through, rather than viewing it through a murky window.

If you do ride on the roof, make sure you are well wedged in, so you don't catapult off when the bus swerves, brakes or lurches. It's also best to sit facing forwards – that way you can see low-hanging wires and branches before you get swatted. Make sure you have sunscreen and appropriate clothing too, as it can be surprisingly cold up there.

insurance may not cover you if you don't.

Road Rules

If you do drive, be aware that you drive on the left-hand side of the road, left turns are allowed without stopping, and that traffic entering a roundabout has priority over traffic already on the roundabout. Locals rarely signal and other vehicles will pull out regardless of whether or not anyone is coming – drive defensively. Try to avoid any dealings with traffic police: locals are routinely stung for bribes and foreigners are increasingly being targeted.

Finally, our best advice is to trust nothing and nobody on the road. Expect kids, chickens, ducks, women, old men, babies, cows, dogs and almost anything else that can move to jump in front of you at any moment, without any kind of warning. Good luck.

Tours

The winding roads of Nepal are glorious for mountain riding (when not potholed) and several international companies run fully supported motorcycle tours, including Asia-Bike-Tours (www.asia-biketours.com) and Blazing

Trails (www.blazingtrails tours.com).

Local operators include the following:

Himalayan Enfielders (Map p70; ☑01-4440462; www.himalayanenfielders.com; Lazimpat, Kathmandu)

Himalayan Offroad (Map p90; ☑01-4700770; www.himalayanoffroad.com; Chaksibari Marg, Thamel)

Himalayan Roadrunners (☑01-5570051; www.ridehigh.com)

Wild Tracks Adventure (Map p70; ☑01-4439590; www.wildtracksnepal.com; Baluwatar, Kathmandu)

Local Transport

Autorickshaw & Cycle-Rickshaw

Cycle-rickshaws are common in the old part of Kathmandu and in towns in the Terai, and they provide an atmospheric way to explore the crowded and narrow streets. Prices are highly negotiable.

Nepal's two-stroke, three-wheeled autorickshaws are being phased out everywhere in favour of electric models, but a few are still hanging on in a couple of Terai towns.

Taxi

Metered taxis are found in larger towns such as Kathmandu and Pokhara, and these can be hired for both local and long-distance journeys. Metered taxis have black licence plates; private cars that operate as taxis for long-distance routes have red or green plates.

Taxis can be flagged down anywhere, and they loiter at official stops in tourist destinations such as Bhaktapur and Patan. On most routes, taxi drivers will refuse to use the meter – this is often an attempt to overcharge tourists, but it may also reflect rising fuel costs and traffic delays. If a driver refuses to use the meter, try another taxi. If no taxis are willing to use the meter, haggle down to reach a reasonable price. As a side note, we can't recall the last time a taxi driver volunteered to use the meter!

In Kathmandu there is a new motorbike ride-hailing app, Tootle (https://tootle.today), that offers a cheaper and faster alternative to taxis, although it only works until 8pm.

Tempo

Tempos are outsized autorickshaws that run on fixed routes in larger cities. Kathmandu's archaic, polluting diesel tempos have been replaced by electric and gas-powered *safa* (clean) tempos and petrol minibuses. Drivers pick up and drop off anywhere along the route; tap on the roof with a coin when you want to stop.

Train

A new narrow-gauge train is due to begin service between Janakpur and Jaynagar, over the Indian border, sometime in 2018. This promises to be an atmospheric way of seeing the countryside of the Terai, and crossing from Janakpur into India.

Health

Kathmandu has the best health facilities in the country, but standards at clinics and hospitals decline the further you get from the capital. In mountainous areas, there may be no health facilities at all. Trekkers who become unwell in the mountains are generally evacuated to Kathmandu, or overseas in the event of something really serious. Always take out travel insurance to cover the costs of hospital treatment and emergency evacuations.

Many of the most popular areas for visitors are remote and inaccessible, so you should read up on the possible health risks. While trekking, it makes sense to carry an emergency medical kit so that you can treat any symptoms until you reach medical care.

BEFORE YOU GO

Insurance

Considering the terrain, potential health risks and high cost of medical evacuation, it is unwise to travel to Nepal without adequate health insurance.

Recommended Vaccinations

You do not officially require any immunisations to enter the country, unless you have

come from an area where yellow fever is present – in which case, you must show proof of immunisation.

It is best to seek medical advice at least six weeks before travelling, since some vaccinations require multiple injections over a period of time. Note that some vaccinations should not be given during pregnancy or to people with allergies.

Vaccinations you might consider:

Diphtheria and tetanus Vaccinations for these two diseases are usually combined and are recommended for everyone. After an initial course of three injections (usually given in childhood), boosters are necessary every 10 years.

Hepatitis A The vaccine for hepatitis A (eg Avaxim, Havrix 1440 or VAQTA) provides long-term immunity (possibly lifelong) after an initial injection and a booster at six to 12 months.

Hepatitis B Vaccination involves three injections, the quickest course being over three weeks with a booster at 12 months.

Influenza 'Flu' is considered by many to be the most common vaccine-preventable illness in travellers. This vaccine is annual.

Japanese encephalitis This is a mosquito-borne viral encephalitis that occurs in the Terai and occasionally in the Kathmandu Valley, particularly during the monsoon (August to early October). The vaccine is given as two injections over four weeks

with a booster within two years if risk persists. Recommended only for prolonged stays to the Terai (especially the west) or Kathmandu Valley.

Meningococcal meningitis This vaccine is not normally recommended for travellers. A single-dose vaccine boosted every three to five years is recommended only for individuals at high risk and for residents.

Polio Nepal was officially declared polio-free by the World Health Organization in 2014 after having no cases for three years. However, everyone should have this vaccination anyway, which is normally given in childhood.

Rabies Vaccination should be considered for long-term visitors, particularly if you plan to travel to remote areas. In Nepal the disease is carried by street dogs and monkeys. Vaccination is strongly recommended for children. Pre-travel rabies vaccination involves having three injections over 21 to 28 days. If someone who has been vaccinated is bitten or scratched by an animal they will require two vaccine booster injections, while those not vaccinated will require five doses of vaccine and immune globulin (expensive). No booster doses are needed for the average traveller.

Tuberculosis (TB) This disease is highly endemic in Nepal, though cases are extremely rare among travellers. Most people in the West are vaccinated during childhood.

Typhoid Drug-resistant typhoid fever is an ongoing problem in Nepal, particularly in the

Terai, and vaccination is recommended. The vaccine is available as a single injection or oral capsules – ask your doctor for advice.

Yellow fever This disease is not endemic in Nepal and a vaccine for yellow fever is required only if you are coming from an infected area. The record of this vaccine should be provided in a World Health Organization (WHO) Yellow Vaccination Booklet and is valid for life.

Other Preparations

Visiting Nepal may take you to some very remote areas, so it makes sense to visit the doctor before you travel for a general check-up.

➡ If you have any pre-existing medical conditions, bring any medication you need from home.

➡ Ask your physician to give you a written description of your condition and your medications with their generic names in case you have to visit a doctor in Nepal.

➡ It pays to get a dental check-up well before embarking on a trek. One of our previous authors cracked a molar on a particularly tough piece of dried beef while on a research trek and had to walk for five days to reach a dentist who performed an emergency root canal operation without anaesthetic! Be warned.

➡ Contact-lens wearers should bring plenty of solution and take extra care with hygiene to avoid eye infections.

➡ Carry backup prescription glasses and sunglasses in case you can't wear your lenses at some point.

Websites

Medex offers a free download of the useful booklet *Travel at High Altitude* (http://medex.org.uk/medex_book/about_book.php), aimed at laypeople and full of good advice for staying healthy in the mountains. A Nepali translation of the booklet is also available on the website.

The following international organisations provide information on health issues that are pertinent to Nepal.

➡ Centers for Disease Control & Prevention (www.cdc.gov)

➡ Fit for Travel (www.fitfortravel.scot.nhs.uk)

➡ International Society for Mountain Medicine (www.ismm.org)

➡ MASTA (www.masta-travel-health.com)

➡ Medex (www.medex.org.uk)

MEDICAL KIT CHECKLIST

Following is a list of items you should consider including in your medical kit – consult your pharmacist for brands available in your country.

➡ aspirin or paracetamol (acetaminophen in the USA) for pain or fever

➡ anti-inflammatory (ibuprofen) for muscle and joint pain, headache and fever

➡ antibiotics, particularly if travelling off the beaten track; in Nepal, antibiotics are sold without prescription, which has led to widespread resistance to some common antibiotics

➡ ondansetron (Zofran) for relief of severe nausea

➡ rehydration mixture to prevent dehydration during bouts of diarrhoea; particularly important when travelling with children

➡ antihistamine for allergies, eg hay fever; for skin conditions, carry hydrocortisone 1% cream

➡ cold and flu tablets, throat lozenges and nasal decongestant

➡ antifungal cream such as clotrimazole 1% for fungal skin infections and thrush

➡ antiseptic (such as povidone-iodine) for cuts and grazes

➡ bandages, crêpe wraps, Band-Aids (plasters) and other wound dressings

➡ water purification tablets

➡ scissors, tweezers and an electric thermometer (mercury thermometers are prohibited by airlines)

➡ sterile kit in case you need injections; discuss with your doctor

➡ motion-sickness tablets, such as Dramamine, for long bus rides

➡ Diamox (Acetazolmide) tablets if trekking above 3500m

Further Reading

Travel with Children from Lonely Planet includes advice on travel health for younger children. A useful health-care overview for travel in remote areas is David Werner's *Where There Is No Doctor*; get the 2015 update.

Specific titles covering trekking and health:

➡ *Medicine for Mountaineering & Other Wilderness Activities* (James A Wilkerson) covers many medical problems typically encountered in Nepal.

➡ *Altitude Illness: Prevention & Treatment* (Stephen Bezruchka) is essential reading for high-altitude trekking, written by an experienced Nepal trekker.

➡ *Pocket Wilderness First Aid & Wilderness Medicine* (Dr Jim Duff and Peter Gormly) is an excellent portable companion.

IN NEPAL

Availability & Cost of Health Care

Kathmandu has several excellent clinics, including the **Nepal International Clinic** (Map p70; ☏01-4435357, 01-4434642; www.nepalinternationalclinic.com; Lal Durbar; ◔9am-1pm & 2-5pm) and **CIWEC Clinic** (Map p70; ☏01-4435232, 01-4424111; www.ciwec-clinic.com; Kapurdhara Marg, Lazimpat; ◔emergency 24hr, clinic 9am-noon & 1-4pm Mon-Fri), which has a **branch** (Map p216; ☏061-463082; www.ciwec-clinic.com; Mansarovar Path, Central Lakeside; ◔24hr) in Pokhara. A basic visit will cost you US$20 or so. A three-day treatment of antibiotics is less than US$3. Medical provision away from large cities is poor – if possible, travel to Kathmandu or Pokhara for treatment.

SUNBURN, CHAPPED LIPS & COLD SORES

Trekking at high altitude means you are more exposed to intense sunlight than normal. A good pair of sunglasses and diligent use of sunscreen makes all the difference in the world. Nevertheless loads of people get sunburned while trekking. Another problem is chapped lips and cold sores. Painful chapping is common in cold, dry mountain air, and this often brings outbreaks of cold sores for those carrying the virus. Use lip balm, and if you suffer from cold sores, bring Zovirax or a similar acyclovir cream.

While trekking, your only option may be small, local health posts, and even these are few and far between.

In remote areas, you should carry an appropriate medical kit and be prepared to treat yourself until you can reach a health professional.

Infectious Diseases

Dengue Fever

Dengue is caused by a family of viruses transmitted by day-biting Aedes mosquitoes. Symptoms include high fever, pain behind the eyes, headache, backache, joint and muscle pains, and sometimes a rash on the back, chest and abdomen. If you develop symptoms, see a doctor to be diagnosed and monitored as the illness can progress to dengue haemorrhagic fever, which is more severe and life-threatening. The risk of this increases substantially if you have previously been infected with dengue fever. Nepal suffered a major outbreak in 2010; a smaller 2016 outbreak was confined mainly to Chitwan and Jhapa. Elsewhere the risk is low.

Hepatitis

There are several different viruses that cause hepatitis (inflammation of the liver). The symptoms are similar in all forms of the illness and include fever, chills, headache, fatigue, feelings of weakness as well as aches and pains, followed by loss of appetite, nausea, vomiting, abdominal pain, dark urine, light-coloured faeces, jaundiced (yellow) skin and yellowing of the whites of the eyes.

Hepatitis A and E are transmitted by contaminated drinking water and food. Hepatitis A is virtually 100% preventable by using any of the current hepatitis A vaccines. Hepatitis E causes an illness very similar to hepatitis A and there is at present no way to immunise against this virus.

Hepatitis B is only spread by blood (unsterilised needles and blood transfusions) or sexual contact. Risky situations include having a shave, tattoo or body piercing with contaminated equipment.

HIV & AIDS

HIV and AIDS are growing problems in Nepal, with an estimated 75,000 Nepalis infected with the virus, so insist on brand-new disposable needles and syringes for injections.

Blood used for transfusions is usually screened for HIV/AIDS. Try to avoid a blood transfusion unless it seems certain you will die without it.

Malaria

Antimalarial tablets are only recommended if you will be spending long periods in the Terai, particularly during the monsoon. There is no risk in Kathmandu or Pokhara, for short visits to Chitwan, or on typical Himalayan trekking routes.

It makes sense to take measures to avoid being bitten by mosquitoes, as dengue fever, another mosquito-borne illness, has been sporadically documented in the lowlands. Use insect repellent if travelling to the Terai, particularly if staying overnight in jungle areas or in cheap hotels.

Plug-in mosquito killers are more effective than combustible mosquito coils, which can cause respiratory problems.

Rabies

The rabies virus causes a severe brain infection that is almost always fatal. Feral dogs and monkeys are the main carriers of the disease in Nepal.

Rabies is different from other infectious diseases in that a person can be immunised after having been exposed. Human rabies immune globulin (HRIG) is stocked at the CIWEC clinic and the Nepal International Clinic in Kathmandu.

In addition to the HRIG, five injections of rabies vaccine are needed over a one-month period. Travellers who have taken a preimmunisation series only need two rabies shots, three days apart, if they are bitten by a possibly rabid animal.

If you receive a bite or a scratch from an animal in Nepal, wash the wound with soap and water, then a disinfectant, such as povidone-iodine, then seek rabies immunisations. Considering the risk, it makes sense to keep your distance from animals in Nepal, particularly street dogs, cats and monkeys.

Respiratory Infections

Upper respiratory tract infections (such as the common cold) are common ailments in Nepal, especially in polluted Kathmandu. Respiratory infections are aggravated by high altitude, cold weather, pollution, smoking and overcrowded conditions, which increase the opportunities for infection.

Most upper respiratory tract infections go away without treatment, but any infection can lead to complications such as bronchitis, ear infections and pneumonia, which may need to be treated with antibiotics.

Fever

If you have a sustained fever (over 38°C/100.4°F) for more than two days while trekking and you cannot get to a doctor, an emergency treatment is a course of the broad-spectrum antibiotic azithromycin (500mg twice a day for seven days), but you should seek professional medical help as soon as possible.

Traveller's Diarrhoea

Even veteran travellers to South Asia seem to come down with the trots in Nepal. It's just one of those things. The main cause of infection is contaminated water and food, due to low standards of hygiene. However, diarrhoea is usually self-limiting and most people recover within a few days.

Dehydration is the main danger with diarrhoea, particularly in children, pregnant women or the elderly. Soda water, weak black tea with a little sugar, or soft drinks allowed to go flat and half-diluted with clean water will help you replace lost liquids.

TAP WATER

Don't drink the water in Nepal. Ice should be avoided except in upmarket tourist-oriented restaurants. While trekking, purify your own water rather than buying purified water in polluting plastic bottles.

Water Purification

The easiest way to purify water is to boil it thoroughly. Chlorine tablets (eg Puritabs or Steritabs) kill many pathogens but are not effective against giardia and amoebic cysts. Follow the directions carefully – filter water through a cloth before adding the chemicals and be sure to wet the thread on the lid to your water bottle. Once the water is purified, vitamin C or neutralising tablets can be added to remove the chemical taste.

Chlorine is more effective against giardia and amoebic cysts when combined with phosphoric acid (eg Aquamira). Iodine can be used as effectively as chlorine, but is now discouraged by medics in the UK.

Trekking filters take out all parasites, bacteria and viruses, and make water safe to drink. However, it is very important to read the specifications so that you know exactly what the filter removes from the water.

Another option is a UV light–based treatment such as a Steripen, but water has to be clear for this to work.

In severe cases, take oral rehydration salts made up with boiled or purified water. In an emergency you can make up a solution of six teaspoons of sugar and half a teaspoon of salt to a litre of boiled or bottled water. Stick to a bland diet as you recover.

Loperamide (Imodium) or diphenoxylate (Lomotil) can be used to bring temporary relief from the symptoms, but they do not cure the problem.

In the case of diarrhoea with blood or mucus (dysentery), any diarrhoea with fever, profuse watery diarrhoea and persistent diarrhoea not improving after 48 hours, you should visit a doctor. If you cannot reach a doctor, the recommended treatment is azithromycin 500mg once a day for one to three days.

These drugs can also be used in children and pregnant women. In children azithromycin is given in a dose of 10mg per kilogram of body weight per day (as a single dose each day for three days).

Amoebic Dysentery

Caused by the protozoan *Entamoeba histolytica*, amoebic dysentery is characterised by a gradual onset of low-grade diarrhoea, often with blood and mucus. Infection persists until treated.

Since diarrhoea due to amoebic infection is very rare in travellers to Nepal (less than 1%) self-medication is not advised.

Cyclospora

This waterborne intestinal parasite infects the upper intestine, causing diarrhoea, fatigue and loss of appetite lasting up to 12 weeks. Fortunately, the illness is a risk in Nepal mainly during the monsoon, when most tourists visit. Iodine is not sufficient to kill the parasite, but it can be removed by water filters and it is easily killed by boiling.

The treatment for *Cyclospora* diarrhoea is trimethoprim and sulfamethoxazole

EMERGENCY TREATMENTS FOR TREKKING

While trekking it may be impossible to reach medical treatment, so consider carrying the following drugs for emergencies (the concentrations in which these drugs are sold in Nepal are noted next to the drug):

➜ azithromycin 250mg – a broad-spectrum antibiotic, useful for traveller's diarrhoea; take the equivalent of 500mg per day for three consecutive days.

➜ tinidazole 500mg – the recommended treatment for giardiasis is four 500mg pills all at once for two days.

(sold commonly as Bactrim) twice a day for seven days. This drug cannot be taken by people who are allergic to sulphur.

Giardiasis

Also known as giardia, giardiasis accounts for around 12% of the diarrhoea among travellers in Nepal. The disease is caused by a parasite, *Giardia lamblia,* found in water that has been contaminated by human or animal waste.

Symptoms include stomach cramps, nausea, a bloated stomach, watery and foul-smelling diarrhoea, and frequent sulphurous burps and farts but no fever.

The best treatment is four 500mg tablets of tinidazole taken as a single dose each day for two consecutive days. Tinidazole cannot be taken with alcohol.

Environmental Hazards

Acute Mountain Sickness (AMS)

Above 2500m, the concentration of oxygen in the air you breathe starts to drop off markedly, reducing the amount of oxygen that reaches your brain and other organs. Decreasing air pressure at altitude has the additional effect of causing liquid to leak from the capillaries into the lungs and brain, which can be fatal. The human body has the ability to adjust to the changes in pressure and

oxygen concentration as you gain altitude, but this is a gradual process.

The health conditions caused by the effects of altitude are known collectively as altitude sickness or acute mountain sickness (AMS). If allowed to develop unchecked, AMS can lead to coma and death. However, you can avoid this potentially deadly condition by limiting your rate of ascent, which will allow your body to adjust to the altitude. There is also a 100% effective treatment if you do experience serious symptoms: descend immediately.

If you go trekking, it is important to read up on the causes, effects and treatment of altitude sickness before you start walking. Attend one of the free lectures on altitude sickness given by the **Himalayan Rescue Association** (☎01-4440292; www.himalayanrescue.org ; Dhobichaur, Lazimpat) in Kathmandu.

The onset of symptoms of AMS is usually gradual, so there is time to adjust your trekking schedule or retreat off the mountain if you start to feel unwell. Most people who suffer severe effects of AMS have ignored obvious warning signs.

ACCLIMATISATION

The process of acclimatisation is still not fully understood, but it is known to involve modifications in breathing patterns and heart rate and an increase in the oxygen-carrying capacity of the blood. Some people have a faster rate of acclimatisation than others, but almost anyone can trek to high altitudes as long as the rate of ascent does not exceed the rate at which their body can adjust.

AMS is a notoriously fickle affliction and it can affect trekkers and walkers who are accustomed to walking at high altitudes as well as people who have never been to altitude before. AMS has been fatal at 3000m, although 3500m to 4500m is the usual range.

SYMPTOMS

On treks above 4000m, almost everyone experiences some symptoms of mild altitude sickness, with breathlessness and fatigue linked to reduced oxygen in the blood being the most common.

Mild symptoms usually pass if you stop ascending and give your body time to 'catch up' with the increase in altitude. Once you have acclimatised at the altitude where you first developed symptoms, you should be able to slowly continue your ascent. Serious symptoms are a different matter – if you develop any of the symptoms described here, you should descend immediately.

MILD SYMPTIONS

Mild symptoms of AMS are experienced by many travellers above 2800m. Symptoms tend to be worse at night and include headache, dizziness, lethargy, loss of appetite, nausea, breathlessness, irritability and difficulty sleeping.

Never ignore mild symptoms of AMS – this is your body giving you an alarm call. You may develop more serious symptoms if you continue to ascend without giving your body time to adjust.

SERIOUS SYMPTOMS

AMS can become more serious without warning and it can be fatal. Serious symptoms are caused by the accumulation of fluid in the

lungs and brain, and include breathlessness at rest, a dry, irritative cough (which may progress to the production of pink, frothy sputum), severe headache, lack of coordination (typically leading to a 'drunken walk'), confusion, irrational behaviour, vomiting and eventually unconsciousness and death.

PREVENTION

If you trek above 2500m, observe the following rules:

Ascend slowly Where possible, do not sleep more than 300m higher than the elevation where you spent the previous night. If any stage on a trek exceeds this increase in elevation, take at least one rest day to acclimatise before you start the ascent. If you or anyone else in your party seems to be struggling, take a rest day as a precaution.

Climb high, sleep low It is always wise to sleep at a lower altitude than the greatest height reached during the day. If you need to cross a high pass, take an extra acclimatisation day before you cross. Be aware that descending to the altitude where you slept the previous night may not be enough to compensate for a very large increase in altitude during the day.

Trek healthy You are more likely to develop AMS if you are tired, dehydrated or malnourished. Drink extra fluids while trekking. Avoid sedatives or sleeping pills and don't smoke – this will further reduce the amount of oxygen reaching your lungs.

If you feel unwell, stop If you start to display mild symptoms of AMS, stop climbing. Take an acclimatisation day and see if things improve. If your symptoms stay the same or get worse, descend immediately. If on an organised trip make sure your tour leader is aware of your conditions. Don't feel pressured to continue ascending just to keep up with your group.

If you show serious symptoms, descend If you show any serious symptoms of AMS, descend immediately to a lower altitude. Ideally this should be below the

altitude where you slept the night before you first developed symptoms. Most lodges can arrange an emergency porter to help you descend quickly to a safe altitude.

TREATMENT

Treat mild symptoms by resting at the same altitude until recovery. Take paracetamol or aspirin for headaches. Diamox (acetazolamide) can be used to reduce mild symptoms of AMS. However, it is not a cure and it will not stop you from developing serious symptoms. The usual dosage of Diamox is 125mg to 250mg twice daily. The medication is a diuretic so you should drink extra liquid to avoid dehydration. Diamox may also cause disturbances to vision and the sense of taste, and it can cause a harmless tingling sensation in the fingers.

If symptoms persist or become worse, descend immediately – even 500m can help. If the victim cannot walk without support, they may need to be carried down. Any delay could be fatal; if you have to descend in the dark, seek local assistance.

In the event of severe symptoms, the victim may need to be flown to a lower altitude by helicopter. Getting the victim to a lower altitude is the priority – get someone else from the group to call for helicopter rescue and start the descent to the pick-up point. Note that a helicopter rescue can cost you US$2500 to US$10,000.

Emergency treatments for serious symptoms of AMS include supplementary oxygen, nifedipine, dexamethasone and repressurisation using a device known as a Gamow bag (this should only be administered by health professionals), but these only reduce the symptoms and they are not a 'cure'. They should never be used to avoid descent or to enable further ascent.

The only effective treatment for sufferers of severe AMS is to descend rapidly to a lower altitude.

Language

Nepali belongs to the Indo-European language family and has about 35 million speakers. It's closely related to Hindi and is written in the Devanagari script (also used for Hindi). Although Nepali is the national language and is used as a lingua franca between Nepal's ethnic groups, many other languages are also spoken in the country. The Newars of the Kathmandu Valley speak Newari. Other languages are spoken by the Tamangs, Sherpas, Rais, Limbus, Magars, Gurungs and other groups. In the Terai (bordering India), Hindi and Maithili are often spoken.

It's quite easy to get by with English in Nepal. Most people visitors have to deal with in the Kathmandu Valley and in Pokhara will speak some English. Along the main trekking trails, particularly the Annapurna Circuit, English is also widely understood.

Most Nepali consonant sounds are quite similar to their English counterparts. The exceptions are the so-called retroflex consonants and the aspirated consonants. Retroflex sounds are made by curling the tongue tip back to touch the roof of the mouth as you make the sound – they are indicated in this chapter by a dot below the letter, eg ṭ or ḍ as in *Kaṭhmanḍu*. Aspirated consonants are pronounced more forcefully than in English and are made with a short puff of air – they are indicated in this chapter by adding h after the consonant, eg ph is pronounced as the 'p' in 'pit', and th is pronounced as the 't' in 'time'.

As for the vowels, a is pronounced as the 'u' in 'hut', ā as the 'ar' in 'garden' (no 'r' sound), e as in 'best' but longer, i as in 'sister' but longer, o as in 'sold', u as in 'put', ai as in 'aisle' and au as the 'ow' in 'cow'. The stressed syllables are indicated with italics.

BASICS

Even if you learn no other Nepali, there is one word every visitor soon picks up – *namaste* (pronounced na·ma·*ste*). Strictly translated it means 'I salute the god in you', but it's used as an everyday greeting that encompasses everything from 'Hello' to 'How are you?' and even 'See you again soon'. It should be accompanied with the hands held in a prayer-like position, the Nepali gesture equivalent to Westerners shaking hands.

Hello./Goodbye.	na·ma·*ste*
How are you?	ta·*pāi*·lai *kas*·to chha
Excuse me.	ha·*jur*
Please (give me).	*di*·nu·hos
Please (you have).	*khā*·nu·hos
Thank you.	*dhan*·ya·bad

Unlike in many other countries, verbal expressions of thanks are not the cultural norm in Nepal. Although neglecting to say 'Thank you' may make you feel a little uncomfortable, it is rarely necessary in simple commercial transactions – foreigners saying *dhanyabad* all the time sound distinctly odd to Nepalis.

Yes. (I have)	chā
No. (I don't have)	*chhai*·na
I	ma
OK.	*theek*·cha
Wait a minute.	ek chhin *par*·kha·nos
good/pretty	*ram*·ro
I don't need it.	ma·lai cha·*hi*·ṇa
I don't have it.	ma *san*·ga *chhai*·na

WANT MORE?

For in-depth language information and handy phrases, check out Lonely Planet's *Nepali Phrasebook*. You'll find it at **shop.lonelyplanet.com**, or you can buy Lonely Planet's iPhone phrasebooks at the Apple App Store.

Do you speak English?	ta·*pāi* an·*gre*·ji *bol*·na *sak*·nu hun·chha
I only speak a little Nepali.	ma *a*·li *a*·li ne·*pā*·li *bol*·chhu
I understand.	ma bujh·chu
I don't understand.	*mai*·le bu·*jhi*·na
Please say it again.	*phe*·ri bha·*nu*·hos
Please speak more slowly.	ta·*pāi* bi·*stā*·rai *bol*·nu·hos

ACCOMMODATION

Where is a ...?	... *ka*·hā chha
campsite	*shi*·vir
guesthouse	*pā*·hu·na ghar
hotel	*ho*·ṭel
lodge	laj

Can I get a place to stay here?	*ya*·hā bās *paun*·chha
Can I look at the room?	*ko*·ṭhā *her*·na *sak*·chhu
How much is it per night?	ek *rāt*·ko *ka*·ti *pai*·sā ho
Does it include breakfast?	bi·*hā*·na·ko *khā*·na *sa*·met ho

clean	sa·*fā*
dirty	*mai*·lo
fan	*pan*·khā
hot water	*tā*·to *pā*·ni
room	*ko*·ṭhā

LANGUAGES OF NEPAL

Language	Estimated % of the Population
Nepali	47.8
Maithili	12.1
Bhojpuri	7.4
Tharu	5.8
Tamang	5.1
Newari	3.6
Magar	3.3
Rai	2.7
Awadhi	2.4
Limbu	1.4
Gurung	1.2
Sherpa	0.7
Other	6.5

EATING & DRINKING

I'm a vegetarian.	ma sāh·*kā*·*ha*·ri hun
I don't eat spicy food.	ma *pi*·ro *khan*·di·na
Please bring me a spoon.	*ma*·lai *cham*·chah *lyau*·nu·hos
Can I have the bill?	bil *pau*·na *sak*·chhu

banana	*ke*·rah
bread	*ro*·ṭi
cauliflower	*go*·bi
chicken	*ku*·kha·ra/murgh
egg	phul
eggplant	*bhaṇ*·ṭa
fish	*mā*·chha
lentils	daal
meat	*ma*·su
mutton	*kha*·si
okra	ram·*to*·ri·ya
peanut	*ba*·dam
potato	*a*·lu
(cooked) rice	bhāt
spinach	sag

cold beer	*chi*·so *bi*·yar
boiled water	u·*māh*·le·ko *pa*·ni
hot lemon	*ta*·to *pa*·ni·mah *ka*·ga·ti
lemon soda	*so*·ḍa·mah *ka*·ga·ti
milk	dudh
sugar	*chi*·ni
tea	*chi*·ya
yoghurt	*da*·hi

EMERGENCIES

Help!	gu·*hār*
It's an emergency!	*ā*·paṭ *par*·yo
There's been an accident!	dur·*gha*·ṭa·nā *bha*·yo
Please call a doctor.	*dāk*·ṭar·lai bo·*lāu*·nu·hos
Where is the (public) toilet?	shau·*chā*·la·ya *ka*·hā chha
I'm lost.	ma ha·*rā*·ye

HEALTH

Where can I find a good doctor?	*rām*·ro *dāk*·ṭar *ka*·hā *pāin*·cha
Where is the nearest hospital?	*ya*·hā as·pa·*tāl ka*·hā chha
I don't feel well.	*ma*·lāi *san*·cho *chhai*·na

I'm having trouble breathing.	sās *pher*·na sak·*di*·na
I have altitude sickness.	lekh *lāg*·yo
I have a fever.	jo·ro *ā*·yo
I have diarrhoea.	di·shā *lāg*·yo

| medicine | au·sa·dhi |
| pharmacy/chemist | au·sa·dhi pa·sal |

I have ...	ma·lāi ... *lāg*·yo
asthma	*dam*·ko bya·thā
diabetes	ma·dhu·*me*·ha
epilepsy	chā·re rog

SHOPPING & SERVICES

Where's the market?	ba·*zār* ka·*hā* chha
What is it made of?	*ke*·le ba·ne·ko
How much?	*ka*·ti
That's enough.	pugyo
I like this.	ma·lai yo *ram*·ro *lag*·yo
I don't like this.	ma·lai yo *ram*·ro lag·*en*·a

cheap	*sas*·to
envelope	kham
expensive	ma·*han*·go
less	kam
little bit	a·li·*ka*·ti
money	*pai*·sa
more	ba·dhi
stamp	*ti*·ka
bank	baink
... embassy	... *rāj*·du·tā·vas
museum	sam·grā·*hā*·la·ya
police	pra·*ha*·ri
post office	post a·*fis*
tourist office	*tu*·rist a·*fis*

What time does it open/close?	*ka*·ti ba·je khol·chha/ ban·da gar·chha
I want to change some money.	*pai*·sā sāt·nu man·*lāg*·chha
Is there a local internet cafe?	ya·hā in·ṭar·neṭ kyah·phe chha
I'd like to get internet access.	ma·lai in·ṭar·neṭ cha·hi·yo
I'd like to check my email.	i·mel chek gar·nu·par·yo
I'd like to send an email.	i·mel pa·ṭhau·nu·par·yo

SIGNS

खुला	Open
बन्द	Closed
प्रवेश	Entrance
निकास	Exit
प्रवेश निषेध	No Entry
धूम्रपान मनाही छ	No Smoking
मनाही/निषेध	Prohibited
शाचालय	Toilets
तातो	Hot
चिसो	Cold
खतरा	Danger
रोक्नुहोस	Stop
बाटो बन्द	Road Closed

TIME & DATES

| What time is it? | *ka*·ti ba·jyo |
| It's one o'clock. | ek ba·jyo |

minute	*mi*·nat
hour	ghan·tā
day	din
week	hap·tā
month	ma·hi·nā

yesterday	hi·jo
today	ā·ja
now	a·hi·le
tomorrow	bho·li

| What day is it today? | ā·ja ke bār |
| Today is ... | ā·ja ... ho |

Monday	som·bār
Tuesday	man·gal bār
Wednesday	budh·bār
Thursday	bi·hi·bār
Friday	su·kra·bār
Saturday	sa·ni·bār
Sunday	āi·ta·bār

TRANSPORT & DIRECTIONS

| Where? | ka·hā |
| here | ya·hā |

NUMBERS

0	sun·ya	शून्य
1	ek	एक
2	du·i	दुइ
3	tin	तीन
4	chār	चार
5	panch	पाँच
6	chha	छ
7	sāt	सात
8	āṭh	आठ
9	nau	नौ
10	das	दस
11	e·ghār·a	एघार
12	bā·hra	बाह्र
13	te·hra	तेह्र
14	chau·dha	चौध
15	pan·dhra	पन्ध्र
16	so·hra	सोह्र
17	sa·tra	सत्र
18	a·ṭhā·ra	अठार
19	un·nais	उन्नाईस
20	bis	बीस
21	ek kais	एककाईस
22	bais	बाईस
23	teis	तेईस
24	chau·bis	चौबीस
25	pach·chis	पच्चीस
26	chhab·bis	छब्बीस
27	sat·tais	सत्ताईस
28	aṭ·thais	अट्ठाईस
29	u·nan·tis	उनन्तीस
30	tis	तीस
40	chā·lis	चालीस
50	pa·chās	पचास
60	sā·ṭhi	साठी
70	sat·ta·ri	सत्तरी
80	a·si	असी
90	nab·be	नब्बे
100	ek say	एक सय
1000	ek ha·jār	एक हजार
10,000	das ha·jār	दस हजार
100,000	ek lākh	एक लाख
200,000	du·i lākh	दुइ लाख
1,000,000	das lākh	दस लाख

there — tya·hā
What is the address? — the·gā·nā ke ho
Please write down the address. — the·gā·nā lekh·nu·hos
How can I get to ...? — ... ko·lā·gi ka·ti pai·sā lāg·chha
Is it far from here? — ya·hā·ba·ta ke tā·dhā chha
Can I walk there? — hi·ḍe·ra jā·na sa·kin·chhu

boat — nāu
bus — bus
taxi — tyakh·si
ticket — ti·kaṭ

I want to go to ... — ma ...·mā jān·chhu
Where does this bus go? — yo bus ka·hā jān·chha
I want a one-way ticket. — jā·ne ti·kaṭ di·nu·hos
I want a return ticket. — jā·ne·āu·ne ti·kaṭ di·nu·hos
How much is it to go to ...? — ... jā·na ka·ti par·chha
Does your taxi have a meter? — ta·pāi ko tyakh·si mā me·ter chha

TREKKING

Which way is ...? — ... jā·ne ba·to ka·ta par·chha
Is there a village nearby? — na·ji·kai gaun par·chha
How many hours to ...? — ... ka·ti ghan·ṭā
How many days to ...? — ... ka·ti din
Where is the porter? — bha·ri·ya ka·ta ga·yo
I want to sleep. — ma·lai sut·na man lag·yo
I'm cold. — ma·lai jā·ḍo lag·yo
Please give me (water). — ma·lai (pa·ni) di·nu·hos

bridge — pul
cold — jā·ḍo
downhill — o·rā·lo
left — bā·yā
right — dā·yā
teahouse — bhat·ti
uphill — u·kā·lo
way/trail — sā·no bā·ṭo

GLOSSARY

Beware of the different methods of transliterating Nepali and the other languages spoken in Nepal. There are many and varied ways of spelling Nepali words. In particular, the letters 'b' and 'v' are often interchanged.

ACAP – Annapurna Conservation Area Project

Aditya – ancient *Vedic* sun god, also known as Suriya

Agni – ancient *Vedic* god of the hearth and fire

Agnipura – Buddhist symbol for fire

AMS – acute mountain sickness, also known as altitude sickness

Annapurna – the goddess of abundance and an incarnation of *Mahadevi*

Ashoka – Indian Buddhist emperor who spread Buddhism throughout the subcontinent

Ashta Matrikas – the eight multi-armed mother goddesses

Avalokiteshvara – Buddhist bodhisattva of compassion, known in Tibetan as Chenresig

bagh chal – traditional Nepali game

bahal – Buddhist monastery courtyard

ban – forest or jungle

bandh – strike; see also *julus* and *chakka jam*

Bhadrakali – Tantric goddess who is also a consort of *Bhairab*

Bhagwati – a form of *Durga*, and thus a form of the goddess *Parvati*

Bhairab – the 'terrific' or fearsome Tantric form of *Shiva* with 64 manifestations

bhanjyang – mountain pass

Bhimsen – one of the Pandava brothers, from the *Mahabharata*, seen as a god of tradesmen

bhojanalaya – basic Nepali restaurant or canteen

Bhote – Nepali term for a Tibetan, used in the names of rivers flowing from Tibet

Bodhi tree – a pipal tree under which the *Buddha* was sitting when he attained enlightenment; also known as 'bo tree'

bodhisattva – a near-*Buddha* who renounces the opportunity to attain *nirvana* in order to aid humankind

Bön – the pre-Buddhist animist religion of Tibet

Brahma – the creator god in the Hindu triad, which also includes *Vishnu* and *Shiva*

Brahmin – the highest Hindu caste, said to originate from *Brahma's* head

Buddha – the 'Awakened One'; the originator of Buddhism

chaitya – small *stupa*

chakka jam – literally 'jam the wheels', in which all vehicles stay off the street during a strike; see also *bandh* and *julus*

chakra – *Vishnu's* disc-like weapon; one of the four symbols he holds

Chandra – moon god

chautara – stone platforms around trees, which serve as shady places for porters to rest

Chhetri – the second caste of Nepali Hindus, said to originate from *Brahma's* arms

chörten – Tibetan Buddhist *stupa*

chowk – historically a courtyard or marketplace; these days used more to refer to an intersection or crossroads

daal – lentil soup; the main source of protein in the Nepali diet

Dalai Lama – spiritual leader of Tibetan Buddhist people

danda – hill

deval – temple

Devi – the short form of *Mahadevi*, the *shakti* to *Shiva*

dhaka – hand-woven cotton cloth

dharma – Buddhist teachings

dhoka – door or gate

Dhyani Buddha – the original Adi *Buddha* created five Dhyani Buddhas, who in turn create the universe of each human era

doko – basket carried by porters

dorje – Tibetan word for the 'thunderbolt' symbol of Buddhist power; *vajra* in Nepali

durbar – palace

Durga – fearsome manifestation of *Parvati*, *Shiva's* consort

gaida – rhinoceros

Ganesh – son of *Shiva* and *Parvati*, instantly recognisable by his elephant head

Ganga – goddess of the Ganges

Garuda – the man-bird *vehicle* of *Vishnu*

Gautama Buddha – the historical Buddha, founder of Buddhism

Gelugpa – one of the four major schools of Tibetan Buddhism

ghat – steps beside a river; a 'burning ghat' is used for cremations

gompa – Tibetan Buddhist monastery

gopi – milkmaids; companions of *Krishna*

gufa – cave

Gurkhas – Nepali soldiers who have long formed a part of the British army; the name comes from the region of Gorkha

Gurung – western hill people from around Gorkha and Pokhara

Hanuman – monkey god

harmika – square base on top of a *stupa's* dome, upon which the eyes of the *Buddha* are painted

hathi – elephant

himal – range or massif with permanent snow

hiti – water conduit or tank with waterspouts

hookah – water pipe for smoking

howdah – riding platform for passengers on an elephant

Indra – king of the *Vedic* gods; god of rain

Jagannath – *Krishna* as Lord of the Universe

janai – sacred thread, which high-caste Hindu men wear looped over their left shoulder

jatra – festival

jayanti – birthday

jhankri – faith healers who perform in a trance while beating drums

Jogini – mystical goddesses and counterparts to the 64 manifestations of *Bhairab*

julus – a procession or demonstration; see also *bandh* and *chakka jam*

Kali – the most terrifying manifestation of *Parvati*

Kalki – *Vishnu's* tenth and as yet unseen incarnation during which he will come riding a white horse and wielding a sword to destroy the world

Kam Dev – *Shiva's* companion

karma – Buddhist and Hindu law of cause and effect, which continues from one life to another

KEEP – Kathmandu Environmental Education Project

Khas – Hindu hill people

khat – see *palanquin*

khata – Tibetan prayer scarf, presented to an honoured guest or Buddhist *lama*

khola – stream or tributary

khukuri – traditional curved knife of the *Gurkhas*

kosi – river

kot – fort

Krishna – fun-loving eighth incarnation of *Vishnu*

Kumari – living goddess; a peaceful incarnation of *Kali*

kunda – water tank fed by springs

la – mountain pass

lama – Tibetan Buddhist monk or priest

lingam – phallic symbol signifying *Shiva's* creative powers

Machhendranath – patron god of the Kathmandu Valley and an incarnation of *Avalokiteshvara*

Mahabharata – one of the major Hindu epics

Mahadeva – literally 'Great God'; *Shiva*

Mahadevi – literally 'Great Goddess', sometimes known as *Devi*; the *shakti* to *Shiva*

Mahayana – the 'greater vehicle' of Buddhism; a later adaptation of the teaching, which lays emphasis on the *bodhisattva* ideal

makara – mythical crocodile-like beast

Malla – royal dynasty of the Kathmandu Valley responsible for most of the important temples and palaces of the valley towns

mandala – geometrical and astrological representation of the path to enlightenment

mandir – temple

mani – stone carved with the Tibetan Buddhist chant *om mani padme hum*

Manjushri – Buddhist *bodhisattva* of wisdom

mantra – prayer formula or chant

Mara – Buddhist god of death; has three eyes and holds the *wheel of life*

math – Hindu priest's house

mela – country fair

misthan bhandar – Indian-style sweet house and snack bar

naga – serpent deity

Nagpura – Buddhist symbol for water

namaste – traditional Hindu greeting (hello or goodbye), with the hands brought together at chest or head level, as a sign of respect

Nandi – *Shiva's* vehicle, the bull

Narayan – *Vishnu* as the sleeping figure on the cosmic ocean; from his navel *Brahma* appeared and went on to create the universe

Narsingha – man-lion incarnation of *Vishnu*

Newar – people of the Kathmandu Valley

nirvana – ultimate peace and cessation of rebirth (Buddhism)

om mani padme hum – sacred Buddhist *mantra*, which means 'hail to the jewel in the lotus'

padma – lotus flower

pagoda – multistoreyed Nepali temple, whose design was exported across Asia

palanquin – portable covered bed usually shouldered by four men; also called a *khat*

Parvati – *Shiva's* consort

pashmina – goat-wool blanket or shawl

Pashupati – *Shiva* as Lord of the Animals

path – small, raised platform to shelter pilgrims

phanta – grass plains

pipal tree – see *Bodhi tree*

pokhari – large water tank, or small lake

prasad – food offering

prayer flag – square of cloth printed with a *mantra* and hung in a string as a prayer offering

prayer wheel – cylindrical wheel inscribed with a Buddhist prayer or *mantra* that is 'said' when the wheel spins

Prithvi – *Vedic* earth goddess

puja – religious offering or prayer

pujari – priest

purnima – full moon

rajpath – road or highway, literally 'king's road'

Ramayana – Hindu epic

Rana – a hereditary line of prime ministers who ruled Nepal from 1846 to 1951

rath – temple chariot in which the idol is conveyed in processions

rudraksha – dried seeds worn in necklaces by *sadhus*

SAARC – South Asian Association for Regional Cooperation; includes Bangladesh, Bhutan, India, Nepal, Pakistan and Sri Lanka

sadhu – wandering Hindu holy man

Sagarmatha – Nepali name for Mt Everest

sal – tree of the lower Himalayan foothills

saligram – a black ammonite fossil of a Jurassic-period sea creature that is also a symbol of *Shiva*

sankha – conch shell, one of *Vishnu's* four symbols

Saraswati – goddess of learning and creative arts, and consort of *Brahma;* carries a lute-like instrument

seto – white

Shaivite – follower of *Shiva*

shakti – dynamic female element in male/female relationships; also a goddess

Sherpa – Buddhist hill people of Tibetan ancestry famed for work with mountaineering expeditions; with a lower-case 's' it refers to a trek staffer or high-altitude porter

shikhara – Indian-style temple with a tall, corn-cob-like spire

Shiva – the most powerful Hindu god, the creator and destroyer; part of the Hindu triad with *Vishnu* and *Brahma*

sindur – red vermilion powder and mustard-oil mixture used for offerings

sirdar – leader/organiser of a trekking party

stupa – bell-shaped Buddhist religious structure, originally designed to hold the relics of the *Buddha*

Sudra – the lowest Nepali caste, said to originate from *Brahma's* feet

sundhara – fountain with golden spout

tabla – hand drum

tahr – wild mountain goat

tal – lake

Taleju Bhawani – Nepali goddess, an aspect of *Mahadevi* and the family deity of the *Malla* kings of the Kathmandu Valley

tappu – island

Tara – White Tara is the consort of the *Dhyani Buddha* Vairocana; Green Tara is associated with Amoghasiddhi

teahouse trek – independent trekking between village inns (ie no camping)

tempo – three-wheeled, automated minivan commonly used in Nepal

Thakali – people of the Kali Gandaki Valley who specialise in running hotels

thali – literally a plate with compartments for different dishes; an all-you-can-eat set meal

thangka – Tibetan religious painting

third eye – symbolic eye on *Buddha* figures, used to indicate the *Buddha's* all-seeing wisdom and perception

thukpa – noodle soup

tika – red sandalwood-paste spot marked on the forehead, particularly for religious occasions

tole – street or quarter of a town; sometimes used to refer to a square

tonga – horse carriage

topi – traditional Nepali cap

torana – carved pediment above temple doors

Tribhuvan – the king who in 1951 ended the *Rana* period and Nepal's long seclusion

trisul – trident weapon that is a symbol of *Shiva*

tunala – carved temple struts

tundikhel – parade ground

Uma Maheshwar – *Shiva* and *Parvati* in a pose where *Shiva* sits cross-legged and *Parvati* sits on his thigh and leans against him

Upanishads – ancient *Vedic* scripts; the last part of the *Vedas*

vahana – a god's animal mount or *vehicle*

Vaishnavite – follower of *Vishnu*

Vaisya – caste of merchants and farmers, said to originate from *Brahma's* thighs

vajra – the 'thunderbolt' symbol of Buddhist power in Nepal; *dorje* in Tibetan

Vedas – ancient orthodox Hindu scriptures

Vedic gods – ancient Hindu gods described in the *Vedas*

vehicle – the animal with which a Hindu god is associated

vihara – Buddhist religious buildings and pilgrim accommodation

Vishnu – the preserver; one of the three main Hindu gods, along with *Brahma* and *Shiva*

wheel of life – Buddhist representation of how humans are chained by desire to a life of suffering

yak – cow-like Nepali beast of burden (only pure-blood animals of the genus *Bos grunniens* can properly be called yaks; crossbreeds have other names)

yaksha – attendant deity or nymph

Yama – *Vedic* god of death; his messenger is the crow

Yellow Hats – name sometimes given to adherents of the *Gelugpa* school of Tibetan Buddhism

yeti – abominable snowman; mythical hairy mountain man of the Himalaya

yogi – yoga master

yoni – female sexual symbol, equivalent of a *lingam*

zamindar – absentee landlord and/or moneylender

Behind the Scenes

SEND US YOUR FEEDBACK

We love to hear from travellers – your comments keep us on our toes and help make our books better. Our well-travelled team reads every word on what you loved or loathed about this book. Although we cannot reply individually to your submissions, we always guarantee that your feedback goes straight to the appropriate authors, in time for the next edition. Each person who sends us information is thanked in the next edition – the most useful submissions are rewarded with a selection of digital PDF chapters.

Visit **lonelyplanet.com/contact** to submit your updates and suggestions or to ask for help. Our award-winning website also features inspirational travel stories, news and discussions.

Note: We may edit, reproduce and incorporate your comments in Lonely Planet products such as guidebooks, websites and digital products, so let us know if you don't want your comments reproduced or your name acknowledged. For a copy of our privacy policy visit lonelyplanet.com/privacy.

OUR READERS

Many thanks to the travellers who used the last edition and wrote to us with helpful hints, useful advice and interesting anecdotes:

Aäron van der Sanden, Albert Horváth, Angelique De Paepe, Anjali Badloe, Anne Tuart, Annebeth Muntinga, Antoinette Heuvel Rijnders, Benjamin Robson, Brigitte Mueller, Caron Dhoju, Dale Golden, Daniela Wicker, David Wells, Eline Bertrums, Emily Coles, Eva van Winsen, Filippo Carlotta FCt, Fleur Davey, Florian Schmid, Frans Wildenborg, Ina Tillema, John Blum, Jonas Bernstein, Julia Sahin, Kate Allberry, Laska Pare, Mara Kuijpers, Michel Geerligs, Nikolaus Schulz, Phil Tennon, Philipp Degenhardt, Sam Scott, Sarah Lennon, Silvia Paola Antonini, Simon Krenger, Stephen King, Tamanna Patel, Tan Gandhara, Tereza Nesnidalova, Tineke van der Wal, Tom Stuart, Tshering Pema Tamang, Valen Pirret, Veronica Benardinelli, Victor Speidel, Virginia Ruiz Albacete.

WRITER THANKS
Bradley Mayhew

Thanks to Niraj and Abhi at Rural Heritage, and Dambar at Nuwakot for showing me the earthquake repairs there. Thanks to Durga Tamang for updates on the Tamang Heritage Trail. Cheers to Rajan of Earthbound Expeditions for the Kakani trip and to Dawa Sherpa of Asian Trekking and Ang Rita Sherpa for updates on the Khumbu. Thanks to Mukhiya and Maya for a base in Kathmandu.

Lindsay Brown

I am very grateful for the assistance provided by numerous friendly folks across Nepal. In particular, I thank Stan Armington and the excellent staff at the Tibet Resort. Thanks to Durga Bhandari at Malla Treks and Jugal Rajbhandari in Bhaktapur. I would also like to acknowledge my fellow authors and partner Jenny Fegent.

Paul Stiles

In the marathon journey that was my research trip, I was helped along by a slew of drivers, guides, hoteliers, and all-around experts of whom Niraj, Mark, Naben, Dhan and Robin stand out. Above all, I wish to thank Abhi for the untiring support that kept me in one piece. How many Shresthas are there, anyway?

ACKNOWLEDGEMENTS

Climate map data adapted from Peel MC, Finlayson BL & McMahon TA (2007) 'Updated World Map of the Köppen-Geiger Climate Classification', Hydrology and Earth System Sciences, 11, 163344.

Cover photograph: Procession of novice monks at Bodhnath Stupa, Felix Hug ©

THIS BOOK

This 11th edition of Lonely Planet's *Nepal* guidebook was researched and written by Bradley Mayhew, Lindsay Brown and Paul Stiles. The previous edition was written by Bradley Mayhew, Lindsay Brown and Stuart Butler. The 9th edition was written by Bradley Mayhew, Lindsay Brown and Trent Holden. This guidebook was produced by the following:

Destination Editor
Joe Bindloss

Product Editors Kate Kiely, Kate Mathews

Senior Cartographer
Valentina Kremenchutskaya

Book Designer Lauren Egan

Assisting Editors Janet Austin, Michelle Bennett, Carolyn Boicos, Pete Cruttenden, Andrea Dobbin, Carly Hall, Rosie Nicholson, Susan Paterson

Assisting Cartographer Julie Dodkins

Cover Researcher Naomi Parker

Thanks to Imogen Bannister, Heather Champion, Shona Gray, Lauren Keith, Claire Naylor, Karyn Noble, Martine Power, Anna Tyler

Index

Map Legend

Sights
- Beach
- Bird Sanctuary
- Buddhist
- Castle/Palace
- Christian
- Confucian
- Hindu
- Islamic
- Jain
- Jewish
- Monument
- Museum/Gallery/Historic Building
- Ruin
- Shinto
- Sikh
- Taoist
- Winery/Vineyard
- Zoo/Wildlife Sanctuary
- Other Sight

Activities, Courses & Tours
- Bodysurfing
- Diving
- Canoeing/Kayaking
- Course/Tour
- Sento Hot Baths/Onsen
- Skiing
- Snorkelling
- Surfing
- Swimming/Pool
- Walking
- Windsurfing
- Other Activity

Sleeping
- Sleeping
- Camping

Eating
- Eating

Drinking & Nightlife
- Drinking & Nightlife
- Cafe

Entertainment
- Entertainment

Shopping
- Shopping

Information
- Bank
- Embassy/Consulate
- Hospital/Medical
- Internet
- Police
- Post Office
- Telephone
- Toilet
- Tourist Information
- Other Information

Geographic
- Beach
- Hut/Shelter
- Lighthouse
- Lookout
- Mountain/Volcano
- Oasis
- Park
- Pass
- Picnic Area
- Waterfall

Population
- Capital (National)
- Capital (State/Province)
- City/Large Town
- Town/Village

Transport
- Airport
- Border crossing
- Bus
- Cable car/Funicular
- Cycling
- Ferry
- Metro station
- Monorail
- Parking
- Petrol station
- Subway station
- Taxi
- Train station/Railway
- Tram
- Underground station
- Other Transport

Note: Not all symbols displayed above appear on the maps in this book

Routes
- Tollway
- Freeway
- Primary
- Secondary
- Tertiary
- Lane
- Unsealed road
- Road under construction
- Plaza/Mall
- Steps
- Tunnel
- Pedestrian overpass
- Walking Tour
- Walking Tour detour
- Path/Walking Trail

Boundaries
- International
- State/Province
- Disputed
- Regional/Suburb
- Marine Park
- Cliff
- Wall

Hydrography
- River, Creek
- Intermittent River
- Canal
- Water
- Dry/Salt/Intermittent Lake
- Reef

Areas
- Airport/Runway
- Beach/Desert
- Cemetery (Christian)
- Cemetery (Other)
- Glacier
- Mudflat
- Park/Forest
- Sight (Building)
- Sportsground
- Swamp/Mangrove

OUR STORY

A beat-up old car, a few dollars in the pocket and a sense of adventure. In 1972 that's all Tony and Maureen Wheeler needed for the trip of a lifetime – across Europe and Asia overland to Australia. It took several months, and at the end – broke but inspired – they sat at their kitchen table writing and stapling together their first travel guide, *Across Asia on the Cheap*. Within a week they'd sold 1500 copies. Lonely Planet was born.

Today, Lonely Planet has offices in Franklin, London, Melbourne, Oakland, Dublin, Beijing and Delhi, with more than 600 staff and writers. We share Tony's belief that 'a great guidebook should do three things: inform, educate and amuse'.

OUR WRITERS

Bradley Mayhew

Kathmandu, Around the Kathmandu Valley, Trekking Routes Bradley has been writing guidebooks for 20 years now. He started travelling while studying Chinese at Oxford University, and has since focused his expertise on China, Tibet, the Himalaya and Central Asia. He is a coauthor of the Lonely Planet guides *Tibet*, *Nepal*, *Trekking in the Nepal Himalaya*, *Bhutan*, *Central Asia* and many others. Bradley has also fronted two TV series for Arte and SWR, one retracing the route of Marco Polo via Turkey, Iran, Afghanistan, Central Asia and China, and the other trekking Europe's 10 most scenic long-distance trails. Bradley also wrote the Plan Your Trip chapters (with the exception of Eat & Drink Like a Local) and the Directory chapter.

Lindsay Brown

Around the Kathmandu Valley; Pokhara; Biking, Rafting & Kayaking Lindsay started travelling as a young bushwalker exploring the Blue Mountains west of Sydney. Then as a marine biologist he dived the coastal and island waters of southeastern Australia. He continued travelling whenever he could while employed at Lonely Planet as an editor and publishing manager. Since becoming a freelance writer and photographer he has coauthored more than 35 Lonely Planet guides to destinations such as Australia, Bhutan, India, Malaysia, Nepal, Pakistan and Papua New Guinea. Lindsay also wrote the Eat & Drink Like a Local chapter plus the Understand chapters.

Paul Stiles

Around the Kathmandu Valley; Kathmandu to Pokhara; The Terai & Mahabharat Range When Paul was 21, he bought an old motorcycle in London and drove it to Tunisia. That did it for him. Since then he's explored around 60 countries and covered many adventure destinations for Lonely Planet, including Morocco, Madagascar, São Tomé & Príncipe, Indonesia, the Philippines, Hawaii, Maui, and Kaua'i. He has also lived for long stretches in America, Scotland and Spain. In all things, he tries to follow the rocking chair rule: when making key life decisions, assume the perspective of an elderly person slowly rocking on his porch. Because some day that will be you. Paul also wrote the Health and Transport chapters.

Published by Lonely Planet Global Limited
CRN 554153
11th edition – Jul 2018
ISBN 978 1 78657 057 4
© Lonely Planet 2018   Photographs © as indicated 2018
10 9 8 7 6 5 4 3 2 1
Printed in Singapore